Scale 1:250,000

or 3.94 miles to 1 inch

24th edition July 2001

© Automobile Association Developments Limited 2001

Revised version of the atlas formerly known as *Complete Atlas of Britain.*

Original edition printed 1979.

Published by AA Publishing (a trading name of Automobile Association Developments Limited, whose registered office is Norfolk House, Priestley Road, Basingstoke, Hampshire RG24 9NY. Registered number 1878835).

Mapping produced by the Cartographic Department of The Automobile Association. This atlas has been compiled and produced from the Automaps database utilising electronic and computer technology.

ISBN 0 7495 2972 5

A CIP catalogue record for this book is available from The British Library.

Printed in Italy by Rotolito, Lombarda.

The contents of this atlas are believed to be correct at the time of the latest revision. However, the publishers cannot be held responsible for loss occasioned to any person acting or refraining from action as a result of any material in this atlas, nor for any errors, omissions or changes in such material. The publishers would welcome information to correct any errors or omissions and to keep this atlas up to date. Please write to the Cartographic Editor, Publishing Division, The Automobile Association, Fanum House, Basing View, Basingstoke, Hampshire RG21 4EA.

Information on National Parks provided by the Countryside Agency for England and the Countryside Council for Wales.

Information on National Scenic Areas in Scotland provided by Scottish Natural Heritage.

Information on Forest Parks provided by the Forestry Commission.

The RSPB sites shown are a selection chosen by the Royal Society for the Protection of Birds.

National Trust properties shown are a selection of those open to the public as indicated in the handbooks of the National Trust and the National Trust for Scotland.

2002 MOTORIST'S AT BRITAI

GW00705990

contents

Map pages			inside front cover
Traffic and travel information			II–III
Route planner and mileage chart			IV–IX
Motorways			**X–XIII**
Restricted junctions	X–XI	M25 and M60	XII–XIII
Map symbols			**XIV–1**
Road maps			**2–116**
The Channel Islands	6–7	Scottish islands	111
The Isle of Man	116	Ireland	112–115
Town plans			**117–129**
Key to town plans	117	Central London street index	152–158
Central London	142–151		
District maps			**130–141**
Birmingham district	130–131	Tyne & Wear district	136–137
Glasgow district	132–133	London district	138–141
Manchester district	134–135		
Index to place names			**159–194**
County map (index opener)			159
Distances and journey times			inside back cover

traffic and travel information

The Automobile Association is Britain's largest motoring organisation, providing accurate and up-to-date information for all motorists. Our information detailing traffic congestion, road conditions and public transport news is collected from more than 8,000 sources, including, among others, local authorities, roadside cameras and our own registered mobile phone service 'Jambusters'.
AA Roadwatch operates 24 hours a day, giving traffic information on all UK motorways, major trunk roads and local roads. The result is one of the most comprehensive and up-to-the-minute traffic report services available.

Instant traffic reports

09003 401 100/401 100 mobile
www.theAA.com

These numbers give you direct access to a range of traffic and travel information services, including: the latest traffic reports for your local area, or for any region of the UK; a traffic report on any motorway or A-road of your choice; and local and national five-day weather forecasts.

UK and european routes

0870 5500 600
www.theAA.com

AA routes are available for the UK, Ireland and continental Europe, to help you map out a detailed plan of the best way to get to your destination. Route planning is also available online and, if you tell us your usual routes, we can send you e-mail alerts at times pre-determined by you to let you know what traffic incidents and delays are occurring.

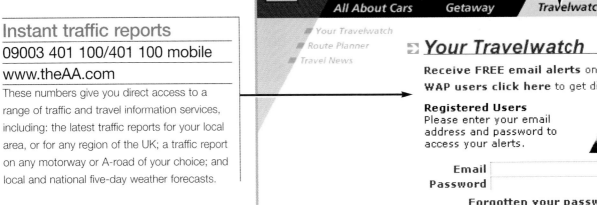

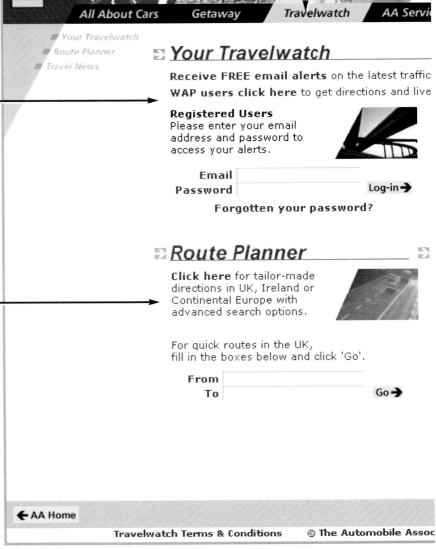

All About Cars   **Getaway**   **Travelwatch**   **AA Servi**

- Your Travelwatch
- Route Planner
- Travel News

Your Travelwatch

Receive FREE email alerts on the latest traffic
WAP users click here to get directions and live

Registered Users
Please enter your email address and password to access your alerts.

Email _____
Password _____   Log-in →

Forgotten your password?

Route Planner

Click here for tailor-made directions in UK, Ireland or Continental Europe with advanced search options.

For quick routes in the UK, fill in the boxes below and click 'Go'.

From _____
To _____   Go →

← AA Home

Travelwatch Terms & Conditions   © The Automobile Assoc

In-car information systems and radio

AA traffic and travel information can also be received by intelligent in-car navigation systems that warn of delays, provide detailed routes and even recommend a suitable hotel for a stopover. Alternatively, use your WAP-enabled mobile device to access this information on the AA's website. AA Roadwatch reports are also available over many local radio stations.

Air ambulance
0800 3899 899

For information about the work of the National Association of Air Ambulance Services, or to make a donation to NAAAS by debit or credit card, call the number above.

Air ambulances are a vital part of emergency services, providing a rapid response and transfer from incident to hospital.

CALL NOW 0800 085 3007

■ Site Map   ■ Contact Us   ■ About the AA

Quick Links : Pick from List ▲▼

problems on your route.
travel news on your phone.

New user
Give us the details of your trip and Travelwatch will **email you** personalised traffic reports.

New User **Register Now →**

Travel News

Click here to search for travel updates in cities, towns & motorways.

For live **traffic & weather information** on the move in Great Britain, call 09003 401 100 or **401 100** from your mobile. (Calls cost 60p per minute.)

12. A4, Major roadworks, Uxbridge Road, E.
13. A4, Temporary traffic lights, Saltford, E.
14. A5, Roadworks. Delays expected, Staples Corner, N.
15. A5, Temporary traffic lights, Dunstable, N.

Pause

✉ **Email Us: customer.services@theAA.com** ℂ
Phone Us: 0870 600 0371
:iation Limited 2001   **Web Site Terms & Conditions**

Road user information line (Highways Agency)
0845 750 040 30

For information on motorways and trunk roads, to make a complaint or comment on road conditions or roadworks, for MoT and vehicle licence enquiries.

AA The Driving School
0800 60 70 80
www.theAA.com

The AA's Driving School is the only national driving school to use fully qualified instructors exclusively. Attractive packages are available to people pre-paying for 12 hours' tuition.

Petrolbusters
www.theAA.com

Click on the Petrolbusters symbol to locate the cheapest petrol in your area.

Call tariffs

0800 – free to caller, 0845 – charged at BT local rate, 0870 – charged at BT national rate, 09003 – 60p per minute at all times. Availability and prices for mobile calls can vary – contact your service provider for details.

Information correct at time of going to press.

route planner

The distances between towns on the mileage chart are given to the nearest mile and are measured along the normal AA-recommended routes. It should be noted that AA-recommended routes do not necessarily follow the shortest distance between places but are based on the quickest travelling time, making maximum use of motorways and dual carriageways.

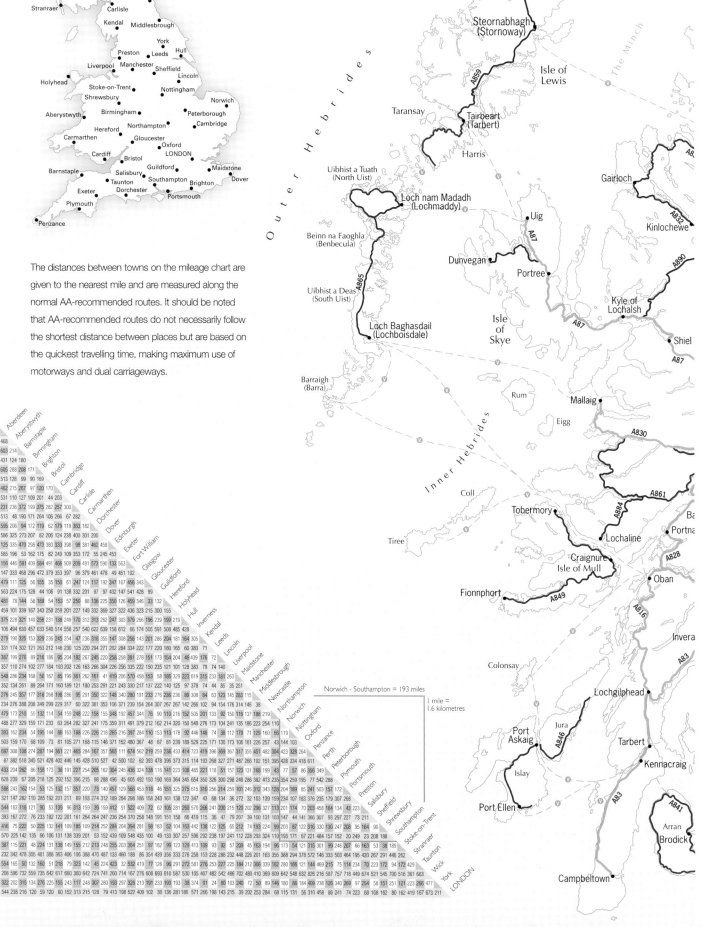

Norwich – Southampton = 193 miles

1 mile = 1.6 kilometres

Mileage chart (diagonal labels, in order): Aberdeen, Aberystwyth, Barnstaple, Birmingham, Brighton, Bristol, Cambridge, Cardiff, Carlisle, Carmarthen, Dorchester, Dover, Edinburgh, Exeter, Fort William, Glasgow, Gloucester, Guildford, Hereford, Holyhead, Hull, Inverness, Kendal, Leeds, Lincoln, Liverpool, Maidstone, Manchester, Middlesbrough, Newcastle, Northampton, Norwich, Nottingham, Oxford, Penzance, Perth, Peterborough, Plymouth, Portsmouth, Preston, Salisbury, Sheffield, Shrewsbury, Southampton, Stoke-on-Trent, Stranraer, Taunton, Wick, York, LONDON

	distances (miles)
Aberystwyth	468
Barnstaple	603 214
Birmingham	431 124 180
Brighton	605 288 208 171
Bristol	513 128 99 90 169
Cambridge	462 215 267 97 120 170
Cardiff	531 110 127 109 201 44 203
Carlisle	231 236 372 199 375 282 257 300
Carmarthen	513 48 190 171 264 105 266 67 282
Dorchester	595 206 94 172 119 62 179 119 363 182
Dover	586 325 273 207 82 206 124 238 400 301 200
Edinburgh	125 335 470 298 473 380 333 398 98 381 462 458
Exeter	585 196 53 162 175 82 249 109 353 172 55 245 453
Fort William	156 446 581 409 584 491 466 509 209 491 573 590 133 563
Glasgow	147 333 468 296 472 379 353 397 96 379 461 478 49 451 102
Gloucester	479 111 125 56 155 35 150 61 247 124 117 347 107 456 343
Guildford	563 224 175 128 44 106 91 138 332 201 97 97 432 147 541 428 99
Hereford	481 78 144 58 189 54 153 57 250 88 136 225 350 126 459 346 33 132
Holyhead	459 101 339 167 343 250 259 201 227 149 332 369 327 322 436 353 215 300 155
Hull	375 228 321 140 258 231 138 249 170 312 313 262 247 303 379 266 196 239 199 219
Inverness	106 494 630 457 633 540 514 558 257 540 622 639 158 612 66 174 505 591 508 485 428
Kendal	279 190 325 153 329 236 254 254 47 236 318 355 147 308 256 147 201 286 204 181 164 305
Leeds	331 174 302 121 263 212 146 230 125 220 294 271 202 284 334 222 177 220 180 165 60 383 71
Lincoln	367 199 276 89 216 186 95 204 182 267 245 220 258 258 391 278 151 173 154 204 46 439 176 72
Liverpool	357 110 277 184 193 202 126 163 266 304 226 256 335 101 128 79 74 140
Maidstone	548 286 234 168 50 167 85 199 361 262 161 41 419 206 570 458 153 58 186 329 223 619 315 233 181 263
Manchester	352 134 261 89 264 171 160 189 121 180 253 291 221 243 330 217 137 222 140 125 97 378 74 44 85 35 251
Middlesbrough	276 245 357 177 318 268 196 286 95 291 350 322 148 340 280 191 233 276 236 89 308 84 63 123 145 283 115
Newcastle	234 276 388 208 349 299 229 317 60 322 381 353 106 371 239 154 264 307 267 142 266 102 94 154 176 314 146 38
Northampton	479 173 210 55 132 114 54 159 248 222 158 155 348 192 457 344 76 90 110 216 152 505 201 133 92 150 116 137 188 219
Norwich	488 277 320 173 233 63 264 282 137 355 359 311 491 359 212 162 214 320 276 104 141 135 186 223 254 116 119
Nottingham	393 162 234 54 195 144 86 163 188 226 226 216 265 216 397 284 110 153 113 178 92 446 148 74 38 112 179 71 129 160 66 119
Oxford	503 159 170 68 109 73 81 105 271 168 115 146 371 152 480 367 48 67 81 239 189 529 225 171 130 173 106 161 226 257 43 144 103
Penzance	697 308 108 274 287 194 361 221 465 284 167 357 565 111 674 562 275 259 238 433 414 723 419 396 373 355 401 355 482 304 423 328 264
Perth	87 382 518 345 521 428 402 446 145 428 510 527 42 500 102 62 393 478 396 373 315 114 193 268 327 271 487 266 192 151 395 428 334 418 611
Peterborough	433 204 262 86 158 173 38 191 227 254 205 162 304 245 436 324 138 116 141 223 108 485 221 118 51 157 123 131 168 199 43 77 57 86 356 349
Plymouth	628 239 67 205 218 125 292 152 396 215 98 288 496 24 605 493 200 190 169 364 345 654 350 326 300 286 332 286 413 235 354 259 195 77 542 288
Portsmouth	588 243 162 154 53 125 132 157 357 220 73 140 457 129 566 453 118 46 151 325 275 615 310 256 214 259 101 246 312 343 122 343 128 204 189 85 241 503 157 172
Preston	321 147 282 110 285 192 201 211 89 193 274 312 189 264 298 186 158 243 161 138 122 347 43 68 134 36 272 32 103 139 234 107 183 376 235 179 307 268
Salisbury	544 183 118 121 90 53 139 92 313 159 39 159 412 91 512 400 70 62 105 281 260 570 266 241 200 245 458 204 309 97 45 107 44 141 141 307 91 57 99 207 227 73 211
Sheffield	393 167 272 76 233 182 122 201 161 264 264 247 236 254 370 258 148 191 151 158 65 419 115 36 47 79 207 39 100 131 103 147 44 141 166 307 93 297 227 73 211
Shrewsbury	416 75 225 52 225 132 141 109 185 109 214 252 284 204 294 281 98 183 52 104 163 442 125 65 112 125 66 72 193 224 199 203 122 316 330 102 297 228 95 164 90
Southampton	570 225 142 135 66 106 131 138 358 227 39 123 475 107 583 452 106 42 128 298 197 611 292 212 184 229 125 217 283 314 83 117 49 173 171 67 221 484 57 152 20 249 23 208 168
Stoke-on-Trent	387 115 221 48 224 131 138 149 149 155 212 214 248 255 203 364 251 97 182 99 123 129 413 109 93 92 57 229 45 163 194 96 173 52 133 225 242 143 300 247 66 163 53 36 189
Stranraer	232 342 478 305 481 388 363 406 106 388 470 487 133 460 188 69 354 439 356 333 278 222 282 402 448 226 570 295 388 294 378 572 146 333 503 464 195 420 267 291 446 262
Taunton	554 165 50 132 160 51 218 73 332 419 77 126 96 291 272 581 253 227 225 184 213 308 184 192 350 186 225 224 107 55 114 234 70 223 192 429
Wick	208 596 732 559 735 642 617 660 360 642 724 741 260 714 167 276 608 693 610 587 530 105 407 482 542 486 702 480 410 369 609 642 548 632 826 216 587 757 718 449 674 521 545 700 516 361 683
York	322 202 315 134 276 225 155 243 117 248 307 280 193 297 326 213 191 233 194 133 38 374 91 24 80 103 240 72 50 89 146 180 86 184 429 238 120 369 269 97 254 58 151 251 121 223 266 477
LONDON	544 238 126 120 59 120 60 152 313 215 128 79 413 198 522 409 102 30 136 281 186 571 266 198 143 215 39 202 253 284 68 115 131 55 310 458 86 241 74 223 88 168 162 80 162 419 167 673 211

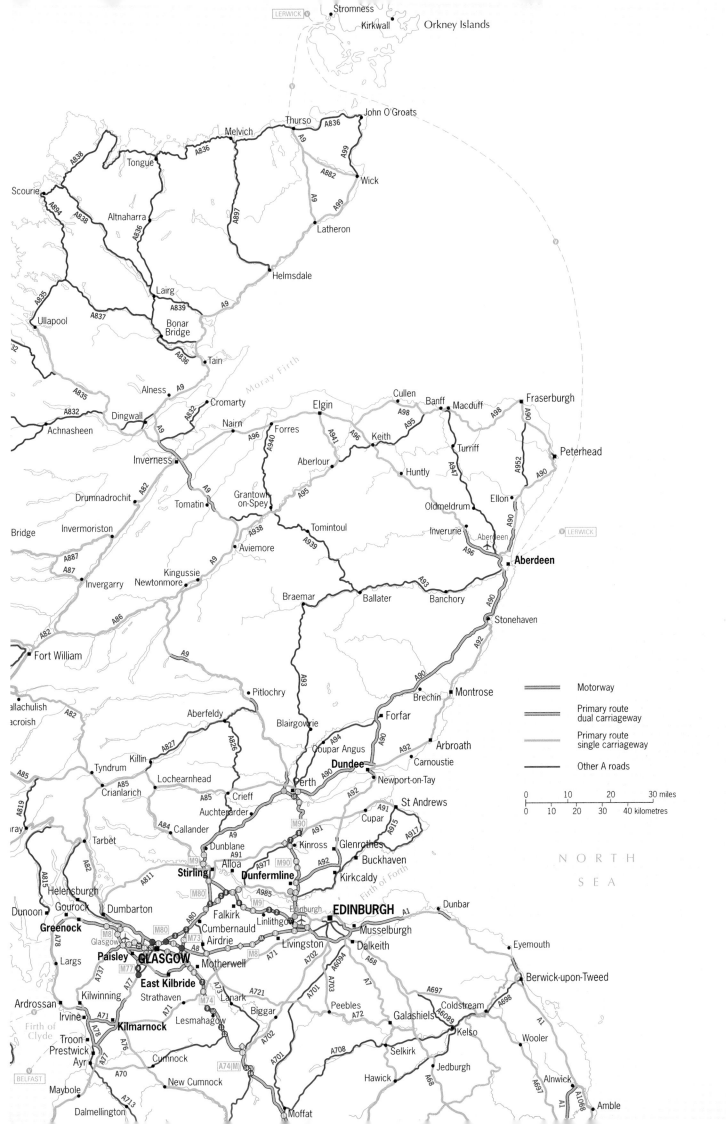

Motorway

Primary route
dual carriageway

Primary route
single carriageway

Other A roads

0   10   20   30 miles
0   10   20   30   40 kilometres

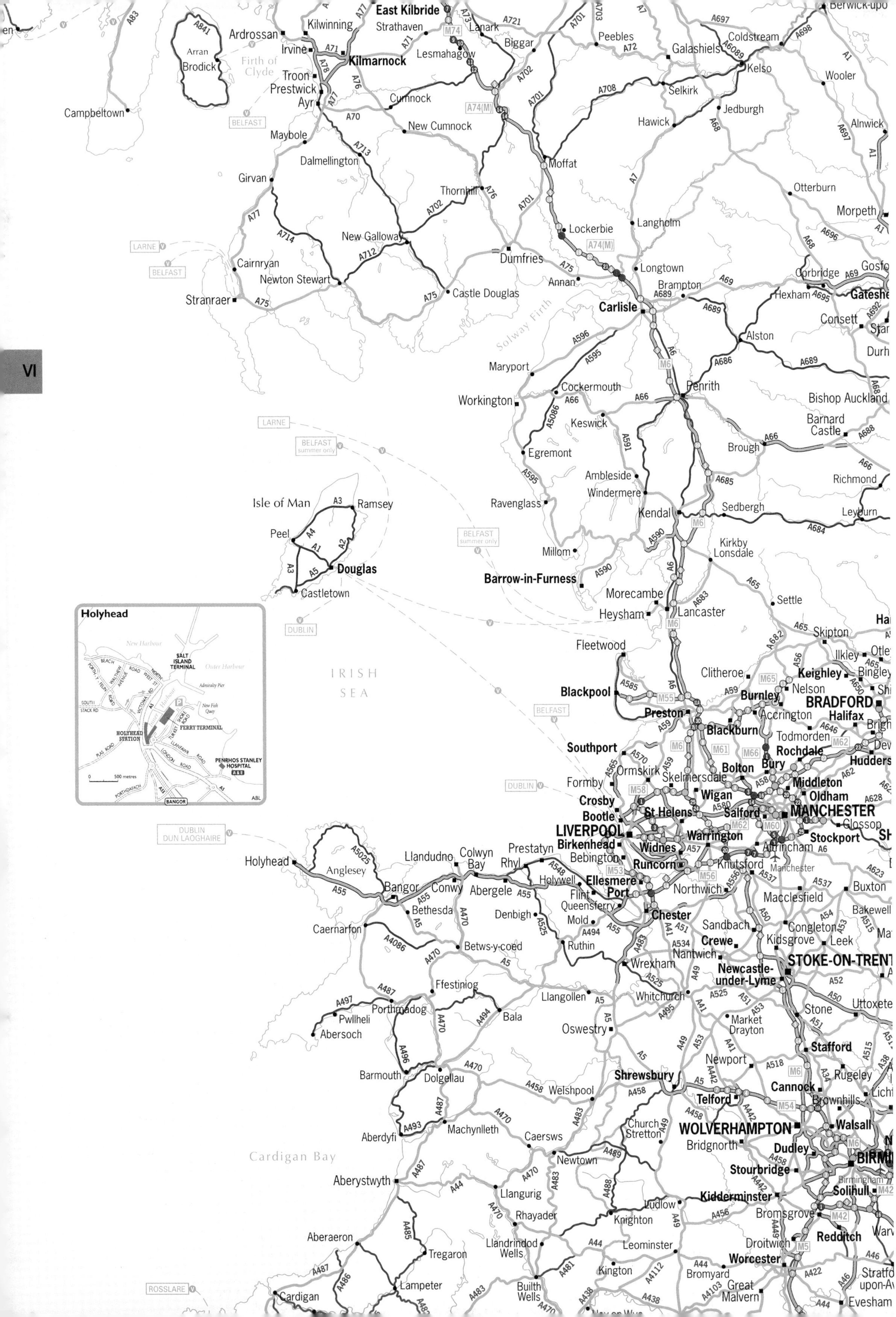

A83 A841 Arran Brodick Campbeltown Firth of Clyde

Kilwinning Strathaven Lanark A721 A703 A701 A702 A697 Coldstream Berwick-upo
East Kilbride A77 M73 A72 Biggar Peebles A72 Galashiels A6089 Kelso Wooler
Ardrossan Kilmarnock Lesmahagow A74(M) A708 Selkirk Jedburgh A68 Alnwick A697
Irvine A71 A76 A701 A7 Hawick A68 A1
Troon Prestwick Ayr A70 New Cumnock Cumnock A702 A74(M) Moffat Langholm Otterburn Morpeth A696 A1
Maybole A713 Thornhill A76 A701 Lockerbie Langholm Corbridge A69 Gosfo Gateshe
Girvan A714 New Galloway A712 Dumfries A75 Longtown Brampton Hexham A695 Consett Star
Dalmellington A702 Annan A689 Carlisle A689 Alston Durh
Cairnryan Newton Stewart A75 Castle Douglas Solway Firth A596 Maryport A595 A66 Penrith Bishop Auckland A688
Stranraer A75 Cockermouth A66 M6 A686 Barnard Castle
Workington A5086 A66 Keswick A591 Brough A66 Richmond
Egremont A595 Ambleside Windermere A685 Leyburn
Ravenglass Kendal Sedbergh A684
Millom A590 Kirkby Lonsdale M6 A590
Barrow-in-Furness A590 A6 A65 Skipton Ha
Morecambe A683 Settle A65 Ilkley Otl
Heysham Lancaster M6 Keighley Bingley Shi
Fleetwood A682 Clitheroe A59 Burnley Nelson A650 BRADFORD
Blackpool A585 A6 Preston Blackburn Accrington Halifax Brigh
M55 M65 Todmorden A646 Dev
Southport A570 M61 M66 Rochdale M62 Huddo
Ormskirk A59 Skelmersdale Bolton Bury Middleton Oldham A628
Formby M58 Wigan A580 Salford MANCHESTER Glossop Sh
Crosby St Helens A58 Stockport
Bootle LIVERPOOL Warrington M60 A6
Birkenhead Widnes Altrincham A623 Buxton
Bebington Runcorn Knutsford Manchester Bakewell Ma
M53 A57 Northwich A556 A537 A537 Macclesfield
Ellesmere Port A54
Holywell Flint Chester Sandbach A50 Congleton Leek
Queensferry Mold Crewe Kidsgrove
Denbigh A494 Nantwich NEWCASTLE-under-Lyme STOKE-ON-TRENT
Ruthin A525 A41 A51 A52
Wrexham A49 A53 Stone Uttoxete
Holyhead Anglesey A5025 Llandudno Colwyn Bay Rhyl Prestatyn A548 A534 Market Drayton A50
Bangor Conwy Abergele A55 Whitchurch A495 Newport A518 Stafford
Bethesda A55 A5 Newport A442 M6
Caernarfon A4086 Betws-y-coed A5 Llangollen A5 Shrewsbury A5 Telford M54 Cannock A34 Rugeley
Ffestiniog A470 Bala A494 A458 Welshpool A458 A458 Church Stretton A442 WOLVERHAMPTON Brownhills Lichf
Porthmadog A497 Pwllheli Abersoch A496 Barmouth Dolgellau Llangurig A489 Newtown Caersws Bridgnorth A458 Dudley Walsall M6
Aberdyfi A493 Machynlleth A470 A483 A488 Ludlow A449 Kidderminster BIRM
Cardigan Bay Aberystwyth A44 Rhayader Knighton A49 Leominster Stourbridge Solihull M42
Aberaeron A487 A485 Llandrindod Wells A483 Kington Bromyard A456 Bromsgrove Birmingham
Tregaron A485 Builth Wells A470 Leominster A44 Great Malvern Droitwich M5 Redditch War
Cardigan A487 A486 Lampeter A482 A438 A4112 A4103 Worcester A422 Strat upon-Av Evesham
ROSSLARE

IRISH SEA

Isle of Man A3 Ramsey Peel A4 A1 A2 A3 A5 Douglas Castletown

LARNE BELFAST BELFAST summer only DUBLIN DUBLIN DUN LAOGHAIRE

Holyhead

New Harbour
SALT ISLAND TERMINAL
Outer Harbour
BEACH NEWRY ST
PORTH-Y-FELIN AVENUE NORTH ROAD WEST ST
Admiralty Pier
SOUTH STACK RD
VICTORIA RD
Harbour
New Fish Quay
HOLYHEAD STATION
P
FERRY TERMINAL
PLAS ROAD LONDON ROAD
PENRHOS STANLEY HOSPITAL
PORTHDAFARCH
0   500 metres
BANGOR   ABL

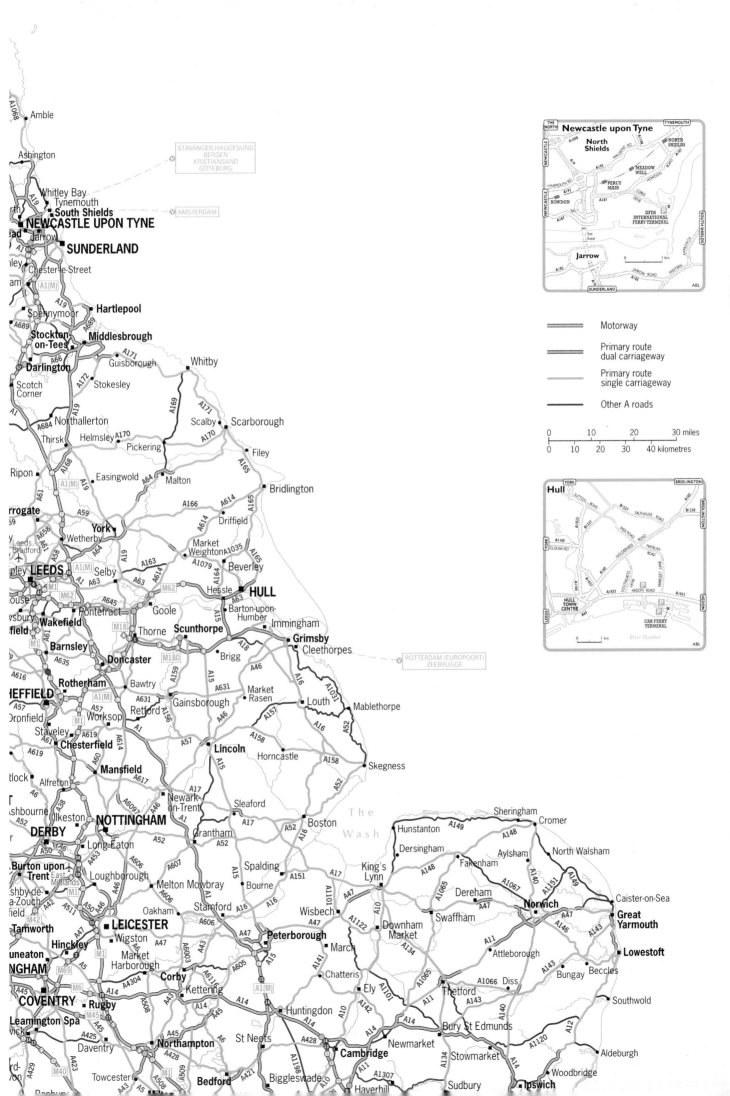

motorways – restricted junctions

Motorway junctions which have access and exit restrictions,
as shown by on atlas pages
(Motorways and Service Areas booklet also available tel: **0870 5500 600**)

M1 LONDON–LEEDS

Junction		
2 (pg 21)	Northbound	No exit. Access only from A1 *(northbound)*
	Southbound	No access. Exit only to A1 *(southbound)*
4 (pg 21)	Northbound	No exit. Access only from A41 *(northbound)*
	Southbound	No access. Exit only to A41 *(southbound)*
6A (pg 20)	Northbound	No exit. Access only from M25
	Southbound	No access. Exit only to M25
7 (pg 20)	Northbound	No exit. Access only from M10
	Southbound	No access. Exit only to M10
17 (pg 41)	Northbound	No access. Exit only to M45
	Southbound	No exit. Access only from M45
19 (pg 41)	Northbound	Exit only to northbound M6
	Southbound	No access from A14. Access only from M6
21A (pg 41)	Northbound	No access. Exit only to A46
	Southbound	No exit. Access only from A46
23A (pg 41)	Northbound	No exit. Access only from A42
	Southbound	No access. Exit only to A42
24A (pg 41)	Northbound	No exit. Access only from A50
	Southbound	No access. Exit only to A50
34 (pg 51)	Staggered junction; follow signs	
	Northbound	No restriction
	Southbound	No restriction
35A (pg 51)	Northbound	No access. Exit only to A616
	Southbound	No exit. Access only from A616
43 (pg 58)	Northbound	No access. Exit only to M621
	Southbound	No exit. Access only from M621
48 (pg 60)	Northbound	No exit. Access only from A1(M)
	Southbound	No access. Exit only to A1(M)

M2 ROCHESTER–FAVERSHAM

Junction		
1 (pg 22)	Westbound	Exit only to A289 *(eastbound)*
	Eastbound	Access only from A289 *(westbound)*

M3 SUNBURY–SOUTHAMPTON

Junction		
8 (pg 19)	Southwestbound	No access. Exit only to A303
	Northeastbound	No exit. Access only from A303
10 (pg 9)	Southwestbound	No exit. Access only from Winchester & A31
	Northeastbound	No access. Exit only to Winchester & A31
11 (pg 9)	Staggered junction; follow signs	
	Southwestbound	No restriction
	Northeastbound	No restriction
13 (pg 9)	Southwestbound	Access only to M27 *(westbound)* & A33
	Northeastbound	No restriction
14 (pg 9)	Southwestbound	No access. Exit only to M27 *(eastbound)* & A33
	Northeastbound	No exit. Access only

M4 LONDON–SOUTH WALES

Junction		
1 (pg 21)	Westbound	Access only from A4 *(westbound)*
	Eastbound	Exit only to A4 *(eastbound)*
2 (pg 21)	Staggered junction; follow signs	
	Westbound	No restriction
	Eastbound	No restriction
4A (pg 20)	Southbound	No exit to A4 *(westbound)*
	Northbound	No restriction
21 (pg 28)	Westbound	No access. Exit only to M48
	Eastbound	No exit. Access only from M48
23 (pg 28)	Westbound	No exit. Access only from M48
	Eastbound	No access. Exit only to M48
25 (pg 28)	Westbound	No access. Exit only to B4596
	Eastbound	No exit. Access only from B4596
25A (pg 28)	Westbound	No access. Exit only to A4042
	Eastbound	No exit. Access only from A4042
29 (pg 28)	Westbound	No access. Exit only to A48(M)
	Eastbound	No exit. Access only from A48(M)
38 (pg 26)	Westbound	No access. Exit only to A48
	Eastbound	No restriction
39 (pg 26)	Westbound	No exit. Access only from A48
	Eastbound	No access or exit
41 (pg 26)	Staggered junction; follow signs	
	Westbound	No restriction
	Eastbound	No restriction
42 (pg 26)	Staggered junction; follow signs	
	Westbound	Exit only to A483
	Eastbound	Access only from A483

M5 BIRMINGHAM–EXETER

Junction		
10 (pg 29)	Southwestbound	No access. Exit only to A4019
	Northeastbound	No exit. Access only from A4019
11A (pg 29)	Southwestbound	Exit only to A417 *(eastbound)*
	Northeastbound	Access only from A417 *(westbound)*
12 (pg 29)	Southwestbound	No exit. Access only from A38
	Northeastbound	No access. Exit only
18A (pg 28)	Southwestbound	No exit. Access only from M49
	Northeastbound	Exit only to M49

M6 RUGBY–CARLISLE

Junction		
4 (pg 40)	Northwestbound	No access from M42 *(southbound)*. No exit to M42 *(northbound)*
	Southeastbound	No access from M42 *(southbound)*. No exit to M42
4A (pg 40)	Northwestbound	No exit. Access only from M42 *(southbound)*
	Southeastbound	No access. Exit only to M42
5 (pg 40)	Northwestbound	No access. Exit only to A452
	Southeastbound	No exit. Access only from A452
10A (pg 40)	Northbound	No access. Exit only to M54
	Southbound	No exit. Access only from M54
20 (with M56) (pg 57)	Staggered junction; follow signs	
	Northbound	No restriction
	Southbound	No restriction
24 (pg 57)	Northbound	No exit. Access only from A58
	Southbound	No access. Exit only to A58
25 (pg 57)	Northbound	No access. Exit only
	Southbound	No exit. Access only
29 (pg 57)	Northbound	No direct access, use adjacent slip road to junction 29A
	Southbound	No direct exit, use adjacent slip road from junction 29A
29A (pg 57)	Northbound	No direct exit, use adjacent slip road from junction 29
	Southbound	No direct access, use adjacent slip road to junction 29
30 (pg 57)	Northbound	No exit. Access only from M61
	Southbound	No access. Exit only to M61
31A (pg 57)	Northbound	No access. Exit only
	Southbound	No exit. Access only

M8 EDINBURGH–GLASGOW–BISHOPTON

Junction		
3A (pg 86)	Staggered junction; follow signs	
	Westbound	No restriction
	Eastbound	No restriction
8 (pg 85)	Westbound	No access from M73 *(southbound)* or from A8 *(eastbound)* & A89
	Eastbound	No exit to M73 *(northbound)* or to A8 *(westbound)* & A89
9 (pg 85)	Westbound	No exit. Access only
	Eastbound	No access. Exit only
13 (pg 85)	Westbound	Access only from M80 *(southbound)*
	Eastbound	Exit only to M80 *(northbound)*
14 (pg 85)	Westbound	No exit. Access only
	Eastbound	No access. Exit only
16 (pg 85)	Westbound	No access. Exit only to A804
	Eastbound	No exit. Access only from A879
17 (pg 85)	Westbound	Exit only to A82
	Eastbound	No restriction
18 (pg 85)	Westbound	Access only from A82 *(eastbound)*
	Eastbound	No access. Exit only to A814
19 (pg 85)	Westbound	No access from A814 *(westbound)*
	Eastbound	No access. Exit only to A814 *(westbound)*
20 (pg 85)	Westbound	No access. Exit only
	Eastbound	No exit. Access only
21 (pg 85)	Westbound	No exit. Access only
	Eastbound	No access. Exit only to A8
22 (pg 85)	Westbound	No access. Exit only to M77 *(southbound)*
	Eastbound	No exit. Access only from M77 *(northbound)*
23 (pg 85)	Westbound	No access. Exit only to B768
	Eastbound	No exit. Access only from B768
25 (pg 85)	Westbound	No access/exit from/to A8
	Eastbound	No access/exit from/to A8
25A (pg 85)	Westbound	No access. Exit only
	Eastbound	No exit. Access only
28 (pg 84)	Westbound	No access. Exit only
	Eastbound	No exit. Access only

M9 EDINBURGH–DUNBLANE

Junction		
1A (pg 86)	Northwestbound	No access. Exit only to A8000
	Southeastbound	No exit. Access only from A8000
2 (pg 86)	Northwestbound	No exit. Access only
	Southeastbound	No access. Exit only
3 (pg 86)	Northwestbound	No access. Exit only
	Southeastbound	No exit. Access only
6 (pg 85)	Northwestbound	No exit. Access only from A904
	Southeastbound	No access. Exit only to A905
8 (pg 85)	Northwestbound	No access. Exit only to M876 *(southwestbound)*
	Southeastbound	No exit. Access only from M876 *(northeastbound)*

M10 ST ALBANS–M1

Junction		
with M1 (jct 7) (pg 20)	Northwestbound	Exit only to M1 *(northbound)*
	Southeastbound	Access only from M1 *(southbound)*

M11 LONDON–CAMBRIDGE

Junction		
4 (pg 21)	Northbound	Access only from A406
	Southbound	Exit only to A406
5 (pg 21)	Northbound	No access. Exit only to A1168
	Southbound	No exit. Access only from A1168
9 (pg 33)	Northbound	No access. Exit only to A11
	Southbound	No exit. Access only from A11
13 (pg 33)	Northbound	No access Exit only to A1303
	Southbound	No exit. Access only from A1303
14 (pg 33)	Northbound	Exit only to A14 *(eastbound)*
	Southbound	Access only from A14

M20 SWANLEY–FOLKESTONE

Junction		
2 (pg 22)	Staggered junction; follow signs	
	Southeastbound	No access. Exit only to A227
	Northwestbound	No exit. Access only from A227
3 (pg 22)	Southeastbound	No exit. Access only from M26 *(eastbound)*
	Northwestbound	No access. Exit only to M26 *(westbound)*
5 (pg 22)	Southeastbound	For access follow signs. Exit only to A20
	Northwestbound	No exit. Access only from A20
6 (pg 22)	Southeastbound	For exit follow signs
	Northwestbound	No restriction
11A (pg 13)	Southeastbound	No access. Exit only
	Northwestbound	No exit. Access only

M23 HOOLEY–CRAWLEY

Junction		
7 (pg 21)	Southbound	Access only from A23 *(southbound)*
	Northbound	Exit only to A23 *(northbound)*
10A (pg 11)	Southbound	No access. Exit only to B2036
	Northbound	No exit. Access only from B2036

M25 LONDON ORBITAL

(refer also to atlas pg xii)

Junction		
1B (pg 21)	Clockwise	No access (use slip road via jct 2).Exit only to A225 & A296
	Anticlockwise	No exit (use slip road via jct 2). Access only from A225 & A296
5 (pg 21)	Clockwise	No exit to M26
	Anticlockwise	No access from M26
9 (pg 21)	Staggered junction; follow signs	
	Clockwise	No restriction
	Anticlockwise	No restriction
19 (pg 20)	Clockwise	No access. Exit only to A41
	Anticlockwise	No exit. Access only from A41
21 (pg 20)	Clockwise	Access only from M1 *(southbound)*. Exit only to M1 *(northbound)*
	Anticlockwise	Access only from M1 *(southbound)*. Exit only to M1 *(northbound)*
21A (pg 20)	Clockwise	No link from M1 to A405
	Anticlockwise	No link from M1 to A405
31 (pg 21)	Clockwise	No exit (use slip road via jct 30)
	Anticlockwise	For access follow signs

M26 SEVENOAKS–WROTHAM

Junction		
with M25 (jct 5) (pg 21)	Eastbound	Access only from anticlockwise M25 *(eastbound)*
	Westbound	Exit only to clockwise M25 *(westbound)*
with M20 (jct 3) (pg 22)	Eastbound	Exit only to M20 *(southeastbound)*
	Westbound	Access only from M20 *(northwestbound)*

M27 CADNAM–PORTSMOUTH

Junction		
4 (pg 9)	Staggered junction; follow signs	
	Eastbound	Access only from M3 *(southbound)*. Exit only to M3 *(northbound)*
	Westbound	Access only from M3 *(southbound)*. Exit only to M3 *(northbound)*
10 (pg 9)	Eastbound	No exit. Access only from A32
	Westbound	No access. Exit only to A32
12 (pg 9)	Staggered junction; follow signs	
	Eastbound	Access only from M275 *(northbound)*
	Westbound	Exit only to M275 *(southbound)*

M40 LONDON–BIRMINGHAM

Junction		
3 (pg 20)	Northwestbound	No access. Exit only to A40
	Southeastbound	No exit. Access only from A40
7 (pg 31)	Northwestbound	No access. Exit only to A329
	Southeastbound	No exit. Access only from A329
8 (pg 31)	Northwestbound	No access. Exit only to A40
	Southeastbound	No exit. Access only from A40
13 (pg 30)	Northwestbound	No access. Exit only to A452
	Southeastbound	No exit. Access only from A452
14 (pg 30)	Northwestbound	No exit. Access only from A452
	Southeastbound	No access. Exit only to A452
16 (pg 40)	Northwestbound	No exit. Access only from A3400
	Southeastbound	No access. Exit only to A3400

M42 BROMSGROVE-MEASHAM

Junction		
1 (pg 40)	Northeastbound	No exit. Access only from A38
	Southwestbound	No access. Exit only to A38
7 (pg 40)	Northeastbound	No access. Exit only to M6 *(northwestbound)*
	Southwestbound	No exit. Access only from M6 *(northwestbound)*
7A (pg 40)	Northeastbound	No access. Exit only to M6 *(southeastbound)*
	Southwestbound	No access or exit
8 (pg 40)	Northeastbound	No exit. Access only from M6 *(southeastbound)*
	Southwestbound	No access. Exit only to M6 *(northwestbound)*

M45 COVENTRY-M1

Junction		
unnumbered (Dunchurch) (pg 41)	Eastbound	No access. Exit only to A45 & B4429
	Westbound	No exit. Access only from A45 & B4429
with M1 (jct 17) (pg 41)	Eastbound	Exit only to M1 *(southbound)*
	Westbound	Access only from M1 *(northbound)*

M53 MERSEY TUNNEL-CHESTER

Junction		
1 (pg 56)	Southwestbound	No exit. Access only from A554 & A5139
	Northeastbound	No access. Exit only to A554 & A5139
11 (pg 48)	Southeastbound	Access only from M56 *(westbound)*. Exit only to M56 *(eastbound)*
	Northwestbound	Access only from M56 *(westbound)*. Exit only to M56 *(eastbound)*

M54 TELFORD

Junction		
with M6 (jct 10A) (pg 40)	Westbound	No exit. Access only from M6 *(northbound)*
	Eastbound	No access. Exit only to M6 *(southbound)*

M56 NORTH CHESHIRE

Junction		
1 (pg 57)	Westbound	No exit. Access only from M60 *(westbound)*
	Eastbound	No access. Exit only to M60 *(eastbound)* & A34 *(northbound)*
2 (pg 57)	Westbound	No access. Exit only to A560
	Eastbound	No exit. Access only from A560
3 (pg 57)	Westbound	No exit. Access only from A5103
	Eastbound	No access. Exit only to A5103 & A560
4 (pg 57)	Westbound	No access. Exit only
	Eastbound	No exit. Access only
7 (pg 57)	Staggered junction; follow signs	
	Westbound	No restriction
	Eastbound	No restriction
9 (pg 57)	Westbound	Exit to M6 *(southbound)* via A50 interchange
	Eastbound	Access from M6 *(northbound)* via A50 interchange
15 (pg 48)	Westbound	No access. Exit only to M53
	Eastbound	No exit. Access only from M53

M57 LIVERPOOL OUTER RING ROAD

Junction		
3 (pg 56)	Northwestbound	No exit. Access only from A526
	Southeastbound	No access. Exit only to A526
5 (pg 56)	Northwestbound	No exit. Access only from A580 *(westbound)*
	Southeastbound	No access. Exit only to A580

M58 LIVERPOOL-WIGAN

Junction		
1 (pg 56)	Eastbound	No exit. Access only
	Westbound	No access. Exit only

M60 MANCHESTER ORBITAL

(refer also to atlas pg xiii)

Junction		
2 (pg 57)	Clockwise	No exit. Access only from A560
	Anticlockwise	No access. Exit only to A560
3 (pg 57)	Clockwise	No access from M56
	Anticlockwise	No exit. Access only from A34 *(northbound)*
4 (pg 57)	Clockwise	Access only from A34 *(northbound)*. Exit only to M56
	Anticlockwise	Access only from M56 *(eastbound)*. Exit only to A34 *(southbound)*
5 (pg 57)	Clockwise	Access/exit only from/to A5103 *(northbound)*
	Anticlockwise	Access/exit only from/to A5103 *(southbound)*
7 (pg 57)	Clockwise	No access (use adjacent slip road to junction 8). Exit only to A56
	Anticlockwise	No exit (use adjacent slip road from junction 8). Access only from A56
14 (pg 57)	Clockwise	No exit. Access to M60 from A580 *(eastbound)*. Access to M61 *(westbound)* from A580 *(westbound)*
	Anticlockwise	No access. Exit from M61 *(eastbound)* to A580 *(eastbound)*. No exit from M60
15 (pg 57)	Clockwise	Access only from M61 *(eastbound)*. Exit to M61 *(westbound)*
	Anticlockwise	No access. Exit to M61 *(westbound)* & A580 *(westbound)*
16 (pg 57)	Clockwise	No exit. Access only from A666
	Anticlockwise	No access. Exit only to A666
20 (pg 57)	Clockwise	No access. Exit only to A664
	Anticlockwise	No exit. Access only from A664
22 (pg 57)	Clockwise	No restriction
	Anticlockwise	No access. Exit only to A62
25 (pg 57)	Clockwise	No access. Exit only to A6017
	Anticlockwise	No restriction
26 (pg 57)	Clockwise	No restriction
	Anticlockwise	No access or exit
27 (pg 57)	Clockwise	No exit. Access only from A626
	Anticlockwise	No access. Exit only to A626

M61 GREATER MANCHESTER-PRESTON

Junction		
1 (pg 57)	No restriction; follow signs	
2 (pg 57)	No restriction; follow signs	
3 (pg 57)	Northwestbound	No access or exit
	Southeastbound	No access. Exit only to A660
with M6 (jct 30) (pg 57)	Northwestbound	Exit only to M6 *(northbound)*
	Southeastbound	Access only from M6 *(southbound)*

M62 LIVERPOOL-HUMBERSIDE

Junction		
23 (pg 58)	Eastbound	No access. Exit only to A640
	Westbound	No exit. Access only from A640

M65 PRESTON-COLNE

Junction		
1 (pg 57)	Northeastbound	Access and exit to M6 only
	Southwestbound	Access and exit to M6 only
9 (pg 57)	Northeastbound	No access. Exit only to A679
	Southwestbound	No exit. Access only from A679
11 (pg 57)	Northeastbound	No exit. Access only
	Southwestbound	No access. Exit only

M66 GREATER MANCHESTER

Junction		
with A56 (pg 57)	Southbound	Access only from A56 *(southbound)*
	Northbound	Exit only to A56 *(northbound)*
1 (pg 57)	Southbound	No exit. Access only from A56
	Northbound	No access. Exit only to A56

M67 HYDE BYPASS

Junction		
1 (pg 50)	Eastbound	No access. Exit only to A6017
	Westbound	No exit. Access only from A6017
2 (pg 50)	Eastbound	No exit. Access only
	Westbound	No access. Exit only to A57
3 (pg 50)	Eastbound	No restriction
	Westbound	No access. Exit only to A627

M69 COVENTRY-LEICESTER

Junction		
2 (pg 41)	Northbound	No exit. Access only from B4669
	Southbound	No access. Exit only to B4669

M73 EAST OF GLASGOW

Junction		
2 (pg 85)	Northbound	No access from or to A89. No access from M8 *(eastbound)*
	Southbound	No access from or to A89. No exit to M8 *(westbound)*
3 (pg 85)	Northbound	Exit only to A80 *(northeastbound)*
	Southbound	Access only from A80 *(southwestbound)*

M74 GLASGOW-ABINGTON

Junction		
2 (pg 85)	Southbound	No exit. Access only from A763
	Northbound	No access. Exit only to A763
3 (pg 85)	Southbound	No access. Exit only
	Northbound	Exit via junction 4. Access only
7 (pg 77)	Southbound	No access. Exit only to A72
	Northbound	No exit. Access only from A72
9 (pg 77)	Southbound	No access. Exit only to B7078
	Northbound	No access or exit
10 (pg 77)	Southbound	No exit. Access only from B7078
	Northbound	No restrictions
11 (pg 77)	Southbound	No access. Exit only to B7078
	Northbound	No exit. Access only from B7078
12 (pg 77)	Southbound	No exit. Access only from A70
	Northbound	No access. Exit only to A70

A74(M) ABINGTON-GRETNA

Junction		
14 (pg 77)	Staggered junction; follow signs	
	Southbound	No restriction
	Northbound	No restriction
18 (pg 79)	Southbound	No exit. Access only from B723
	Northbound	No access. Exit only to B723
21 (pg 71)	Southbound	No access. Exit only to B6357
	Northbound	No exit. Access only from B6357
with B7076 (pg 71)	Southbound	No exit. Access only
	Northbound	No access. Exit only
Gretna Green (pg 71)	Southbound	No access. Exit only (use B7076 through Gretna to access A75)
	Northbound	No exit. Access only
with A75 (pg 71)	Southbound	No exit. Access only from A75
	Northbound	No access. Exit only to A75
with A6071 (pg 71)	Southbound	Exit only to A74 *(southbound)*
	Northbound	Access only from A74 *(northbound)*

M77 WEST OF GLASGOW

Junction		
with M8 (pg 85)	Southbound	No access from M8 *(eastbound)*
	Northbound	No exit to M8 *(westbound)*
4 (pg 85)	Southbound	No access. Exit only
	Northbound	No exit. Access only
with A77 (pg 85)	Southbound	Exit only to A77 *(southbound)*
	Northbound	Access only from A77 *(northbound)*

M80 STEPPS BYPASS

Junction		
3 (pg 85)	Northeastbound	No access. Exit only
	Southwestbound	No exit. Access only

M80 BONNYBRIDGE-STIRLING

Junction		
5 (pg 85)	Northbound	No access. Exit only to M876 *(northeastbound)*
	Southbound	No exit. Access only from M876 *(southwestbound)*

M90 FORTH ROAD BRIDGE-PERTH

Junction		
2A (pg 86)	Northbound	No access. Exit only to A92 *(eastbound)*
	Southbound	No exit. Access only from A92 *(westbound)*
7 (pg 86)	Northbound	No exit. Access only from A91
	Southbound	No access. Exit only to A911
8 (pg 86)	Northbound	No access. Exit only to A91
	Southbound	No exit. Access only from A91
10 (pg 92)	Northbound	No access from A912. No exit to A912 *(southbound)*
	Southbound	No access from A912 *(northbound)*. No exit to A912

M180 SOUTH HUMBERSIDE

Junction		
1 (pg 59)	Eastbound	No access. Exit only to A18
	Westbound	No exit. Access only from A18

M606 BRADFORD SPUR

Junction		
2 (pg 58)	Northbound	No access. Exit only
	Southbound	No restriction

M621 LEEDS-M1

Junction		
2A (pg 58)	Eastbound	No exit. Access only
	Westbound	No access. Exit only
4 (pg 58)	Southeastbound	No access. Exit only
	Northwestbound	No restriction
5 (pg 58)	Southeastbound	No exit. Access only
	Northwestbound	No access. Exit only
6 (pg 58)	Southeastbound	No access. Exit only
	Northwestbound	No exit. Access only
with M1 (jct 43) (pg 58)	Southbound	Exit only to M1 *(southbound)*
	Northbound	Access only from M1 *(northbound)*

M876 BONNYBRIDGE-KINCARDINE BRIDGE

Junction		
with M80 (jct 5) (pg 85)	Northeastbound	Access only from M80 *(northbound)*
	Southwestbound	Exit only to M80 *(southbound)*
2 (pg 85)	Northeastbound	No access. Exit only to A9
	Southwestbound	No exit. Access only from A9
with M9 (jct 8) (pg 85)	Northeastbound	Exit only to M9 *(eastbound)*
	Southwestbound	Access only from M9 (westbound)

A1(M) SOUTH MIMMS-BALDOCK

Junction		
2 (pg 21)	Northbound	No access. Exit only to A1001
	Southbound	No exit. Access only from A1001
3 (pg 21)	Northbound	No restriction
	Southbound	No access. Exit only to A414
5 (pg 21)	Northbound	No exit. Access only
	Southbound	No access or exit

A1(M) ALCONBURY-PETERBOROUGH

Junction		
14 (pg 32)	Staggered junction; follow signs	
	Northbound	No restriction
	Southbound	No restriction
15 (pg 42)	Staggered junction; follow signs	
	Northbound	No restriction
	Southbound	No restriction

A1(M) EAST OF LEEDS

Junction		
44 (pg 59)	Northbound	Access only from M1 *(northbound)*
	Southbound	Exit only to M1 *(southbound)*

A1(M) SCOTCH CORNER-TYNESIDE

Junction		
57 (with A66(M)) (pg 65)	Northbound	No access. Exit only to A66(M) *(eastbound)*
	Southbound	No exit. Access only from A66(M) *(westbound)*
65 (with A194(M)) (pg 73)	Northbound	No access. Exit only to A194(M) & A1 *(northbound)*
	Southbound	No exit. Access only from A194(M) *(southbound)*

A3(M) HORNDEAN-HAVANT

Junction		
1 (pg 10)	Southbound	No access. Exit only to A3
	Northbound	No exit. Access only from A3
4 (pg 10)	Southbound	No exit. Access only
	Northbound	No access. Exit only

A48(M) CARDIFF SPUR

Junction		
29 (with M4) (pg 28)	Westbound	Access only from M4 *(westbound)*
	Eastbound	Exit only to M4 *(eastbound)*
29A (pg 28)	Westbound	Exit only to A48 *(westbound)*
	Eastbound	Access only from A48 *(eastbound)*

A66(M) DARLINGTON SPUR

Junction		
with A1(M) (jct 57) (pg 65)	Eastbound	Access only from A1(M) *(northbound)*
	Westbound	Exit only to A1(M) *(southbound)*

A194(M) TYNESIDE

Junction		
with A1(M) (jct 65) (pg 73)	Northbound	Access only from A1(M) *(northbound)*
	Southbound	Exit only to A1(M) *(southbound)*

M25 London orbital motorway

Refer also to atlas page 20–21

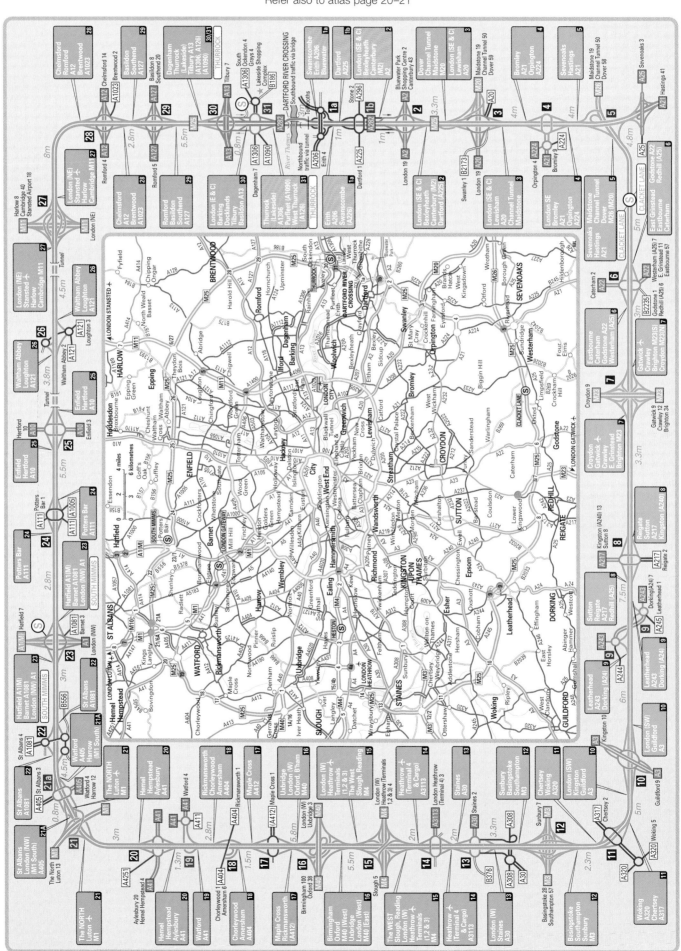

M60 Manchester orbital motorway

Refer also to atlas page 57

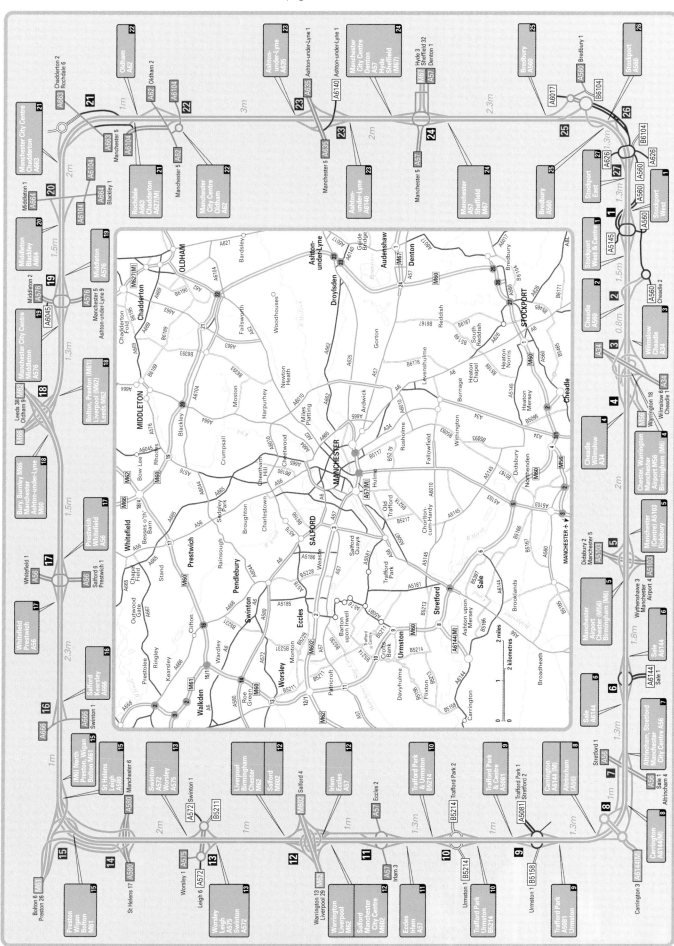

map symbols

Motoring information

Motorway with number	Unclassified road single/dual carriageway	Vehicle ferry	AA telephone
Motorway junction with and without number	Roundabout	Railway line/in tunnel	Urban area and village
Restricted motorway junctions	Interchange/junction	Railway station and level crossing	Spot height in metres
Motorway service area	Narrow primary/other A/B road with passing places (Scotland)	Tourist railway	Pass
Motorway and junction under construction	Road under construction	Airport	River, canal, lake
Primary route single/dual carriageway	Road tunnel	Heliport	Sandy beach
Primary route service area	Steep gradient (arrows point downhill)	International freight terminal	County/County Borough/Council Area boundary
Primary route destination	Road toll	Major shopping centre	National boundary
Other A road single/dual carriageway	Distance in miles between symbols	Park and Ride location (at least 6 days)	Page overlap and number
B road single/dual carriageway			

Tourist information Places of interest are also shown on town plans. See pages 117–129

Tourist Information Centre	Agricultural showground	Prehistoric monument	Ski slope – natural
Tourist Information Centre (seasonal)	Theme park	Battle site with year	Ski slope – artificial
Visitor or heritage centre	Farm or animal centre	Steam centre (railway)	National Trust property
Abbey, cathedral or priory	Zoological or wildlife collection	Cave	National Trust for Scotland property
Ruined abbey, cathedral or priory	Bird collection	Windmill	Other place of interest
Castle	Aquarium	Monument	Boxed symbols indicate attractions within urban areas
Historic house or building	Nature reserve	Golf course	National Park (England & Wales)
Museum or art gallery	RSPB site	County cricket ground	National Scenic Area (Scotland)
Industrial interest	Forest drive	Rugby Union national stadium	Forest Park
Aqueduct or viaduct	National trail	International athletics stadium	Heritage coast
Garden	Viewpoint	Horse racing	Little Chef Restaurant (7am–10pm)
Arboretum	Picnic site	Show jumping/equestrian circuit	Travelodge
Vineyard	Hill-fort	Motor-racing circuit	Little Chef Restaurant and Travelodge
Country park	Roman antiquity	Air show venue	Granada Burger King site

XIV

Ireland

(see pages 112–115) For tourist information see opposite page

Motorway	National primary route (Republic of Ireland)	Primary route (Northern Ireland)	Road under construction
Motorway junction with and without number	National secondary route (Republic of Ireland)	A road (Northern Ireland)	Distance in miles between symbols
Restricted motorway junctions	Regional road (Republic of Ireland)	B road (Northern Ireland)	International boundary

1

District maps

(see pages 130–141) For tourist information see opposite page

Motorway	Unclassified road single/dual	Railway station	24-hour Accident & Emergency hospital
Motorway under construction	Road under construction	Inner London Regional Transport (LRT) station	Hospital
Primary route single/dual	Restricted road	Outer London Regional Transport (LRT) station	Crematorium
Other A road single/dual	Railway line/in tunnel	Railway station/LRT interchange	Shopping centre
B road single/dual	Tourist railway	Light railway/tramway station	Sports stadium

Central London

(see pages 142–151)

Motorway	Restricted road (access only/private)	Banned turn (restricted periods only)	Post Office
Primary route single/dual	Footpath	Ahead only	Police station
Other A road single/dual	Track	Mini-roundabout	24-hour Accident & Emergency hospital
B road single/dual	Pedestrian street	Barrier	Steps
Unclassified road single/dual	Railway line/in tunnel	Railway station	Church
Unclassified road wide/narrow	One-way street	London Regional Transport (LRT) station	Tourist Information Centre
Road under construction	Compulsory turn	Docklands Light Railway (DLR) station	Tourist Information Centre (seasonal)
Road tunnel wide/narrow	Banned turn	Parking	

Royal Parks (opening and closing times for traffic)

Green Park	Constitution Hill: closed Sundays, 08.00–dusk
Hyde Park	Open 05.00–midnight
Regent's Park	Open 05.00–midnight
St James's Park	The Mall: closed Sundays, 08.00–dusk

Traffic regulations in the City of London include security checkpoints and restrict the number of entry and exit points.

Note: Oxford Street is closed to through-traffic (except buses & taxis) 07.00–19.00, Monday–Saturday. Restricted parts of Frith Street/Old Compton Street are closed to vehicles 12.00–01.00 daily.

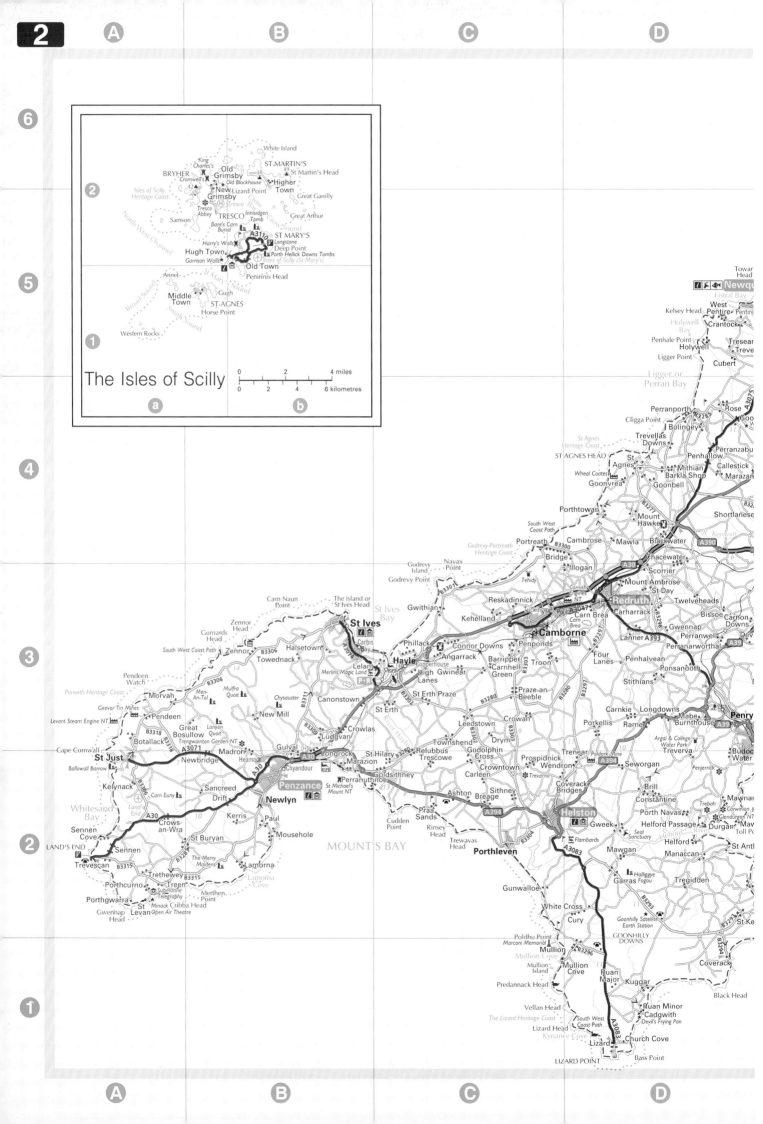

The Isles of Scilly

White Island
ST·MARTIN'S
'King Charles's
Old Grimsby
St Martin's Head
BRYHER
Cromwell's
Old Blockhouse
Lizard Point
Higher Town
New Grimsby
Great Ganilly
Isles of Scilly Heritage Coast
Tresco Abbey
TRESCO
Innisidgen Tomb
Great Arthur
Samson
Bant's Carn Burial
A3110
ST MARY'S
Harry's Walls
Longstone
Deep Point
Hugh Town
Porth Hellick Downs Tombs
Garrison Walls
Isles of Scilly (St Mary's)
Old Town
North West Channel
Annet
Peninnis Head
Towar Head
Middle Town
Gugh
ST·AGNES
Horse Point
Broad Sound
Smith Sound
St Mary's Sound
Western Rocks

0		2		4 miles
0	2	4		6 kilometres

a

b

Newqu
Fistral Bay
West Pentire
Pentire
Kelsey Head
Holywell Bay
Crantock
Penhale Point
Tresear
Treve
Holywell
Ligger Point
Cubert
Ligger or Perran Bay
Perranporth
Rose
Goo
Cligga Point
Bolingey
A3075
St Agnes Heritage Coast
Trevellas Downs
Perranzabu
ST AGNES HEAD
St Agnes
Penhallow
Wheal Coates
Mithian
Callestick
Marazan
Goonvrea
Barkla Shop
Goonbell
South West Coast Path
Mount Hawke
Shortlanes
Godrevy-Portreath Heritage Coast
Portreath
Cambrose
Mawla
Blackwater
A390
Godrevy Island
Navax Point
Bridge
Illogan
A30
Chacewater
Godrevy Point
Tehidy
Cornish Engines NT
Mount Ambrose
St Day
Scorrier
B3301
Reskadinnick
Redruth
Twelveheads
Carn Naun Point
The Island or St Ives Head
Gwithian
Tuckingmill
Pool A3047
Carn Brea
Carharrack
Bissoe
Carnon Downs
St Ives Bay
Kehelland
Camborne
Gwennap
Perranwell
St Ives
Penponds
Carn Brea
Zennor Head
Carbis Bay
Phillack
Lanner A393
Penhalvean
Gurnards Head
Connor Downs
Four Lanes
Ponsanooth
Dev
South West Coast Path
Zennor
B3306
Halsetown
Hayle
Angarrack
Barripper
Troon
Pendeen Watch
Towednack
Copperhouse
High Gwinear
Carnhell Green
Stithians
B3306
Lelant
Penwith Heritage Coast
Merlins Magic Land
Lanes
Praze-an-Beeble
Carnkie
Longdowns
Mabe
Penry
Morvah
Men-An-Tol
P+R
St Erth Praze
B3280
Burnthouse
A39
Geevor Tin Mines
Mulfra Quoit
Canonstown
Leedstown
Crowan
Porkellis
Ramel
Pendeen
Chysauster
St Erth
Argal & College Water Park
Treverva
Levant Steam Engine NT
Lanyon Quoit
New Mill
Crowlas
Townshend
Drym
Godolphin Cross
Trenear
Poldark Mine
Penjerrick
Great Bosullow
Trengwainton Garden NT
Ludgvan
Prospidnick
Wendron
Budoc
Botallack
B3318
Madron
Gulval
Longrock
Relubbus
Crowntown
Water
Cape Cornwall
A3071
Newbridge
Heamoor
A30
St Hilary
Trescowe
Carleen
Coverack Bridges
Brill
St Just
Chyandour
Marazan
Sithney
Constantine
Porth Navas
Mawnan
Ballowall Barrow
Penzance
Perranuthnoe
Goldsithney
Breage
Helston
Trebah
Glendurgan NT
Mav
Kelynack
Sancreed
Newlyn
St Michael's Mount NT
Ashton
A394
Gweek
Helford Passage
Durgan
Toll Po
Whitesand Bay
Drift
Praa Sands
Flambards
Seal Sanctuary
Helford
Carn Euny
Kerris
Paul
Cudden Point
Manaccan
St Antl
Sennen Cove
A30
Crows-an-Wra
Rinsey Head
Porthleven
Mawgan
St Buryan
Mousehole
Trewavas Head
A3083
Halliggye Garras Fogou
Tregidden
LAND'S END
Sennen
MOUNT'S BAY
Gunwalloe
Trevescan
The Merry Maidens
Lamorna
White Cross
Porthcurno
Tretheway
Treen
B3315
Lamorna Cove
Cury
Goonhilly Satellite Earth Station
St Ke
Porthgwarra
Merthen Point
Poldhu Point
GOONHILLY DOWNS
Gwennap Head
St Levan
Submarine Telegraphy
Marconi Memorial
B3296
Minack Cribba Head Open Air Theatre
Mullion
Mullion Cove
Mullion Island
Mullion Cove
Ruan Major
Kuggar
Coverack
Predannack Head
Ruan Minor
Black Head
Vellan Head
Cadgwith
The Lizard Heritage Coast
South West Coast Path
Devil's Frying Pan
Lizard Head
A3083
Church Cove
Kynance Cove
Lizard
Bass Point
LIZARD POINT

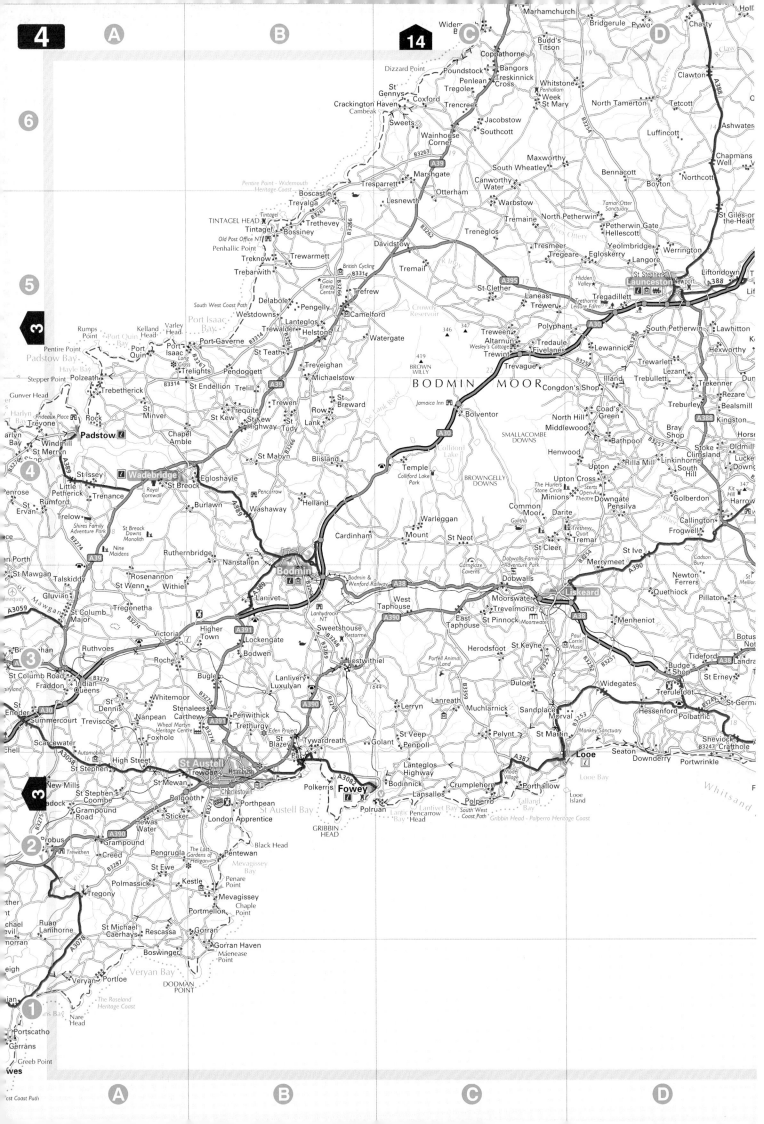

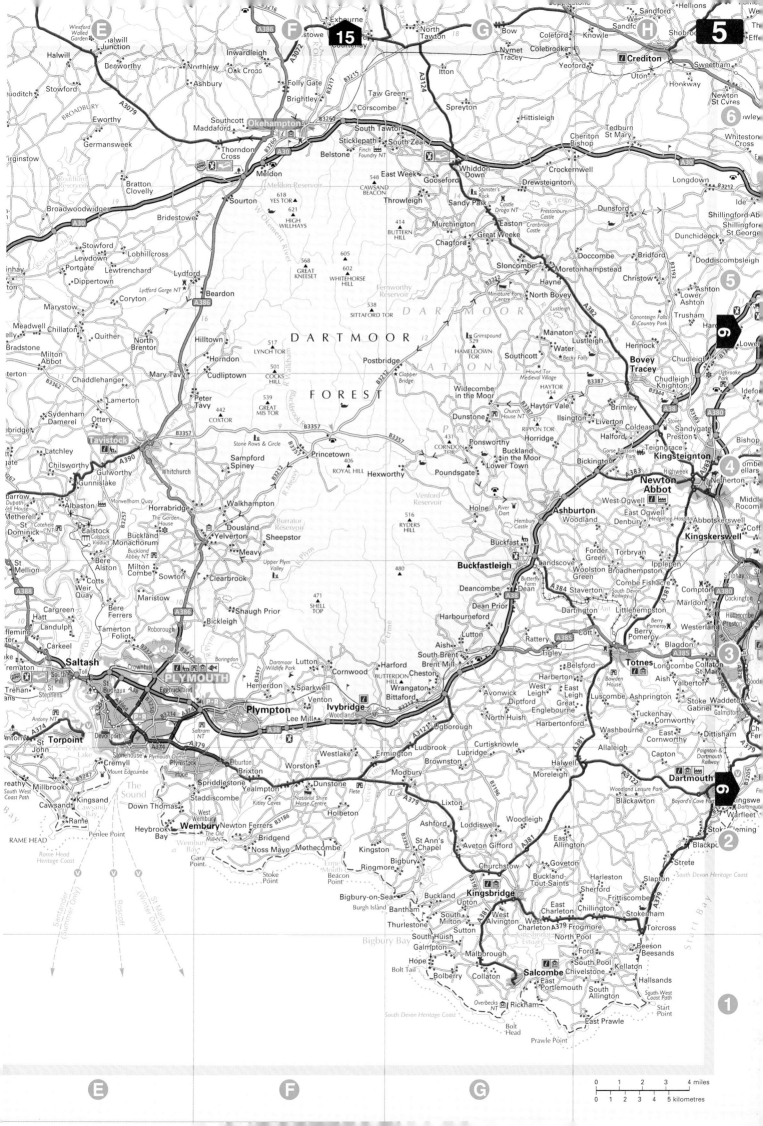

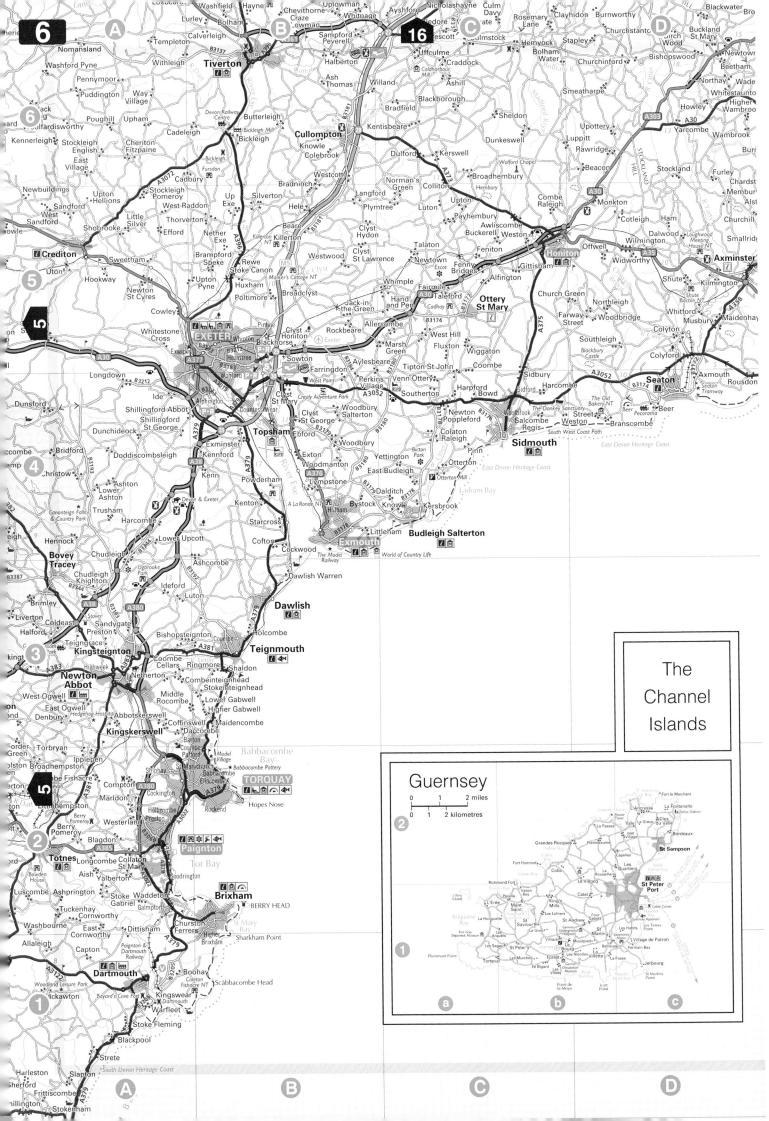

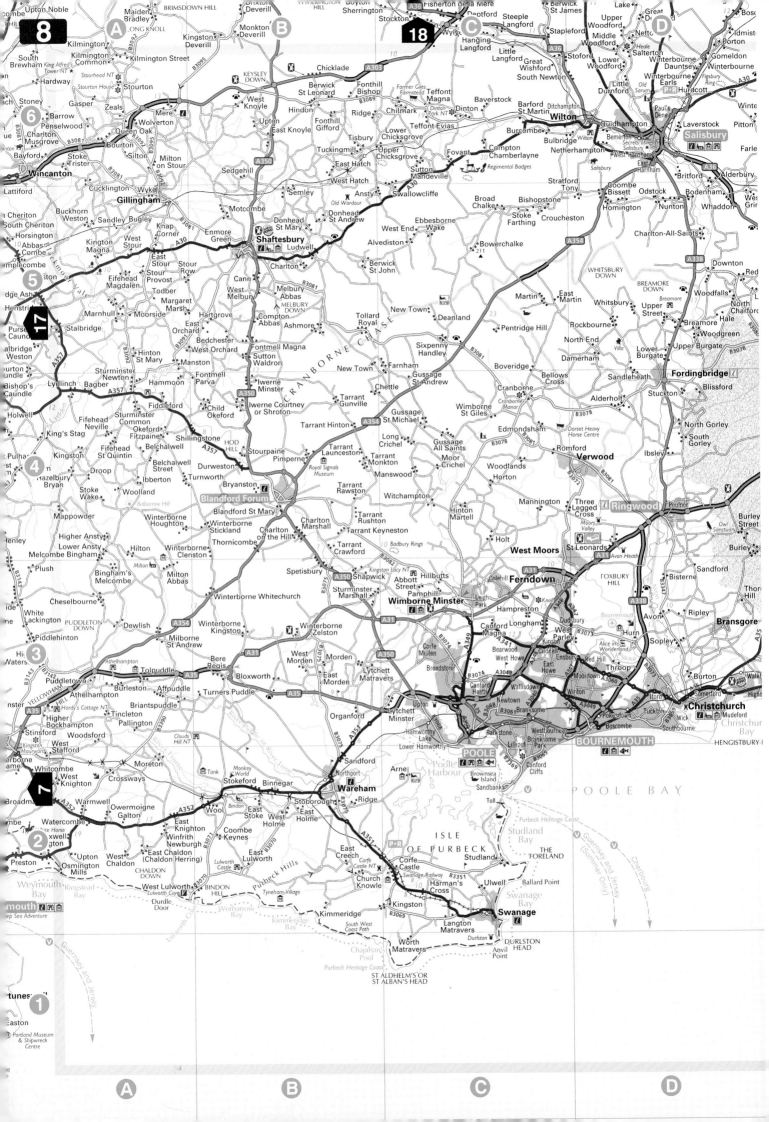

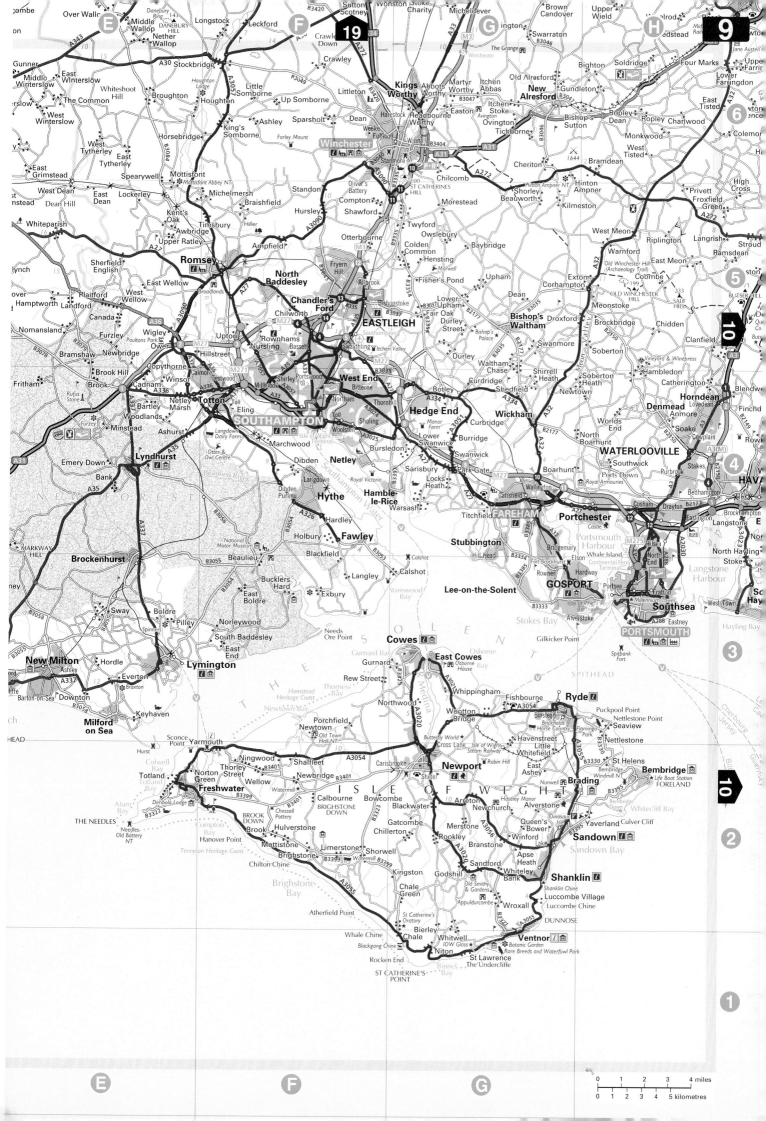

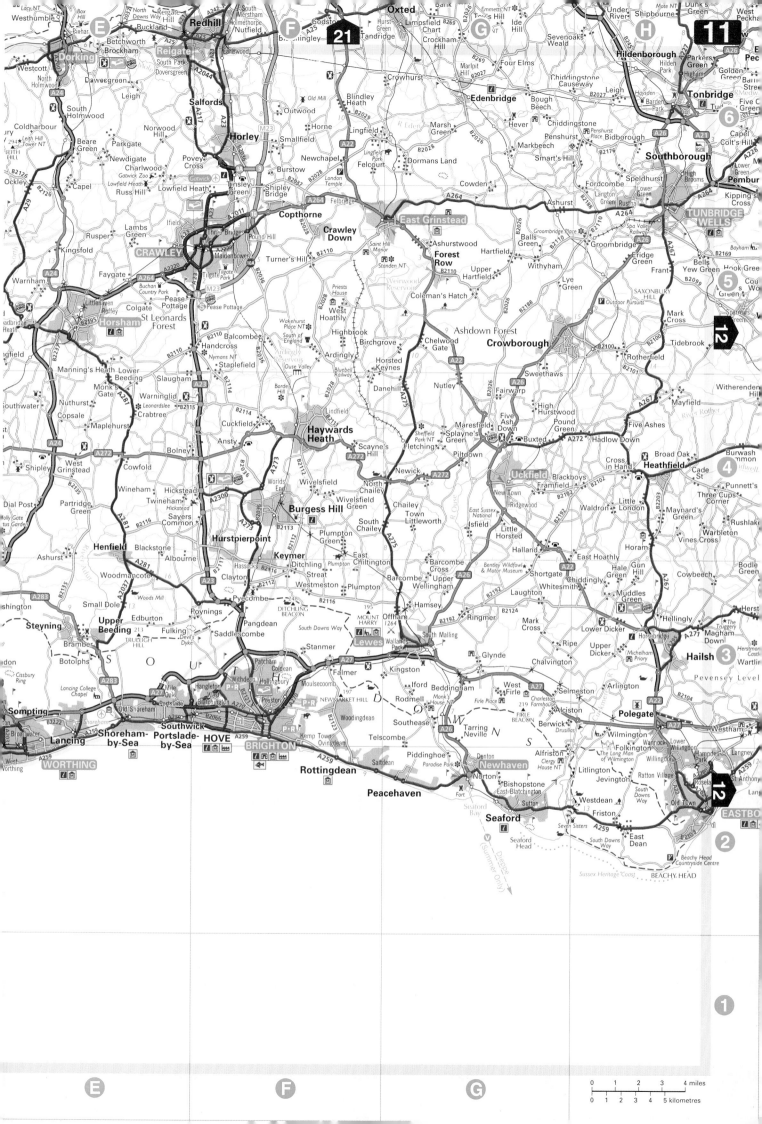

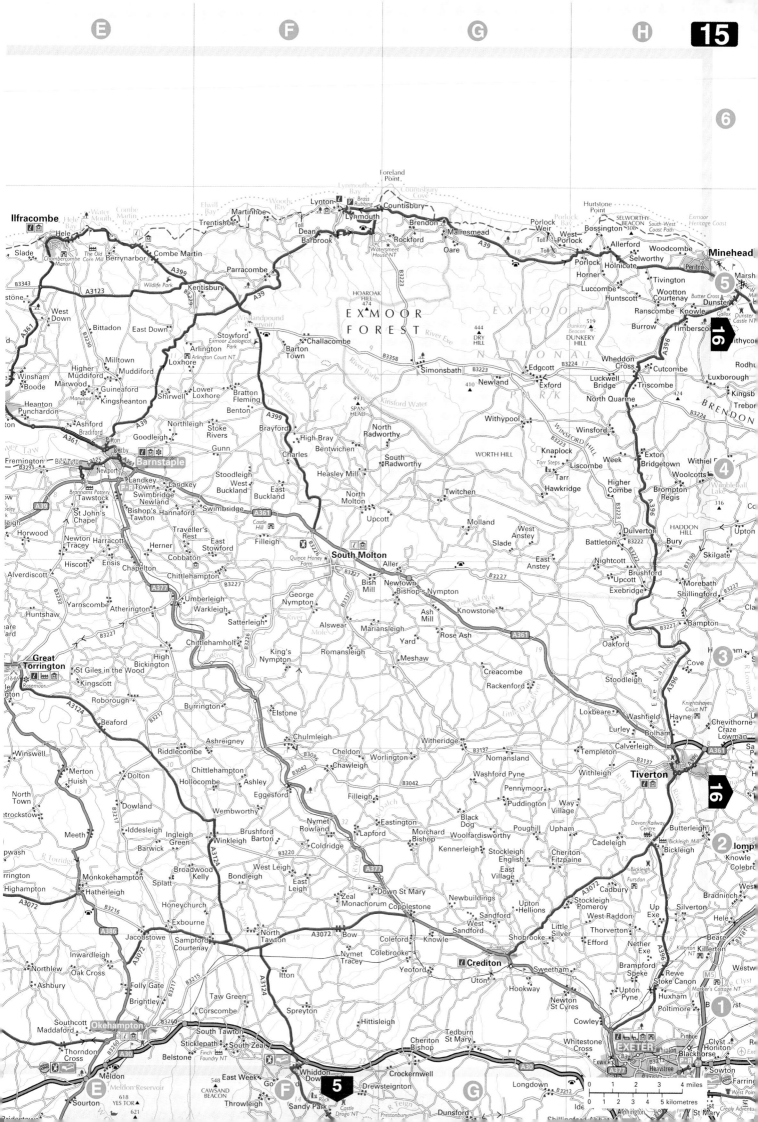

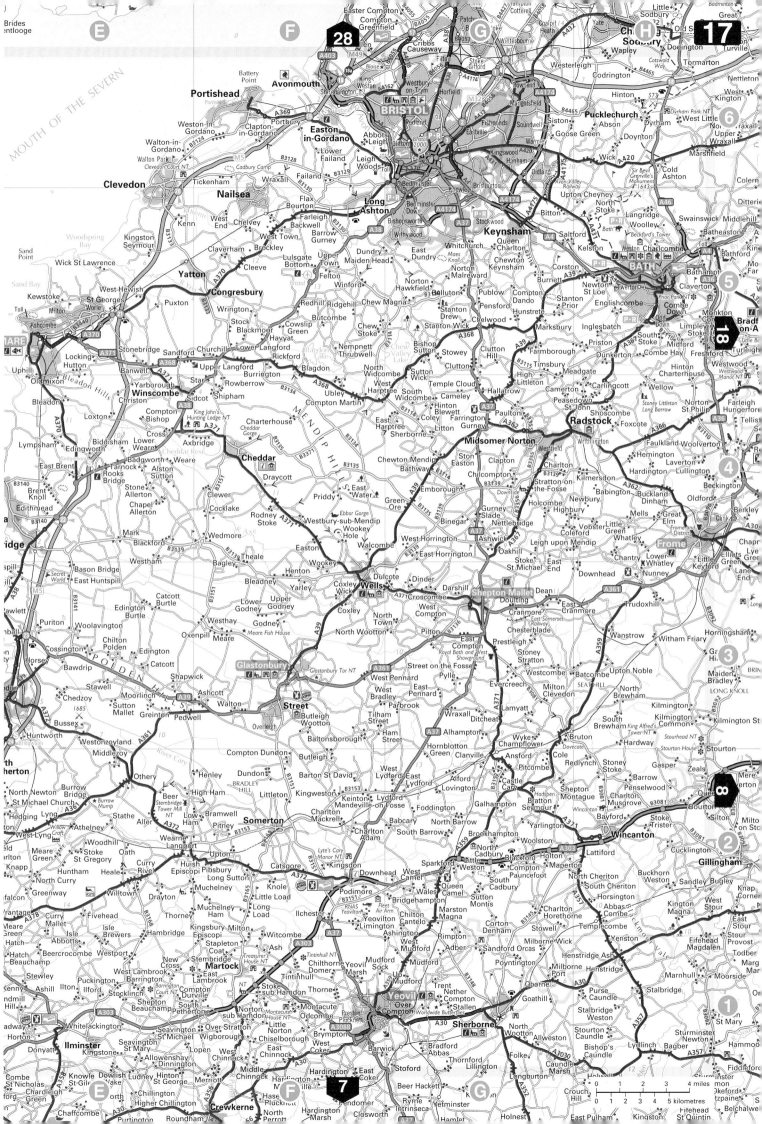

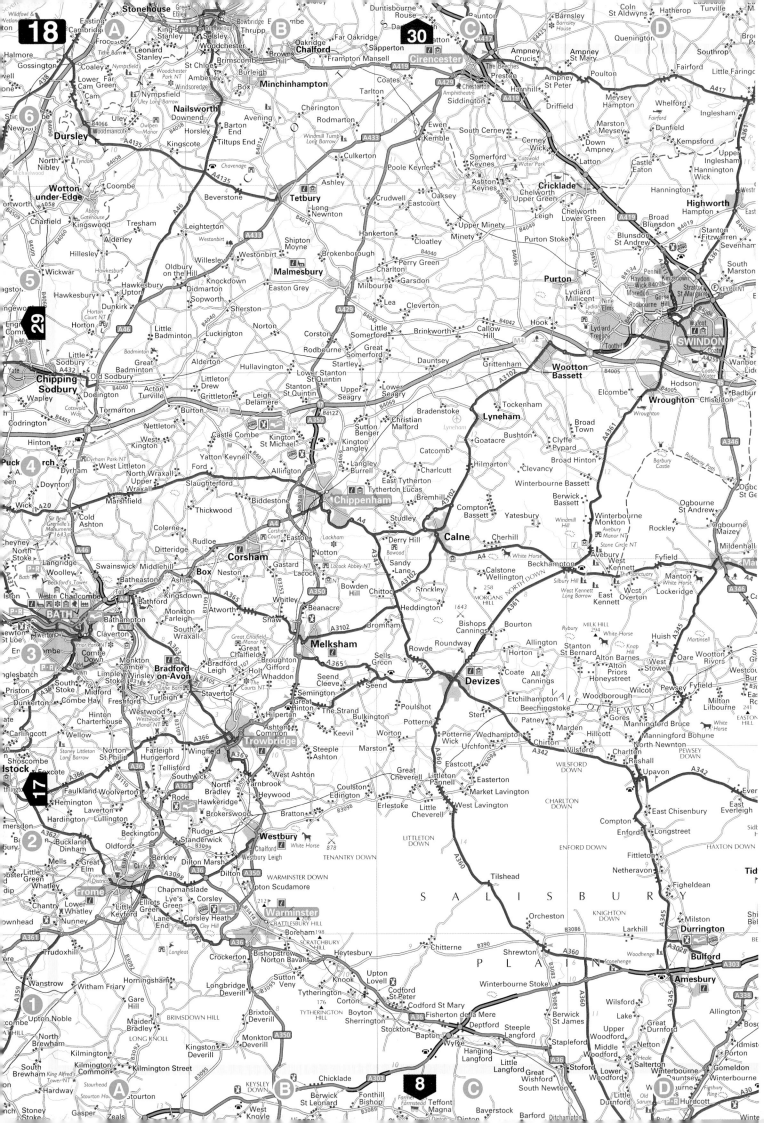

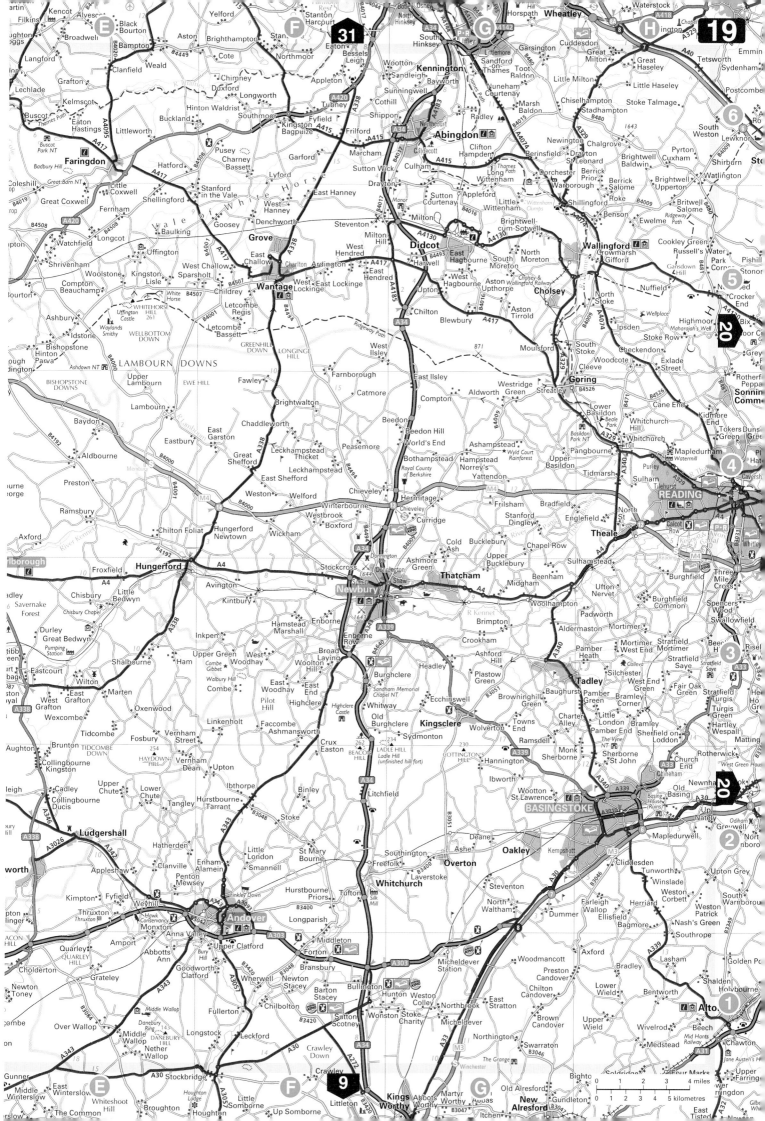

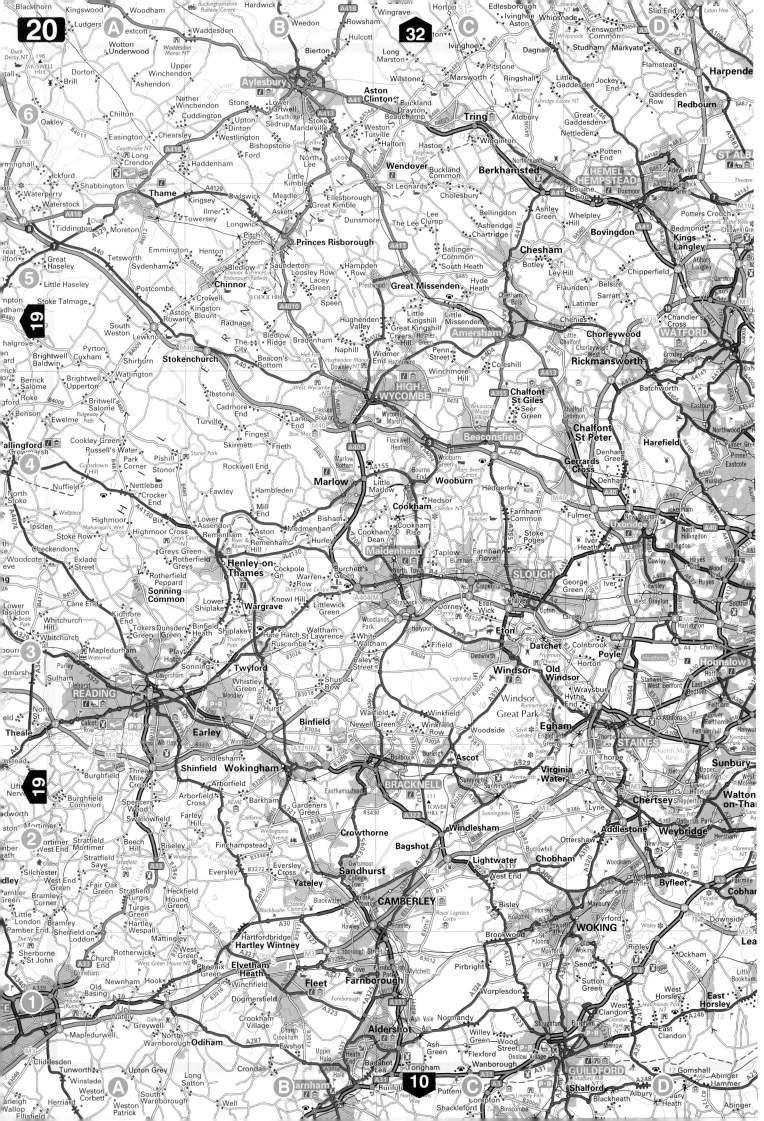

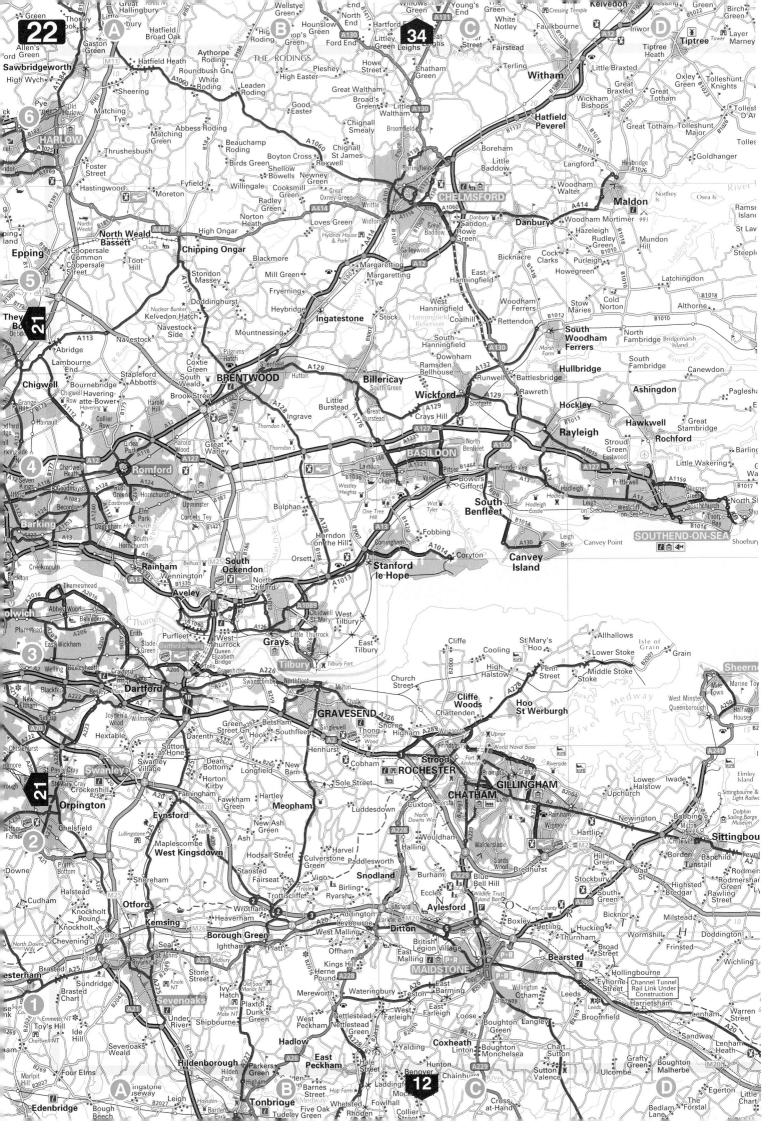

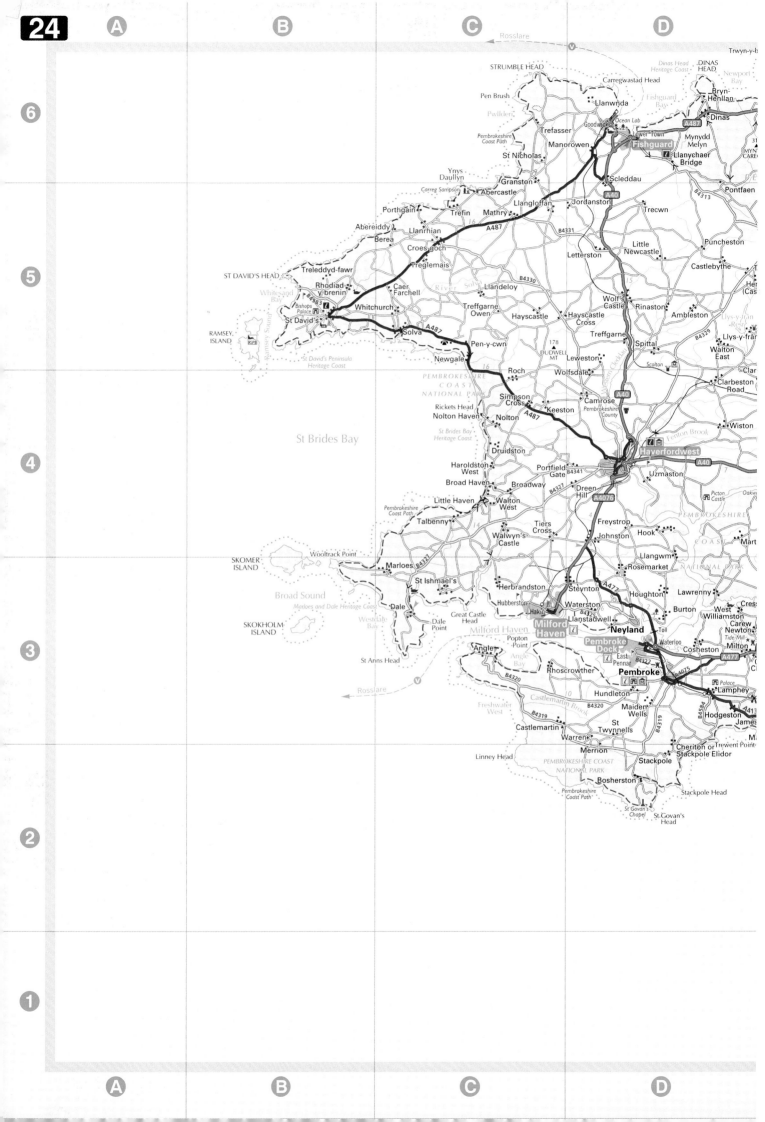

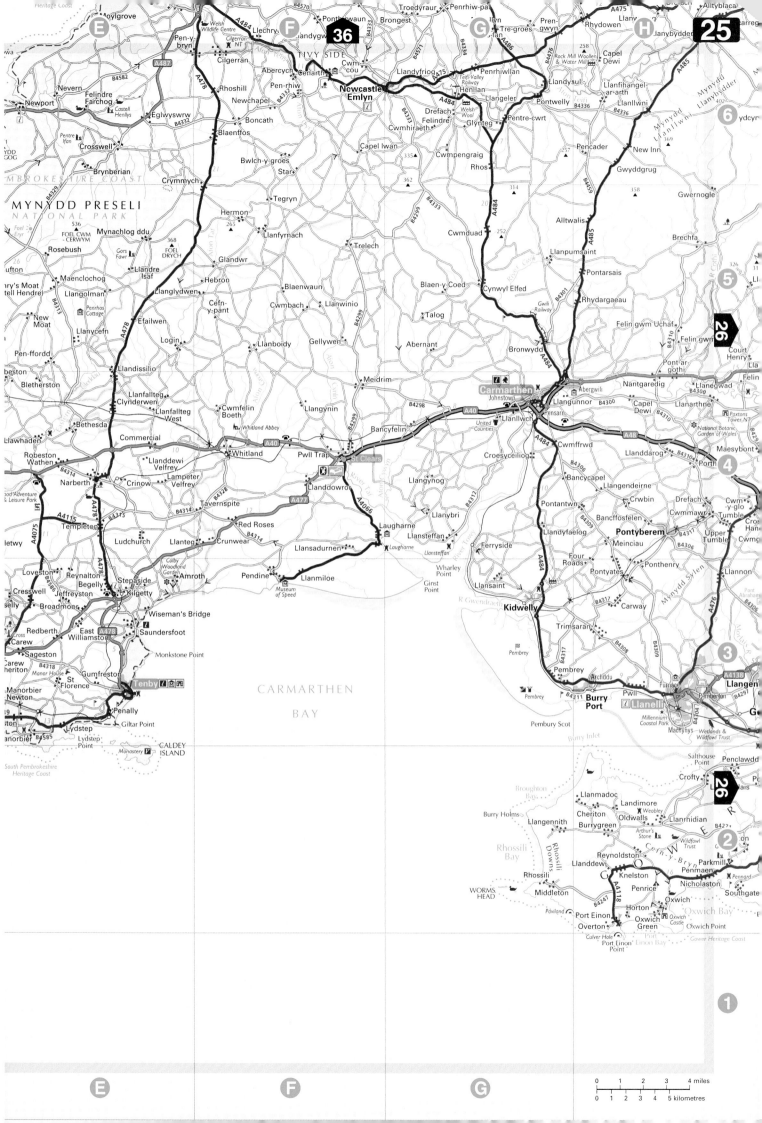

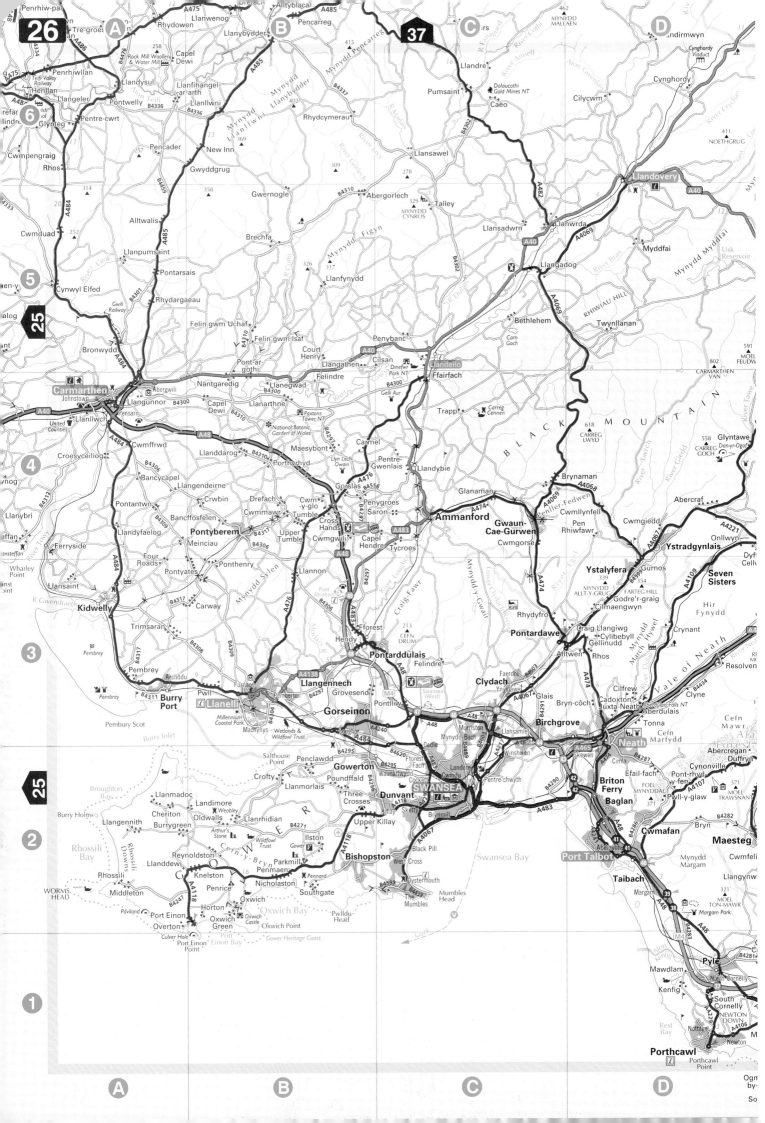

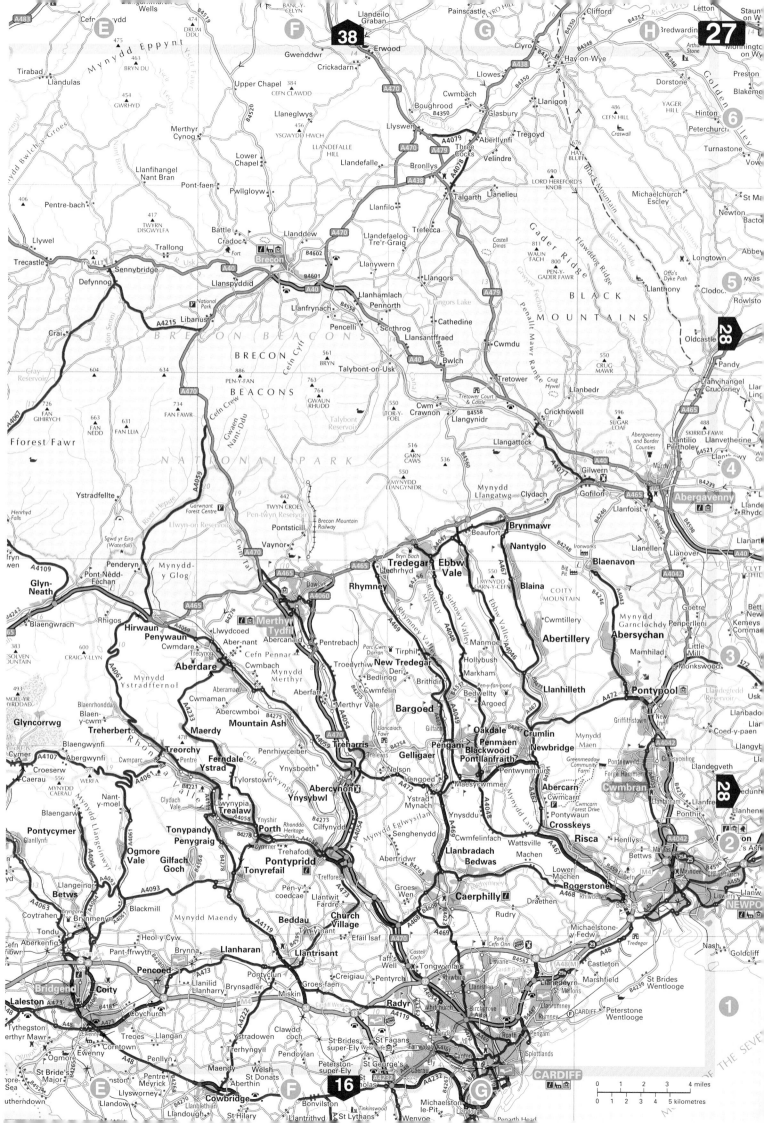

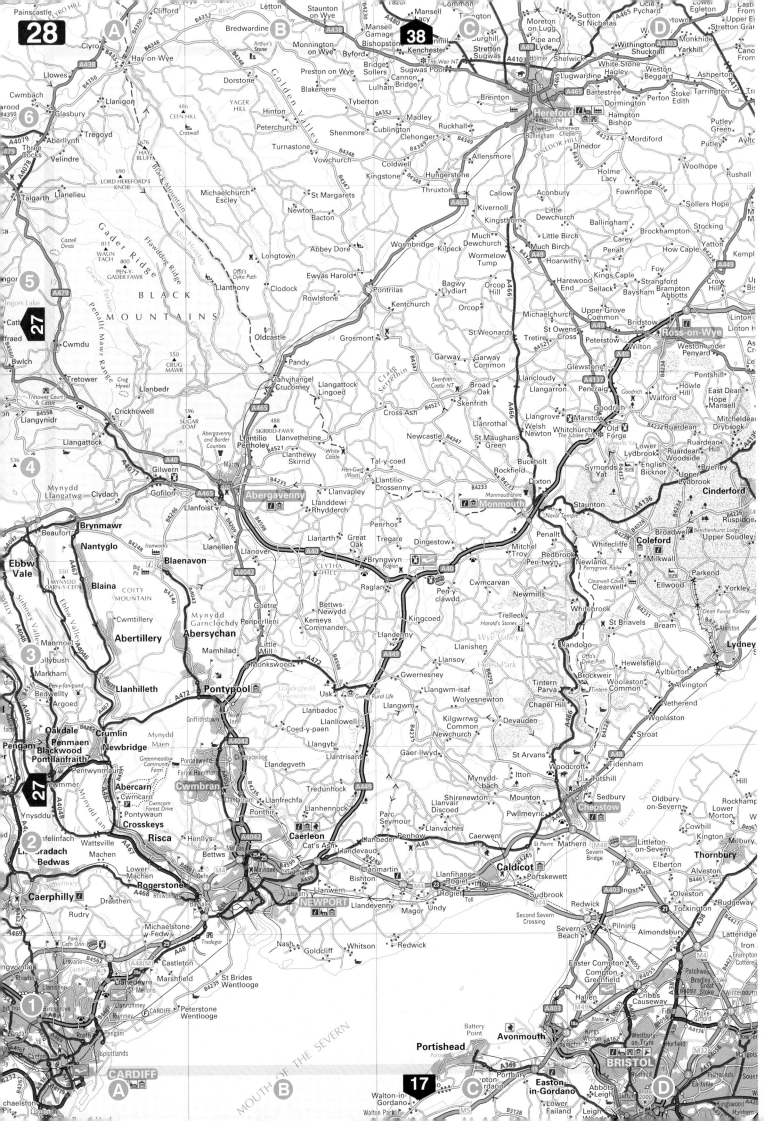

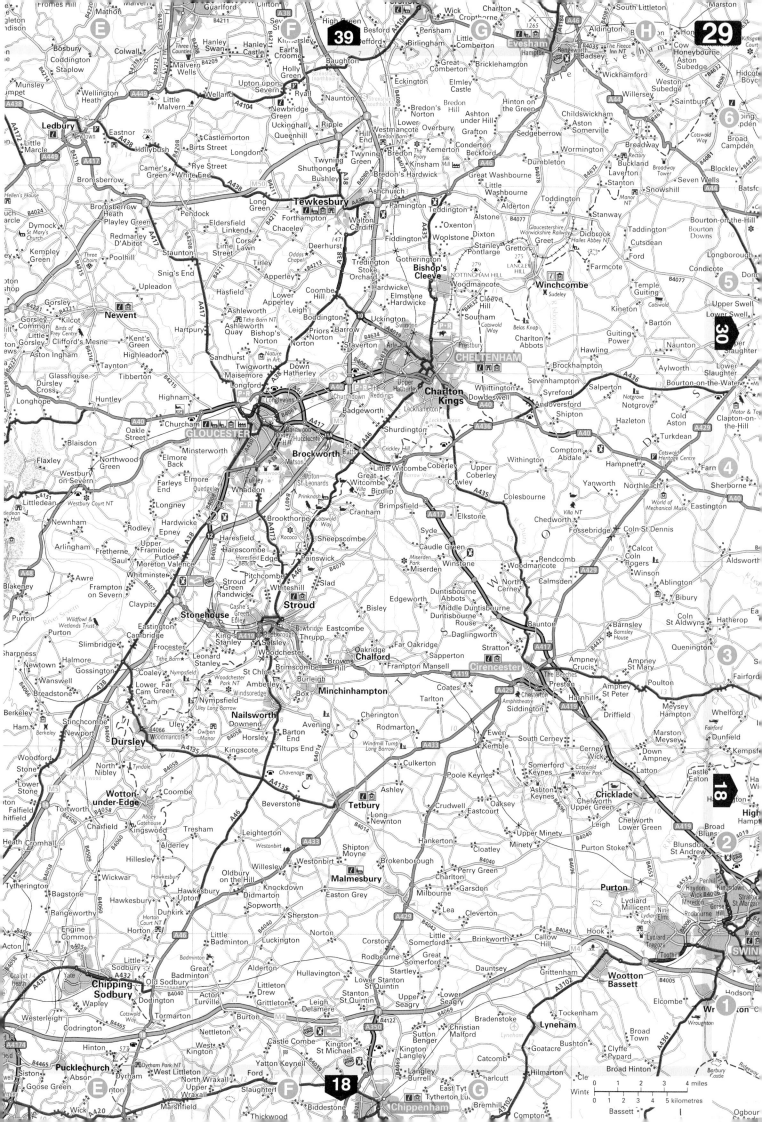

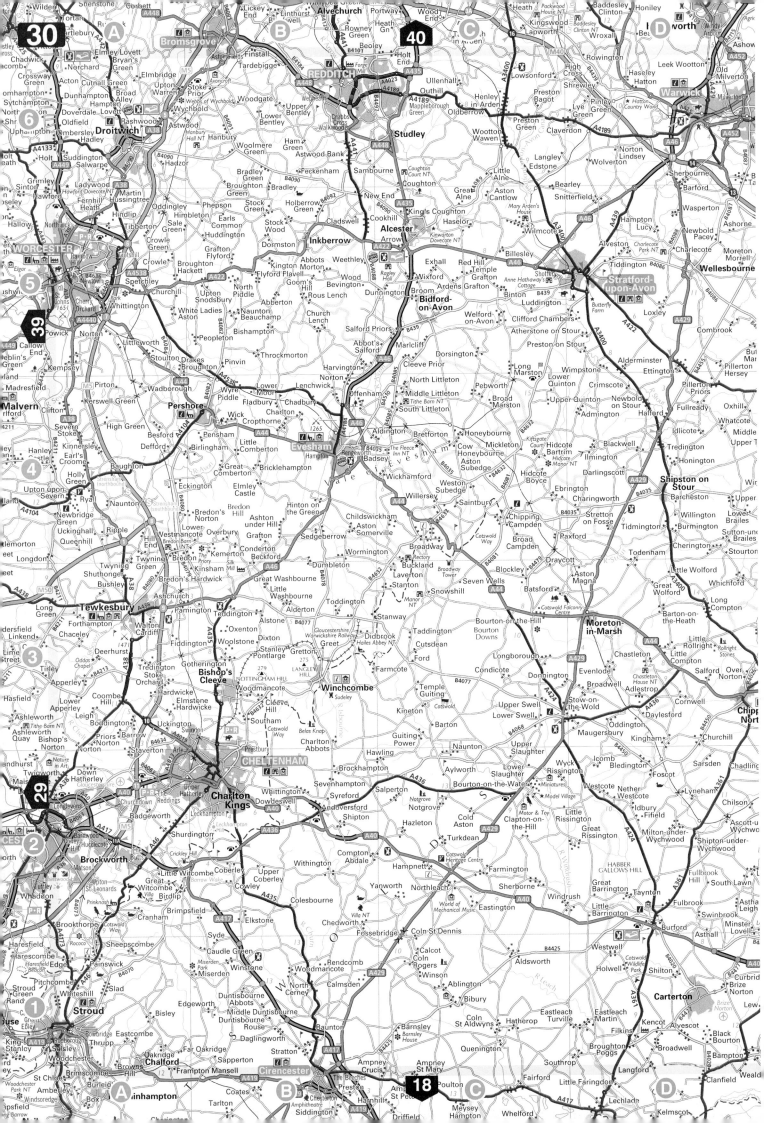

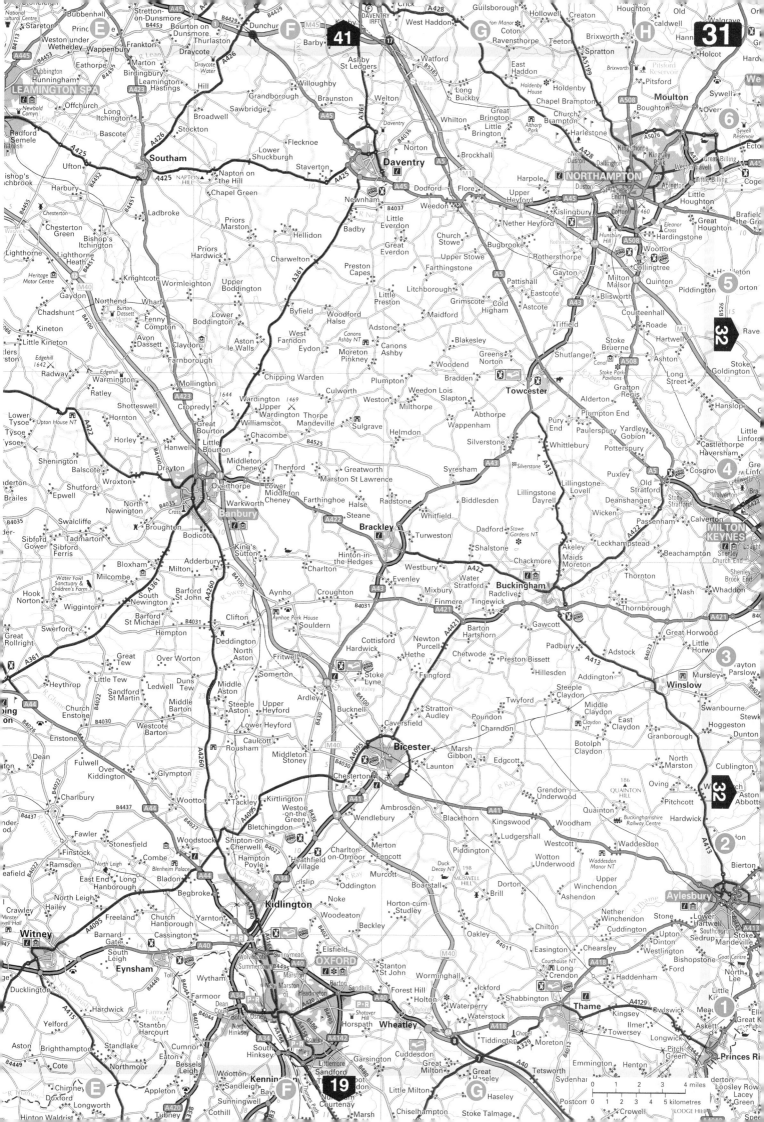

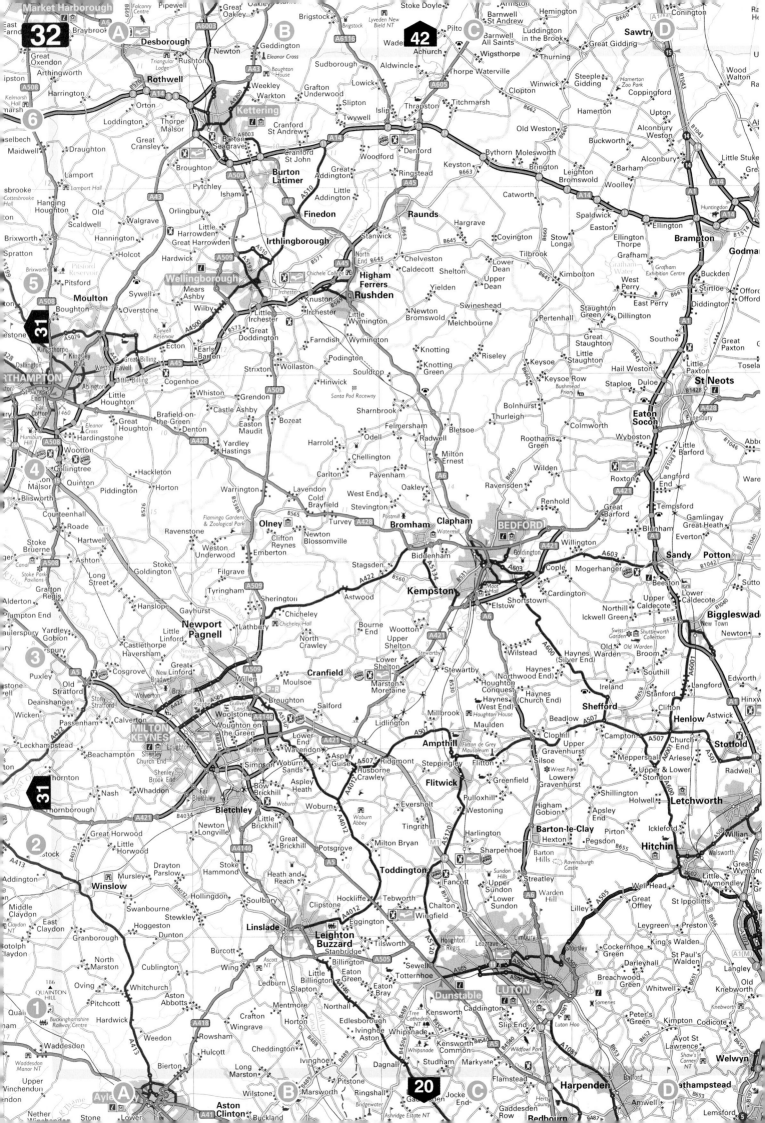

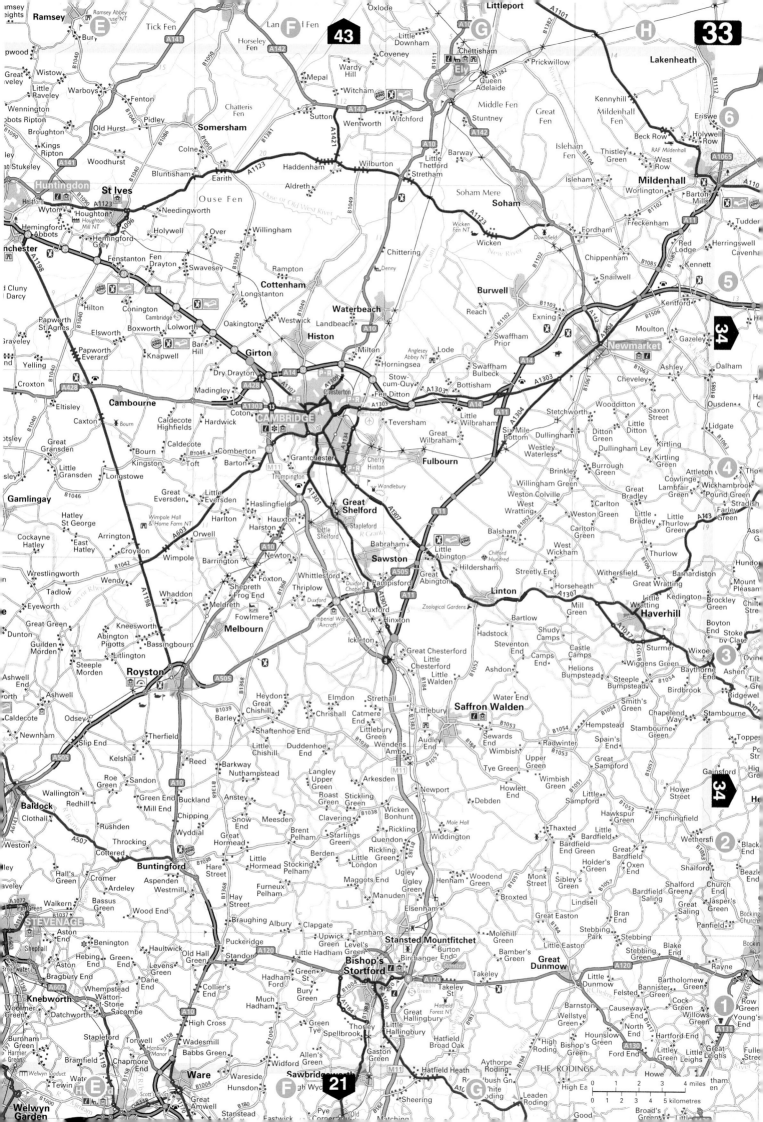

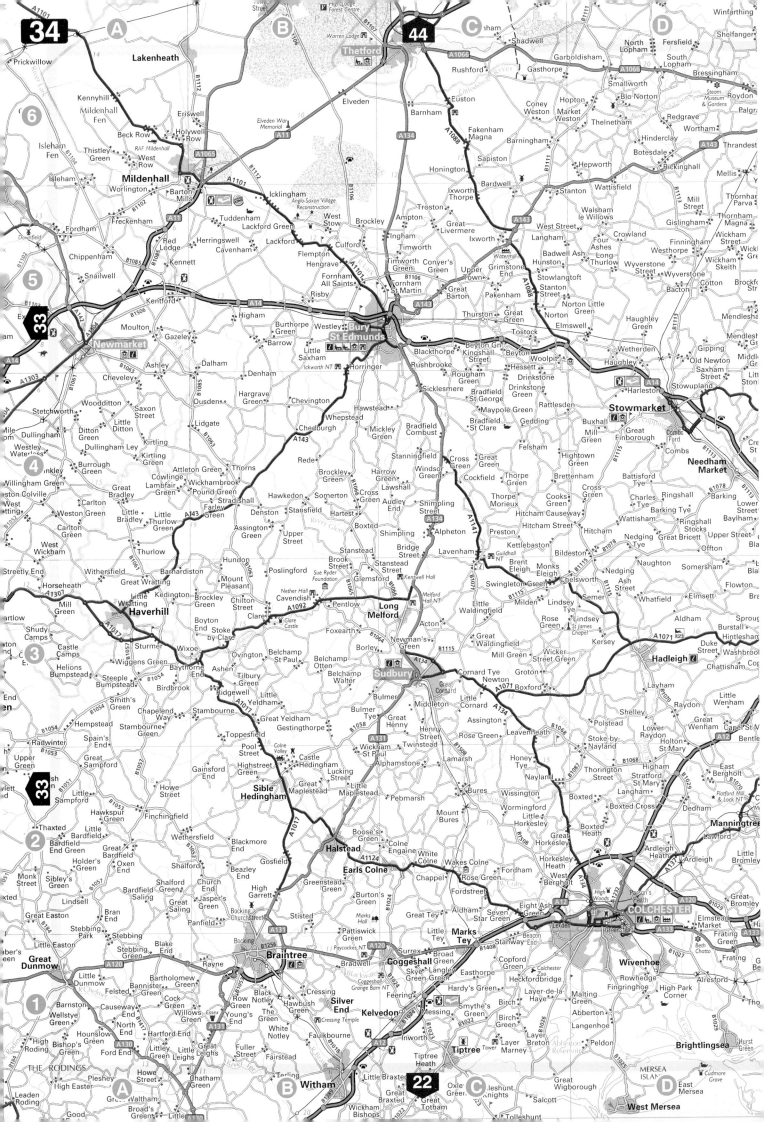

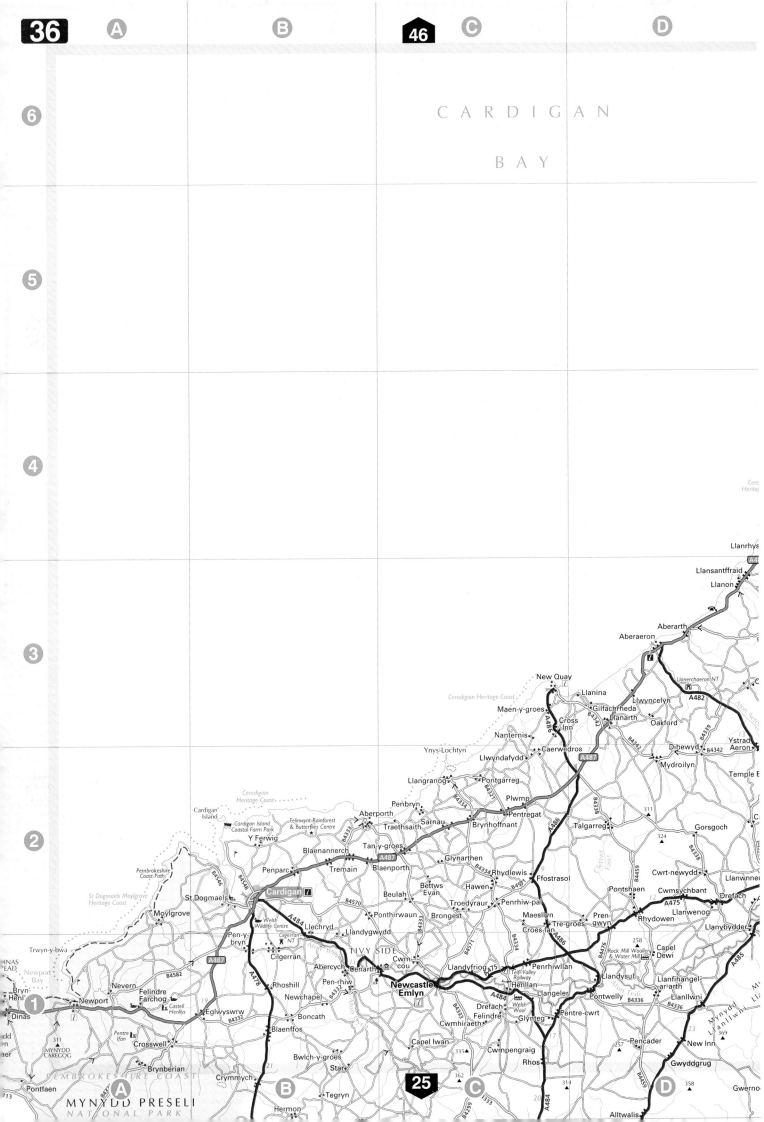

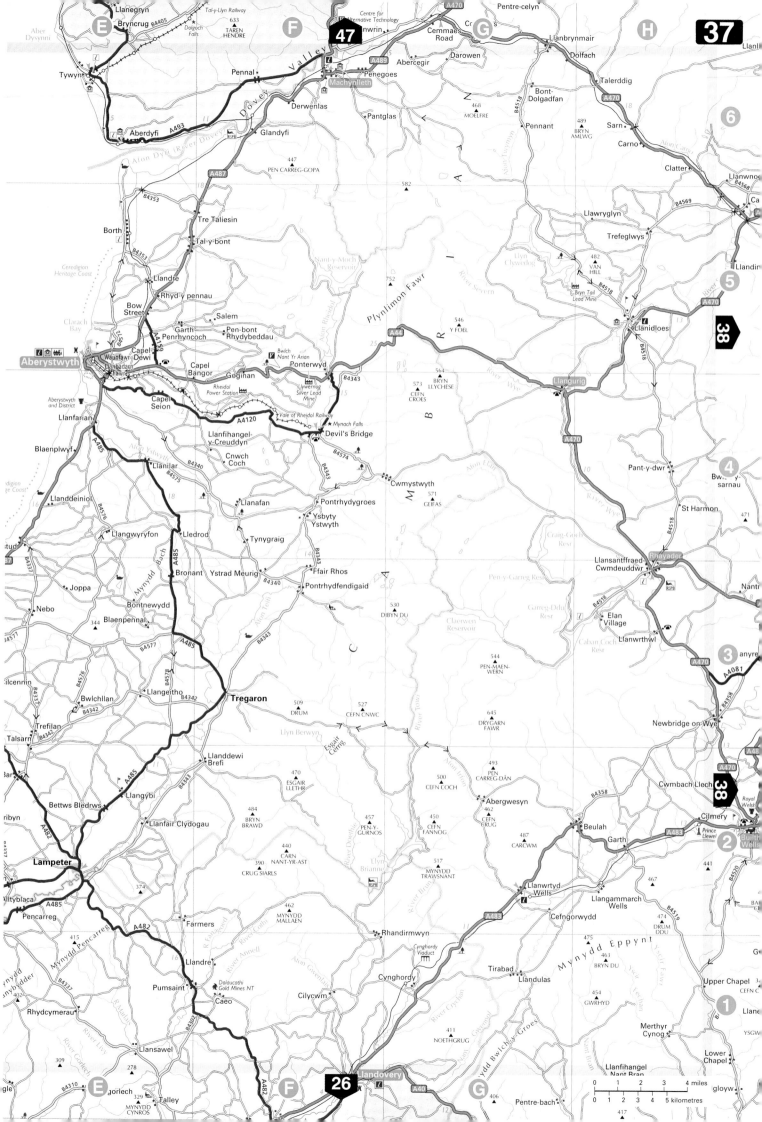

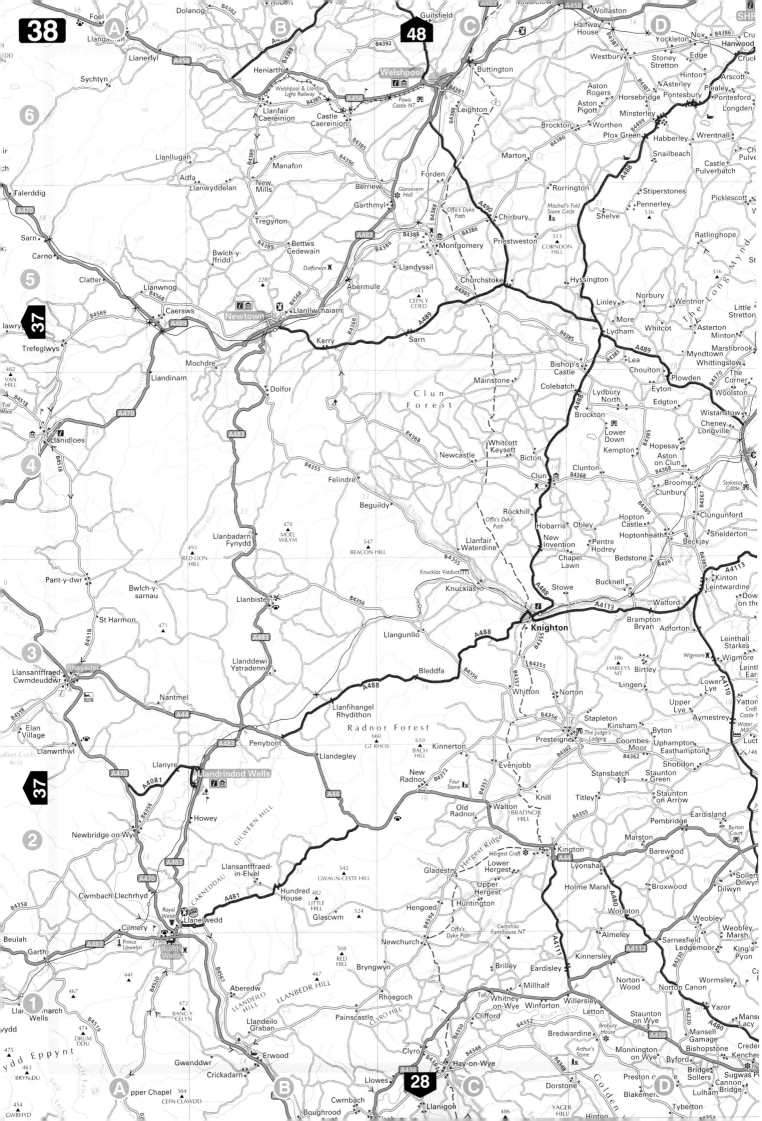

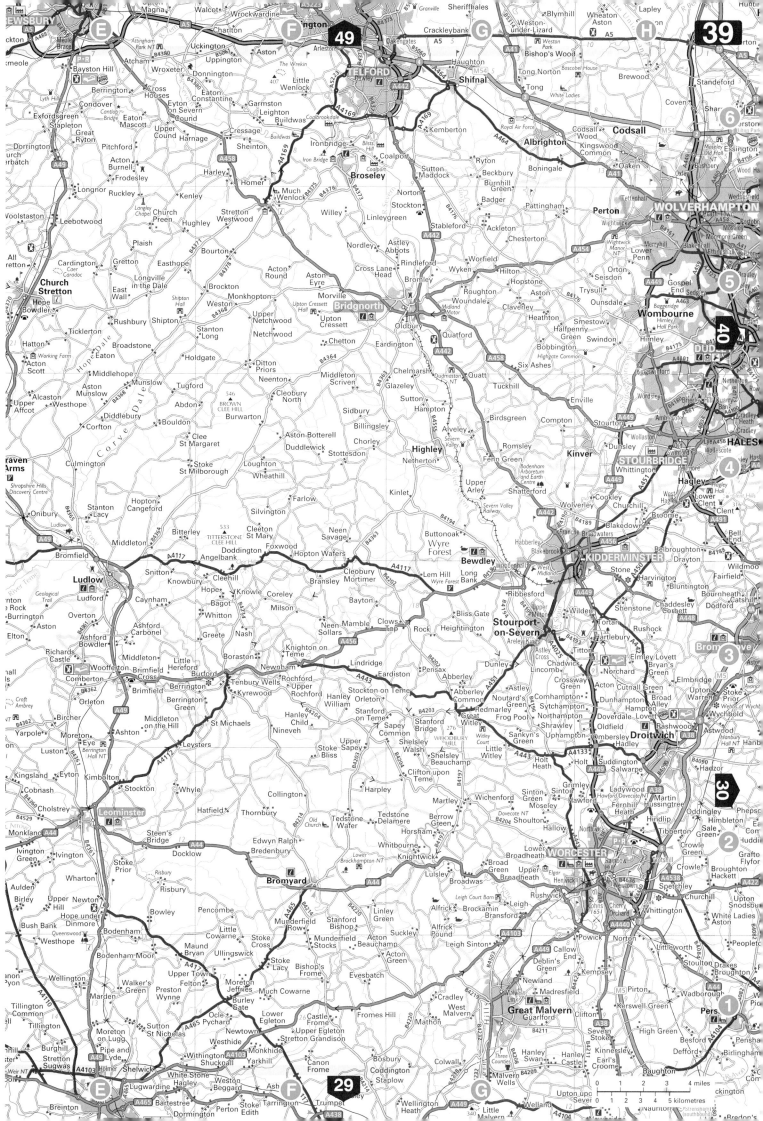

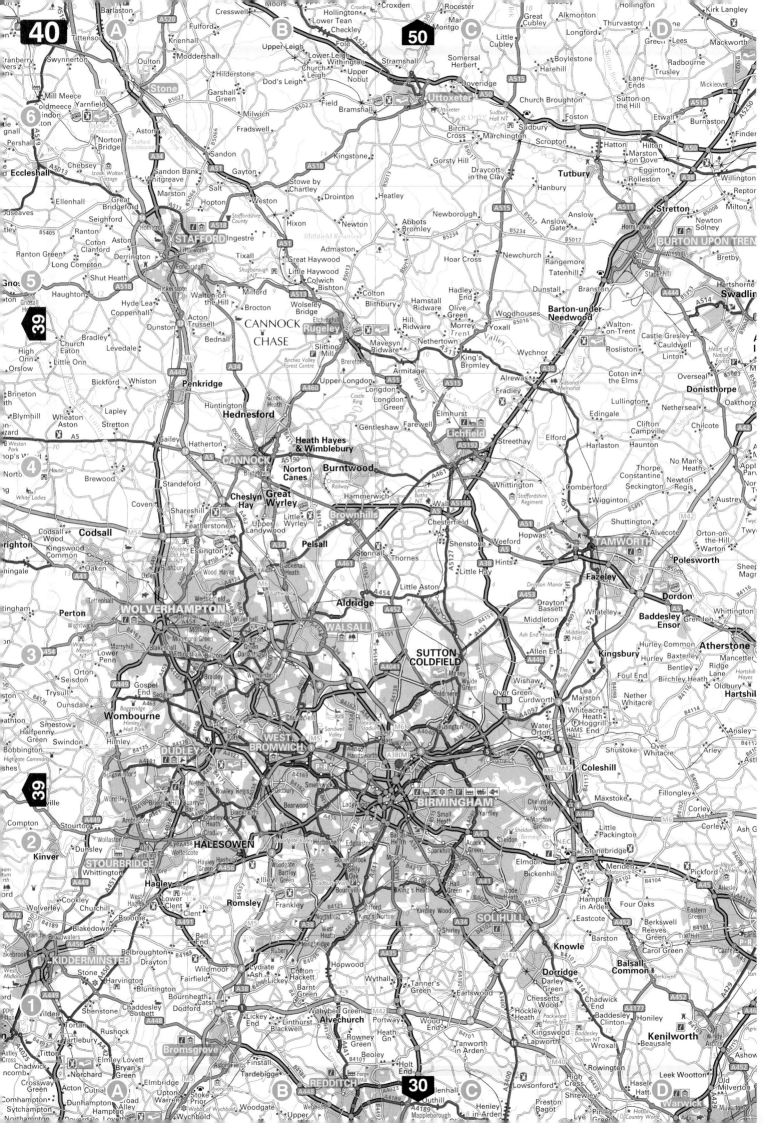

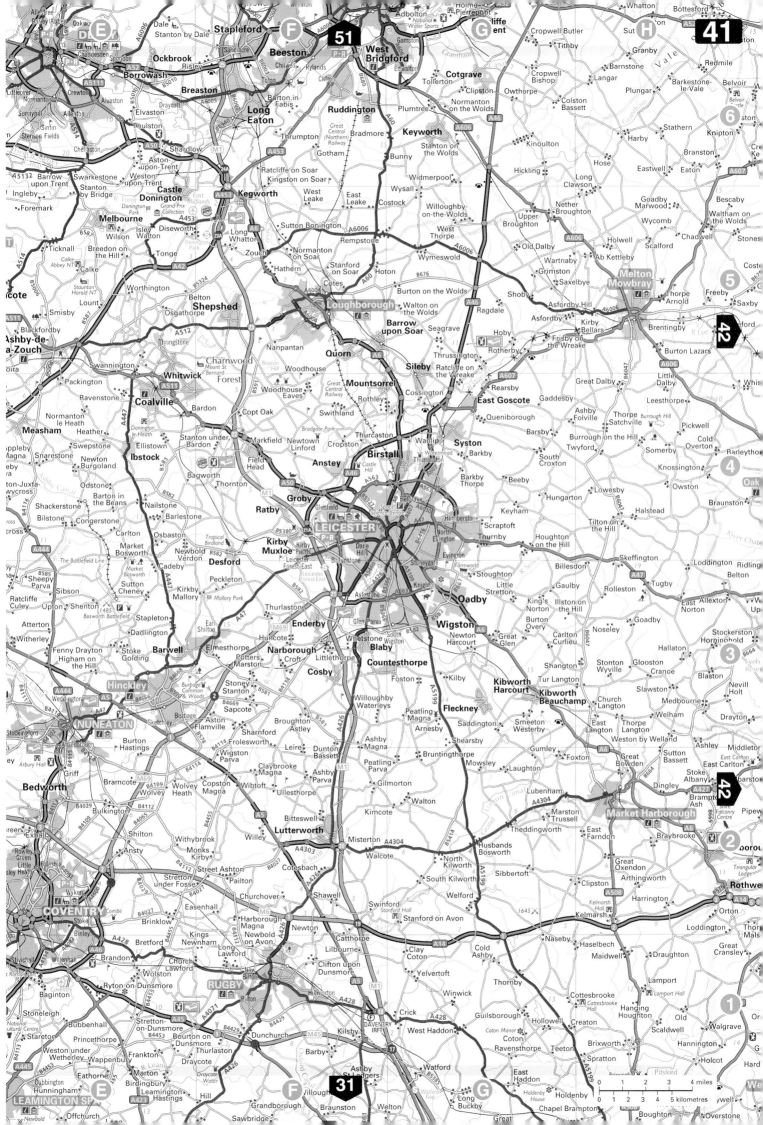

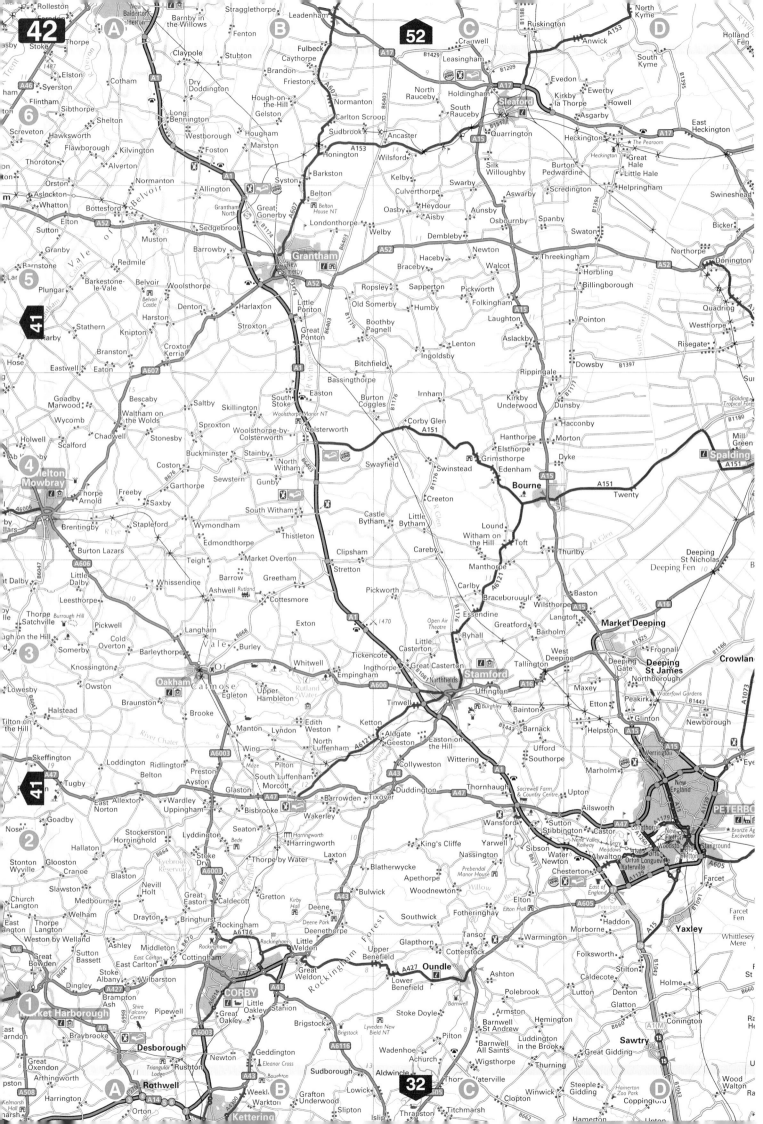

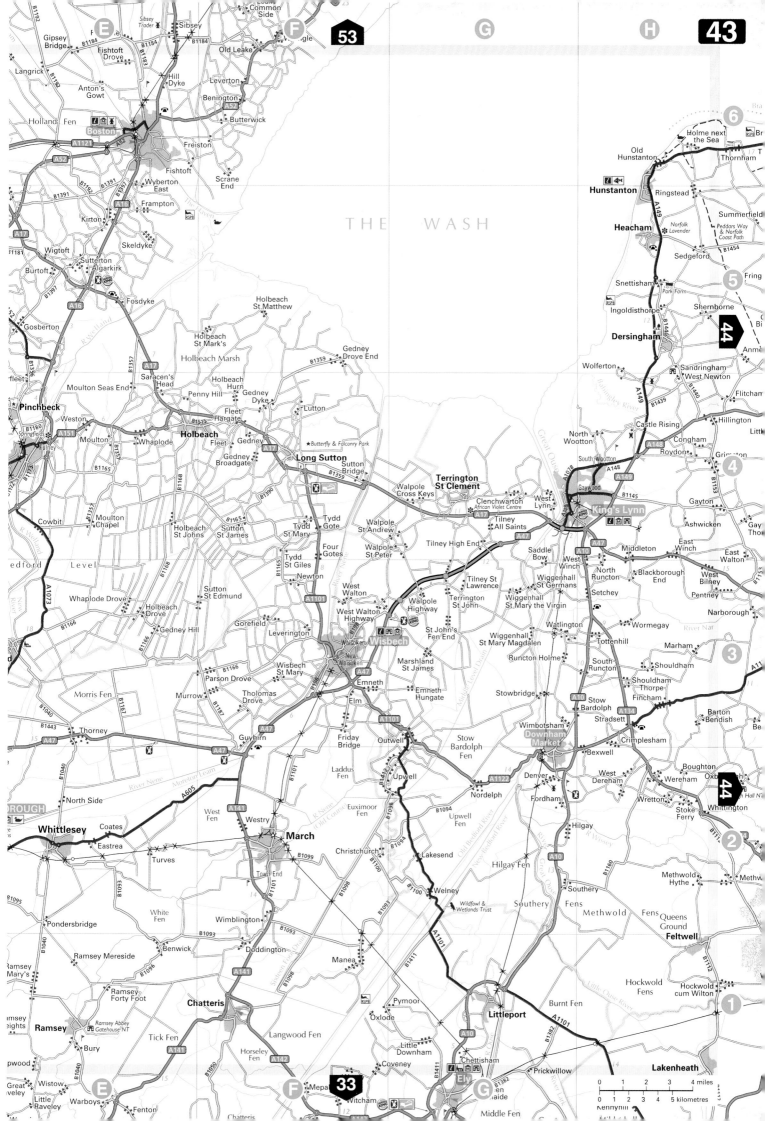

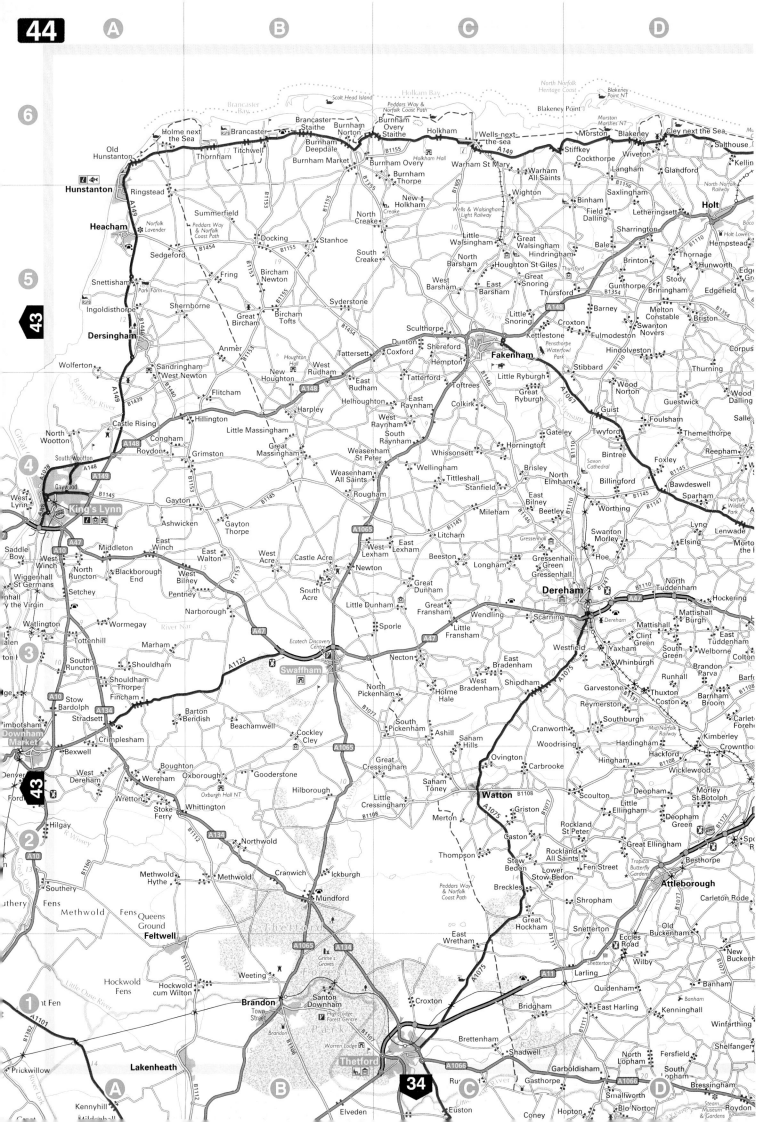

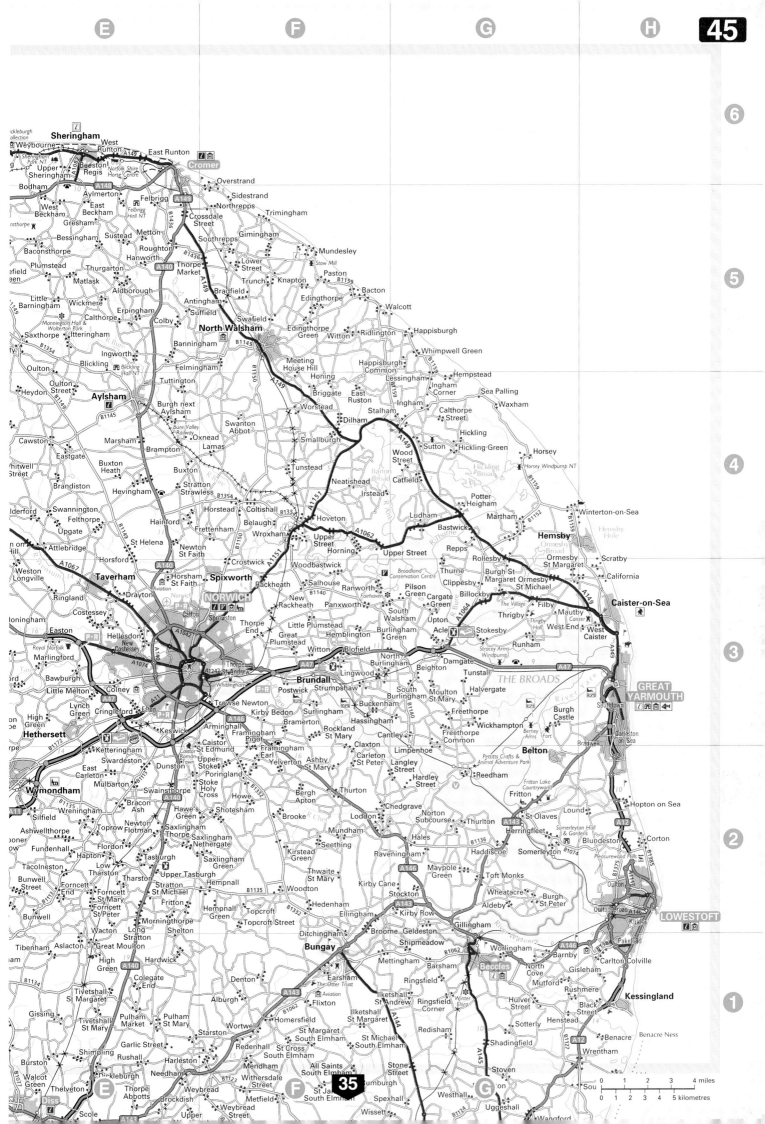

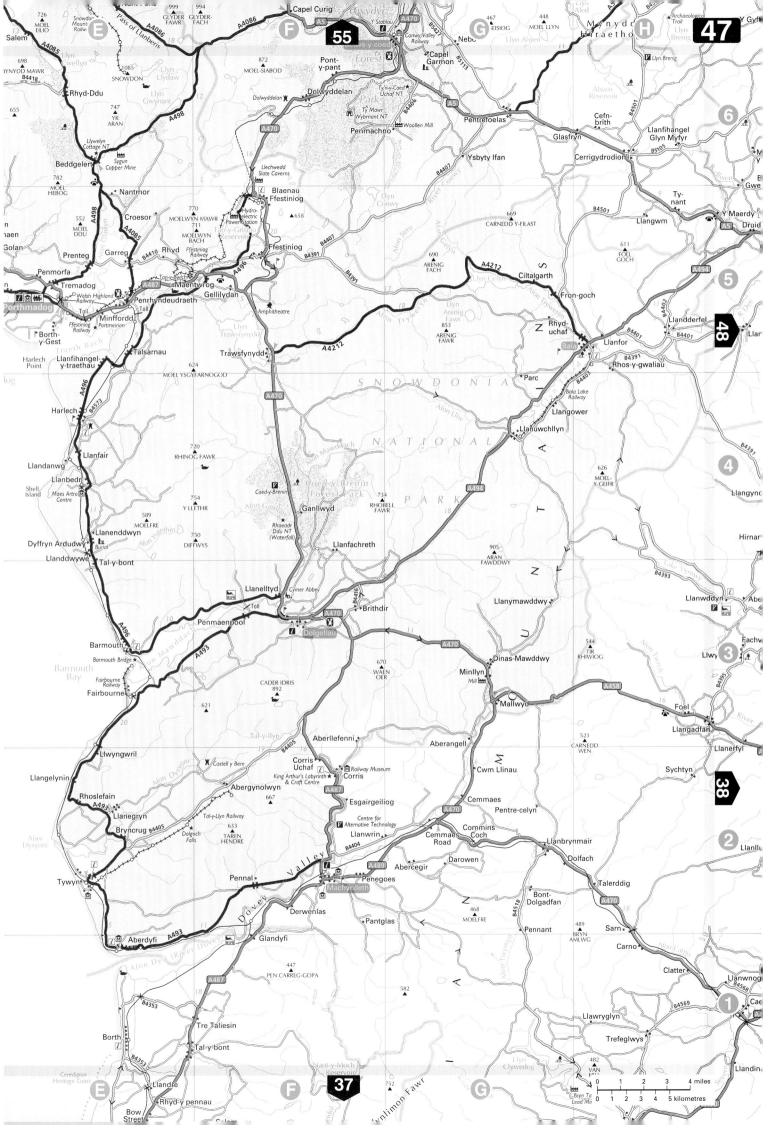

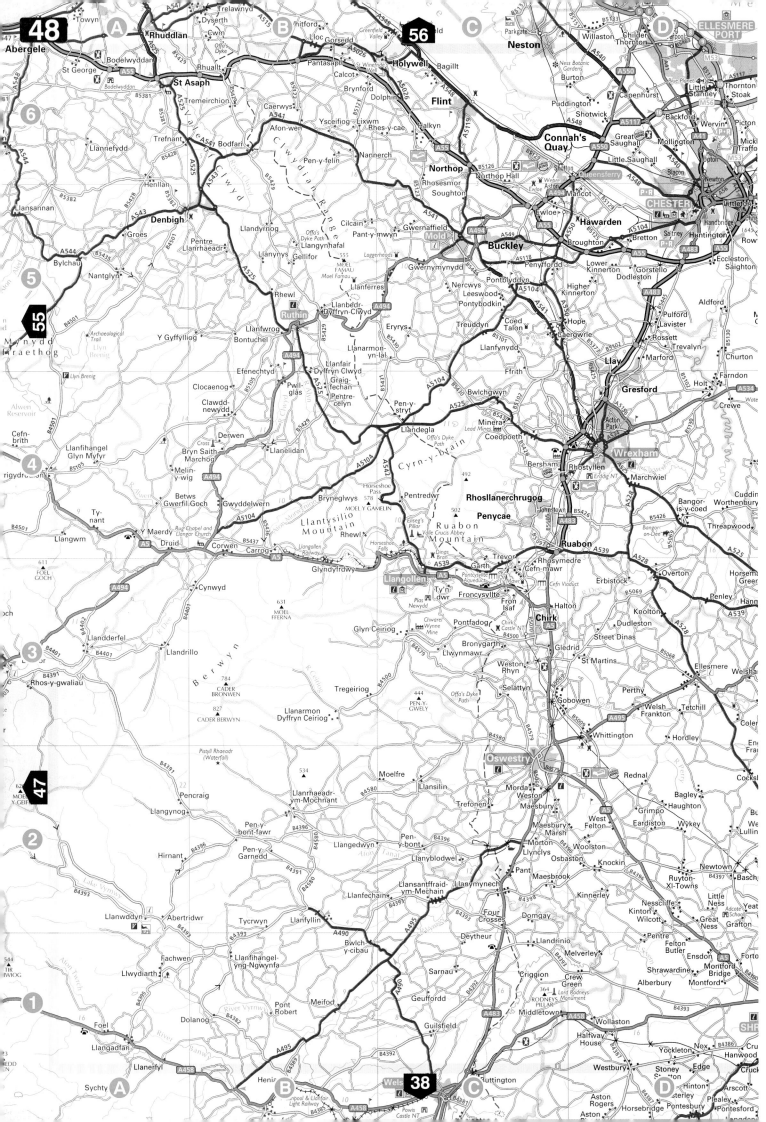

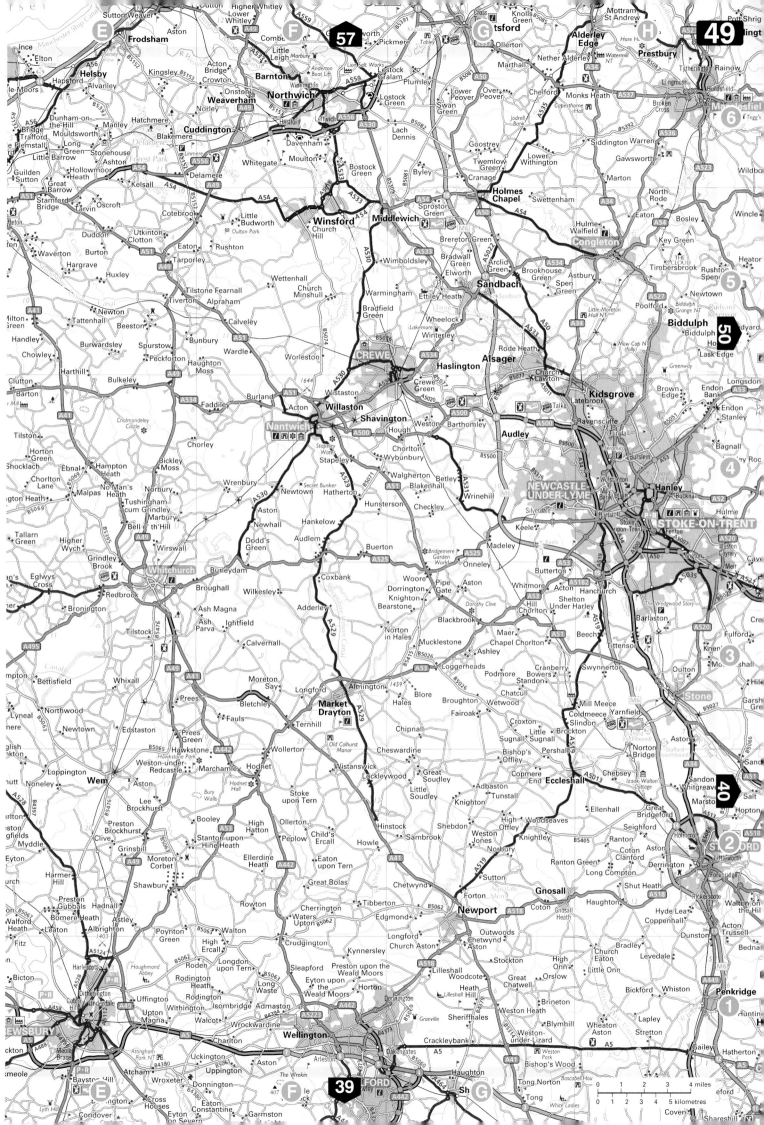

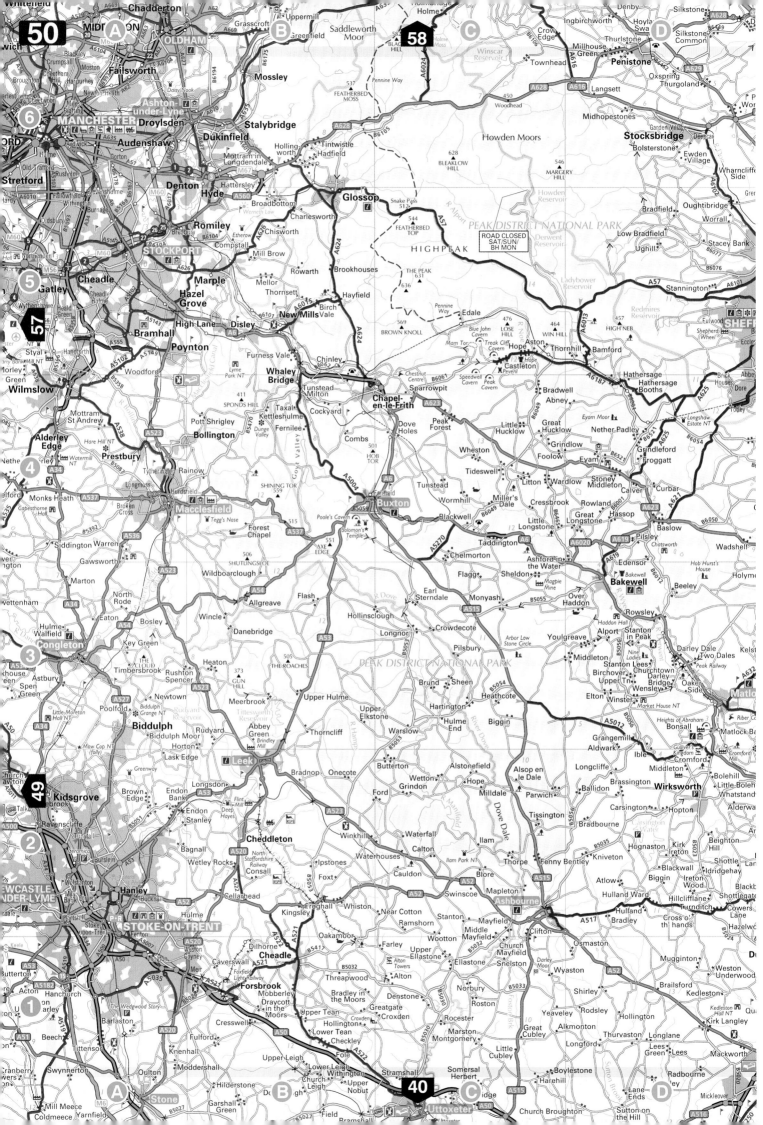

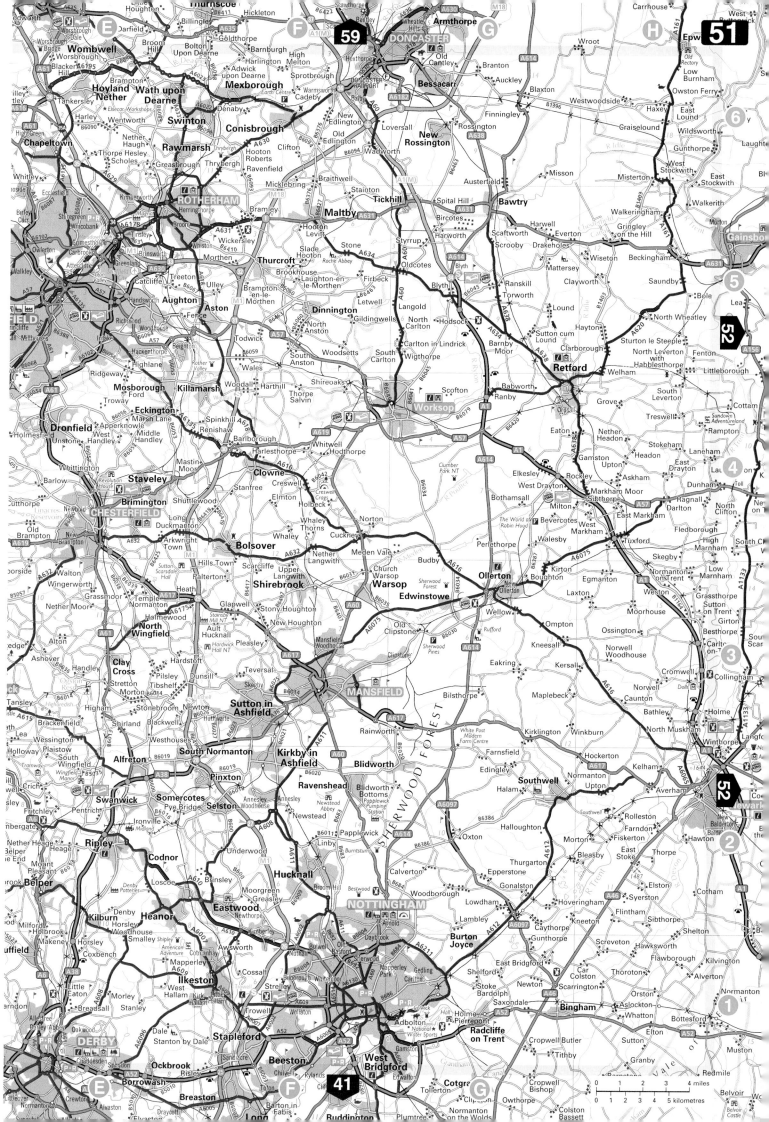

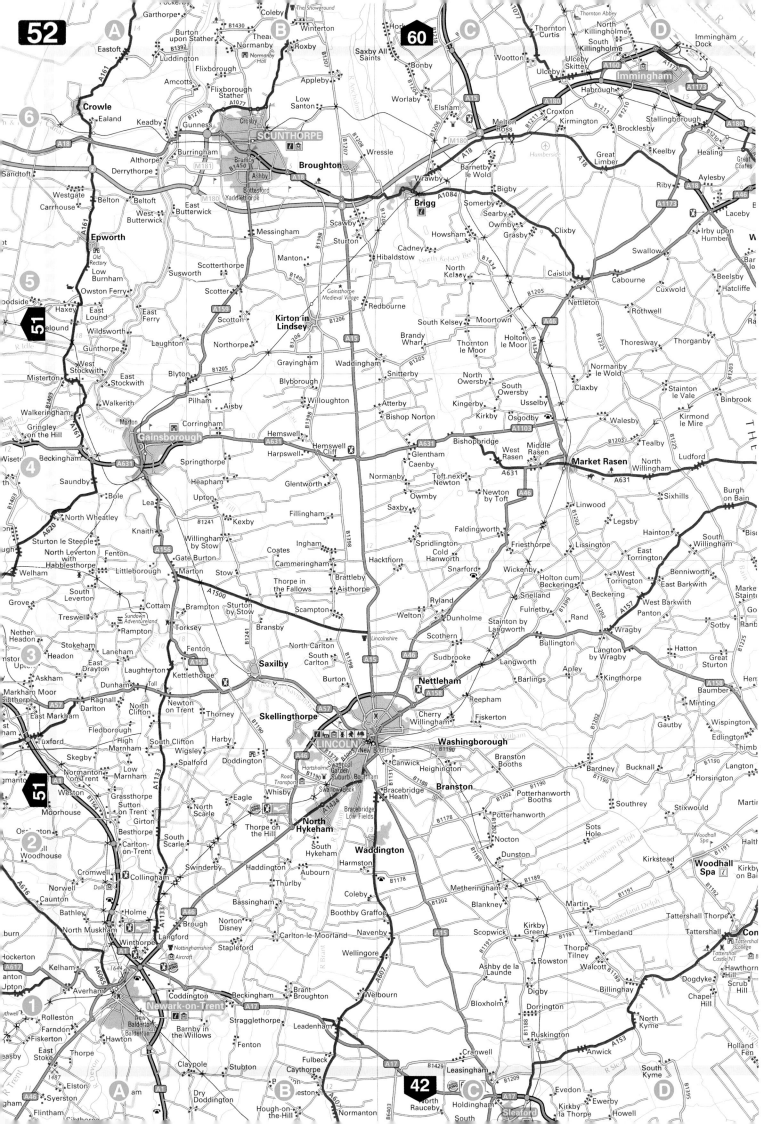

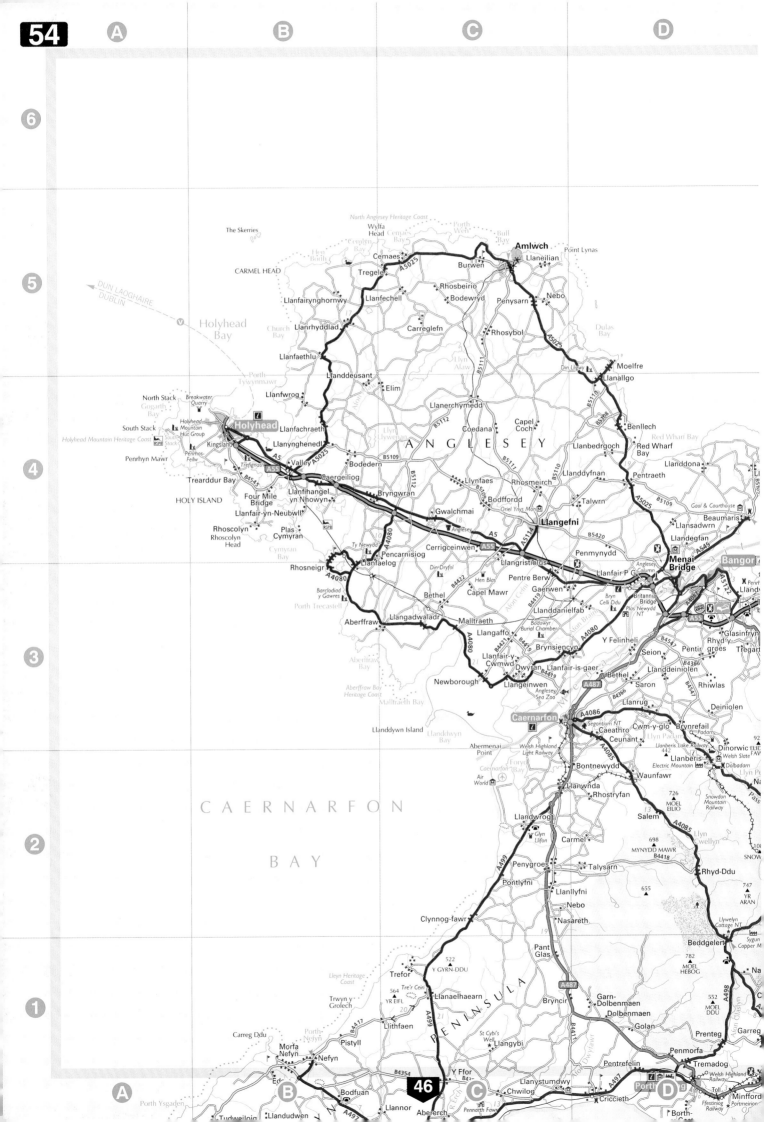

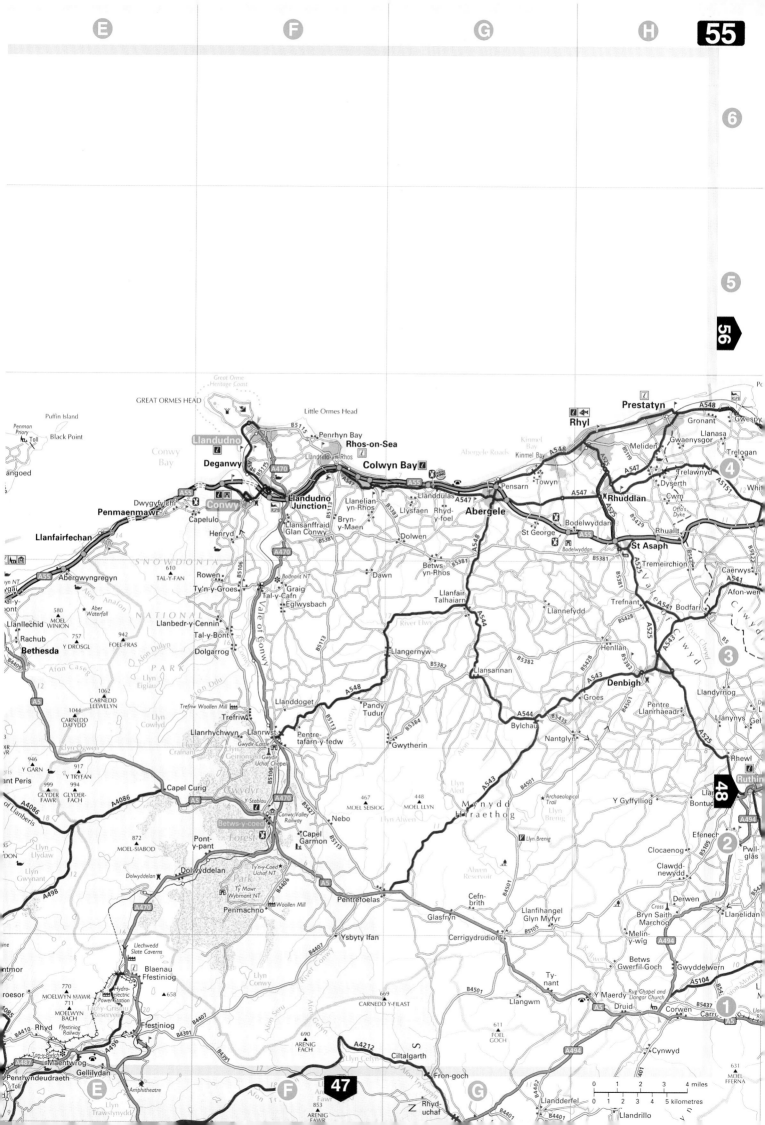

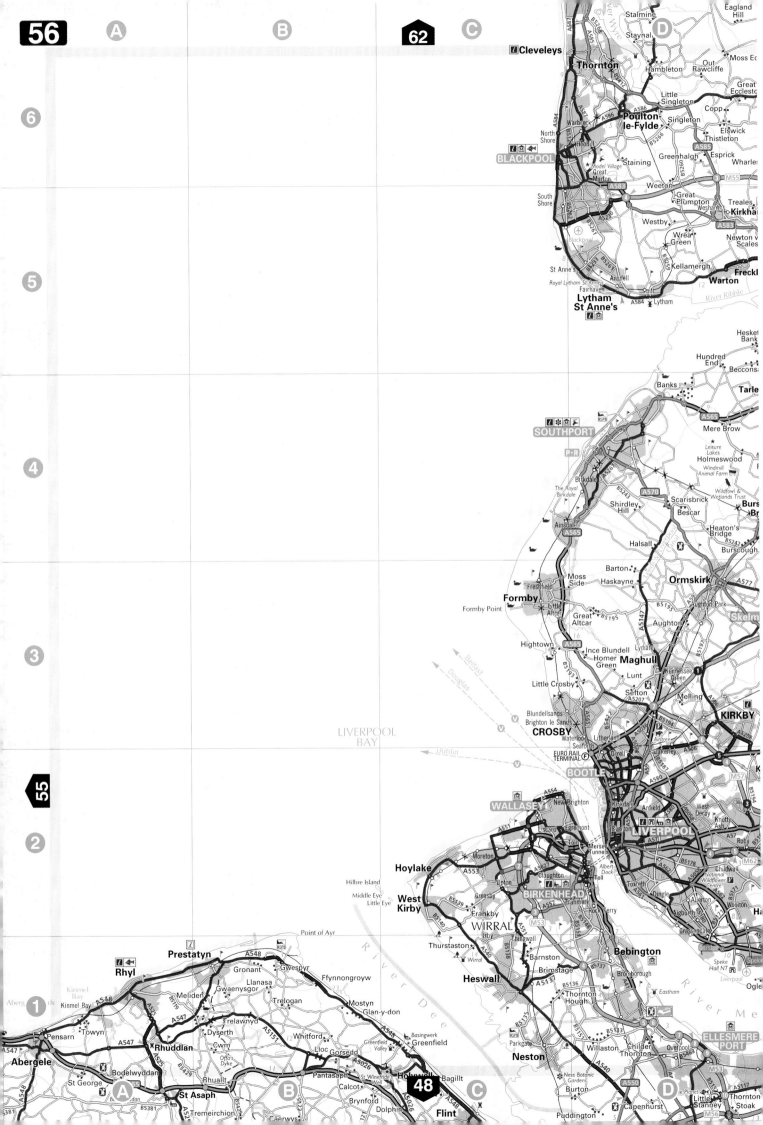

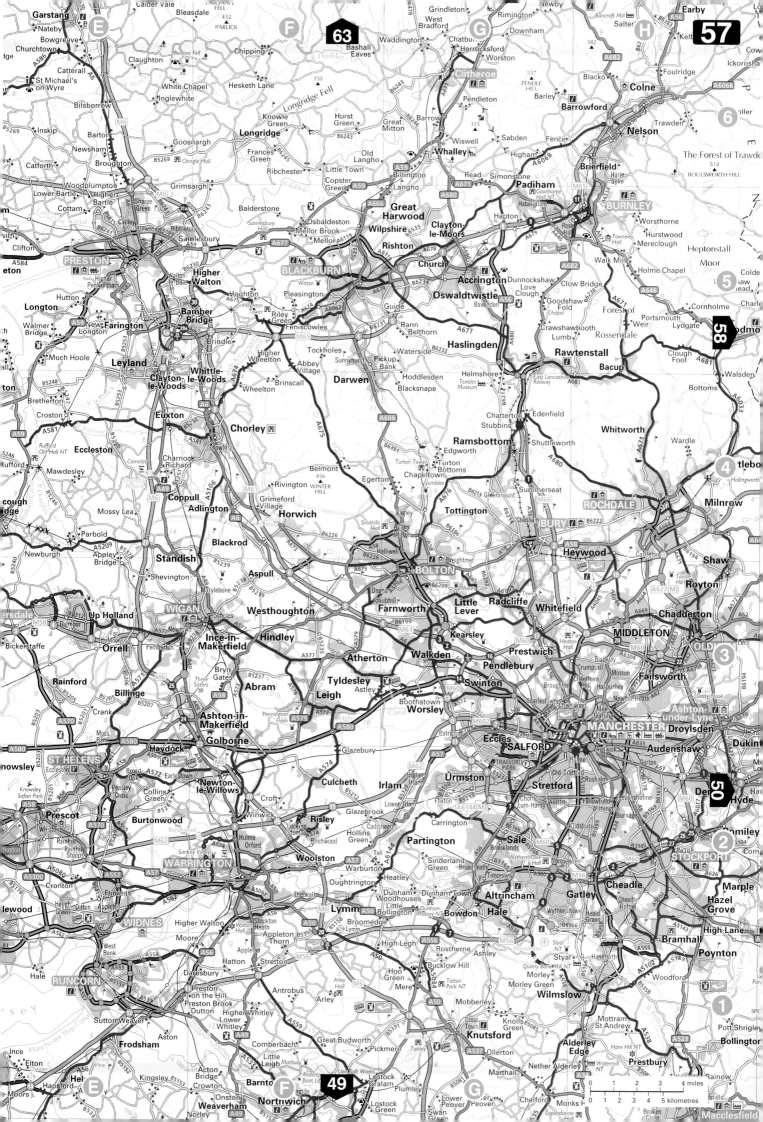

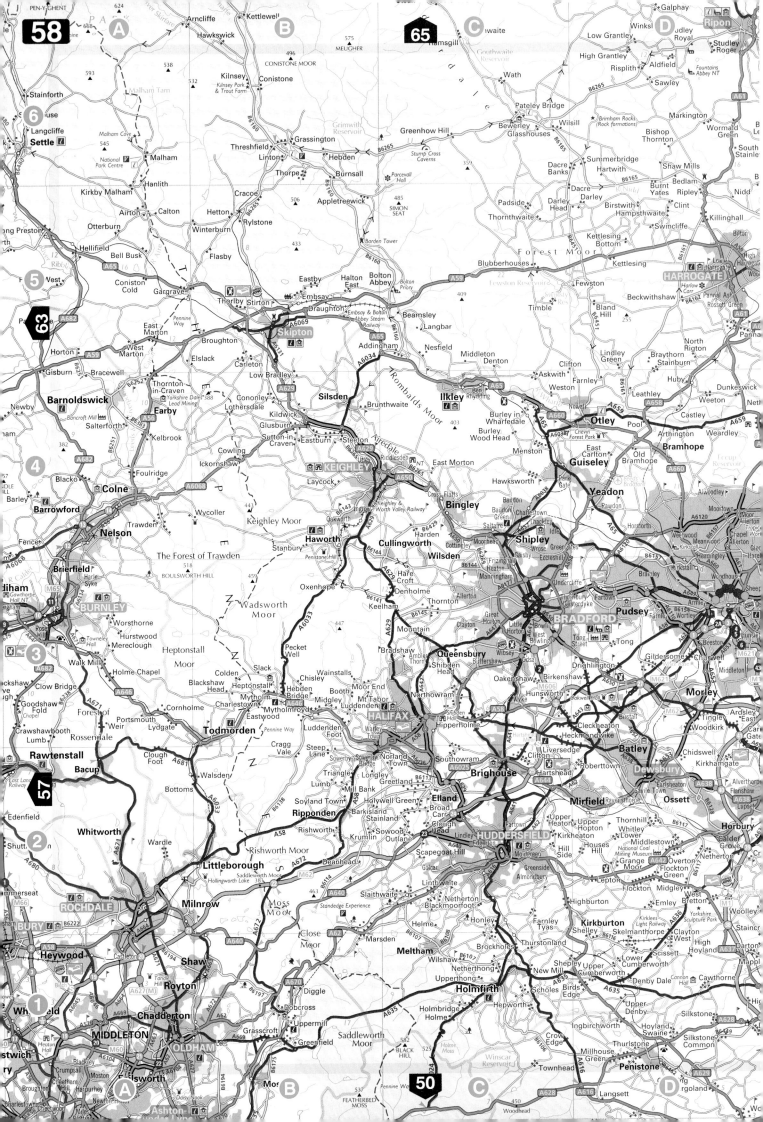

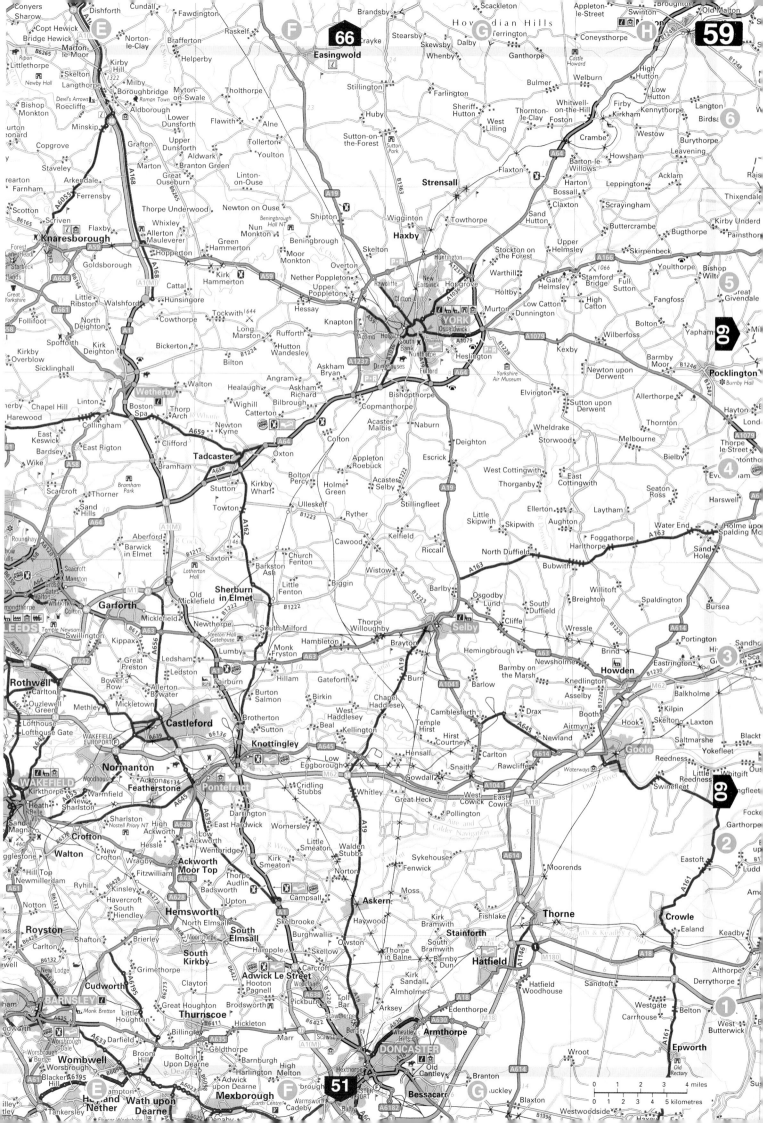

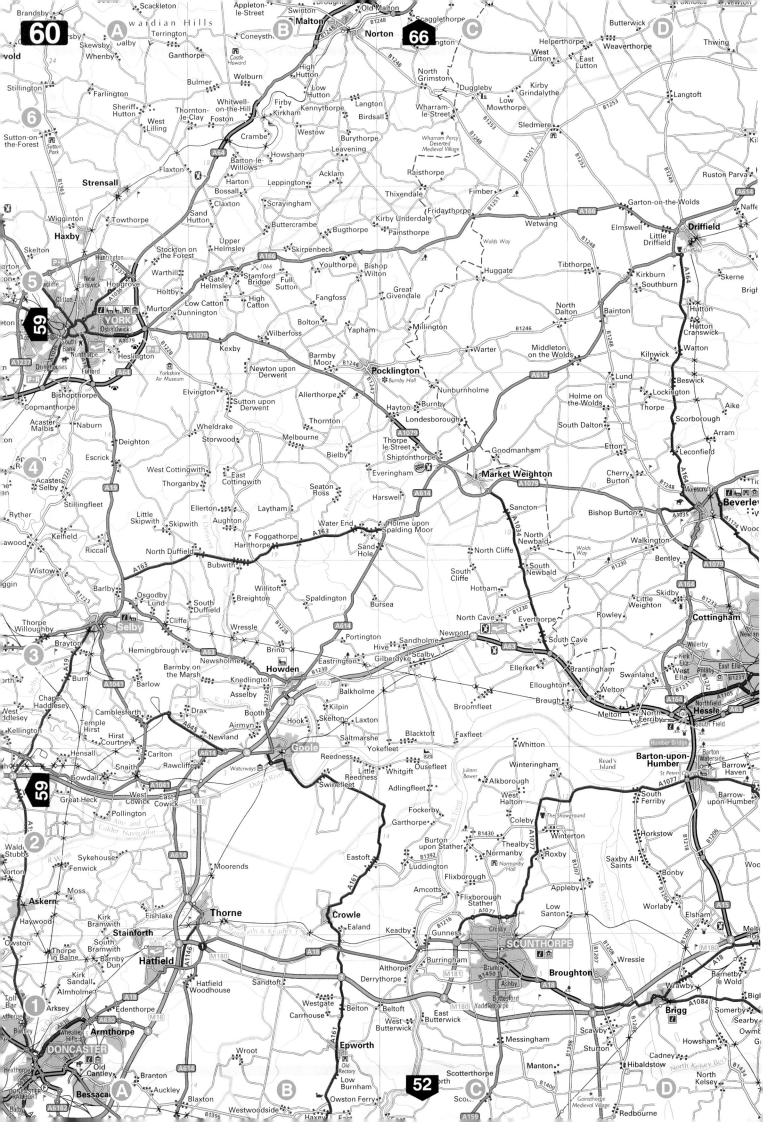

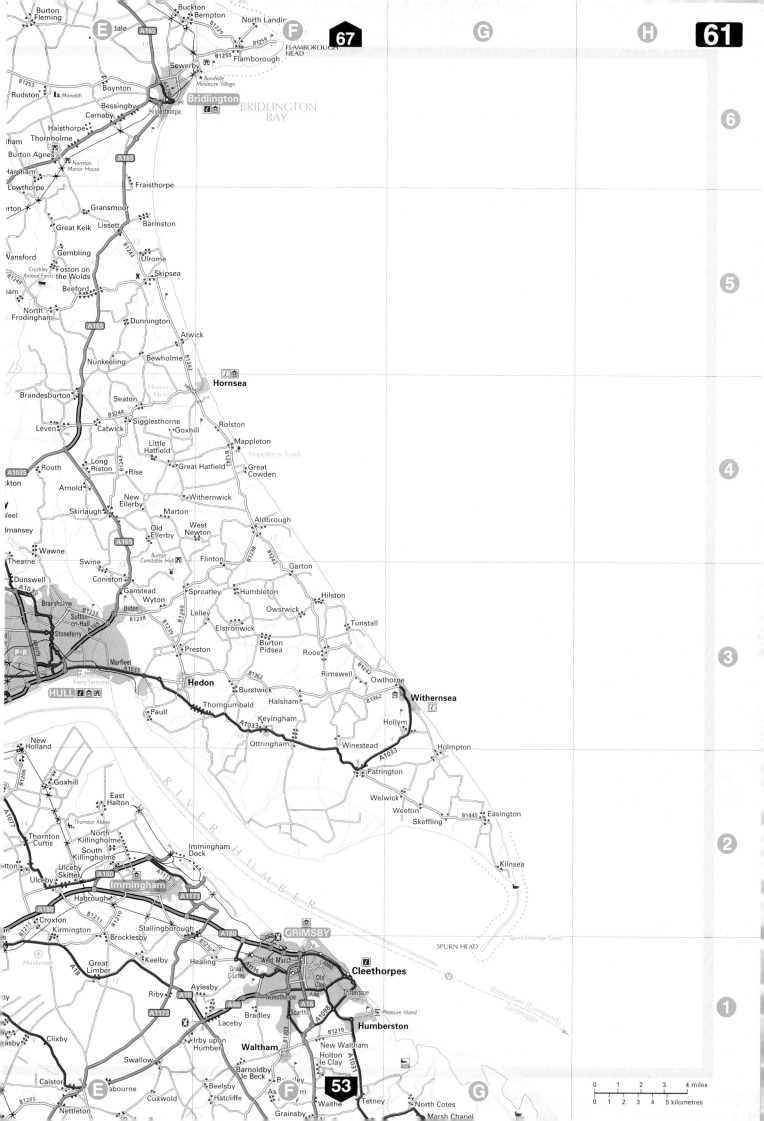

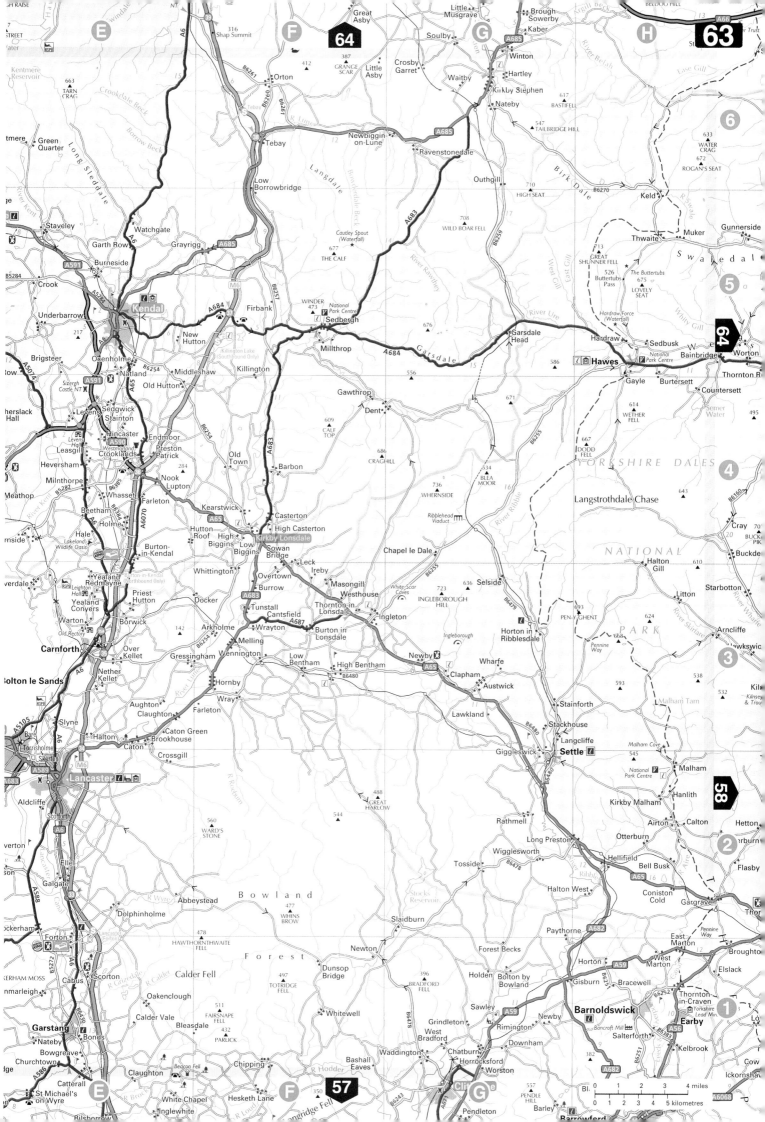

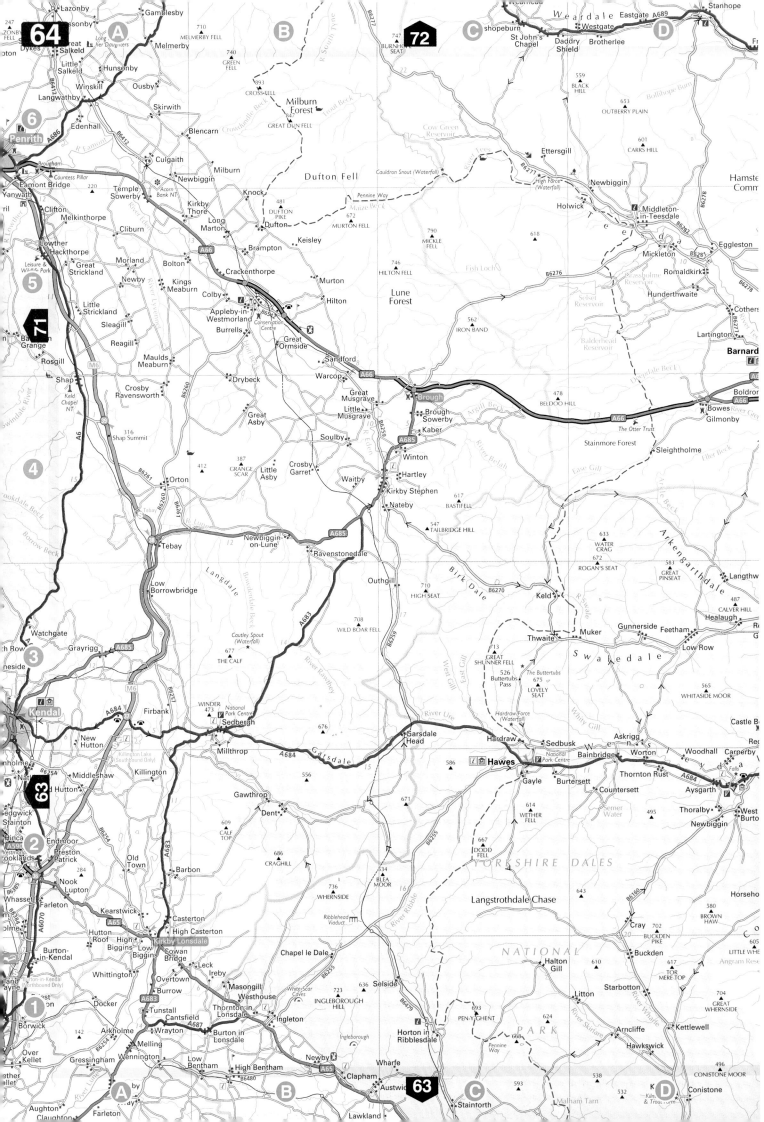

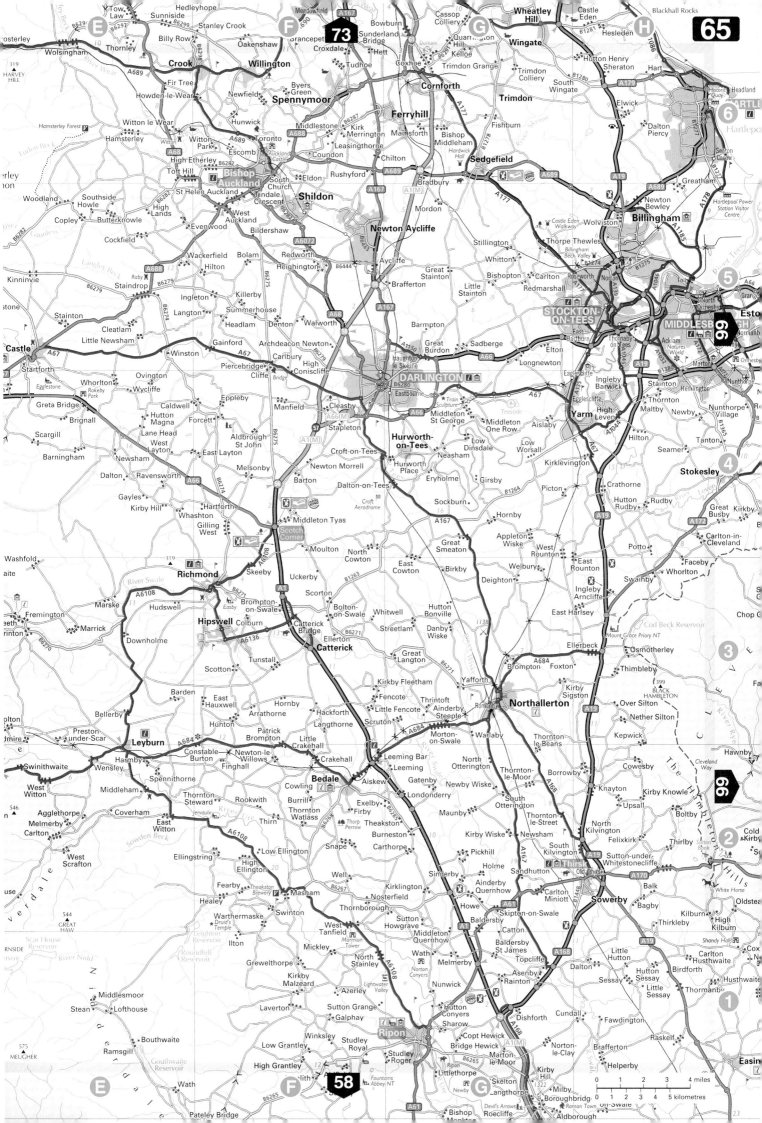

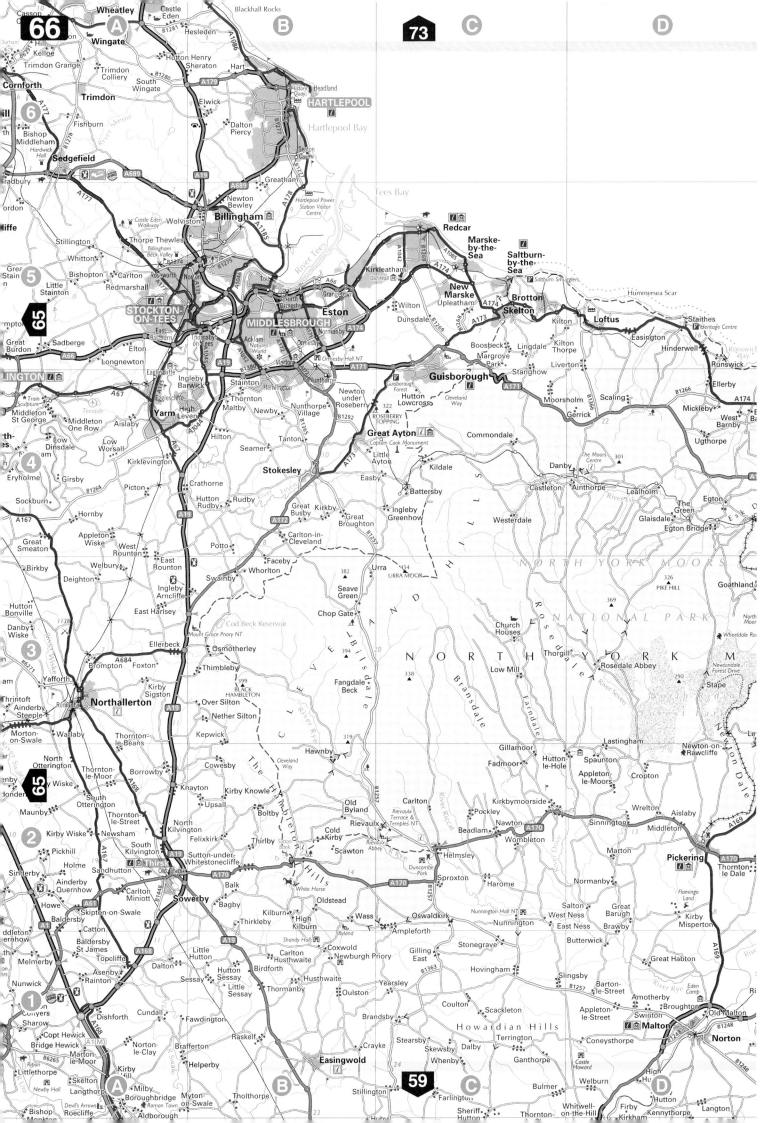

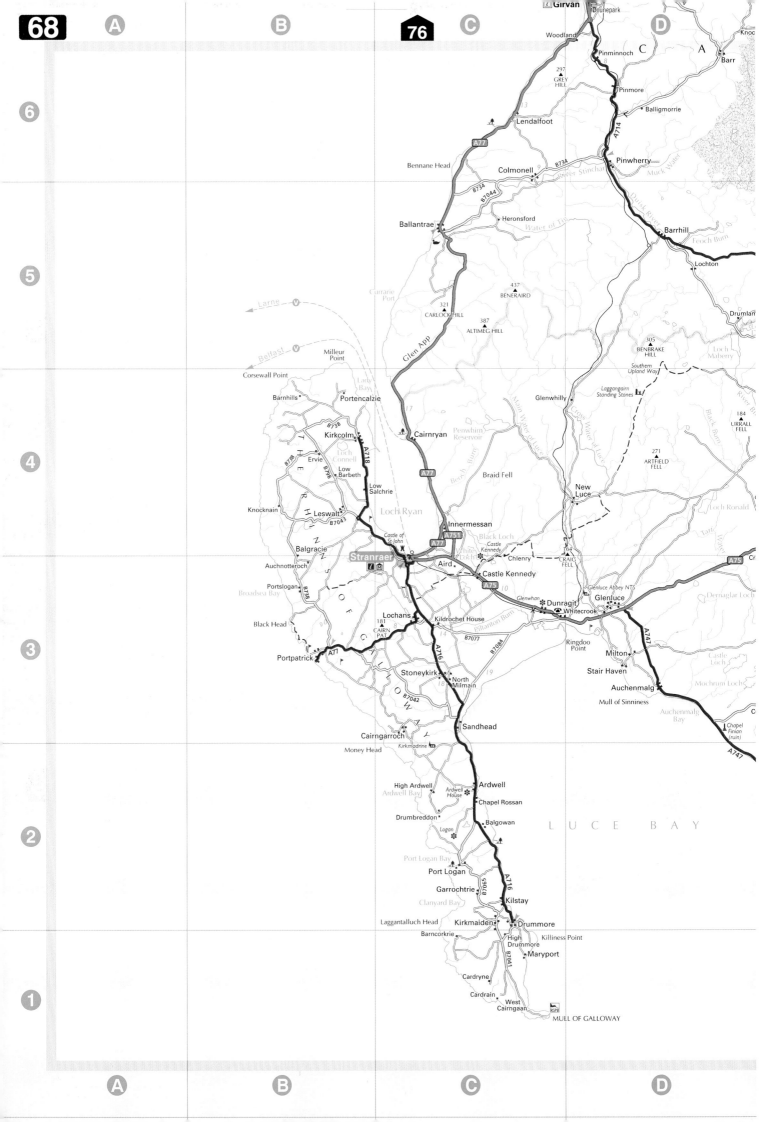

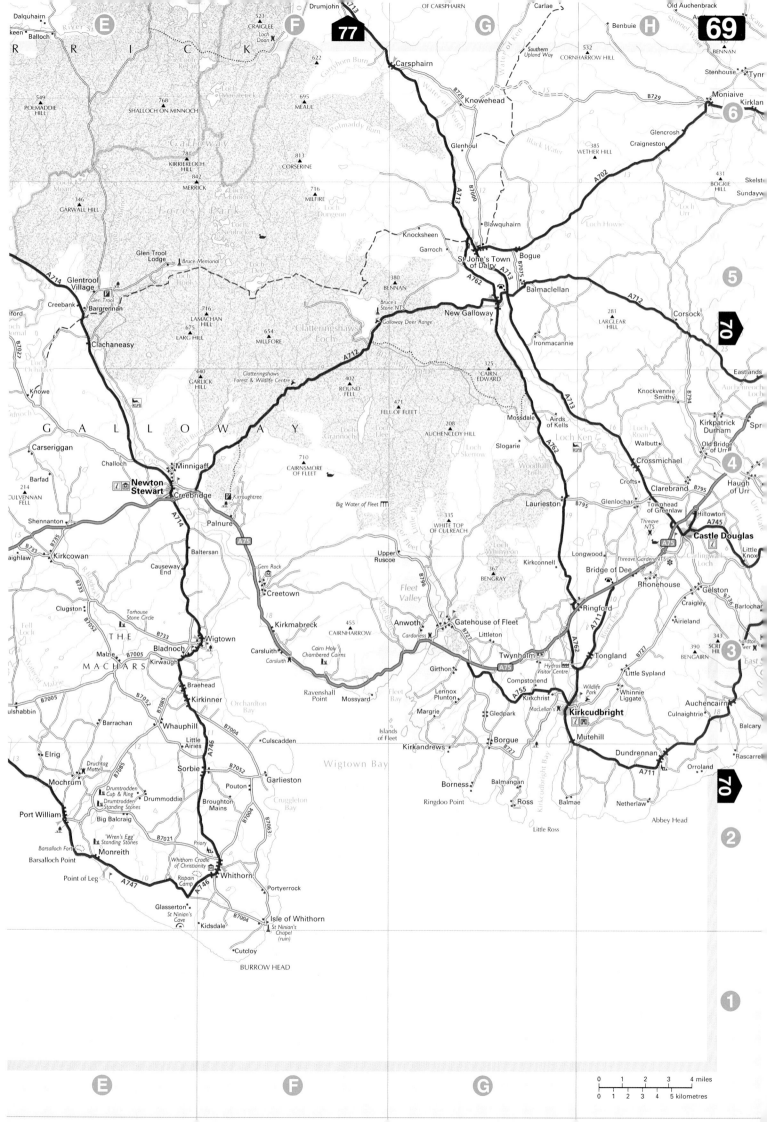

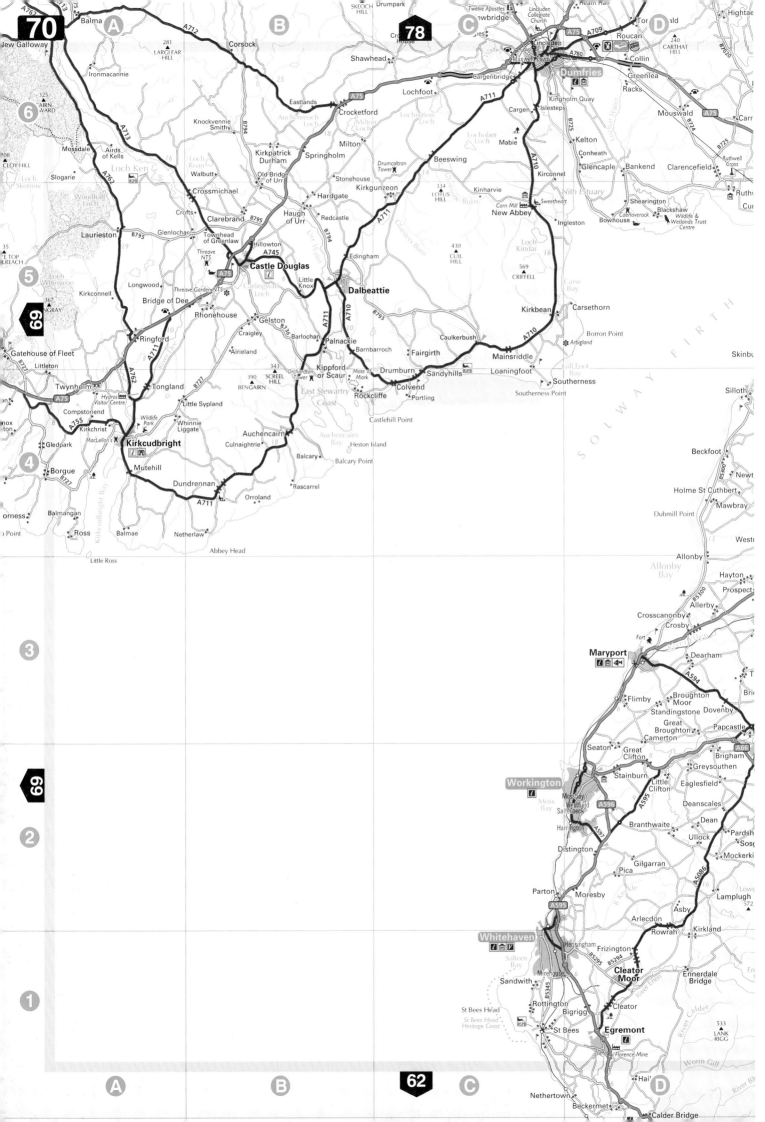

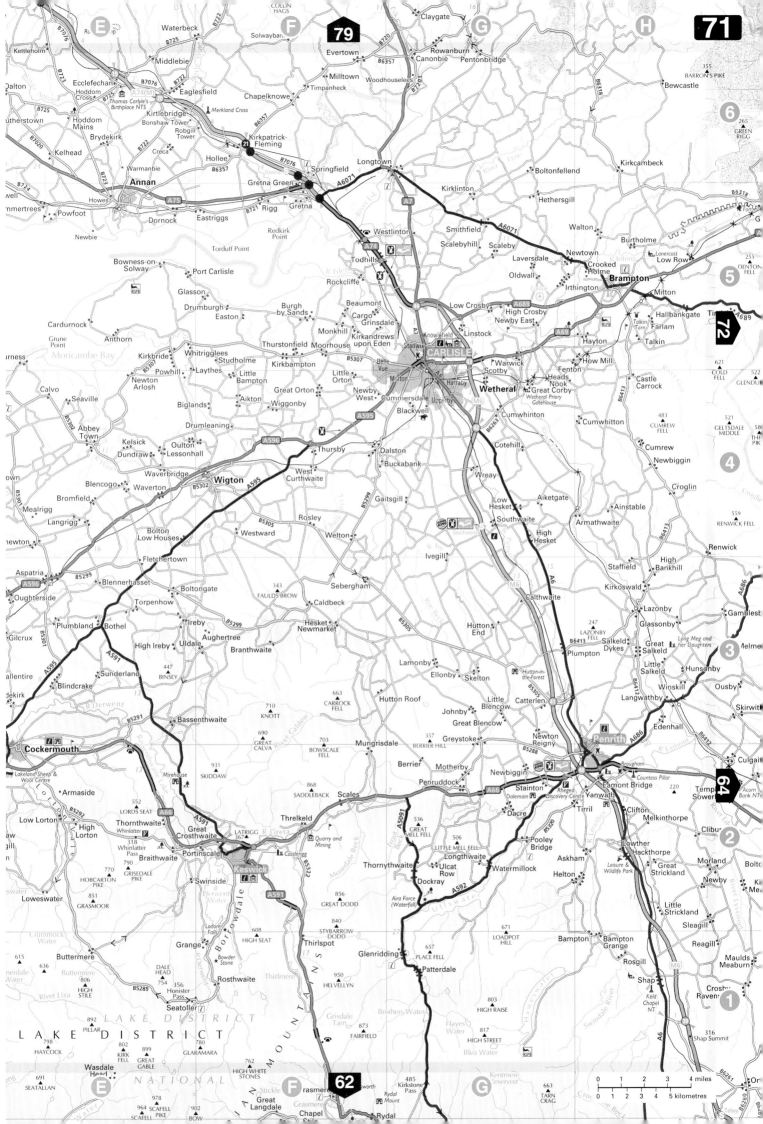

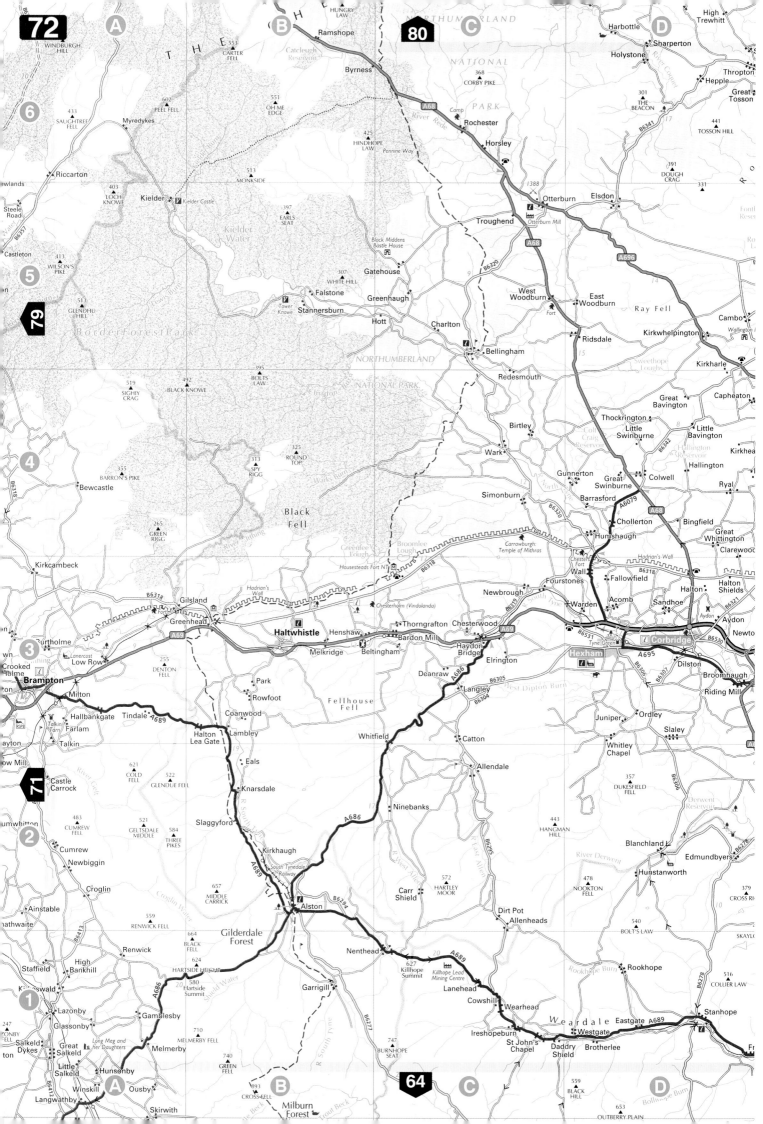

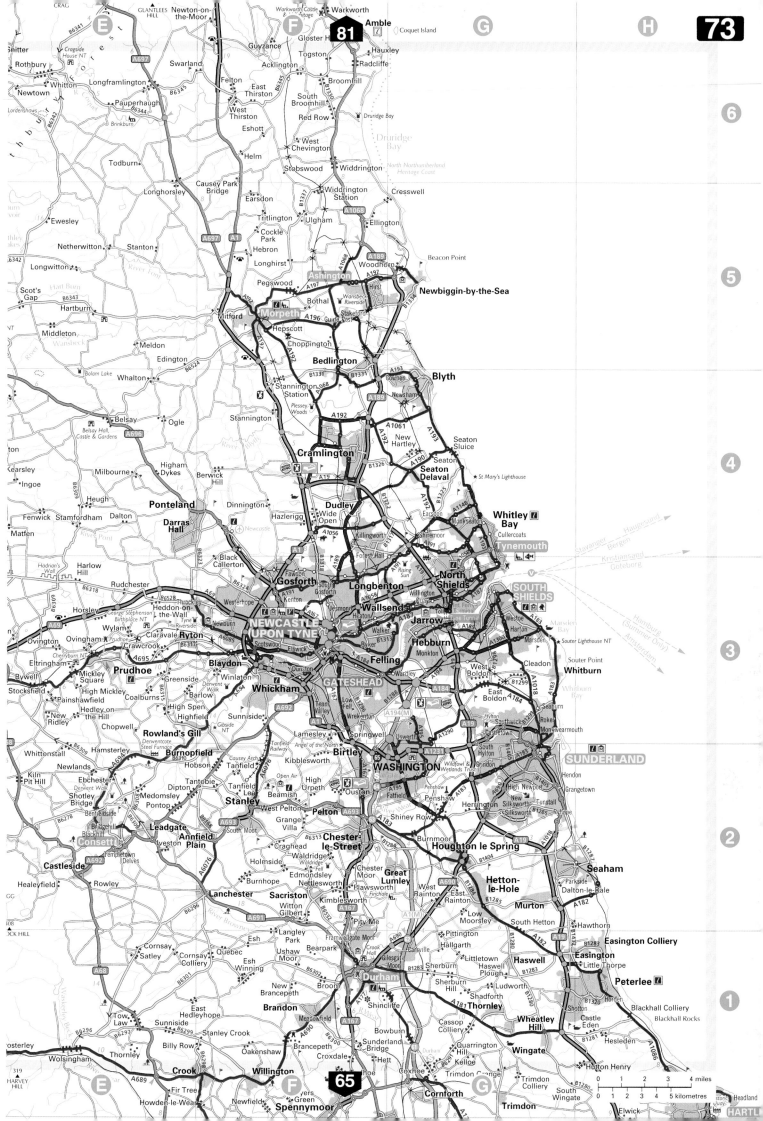

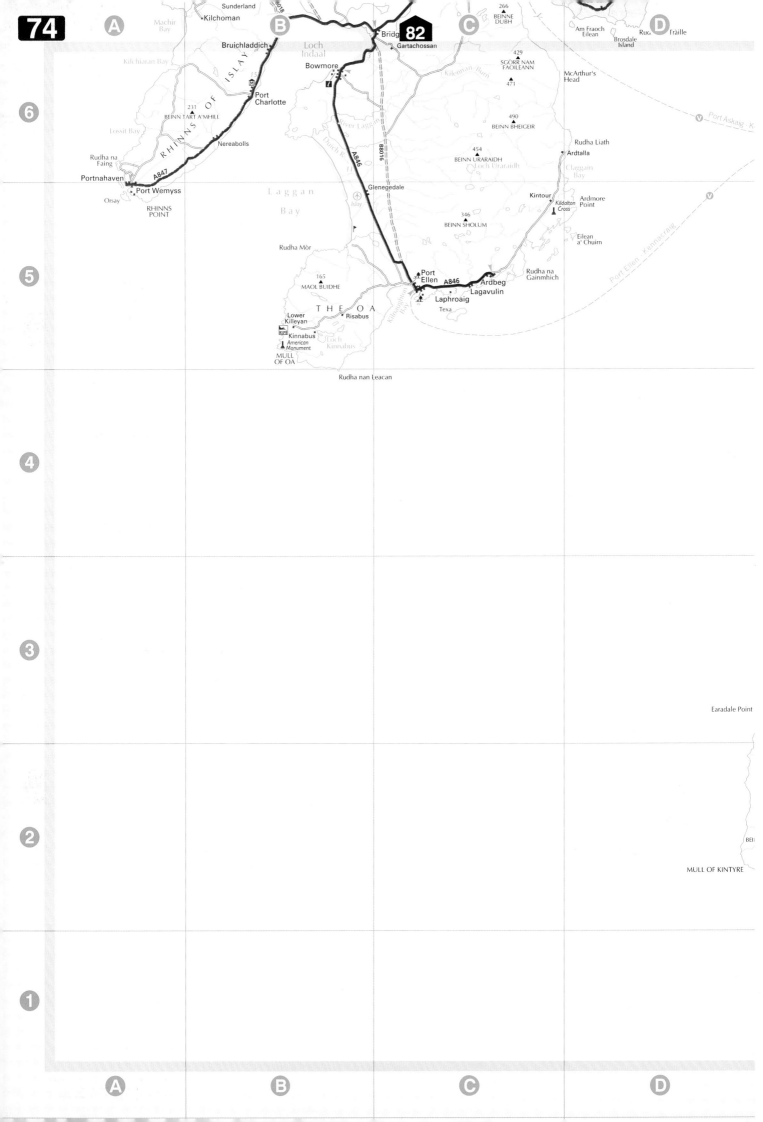

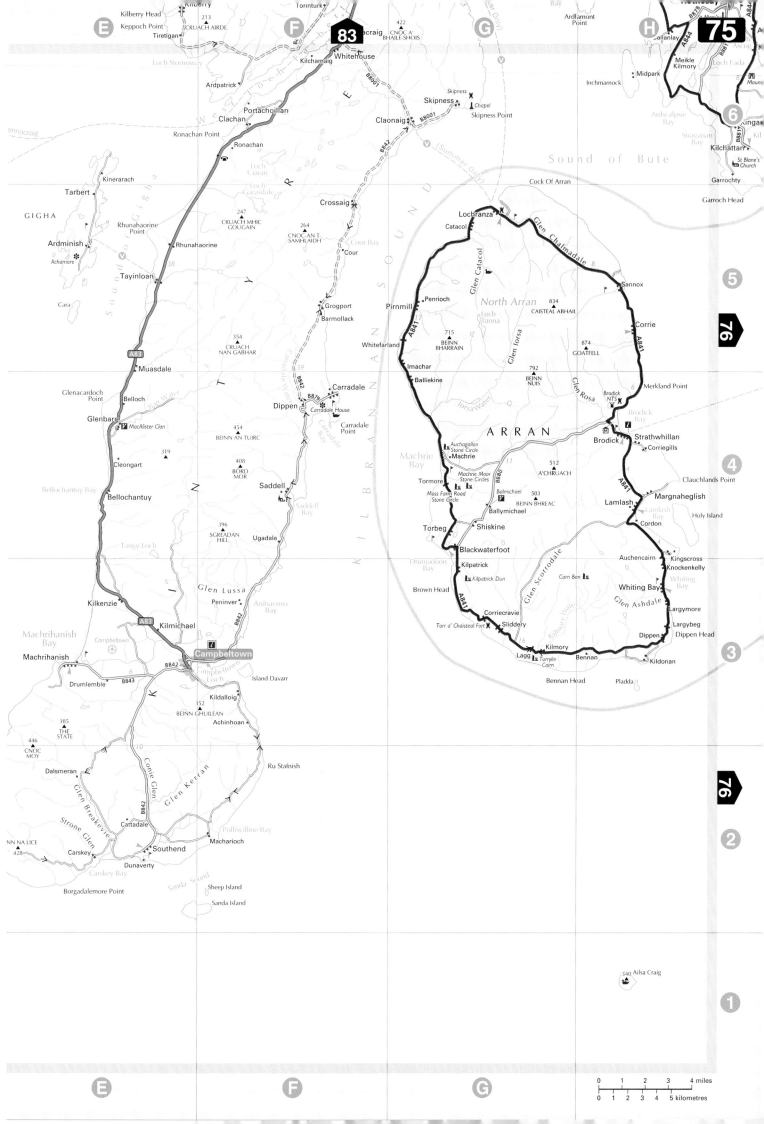

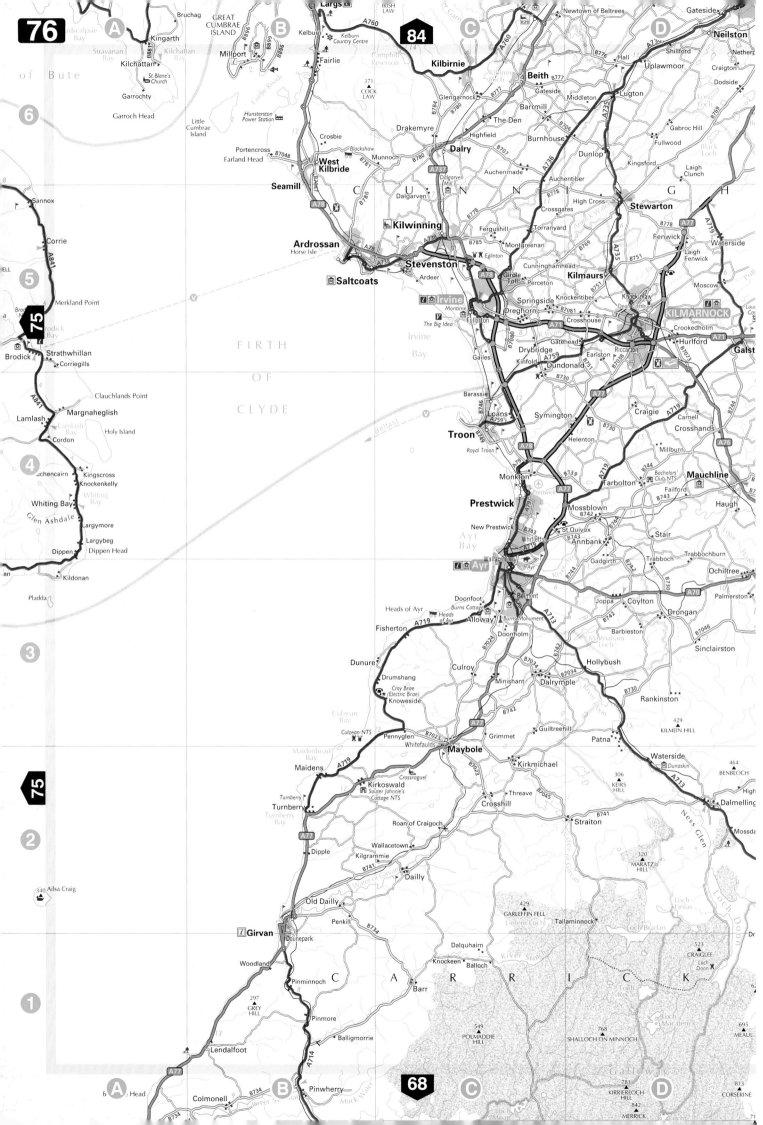

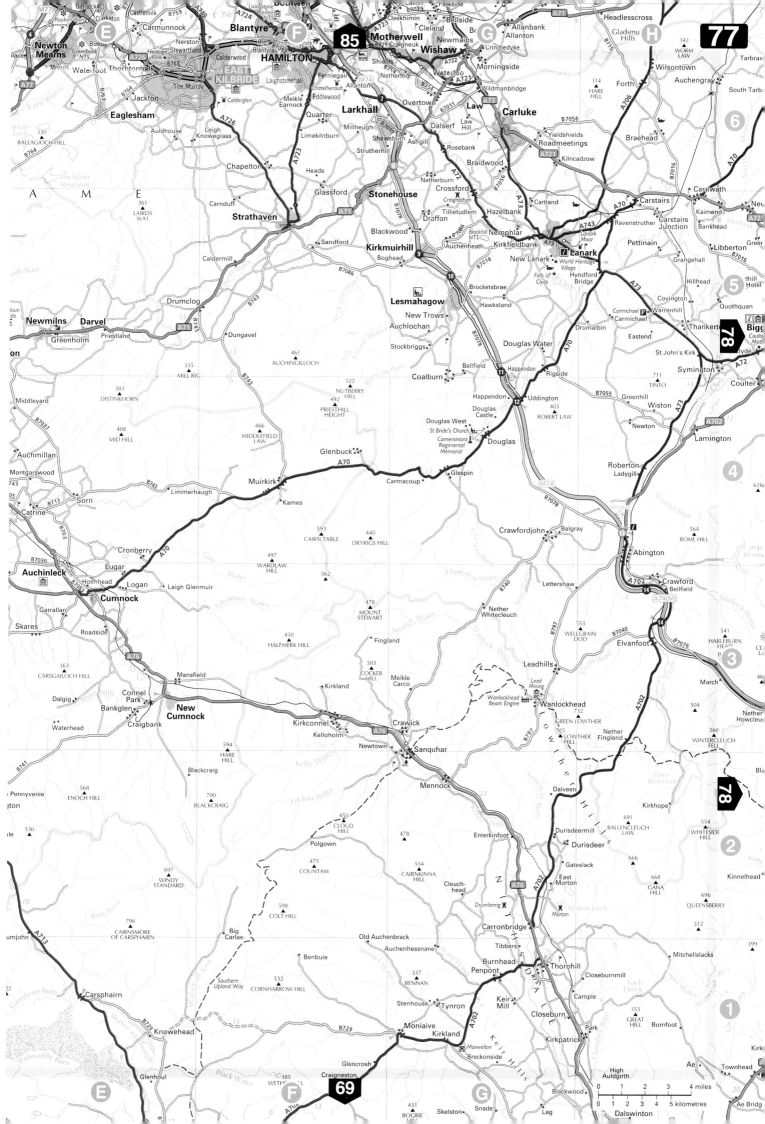

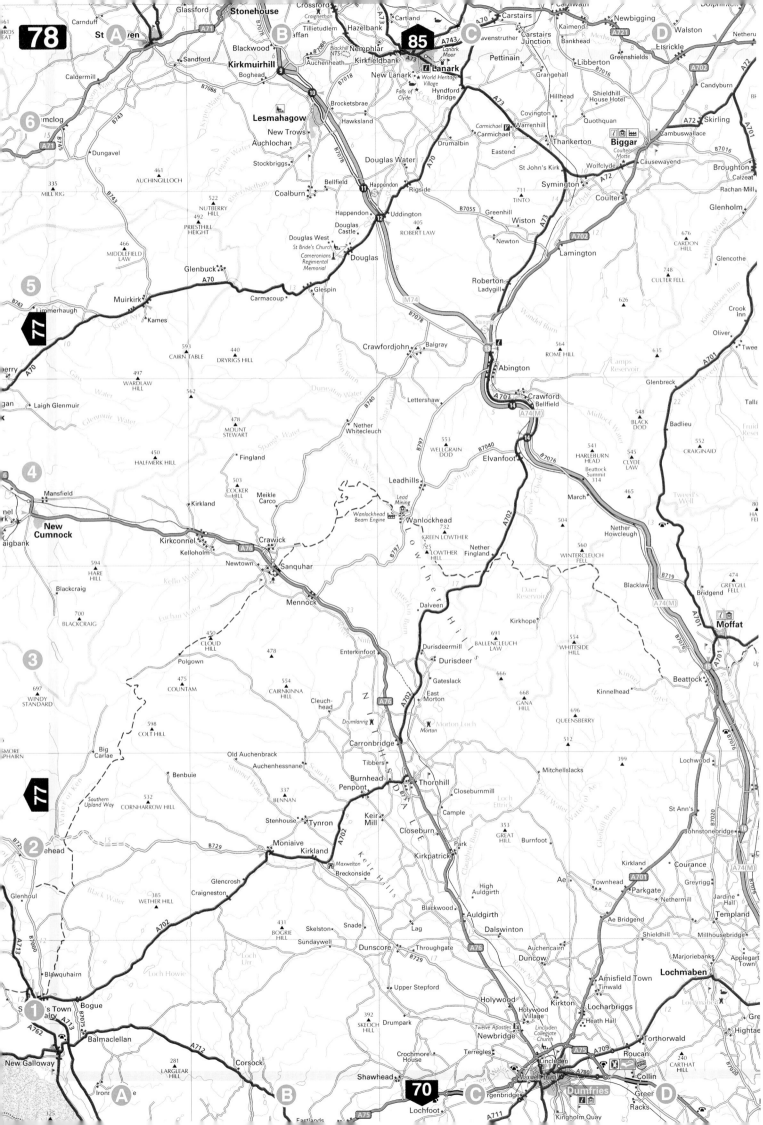

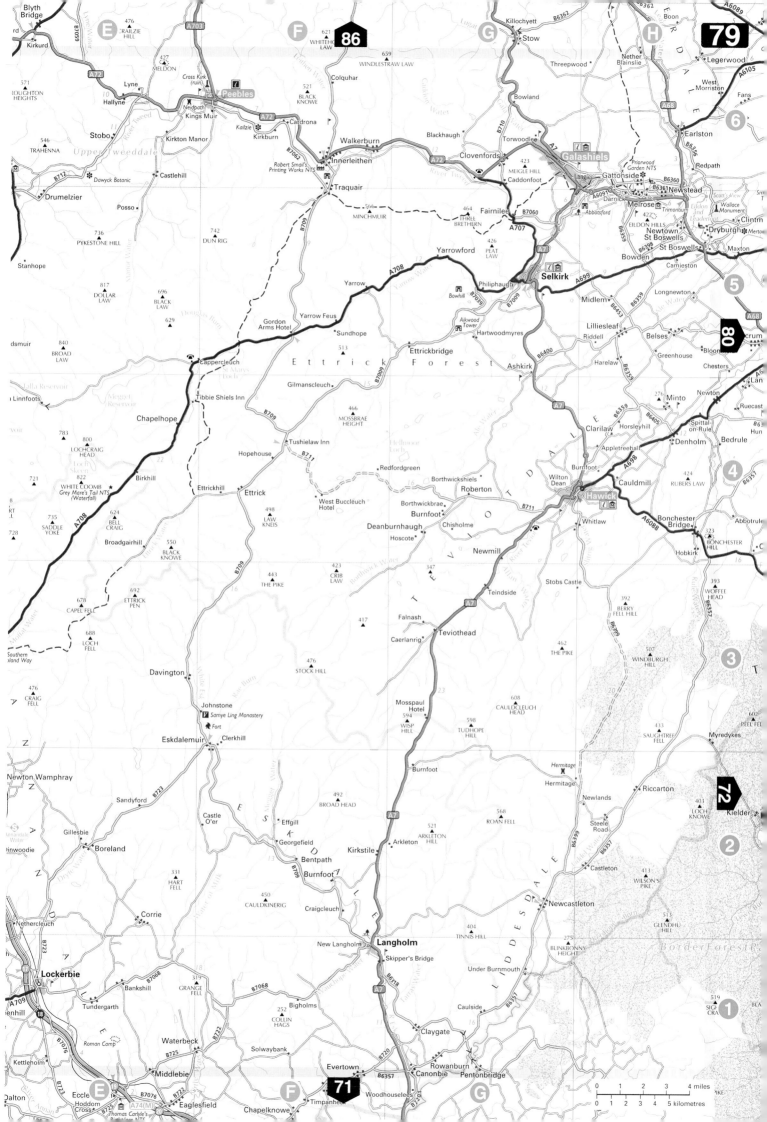

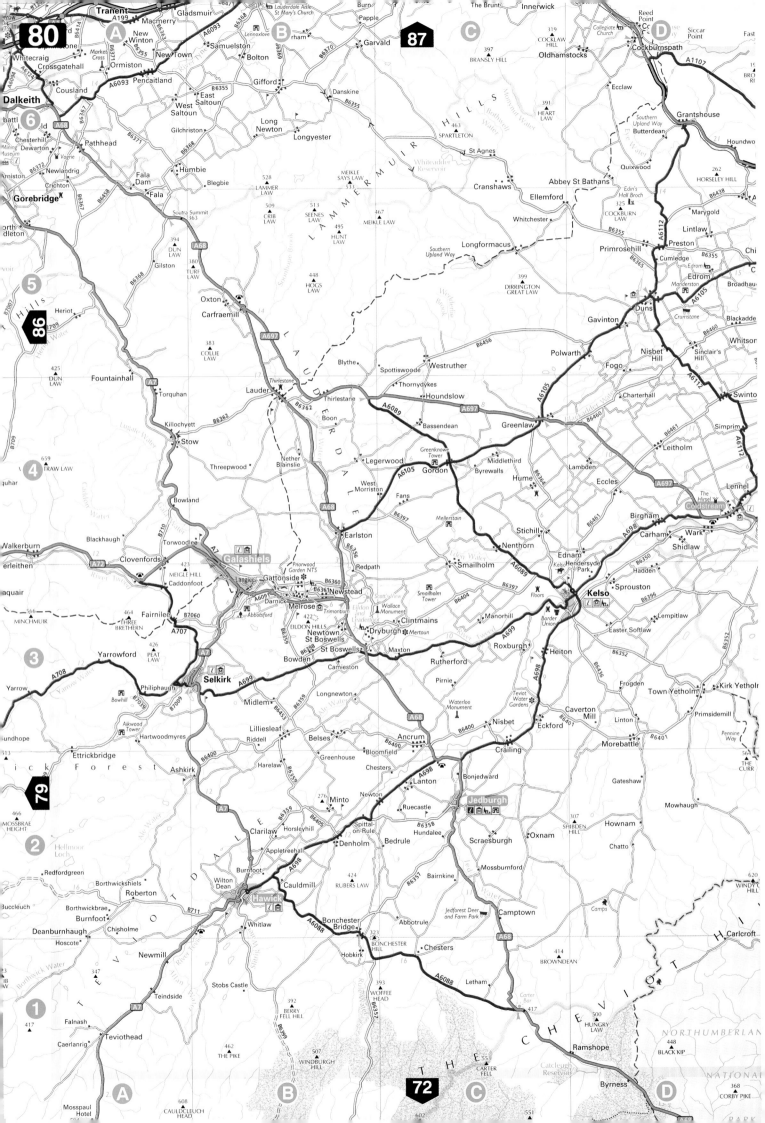

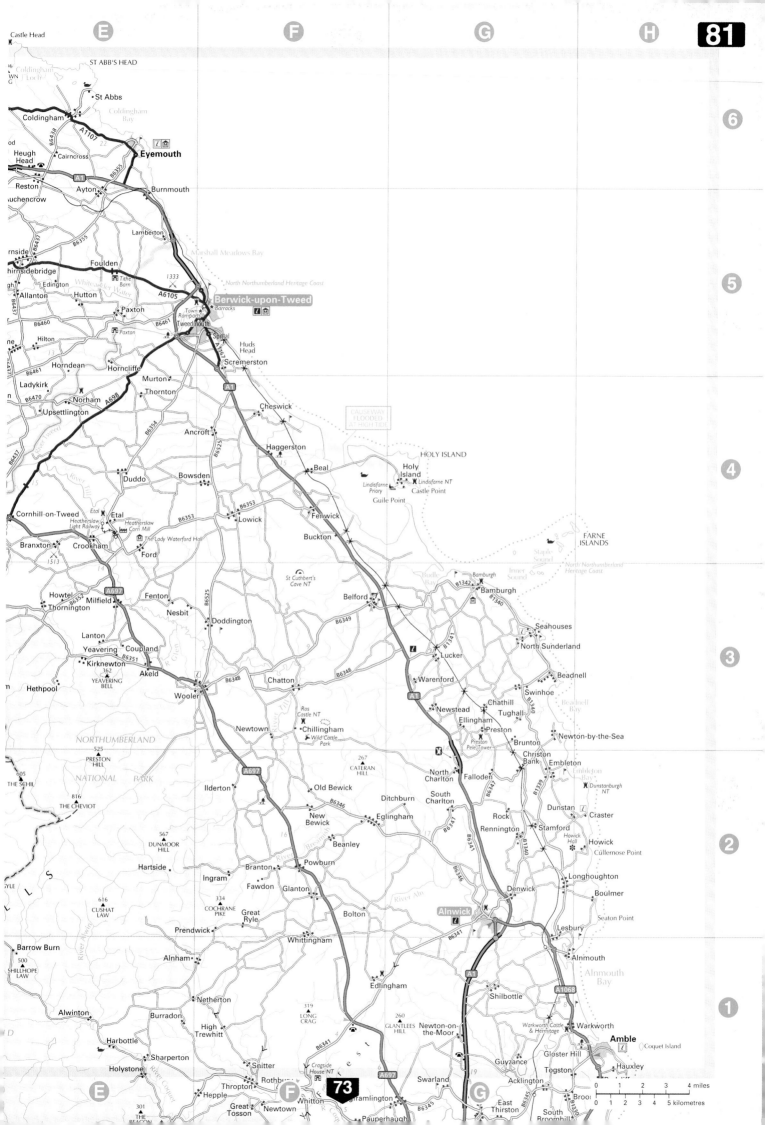

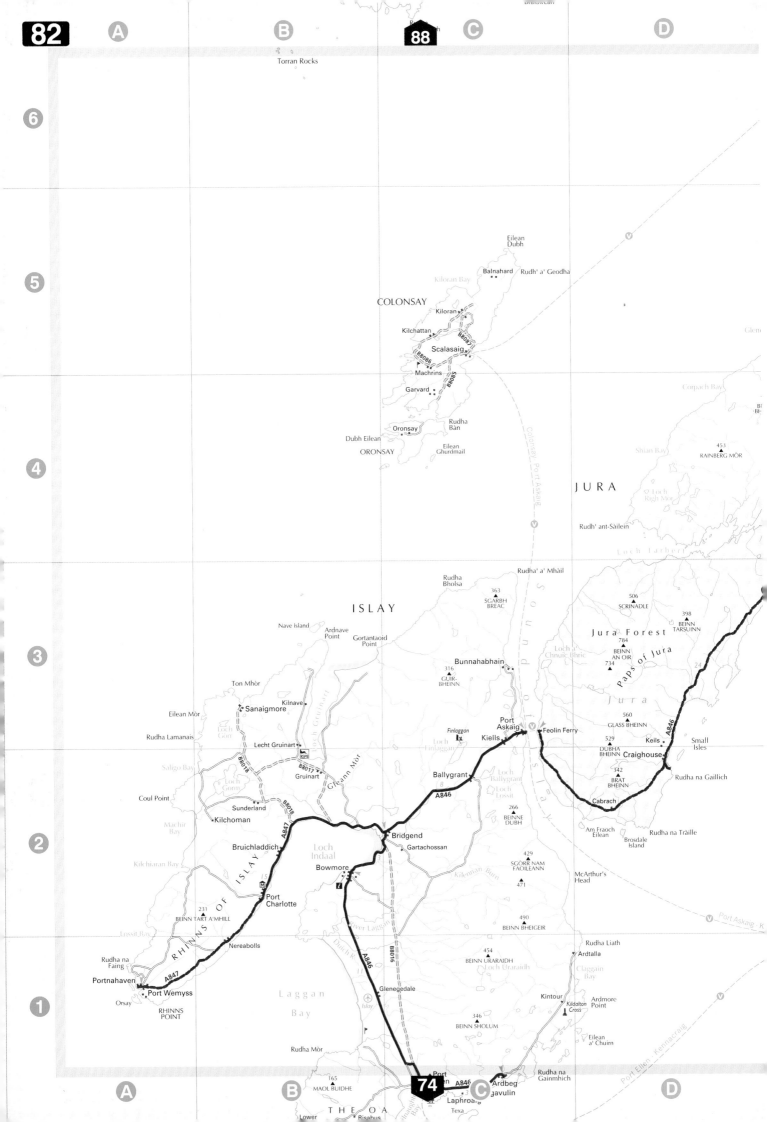

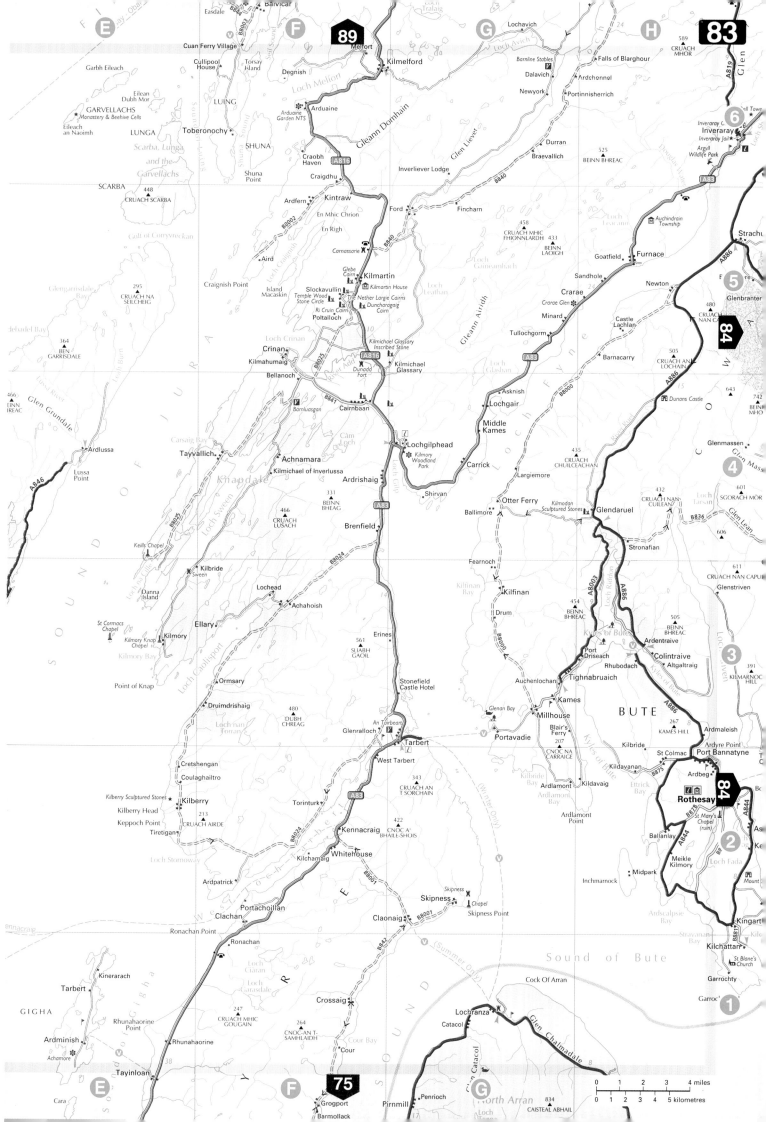

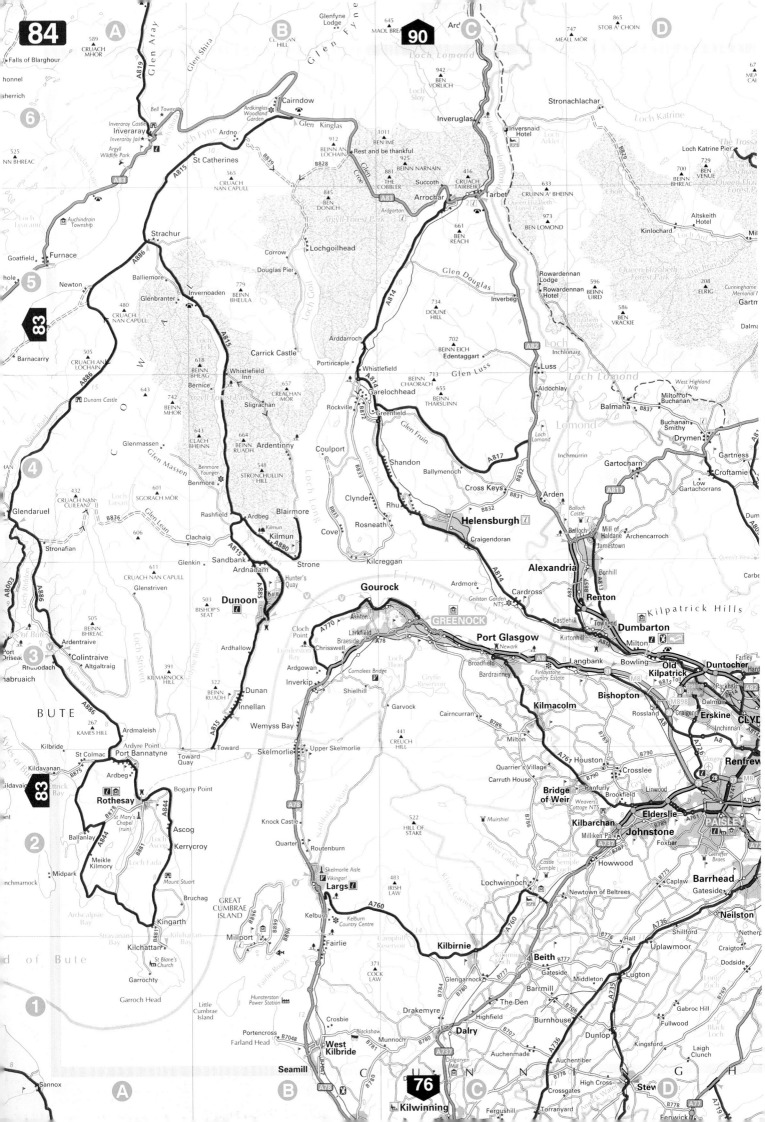

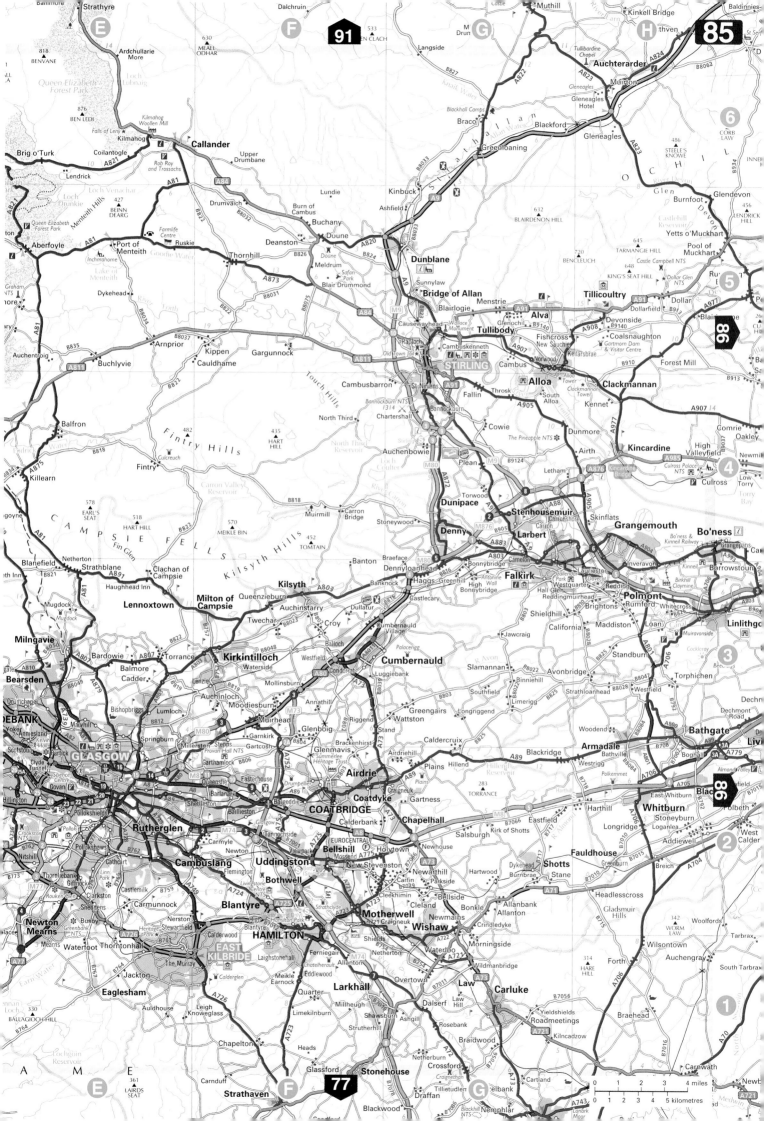

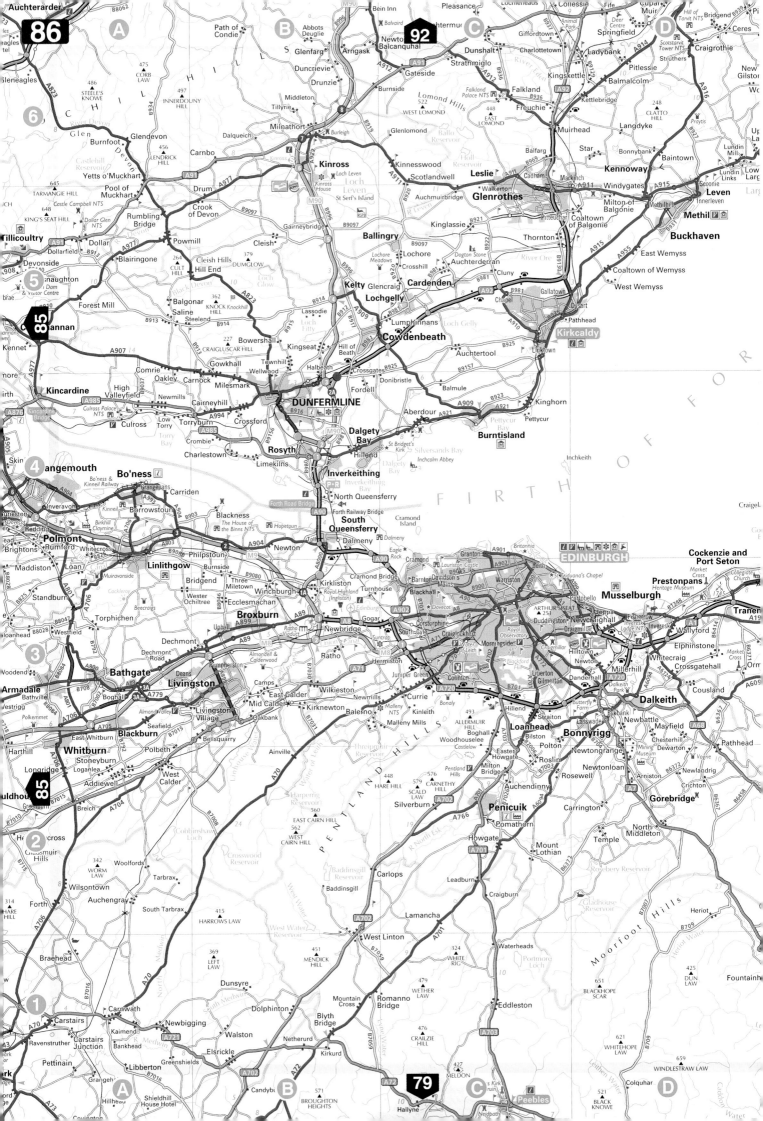

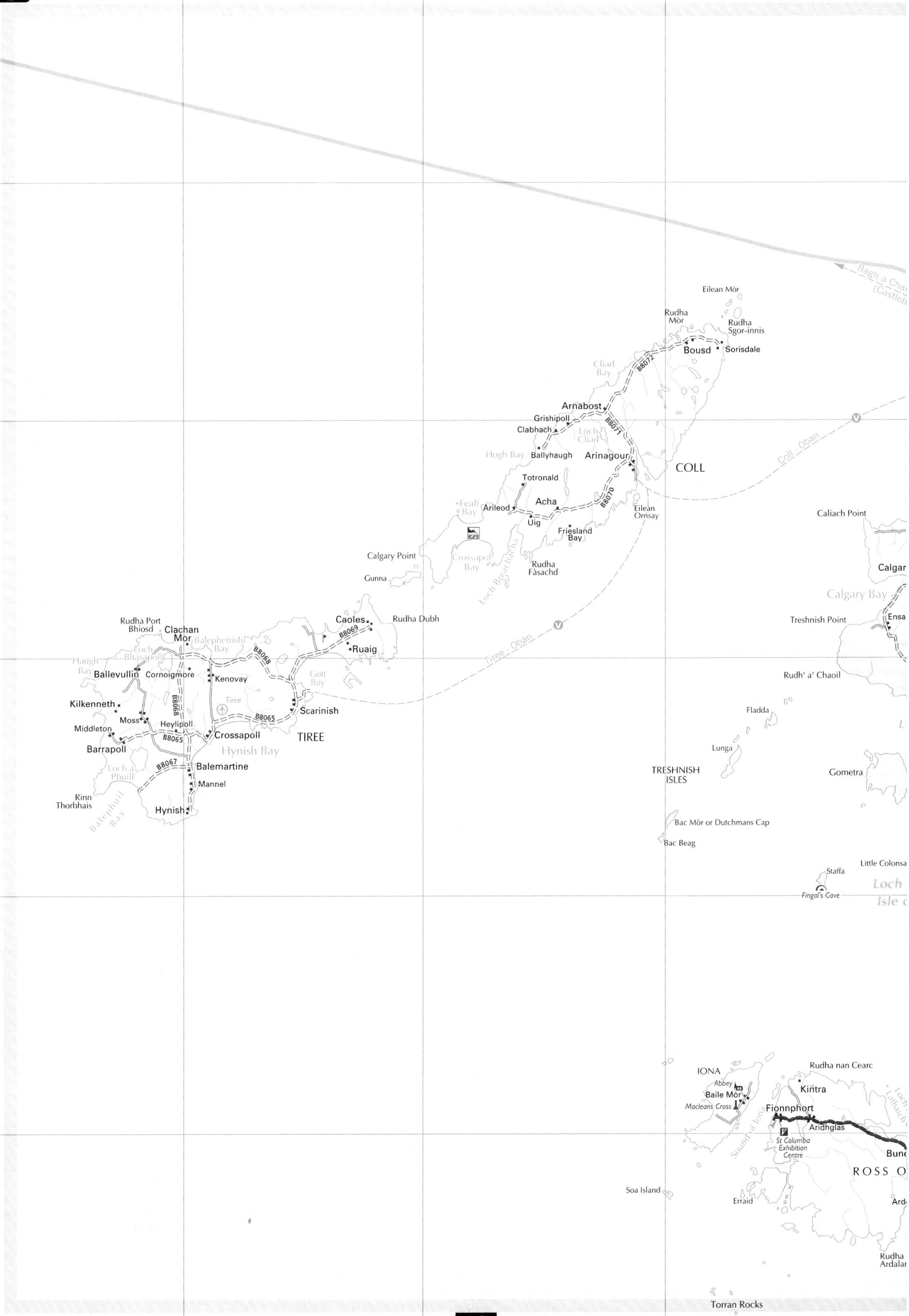

A B C D

6

5

Eilean Mòr

Rudha
Mòr
Rudha
Sgor-innis
Bousd Sorisdale

Cliad
Bay

B8072

Arnabost
Grishipoll
Clabhach
Loch
Cliad
Hogh Bay Ballyhaugh
Arinagour
COLL
Coll - Oban

Totronald

Feall
Bay
Calgary Point
RSPB
Crossapol
Bay

Arileod **Acha**
Uig
Friesland
Bay
Eilean
Ornsay

4

Caliach Point

Calga

Gunna
Rudha
Fàsachd

Loch Bìgearbhui

Calgary Bay

Rudha Port
Bhiosd **Clachan**
Mòr
Balephetrish
Bay
Caoles
Rudha Dubh
B8069
Ruaig

Treshnish Point
Ensa

Loch
Bhasapoll
Haugh
Bay
Ballevullin Cornoigmore
B8068
Kenovay
Gott
Bay
Tiree - Oban

Rudh' a' Chaoil

B8068
Kilkenneth
Moss
Heylipoll
B8065
Tiree
Scarinish

Fladda

Lunga

Middleton
Barrapoll
B8065 **Crossapoll**
TIREE

TRESHNISH
ISLES
Gometra

3

Rinn
Thorbhais
Loch a'
Phuill
B8067
Balemartine
Mannel
Hynish Bay

Balephuill
Bay
Hynish

Bac Mòr or Dutchmans Cap

Bac Beag

Staffa
Little Colonsa

Fingal's Cave
Loch
Isle o

2

IONA
Rudha nan Cearc

Abbey
Baile Mòr
Kintra
Fionnphort

Macleans Cross
Aridhglas
St Columba
Exhibition
Centre
Bune

ROSS O

Soa Island
Erraid
Ard

1

Rudha
Ardalar

Torran Rocks

A B C D

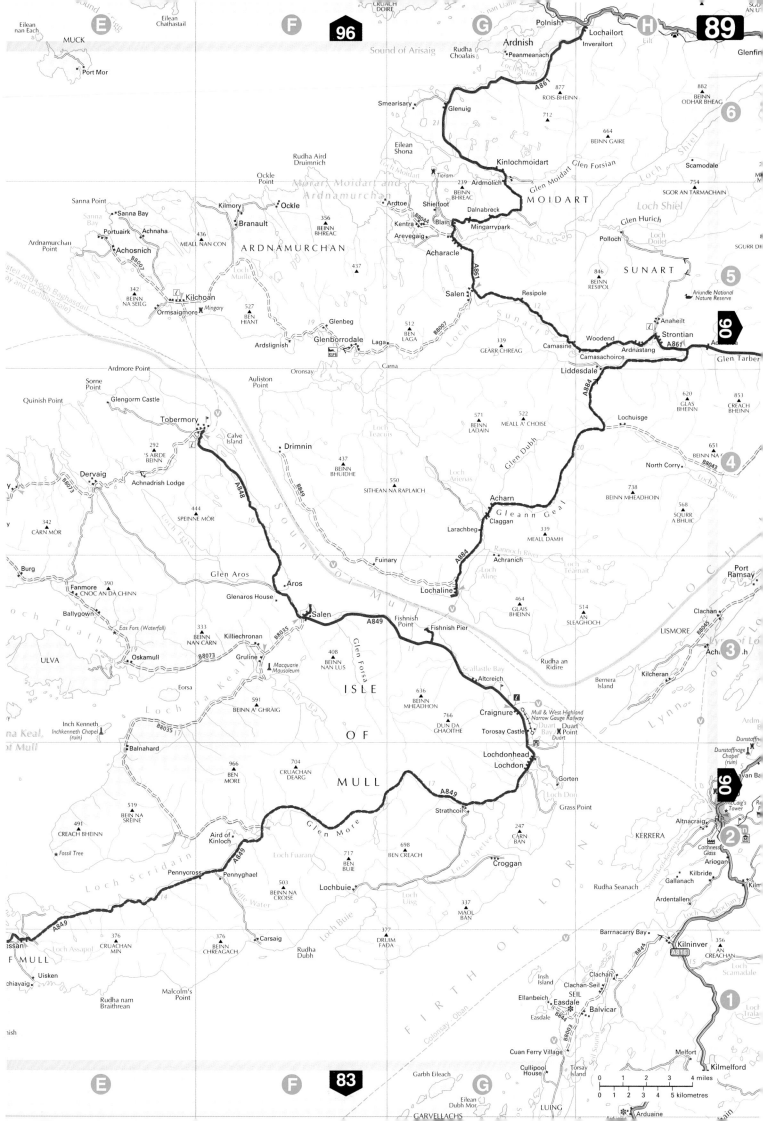

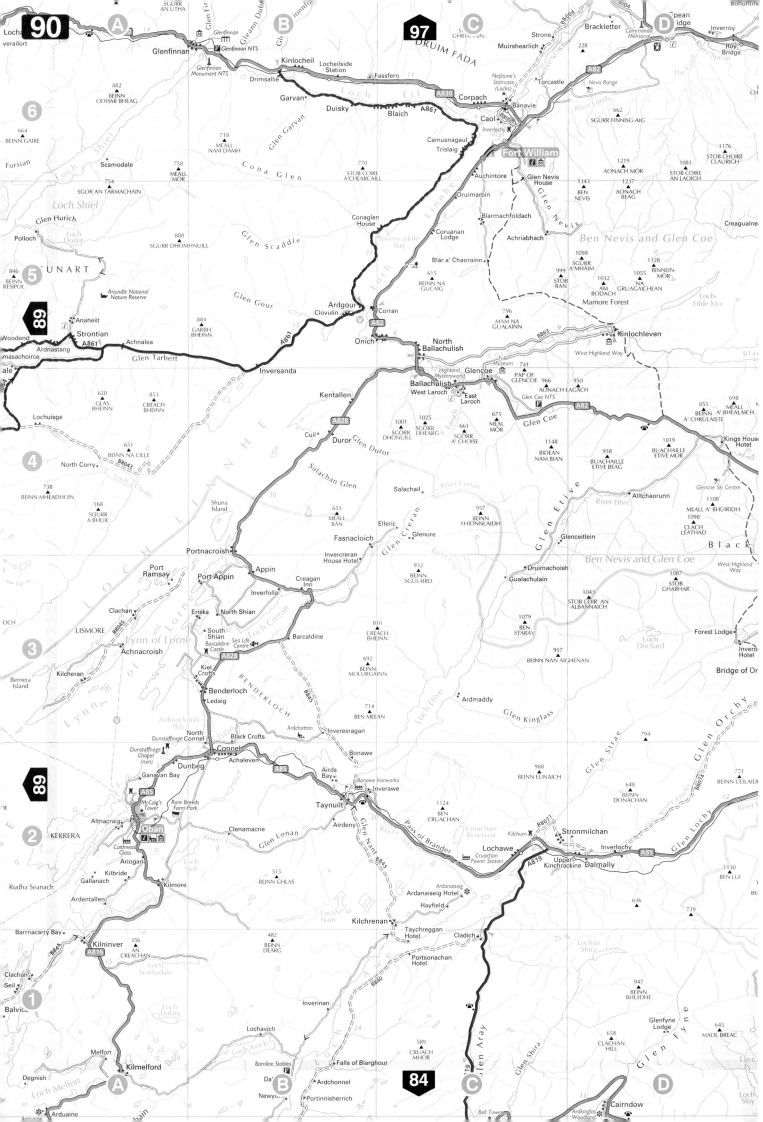

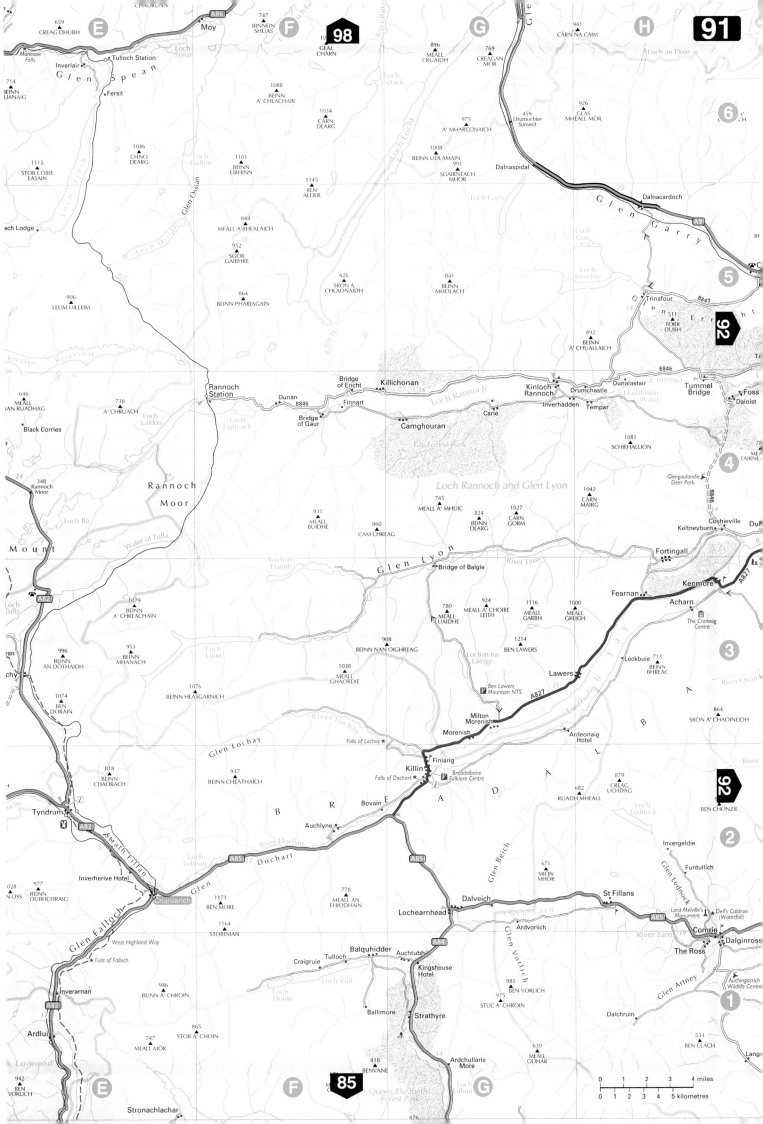

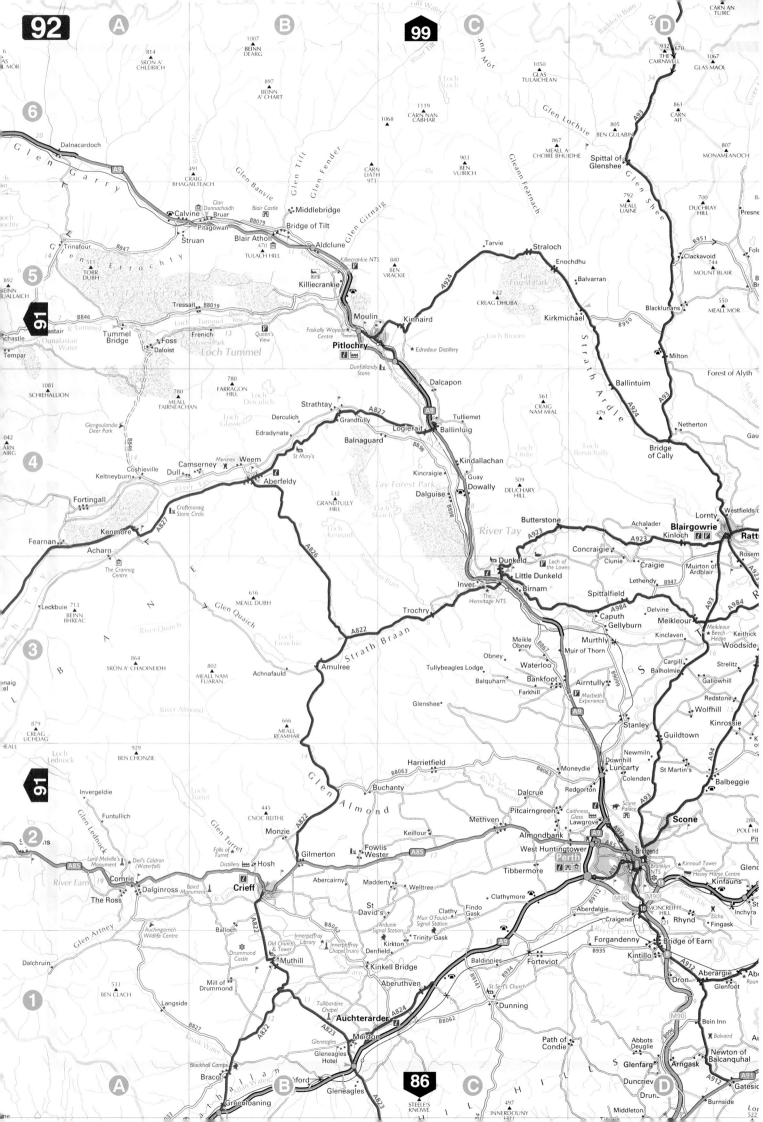

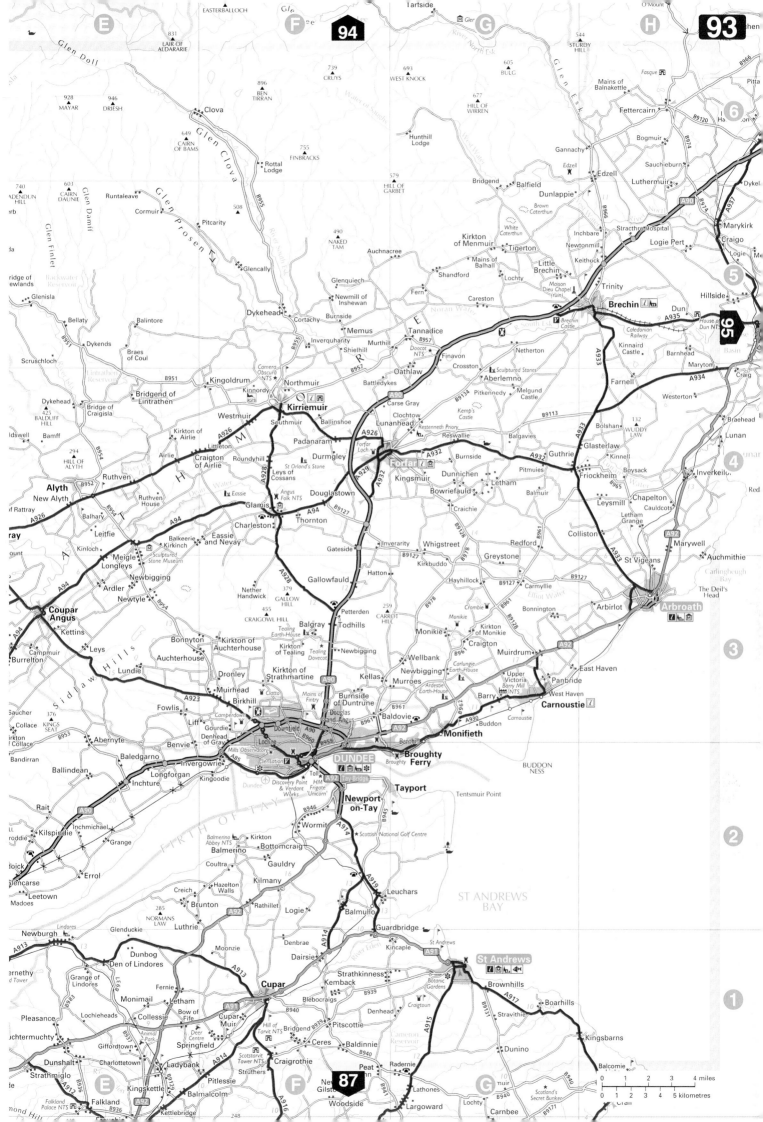

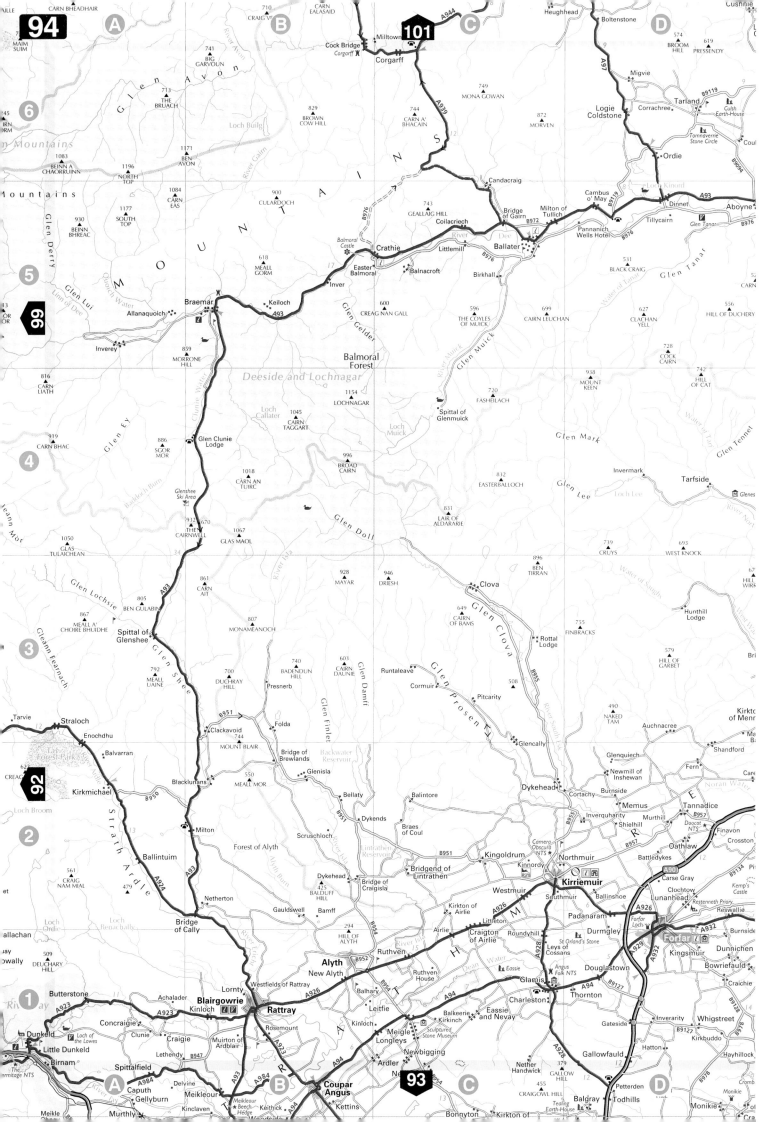

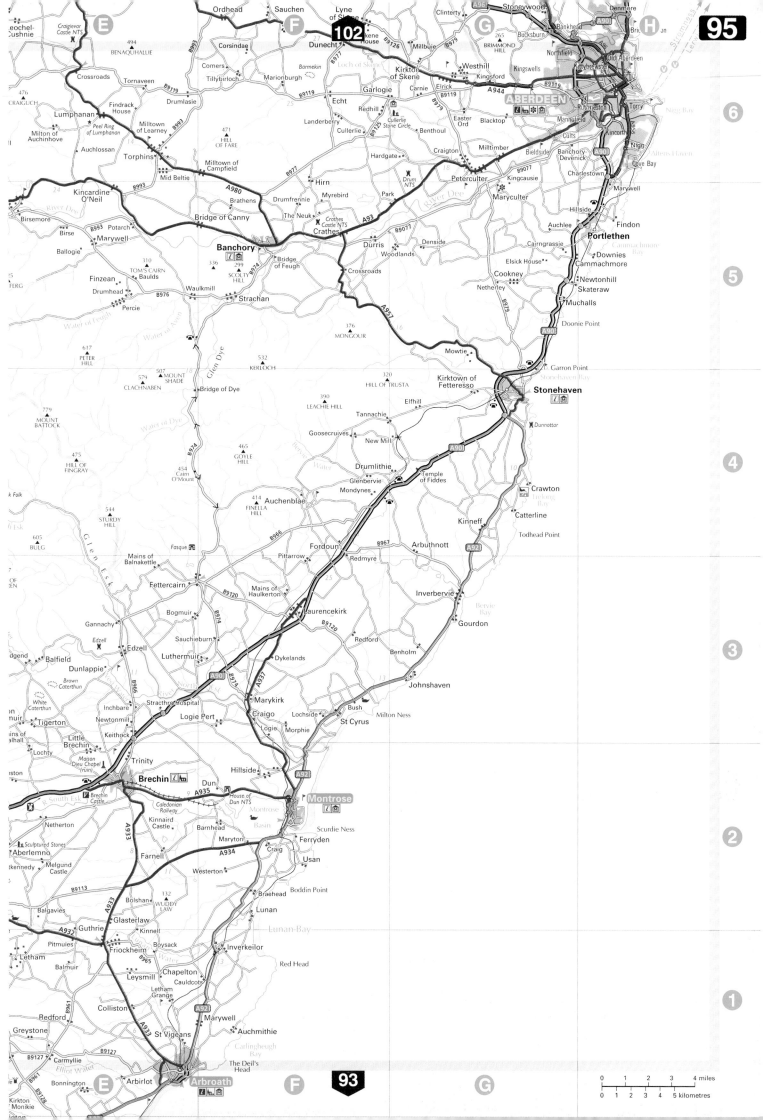

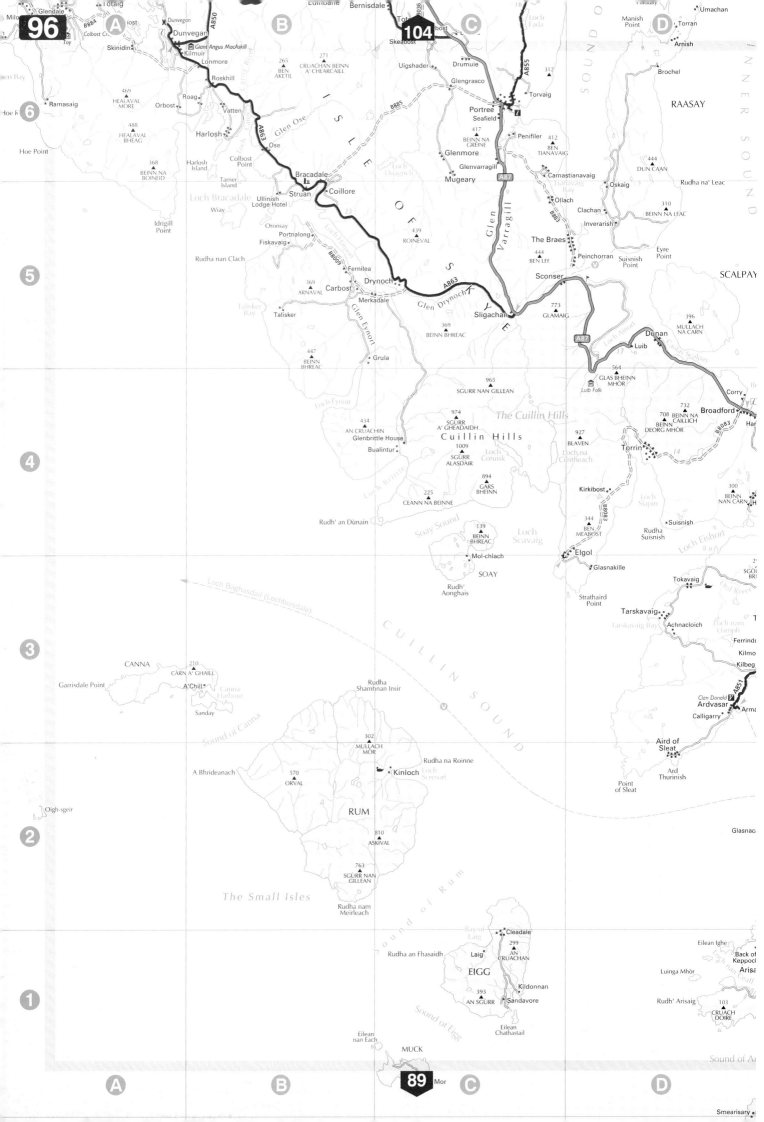

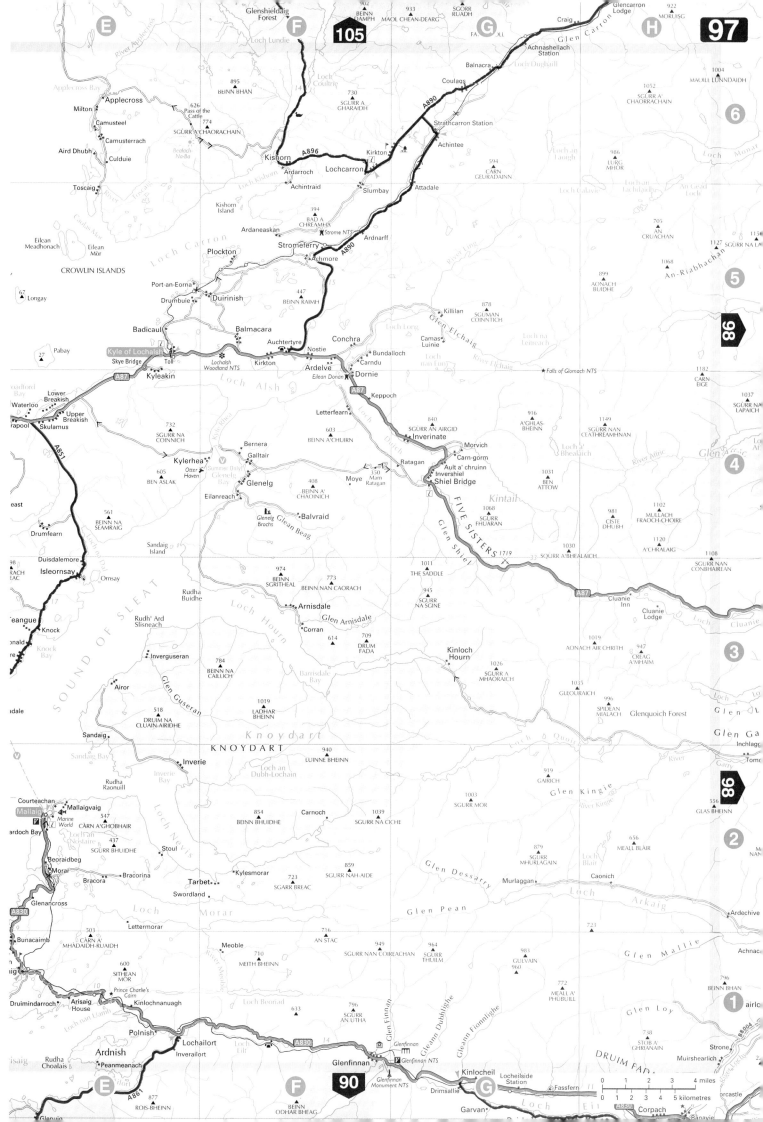

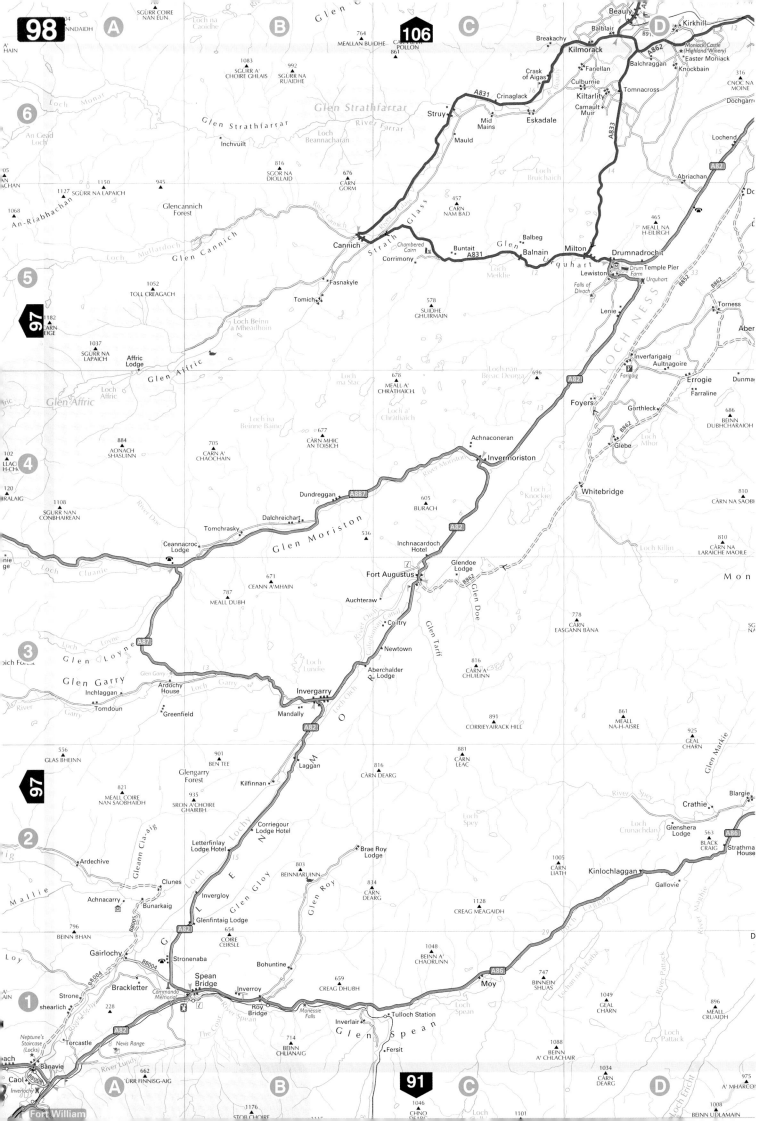

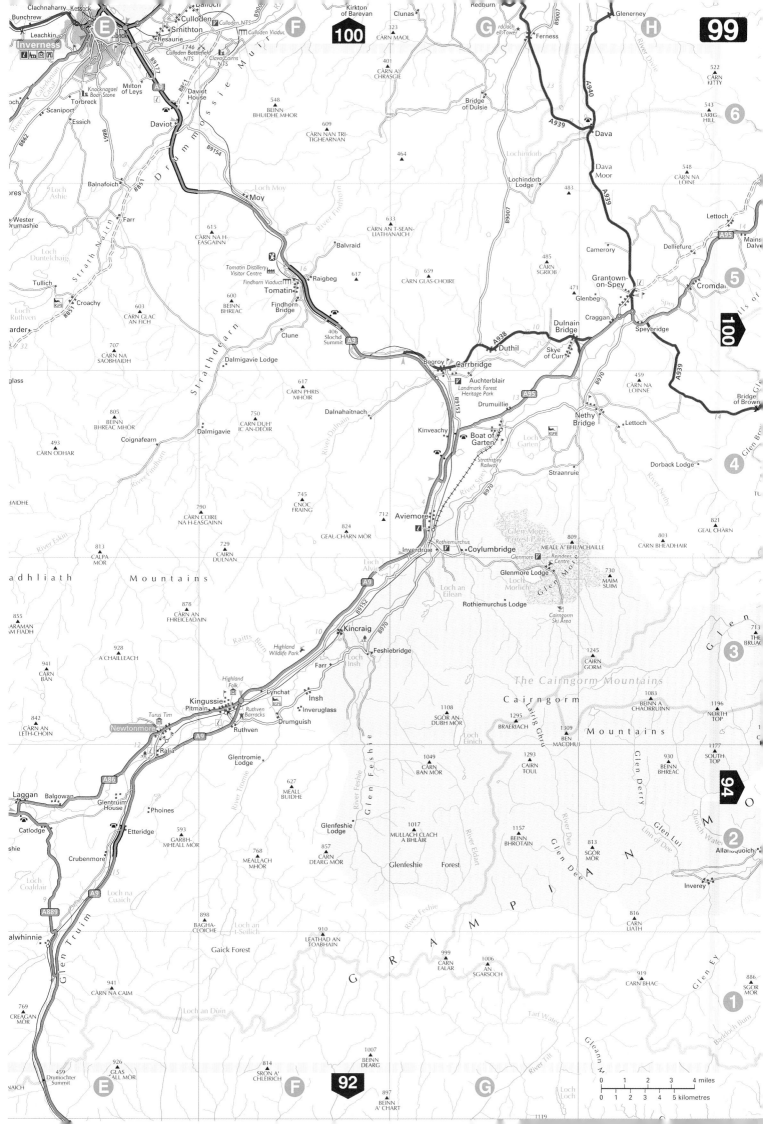

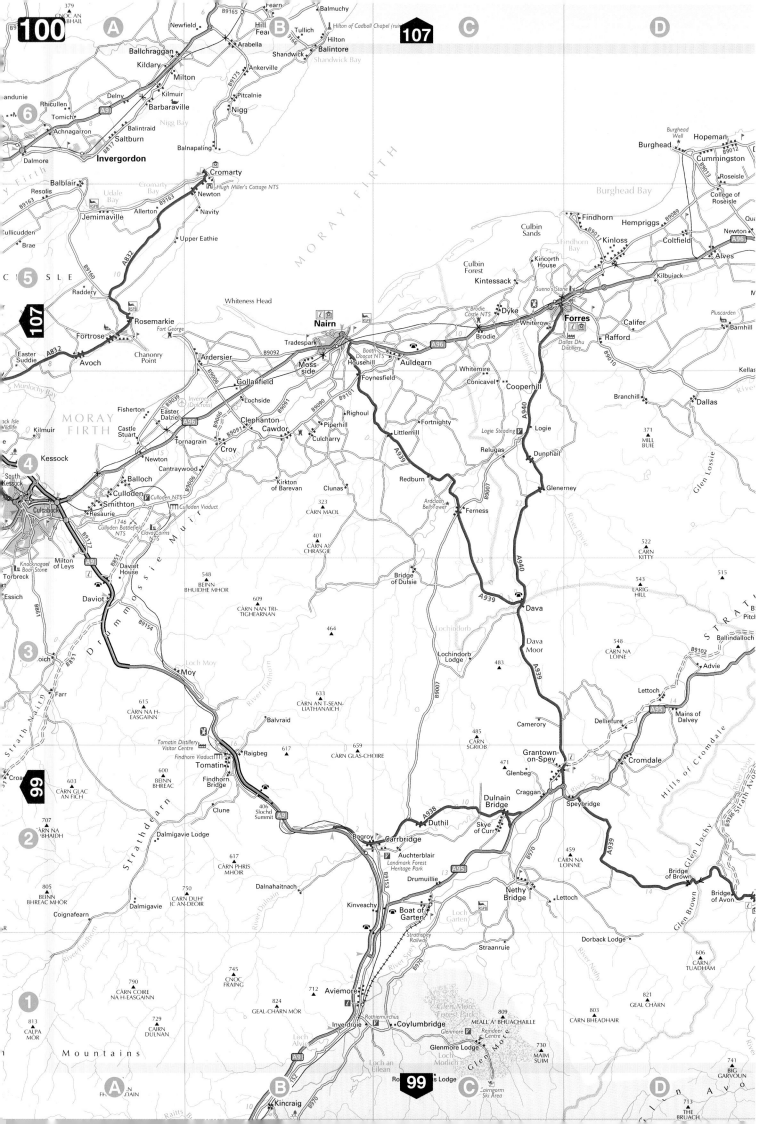

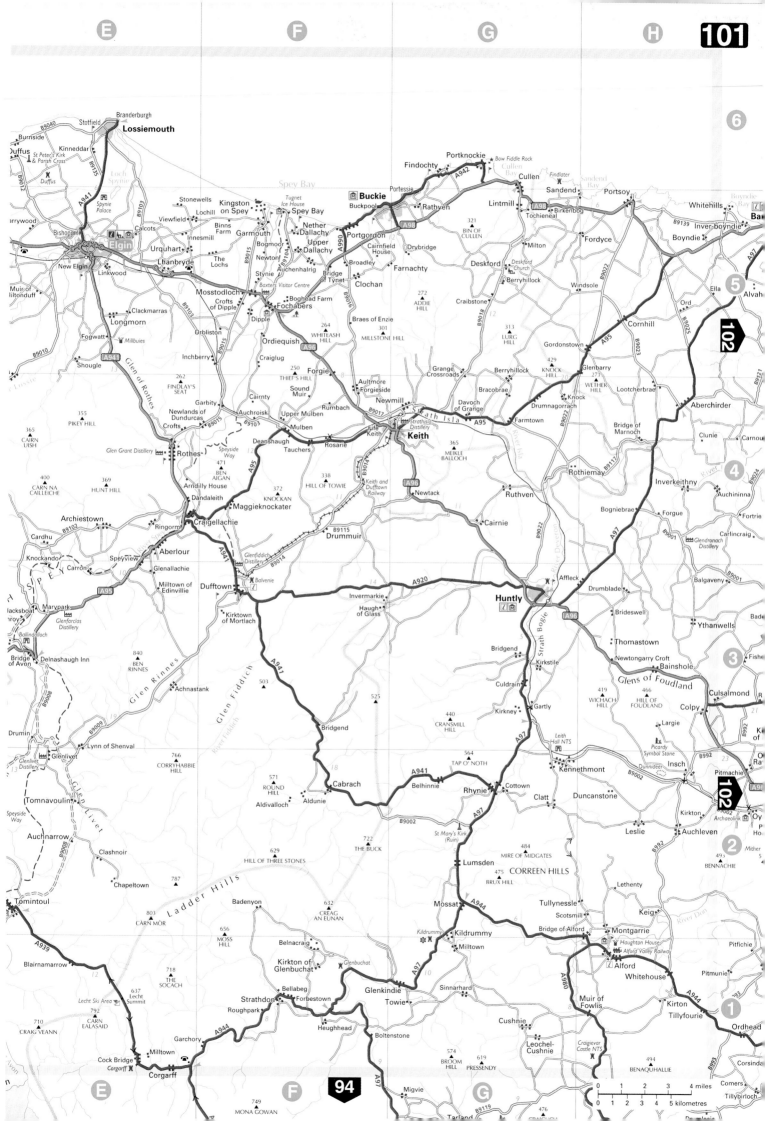

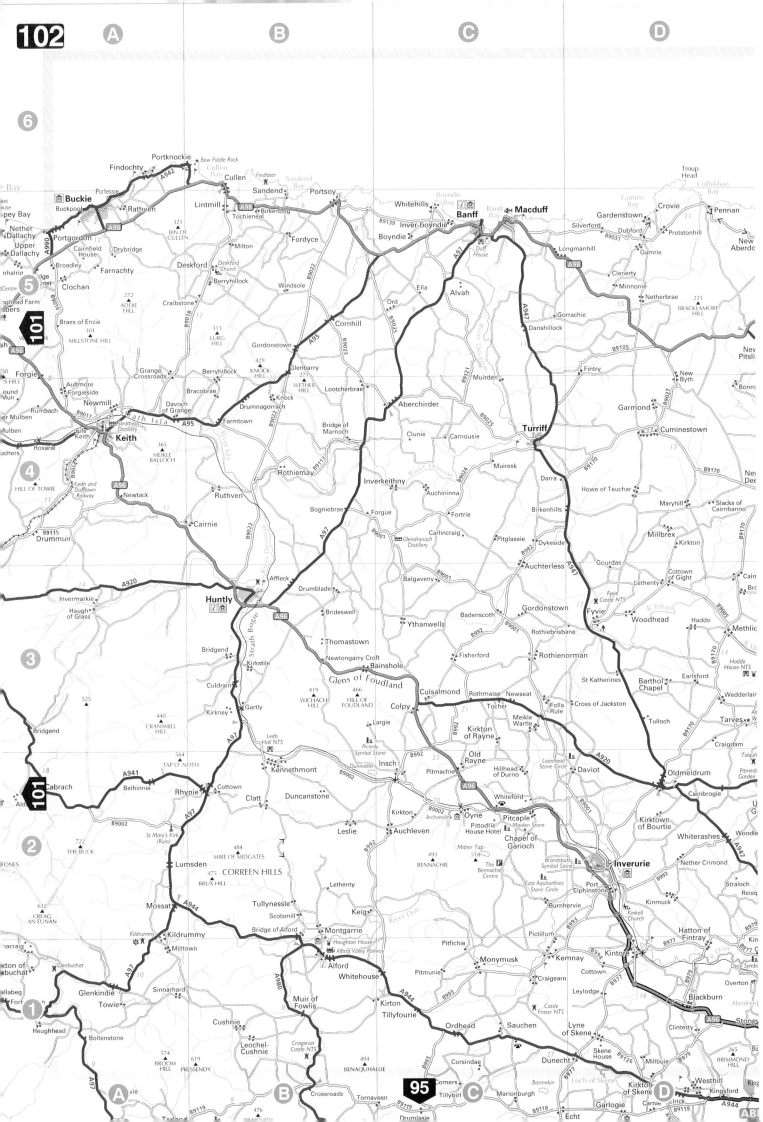

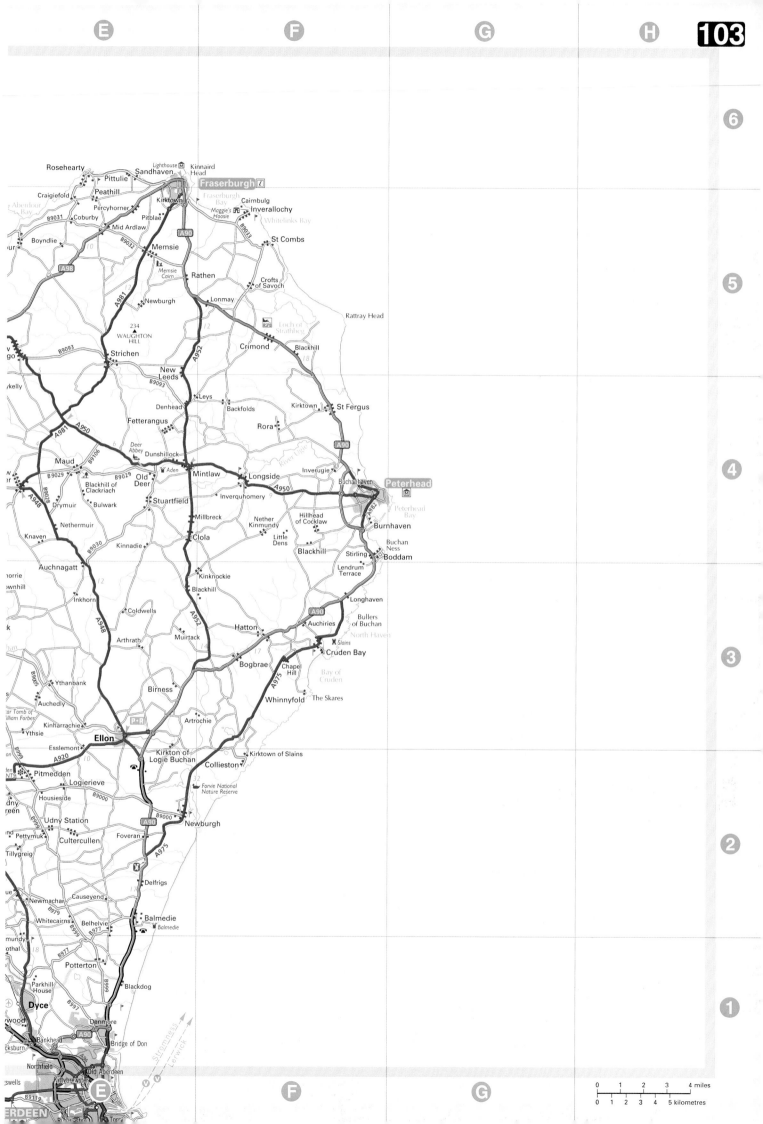

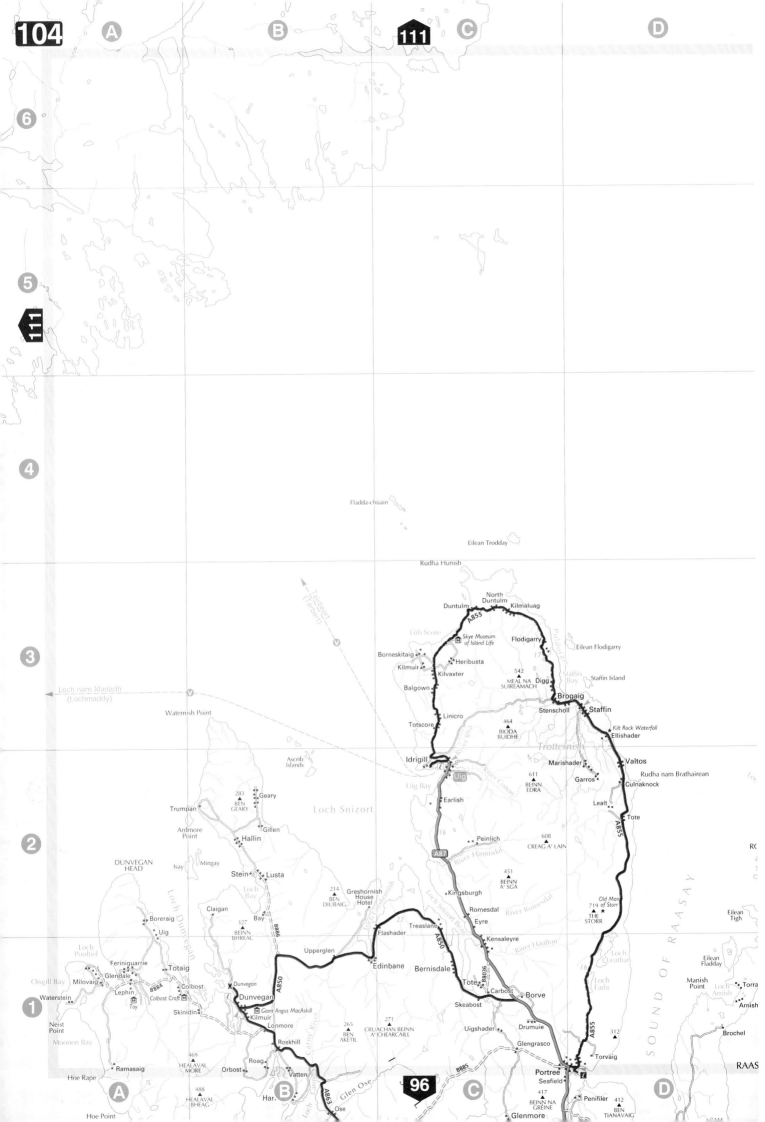

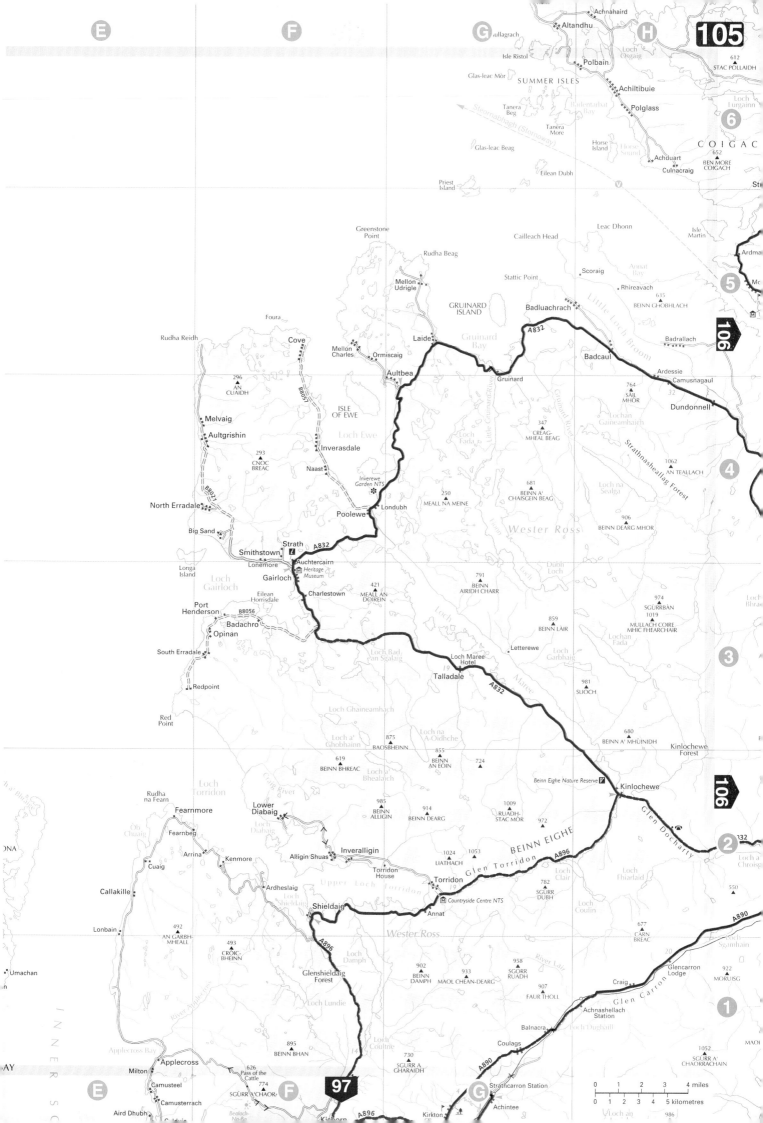

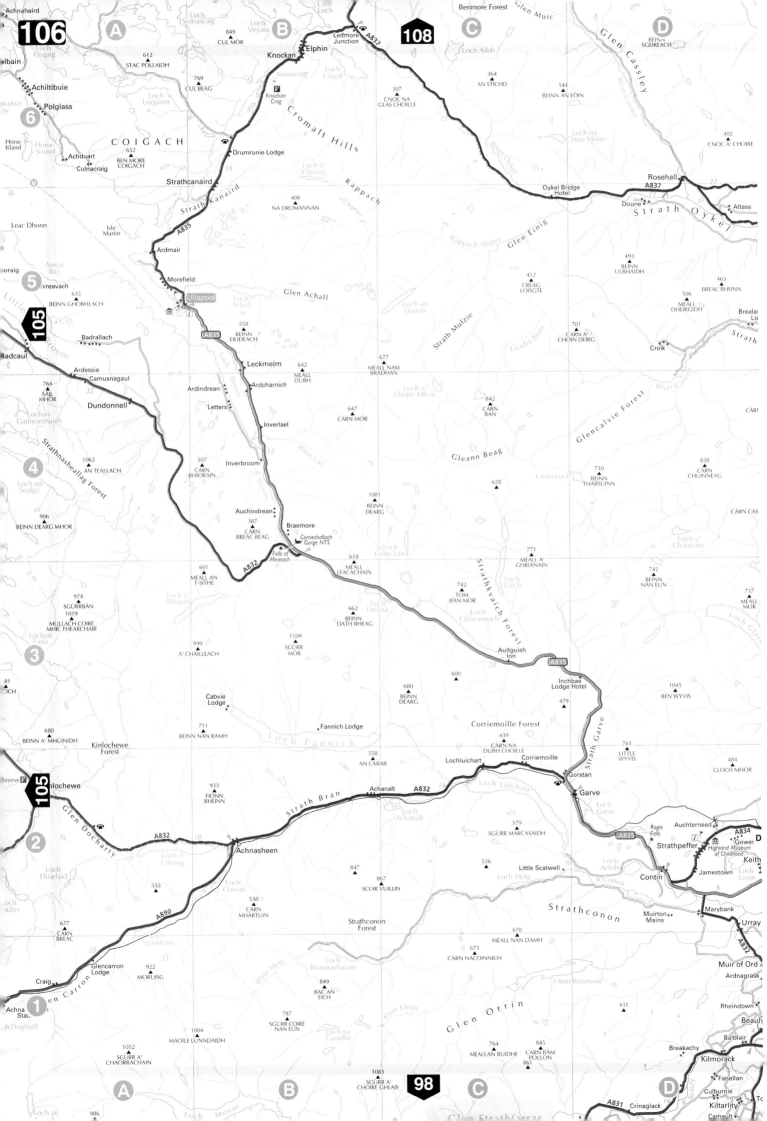

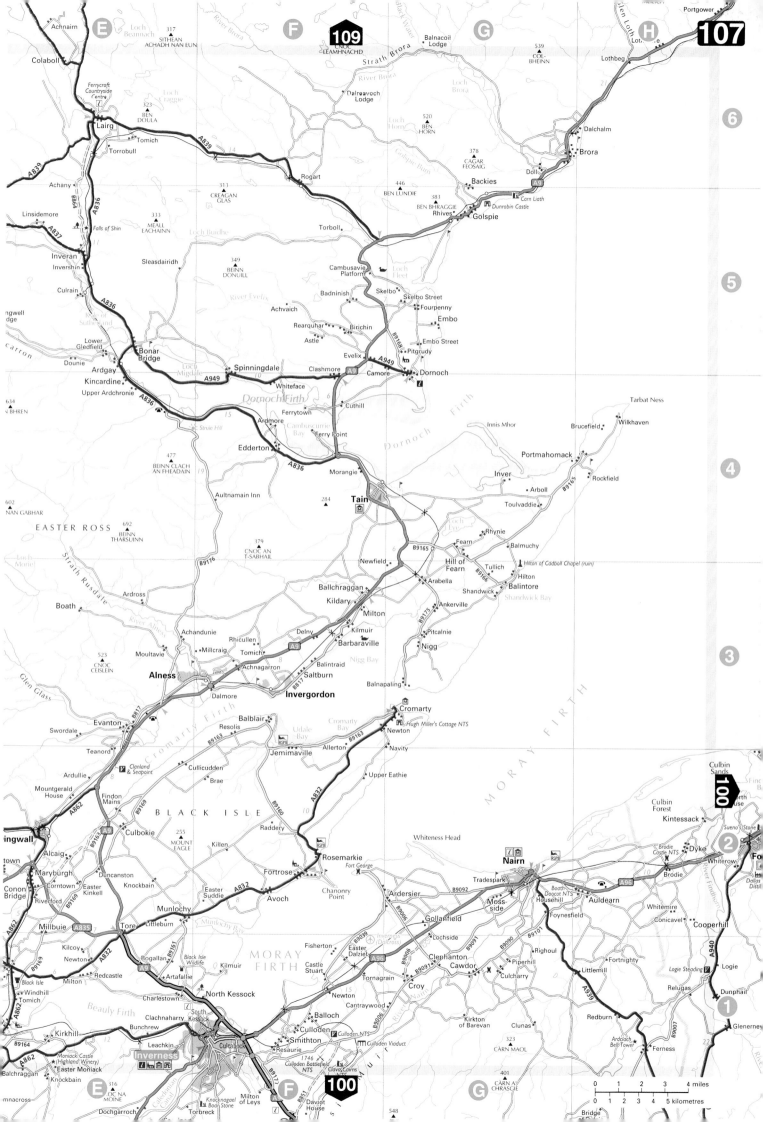

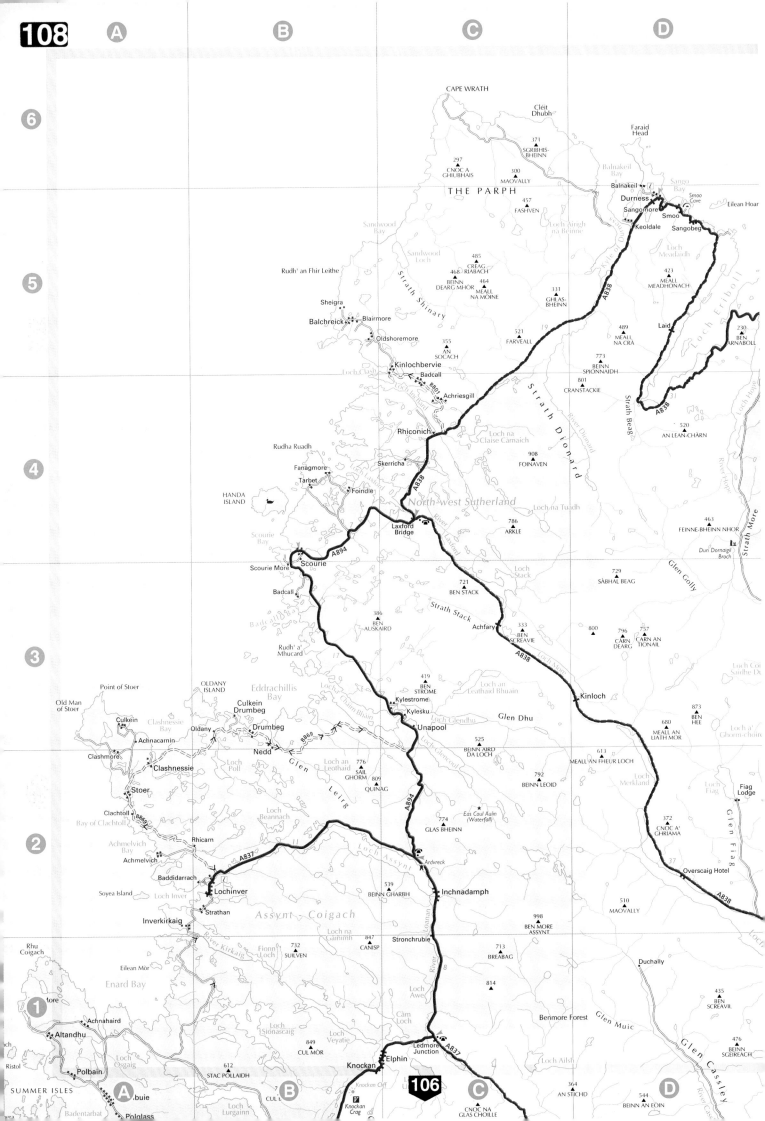

A B C D

6

CAPE WRATH

Cléit
Dhubh

371
SGRIBHIS-
BHEINN

Faraid
Head

297
CNOC A
GHIUBHAIS

300
MAOVALLY

Balnakeil
Bay

THE PARPH

457
FASHVEN

Balnakeil

Sango
Bay

Smoo
Cave

Eilean Hoar

5

Sandwood
Bay

Durness
Sangomore
Keoldale
Smoo
Sangobeg

Rudh' an Fhir Leithe

Sandwood
Loch

Loch Airigh
na Beinne

485
CREAG
RIABACH

423
MEALL
MEADHONACH

Sheigra

468
BEINN
DEARG MHÒR

464
MEALL
NA MÒINE

Strath Shinary

331
GHLAS-
BHEINN

Laid

Balchreick Blairmore

521
FARVEALL

489
MEALL
NA CRÀ

230
BEN
ARNABOLL

Oldshoremore

355
AN
SOCACH

773
BEINN
SPIONNAIDH

520
AN LEAN-CHÀRN

Kinlochbervie
Badcall

801
CRANSTACKIE

Strath Beag

Achriesgill

Strath Dionard

4

Rudha Ruadh

Rhiconich

Loch na
Claise Carnaich

908
FOINAVEN

Fanagmore
Tarbet

Skerricha

Foindle

North-west Sutherland

HANDA
ISLAND

786
ARKLE

Laxford
Bridge

463
FEINNE-BHEINN NHOR

Loch na Tuadh

Scourie
Bay

Dun Dornaigil
Broch

Glen Golly

Scourie More Scourie

Loch
Stack

729
SÀBHAL BEAG

3

Badcall

721
BEN STACK

Strath Stack

800

796
CARN
DEARG

757
CARN AN
TIONAIL

386
BEN
AUSKAIRD

Achfary

333
BEN
SCREAVIE

Rudh' a'
Mhucard

Kinloch

873
BEN
HEE

OLDANY
ISLAND

Eddrachillis
Bay

419
BEN
STROME

680
MEALL
AN LIATH MOR

Point of Stoer

Culkein
Drumbeg

Kylestrome
Kylesku

Glen Dhu

613
MEALL AN FHEUR LOCH

Old Man
of Stoer

Drumbeg

Unapool

525
BEINN AIRD
DA LOCH

792
BEINN LEOID

372
CNOC A'
GHRIAMA

Culkein

Oldany

Nedd

Loch an
Leothaid

776
SAIL
GHORM

809
QUINAG

774
GLAS BHEINN

Eas Coul Aulin
(Waterfall)

Fiag
Lodge

Achnacarnin

2

Clashmore

Clashnessie

Stoer

Loch
Beannach

Rhicarn

Ardvreck

539
BEINN GHARBH

Inchnadamph

Overscaig Hotel

Achmelvich
Bay

Achmelvich

Baddidarrach

Lochinver

Strathan

998
BEN MORE
ASSYNT

510
MAOVALLY

Soyea Island

Loch Inver

Assynt · Coigach

Stronchrubie

Inverkirkaig

Loch na
Gainmh

847
CANISP

713
BREABAG

Duchally

Rhu
Coigach

Enard Bay

732
SUILVEN

814

1

Achnahaird

Altandhu

Càm
Loch

435
BEN
SCREAVIL

Loch
Sionascaig

Loch
Awe

Benmore Forest

Glen Muic

Ristol

849
CUL MÒR

Ledmore
Junction

476
BEINN
SGEIREACH

Polbain

612
STAC POLLAIDH

Knockan Elphin

AN STICHD

Loch Ailsh

364

SUMMER ISLES

buie

A

CUL

B

106

C

364
AN STICHD

544
BEINN AN EÒIN

D

Polglass

Badentarbat

Knockan Cliff

Loch
Lurganin

Knockan
Crag

CNOC NA
GLAS CHOILLE

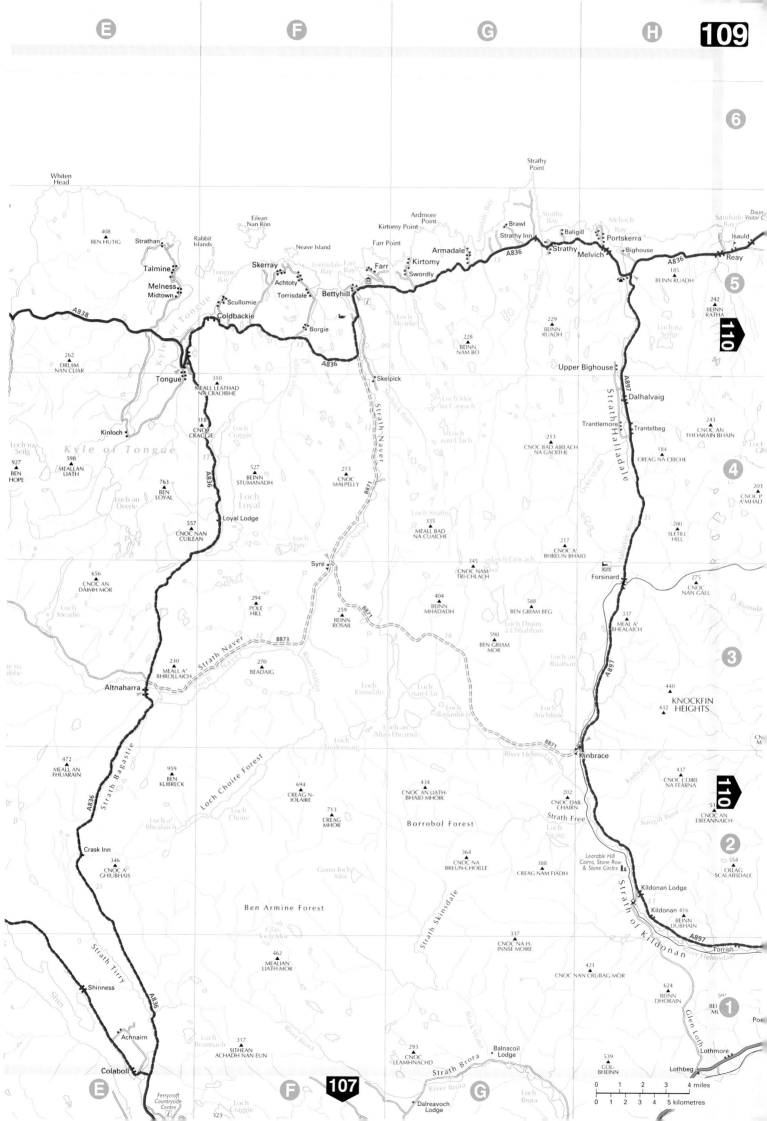

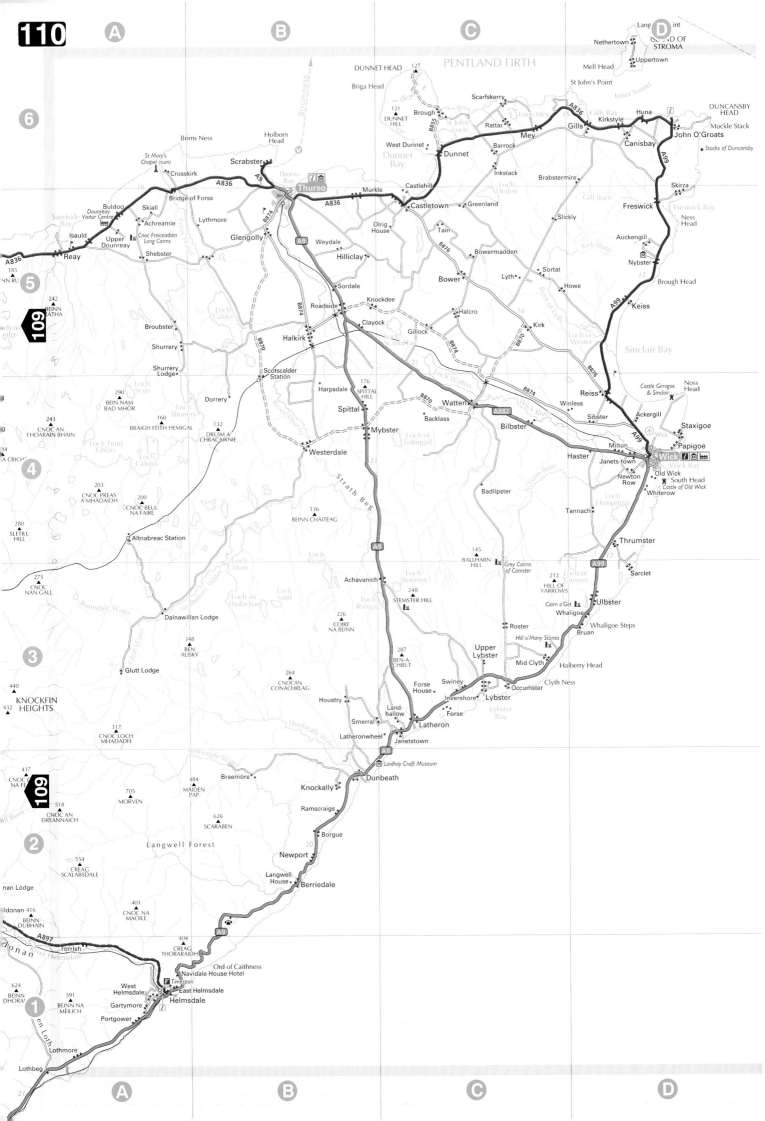

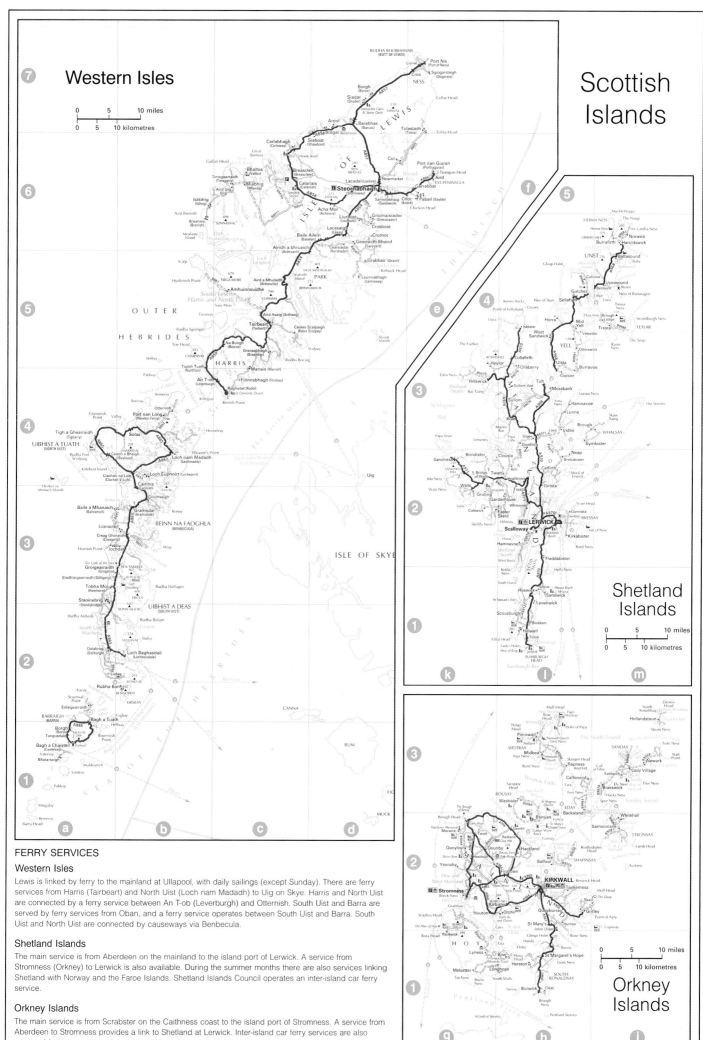

Scottish Islands

Western Isles

Shetland Islands

Orkney Islands

FERRY SERVICES

Western Isles

Lewis is linked by ferry to the mainland at Ullapool, with daily sailings (except Sunday). There are ferry services from Harris (Tairbeart) and North Uist (Loch nam Madadh) to Uig on Skye. Harris and North Uist are connected by a ferry service between An T-ob (Leverburgh) and Otternish. South Uist and Barra are served by ferry services from Oban, and a ferry service operates between South Uist and Barra. South Uist and North Uist are connected by causeways via Benbecula.

Shetland Islands

The main service is from Aberdeen on the mainland to the island port of Lerwick. A service from Stromness (Orkney) to Lerwick is also available. During the summer months there are also services linking Shetland with Norway and the Faroe Islands. Shetland Islands Council operates an inter-island car ferry service.

Orkney Islands

The main service is from Scrabster on the Caithness coast to the island port of Stromness. A service from Aberdeen to Stromness provides a link to Shetland at Lerwick. Inter-island car ferry services are also operated (advance reservations recommended).

Ireland

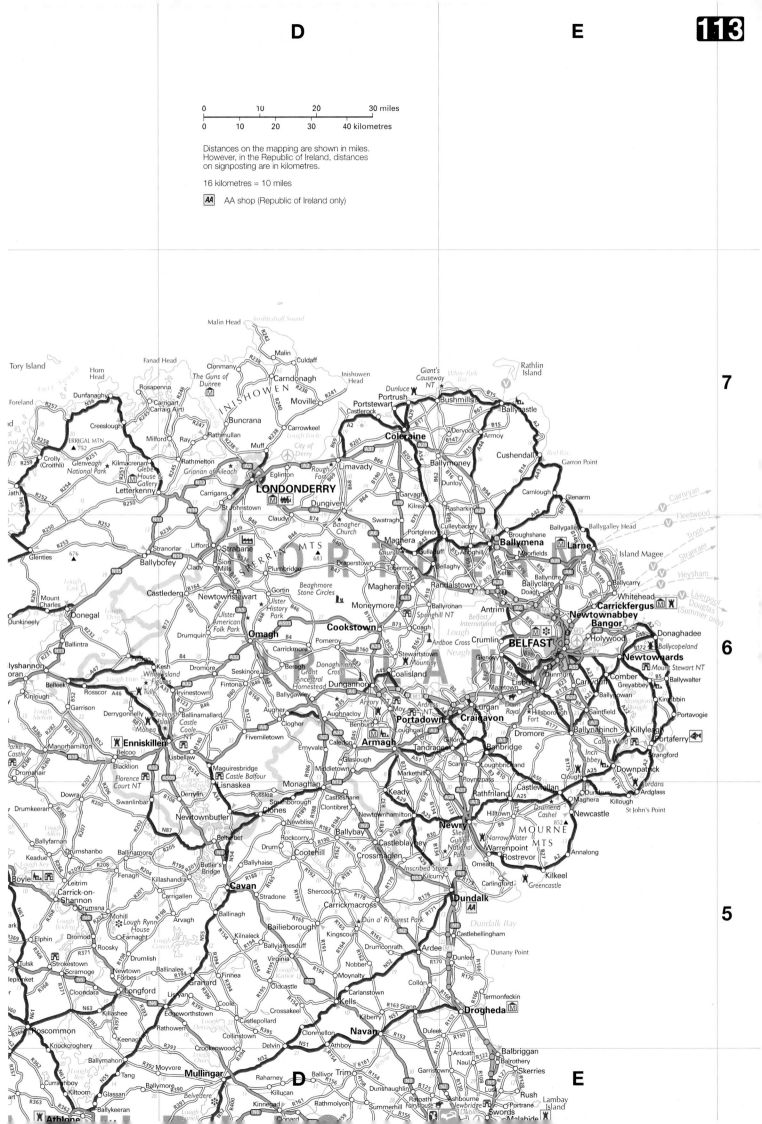

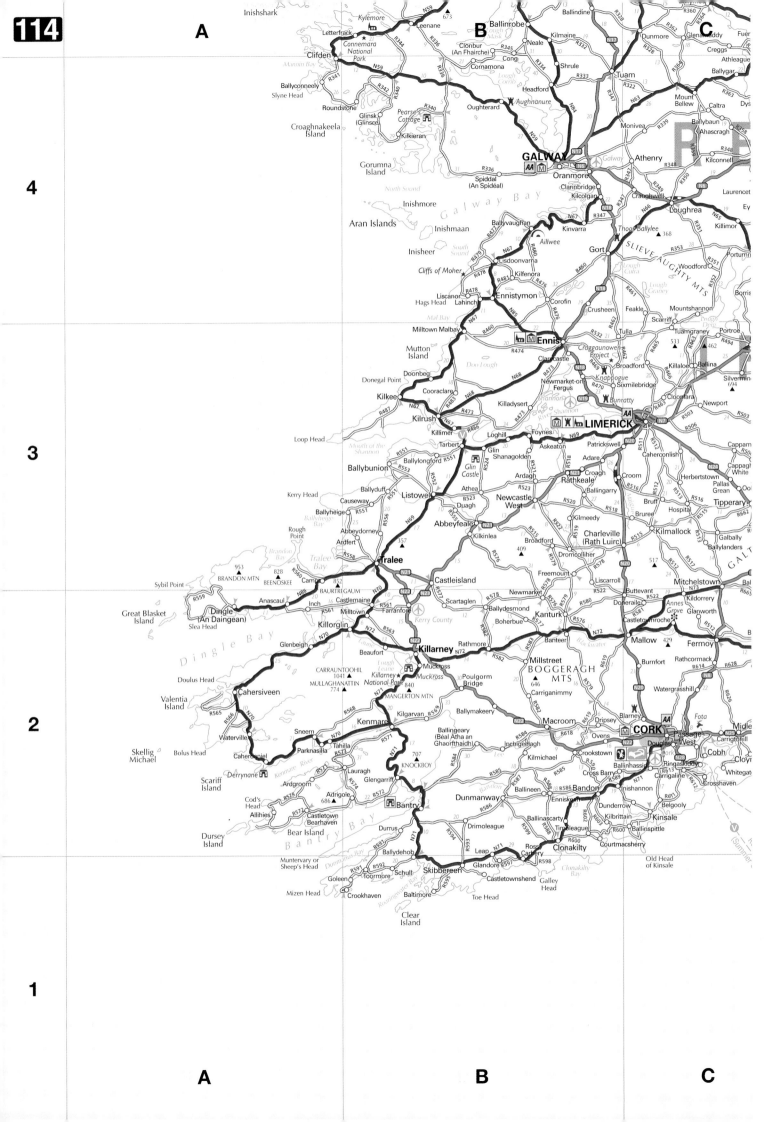

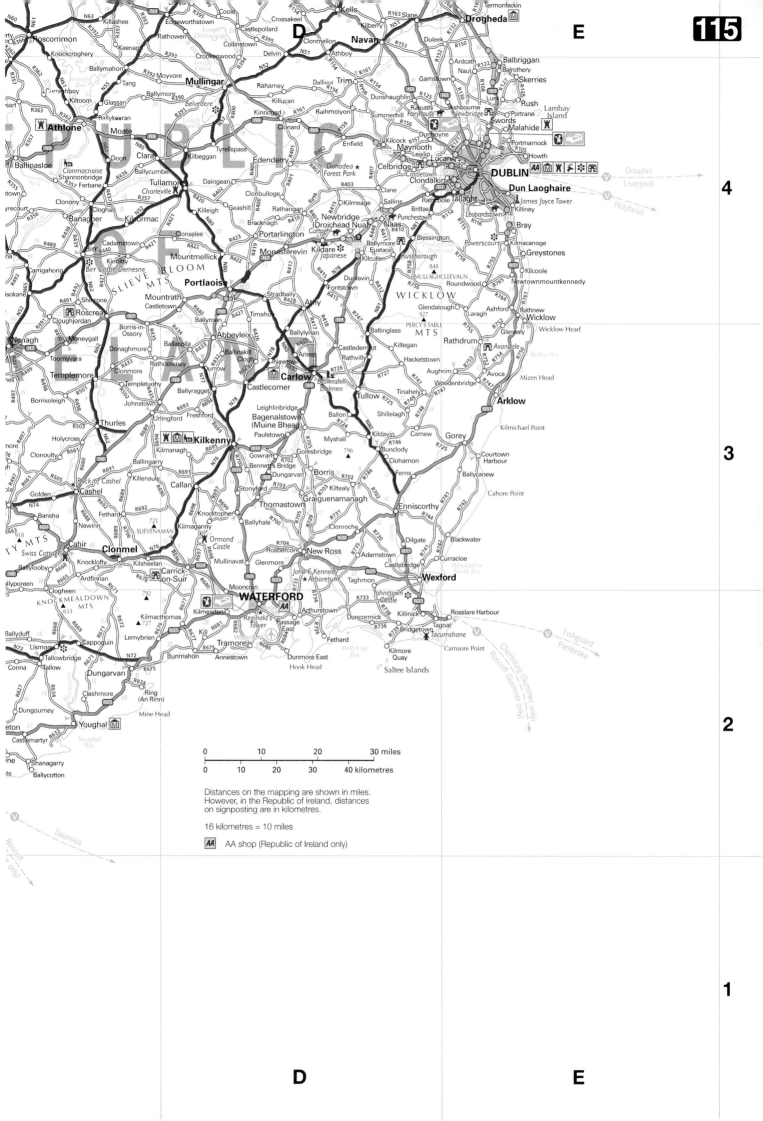

Distances on the mapping are shown in miles.
However, in the Republic of Ireland, distances
on signposting are in kilometres.

16 kilometres = 10 miles

AA AA shop (Republic of Ireland only)

The Isle of Man

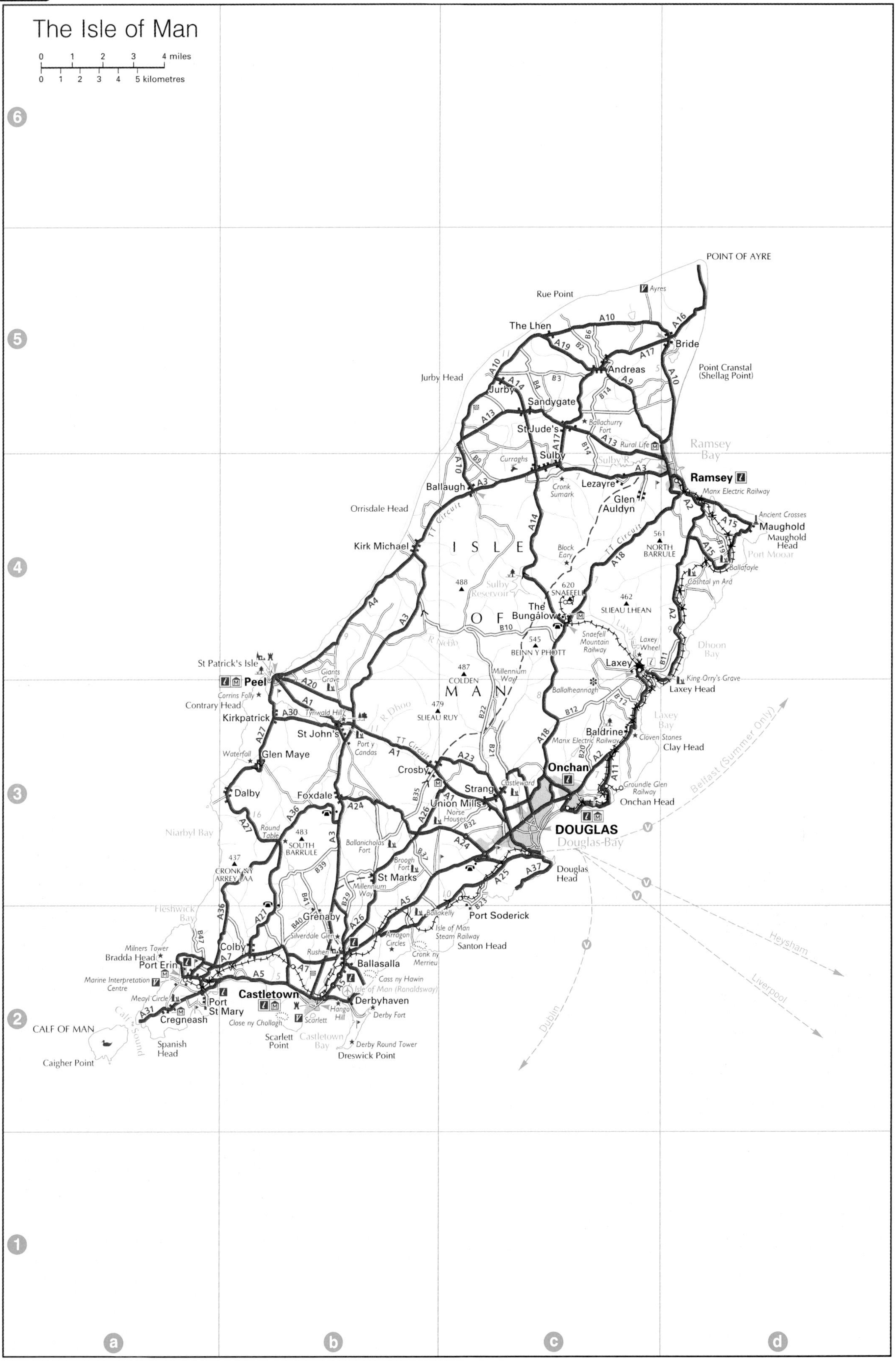

0 1 2 3 4 miles
0 1 2 3 4 5 kilometres

6

5

POINT OF AYRE

Rue Point

Ayres

The Lhen

A10

A16

Bride

A19

B2

B9

A17

Jurby Head

A10

A14

Andreas

A9

Point Cranstal
(Shellag Point)

Jurby

B4

B3

B14

A10

Sandygate

St Jude's

A13

A17

Ballachurry Fort

A13

Rural Life

Ramsey Bay

A10

B9

Sulby

Curraghs

B14

Sulby R.

A3

Ramsey

Manx Electric Railway

Ballaugh

A3

Lezayre

A2

A15

Ancient Crosses

Cronk Sumark

Glen Auldyn

A15

A19

Maughold

Orrisdale Head

ISLE

Block Eary

NORTH BARRULE

561

Ballafayle

Cashtal yn Ard

Maughold Head

Port Mooar

Kirk Michael

TT Circuit

A14

A18

TT Circuit

488

620
SNAEFELL

462
SLIEAU LHEAN

A2

4

A4

A3

OF

Sulby Reservoir

The Bungalow

B10

Snaefell Mountain Railway

R. Neb

545
BEINN Y PHOTT

Laxey

Dhoon Bay

St Patrick's Isle

Giants Grave

487

MAN

Laxey Wheel

Peel

Corrins Folly

Millennium Way

Laxey Head

King Orry's Grave

Contrary Head

A20

COLDEN

A1

Ballalheannagh

Laxey Bay

Kirkpatrick

A30

Tynwald Hill

479
SLIEAU RUY

B22

B12

Laxey Bay

St John's

A27

Port y Candas

A1

B12

Baldrine

Waterfall

Glen Maye

TT Circuit

A23

A18

Manx Electric Railway

Cloven Stones

R. Dhoo

B21

A2

Clay Head

Dalby

Foxdale

Crosby

B35

A1

Strang

Castleward

Onchan

Groudle Glen Railway

3

A27

A24

Norse Houses

Union Mills

B32

A14

Onchan Head

Round Table

483
SOUTH BARRULE

A3

Ballanicholas Fort

B37

DOUGLAS

Niarbyl Bay

B39

Brough Fort

Douglas Bay

437
CRONK NY ARREY LAA

St Marks

Millennium Way

A5

A25

A37

Douglas Head

A36

B40

Grenaby

A26

Ballakelly

Port Soderick

B45

Belfast (Summer only)

Heswick Bay

A27

B41

Silverdale Glen

Arragon Circles

Isle of Man Steam Railway

Santon Head

Heysham

Colby

Rushen Abbey

Cronk ny Merriu

Liverpool

Milners Tower

Bradda Head

A7

A5

Ballasalla

Cass ny Hawin

Dublin

Marine Interpretation Centre

Port Erin

A5

A37

Isle of Man (Ronaldsway)

Meayl Circle

A31

Port St Mary

Castletown

Derbyhaven

2

CALF OF MAN

Cregneash

St Mary

Close ny Chollagh

Scarlett

Hango Hill

Derby Fort

Spanish Head

Scarlett Point

Castletown Bay

Derby Round Tower

Caigher Point

Dreswick Point

1

a **b** **c** **d**

key to town plans

Town plan legend

▨	AA-recommended routes
▨▨	Restricted roads / pedestrians only
—	Other roads
COLLEGE ▨	Buildings of interest
†	Churches
▨	Parks and open spaces
P	Car parks
🚻 C	Toilets
←	One-way streets
▨	Shopmobility
P+◉	Park and ride
M	Metrolink stations

Aberdeen	Page 117	Manchester	Page 123
Aberystwyth	117	Middlesbrough	123
Bath	118	Milton Keynes	124
Birmingham	118	Newcastle upon Tyne	124
Blackpool	118	Newquay	124
Bradford	118	Norwich	124
Brighton	119	Nottingham	125
Bristol	119	Oxford	125
Cambridge	119	Peterborough	125
Canterbury	119	Plymouth	125
Cardiff	120	Portsmouth	126
Carlisle	120	Reading	126
Chester	120	Salisbury	126
Coventry	120	Sheffield	126
Derby	121	Shrewsbury	127
Dundee	121	Southampton	127
Edinburgh	121	Stratford-upon-Avon	127
Exeter	121	Sunderland	127
Glasgow	122	Swansea	128
Hull	122	Taunton	128
Ipswich	122	Tunbridge Wells	128
Leeds	122	Warwick	128
Leicester	123	Watford	129
Liverpool	123	Winchester	129
LONDON	142–151	Worcester	129
		York	129

Central London

Aberdeen
Aberystwyth

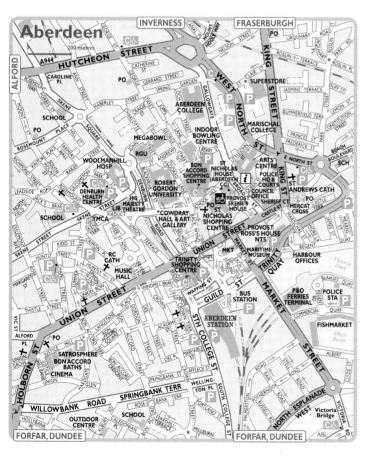

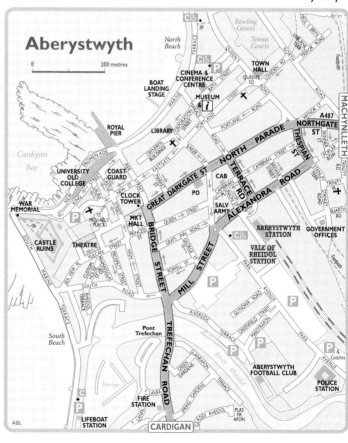

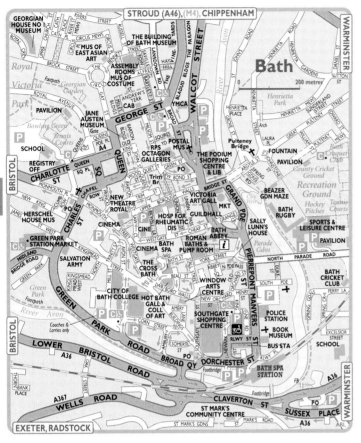

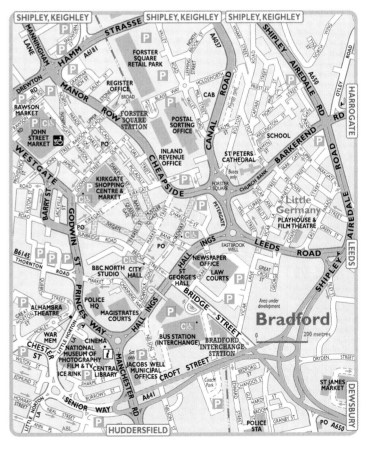

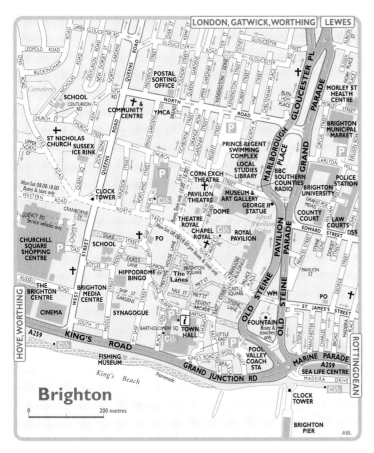

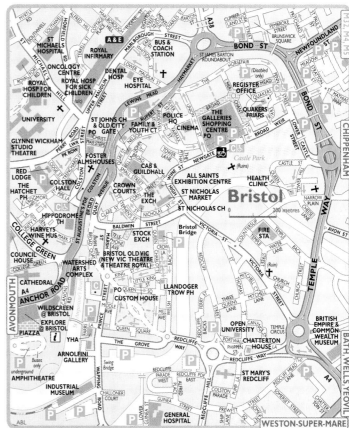

119

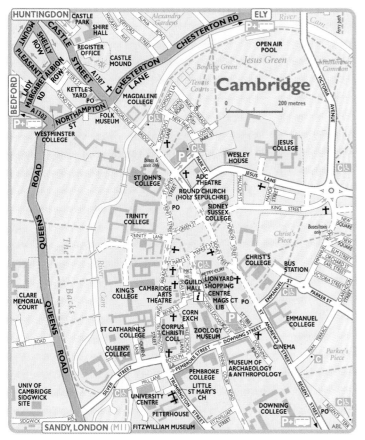

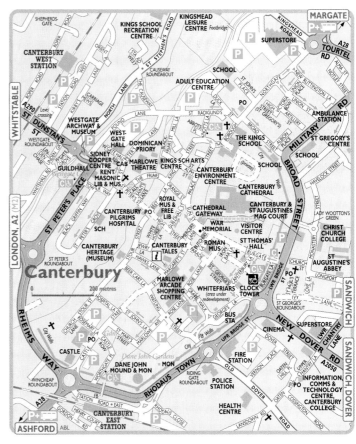

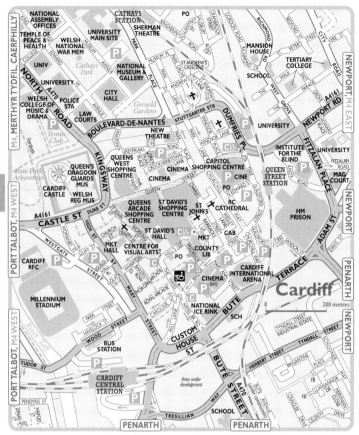

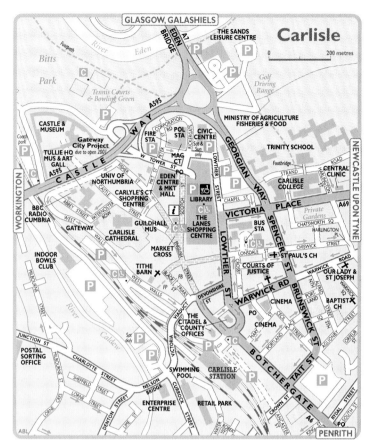

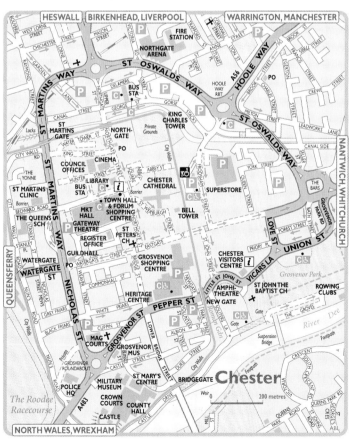

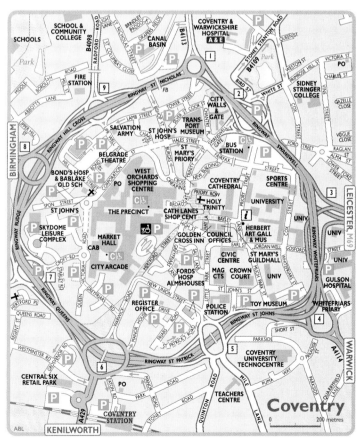

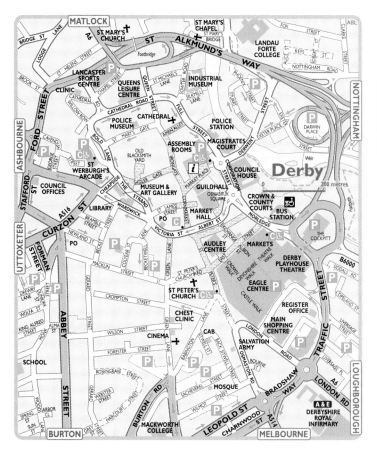

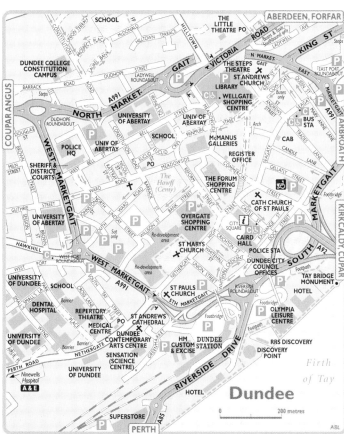

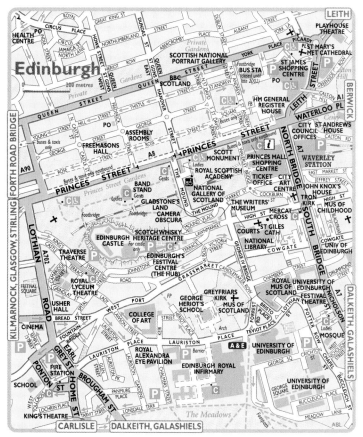

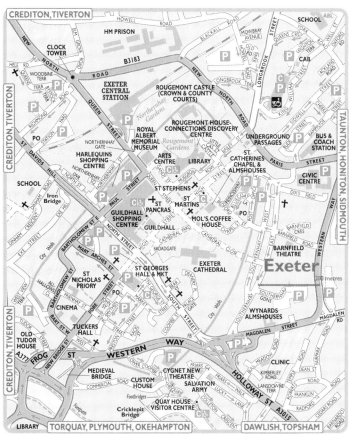

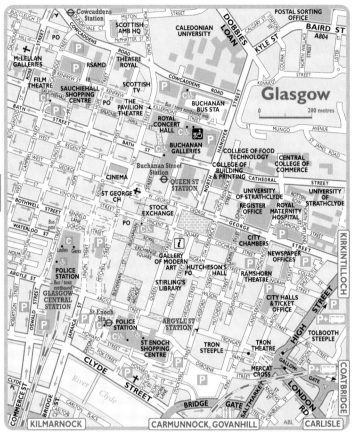

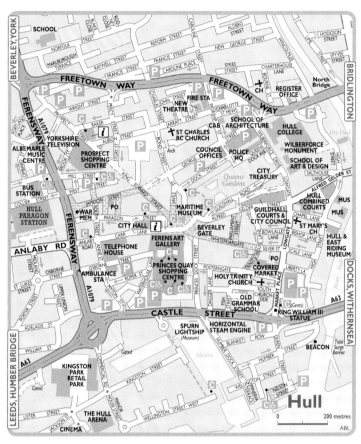

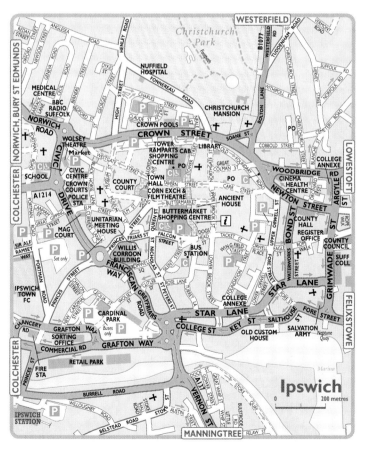

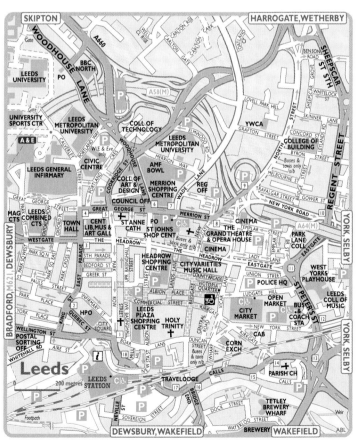

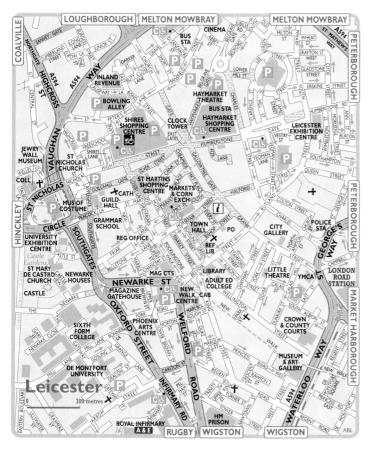

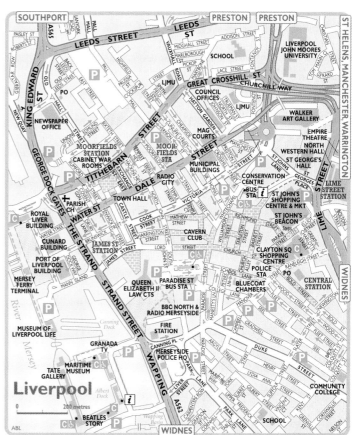

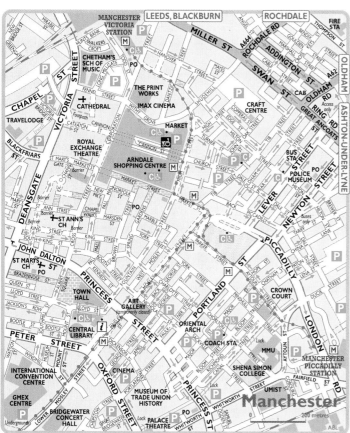

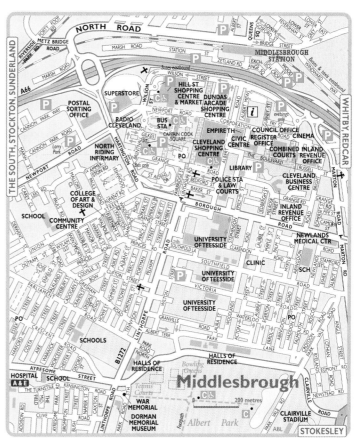

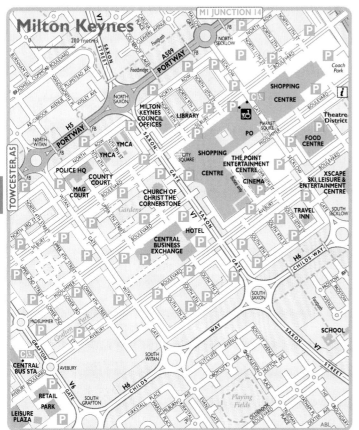

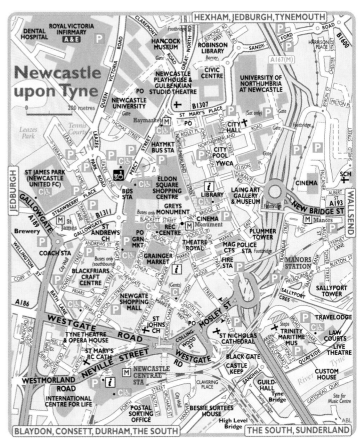

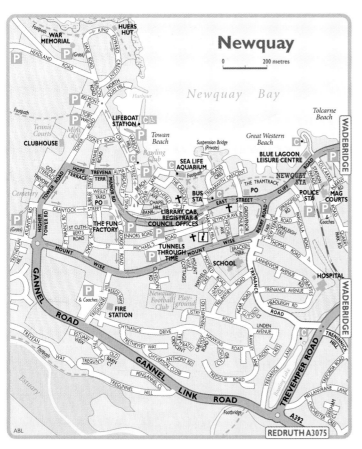

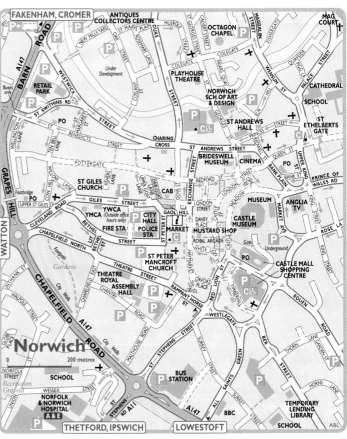

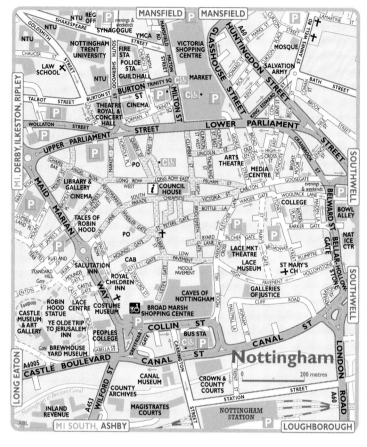

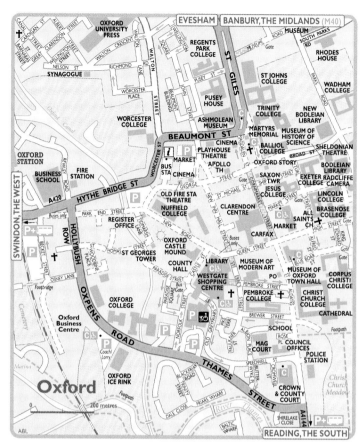

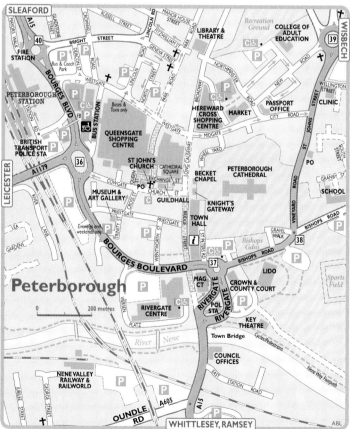

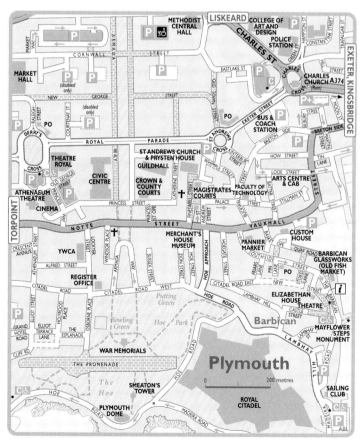

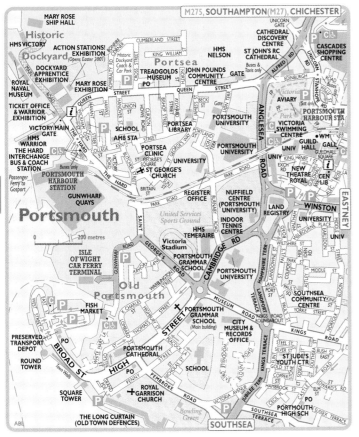

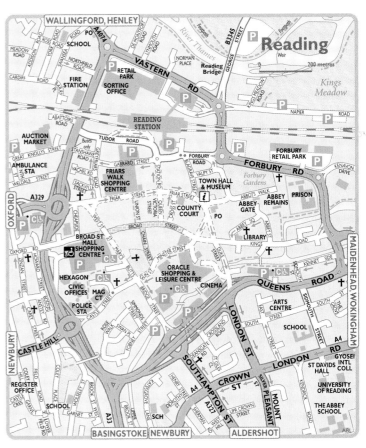

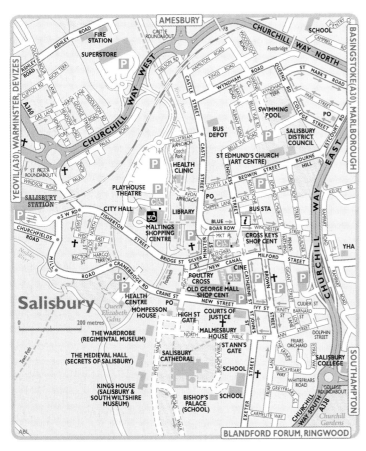

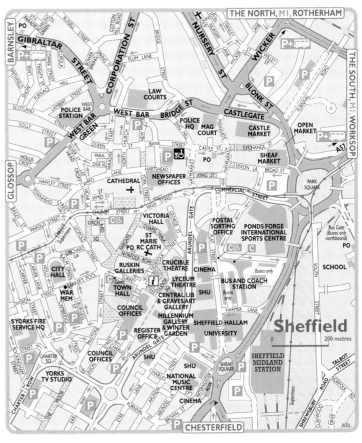

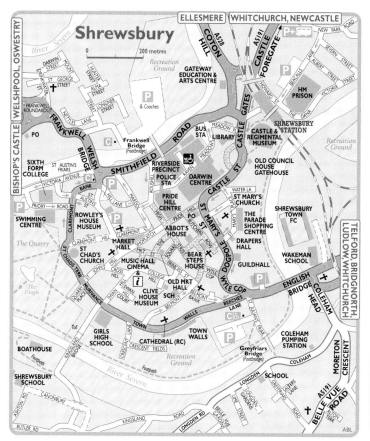

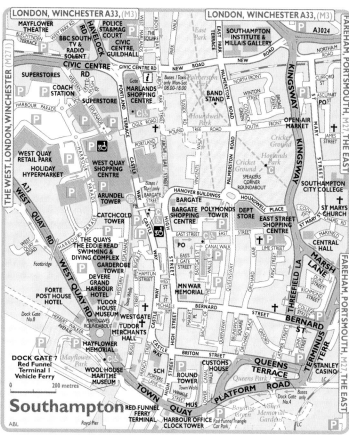

127

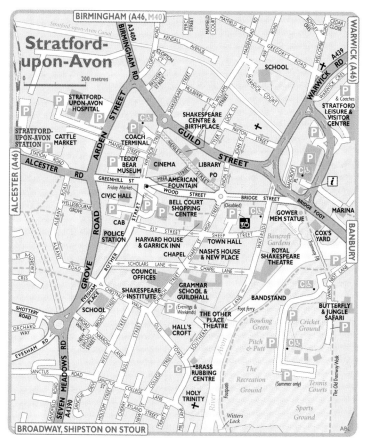

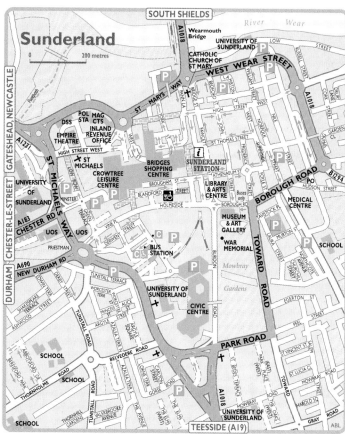

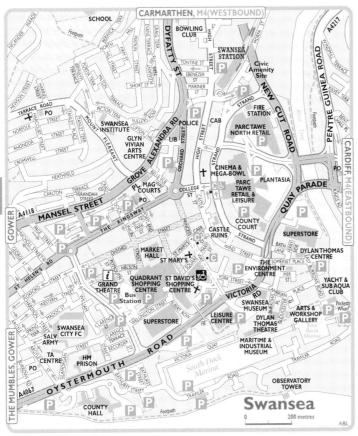

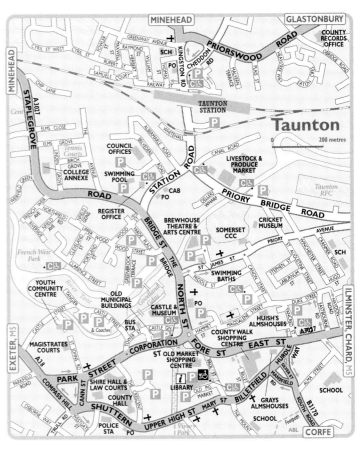

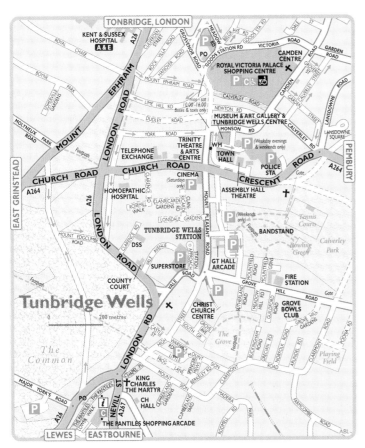

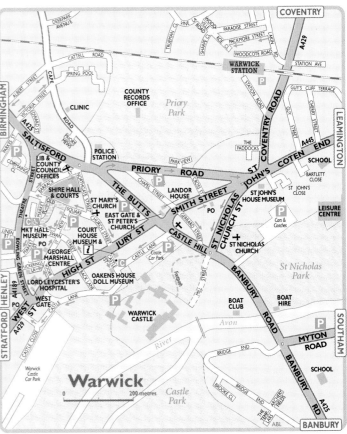

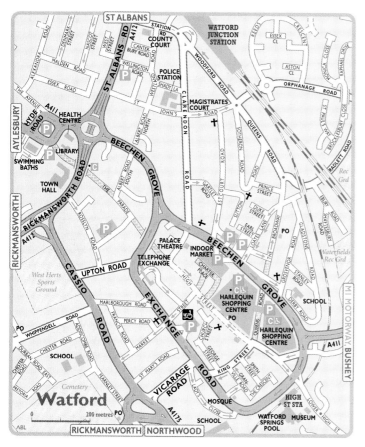

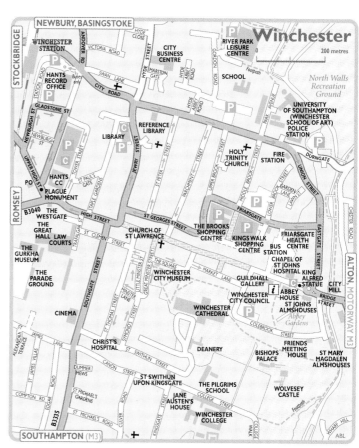

129

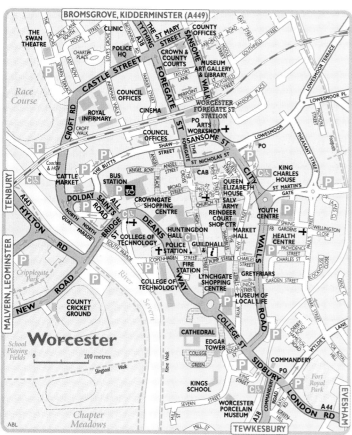

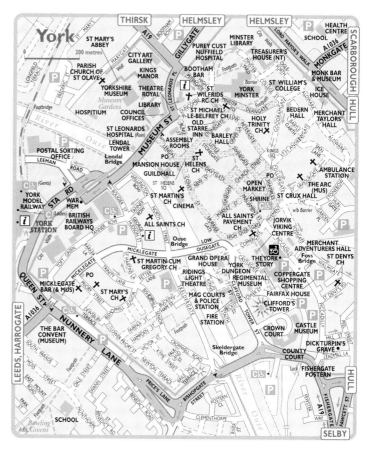

Glasgow district

0   1   2 miles
0   1   2   3 kilometres

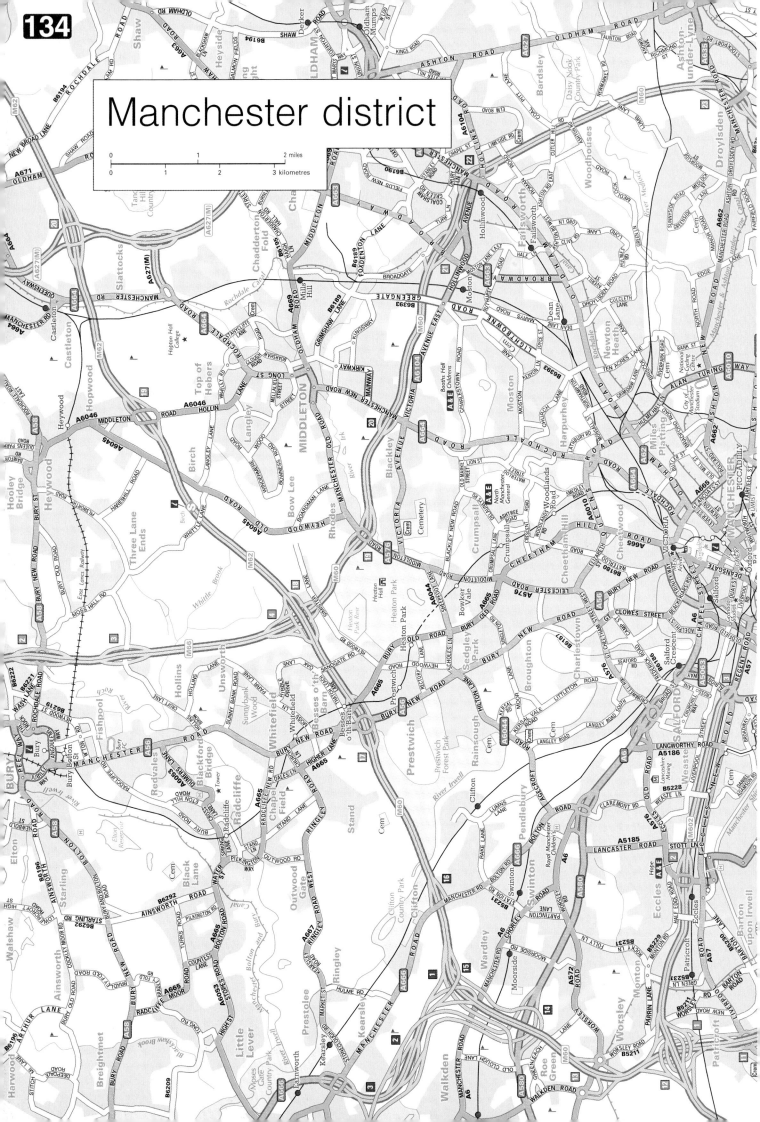

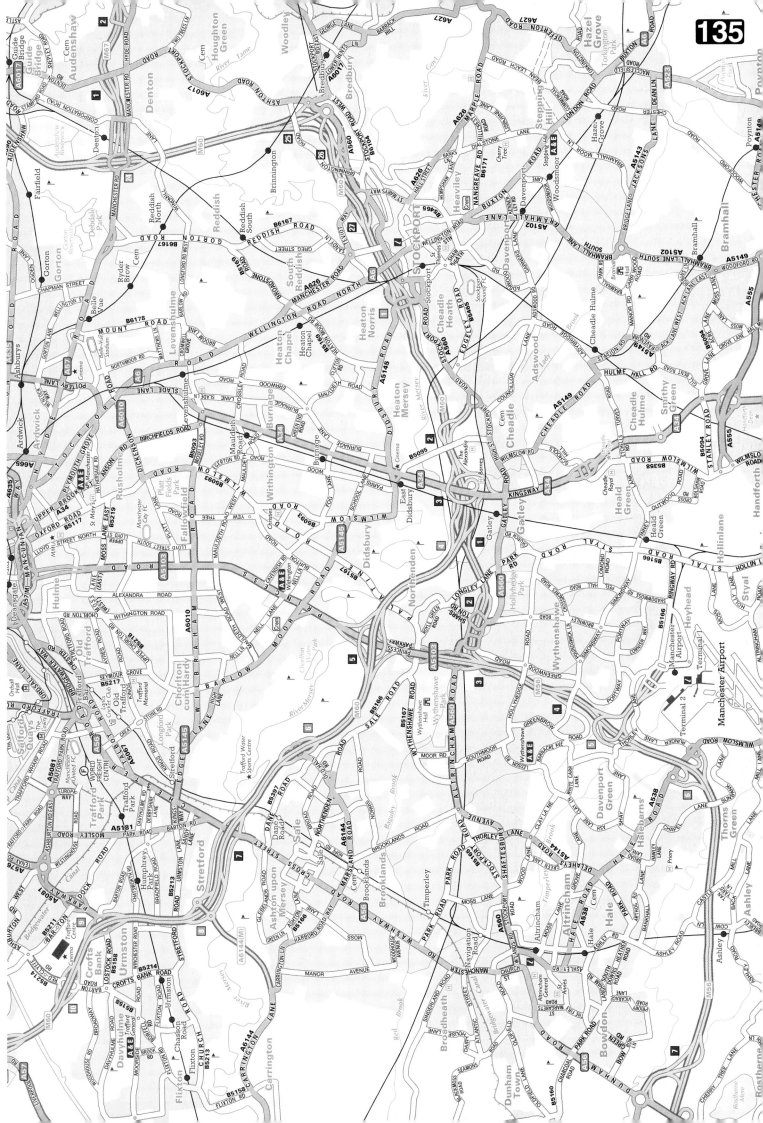

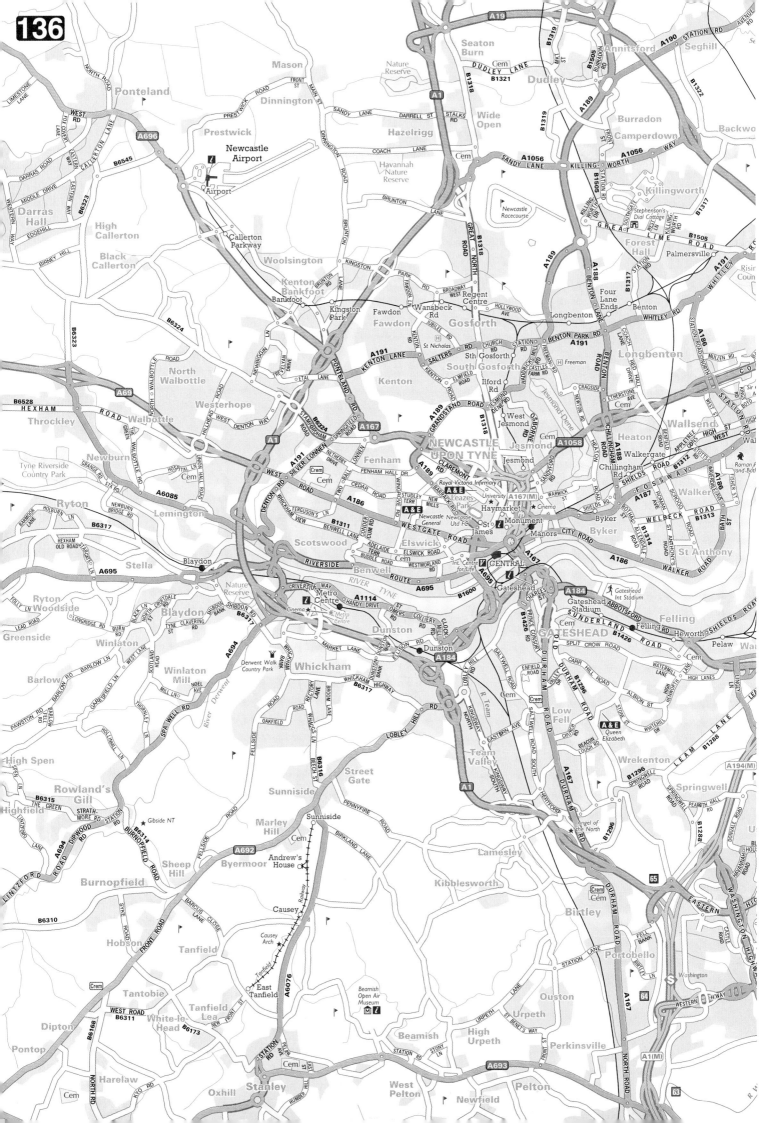

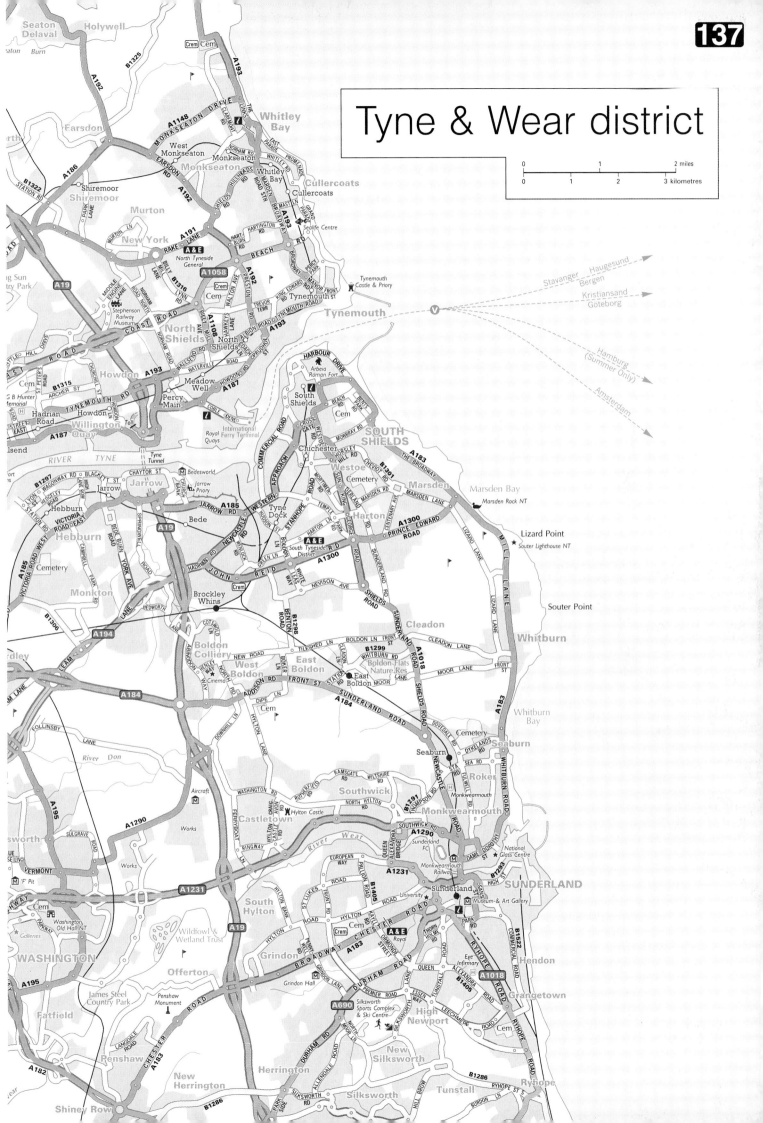

Tyne & Wear district

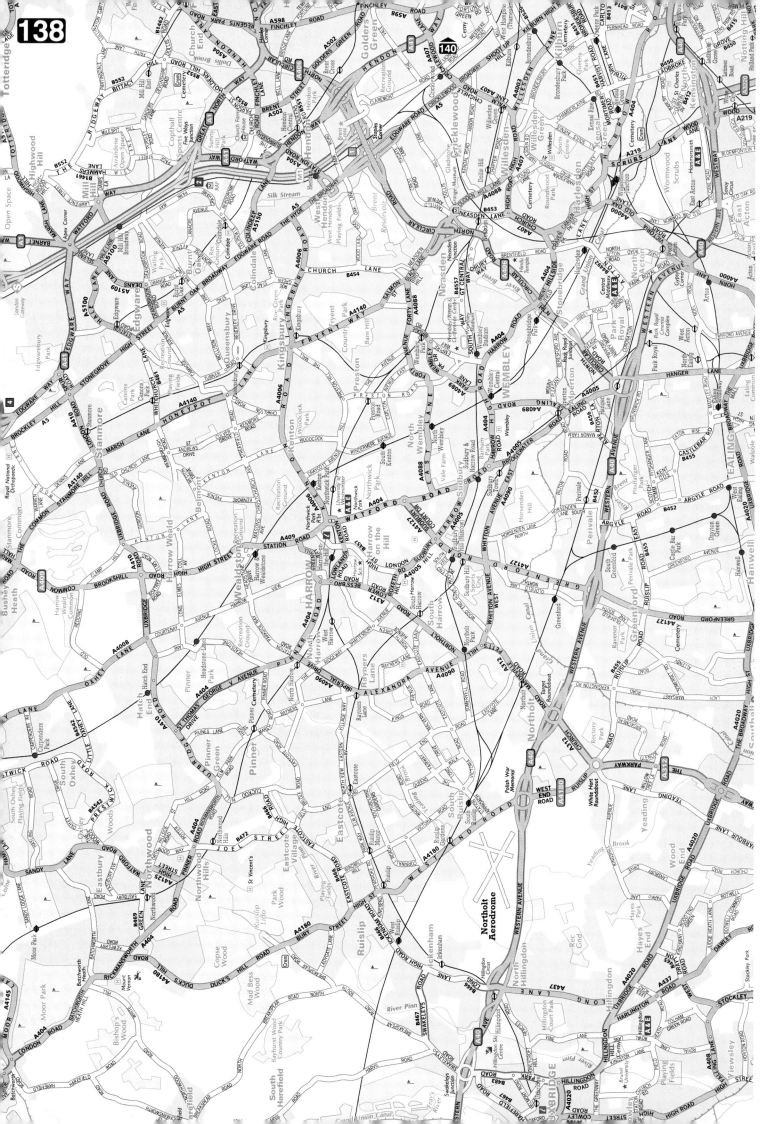

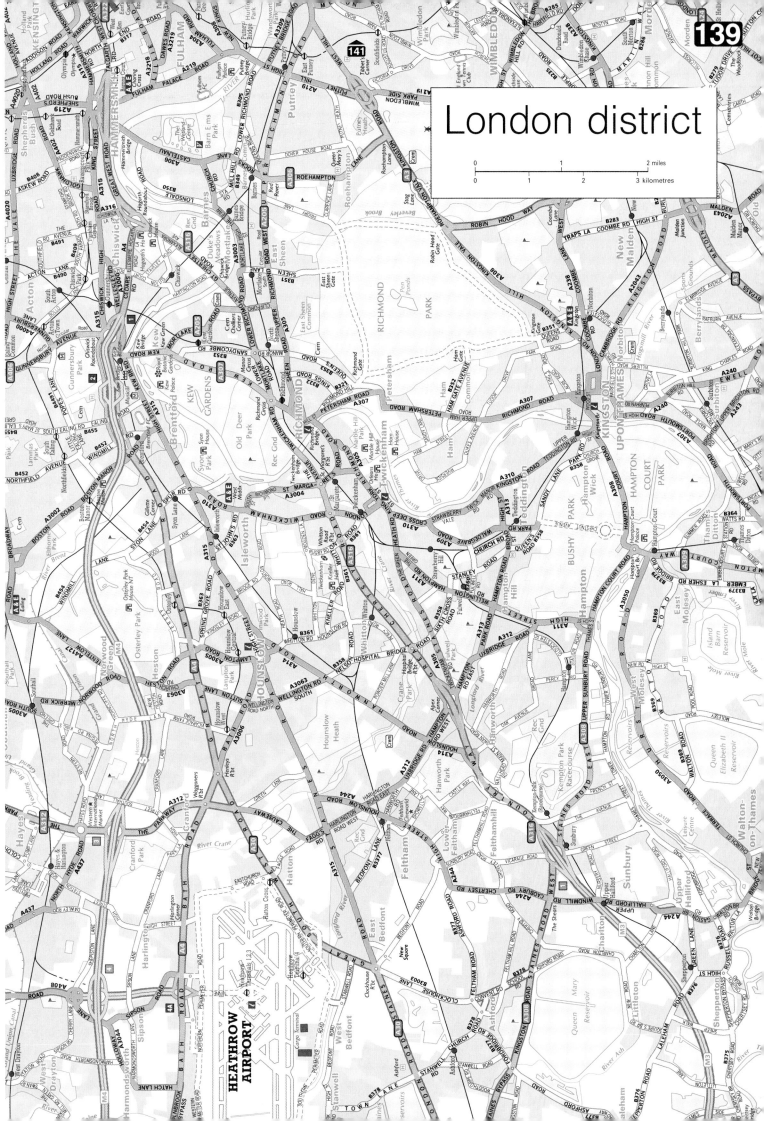

London district

141

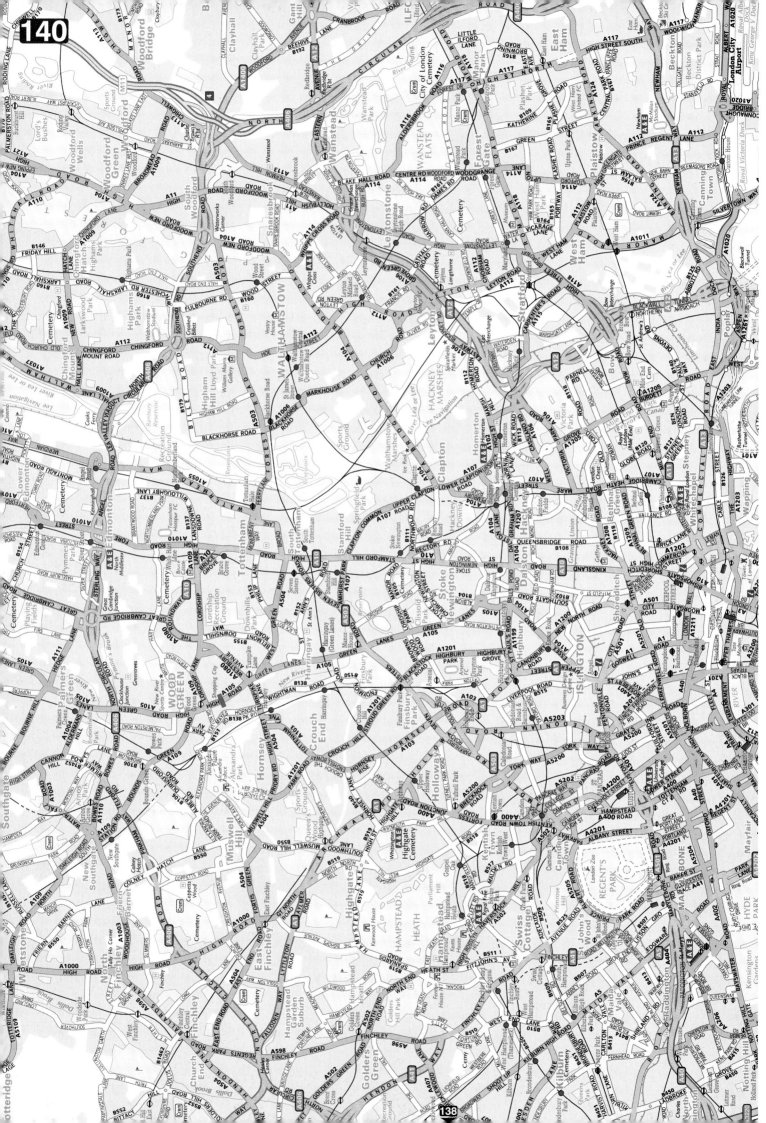

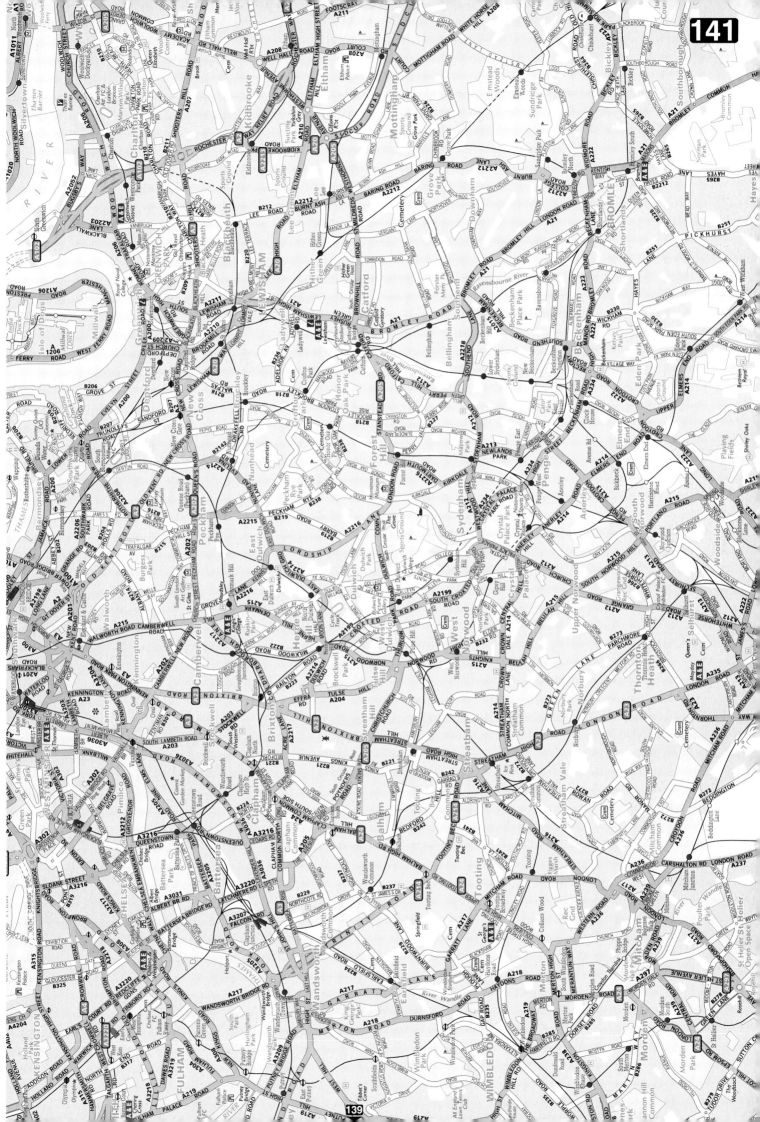

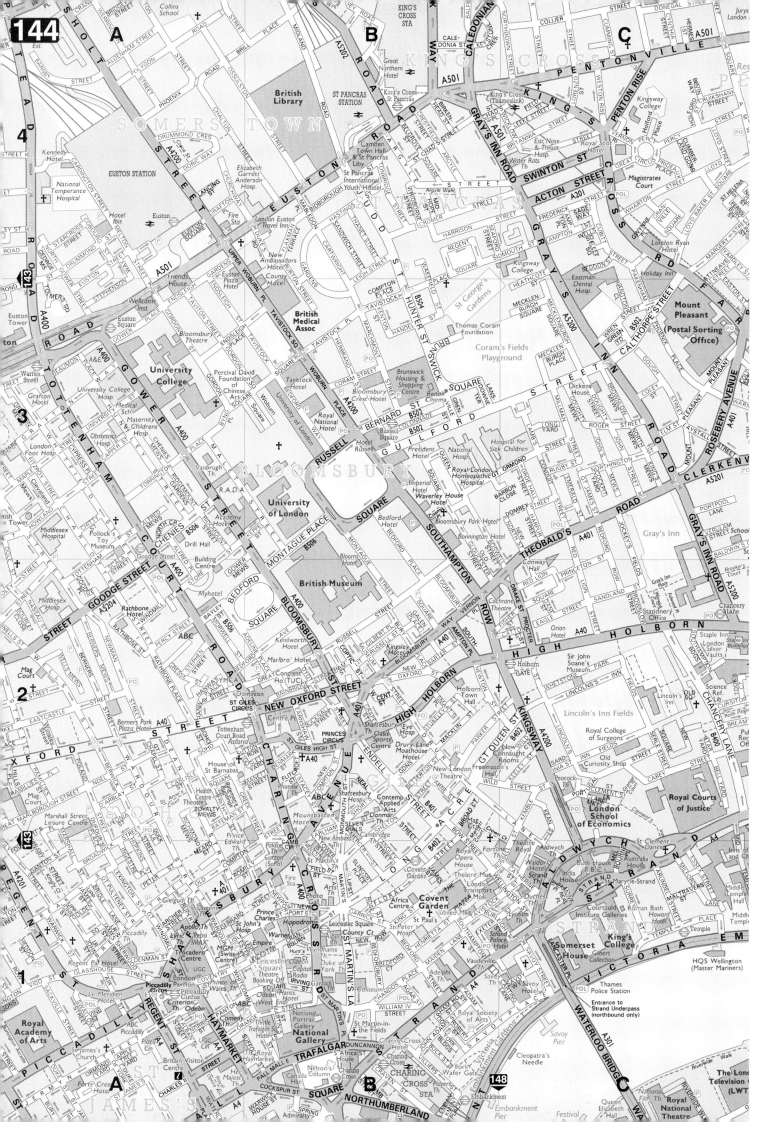

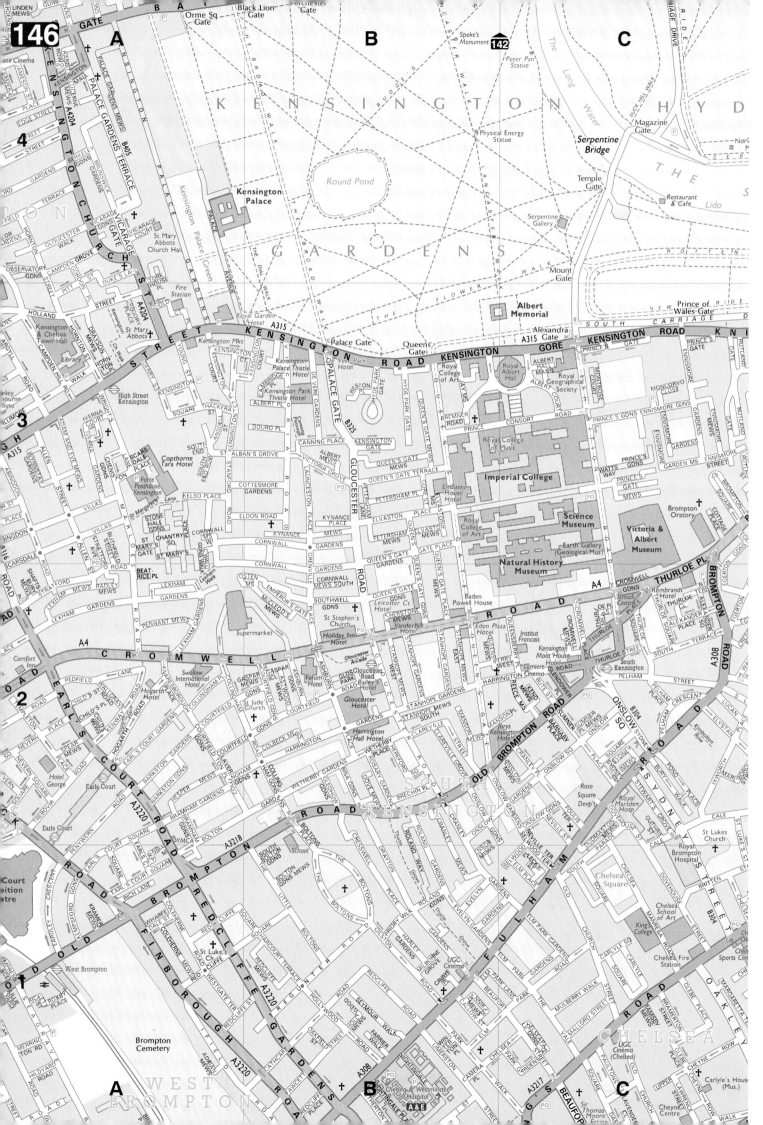

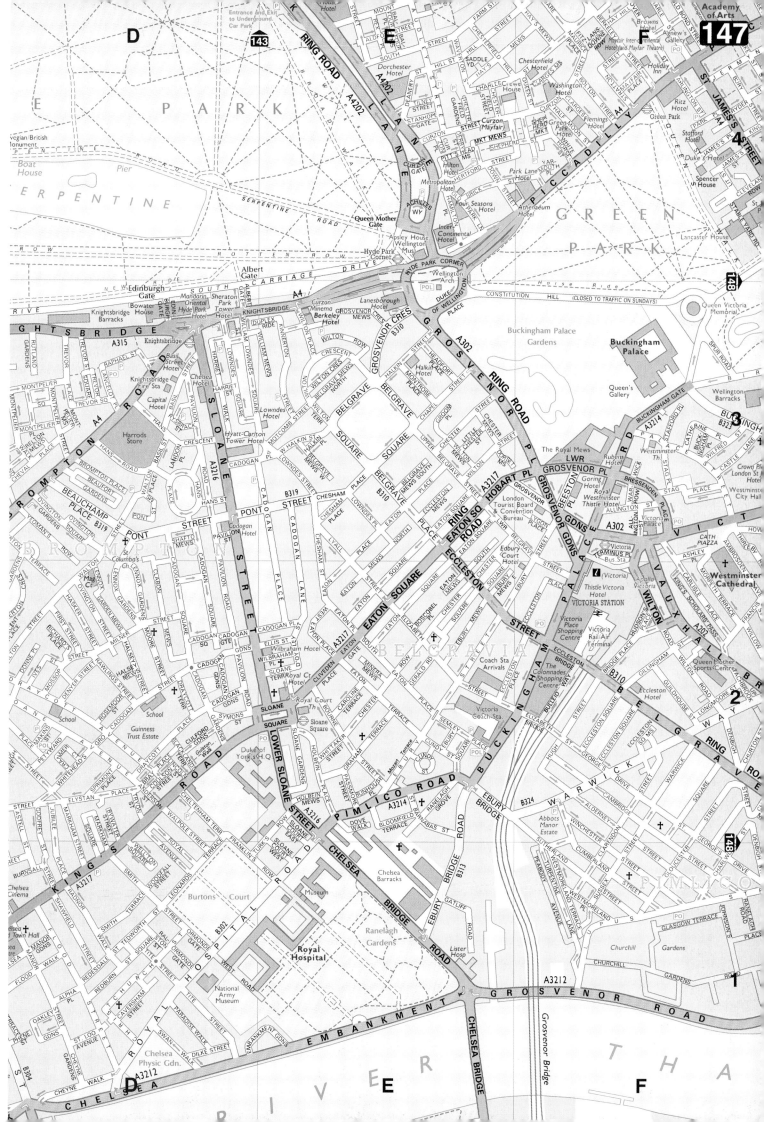

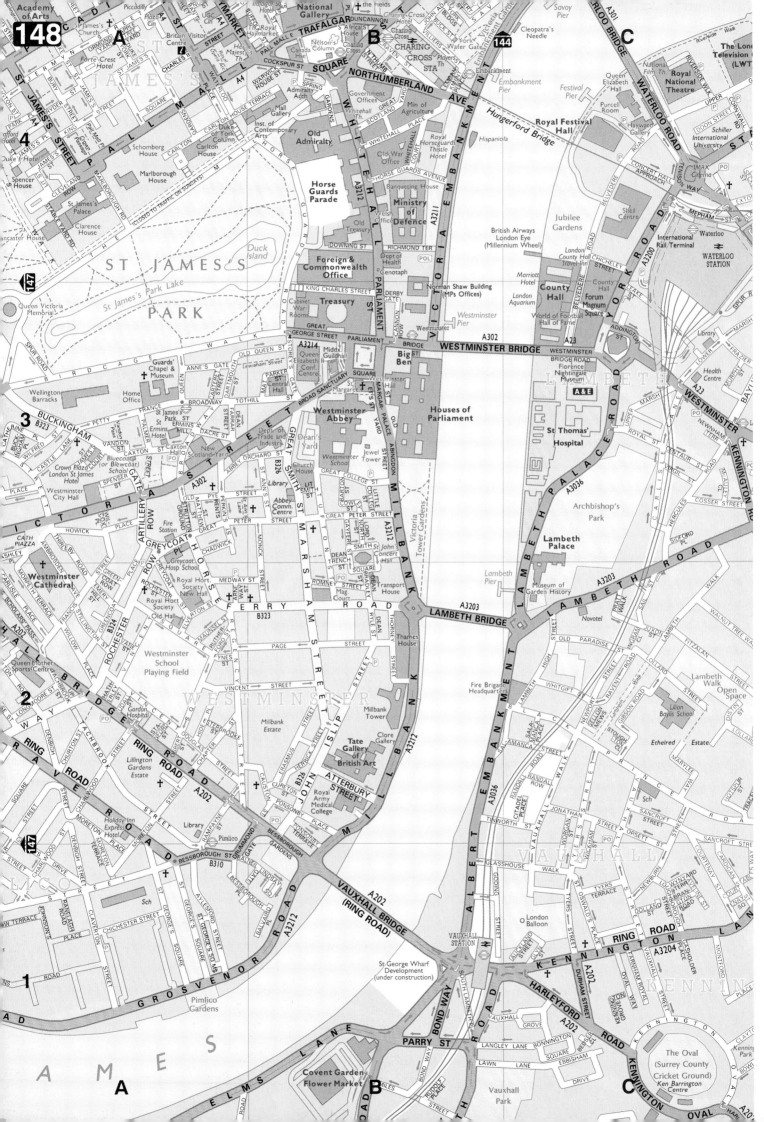

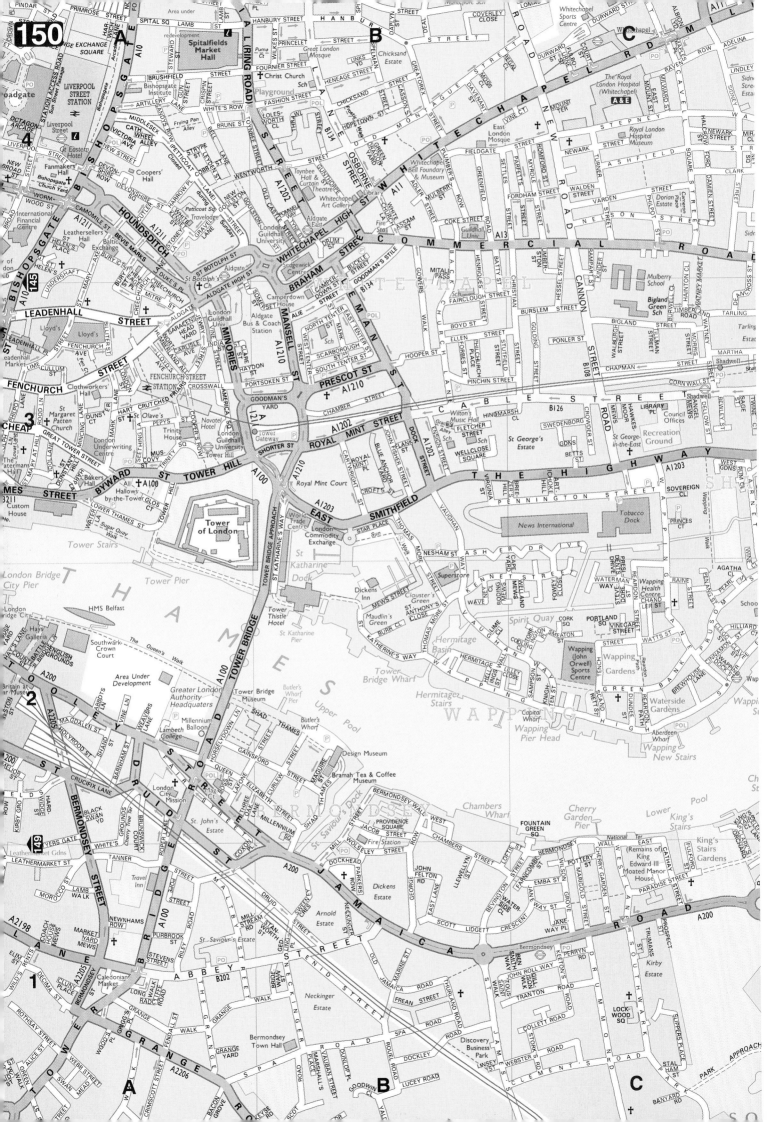

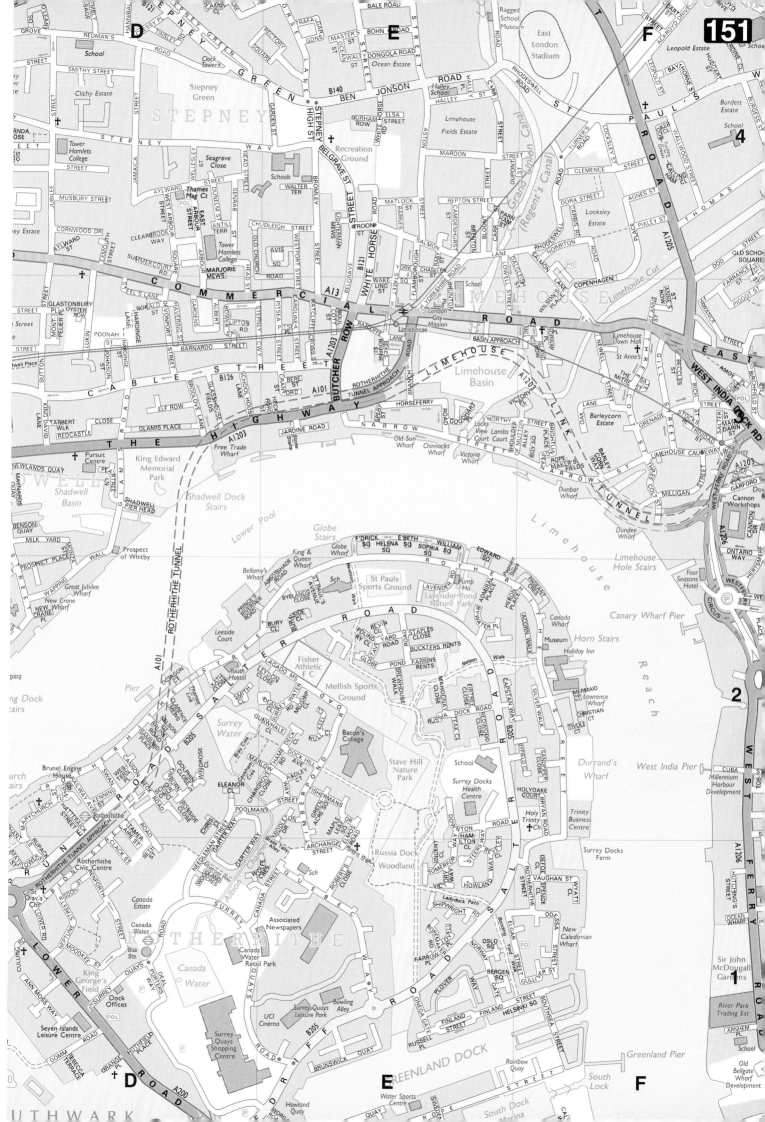

Central London street index

In the index the street names are listed in alphabetical order and written in full, but may be abbreviated on the map. Postal codes are listed where information is available. Each entry is followed by its map page number in bold type, and an arbitrary letter and grid reference number. For example, for Exhibition Road SW7 **146** C3, turn to page 146. The letter 'C' refers to the grid square located at the bottom of the page; the figure '3' refers to the grid square located at the left-hand side of the page. Exhibition Road is found within the intersecting square. SW7 is the postcode. A proportion of street names and their references are also followed by the name of another street in italics. These entries do not appear on the map due to insufficient space but can be located adjacent to the name of the road in italics.

A

Abbey Orchard Street *SW1* **148** B3
Abbey Street *SE1* **150** A1
Abbots Gardens *W8* **146** A3
St Mary's Place
Abbots Lane *SE1* **150** A2
Abbots Walk *W8* **146** A3
St Mary's Place
Abbotshade Road *SE16* **151** E2
Abchurch Lane *EC4* **145** F1
Abercorn Close *NW8* **142** B4
Abercorn Place *NW8* **142** B4
Aberdeen Place *NW8* **142** C3
Aberdour Street *SE1* **149** F2
Abingdon Road *W8* **146** A3
Abingdon Street *SW1* **148** B3
Abingdon Villas *W8* **146** A3
Achilles Way *W1* **147** E4
Ackroyd Drive *E3* **151** F4
Acorn Walk *SE16* **151** F2
Acton Street *WC1* **144** C4
Adam and Eve Court *W1* **143** E1
Oxford Street
Adam And Eve Mews *W8* **146** A3
Adam Street *WC2* **144** B1
Adam's Row *W1* **143** E1
Addington Street *SE1* **148** C3
Addle Hill *EC4* **145** E1
Addle Street *EC2* **145** E2
Adelaide Street *WC2* **144** B1
William IV Street
Adelina Grove *E1* **150** D4
Adeline Place *WC1* **144** B2
Adelphi Terrace *WC2* **144** B1
Adams Street
Adler Street *E1* **150** B4
Admiral Place *SE16* **151** E2
Admiral Way *W9* **142** A3
Adpar Street *W2* **142** C3
Adrian Mews *SW10* **146** A1
Agar Street *WC2* **144** B1
Agatha Close *E1* **150** C2
Agdon Street *EC1* **145** D3
Agnes Street *E14* **151** F4
Ainstey Street *SE16* **151** D1
Brunel Road
Air Street *W1* **144** A1
Alaska Street *SE1* **148** C4
Albany Mews *SE5* **149** E1
Albany Road *SE5* **149** E1
Albany Street *NW1* **143** F4
Albatross Way *SE16* **151** D1
Albemarle Street *W1* **143** F1
Albemarle Way *EC1* **144** C3
Clerkenwell Road
Albert Court *SW7* **146** C3
Albert Embankment *SE1* **148** B1
Albert Gardens *E1* **151** D3
Albert Hall Mansions *SW7* **146** C3
Albert Mews *W8* **146** B3
Albert Place *W8* **146** B3
Alberta Street *SE17* **149** D1
Albion Close *W2* **143** D1
Albion Mews *W2* **143** D1
Albion Place *EC1* **145** D3
Albion Street *SE16* **151** D1
Albion Street *W2* **143** D1
Albion Way *EC1* **145** E2
Albion Yard *E1* **150** C4
Aldburgh Mews *W1* **143** E2
Marylebone Lane
Aldenham Street *NW1* **144** A4
Aldermanbury *EC2* **145** E2
Aldermanbury Square *EC2* **145** E2
Aldermanbury
Alderney Street *SW1* **147** F2
Aldersgate Street *EC1* **145** E3
Aldford Street *W1* **143** E1
Aldgate *EC3* **150** A3
Aldgate High Street *EC3* **150** A3
Aldsworth Close *W9* **142** A3
Aldwych *WC2* **144** C1
Alexander Place *SW7* **146** C2
Alexander Square *SW3* **146** C2
Alexander Street *W2* **142** A2
Alford Place *N1* **145** E4
Alfred Mews *W1* **144** A3
Alfred Place *WC1* **144** A3
Alfred Road *W2* **142** A2
Alice Street *SE1* **149** F3
Alie Street *E1* **150** B3
All Hallows Lane *EC4* **145** F1
All Soul's Place *W1* **143** F2
Langham Street
Allen Street *W8* **146** A3
Allington Street *SW1* **147** F3
Allsop Place *NW1* **143** D3
Alma Square *NW8* **142** B4
Alpha Place *SW3* **147** D1
Alsace Road *SE17* **149** F1
Alscot Road *SE1* **150** B1
Alvey Street *SE17* **149** F2
Ambergate Street *SE17* **149** D1
Amberley Road *W9* **142** A3
Ambrosden Avenue *SW1* **148** A3
Amelia Street *SE17* **149** E2
Amen Corner *EC4* **145** D2
Amen Court *EC4* **145** D2
America Square *EC3* **150** A3
America Street *SE1* **149** E4
Amoy Place *E14* **151** F3
Ampton Place *WC1* **144** C4
Ampton Street *WC1* **144** C4
Amwell Street *EC1* **144** C4
Anderson Street *SW3* **147** D2
Andrew Borde Street *WC2* **144** B2
Charing Cross Road
Angel Court *EC2* **145** F2
Angel Court *SW1* **148** A4
King Street
Angel Mews *E1* **150** C3
Angel Passage *EC4* **145** F1
Angel Place *SE1* **149** E4
Angel Street *EC1* **145** E2
Ann Moss Way *SE16* **151** D1
Ansdell Street *W8* **146** A3
Antill Terrace *E1* **151** D4
Apothecary Street *EC4* **145** D2
New Bridge Street
Apple Tree Yard *SW1* **144** A1
Appold Street *EC2* **145** F3
Aquinas Street *SE1* **149** D4
Arbour Square *E1* **151** D4
Archangel Street *SE16* **151** E1
Archer Street *W1* **144** A1
Argent Street *SE1* **149** E4
Loman Street
Argyle Square *WC1* **144** B4
Argyle Street *WC1* **144** B4
Argyle Walk *WC1* **144** B4
Argyll Road *W8* **146** A3
Argyll Street *W1* **143** F2
Arlington Street *SW1* **147** F4
Arlington Way *EC1* **145** D4
Arne Street *WC2* **144** B2
Arneway Street *SW1* **148** A2
Arnside Street *SE17* **149** E1
Arthur Street *EC4* **145** F1
Artichoke Hill *E1* **150** C3
Artillery Lane *E1* **150** A4
Artillery Passage *E1* **150** A4
Artillery Lane
Artillery Row *SW1* **148** A3
Artizan Street *E1* **150** A4
Harrow Place
Arundel Street *WC2* **144** C1
Ashbridge Street *NW8* **142** C3
Ashburn Gardens *SW7* **146** B2
Ashburn Mews *SW7* **146** B2
Ashburn Place *SW7* **146** B2
Ashby Street *EC1* **145** D4
Asher Drive *E1* **150** B3
Ashfield Street *E1* **150** C4
Ashfield Yard *E1* **151** D4
Ashfield Street
Ashland Place *W1* **142** E3
Ashley Place *SW1* **147** F3
Ashmill Street *NW1* **142** C3
Ashworth Road *W9* **142** A4
Aske Street *N1* **145** F4
Asolando Drive *SE17* **149** E2
King & Queen Street
Assam Street *E1* **150** B4
Assembly Passage *E1* **151** D4
Astell Street *SW3* **147** D2
Aston Street *E14* **151** E4
Astwood Mews *SW7* **146** B2
Atherstone Mews *SW7* **146** B2
Atterbury Street *SW1* **148** B2
Attneave Street *WC1* **144** C4
Aubrey Place *NW8* **142** B4
Auckland Street *SE11* **148** C1
Augustus Street *NW1* **143** F4
Aulton Place *SE11* **149** D1
Austin Friars *EC2* **145** F2
Austin Friars Square *EC2* **145** F2
Austin Friars
Austral Street *SE11* **149** D2
Ave Maria Lane *EC4* **145** E2
Aveline Street *SE11* **148** C1
Avery Row *W1* **143** F1
Avis Square *E1* **151** E4
Avon Place *SE1* **149** E3
Avonmouth Street *SE1* **149** E3
Aybrook Street *W1* **143** E2
Aylesbury Road *SE17* **149** F1
Aylesbury Street *EC1* **145** D3
Aylesford Street *SW1* **148** A1
Aylward Street *E1* **151** D4
Ayres Street *SE1* **149** E4

B

Babmaes Street *SW1* **148** A4
Jermyn Street
Bacchus Walk *N1* **145** F4
Bache's Street *N1* **145** F4
Back Church Lane *E1* **150** B4
Back Hill *EC1* **145** D3
Bacon Grove *SE1* **150** A1
Bainbridge Street *WC1* **144** B2
Baker Street *W1 & NW1* **143** D3
Baker's Mews *W1* **143** E2
Baker's Row *EC1* **145** F3
Baker's Yard *EC1* **145** D3
Baker's Row
Bakers Hall Court *EC3* **150** A3
Harp Lane
Balcombe Street *NW1* **143** D3
Balderton Street *W1* **143** E1
Baldwin Street *EC1* **145** F4
Baldwin's Gardens *EC1* **144** C3
Bale Road *E1* **151** F4
Balfe Street *N1* **144** B4
Balfour Mews *W1* **143** E1
Balfour Place *W1* **143** E1
Balfour Street *SE17* **149** F2
Balneil Gate *SW1* **148** A1
Baltic Street East *EC1* **145** E3
Baltic Street West *EC1* **145** E3
Balvaird Place *SW1* **148** B2
Bancroft Road *E1* **148** C1
Bank End *SE1* **149** E4
Bankside *SE1* **149** E4
Bankside Jetty *SE1* **145** E1
Banner Street *EC1* **145** E3
Banyard Road *SE16* **150** C1
Barbon Close *WC1* **144** C3
Barge House Street *SE1* **145** D1
Bark Place *W2* **142** A1
Barkston Gardens *SW5* **146** A2
Barleycorn Way *E14* **151** F3
Barlow Place *W1* **143** F1
Barlow Street *SE17* **149** F2
Barnaby Place *SW7* **146** C2
Barnardo Street *E1* **151** D3
Barnby Street *NW1* **144** A4
Barnes Street *E14* **151** E4
Barnham Street *SE1* **150** A2
Barnwood Close *W9* **142** A3
Baron's Place *SE1* **149** D3
Barrett Street *W1* **143** E2
Barrie Street *W2* **142** B1
Barrow Hill Road *NW8* **142** C4
St Johns Wood High Street
Barter Street *WC1* **144** B2
Barth Lane *EC2* **145** F2
Bartholomew Close *EC1* **145** E2
Bartholomew Square *EC1* **145** E3
Bartholomew Street *SE1* **149** F2
Barton Street *SW1* **148** B3
Basil Street *SW3* **147** D3
Basin Approach *E14* **151** E3
Basinghall Avenue *EC2* **145** E2
Basinghall Street *EC2* **145** E2
Bastwick Street *EC1* **145** E3
Bate Street *E14* **151** F3
Bateman Street *W1* **144** A2
Bateman's Buildings *W1* **144** A2
Bath Court *EC1* **144** C3
Warner Street
Bath Place *N1* **145** F4
Bath Street *EC1* **145** E4
Bath Terrace *SE1* **149** E3
Bathurst Mews *W2* **142** C1
Bathurst Street *W2* **142** C1
Battle Bridge Lane *SE1* **149** F4
Batty Street *E1* **150** B4
Bayley Street *WC1* **144** A2
Baylis Road *SE1* **148** C3
Bayswater Road *W2* **142** A1
Baythorne Street *E3* **151** F4
Beaconsfield Road *SE17* **149** F1
Beak Street *W1* **144** A1
Bear Alley *EC4* **145** D2
Farringdon Street
Bear Gardens *SE1* **145** E1
Bear Lane *SE1* **149** D4
Bear Street *WC2* **144** B1
Cranbourn Street
Beatrice Place *W8* **146** A2
Beauchamp Place *SW3* **147** D3
Beauchamp Street *EC1* **145** D3
Brooke Street
Beaufort Gardens *SW3* **147** D3
Beaufort Street *SW3* **146** B1
Beaumont Mews *W1* **143** E2
Beaumont Place *W1* **144** A3
Beaumont Street *W1* **143** E3
Beccles Street *E14* **151** F3
Beckway Street *SE17* **149** F2
Bedale Street *SE1* **149** E3
Borough High Street
Bedford Avenue *WC1* **144** B2
Bedford Court *WC2* **144** B1
Bedford Gardens *W8* **146** A4
Bedford Place *WC1* **144** B3
Bedford Row *WC1* **144** C3
Bedford Square *WC1* **144** B2
Bedford Street *WC2* **144** B1
Bedford Way *WC1* **144** B3
Bedfordbury *WC2* **144** B1
Bedser Close *SE11* **148** C1
Beech Street *EC2* **145** E3
Beeston Place *SW1* **147** F3
Bekesbourne Street *E14* **151** E3
Belgrave Mews North *SW1* **147** E3
Belgrave Mews South *SW1* **147** E3
Belgrave Mews West *SW1* **147** E3
Belgrave Place *SW1* **147** E3
Belgrave Road *SW1* **147** F2
Belgrave Square *SW1* **147** E3
Belgrave Street *E1* **151** E3
Belgrove Street *WC1* **144** B4
Bell Lane *E1* **150** A4
Bell Street *NW1* **142** C3
Bell Yard *WC2* **144** C2
Belvedere Buildings *SE1* **149** E3
Belvedere Road *SE1* **148** C4
Ben Jonson Road *E1* **151** E4
Ben Smith Way *SE16* **150** C1
Bendall Mews *W1* **143** D3
Bennet's Hill *EC4* **145** E1
Castle Baynard Street
Benson Quay *E1* **151** D3
Bentinck Mews *W1* **143** E2
Marylebone Lane
Bentinck Street *W1* **143** E2
Bere Street *E1* **151** E3
Bergen Square *SE16* **151** E1
Berkeley Gardens *W8* **146** A4
Berkeley Mews *W1* **143** D2
Berkeley Square *W1* **143** F1
Berkeley Street *W1* **143** F1
Bermondsey Square *SE1* **145** E2
Long Lane
Bermondsey Street *SE1* **150** A2
Bermondsey Wall East *SE16* **150** B1
Bermondsey Wall West *SE16* **150** B2
Bernard Street *WC1* **144** B3
Berners Mews *W1* **144** A2
Berners Street *W1* **144** A2
Berry Street *EC1* **145** E3
Berryfield Road *SE17* **149** E1
Berwick Street *W1* **144** A2
Bessborough Gardens *SW1* **148** B2
Bessborough Place *SW1* **148** A1
Bessborough Street *SW1* **148** A1
Betterton Street *WC2* **144** B2
Betts Street *E1* **150** C3
Bevenden Street *N1* **145** F4
Beverston Mews *W1* **143** D2
Bevin Close *SE16* **151** E2
Bevin Way *WC1* **144** C4
Bevington Street *SE16* **150** B1
Bevis Marks *EC3* **150** A4
Bewley Street *E1* **150** C3
Bickenhall Street *W1* **143** D3
Bidborough Street *WC1* **144** B4
Biddulph Road *W9* **142** A4
Bigland Street *E1* **150** C3
Billiter Square *EC3* **150** A3
Fenchurch Avenue
Billiter Street *EC3* **150** A3
Bina Gardens *SW5* **146** B2
Bingham Place *W1* **143** E3
Binney Street *W1* **143** E1
Birchfield Street *E14* **151** E3
Birchin Lane *EC3* **145** F1
Bird Street *W1* **143** E2
Birdcage Walk *SW1* **148** A3
Birkenhead Street *WC1* **144** B4
Bishop's Court *EC4* **145** D2
Old Bailey
Bishop's Court *WC2* **144** C2
Chancery Lane
Bishop's Terrace *SE11* **149** D2
Bishops Bridge Road *W2* **142** B2
Bishopsgate *EC2* **145** F2
Bishopsgate Arcade *EC2* **150** A4
Bishopsgate Churchyard *EC2* **145** F2
Bittern Street *SE1* **149** E3
Black Prince Road *SE1 & SE11* **148** C2
Black Swan Yard *SE1* **150** A2
Blackall Street *EC2* **145** F3
Blackburne's Mews *W1* **143** E1
Blackfriars Bridge *EC4 & SE1* **145** D1
Blackfriars Lane *EC4* **145** D1
Blackfriars Passage *EC4* **145** D1
Blackfriars Road *SE1* **149** D4
Blacklands Terrace *SW3* **147** D2
Blackwood Street *SE17* **149** F1
Blandford Square *NW1* **143** D3
Blandford Street *W1* **143** F2
Bleeding Heart Yard *EC1* **145** D2
Greville Street
Blenheim Street *W1* **143** F1
New Bond Street
Bletchley Street *N1* **145** E4
Blithfield Street *W8* **146** A3
Blomfield Road *W9* **142** A3
Blomfield Street *EC2* **145** F2
Blomfield Villas *W2* **142** B2
Bloomburg Street *SW1* **147** F2
Vauxhall Bridge Road
Bloomfield Place *W1* **143** F1
Bourdon Street
Bloomfield Terrace *SW1* **147** E2
Bloomsbury Court *WC1* **144** B2
High Holborn
Bloomsbury Place *WC1* **144** B3
Southampton Row
Bloomsbury Square *WC1* **144** B2
Bloomsbury Street *WC1* **144** B2
Bloomsbury Way *WC1* **144** B2
Blount Street *E14* **151** E4
Blue Anchor Yard *E1* **150** B3
Blue Ball Yard *SW1* **148** A4
St James's Street
Bohn Road *E1* **151** F4
Bolsover Street *W1* **143** F3
Bolt Court *EC4* **145** D2
Bolton Gardens *SW5* **146** A2
Bolton Gardens Mews *SW10* **146** B1
Bolton Street *W1* **147** F4
Boltons Place *SW10* **146** B2
Bond Way *SW8* **148** B1
Bonding Yard Walk *SE16* **151** E1
Bonhill Street *EC2* **145** F3
Bonnington Square *SW8* **148** C1
Booker Close *E14* **151** F4
Boot Street *N1* **145** F4
Booth's Place *W1* **143** F2
Wells Street
Boreas Walk *N1* **145** E4
Nelson Place
Borough High Street *SE1* **149** E3
Borough Road *SE1* **149** E3
Borrett Close *SE17* **149** E1
Boscobel Place *SW1* **147** E2
Boscobel Street *NW8* **142** C3
Boss Street *SE1* **150** A2
Boston Place *NW1* **142** D3
Boswell Court *WC1* **144** B3
Boswell Street
Boswell Street *WC1* **144** B3
Botolph Lane *EC3* **145** F1
Bott's Mews *W2* **142** A2
Boulcott Street *E1* **151** E3
Boundary Lane *SE17* **149** E1
Boundary Road *SE1* **149** D4
Bourdon Street *W1* **143** F1
Bourlet Close *W1* **143** F2
Bourne Street *SW1* **147** E2
Bourne Terrace *W2* **142** A2
Bouverie Street *EC4* **145** D1
Bow Lane *EC4* **145** E1
Bow Street *WC2* **144** B2
Bowden Street *SE11* **149** D1
Bower Street *E1* **151** D3
Bowling Green Lane *EC1* **145** D3
Bowling Green Place *SE1* **149** F4
Newcomen Street
Bowling Green Street *SE11* **148** C1
Bowling Green Walk *N1* **145** F4
Boyd Street *E1* **150** B3
Boyfield Street *SE1* **149** D3
Boyle Street *W1* **143** F1
Savile Row
Boyson Road *SE17* **149** E1
Brackley Street *EC1* **145** E3
Brad Street *SE1* **149** D4
Braden Street *W9* **142** A3
Bradenham Close *SE17* **149** F1
Braganza Street *SE17* **149** D1
Braham Street *E1* **150** B3
Bramerton Street *SW3* **146** C1
Bramham Gardens *SW5* **146** A2
Branch Road *E14* **151** E3
Brandon Street *SE17* **149** E2
Brangton Road *SE11* **148** C1
Brass Tally Alley *SE16* **151** E1
Bray Crescent *SE16* **151** D2
Bray Place *SW3* **147** D2
Bread Street *EC4* **145** E1
Bream's Buildings *EC4* **144** C2
Brechin Place *SW7* **146** B2
Breezer's Hill *E1* **150** C3
Bremner Road *SW7* **146** B3
Brendon Street *W1* **143** D2
Brenton Street *E14* **151** E4
Bressenden Place *SW1* **147** F3
Brettell Street *SE17* **149** F1
Brewer Street *W1* **144** A1
Brewers' Green *SW1* **148** A3
Caxton Street
Brewhouse Lane *E1* **150** C2
Brewhouse Walk *SE16* **151** E2
Brick Court *EC4* **144** C2
Middle Temple Lane
Brick Street *W1* **147** E4
Bride Lane *EC4* **145** D2
Bridewain Street *SE1* **150** B1
Bridewell Place *EC4* **145** D1
Bridford Mews *W1* **143** F3
Bridge Place *SW1* **147** F2
Bridge Street *SW1* **148** B3
Bridge Yard *SE1* **149** F4
Bridgeport Place *E1* **150** B2
Kennet Street
Bridgewater Square *EC2* **145** E3
Beech Street
Bridgewater Street *EC2* **145** E3
Beech Street
Bridgeway Street *NW1* **144** A2
Bridle Lane *W1* **144** A1
Bridstow Place *W2* **142** A2
Brightlingsea Place *E14* **151** F3
Brill Place *NW1* **144** A4
Briset Street *EC1* **145** D3
Bristol Gardens *W9* **142** A3
Bristol Mews *W9* **142** B3
Britannia Street *WC1* **144** C4
Britannia Walk *N1* **145** F4
Britten Street *SW3* **146** C1
Britton Street *EC1* **145** D3
Broad Court *WC2* **144** B2
Broad Sanctuary *SW1* **148** B3
Broad Walk *W2* **147** E4
Broadbent Street *W1* **143** F1
Broadley Street *NW8* **142** C4
Broadley Terrace *NW1* **143** D3
Broadstone Place *W1* **143** E3
Broadwall *SE1* **149** D4
Broadway *SW1* **148** A3
Broadwick Street *W1* **144** A1
Brockham Street *SE1* **149** E3
Brodlove Lane *E1* **151** D3
Bromley Street *E1* **151** E4
Brompton Place *SW3* **147** D3
Brompton Road *SW3* **147** D3
Brompton Square *SW3* **146** C3
Bronti Close *SE17* **149** E1
Brook Drive *SE11* **149** D2
Brook Gate *W1* **143** E1
Brook Mews North *W2* **142** B1
Brook Street *W1* **143** E1
Brook Street *W2* **142** C1
Brook's Mews *W1* **143** F1
Brooke Street *EC1* **145** D2
Brooke's Court *EC1* **144** C2
Brooke's Market *EC1* **145** D2
Brooke Street
Brown Hart Gardens *W1* **143** E1
Brown Street *W1* **143** D2
Browning Close *W9* **142** B3
Browning Street *SE17* **149** E2
Brownlow Mews *WC1* **144** C3
Brownlow Street *WC1* **144** C2

Brune Street

Dombey Street

153

Brune Street E1 150 A4
Brunel Road SE16 151 D1
Brunswick Gardens W8 146 A4
Brunswick Mews W1 143 D2
Brunswick Place N1 145 F4
Brunswick Quay SE16 151 E1
Brunswick Square WC1 144 B3
Brunton Place E14 151 E3
Brushfield Street E1 150 A4
Bruton Lane W1 143 F1
Bruton Place W1 143 F1
Bruton Street W1 143 F1
Bryan Road SE16 151 F2
Bryanston Mews East W1 143 D2
Bryanston Mews West W1 143 D2
Bryanston Place W1 143 D2
Bryanston Square W1 143 D2
Bryanston Street W1 143 D2
Buck Hill Walk W2 142 C1
Buck Street WC2 144 B1
Buckingham Gate SW1 147 F3
Buckingham Palace Road SW1 147 F2
Buckingham Place SW1 147 F3
Buckland Street N1 145 F4
Buckle Street E1 150 B4
Bucklersbury EC4 145 E2
Bucknall Street WC2 144 B2
Buckters Rents SE16 151 E2
Budge's Walk W2 142 B4
Bulleid Way SW1 147 F2
Bulstrode Place W1 143 E2
Marylebone Lane
Bulstrode Street W1 143 E2
Bunhill Row EC1 145 F3
Bunhouse Place SW1 147 E2
Burbage Close SE1 149 F3
Burdett Street SE1 149 D3
Burge Street SE1 149 F3
Burgess Street E14 151 F4
Burgon Street EC4 145 E2
Carter Lane
Burleigh Street WC2 144 B1
Burlington Arcade W1 143 F1
Burlington Gardens W1 143 F1
Burne Street NW1 142 C3
Burnsall Street SW3 147 D1
Burnside Close SE16 151 E2
Burr Close E1 150 B2
Burrell Street SE1 149 D4
Burrows Mews SE1 149 D4
Bursar Street SE1 150 A2
Tooley Street
Burslem Street E1 150 C3
Burton Grove SE17 149 F1
Burton Street WC1 144 B4
Burwell Close E1 150 C3
Burwood Place W2 143 D2
Bury Close SE16 151 E2
Bury Court EC3 150 A4
Bury Place WC1 144 B2
Bury Street EC3 150 A3
Bury Street SW1 148 A4
Bury Walk SW3 146 C2
Bush Lane EC4 145 E1
Bushell Street E1 150 B2
Wapping High Street
Butcher Row E1 151 E3
Bute Street SW7 146 C1
Butler Place SW1 147 F3
Buckingham Gate
Butterfield Close SE16 150 C1
Buttesland Street N1 145 F4
Byelands Close SE16 151 E2
Byfield Close SE16 151 F2
Byng Place WC1 144 A3
Byward Street EC3 150 A3
Bywater Place SE16 151 E2
Bywater Street SW3 147 D2

C

Cabbell Street NW1 142 C2
Cable Street E1 150 B3
Cadiz Street SE17 149 E1
Cadogan Gardens SW3 147 D2
Cadogan Gate SW1 147 D2
Cadogan Lane SW1 147 E3
Cadogan Place SW1 147 E2
Cadogan Square SW1 147 D2
Cadogan Street SW3 147 D2
Cahill Street EC1 145 E3
Dufferin Street
Cale Street SW3 146 C2
Caleb Street SE1 149 E4
Marshalsea Road
Caledonia Street N1 144 B4
Caledonian Road N1 & N7 144 B4
Callingham Close E14 151 F4
Callow Street SW3 146 B1
Calthorpe Street WC1 144 C3
Camberwell Road SE5 149 E1
Cambridge Circus WC2 144 B1
Cambridge Gate NW1 143 F3
Cambridge Gate Mews NW1 143 F4
Albany Street
Cambridge Place W8 146 B3
Cambridge Road NW6 142 A4
Cambridge Square W2 142 C2
Cambridge Street SW1 147 F2
Cambridge Terrace Mews NW1 144 F4
Chester Gate
Camdenhurst Street E14 151 E4
Camera Place SW10 146 B1
Cameron Place E1 150 C4
Camomile Street EC3 150 A4
Campden Grove W8 146 A4
Campden Hill Road W8 146 A3
Camperdown Street E1 150 B3
Canada Street SE16 151 E1
Canal Street SE5 149 F1
Candover Street W1 143 F2
Foley Street
Canning Passage W8 146 B3
Canning Place W8 146 B3
Cannon Beck Road SE16 151 D2
Cannon Drive E14 151 F3
Cannon Row SW1 148 B3
Cannon Street EC4 145 E2
Cannon Street Road E1 150 C3
Canterbury Place SE17 149 E2
Canvey Street SE1 149 E4
Cape Yard E1 150 B3
Capland Street NW8 142 C3
Capper Street WC1 144 A3
Capstan Way SE16 151 E2
Carbis Road E14 151 F4
Carburton Street W1 143 F3
Cardigan Street SE11 148 C1
Cardington Street NW1 144 A4
Carey Lane EC2 145 E2
Carey Street WC2 144 C2
Carlisle Avenue EC3 150 A3
Carlisle Lane SE1 148 C3
Carlisle Place SW1 147 F2
Carlisle Street W1 144 A2
Carlos Place W1 143 E1
Carlton Gardens SW1 148 A4
Carlton House Terrace SW1 148 A4
Carlton Vale NW6 142 A4
Carlyle Square SW3 146 C1
Carmelite Street EC4 145 D1
Carnaby Street W1 144 A1
Caroline Place Mews W2 142 A1
Caroline Street E1 151 E3
Caroline Terrace SW1 147 E2
Carpenter Street W1 143 E1
Carr Street E14 151 E4
Carrington Street W1 147 E4
Shepherd Street
Carter Lane EC4 145 E2
Carter Place SE17 149 E1
Carter Street SE17 149 E1
Carteret Street SW1 148 A3
Carthusian Street EC1 145 E3
Carting Lane WC2 144 C1
Cartwright Gardens WC1 144 B4
Cartwright Street E1 150 B3
Casson Street E1 150 B4
Castellain Road W9 142 A3
Castle Baynard Street EC4 145 E1
Castle Lane SW1 148 A3
Castle Yard SE1 149 D4
Castlebrook Close SE11 149 D2
Brook Drive
Castlereagh Street W1 143 D2
Catesby Street SE17 149 F2
Cathay Street SE16 150 C1
Cathcart Road SW10 146 B1
Cathedral Piazza SW1 147 F3
Cathedral Street SE1 149 F4
Winchester Walk
Catherine Place SW1 147 F3
Catherine Street WC2 144 C1
Catherine Wheel Alley E1 150 A4
Catherine Wheel Yard SW1 148 A4
Little St James's Street
Cato Street W1 143 D2
Catton Street WC1 144 C2
Causton Street SW1 148 B2
Cavaye Place SW10 146 B1
Cavell Street E1 150 C4
Cavendish Avenue NW8 142 C4
Cavendish Close NW8 142 C4
Cavendish Mews North W1 143 F3
Hallam Street
Cavendish Mews South W1 143 F2
Hallam Street
Cavendish Place W1 143 F2
Cavendish Square W1 143 F2
Caversham Street SW3 147 D1
Caxton Street SW1 148 A3
Cayton Place EC1 145 E4
Cayton Street
Cayton Street EC1 145 E4
Cecil Court WC2 144 B1
St Martin's Lane
Centaur Street SE1 148 C3
Central Street EC1 145 E4
Chadwell Street EC1 145 D4
Chadwick Street SW1 148 A3
Chagford Street NW1 143 D3
Chalton Street NW1 144 A4
Chamber Street E1 150 B3
Chambers Street SE16 150 B1
Chancel Street SE1 149 D4
Chancery Lane WC2 144 C2
Chandler Street E1 150 C2
Chandos Place WC2 144 B1
Chandos Street W1 143 F2
Chantry Square W8 146 A3
Chapel Court SE1 149 E4
Chapel Place W1 143 F2
Chapel Side W2 142 A1
Chapel Street NW1 142 C2
Chapel Street SW1 147 E3
Chapman Street E1 150 C3
Chapter Road SE17 149 E1
Chapter Street SW1 148 A2
Chapter Terrace SE17 149 D1
Chargrove Close SE16 151 D2
Charing Cross Road WC2 144 B2
Charles II Street SW1 148 A4
Charles Square N1 145 F4
Charles Street W1 147 E4
Charleston Street SE17 149 E2
Charlie Chaplin Walk SE1 148 C4
Waterloo Road
Charlotte Place W1 144 A2
Goodge Street
Charlotte Place SW1 147 F2
Wilton Road
Charlotte Road EC2 145 F4
Charlotte Street W1 144 A3
Charlwood Street SW1 148 A1
Chart Street N1 145 F4
Charterhouse Square EC1 145 E2
Charterhouse Street EC1 145 D2
Chaseley Street E14 151 E4
Chatham Street SE17 149 F2
Cheapside EC4 145 E2
Chelsea Bridge SW1 & SW8 147 E1
Chelsea Bridge Road SW1 147 E1
Chelsea Embankment SW3 147 D1
Chelsea Manor Gardens SW3 147 D1
Chelsea Manor Street SW3 147 D1
Chelsea Park Gardens SW3 146 C1
Chelsea Square SW3 146 C1
Cheltenham Terrace SW3 147 D2
Chenies Mews WC1 144 A3
Chenies Street WC1 144 E3
Cheniston Gardens W8 146 A3
Chepstow Place W2 142 A1
Chepstow Road W2 142 A2
Chequer Street EC1 145 E3
Cherbury Street N1 145 F4
Cherry Garden Street SE16 150 C1
Cherry Tree Terrace SE1 150 A2
Chesham Place SW1 147 E3
Chesham Street SW1 147 E3
Chester Close North NW1 143 F4
Chester Close South NW1 143 F4
Chester Court NW1 143 F4
Albany Street
Chester Gate NW1 143 F4
Chester Mews SW1 147 E3
Chester Place NW1 143 F4
Chester Row SW1 147 E2
Chester Square SW1 147 E2
Chester Street SW1 147 E3
Chester Terrace NW1 143 F4
Chester Way SE11 149 D2
Chesterfield Gardens W1 147 E4
Chesterfield Hill W1 143 E1
Chesterfield Street W1 147 E4
Cheval Place SW7 147 D3
Cheyne Gardens SW3 146 D1
Cheyne Walk SW3 & SW10 146 C1
Chicheley Street SE1 148 C4
Chichester Rents WC2 144 C2
Chancery Lane
Chichester Road W2 142 A3
Chichester Street SW1 148 A1
Chicksand Street E1 150 B4
Chigwell Hill E1 150 C3
The Highway
Child's Place SW5 146 A2
Child's Street SW5 146 A2
Childs Mews SW5 146 A2
Chiltern Street W1 143 E3
Chilworth Mews W2 142 B2
Chilworth Street W2 142 B2
Chiswell Street EC1 145 E3
Chitty Street W1 144 A3
Christchurch Street SW3 147 D1
Christian Court SE16 151 F2
Christian Street E1 150 C3
Christopher Close SE16 150 D1
Christopher Street EC2 145 F3
Chudleigh Street E1 151 E4
Chumleigh Street SE5 149 F1
Church Place SW1 147 F4
Piccadilly
Church Street NW8 142 C3
Church Yard Row SE11 149 D2
Churchill Gardens Road SW1 147 F1
Churchway NW1 144 A4
Churton Street SW1 148 A2
Cinnamon Street E1 150 C2
Circus Mews W1 143 D3
Enford Street
Circus Place EC2 145 F2
Finsbury Circus
Circus Road NW8 142 C4
Cirencester Street W2 142 A3
Citadel Place SE11 148 C2
City Garden Row N1 145 E4
City Road EC1 145 F3
Clabon Mews SW1 147 D2
Clack Street SE16 151 D1
Clanricarde Gardens W2 142 A1
Clare Market WC2 144 C2
Claremont Close N1 145 D4
Claremont Square N1 145 D4
Clarence Gardens NW1 143 F4
Clarence Mews SE16 151 D2
Clarendon Close W2 142 C1
Clarendon Gardens W9 142 B3
Clarendon Place W2 142 C1
Clarendon Road W11 147 F1
Clarendon Street SW1 147 F1
Clarendon Terrace W9 142 B3
Clareville Grove SW7 146 B2
Clareville Street SW7 146 B2
Clarges Mews W1 147 F4
Clarges Street W1 147 F4
Clark Street E1 150 C4
Clark's Orchard SE16 150 C1
Clave Street E1 150 C2
Claverton Street SW1 148 A1
Clay Street W1 143 D2
Clayton Street SE11 148 C1
Clearbrook Way E1 151 D4
Clearwell Drive W9 142 A3
Cleaver Square SE11 149 D1
Cleaver Street SE11 149 D1
Clegg Street E1 150 C2
Clemence Street E14 151 F4
Clement's Inn WC2 144 C2
Clement's Road SE16 150 C1
Clements Lane EC4 145 F1
Clenston Mews W1 143 D2
Clere Street EC2 145 F3
Clerkenwell Close EC1 145 D3
Clerkenwell Green EC1 145 D3
Clerkenwell Road EC1 144 C3
Cleveland Gardens W2 142 B2
Cleveland Mews W1 143 F3
Cleveland Place SW1 148 A4
King Street
Cleveland Row SW1 148 A4
Cleveland Square W2 142 B2
Cleveland Street W1 143 F3
Cleveland Terrace W2 142 B2
Clifford Street W1 143 F1
Clifton Gardens W9 142 B3
Clifton Place W2 142 C1
Clifton Road W9 142 B3
Clifton Street EC2 145 F3
Clifton Villas W9 142 B3
Clink Street SE1 149 E4
Clipper Close SE16 151 D2
Kinburn Street
Clipstone Mews W1 143 F3
Clipstone Street W1 143 F3
Cliveden Place SW1 147 E2
Cloak Lane EC4 145 E1
Cloth Fair EC1 145 E2
Cloth Street EC1 145 E3
Clunbury Street N1 145 F4
Cherbury Street
Cluny Place SE1 149 F3
Coach & Horses Yard W1 143 F1
Old Burlington Street
Coach House Mews SE1 149 F3
Cobb Street E1 150 A4
Cobourg Street NW1 144 A4
Cock Lane EC1 145 D2
Cockpit Yard WC1 144 C3
Cockspur Street SW1 148 B4
Codling Close E1 150 C1
Coin Street SE1 149 D4
Coke Street E1 150 B4
Colbeck Mews SW7 146 B2
Colchester Street E1 150 B4
Drum Street
Coldbath Square EC1 144 C3
Cole Street SE1 149 E3
Colebrooke Row N1 145 D1
Coleherne Mews SW10 148 A1
Coleherne Road SW10 146 A1
Coleman Street EC2 145 E2
Coley Street WC1 144 C3
College Hill EC4 145 E1
College Street
College Street EC4 145 E1
Collett Road SE16 150 C1
Collier Street N1 144 C4
Collingham Gardens SW5 146 A2
Collingham Place SW4 146 A2
Collingham Road SW5 146 A2
Collinson Street SE1 149 E3
Colnbrook Street SE1 149 D3
Colombo Street SE1 149 D4
Colonnade WC1 144 B3
Colworth Grove SE17 149 E2
Commercial Road E1 & E14 150 B4
Commercial Street E1 150 A4
Compton Passage EC1 145 D3
Compton Place WC1 144 B3
Compton Street EC1 145 D3
Comus Place SE17 149 F2
Concert Hall Approach SE1 148 C4
Conder Street E14 151 E4
Salmon Lane
Conduit Mews W2 142 C4
Conduit Place W2 142 C2
Conduit Street W1 143 F1
Congreve Street SE17 149 F2
Connaught Place W2 143 D1
Connaught Square W2 143 D2
Connaught Street W2 142 C2
Cons Street SE1 149 D4
Constitution Hill SW1 147 E3
Content Street SE17 149 E2
Conway Street W1 143 F3
Cook's Road E15 149 D1
Cookham Crescent SE16 151 D2
Coombs Street N1 145 E4
Cooper Close SE1 149 D3
Cooper's Row EC3 150 A3
Cope Place W8 146 A3
Copenhagen Place E14 151 F3
Copley Close SE17 149 E1
Copperfield Street SE1 149 E4
Copthall Avenue EC2 145 F2
Coptic Street WC1 144 B2
Coral Street SE1 149 D3
Coram Street WC1 144 B3
Cork Square E1 150 C2
Cork Street W1 143 F1
Corlett Street NW1 142 C3
Bell Street
Corner House Street WC2 148 B4
Northumberland Street
Cornhill EC3 145 F2
Cornwall Gardens SW7 146 B3
Cornwall Gardens Walk SW7 146 A2
Cornwall Mews South SW7 146 B2
Cornwall Mews West SW7 146 A3
Cornwall Road SE1 148 C4
Cornwall Square SE11 149 D1
Cornwall Street E1 150 C3
Cornwall Terrace NW1 143 D3
Cornwood Drive E1 151 D4
Coronet Street N1 145 F4
Corporation Row EC1 145 D3
Corsham Street N1 145 F4
Cosmo Place WC1 144 B3
Cosser Street SE1 148 C3
Cosway Street NW1 143 D3
Cotham Street SE17 149 E2
Cottage Place SW3 146 C3
Cottesloe Mews SE1 149 D3
Cottesmore Gardens W8 146 B3
Cottingham Close SE11 149 D2
Cottington Street SE11 149 D2
Cottons Lane SE1 149 F4
Counter Street SE1 149 F4
County Street SE1 149 E2
Court Street E1 150 C4
Courtenay Square SE11 148 C1
Courtenay Street SE11 148 C1
Courtfield Gardens SW5 146 A2
Courtfield Road SW7 146 B2
Cousin Lane EC4 145 F1
Coventry Street W1 144 A1
Coverley Close E1 150 B4
Cowcross Street EC1 145 D3
Cowley Street SW1 148 B3
Cowper Street EC2 145 F3
Coxon Place SE1 150 A1
Crace Street NW1 144 A4
Crail Row SE17 149 F2
Cramer Street W1 143 E2
Crampton Street SE17 149 C2
Cranbourn Street WC2 144 B1
Cranford Street E1 151 E3
Cranley Gardens SW7 146 B2
Cranley Mews SW7 146 B2
Cranley Place SW7 146 C2
Cranmer Court SW3 147 D2
Cranwood Street EC1 145 F4
Craven Hill W2 142 B1
Craven Hill Gardens W2 142 B1
Craven Hill Mews W2 142 B1
Craven Road W2 142 B1
Craven Street WC2 144 B1
Craven Terrace W2 142 B1
Crawford Passage EC1 145 D3
Crawford Place W1 143 D2
Crawford Street W1 143 D2
Creasy Street SE1 149 F3
Swan Mead
Creechurch Lane EC3 150 A3
Creechurch Place EC3 150 A3
Creed Lane EC4 145 E2
Crescent EC3 150 A3
America Square
Crescent Place SW3 147 D2
Crescent Row EC1 145 E3
Cresswell Place SW10 146 B1
Cressy Place E1 151 D4
Crestfield Street WC1 144 B4
Cricketers' Court SE11 149 D1
Kennington Park Road
Crimscott Street SE1 150 A1
Cripplegate Street EC1 143 E3
Viscount Street
Crispin Street E1 150 A4
Crofts Street E1 150 B3
Cromer Street WC1 144 B3
Crompton Street W2 142 B3
Cromwell Mews SW7 146 C2
Cromwell Place SW7 146 C2
Cromwell Road SW7 & SW5 146 A1
Crondall Street N1 145 F4
Crosby Row SE1 149 F3
Crosby Square EC3 145 F2
Great St Helen's
Cross Keys Close W1 143 E2
Marylebone Lane
Cross Lane EC3 150 A3
St Dunstan's Hill
Crosslet Street SE17 149 F2
Crosswall EC3 150 A3
Crowder Street E1 150 C3
Crown Court WC2 144 B2
Crown Office Row EC4 145 D1
Crown Passage SW1 148 A4
Crown Place EC2 145 F3
Crucifix Lane SE1 150 A2
Cruikshank Street WC1 144 C4
Crutched Friars EC3 150 A3
Cubitt Street WC1 144 C4
Cubitts Yard WC2 144 B1
James Street
Culford Gardens SW3 147 D2
Culling Road SE16 151 D1
Cullum Street EC3 150 A3
Culross Street W1 143 E1
Culworth Street NW8 142 C4
Cumberland Gardens WC1 144 C4
Great Percy Street
Cumberland Gate W1 & W2 143 D1
Cumberland Market NW1 143 F4
Cumberland Street SW1 147 F1
Cumberland Terrace NW1 143 E4
Cumberland Terrace Mews NW1 143 F4
Albany Street
Cumming Street N1 144 C4
Cundy Street SW1 147 E2
Cunningham Place NW8 142 C3
Cureton Street SW1 148 B2
Curlew Street SE1 150 B2
Cursitor Street EC4 144 C2
Curzon Gate W1 147 E4
Curzon Place W1 147 E4
Curzon Street W1 147 E4
Cuthbert Street W2 142 C3
Cutler Street E1 150 A4
Cynthia Street N1 144 C4
Cypress Place W1 144 A3
Cyrus Street EC1 145 D3

D

D'Arblay Street W1 144 A2
D'Oyley Street SW1 147 E2
Dacre Street SW1 148 A3
Dalgleish Street E14 151 E4
Dallington Square EC1 145 E3
Dallington Street EC1 145 D3
Damien Street E1 150 C4
Dane Street WC1 144 C2
Dante Road SE11 149 D2
Daplyn Street E1 150 B4
Dark House Walk EC3 145 F1
Dartford Street SE17 149 E1
Dartmouth Street SW1 148 A3
Darwin Street SE17 149 F2
Date Street SE17 149 E1
Davenant Street E1 150 B4
Daventry Street NW1 142 C3
Davidge Street SE1 149 D3
Davies Mews W1 143 E1
Davies Street W1 143 E1
Dawes Street SE17 149 F2
Dawson Place W2 142 A1
De Laune Street SE17 149 D1
De Vere Gardens W8 146 B3
De Walden Street W1 143 E2
Westmorland Street
Deacon Way SE17 149 E2
Deal Porters Way SE16 151 D1
Deal Street E1 150 B4
Dean Bradley Street SW1 148 B2
Dean Close SE16 151 E2
Dean Farrar Street SW1 148 A3
Dean Ryle Street SW1 148 B2
Dean Stanley Street SW1 148 B2
Millbank
Dean Street W1 144 A2
Dean Trench Street SW1 148 B3
Dean's Buildings SE17 149 F2
Dean's Court EC4 145 E2
Carter Lane
Dean's Mews W1 143 F2
Deancross Street E1 150 C3
Deanery Street W1 147 E4
Decima Street SE1 149 F3
Deck Close SE16 151 E2
Defoe Close SE16 151 F1
Delamere Terrace W2 142 A3
Delaware Road W9 142 A3
Dellow Street E1 150 C3
Delverton Road SE17 149 E1
Denbigh Street SW1 148 A2
Denman Street W1 144 A1
Denmark Place WC2 144 B2
Charing Cross Road
Denmark Street WC2 144 B2
Denning Close NW8 142 B4
Denny Crescent SE11 149 D2
Denny Street SE11 149 D2
Denyer Street SW3 147 D2
Derby Gate SW1 148 B3
Derby Street W1 147 E4
Dering Street W1 143 F2
Deverell Street SE1 149 F3
Devereux Court WC2 144 B1
Strand
Devonport Street E1 151 D3
Devonshire Close W1 143 F3
Devonshire Mews South W1 143 E3
Devonshire Mews West W1 143 E3
Devonshire Place W1 143 E3
Devonshire Place W8 146 A3
St Mary's Place
Devonshire Place Mews W1 143 E3
Devonshire Row EC2 150 A4
Devonshire Square EC2 150 A4
Devonshire Street W1 143 E3
Devonshire Terrace W2 142 B1
Diadem Court W1 144 A2
Dean Street
Dickens Square SE1 149 E3
Dilke Street SW3 147 D1
Dingley Place EC1 145 E4
Dingley Road EC1 145 E4
Disney Place SE1 149 E3
Disney Street SE1 149 E4
Redcross Way
Distaff Lane EC4 145 E1
Distin Street SE11 148 C2
Dixon's Alley SE16 150 C1
West Lane
Dock Hill Avenue SE16 151 E2
Dock Street E1 150 B3
Dockhead SE1 150 B1
Dockley Road SE16 150 B1
Dod Street E14 151 F4
Doddington Grove SE17 149 D1
Doddington Place SE17 149 D1
Dodson Street SE1 149 D3
Dolben Street SE1 149 D4
Dolland Street SE11 148 C1
Dolphin Close SE16 151 D2
Dombey Street WC1 144 C3

Domingo Street
Hardwick Street
154

Domingo Street *EC1* 145 E3
Old Street
Dominion Street *EC2* 145 F2
Donegal Street *N1* 144 C4
Dongola Road *E1* 151 F4
Donne Place *SW3* 147 D2
Doon Street *SE1* 148 C4
Dora Street *E14* 151 F4
Doric Way *NW1* 144 A4
Dorrington Street *EC1* 145 D3
Brooke Street
Dorset Close *NW1* 143 D3
Dorset Mews *SW1* 147 E3
Dorset Rise *EC4* 145 D1
Dorset Square *NW1* 143 D3
Dorset Street *W1* 143 D2
Doughty Mews *WC1* 144 C3
Doughty Street *WC1* 144 C3
Douglas Place *SW1* 148 A2
Douglas Street
Douglas Street *SW1* 148 A2
Douro Place *W8* 146 B3
Dove Mews *SW5* 146 B2
Dove Walk *SW1* 147 E2
Dovehouse Street *SW3* 146 C1
Dover Street *W1* 143 F1
Dowgate Hill *EC4* 145 F1
Down Street *W1* 147 E4
Downfield Close *W9* 142 A3
Downing Street *SW1* 148 B4
Downton Road *SE16* 151 E2
Doyce Street *SE1* 149 E4
Draco Street *SE17* 149 E1
Drake Street *WC1* 144 C2
Draycott Avenue *SW3* 147 D2
Draycott Place *SW3* 147 D2
Draycott Terrace *SW3* 147 D2
Drayson Mews *W8* 146 A3
Drayton Gardens *SW10* 146 B1
Druid Street *SE1* 150 A2
Drum Street *E1* 150 B4
Drummond Crescent *NW1* 144 A4
Drummond Gate *SW1* 148 A1
Drummond Road *SE16* 150 C1
Drummond Street *NW1* 143 F3
Drury Lane *WC2* 144 B2
Dryden Court *SE11* 149 D2
Duchess Mews *W1* 143 F2
Duchess Street *W1* 143 F2
Duchy Street *SE1* 149 D4
Duck Lane *W1* 144 A2
Dudley Street *W2* 142 B2
Dudmaston Mews *SW3* 146 C2
Dufferin Street *EC1* 145 E3
Dufour's Place *W1* 144 A4
Dugard Way *SE11* 149 D2
Renfrew Road
Duke of Wellington Place *SW1* 147 E3
Duke of York Street *SW1* 144 A1
Duke Street *W1* 143 E2
Duke Street Hill *SE1* 149 F4
Duke's Lane *W8* 146 A4
Duke's Place *EC3* 150 A4
Duke's Road *WC1* 144 B4
Duke's Yard *W1* 143 E2
Duke Street
Duncannon Street *WC2* 144 B1
Dundee Street *E1* 150 C2
Dundee Wharf *E14* 151 F3
Dunelm Street *E1* 151 D4
Dunlop Place *SE16* 150 B1
Dunraven Street *W1* 143 E1
Dunstable Mews *W1* 143 E3
Dunster Court *EC3* 150 A3
Dunsterville Way *SE1* 149 F3
Duplex Ride *SW1* 147 E3
Dupont Street *E14* 151 E4
Durham House Street *WC2* 144 B1
Durham Row *E1* 151 E4
Durham Street *SE11* 148 C1
Durham Terrace *W2* 142 A2
Durward Street *E1* 150 C4
Durweston Street *W1* 143 D2
Crawford Street
Dyott Street *WC1* 144 B2
Dysart Street *EC2* 145 F3

E

Eagle Court *EC1* 145 D3
Eagle Place *SW1* 148 A4
Piccadilly
Eagle Street *WC2* 144 C2
Eardley Crescent *SW5* 146 A1
Earl Street *EC2* 145 F3
Earl's Court Gardens *SW5* 146 A2
Earl's Court Square *SW5* 146 A1
Earlham Street *WC2* 144 B2
Earls Court Road *W8* 146 A2
Earlstoke Street *EC1* 145 D4
Spencer Street
Earnshaw Street *WC2* 144 B2
Easley's Mews *W1* 143 E2
Wigmore Street
East Arbour Street *E1* 151 D4
East Harding Street *EC4* 145 D2
East India Dock Wall Road *E14* 145 D2
East Lane *SE16* 150 B1
East Mount Street *E1* 150 C4
East Road *N1* 145 F4
East Smithfield *E1* 150 B3
East Street *SE17* 149 E1
East Tenter Street *E1* 150 B3
Eastbourne Mews *W2* 142 B2
Eastbourne Terrace *W2* 142 B2
Eastcastle Street *W1* 144 A2
Eastcheap *EC3* 145 F1
Easton Street *WC1* 144 C3
Eaton Gate *SW1* 147 E2
Eaton Mews North *SW1* 147 E2
Eaton Mews South *SW1* 147 E2
Eaton Place *SW1* 147 E2
Eaton Square *SW1* 147 E2
Eaton Terrace *SW1* 147 E2
Ebbisham Drive *SW8* 148 C1
Ebenezer Street *N1* 145 F4
Ebury Bridge *SW1* 147 E2
Ebury Bridge Road *SW1* 147 E1
Ebury Mews *SW1* 147 E2
Ebury Mews East *SW1* 147 E2
Ebury Square *SW1* 147 E2
Ebury Street *SW1* 147 E2
Eccleston Bridge *SW1* 147 F2
Eccleston Mews *SW1* 147 E3
Eccleston Place *SW1* 147 E2
Eccleston Square *SW1* 147 F2
Eccleston Square Mews *SW1* 147 F2
Eccleston Street *SW1* 147 E2
Edbrooke Road *W9* 142 A3
Edge Street *W8* 146 A4
Edgware Road *W2* 142 C3
Edward Mews *NW1* 143 F4
Edward Mews *W1* 143 E2
Edward Square *SE16* 151 F3
Egerton Crescent *SW3* 147 D2
Egerton Gardens *SW3* 146 C2
Egerton Terrace *SW3* 147 D3
Elba Place *SE17* 149 E2
Eldon Road *W8* 146 B3
Eldon Street *EC2* 145 F2
Eleanor Close *SE16* 151 D2
Elephant and Castle *SE1* 149 E2
Elephant Lane *SE16* 150 C2
Elephant Road *SE17* 149 E2
Elf Row *E1* 151 D3
Elgar Street *SE16* 151 F1
Elgin Avenue *W9* 142 A3
Elgin Mews North *W9* 142 A4
Elgin Mews South *W9* 142 B4
Elia Street *N1* 145 D4
Elim Street *SE1* 149 F3
Eliot Mews *NW8* 142 B4
Elizabeth Bridge *SW1* 147 F2
Elizabeth Close *W9* 142 B3
Elizabeth Square *SE16* 151 E3
Elizabeth Street *SW1* 147 E2
Ellen Street *E1* 150 B3
Elliott Road *SE9* 149 D2
Ellis Street *SW1* 147 E2
Elm Park Gardens *SW10* 146 C1
Elm Park Lane *SW3* 146 B1
Elm Park Road *SW3* 146 B1
Elm Place *SW7* 146 C1
Elm Street *WC1* 144 C3
Elm Tree Close *NW8* 142 C4
Elm Tree Road *NW8* 142 C4
Elmfield Way *W9* 142 A3
Elmos Road *SE16* 151 E1
Elms Mews *W2* 142 C1
Elnathan Mews *W9* 142 A3
Elsa Street *E1* 151 E4
Elsted Street *SE17* 149 F2
Elvaston Mews *SW7* 146 B3
Elvaston Place *SW7* 146 B3
Elverton Street *SW1* 148 A2
Ely Place *EC1* 145 D2
Elystan Place *SW3* 147 D2
Elystan Street *SW3* 146 C2
Emba Street *SE16* 150 C1
Embankment Gardens *SW3* 147 D1
Embankment Place *WC2* 148 B4
Emerald Street *WC1* 144 C3
Emerson Street *SE1* 149 E4
Emery Hill Street *SW1* 148 A2
Emery Street *SE1* 149 D3
Emmett Street *E14* 151 F3
Emperor's Gate *SW7* 146 B2
Empress Place *SW6* 146 A1
Empress Street *SE17* 149 E1
Endell Street *WC2* 144 B2
Endsleigh Gardens *WC1* 144 A3
Endsleigh Place *WC1* 144 A3
Endsleigh Street *WC1* 144 A3
Enford Street *W1* 143 D3
English Grounds *SE1* 150 A2
Enid Street *SE16* 150 B1
Ennismore Garden Mews *SW7* 146 C3
Ennismore Gardens *SW7* 146 C3
Ennismore Mews *SW7* 146 C3
Ennismore Street *SW7* 146 C3
Ensign Street *E1* 150 B3
Ensor Mews *SW7* 146 B1
Epworth Street *EC2* 145 F3
Erasmus Street *SW1* 148 B2
Errol Street *EC1* 145 E3
Essendine Road *W9* 142 A4
Essex Street *WC2* 144 C1
Esterbrooke Street *SW1* 148 A2
Ethel Street *SE17* 149 E2
Europa Place *EC1* 145 E4
Euston Road *NW1* 143 F3
Euston Square *NW1* 144 A4
Euston Street *NW1* 144 A4
Evelyn Gardens *SW7* 148 B1
Evelyn Walk *N1* 145 F4
Evelyn Yard *W1* 144 A2
Gresse Street
Eversholt Street *NW1* 144 A4
Ewer Street *SE1* 149 E4
Exchange Place *EC2* 150 A4
Exchange Square *EC2* 150 A4
Exeter Street *WC2* 144 B1
Exhibition Road *SW7* 146 C3
Exmouth Market *EC1* 145 D3
Exmouth Street *E1* 151 D4
Exon Street *SE17* 149 F2
Exton Street *SE1* 148 C4
Eyre Street Hill *EC1* 145 D3

F

Fair Street *SE1* 150 A2
Fairclough Street *E1* 150 B3
Falcon Close *SE1* 149 E4
Falconberg Mews *W1* 144 A2
Sutton Row
Falmouth Road *SE1* 149 E3
Fann Street *EC1* 145 E3
Fanshaw Street *N1* 145 F4
Fareham Street *W1* 144 B1
Dean Street
Farm Street *W1* 143 E1
Farmer Street *W8* 146 A4
Farncombe Street *SE16* 150 C1
Farnell Mews *SW5* 146 A1
Farnham Place *SE1* 149 E4
Farnham Royal *SE11* 148 C1
Farrance Street *E14* 151 F3
Farrier Walk *SW10* 146 B1
Farringdon Lane *EC1* 145 D3
Farringdon Road *EC1* 144 C3
Farringdon Street *EC4* 145 D2
Farrins Rents *SE16* 151 E2
Farrow Place *SE16* 151 E1
Farthing Alley *SE1* 150 B1
Wolseley Street
Farthing Fields *E1* 150 C2
Raine Street
Fashion Street *E1* 150 B4
Faunce Street *SE17* 149 D1
Fawcett Street *SW10* 146 B1
Featherstone Street *EC1* 145 F3
Fen Court *EC3* 150 A3
Fenchurch Avenue *EC3* 150 A3
Fenchurch Buildings *EC3* 145 F1
Fenchurch Street
Fenchurch Place *EC3* 145 F1
Fenchurch Street
Fenchurch Street *EC3* 145 F1
Fendall Street *SE1* 150 A1
Fenning Street *SE1* 149 F4
St Thomas Street
Fennings Circus *W1* 144 A2
Fernsbury Street *WC1* 144 C4
Fetter Lane *EC4* 145 D2
Field Street *WC1* 144 C4
Fieldgate Street *E1* 150 B4
Fielding Street *SE17* 149 E1
Finborough Road *SW10* 146 A1
Finch Lane *EC3* 145 F2
Finland Street *SE16* 151 E1
Finsbury Avenue *EC2* 145 F2
Finsbury Circus *EC2* 145 F2
Finsbury Market *EC2* 145 F3
Finsbury Pavement *EC2* 145 F3
Finsbury Square *EC2* 145 F3
Finsbury Street *EC2* 145 F3
First Street *SW3* 147 D2
Firtree Close *SE16* 151 E2
Fish Street Hill *EC3* 145 F1
Fish Wharf *EC3* 145 F1
Fisher Street *WC1* 144 C2
Fishermans Drive *SE16* 151 E2
Fisherton Street *NW8* 142 C3
Fishmongers' Hall Wharf *EC4* 145 F1
Fitzalan Street *SE11* 148 C2
Fitzhardinge Street *W1* 143 E2
Fitzmaurice Place *W1* 143 F1
Fitzroy Square *W1* 143 F3
Fitzroy Street *W1* 143 F3
Flamborough Street *E14* 151 E3
Flank Street *E1* 150 B3
Flaxman Terrace *WC1* 144 B4
Fleet Square *WC1* 144 C4
Fleet Street *EC4* 145 D2
Fleming Road *SE17* 149 D1
Fletcher Street *E1* 150 B3
Flint Street *SE17* 149 F2
Flitcroft Street *WC2* 144 B2
Flood Street *SW3* 147 D1
Flood Walk *SW3* 147 D1
Floral Street *WC2* 144 B1
Flower and Dean Walk *E1* 150 B4
Thrawl Street
Foley Street *W1* 143 F2
Forbes Street *E1* 150 B3
Ford Square *E1* 150 C4
Fordham Street *E1* 150 C4
Fore Street *EC2* 145 E2
Fore Street Avenue *EC2* 145 E2
Formosa Street *W9* 142 A3
Forset Street *W1* 143 D2
Forsyth Gardens *SE17* 149 D1
Fort Street *E1* 150 A4
Artillery Lane
Fortune Street *EC1* 145 E3
Foscote Mews *W9* 142 A3
Foster Lane *EC2* 145 E2
Foubert's Place *W1* 143 F1
Foulis Terrace *SW7* 146 C2
Foundry Close *SE16* 151 E2
Fountain Green Square *SE16* 150 C1
Fournier Street *E1* 150 B4
Fowey Close *E1* 150 C2
Fox and Knot Street *EC1* 145 E2
Charterhouse Square
Frampton Street *NW8* 142 C3
Francis Street *SW1* 148 A2
Franklin's Row *SW3* 147 D1
Frazier Street *SE1* 148 C3
Frean Street *SE16* 150 B1
Frederick Close *W2* 143 D1
Frederick Road *SE17* 149 E1
Frederick Square *SE16* 151 E3
Frederick Street *WC1* 144 C4
Fredericks Row *EC1* 145 D4
Goswell Road
Fremantle Street *SE17* 149 F2
French Ordinary Court *EC3* 150 A3
Hart Street
Friar Street *EC4* 145 E2
Carter Lane
Friday Street *EC4* 145 E1
Friend Street *EC1* 145 D4
Frith Street *W1* 144 A2
Frostic Walk *E1* 150 B4
Frying Pan Alley *E1* 150 A4
Fulbourne Street *E1* 150 C4
Fulford Street *SE16* 150 C1
Fulham Road *SW3, SW6 & SW10* 146 C1
Fulwood Place *WC1* 144 C2
Furnival Street *EC4* 145 D2
Fynes Street *SW1* 148 A2

G

Gabriels Wharf *SE1* 149 D4
Gainsford Street *SE1* 150 A2
Galen Place *WC1* 144 B2
Galleon Close *SE16* 151 D2
Kinburn Street
Galway Street *EC1* 145 E4
Gambia Street *SE1* 149 D4
Ganton Street *W1* 144 A1
Garbutt Place *W1* 143 E2
Gard Street *EC1* 145 E4
Garden Mews *W2* 142 A1
Garden Road *NW8* 142 B4
Garden Row *SE1* 149 D3
Garden Street *E1* 151 E4
Gardeners Lane *EC4* 145 E1
High Timber Street
Garford Street *E14* 151 F3
Garlick Hill *EC4* 145 F1
Garnault Mews *EC1* 145 D4
Garnet Street *E1* 150 C3
Garrett Street *EC1* 145 E3
Garrick Street *WC2* 144 B1
Garter Way *SE16* 151 D1
Garway Road *W2* 142 A2
Gasholder Place *SE11* 148 C1
Gaspar Close *SW5* 146 B2
Gaspar Mews *SW5* 146 B2
Gate Street *WC2* 144 C2
Gateway *SE17* 149 E1
Gatliff Road *SW1* 147 E1
Gaunt Street *SE1* 149 E3
Gavel Street *SE17* 149 F2
Gayfere Street *SW1* 148 B3
Gaywood Street *SE1* 149 D3
Gaza Street *SE17* 149 D1
Gedling Place *SE1* 150 B1
Gee Street *EC1* 145 E3
Gees Court *W1* 143 E2
George Mathers Road *SE11* 149 D2
George Mews *NW1* 144 A4
George Row *SE16* 150 B1
George Street *W1* 143 D2
George Yard *EC3* 145 F1
George Yard *W1* 143 E1
Gerald Road *SW1* 147 E2
Geraldine Street *SE11* 149 D3
Gerrard Place *W1* 144 B1
Gerrard Street
Gerrard Street *W1* 144 A1
Gerridge Street *SE1* 149 D3
Gibson Road *SE11* 149 D3
Gilbert Place *WC1* 144 B2
Gilbert Road *SE11* 149 D2
Gilbert Street *W1* 143 E1
Gildea Street *W1* 143 F2
Gill Street *E14* 151 F3
Gillingham Street *SW1* 147 F2
Gillison Walk *SE16* 150 C1
Gilpin Close *W2* 142 B2
Porteus Road
Gilston Road *SW10* 146 B1
Giltspur Street *EC1* 145 D2
Gladstone Street *SE1* 149 D3
Glamis Place *E1* 151 D3
Glamis Road *E1* 151 D3
Glasgow Terrace *SW1* 147 F1
Glasshill Street *SE1* 149 E3
Glasshouse Fields *E1* 151 D3
Glasshouse Street *W1* 144 A1
Glasshouse Walk *SE11* 148 B1
Glastonbury Place *E1* 151 D3
Glebe Place *SW3* 146 C1
Gledhow Gardens *SW5* 146 B2
Glendower Place *SW7* 146 C2
Glentworth Street *NW1* 143 D3
Globe Pond Road *SE16* 151 E2
Globe Street *SE1* 149 E3
Gloucester Arcade *SW7* 146 B2
Gloucester Court *EC3* 150 A3
Gloucester Gate Mews *NW1* 144 F4
Albany Street
Gloucester Mews *W2* 142 B2
Gloucester Mews West *W2* 142 B2
Gloucester Park *SW7* 146 B2
Gloucester Place *NW1 & W1* 143 D3
Gloucester Place Mews *W1* 143 D2
Gloucester Road *SW7* 146 B3
Gloucester Square *W2* 142 C2
Gloucester Street *SW1* 147 F1
Gloucester Terrace *W2* 142 B2
Gloucester Walk *W8* 146 A4
Gloucester Way *EC1* 145 D4
Glyn Street *SE11* 148 C1
Goat Street *SE1* 150 A2
Lafone Street
Godfrey Street *SW3* 147 D2
Goding Street *SE11* 148 B1
Godliman Street *EC4* 145 E1
Golden Lane *EC1* 145 E3
Golden Square *W1* 144 A1
Golding Street *E1* 150 C3
Gomm Road *SE16* 151 D1
Goodge Place *W1* 144 A2
Goodge Street *W1* 144 A2
Goodhart Place *E14* 151 E3
Goodman's Stile *E1* 150 B4
Goodman's Yard *E1* 150 B3
Goodwin Close *SE16* 150 B1
Gophir Lane *EC4* 145 F1
Bush Lane
Gordon Place *W8* 146 A4
Gordon Square *WC1* 144 A3
Gordon Street *WC1* 144 A3
Gore Street *SW7* 146 B3
Goring Street *E1* 150 A4
Bevis Marks
Gosfield Street *W1* 143 F2
Goslett Yard *WC2* 144 B2
Goswell Road *EC1* 145 D4
Gough Square *EC4* 145 D2
Gough Street *WC1* 144 C3
Goulston Street *E1* 150 B4
Gower Mews *WC1* 144 A2
Gower Place *WC1* 144 A3
Gower Street *WC1* 144 A3
Gowers Walk *E1* 150 B3
Grace's Alley *E1* 150 B3
Gracechurch Street *EC3* 145 F1
Graces Mews *NW8* 142 B4
Grafton Mews *W1* 143 F3
Grafton Place *NW1* 144 A4
Grafton Street *W1* 143 F1
Grafton Way *W1* 143 A3
Graham Street *N1* 145 E4
Graham Terrace *SW1* 147 E2
Granby Terrace *NW1* 143 F4
Grand Avenue *EC1* 145 D2
Grand Junction Wharf *N1* 145 E4
Grange Court *WC2* 144 C2
Grange Road *SE1* 150 A1
Grange Walk *SE1* 150 A1
Grange Yard *SE1* 150 A1
Grant's Quay Wharf *EC3* 145 F1
Grantully Road *W9* 142 A4
Granville Place *W1* 143 E2
Granville Road *NW6* 142 A4
Granville Square *WC1* 144 C4
Granville Street *WC1* 144 C4
Granville Square
Grape Street *WC2* 144 B2
Gravel Lane *E1* 150 A4
Gray Street *SE1* 149 D3
Gray's Inn Place *WC1* 144 C2
Gray's Inn Road *WC1* 144 B4
Great Castle Street *W1* 143 F2
Great Central Street *NW1* 143 D3
Great Chapel Street *W1* 144 A2
Great College Street *SW1* 143 D1
Seymour Street
Great Cumberland Place *W1* 143 D2
Great Dover Street *SE1* 149 F3
Great Eastern Street *EC2* 145 F3
Great George Street *SW1* 148 B3
Great Guildford Street *SE1* 149 E4
Great James Street *WC1* 144 C3
Great Marlborough Street *W1* 143 F2
Great Maze Pond *SE1* 149 F4
Great New Street *EC4* 145 D2
Great Newport Street *WC2* 144 B1
Charing Cross Road
Great Ormond Street *WC1* 144 C3
Great Percy Street *WC1* 144 C4
Great Peter Street *SW1* 148 A3
Great Portland Street *W1* 143 F3
Great Pulteney Street *W1* 144 A1
Great Queen Street *WC2* 144 B2
Great Russell Street *WC1* 144 B2
Great Scotland Yard *SW1* 148 B4
Great Smith Street *SW1* 148 B3
Great St Helen's *EC3* 145 F2
Great St Thomas Apostle *EC4* 145 E1
Queen Street
Great Suffolk Street *SE1* 149 E3
Great Sutton Street *EC1* 145 D3
Great Swan Alley *EC2* 145 F2
Great Tower Street *EC3* 150 A3
Great Trinity Lane *EC4* 145 E1
Garlick Hill
Great Turnstile *WC1* 144 B2
High Holborn
Great Winchester Street *EC2* 145 F2
Great Windmill Street *W1* 144 A1
Greatorex Street *E1* 150 B4
Greek Street *W1* 144 B2
Green Bank *E1* 150 C2
Green Dragon Court *SE1* 149 F4
Green Dragon Yard *E1* 150 B4
Green Street *W1* 143 E1
Green Walk *SE1* 149 F3
Green Yard *WC1* 144 C3
Greenacre Square *SE16* 151 E2
Greenberry Street *NW8* 142 C4
Greencoat Place *SW1* 148 A2
Greencoat Row *SW1* 148 A2
Greenfield Road *E1* 150 B4
Greenham Close *SE1* 149 D3
Greenwell Street *W1* 143 F3
Greet Street *SE1* 149 D4
Gregory Place *W8* 146 A3
Greig Terrace *SE17* 149 E1
Grenade Street *E14* 151 F3
Grendon Street *NW8* 142 C3
Grenville Place *SW7* 146 B2
Grenville Street *WC1* 144 B3
Gresham Street *EC2* 145 E2
Gresse Street *W1* 144 A2
Greville Street *EC1* 145 D2
Greycoat Place *SW1* 148 A3
Greycoat Street *SW1* 148 A2
Greystoke Place *EC4* 145 D2
Fetter Lane
Grigg's Place *SE1* 150 A1
Groom Place *SW1* 147 E3
Grosvenor Crescent *SW1* 147 E3
Grosvenor Crescent Mews *SW1* 147 E3
Grosvenor Gardens *SW1* 147 F3
Grosvenor Gate *W1* 143 E1
Park Lane
Grosvenor Hill *W1* 143 F1
Grosvenor Place *SW1* 147 E3
Grosvenor Road *SW1* 147 F1
Grosvenor Square *W1* 143 E1
Grosvenor Street *W1* 143 E1
Grove End Road *NW8* 142 B4
Grove Gardens *NW8* 143 D4
Grove Hall Court *NW8* 142 B4
Guildhall Buildings *EC2* 145 E2
Basinghall Street
Guildhall Yard *EC2* 145 E2
Guildhouse Street *SW1* 147 F2
Guilford Place *WC1* 144 B3
Guilford Street
Guilford Street *WC1* 144 B3
Guinness Square *SE1* 149 F2
Gulliver Street *SE16* 151 F1
Gulston Walk *SW3* 147 D2
Gun Street *E1* 150 A4
Gunthorpe Street *E1* 150 B4
Gunwhale Close *SE16* 151 E2
Guthrie Street *SW3* 146 C2
Gutter Lane *EC2* 145 E2
Guy Street *SE1* 149 F3
Gwynne Place *WC1* 144 C4

H

Haberdasher Street *N1* 145 F4
Hainton Close *E1* 150 C3
Halcrow Street *E1* 150 C4
Half Moon Court *EC1* 145 E2
Bartholomew Close
Half Moon Street *W1* 147 F4
Halkin Place *SW1* 147 E3
Halkin Street *SW1* 147 E3
Hall Gate *NW8* 142 B4
Hall Place *W2* 142 C3
Hall Road *NW8* 142 B4
Hall Street *EC1* 145 D4
Hallam Mews *W1* 143 F3
Hallam Street *W1* 143 F3
Halley Place *E14* 151 E4
Halley Street *E14* 151 E4
Halsey Mews *SW3* 147 D2
Halsey Street *SW3* 147 D2
Hamilton Close *NW8* 142 B4
Hamilton Close *SE16* 151 E1
Hamilton Gardens *NW8* 142 B4
Hamilton Place *W1* 147 E4
Hamilton Square *SE1* 149 F3
Hamilton Terrace *NW8* 142 B4
Hammett Street *EC3* 150 A3
America Square
Hampstead Road *NW1* 143 F4
Hampton Street *SE1 & SE17* 149 E2
Hanbury Street *E1* 150 B4
Handel Street *WC1* 144 B3
Hankey Place *SE1* 149 F3
Hannibal Road *E1* 151 D4
Hanover Place *WC2* 144 B1
Long Acre
Hanover Square *W1* 143 F2
Hanover Street *W1* 143 F2
Hanover Terrace *NW1* 143 D4
Hanover Terrace Mews *NW1* 143 D4
Hans Crescent *SW1* 147 D3
Hans Place *SW1* 147 D3
Hans Road *SW3* 147 D3
Hans Street *SW1* 147 D3
Hanson Street *W1* 143 F2
Hanway Place *W1* 144 A2
Hanway Street *W1* 144 A2
Harbert Road *W2* 142 C2
Harcourt Street *W1* 143 D2
Harcourt Terrace *SW10* 146 B1
Harding Close *SE17* 149 E1
Hardinge Lane *E1* 151 D3
Hardinge Street
Hardinge Street *E1* 151 D3
Hardwick Street *EC1* 145 D4

Hardwicke Mews WC1 .... 144 C4
  Lloyd Baker Street
Hardwidge Street SE1 .... 149 F4
Harewood Avenue NW1 .... 143 D3
Harewood Place W1 .... 143 F2
Harley Gardens SW10 .... 146 B1
Harley Place W1 .... 143 E3
Harley Street W1 .... 143 E3
Harleyford Road SE11 .... 148 C1
Harmsworth Mews SE11 .... 149 D4
  West Square
Harmsworth Street SE17 .... 149 D1
Harp Alley EC4 .... 145 D2
  Farringdon Street
Harp Lane EC3 .... 150 A3
Harper Road SE1 .... 149 E3
Harpur Street WC1 .... 144 C3
Harriet Street SW1 .... 147 D3
Harriet Walk SW1 .... 147 D3
Harrington Gardens SW7 .... 146 B2
Harrington Road SW7 .... 146 C2
Harrington Street NW1 .... 143 F4
Harrison Street WC1 .... 144 B4
Harrow Place E1 .... 150 A4
Harrow Road W2, W9, W10 & NW10 .... 142 B2
Harrow Road Bridge W2 .... 142 B2
Harrowby Street W1 .... 143 D2
Hart Street EC3 .... 150 A3
Harwich Lane EC2 .... 150 A4
Harwood Row NW1 .... 143 D3
Hasker Street SW3 .... 147 D2
Hastings Street WC1 .... 144 B4
Hatfields SE1 .... 149 D4
Hatherley Grove W2 .... 142 A2
Hatherley Street SW1 .... 148 A2
Hatteraick Street SE16 .... 151 D2
Hatton Garden EC1 .... 145 D3
Hatton Place EC1 .... 145 D3
Hatton Place EC1 .... 145 D3
Hatton Street NW8 .... 142 C3
Hatton Wall EC1 .... 145 D3
Haunch of Venison Yard W1 .... 142 C1
  Brook Street
Havering Street E1 .... 151 D3
Haverstock Street N1 .... 145 E4
Hawkesmoor Mews E1 .... 150 C3
Hay Hill W1 .... 143 F1
Hay's Lane SE1 .... 149 F4
Hay's Mews W1 .... 143 F1
Hayes Place NW1 .... 143 D3
Hayles Street SE11 .... 149 D2
Haymarket SW1 .... 144 A1
Hayne Street EC1 .... 145 E3
Hayward's Place EC1 .... 145 D3
Headfort Place SW1 .... 147 E3
Heathcote Street WC1 .... 144 C3
Heckford Street E1 .... 151 E3
Heddon Street W1 .... 143 F1
Hedger Street SE11 .... 149 D2
Heiron Street SE17 .... 149 E1
Helena Square SE16 .... 151 E3
Hellings Street E1 .... 150 B2
Helmet Row EC1 .... 145 E3
Helsinki Square SE16 .... 151 E3
Hemp Walk SE17 .... 149 F2
Henderson Drive NW8 .... 142 C3
Heneage Lane EC3 .... 150 A4
Heneage Place EC3 .... 150 A4
Heneage Street E1 .... 150 B4
Henniker Mews SW3 .... 146 B1
Henrietta Place W1 .... 143 E2
Henrietta Street WC2 .... 144 B1
Henriques Street E1 .... 150 B4
Henshaw Street SE17 .... 149 F2
Herald's Place SE11 .... 149 D2
Herbal Hill EC1 .... 145 D3
Herbrand Street WC1 .... 144 B3
Hercules Road SE1 .... 148 C3
Hereford Road W2 .... 145 A2
Hereford Square SW7 .... 146 B2
Hermes Street N1 .... 144 C4
Hermit Street EC1 .... 145 D4
Hermitage Street W2 .... 142 C2
Hermitage Wall E1 .... 150 B2
Heron Place SE16 .... 151 E2
Herrick Street SW1 .... 148 B2
Hertford Street W1 .... 147 E4
Hesper Mews SW5 .... 146 A2
Hessel Street E1 .... 150 C3
Heygate Street SE17 .... 149 E2
Hide Place SW1 .... 148 A2
High Holborn WC1 .... 144 B2
High Timber Street EC4 .... 145 E1
Hildyard Road SW6 .... 146 A1
Hill Road W9 .... 142 B4
Hill Street W1 .... 143 F2
Hillery Close SW1 .... 149 F2
Hilliard's Court E1 .... 150 C2
Hillingdon Street SE5 & SE17 .... 149 E1
  Pelier Street
Hind Court EC4 .... 145 D2
Hinde Street W1 .... 143 E2
Hindmarsh Close E1 .... 150 B3
Hobart Place SW1 .... 147 F3
Hogarth Court EC3 .... 145 F1
  Fenchurch Street
Hogarth Place SW5 .... 146 A2
Hogarth Road SW5 .... 146 A2
Holbein Mews SW1 .... 147 E2
Holbein Place SW1 .... 147 E2
Holborn EC1 .... 145 D2
Holborn Circus EC1 .... 145 D2
Holborn Viaduct EC1 .... 145 D2
Holford Place WC1 .... 144 C4
Holford Street WC1 .... 144 C4
Holland Street SE1 .... 149 D4
Holland Street W8 .... 146 A3
Hollen Street W1 .... 144 A2
  Wardour Street
Holles Street W1 .... 143 F2
Holley Mews SW10 .... 146 B1
  Drayton Gardens
Hollywood Mews SW10 .... 146 B1
Hollywood Road SW10 .... 146 B1
Holyoak Road SE11 .... 149 D2
Holyoake Court SE16 .... 151 F2
Holyrood Street SE1 .... 150 A2
Holywell Row EC2 .... 145 F3
Homer Row W1 .... 143 D2
Homer Street W1 .... 143 D2
Honduras Street EC1 .... 145 E3
  Old Street
Hooper Street E1 .... 150 B3
Hop Gardens WC2 .... 144 B1
  St Martin's Lane
Hope Wharf SE16 .... 151 E2
Hopetown Street E1 .... 150 B4
Hopkins Street W1 .... 144 A1
Hopton Street SE1 .... 149 D4
Hopwood Road SE17 .... 149 F1

Horley Crescent SE16 .... 151 D2
  Marlow Way
Hornton Place W8 .... 146 A3
Hornton Street W8 .... 146 A3
Horse Guards Avenue SW1 .... 148 B4
Horse Guards Road SW1 .... 148 B4
Horse Ride SW1 .... 147 F3
Horseferry Road E14 .... 151 E3
Horseferry Road SW1 .... 148 A3
Horselydown Lane SE1 .... 150 A2
Hosier Lane EC1 .... 145 D2
Hothfield Place SE16 .... 151 D1
Hotspur Street SE11 .... 148 C2
Houghton Street WC2 .... 144 C1
  Aldwych
Houndsditch EC3 .... 150 A4
Howard Place SW1 .... 144 A2
  Carlisle Street
Howell Walk SE1 .... 149 E2
Howick Place SW1 .... 148 A3
Howland Street W1 .... 144 A3
Howland Way SE16 .... 151 E1
Howley Place W2 .... 142 B3
Hoxton Market N1 .... 145 F4
Hoxton Square N1 .... 145 F4
Huddart Street E3 .... 151 F4
Hudson's Place SW1 .... 147 F2
Huggin Hill EC4 .... 145 E1
Hugh Street W1 .... 147 F2
Hull Close SE16 .... 151 E2
Hull Street EC1 .... 145 E4
Hunt's Court WC2 .... 144 B1
Hunter Close SE1 .... 149 F3
  Prioress Street
Hunter Street WC1 .... 144 B3
Huntley Street WC1 .... 144 A3
Huntsman Street SE17 .... 149 F2
Huntsworth Mews NW1 .... 143 D3
Hutton Street EC4 .... 145 D1
Hyde Park Corner W1 .... 147 E4
Hyde Park Crescent W2 .... 142 C2
Hyde Park Gardens W2 .... 142 C1
Hyde Park Gardens Mews W2 .... 142 C1
Hyde Park Gate SW7 .... 146 B3
Hyde Park Square W2 .... 142 C2
Hyde Park Street W2 .... 142 C2

Idol Lane EC3 .... 150 A3
Ifield Road SW10 .... 146 A1
Ilchester Gardens W2 .... 142 A1
Iliffe Street SE17 .... 149 E2
India Place WC2 .... 144 C1
  Montreal Place
India Street EC3 .... 150 A3
Ingestre Place W1 .... 144 A1
Inglebert Street EC1 .... 145 D4
Ingram Close SE11 .... 148 C2
Inigo Place WC2 .... 144 B1
  Bedford Street
Inner Temple Lane EC4 .... 145 D2
Inverness Gardens W8 .... 146 A4
  Palace Garden Terrace
Inverness Mews W2 .... 142 B1
Inverness Place W2 .... 142 B1
Inverness Terrace W2 .... 142 B1
Invicta Plaza SE1 .... 149 D4
Inville Road SE17 .... 149 F1
Ireland Yard EC4 .... 145 D1
  St Andrew's Hill
Ironmonger Lane EC2 .... 145 E2
Ironmonger Row EC1 .... 145 E4
Ironside Close SE16 .... 151 D2
Irving Street WC2 .... 144 B1
Isambard Place SE16 .... 151 D2
Island Row E14 .... 151 F3
Iverna Court W8 .... 146 A3
Iverna Gardens W8 .... 146 A3
Ives Street SW3 .... 147 D2
Ivor Place NW1 .... 143 D3
Ixworth Place SW3 .... 146 C2

Jacob Street SE1 .... 150 B2
Jamaica Road SE1 & SE16 .... 150 B1
Jamaica Street E1 .... 151 D4
James Street W1 .... 143 E2
James Street WC2 .... 144 B1
  Long Acre
Jameson Street W8 .... 146 A4
Janeway Place SE16 .... 150 C1
Janeway Street SE16 .... 150 C1
Jardine Road E1 .... 151 E3
Jay Mews SW7 .... 146 B3
Jermyn Street SW1 .... 148 A4
Jerome Crescent NW8 .... 143 D3
Jewry Street EC3 .... 150 A3
Joan Street SE1 .... 149 D4
Jockey's Fields WC1 .... 144 C3
John Adams Street WC2 .... 144 B1
John Aird Court W2 .... 142 B3
John Carpenter Street EC4 .... 145 D1
John Felton Road SE16 .... 150 B2
John Fisher Street E1 .... 150 B3
John Islip Street SW1 .... 148 B2
John Maurice Close SE17 .... 149 F2
John Princes Street W1 .... 143 F2
John Roll Way SE16 .... 150 C1
John Street WC1 .... 144 C3
John's Mews WC1 .... 144 C3
Johnson Street E1 .... 151 D3
Johnson's Place SW1 .... 148 A1
Joiner Street SE1 .... 149 F4
Jonathan Street SE11 .... 148 C2
Jones Street W1 .... 143 A3
  Bourdon Street
Jubilee Place SW3 .... 147 D2
Jubilee Street E1 .... 151 D4
Judd Street WC1 .... 144 B4
Junction Mews W2 .... 142 C2
Juxon Street SE11 .... 148 C2

Katherine Close SE16 .... 151 D2
Kean Street WC2 .... 144 C2
Keel Close SE16 .... 151 E2
Keeley Street WC2 .... 144 C2
Keeton's Road SE16 .... 150 C1
Kelso Place W8 .... 146 A3
Kemble Street WC2 .... 144 C2
Kempsford Gardens SW5 .... 146 A1
Kempsford Road SE11 .... 149 D2
Kempton Court E1 .... 150 C4
  Durward Street
Kendal Street W2 .... 143 C2
Kendall Place W1 .... 143 D2
Kendrick Mews SW7 .... 146 C2
Kendrick Place SW7 .... 146 C2
  Reece Mews
Kennet Street E1 .... 150 B2
Kennet Wharf Lane EC4 .... 145 E1
Kenning Street SE16 .... 151 D2
Kennings Way SE11 .... 149 D1
Kennington Green SE11 .... 149 D1
Kennington Grove SE11 .... 148 C1
Kennington Lane SE11 .... 148 C1
Kennington Oval SE11 .... 148 C1
Kennington Park Gardens SE11 .... 149 D1
Kennington Park Place SE11 .... 149 D1
Kennington Park Road SE11 .... 149 D1
Kennington Road SE1 & SE11 .... 148 C3
Kenrick Place W1 .... 143 E2
Kensington Church Street W8 .... 146 A4
Kensington Church Walk W8 .... 146 A3
Kensington Court W8 .... 146 A3
Kensington Court Place W8 .... 146 A3
Kensington Gardens Square W2 .... 142 A2
Kensington Gate W8 .... 146 B3
Kensington Gore SW7 .... 146 B3
Kensington High Street W8 & W14 .... 146 A3
Kensington Mall W8 .... 146 A4
Kensington Palace Gardens W8 .... 146 A4
Kensington Road W8 & SW7 .... 146 B3
Kensington Square W8 .... 146 A3
Kent Passage NW1 .... 143 D4
Kent Terrace NW1 .... 143 D4
Kenton Street WC1 .... 143 D3
Kenway Road SW5 .... 145 A2
Keppel Row SE1 .... 149 E4
Keppel Street WC1 .... 144 B3
Keyse Road SE1 .... 150 B1
Keystone Crescent N1 .... 144 B4
Keyworth Street SE1 .... 149 D3
Kilburn Park Road NW6 .... 142 A4
Kildare Gardens W2 .... 142 A2
Kildare Terrace W2 .... 142 A2
Kimbolton Row SW3 .... 146 C2
  Fulham Road
Kinburn Street SE16 .... 151 D2
Kinder Street E1 .... 150 C4
King and Queen Street SE17 .... 149 E2
King Charles Street SW1 .... 148 B3
King David Lane E1 .... 151 D3
King Edward III Mews SE16 .... 150 C1
  Paradise Street
King Edward Street EC1 .... 145 E2
King Edward Walk SE1 .... 149 D3
King James Street SE1 .... 149 E3
King Square EC1 .... 145 E4
King Street EC2 .... 145 E2
King Street SE1 .... 148 A4
King Street SW1 .... 148 A4
King Street WC2 .... 144 B1
King William Street EC4 .... 145 F1
King's Bench Walk EC4 .... 145 D1
King's Cross Road WC1 .... 144 C4
King's Mews WC1 .... 144 C3
King's Road SW3, SW6 & SW10 .... 147 D1
King's Scholars' Passage SW1 .... 147 F2
King's Stairs Close SE16 .... 150 C2
Kinghorn Street EC1 .... 145 E3
Kinglake Street SE17 .... 149 F2
Kingly Court W1 .... 144 A1
Kingly Street W1 .... 143 F1
Kings Arms Yard EC2 .... 145 F2
Kings Bench Street SE1 .... 149 D3
Kingscote Street EC4 .... 145 D1
Kingsway WC2 .... 144 C2
Kinnerton Street SW1 .... 147 E3
Kipling Street SE1 .... 149 F4
Kirby Grove SE1 .... 150 A1
Kirby Street EC1 .... 145 D3
Knaresborough Place SW5 .... 146 A2
Knight's Walk SE11 .... 149 D2
Knighten Street E1 .... 150 C2
Knightrider Street EC4 .... 145 E1
  Godliman Street
Knightsbridge SW1 & SW7 .... 147 D3
Knightsbridge Green SW1 .... 147 D3
  Brompton Road
Knox Street W1 .... 143 D3
Kramer Mews SW5 .... 146 A1
Kynance Mews SW7 .... 146 B3

Lackington Street EC2 .... 145 F3
Lafone Street SE1 .... 150 A2
Lagado Mews SE16 .... 151 E2
Lamb Street E1 .... 150 A4
Lamb Walk SE1 .... 149 F3
Lamb's Conduit Street WC1 .... 144 C3
Lamb's Passage EC1 .... 145 F3
Lambeth Bridge SW1 & SE11 .... 148 B2
Lambeth High Street SE1 .... 148 C2
Lambeth Hill EC4 .... 145 E1
Lambeth Palace Road SE1 .... 148 C2
Lambeth Road SE1 .... 148 C2
Lambeth Walk SE11 .... 148 C2
Lamlash Street SE11 .... 149 D2
Lanark Place W9 .... 142 B3
Lanark Road W9 .... 142 A4
Lancaster Gate W2 .... 142 B1
Lancaster Mews W2 .... 142 B1
Lancaster Place WC2 .... 147 D3
Lancaster Street SE1 .... 149 D3
Lancaster Terrace W2 .... 142 C1
Lancaster Walk W2 .... 142 B1
Lancelot Place SW7 .... 147 D3
Lancing Street NW1 .... 144 A4
Landon Place SW1 .... 147 D3
Langdale Close SE17 .... 149 E1
Langham Place W1 .... 143 F2

Langham Street W1 .... 143 F2
Langley Lane SW8 .... 148 B1
Langley Street WC2 .... 144 B1
Langton Close WC1 .... 144 C3
Lansdowne Row W1 .... 143 F1
Lansdowne Terrace WC1 .... 144 B3
Lant Street SE1 .... 149 E3
Larcom Street SE17 .... 149 E2
Lauderdale Road W9 .... 142 A4
Launcelot Street SE1 .... 148 C3
  Lower Marsh
Launceston Place W8 .... 146 B3
Laurence Pountney Lane EC4 .... 145 F1
Lavender Close SE16 .... 151 D1
Lavender Road SE16 .... 151 D2
Laverton Place SW5 .... 146 A2
Lavington Street SE1 .... 149 E4
Law Street SE1 .... 149 F3
Lawn Lane SW8 .... 148 B1
Lawrence Lane EC2 .... 145 E2
  Trump Street
Lawrence Street SW3 .... 146 C1
Laxton Place NW1 .... 143 F3
Laystall Street EC1 .... 144 C3
Layton's Buildings SE1 .... 149 E4
  Borough High Street
Leadenhall Place EC3 .... 145 F1
Leadenhall Street EC3 .... 145 F2
Leake Street SE1 .... 148 C3
Leather Lane EC1 .... 145 D3
Leathermarket Court SE1 .... 149 F3
  Leathermarket Street
Leathermarket Street SE1 .... 149 F3
Lecky Street SW7 .... 146 C2
Lees Place W1 .... 143 E1
Leicester Court WC2 .... 144 B1
  Cranbourn Street
Leicester Place WC2 .... 144 A1
  Lisle Street
Leicester Square WC2 .... 144 B1
Leicester Street WC2 .... 144 B1
Leigh Hunt Street SE1 .... 149 E3
Leigh Street WC1 .... 144 B4
Leinster Gardens W2 .... 142 B1
Leinster Mews W2 .... 142 B1
Leinster Place W2 .... 142 B1
Leinster Square W2 .... 142 A1
Leinster Terrace W2 .... 142 B1
Leman Street E1 .... 150 B3
Lennox Gardens SW1 .... 147 D2
Lennox Gardens Mews SW1 .... 147 D2
Leonard Street EC2 .... 145 F3
Leopold Street E3 .... 151 F4
Leroy Street SE1 .... 149 F2
Lett Street SE1 .... 145 E4
Leverett Street SW3 .... 147 D2
  Mossop Street
Lewisham Street SW1 .... 148 B3
Lexham Gardens W8 .... 146 A2
Lexham Mews W8 .... 146 A2
Lexham Walk W8 .... 146 A2
Lexington Street W1 .... 144 A1
Leyden Street E1 .... 150 A4
Leydon Close SE16 .... 151 E2
Library Place E1 .... 150 C3
Library Street SE1 .... 149 D3
Lighterman Mews E1 .... 151 E4
Lilestone Street NW8 .... 142 C3
Lilley Close E1 .... 150 B2
Lillie Road SW6 .... 146 A1
Lillie Yard SW6 .... 146 A1
Lime Close E1 .... 150 B2
Lime Street EC3 .... 145 F1
Lime Street Passage EC3 .... 145 F1
  Lime Street
Limeburner Lane EC4 .... 145 D2
Limehouse Causeway E14 .... 151 F3
Limehouse Link Tunnel E14 .... 151 F3
Limerston Street SW10 .... 146 B1
Lincoln Street SW3 .... 147 D2
Lincoln's Inn Fields WC2 .... 144 C2
Linden Gardens W2 .... 142 A1
Linden Mews W2 .... 142 A1
Lindley Street E1 .... 150 C4
Lindsay Square SW1 .... 148 B2
Lindsey Street EC1 .... 145 E3
Linhope Street NW1 .... 142 D3
Links Yard E1 .... 150 B4
Linsey Street SE16 .... 150 B1
Lipton Road E1 .... 151 D3
Lisle Street WC2 .... 144 A1
Lisson Grove NW1 & NW8 .... 142 C3
Lisson Street NW1 .... 142 C3
Litchfield Street WC2 .... 144 B1
Little Argyll Street W1 .... 148 A2
  Regent Street
Little Britain EC1 .... 145 E2
Little Chester Street SW1 .... 147 E3
Little College Street SW1 .... 148 B3
Little Dorrit Close SE1 .... 149 E4
Little Edward Street NW1 .... 143 F4
Little George Street SW1 .... 148 B3
  Great George Street
Little London Court SE1 .... 150 B1
  Mill Street
Little Marlborough Street W1 .... 143 F1
  Kingly Street
Little New Street EC4 .... 145 D2
  New Street Square
Little Newport Street WC2 .... 144 B1
Little Portland Street W1 .... 143 F2
Little Russell Street WC1 .... 144 B2
Little Sanctuary SW1 .... 148 B3
  Broad Sanctuary
Little Smith Street SW1 .... 148 B3
Little Somerset Street E1 .... 148 A3
Little St James's Street SW1 .... 148 A4
Little Titchfield Street W1 .... 143 F2
Little Trinity Lane EC4 .... 145 E1
Liverpool Grove SE17 .... 149 E1
Liverpool Street EC2 .... 145 F2
Livonia Street W2 .... 143 F2
Lizard Street EC1 .... 145 E4
Llewellyn Street SE16 .... 150 B1
Lloyd Baker Street WC1 .... 144 C4
Lloyd Square WC1 .... 144 C4
Lloyd Street WC1 .... 144 C4
Lloyd's Avenue EC3 .... 150 A3
Lloyd's Row EC1 .... 145 D4
Locksley Street E14 .... 151 F4
Lockwood Square SE16 .... 150 C1
Lodge Road NW8 .... 142 C4
Loftie Street SE16 .... 150 B1
Lolesworth Close E1 .... 150 B4
Lollard Street SE11 .... 148 C2
Loman Street SE1 .... 149 E4
Lomas Street E1 .... 150 C4
Lombard Court EC4 .... 145 F1
Lombard Lane EC4 .... 145 A2
  Temple Lane
London Bridge EC4 & SE1 .... 145 F1
London Bridge Street SE1 .... 149 F4
London Road SE1 .... 149 D3

London Street EC3 .... 150 A3
London Street W2 .... 142 C2
London Wall EC2 .... 145 E2
Long Acre WC2 .... 144 B1
Long Lane EC1 .... 145 E2
Long Lane SE1 .... 149 F3
Long Walk SE1 .... 150 A1
Long Yard WC1 .... 144 C3
Longford Street NW1 .... 143 F3
Longmoore Street SW1 .... 147 F2
Longville Road SE11 .... 149 D2
Lord Hill's Bridge W2 .... 142 A2
Lord Hill's Road W2 .... 142 A3
Lord North Street SW1 .... 148 B3
Lordship Place SW3 .... 146 C1
Lorenzo Street WC1 .... 144 C4
Lorrimore Road SE17 .... 149 E1
Lorrimore Square SE17 .... 149 E1
Lothbury EC2 .... 145 F2
Loughborough Street SE11 .... 148 C1
Lovat Lane EC3 .... 145 F1
Love Lane EC2 .... 145 E2
Lovell Place SE16 .... 151 E1
Lovers' Walk W1 .... 147 E4
Lowell Street E14 .... 151 E4
Lower Belgrave Street SW1 .... 147 E3
Lower Grosvenor Place SW1 .... 147 F3
Lower James Street W1 .... 144 A1
Lower John Street W1 .... 144 A1
Lower Marsh SE1 .... 148 C3
Lower Road SE8 & SE16 .... 151 D1
Lower Robert Street WC2 .... 144 B1
  Savoy Place
Lower Sloane Street SW1 .... 147 E1
Lower Thames Street EC3 .... 145 F1
Lowndes Place SW1 .... 147 E3
Lowndes Square SW1 .... 147 D3
Lowndes Street SW1 .... 147 E3
Lowood Street E1 .... 150 C3
  Bewley Street
Loxham Street WC1 .... 144 B3
  Cromer Street
Lucan Place SW3 .... 146 C2
Lucerne Mews W8 .... 146 A4
Lucey Road SE16 .... 150 B1
Ludgate Broadway EC4 .... 145 D2
  Pilgrim Street
Ludgate Circus EC4 .... 145 D2
Ludgate Square EC4 .... 145 D2
Luke Street EC2 .... 145 F3
Lukin Street E1 .... 151 D3
Lumley Street W1 .... 143 E1
  Brown Hart Garden
Lupus Street SW1 .... 147 E1
Luton Street NW8 .... 142 C3
Luxborough Street W1 .... 143 E3
Lyall Street SW1 .... 147 E3
Lygon Place SW1 .... 147 F3
Lyons Place NW8 .... 142 C3
Lytham Street SE17 .... 149 F1

Mabledon Place WC1 .... 144 B4
Macclesfield Road EC1 .... 145 E4
Macklin Street WC2 .... 144 B2
Mackworth Street NW1 .... 143 F4
Macleod Street SE17 .... 149 E1
Maddock Way SE17 .... 149 D1
Maddox Street W1 .... 143 F1
Magdalen Street SE1 .... 150 A2
Magee Street SE11 .... 149 D1
Maguire Street SE1 .... 150 B2
Mahogany Close SE16 .... 151 E2
Maida Avenue W2 .... 142 B3
Maida Vale W9 .... 142 B4
Maiden Lane WC2 .... 144 B1
Maiden Lane SE1 .... 149 E4
Makins Street SW3 .... 150 D2
Malet Street WC1 .... 144 A3
Mallord Street SW3 .... 146 C1
Mallory Street NW8 .... 142 C3
Mallow Street EC1 .... 145 F3
Malta Street EC1 .... 145 D3
Maltby Street SE1 .... 150 A1
Maltravers Street WC2 .... 144 C1
Manchester Square W1 .... 143 E2
Manchester Street W1 .... 143 E2
Manciple Street SE1 .... 149 F3
Mandarin Street E14 .... 151 F3
Mandeville Place W1 .... 143 E2
Manette Street W1 .... 144 B2
Manningford Close EC1 .... 145 D4
Manningtree Street E1 .... 150 B4
  Commercial Road
Manor Place SE17 .... 149 E1
Manresa Road SW3 .... 146 C1
Mansell Street E1 .... 150 B3
Mansfield Mews W1 .... 143 F2
  Mansfield Street
Mansfield Street W1 .... 143 F2
Mansion House Place EC4 .... 145 A1
  St Swithun's Lane
Manson Mews SW7 .... 146 B2
Manson Place SW7 .... 146 C2
Maple Leaf Square SE16 .... 151 E2
Maple Street W1 .... 143 F3
Maples Place E1 .... 150 C4
Marble Arch W1 .... 143 D1
Marchmont Street WC1 .... 144 B3
Margaret Court W1 .... 143 F2
  Margaret Street
Margaret Street W1 .... 143 F2
Margaretta Terrace SW3 .... 146 C1
Margery Street WC1 .... 144 C4
Marigold Street SE16 .... 150 C1
Marjorie Mews E1 .... 151 D4
Mark Lane EC3 .... 150 A3
Market Court W1 .... 143 E1
  Oxford Street
Market Mews W1 .... 147 E4
Market Place W1 .... 143 F2
Market Yard Mews SE1 .... 150 A1
Markham Place SW3 .... 147 D2
  Elystan Place
Markham Square SW3 .... 147 D2
Markham Street SW3 .... 147 D2
Marlborough Close SE17 .... 149 E2
Marlborough Road SW1 .... 148 A4
Marlborough Street SW3 .... 146 C2
Marloes Road W8 .... 146 A3
Marlow Way SE16 .... 151 D2
Marne Street W10 .... 150 B1
Maroon Street E14 .... 151 E4
Marshall Street W1 .... 144 A1

155

Marshall's Place SE16 — 150 B1
Marshalsea Road SE1 — 149 E4
Marsham Street SW1 — 148 B3
Marsland Close SE17 — 149 E1
Martha Street E1 — 150 C3
Martin Lane EC4 — 145 F1
Martin's Street WC2 — 144 B1
Martlett Court WC2 — 144 B2
Marylands Road W9 — 142 A3
Marylebone High Street W1 — 143 E3
Marylebone Lane W1 — 143 E2
Marylebone Mews W1 — 143 E2
Marylebone Road NW1 — 143 D3
Marylebone Street W1 — 143 E2
Marylee Way SE11 — 148 C2
Mason Street SE17 — 149 F2
Mason's Arms Mews W1 — 143 F1
Maddox Street
Mason's Place EC1 — 145 E4
Mason's Yard SW1 — 143 E2
Duke Street
Massinger Street SE17 — 149 F2
Master's Street E1 — 151 E4
Matlock Street E14 — 151 E4
Matthew Parker Street SW1 — 148 B3
Maunsel Street SW1 — 148 A2
May's Court WC2 — 144 B1
St Martin's Lane
Mayfair Place W1 — 147 F4
Mayflower Street SE16 — 151 D1
Maynards Quay E1 — 150 C3
McAuley Close SE1 — 148 C3
McCleod's Mews SW7 — 146 B2
Mead Row SE1 — 149 D3
Meadcroft Road SE11 — 149 D1
Meadow Row SE1 — 149 E2
Meard Street W1 — 144 A2
Mecklenburgh Place WC1 — 144 C3
Mecklenburgh Square WC1 — 144 C3
Mecklenburgh Street WC1 — 144 C3
Mecklenburgh Square
Medway Street SW1 — 148 A2
Melbury Street NW1 — 143 D3
Melcombe Place NW1 — 143 D3
Melcombe Street NW1 — 143 D3
Melina Place NW8 — 142 B4
Melior Place SE1 — 149 F4
Snowsfields
Melon Place W8 — 146 A4
Kensington Church Street
Melton Street NW1 — 144 A4
Memel Court EC1 — 145 E3
Baltic Street
Mepham Street SE1 — 148 C4
Mercer Street WC2 — 144 B1
Meredith Street EC1 — 145 D4
Merlin Street WC1 — 145 D4
Mermaid Court SE1 — 149 F4
Mermaid Court SE16 — 151 F1
Mermaid Row SE1 — 149 F3
Merrick Square SE1 — 149 E3
Merrington Road SW6 — 146 A1
Merrow Street SE17 — 149 E1
Methley Street SE11 — 149 D1
Mews Street E1 — 150 B3
Meymott Street SE1 — 149 D4
Micawber Street N1 — 145 E4
Middle Street EC1 — 145 E2
Middle Temple Lane EC4 — 144 C2
Middle Yard SE1 — 149 F4
Middlesex Street E1 — 150 A4
Middleton Drive SE16 — 151 E2
Midford Place W1 — 144 A3
Tottenham Court Road
Midhope Street WC1 — 144 B4
Midland Road NW1 — 144 B4
Midship Close SE16 — 151 E2
Milborne Grove SW10 — 146 B1
Milcote Street SE1 — 149 D3
Mile End Road E1 — 150 C4
Miles Street SW8 — 148 B1
Milford Lane WC2 — 144 C1
Milk Street EC2 — 145 E2
Milk Yard E1 — 151 D3
Mill Place E14 — 151 F3
Mill Street SE1 — 150 B1
Mill Street W1 — 143 F1
Millbank SW1 — 148 B2
Millennium Square SE1 — 150 B2
Milligan Street E14 — 151 F3
Millman Street WC1 — 144 C3
Millstream Road SE1 — 150 A1
Milner Street SW3 — 147 D2
Milton Court EC2 — 145 F3
Milton Street EC2 — 145 F3
Milverton Street SE11 — 149 D1
Milward Street E1 — 150 C4
Mincing Lane EC3 — 150 A3
Minera Mews SW1 — 147 E2
Minories EC3 — 150 A3
Mint Street SE1 — 149 E3
Miranda Close E1 — 150 C4
Mitali Passage E1 — 150 B4
Mitchell Street EC1 — 145 E3
Mitre Road SE1 — 149 D3
Mitre Square EC3 — 150 A3
Mitre Street
Mitre Street EC3 — 150 A3
Molyneux Street W1 — 143 D2
Monck Street SW1 — 148 B3
Moncorvo Close SW7 — 146 C3
Monkton Street SE11 — 149 D2
Monkwell Square EC2 — 145 E2
Monmouth Road W2 — 142 A2
Monmouth Street WC2 — 144 B1
Montagu Mansions W1 — 143 D3
Montagu Mews North W1 — 143 D2
Montagu Mews South W1 — 143 D2
Montagu Mews West W1 — 143 D2
Montagu Place W1 — 143 D2
Montagu Row W1 — 143 D2
Montagu Square W1 — 143 D2
Montagu Street W1 — 143 D2
Montague Close SE1 — 149 F4
Montague Place WC1 — 144 B3
Montague Street EC1 — 145 E2
Montague Street WC1 — 144 B3
Montford Place SE11 — 148 C1
Montpelier Mews SW7 — 147 D3
Montpelier Place SW7 — 147 D3
Montpelier Place E1 — 151 D3
Montpelier Square SW7 — 147 D3
Montpelier Street SW7 — 147 D3
Montpelier Walk SW7 — 147 D3
Montreal Place WC2 — 144 C1
Montrose Court SW7 — 146 C3
Montrose Place SW1 — 147 E3
Monument Street EC3 — 145 F1
Monza Street E1 — 151 D3
Moodkee Street SE16 — 151 D1
Moor Lane EC2 — 145 F2

Moor Place EC2 — 145 F2
Moorfields
Moore Street SW3 — 147 A1
Old Compton Street
Moorfields EC2 — 145 F2
Moorgate EC2 — 145 F2
Mora Street EC1 — 145 E4
Morecambe Close E1 — 151 D4
Morecambe Street SE17 — 149 E2
Moreland Street EC1 — 145 E4
Moreton Place SW1 — 148 A2
Moreton Street SW1 — 148 A2
Moreton Terrace SW1 — 148 A1
Morley Street SE1 — 149 D3
Morocco Street SE1 — 149 F3
Morpeth Terrace SW1 — 147 F2
Morris Street E1 — 150 C3
Morshead Road W9 — 142 A4
Mortimer Market WC1 — 144 A3
Capper Street
Mortimer Street W1 — 143 F2
Morton Mews SW5 — 146 A2
Earl's Court Gardens
Morwell Street WC1 — 144 A2
Moscow Place W2 — 142 A1
Moscow Road W2 — 142 A1
Moss Close E1 — 150 B4
Mossop Street SW3 — 147 D2
Motcomb Street SW1 — 147 E3
Mount Pleasant WC1 — 144 C3
Mount Row W1 — 143 E1
Mount Street W1 — 143 E1
Mount Terrace E1 — 150 C4
Moxon Street W1 — 143 E2
Mozart Terrace SW1 — 147 E2
Mulberry Street E1 — 150 B4
Mulberry Walk SW3 — 146 C1
Mulready Street NW8 — 142 C3
Mulvaney Way SE1 — 149 F3
Mumford Court EC2 — 145 E2
Milk Street
Mundy Street N1 — 145 F4
Munster Square NW1 — 143 F4
Munton Road SE17 — 149 E2
Murphy Street SE1 — 148 C3
Murray Grove N1 — 145 E4
Musbury Street E1 — 151 D4
Muscovy Street EC3 — 150 A3
Museum Street WC1 — 144 B2
Myddelton Passage EC1 — 145 D4
Myddelton Square EC1 — 145 D4
Myddelton Street EC1 — 145 D4
Mylne Street EC1 — 145 D4
Myrdle Street E1 — 150 C4
Myrtle Walk N1 — 145 F4

N

Naoroji Street WC1 — 144 C4
Narrow Street E14 — 151 E3
Nash Street NW1 — 143 F4
Nassau Street W1 — 143 F2
Nathaniel Close E1 — 150 B4
Thrawl Street
National Terrace SE16 — 150 C1
Bermondsey Wall East
Neal Street WC2 — 144 B2
Neathouse Place SW1 — 147 F2
Wilton Road
Nebraska Street SE1 — 149 E3
Neckinger SE1 — 150 B1
Neckinger Street SE1 — 150 B1
Nelson Court SE16 — 151 D2
Nelson Passage EC1 — 145 E4
Mora Street
Nelson Place N1 — 145 E4
Nelson Square SE1 — 149 D4
Nelson Street E1 — 150 C4
Nelson Terrace N1 — 145 D4
Nelson Walk SE16 — 151 E2
Nesham Street E1 — 150 B3
Netherton Grove SW10 — 146 B1
Netley Street NW1 — 143 F4
Nevern Place SW5 — 146 A2
Nevern Square SW5 — 146 A2
Neville Court EC4 — 145 D2
Neville Street SW7 — 146 C2
Neville Terrace SW7 — 146 C1
New Bond Street W1 — 143 F1
New Bridge Street EC4 — 145 D2
New Broad Street EC2 — 145 F2
New Burlington Mews W1 — 150 A3
Hart Street
New Burlington Place W1 — 143 F1
New Burlington Street W1 — 143 F1
New Cavendish Street W1 — 143 E2
New Change EC4 — 145 E2
New Compton Street WC2 — 144 B2
New Crane Place E1 — 151 D3
New Fetter Lane EC4 — 145 D2
New Globe Walk SE1 — 149 E4
New Goulston Street E1 — 150 A4
New Kent Road SE1 — 149 E2
New North Place EC2 — 145 F3
New North Road N1 — 145 F4
New North Street WC1 — 144 C3
New Oxford Street WC1 — 144 B2
New Quebec Street W1 — 143 D2
New Ride SW7 — 146 C3
New Road E1 — 150 C4
New Row WC2 — 144 B1
New Spring Gardens Walk SE11 — 148 B1
Goding Street
New Square WC2 — 144 C2
New Street EC2 — 150 A4
New Street Square EC4 — 145 D2
New Turnstile WC1 — 144 C2
High Holborn
New Union Street EC2 — 145 F2
Newark Street E1 — 150 C4
Newburgh Street W1 — 144 F1
Foubert's Place
Newburn Street SE11 — 148 C1
Newbury Street EC1 — 145 E2
Newcastle Place W2 — 142 C2
Newcomen Street SE1 — 149 F4
Newell Street E14 — 151 F3
Newgate Street EC1 — 145 E2
Newington Butts SE1 & SE11 — 149 D2
Newington Causeway SE1 — 149 E3
Newlands Quay E1 — 151 D3
Newman Street W1 — 144 A2
Newman's Row WC2 — 144 C2
Lincoln's Inn Fields
Newnham Terrace SE1 — 148 C3

Newnhams Row SE1 — 150 A1
Newport Place WC2 — 144 B1
Newport Street SE11 — 148 C2
Newton Road W2 — 142 A2
Newton Street WC2 — 144 B2
Nicholas Lane EC4 — 145 F1
Nicholson Street SE1 — 149 D4
Nightingale Place SW10 — 146 B1
Nile Street N1 — 145 E4
Nine Elms Lane SW8 — 148 A1
Noble Street EC2 — 145 E2
Noel Street W1 — 144 A2
Norbiton Road E14 — 151 F4
Norfolk Crescent W2 — 142 C2
Norfolk Place W2 — 142 C2
Norfolk Square W2 — 142 C2
Norman Street EC1 — 145 E4
Norris Street SW1 — 144 A1
North Audley Street W1 — 143 E1
North Bank NW8 — 142 C4
North Crescent WC1 — 144 A3
North Flockton Street SE16 — 150 B1
Chambers Street
North Gower Street NW1 — 144 A4
North Mews WC1 — 144 C3
North Ride W2 — 142 C1
North Row W1 — 143 E1
North Tenter Street E1 — 150 B3
North Terrace SW3 — 146 C2
North Wharf Road W2 — 142 B2
Northampton Road EC1 — 145 D3
Northampton Row EC1 — 145 D3
Exmouth Market
Northampton Square EC1 — 145 D4
Northburgh Street EC1 — 145 D3
Northchurch SE17 — 149 F2
Northdown Street N1 — 144 C4
Northington Street WC1 — 144 C3
Northumberland Alley EC3 — 150 A3
Northumberland Avenue WC2 — 148 B4
Northumberland Street WC2 — 148 B4
Northwick Close NW8 — 142 C3
Northwick Terrace NW8 — 142 B3
Northy Street E14 — 151 E3
Norton Folgate E1 — 150 A4
Norway Gate SE16 — 151 E1
Norway Place E14 — 151 F3
Norwich Street EC4 — 145 D2
Notting Hill Gate W11 — 142 A1
Nottingham Place W1 — 143 E3
Nottingham Street W1 — 143 E3
Nugent Terrace NW8 — 142 B4

O

O'Leary Square E1 — 151 D4
O'Meara Street SE1 — 149 E4
Oak Lane E14 — 151 F3
Oak Tree Road NW8 — 142 C4
Oakden Street SE11 — 149 D2
Oakfield Street SW10 — 146 B1
Oakington Road W9 — 142 A3
Oakley Crescent EC1 — 145 E4
Oakley Gardens SW3 — 147 D1
Oakley Street SW3 — 146 C1
Oat Lane EC2 — 145 E2
Observatory Gardens W8 — 146 A4
Occupation Road SE17 — 149 E1
Ocean Street E1 — 151 E4
Octagon Arcade EC2 — 145 F2
Octagon Court SE16 — 151 D2
Odessa Street SE16 — 151 F1
Ogle Street W1 — 143 F2
Old Bailey EC4 — 145 D2
Old Bond Street W1 — 143 F1
Old Broad Street EC2 — 145 F2
Old Brompton Road SW5 & SW7 — 146 A1
Old Burlington Street W1 — 143 F1
Old Castle Street E1 — 150 B4
Old Cavendish Street W1 — 143 F2
Old Church Road E1 — 151 D4
Old Church Street SW3 — 146 C1
Old Compton Street W1 — 144 A1
Old Court Place W8 — 146 A3
Old Fleet Lane EC4 — 145 D2
Old Gloucester Street WC1 — 144 B3
Old Jamaica Road SE16 — 150 B1
Old Jewry EC2 — 145 F2
Old Marylebone Road NW1 — 143 D2
Old Mitre Court EC4 — 145 D2
Fleet Street
Old Montagu Street E1 — 150 B4
Old North Street WC1 — 144 C3
Theobalds Road
Old Palace Yard SW1 — 148 B3
Old Paradise Street SE11 — 148 C2
Old Park Lane W1 — 147 E4
Old Pye Street SW1 — 148 A3
Old Quebec Street W1 — 143 D2
Old Queen Street SW1 — 148 A3
Old School Square E14 — 151 F4
Old Square WC2 — 144 C2
Old Street EC1 — 145 E3
Old Theatre Court SE1 — 149 E4
Park Street
Oldbury Place W1 — 143 E3
Olivers Yard EC1 — 145 F3
Olney Road SE17 — 149 E1
Olympia Mews W2 — 142 B1
Onega Gate SE16 — 151 E1
Ongar Road SW6 — 146 A1
Onslow Gardens SW7 — 146 B2
Onslow Mews SW7 — 146 C2
Onslow Square SW7 — 146 C2
Onslow Street EC1 — 145 D3
Saffron Street
Ontario Street SE1 — 149 E3
Opal Street SE11 — 149 D2
Orange Place SE16 — 151 D1
Orange Street WC2 — 144 B1
Orb Street SE17 — 149 F2
Orchard Street W1 — 143 E2
Orchardson Street NW8 — 142 C3
Orde Hall Street WC1 — 144 C3
Orient Street SE11 — 149 D2
Orme Court W2 — 142 A1
Orme Lane W2 — 142 A1
Orme Square W2 — 142 A1
Ormond Yard SW1 — 144 A1
Ormonde Gate SW3 — 147 D1
Orsett Street SE11 — 148 C2
Orsett Terrace W2 — 142 A2
Orton Street E1 — 150 B2
Wapping High Street
Osbert Street SW1 — 148 A2

Osborne Street E1 — 150 B4
Oslo Square SE16 — 151 E1
Osnaburgh Street NW1 — 143 F3
Osnaburgh Terrace NW1 — 143 F3
Albany Street
Ossington Buildings W1 — 143 E2
Moxon Street
Ossington Street W2 — 142 A1
Ossulston Street NW1 — 144 A4
Osten Mews SW7 — 146 B2
Oswin Street SE11 — 149 D2
Othello Close SE1 — 149 D2
Otto Street SE17 — 149 D1
Oval Way SE11 — 148 C1
Ovington Gardens SW3 — 147 D3
Ovington Square SW3 — 147 D3
Ovington Street SW3 — 147 D2
Owen Street EC1 — 145 D4
Oxendon Street SW1 — 144 A1
Oxford Circus W1 — 143 F2
Regent Street
Oxford Square W2 — 142 C2
Oxford Street W1 — 143 E1
Oyster Row E1 — 151 D3
Oystergate Walk EC4 — 145 F1

P

Paddington Green W2 — 142 C3
Paddington Street W1 — 143 E3
Page Street SW1 — 148 B2
Pageant Crescent SE16 — 151 F2
Pageant Steps SE16 — 151 E2
Pageantmaster Court EC4 — 145 D2
Ludgate Hill
Paget Street EC1 — 145 D4
Pakenham Street WC1 — 144 C3
Palace Avenue W8 — 146 A4
Palace Court W2 — 142 A1
Palace Gardens Mews W8 — 146 A4
Palace Gardens Terrace W8 — 146 A4
Palace Gate W8 — 146 B3
Palace Street SW1 — 147 F3
Pall Mall SW1 — 148 A4
Pall Mall East SW1 — 144 B1
Pall Mall Place SW1 — 148 A4
Palmer Street SW1 — 148 A3
Pancras Lane EC4 — 145 E2
Panton Street SW1 — 144 A1
Paradise Street SE16 — 150 C1
Paradise Walk SW3 — 147 D1
Paragon Mews SE1 — 149 F2
Searles Road
Pardoner Street SE1 — 149 F3
Parfetts Street E1 — 150 C4
Paris Garden SE1 — 149 D4
Park Approach SE16 — 150 C1
Park Crescent W1 — 143 E3
Park Crescent Mews East W1 — 143 F3
Park Crescent Mews West W1 — 143 E3
Park Lane W1 — 143 E1
Park Place SW1 — 147 F4
Park Place Villas W2 — 142 B3
Park Road NW1 & NW8 — 143 D4
Park Square East NW1 — 143 F3
Park Square Mews W1 — 143 E3
Harley Street
Park Square West NW1 — 143 E3
Park Street SE1 — 149 E4
Park Street W1 — 143 E1
Park Walk SW10 — 146 B1
Park West Place W2 — 143 D2
Parker Street WC2 — 144 B2
Parkers Row SE1 — 150 B1
Parliament Square SW1 — 148 B3
Parliament Street SW1 — 148 B4
Parnham Street E14 — 151 E4
Parry Street SW8 — 148 B1
Pasley Close SE17 — 149 E1
Passmore Street SW1 — 147 E2
Pastor Street SE11 — 149 D2
Pater Street W8 — 146 A3
Paternoster Row EC4 — 145 E2
Paternoster Square EC4 — 145 E2
Paton Street EC1 — 145 E3
Paul Street EC2 — 145 F3
Paul's Walk EC4 — 145 E1
Paultons Square SW3 — 146 C1
Paveley Street NW8 — 142 C4
Pavilion Road SW1 — 147 D2
Pavilion Street SW1 — 147 D3
Peabody Avenue SW1 — 147 F1
Peacock Street SE17 — 149 E2
Pear Tree Court EC1 — 145 D3
Pear Tree Street EC1 — 145 E3
Pearl Street E1 — 150 C2
Pearman Street SE1 — 149 D3
Peartree Lane E1 — 151 D3
Peerless Street EC1 — 145 F4
Pelham Crescent SW7 — 146 C2
Pelham Place SW7 — 146 C2
Pelham Street SW7 — 146 C2
Pelier Street SE17 — 149 E1
Pelling Street E14 — 151 F4
Pemberton Row EC4 — 145 D2
Pembridge Gardens W2 — 142 A1
Pembridge Place W2 — 142 A1
Pembridge Road W11 — 142 A1
Pembridge Square W2 — 142 A1
Pembroke Mews W8 — 146 A2
Penang Street E1 — 150 C2
Penfold Place NW1 — 142 C3
Penfold Street NW1 & NW8 — 142 C3
Pennant Mews W8 — 146 A2
Pennington Street E1 — 150 C3
Penrose Grove SE17 — 149 E1
Penrose Street SE17 — 149 E1
Penryn Street NW1 — 144 A4
Penton Place SE17 — 149 D2
Penton Rise WC1 — 144 C4
Pentonville Road N1 — 144 C4
Pepper Street SE1 — 149 E4
Pepys Street EC3 — 150 A3
Percival Street EC1 — 145 D3
Percy Circus WC1 — 144 C4
Percy Street W1 — 144 A2
Perkin's Rents SW1 — 148 A3
Perkins Square SE1 — 149 E4
Perry's Place W1 — 144 A2
Perryn Road SE16 — 150 C1
Peter Street W1 — 144 A1
Peter's Hill EC4 — 145 E1
Peter's Lane EC1 — 145 D3
Petersham Lane SW7 — 146 B3

Petersham Mews SW7 — 146 B3
Petersham Place SW7 — 146 B3
Peto Place NW1 — 143 F3
Petticoat Lane E1 — 150 B4
Petticoat Square E1 — 150 A4
Petty France SW1 — 147 F3
Petyward SW3 — 147 D2
Phelp Street SE17 — 149 F1
Phene Street SW3 — 147 D1
Philchurch Place E1 — 150 B3
Phillimore Walk W8 — 146 A3
Philpot Lane EC3 — 145 F1
Philpot Street E1 — 150 C4
Phipp Street EC2 — 145 F3
Phoenix Place WC1 — 144 C3
Phoenix Road NW1 — 144 A4
Phoenix Street WC2 — 144 B2
Charing Cross Road
Piccadilly W1 — 147 F4
Piccadilly Arcade SW1 — 148 A4
Piccadilly
Piccadilly Circus W1 — 144 A1
Piccadilly Place W1 — 144 A1
Vine Street
Pickard Street EC1 — 145 E4
Pickford Wharf N1 — 145 E4
Pickwick Street SE1 — 149 E3
Picton Place W1 — 143 E2
Piggot Street E14 — 151 F3
Pilgrim Street EC4 — 145 D2
Pilgrimage Street SE1 — 149 F3
Pimlico Road SW1 — 147 E2
Pinchin Street E1 — 150 B3
Pindar Street EC2 — 145 F3
Pindock Mews W9 — 142 A3
Pine Street EC1 — 145 D3
Pitfield Street N1 — 145 F4
Pitsea Place E1 — 151 E3
Pitsea Street E1 — 151 E3
Pitt Street W8 — 146 A3
Pitt's Head Mews W1 — 147 E4
Pixley Street E14 — 151 F4
Platina Street EC2 — 145 F3
Playhouse Yard EC4 — 145 D1
Pleydell Court EC4 — 145 D1
Bouverie Street
Plough Place EC4 — 145 D2
Fetter Lane
Plover Way SE16 — 151 E1
Plumber's Row E1 — 150 B4
Plumtree Court EC4 — 145 D2
Plympton Street NW8 — 142 C3
Pocock Street SE1 — 149 D3
Poland Street W1 — 144 A2
Pollen Street W1 — 143 F1
Pollitt Drive NW8 — 142 C4
Polygon Road NW1 — 144 A4
Pomwell Way E1 — 150 B4
Pond Place SW3 — 146 C2
Ponler Street E1 — 150 C3
Ponsonby Place SW1 — 148 B2
Ponsonby Terrace SW1 — 148 B2
Pont Street SW1 — 147 D3
Pont Street Mews SW1 — 147 D3
Poolmans Street SE16 — 151 D2
Poonah Street E1 — 151 D3
Pope Street SE1 — 150 A1
Poplar Place W2 — 142 A1
Poppins Court EC4 — 145 D2
Fleet Street
Porchester Gardens W2 — 142 A1
Porchester Place W2 — 143 D2
Porchester Road W2 — 142 A2
Porchester Square W2 — 142 A2
Porchester Terrace W2 — 142 B1
Porlock Street SE1 — 149 F3
Porter Street W1 — 143 E3
Porter Street SE1 — 149 E4
Porteus Road W2 — 142 B2
Portland Mews W1 — 144 A2
D'Arblay Street
Portland Place W1 — 143 F2
Portland Square E1 — 150 C2
Portland Street SE17 — 149 F1
Portman Close W1 — 143 E2
Portman Mews South W1 — 143 E2
Portman Square W1 — 143 E2
Portman Street W1 — 143 E2
Portpool Lane EC1 — 144 C3
Portsea Place W2 — 143 D2
Portsmouth Street WC2 — 144 C2
Portugal Street
Portsoken Street EC3 — 150 B3
Portugal Street WC2 — 144 C2
Potier Street SE1 — 149 F3
Pottery Street SE16 — 150 C1
Poultry EC2 — 145 F2
Praed Street W2 — 142 C2
Pratt Walk SE11 — 148 C2
Prescot Street E1 — 150 B3
President Street EC1 — 145 E4
Central Street
Presidents Drive E1 — 150 C2
Prestwood Street N1 — 145 E4
Wenlock Road
Price's Street SE1 — 149 D4
Prideaux Place WC1 — 144 C4
Primrose Hill EC4 — 145 D1
Hutton Street
Primrose Street EC2 — 150 A4
Prince Albert Road NW1 & NW8 — 142 C4
Prince Consort Road SW7 — 146 C3
Prince of Wales Terrace W8 — 146 B1
Kensington Road
Prince's Gardens SW7 — 146 C3
Prince's Gate SW7 — 146 C3
Prince's Gate Mews SW7 — 146 C3
Prince's Mews W2 — 142 A1
Prince's Square W2 — 142 A1
Princelet Street E1 — 150 B4
Princes Arcade SW1 — 148 A4
Piccadilly
Princes Circus WC2 — 144 B2
Princes Court E1 — 150 C3
Princes Riverside Road SE16 — 151 D2
Princes Street EC2 — 145 F2
Princes Street W1 — 143 F2
Princess Street SE1 — 149 D3
Princeton Street WC1 — 144 C3
Printer Street EC4 — 145 D2
Prioress Street SE1 — 149 F3
Priory Walk SW10 — 146 B1
Procter Street WC1 — 144 C2
Prospect Place E1 — 151 D2
Prospect Street SE16 — 150 C1
Providence Court W1 — 143 E1
Providence Square SE1 — 150 B2
Provost Street N1 — 145 F4
Prusom Street E1 — 150 C2
Pudding Lane EC3 — 145 F1
Puddle Dock EC4 — 144 D1

Puma Court
Suffolk Lane
157

Puma Court E1 150 B4
Purbrook Street SE1 150 A1

Q

Quarley Way SE15 143 D2
New Quebec Street
Quebec Way SE16 151 E1
Queen Anne Mews W1 143 F2
Chandos Street
Queen Anne Street W1 143 E2
Queen Anne's Gate SW1 148 A3
Queen Elizabeth Street SE1 150 A2
Queen Square WC1 144 B3
Queen Street EC4 145 E1
Queen Street W1 145 F4
Queen Street Place EC4 145 E1
Queen Victoria Street EC4 145 D1
Queen's Gardens SW1 147 F3
Queen's Gardens W2 142 B1
Queen's Gate SW7 146 B3
Queen's Gate Gardens SW7 146 B2
Queen's Gate Mews SW7 146 B3
Queen's Gate Place SW7 146 B3
Queen's Gate Place Mews SW7 146 B2
Queen's Gate Terrace SW7 146 B3
Queen's Mews W2 142 A1
Queen's Row SE17 149 E1
Queen's Walk SW1 147 F4
Queenhithe EC4 145 E1
Queensberry Mews West SW7 146 B2
Queensberry Place SW7 143 F4
Harrington Street
Queensborough Terrace W2 142 B1
Queensway W2 142 A2
Quick Street N1 145 D4

R

Rabbit Row W8 146 A4
Raby Street E14 151 E4
Radcliffe Road SE1 150 A1
Radcot Street SE11 149 D1
Radley Court SE16 151 E2
Radley Mews W8 146 A2
Radnor Mews W2 142 C2
Radnor Place W2 142 C2
Radnor Street EC1 145 D3
Radnor Walk SW3 147 D1
Railway Approach SE1 149 F4
Railway Avenue SE16 151 D2
Raine Street E1 150 C2
Rainsford Street W2 142 C2
Ralston Street SW3 147 D1
Ramillies Place W1 143 F2
Ramillies Street W1 144 A2
Rampart Street E1 150 C4
Rampayne Street SW1 148 A2
Ramsey Mews SW3 146 C1
Randall Road SE11 148 C2
Randall Row SE11 148 C2
Randolph Avenue W9 142 A4
Randolph Crescent W9 142 B3
Randolph Mews W9 142 B3
Randolph Road W9 142 B3
Ranelagh Bridge W2 142 B2
Ranelagh Grove SW1 147 E2
Ranelagh Road SW1 148 A1
Ranston Street NW1 142 C3
Raphael Street SW7 147 D3
Ratcliff Grove EC1 145 E4
Ratcliffe Cross Street E1 151 E3
Ratcliffe Lane E14 151 E3
Rathbone Place W1 144 A2
Raven Row E1 150 C4
Ravensdon Street SE11 149 D1
Ravent Road SE11 148 C2
Ravey Street EC2 145 F3
Rawlings Street SW3 147 D2
Rawstorne Place EC1 145 D4
Rawstorne Street
Rawstorne Street EC1 145 D4
Ray Street EC1 145 D3
Reardon Path E1 150 C2
Reardon Street E1 150 C2
Rebecca Terrace SE16 151 D1
Rectory Square E1 151 E4
Red Lion Row SE17 149 E1
Red Lion Square WC1 144 C2
Red Lion Street WC1 144 C2
Redan Place W2 142 A2
Redburn Street SW3 147 D1
Redcastle Close E1 151 D3
Redcliffe Gardens SW10 & SW5 146 A1
Redcliffe Mews SW10 146 B1
Redcliffe Place SW10 146 B1
Redcliffe Road SW10 146 B1
Redcliffe Square SW10 146 A1
Redcliffe Street SW10 146 A1
Redcross Way SE1 149 E4
Rede Place W2 142 A1
Redesdale Street SW3 147 D1
Redfield Lane SW5 146 A2
Redhill Street NW1 143 F4
Redman's Road E1 151 D4
Redmead Lane E1 150 B2
Wapping High Street
Redriff Road SE16 151 E1
Redwood Close SE16 151 E2
Reece Mews SW7 146 C1
Reedworth Street SE11 149 D2
Reeves Mews W1 143 E1
Regal Close E1 150 C4
Regan Way N1 145 F4
Regency Street SW1 148 A2
Regent Square WC1 144 B4
Regent Street W1 & SW1 143 F2
Regnart Buildings NW1 144 A4
Euston Street
Relton Mews SW7 147 D3
Remington Street N1 145 E4
Remnant Street WC2 144 C2
Kingsway
Renforth Street SE16 151 D1
Renfrew Road SE11 149 D2
Rennie Street SE1 145 E1
Rephidim Street SE1 149 F3
Repton Street E14 151 E4
Reston Place SW7 146 B3
Reveley Close SE16 151 E1
Rex Place W1 143 E1
Rhodeswell Road E14 151 F4
Rich Lane SW5 146 A1
Rich Street E14 151 F3
Richard's Place SW3 147 D2
Richbell Place WC1 144 C3
Emerald Street
Richmond Buildings W1 144 A2
Dean Street
Richmond Mews W1 144 A2
Richmond Terrace SW1 148 B4
Rickett Street SW6 146 A1
Ridgmount Gardens WC1 144 A3
Ridgmount Street WC1 144 A3
Riding House Street W1 143 F2
Riley Road SE1 150 A1
Risborough Street SE1 149 E4
Risdon Street SE16 151 D1
River Street EC1 145 D4
Riverside Walk SE1 148 C4
Rivington Street EC2 145 F3
Robert Adam Street W1 143 E2
Robert Close W9 142 B3
Robert Dashwood Way SE17 149 E2
Robert Street NW1 143 F4
Robert Street WC2 144 B1
Roberts Close SE16 151 E1
Roberts Place EC1 145 D3
Bowling Green Lane
Robinson Street SW3 147 D1
Flood Street
Rochester Row SW1 148 A2
Rochester Street SW1 148 A2
Rockingham Street SE1 149 E3
Rocliffe Street N1 145 E4
Roding Mews E1 150 B2
Rodmarton Street W1 143 D2
Rodney Place SE17 149 E2
Rodney Road SE17 149 E2
Roger Street WC1 144 C3
Roland Gardens SW7 146 B1
Roland Way SE17 149 F1
Roland Way SW7 146 B1
Rolls Buildings EC4 145 D2
Rolls Passage EC4 144 C2
Romford Street E1 150 C4
Romilly Street W1 144 A1
Romney Mews W1 143 E3
Chiltern Street
Romney Street SW1 148 B2
Ronald Street E1 151 D3
Rood Lane EC3 145 F1
Rope Street SE16 151 E1
Ropemaker Road SE16 151 E1
Ropemaker Street EC2 145 F3
Ropemaker's Fields E14 151 F3
Roper Lane SE1 150 A1
Rosary Gardens SW7 146 B2
Roscoe Street EC1 145 E3
Rose & Crown Yard SW1 148 A4
King Street
Rose Alley SE1 149 E4
Rose Street WC2 144 B1
Rosebery Avenue EC1 147 D3
Rosemoor Street SW3 147 D2
Rosoman Place EC1 145 D4
Rosoman Street
Rosoman Street EC1 145 D4
Rossmore Road NW1 143 D3
Rotary Street SE1 149 D3
Rotherhithe Street SE16 151 D2
Rotherhithe Tunnel Approach E14 151 E3
Rotherhithe Tunnel Approach SE16 151 F1
Rothsay Street SE1 149 F3
Rotten Row SW7 & SW1 146 C4
Rouel Road SE16 150 B1
Roupell Street SE1 149 D4
Rowington Close W2 142 A3
Roxby Place SW6 146 A1
Roy Square E14 151 F3
Royal Avenue SW3 147 D1
Royal Exchange Buildings EC3 145 F2
Cornhill
Royal Hospital Road SW3 147 D1
Royal Mint Place E1 150 B3
Royal Mint Street E1 150 B3
Royal Opera Arcade SW1 148 A4
Royal Road SE17 149 D1
Royal Street SE1 148 C3
Royalty Mews W1 144 A2
Royalty Mews W1 144 A2
Rudolf Place SW8 148 B1
Rudolph Road NW6 142 A4
Rufus Street N1 145 F4
Rugby Street WC1 144 C3
Rugg Street E14 151 F3
Rum Close E1 150 C3
Rupack Street SE16 151 D1
Rupert Street W1 144 A1
Rushworth Street SE1 149 D3
Russell Court SW1 148 A4
Cleveland Row
Russell Place SE16 151 E1
Russell Square WC1 144 B3
Russell Street WC2 144 C1
Russia Dock Road SE16 151 E2
Russia Row EC2 145 E2
Russia Walk SE16 151 E1
Rutherford Street SW1 148 A2
Rutland Gardens SW7 147 D3
Rutland Gate SW7 146 C3
Rutland Gate Mews SW7 146 C3
Rutland Gate
Rutland Mews East SW7 146 C3
Ennismore Street
Rutland Mews South SW7 146 C3
Ennismore Street
Rutland Place EC1 145 E3
Rutland Street SW7 146 C3
Rysbrack Street SW3 147 D3

S

Sackville Street W1 144 A1
Saddle Yard W1 147 E4
Saffron Hill EC1 145 D3
Saffron Street EC1 145 D3
Sage Street E1 150 C3
Sage Way WC1 144 C4
Sail Street SE11 148 C2
St Agnes Place SE11 149 D1
St Alban's Grove W8 146 A3
St Alban's Street SW1 144 A1
St Albans Mews W2 142 C3
St Alphage Garden EC2 145 E2
St Andrew Street EC4 145 D2
St Andrew's Hill EC4 145 D1
St Ann's Lane SW1 148 A3
St Ann's Row E14 151 F3
St Ann's Street SW1 148 B3
St Anne Street E14 151 F3
St Anne's Court W1 144 A2
St Anselm's Place W1 143 E1
St Anthony's Close E1 150 B2
St Barnabas Street SW1 147 E2
St Botolph Street EC3 150 A4
St Bride Street EC4 145 D2
St Catherines Mews SW3 147 D2
Milner Street
St Chad's Place WC1 144 B4
St Chad's Street WC1 144 B4
St Christopher's Place W1 143 E2
St Clare Street EC3 150 A3
St Clement's Lane WC2 144 C2
St Clements Court EC4 145 F1
St Cross Street EC1 145 D3
St Dunstan's Court EC4 145 D2
Fleet Street
St Dunstan's Lane EC3 145 F1
St Mary at Hill
St Dunstans Alley EC3 150 A3
St Dunstans Hill
St Dunstans Hill EC3 150 A3
St Ermins Hill SW1 148 A3
St George Street W1 143 F1
St George's Circus SE1 149 D3
St George's Court EC4 145 D2
St George's Drive SW1 147 F2
St George's Mews SE1 149 D3
St George's Road SE1 149 D3
St George's Square SW1 148 A1
St George's Square E14 151 E3
St George's Square Mews SW1 148 A1
St Georges Fields W2 143 D1
St Giles High Street WC2 144 B2
St Helen's Place EC3 145 F2
St Helena Street WC1 144 C4
St James's Court SW1 148 A3
St James's Market SW1 144 A1
Haymarket
St James's Place SW1 147 F4
St James's Road SE1 & SE16 150 B1
St James's Row EC1 145 D3
St James's Walk
St James's Square SW1 148 A4
St James's Street SW1 148 A4
St James's Walk EC1 145 D3
St John Street EC1 145 D4
St John's Lane EC1 145 D3
St John's Place EC1 145 D3
St John's Square EC1 145 D3
St John's Villas W8 146 A3
St Mary's Place
St John's Wood High Street NW8 142 C4
St John's Wood Road NW8 142 C4
St Katherine's Row EC3 145 F1
Fenchurch Street
St Katherine's Way E1 150 B1
St Leonard's Terrace SW3 147 D1
St Loo Avenue SW3 147 D1
St Luke's Close EC1 145 E3
St Luke's Street SW3 146 C1
St Margaret's Lane W8 146 A3
St Margaret's Street SW1 148 B3
St Mark Street E1 150 B3
St Martin's Court WC2 144 B1
St Martin's Lane
St Martin's Lane WC2 144 B1
St Martin's Place WC2 144 B1
St Martin's Street WC2 144 B1
St Martin's-le-Grand EC1 145 E2
St Mary at Hill EC3 145 F1
St Mary Axe EC3 150 A3
St Mary's Gardens SE11 149 D2
St Mary's Gate W8 146 A3
St Mary's Mansions W2 142 B3
St Mary's Place W8 146 A3
St Mary's Square W2 142 C3
St Mary's Terrace W2 142 B3
St Mary's Walk SE11 149 D2
St Marychurch Street SE16 151 D1
St Matthew Street SW1 148 A3
St Michael's Street W2 142 C2
St Olav's Square SE16 151 D1
Lower Road
St Oswald's Place SE11 148 C1
St Paul's Avenue SE16 151 E2
St Paul's Churchyard EC4 145 E2
St Paul's Terrace SE17 149 E1
St Paul's Way E3 151 F4
St Peter's Place W9 142 A3
St Petersburgh Mews W2 142 A1
St Petersburgh Place W2 142 A1
St Stephen's Crescent W2 142 A2
St Stephen's Gardens W2 142 A2
St Stephen's Mews W2 142 A2
St Swithin's Lane EC4 145 F1
St Thomas Street SE1 149 F4
St Vincent Street W1 143 E2
Salamanca Place SE1 148 C2
Salamanca Street SE1 & SE11 148 C2
Salem Road W2 142 A1
Salisbury Close SE17 149 F2
Salisbury Court EC4 145 D2
Salisbury Place W1 143 D3
Salisbury Square EC4 145 D2
Salisbury Court
Salisbury Street NW8 142 C3
Salmon Lane E14 151 E4
Salter Road SE16 151 E1
Salter Street E14 151 F3
Samford Street NW8 142 C3
Sampson Street E1 150 C2
Sancroft Street SE11 148 C2
Sanctuary Street SE1 149 E4
Marshalsea Road
Sandell Street SE1 149 D4
Sandland Street WC1 144 C2
Sandpiper Close SE16 151 F2
Sandwich Street WC1 144 B4
Sandys Row E1 150 A4
Sans Walk EC1 147 D3
Saracens Head Yard EC3 150 A3
Sardinia Street WC2 144 C2
Saunders Court E14 151 F3
Limehouse Causeway
Savage Gardens EC3 150 A3
Pepys Street
Savile Row W1 143 F1
Savoy Buildings WC2 144 C1
Savoy Hill WC2 144 C1
Savoy Way
Savoy Place WC2 144 B1
Savoy Row WC2 144 C1
Savoy Street
Savoy Steps WC2 144 C1
Savoy Way
Savoy Street WC2 144 C1
Savoy Way WC2 144 C1
Sawyer Street SE1 149 E4
Scala Street W1 144 A2
Scandrett Street E1 150 C2
Scarborough Street E1 150 B3
Scarsdale Place W8 146 A3
Scarsdale Villas W8 146 A3
School House Lane E1 151 D3
Schooner Close SE16 151 D2
Scoresby Street SE1 149 D4
Scotswood Street EC1 147 D3
Sans Walk
Scott Ellis Gardens NW8 142 B4
Scott Lidgett Crescent SE16 150 B1
Scovell Road SE1 149 E3
Scrutton Street EC2 145 F3
Seagrave Road SW6 146 A1
Searles Road SE1 149 F2
Sebastian Street EC1 145 D4
Secker Street SE1 148 C4
Sedan Way SE17 149 F2
Sedding Street SW1 147 E2
Sloane Square
Seddon Street WC1 144 C4
Sedley Place W1 143 F2
Woodstock Street
Seething Lane EC3 150 A3
Sekforde Street EC1 145 D3
Sellon Mews SE11 148 C2
Selsey Street E14 151 F4
Selwood Terrace SW7 146 C2
Selwood Place SW7 146 C1
Semley Place SW1 147 E2
Senior Street W2 142 A3
Senrab Street E1 151 D4
Serle Street WC2 144 C2
Serpentine Road W2 146 C1
Seth Street SE16 151 D1
Settles Street E1 150 C4
Seven Dials WC2 144 B2
Seville Street SW1 147 D3
Knightsbridge
Sevington Street W9 142 A3
Seward Street EC1 145 E3
Seymour Mews W1 143 E2
Seymour Place W1 143 D2
Seymour Street W2 143 D1
Seymour Walk SW10 146 B1
Shad Thames SE1 150 A2
Shadwell Pier Head E1 151 D3
Shadwell Place E1 150 C3
Shaftesbury Avenue W1 & WC2 144 A1
Shaftesbury Mews W8 146 A2
Shafto Mews SW1 147 D3
Shand Street SE1 150 A2
Sharsted Street SE17 149 D1
Shawfield Street SW3 147 D1
Sheffield Street WC2 144 C2
Portugal Street
Sheffield Terrace W8 146 A4
Shelmerdine Close E3 151 F4
Shelton Street WC2 144 B2
Shepherd Market W1 147 F4
Shepherd Street W1 147 E4
Shepherd's Place W1 143 E1
Shepherdess Place N1 145 E4
Shepherdess Walk
Shepherdess Walk N1 145 E4
Sheraton Street W1 144 A2
Wardour Street
Sherlock Mews W1 143 E3
Sherwood Street W1 144 A1
Shillibeer Place W1 143 D2
Shipwright Road SE16 151 E1
Shirland Road W9 142 A3
Shoe Lane EC4 145 D2
Short Street SE1 149 D4
Short's Gardens WC2 144 B2
Shorter Street E1 150 B3
Shoulder of Mutton Alley E14 151 F2
Shouldham Street W1 143 D2
Shroton Street NW1 142 C3
Sicilian Avenue WC1 144 B2
Vernon Place
Siddons Lane NW1 143 D3
Sidford Place SE1 148 C2
Sidmouth Street WC1 144 C4
Sidney Square E1 151 D4
Sidney Street E1 150 C4
Silex Street SE1 149 D3
Silk Street EC2 145 E3
Silver Walk SE16 151 F2
Silvester Street SE1 149 E3
Singer Street EC2 145 F3
Sise Lane EC4 145 E2
Pancras Lane
Skinner Street EC1 145 D3
Skinners Lane EC4 145 F4
Queen Street
Sleaford Street SW8 144 B4
Slingsby Place WC2 144 B1
Slippers Place SE16 150 C1
Sloane Avenue SW3 147 D2
Sloane Court East SW3 147 E2
Sloane Court West SW3 147 E1
Sloane Gardens SW1 147 E2
Sloane Square SW1 147 E2
Sloane Street SW1 147 D3
Sloane Terrace SW1 147 E2
Sly Street E1 150 C3
Cannon Street Road
Smart's Place WC2 144 B2
Smeaton Street E1 150 C2
Smith Close SE16 151 D2
Smith Square SW1 148 B3
Smith Street SW3 147 D1
Smith Terrace SW3 147 D1
Smithfield Street EC1 145 D2
Smithy Street E1 151 D4
Snow Hill EC1 145 D2
Snowsfields SE1 149 F4
Soho Square W1 144 A2
Soho Street W1 144 A2
Somerford Way SE16 151 E1
Somers Crescent W2 142 C2
Somers Mews W2 142 C2
Sondes Street SE17 149 F1
Sophia Square SE16 151 E3
South Audley Street W1 143 E1
South Bolton Gardens SW5 146 B1
South Carriage Drive SW1 & SW7 146 C3
South Crescent WC1 144 A2
Store Street
South Eaton Place SW1 147 E2
South End W8 146 A3
South End Row W8 146 A3
South Lambeth Place SW8 148 B1
South Molton Lane W1 143 E1
South Molton Street W1 143 E2
South Parade SW3 146 C1
South Place EC2 145 F2
South Street W1 147 E1
South Tenter Street E1 150 B3
South Terrace SW7 146 C2
South Wharf Road W2 142 C2
Southall Place SE1 149 F3
Long Lane
Southampton Buildings WC2 144 C2
Southampton Place WC1 144 B2
Southampton Row WC1 144 B3
Southampton Street WC2 144 B1
Southsea Street SE16 151 F1
Southwark Bridge EC4 & SE1 145 E1
Southwark Bridge Road SE1 149 E3
Southwark Park Road SE16 150 C1
Southwark Street SE1 149 D4
Southwell Gardens SW7 146 B2
Southwick Street W2 142 C2
Hyde Park Crescent
Sovereign Close E1 150 C3
Spa Road SE16 150 B1
Spanish Place W1 143 E2
Spear Mews SW5 146 A2
Spelman Street E1 150 B4
Spence Close SE16 151 F1
Spencer Street EC1 145 D4
Spenser Street SW1 148 A3
Spert Street E14 151 E3
Spital Square E1 150 A4
Spital Street E1 150 B4
Sprimont Place SW3 147 D2
Spring Gardens SW1 148 B4
Spring Mews W1 143 D3
Spring Street W2 142 C2
Spur Road SW1 147 F3
Spur Road SE1 148 C3
Lower Marsh
Spurgeon Street SE1 149 F3
Squire Gardens NW8 142 C4
Stable Yard Road SW1 148 A4
Stables Way SE11 148 C1
Stacey Street WC2 144 B2
Staff Street EC1 145 F4
Vince Street
Stafford Place SW1 147 F3
Stag Place SW1 147 F3
Stainer Street SE1 149 F4
Staining Lane EC2 145 E2
Stalbridge Street NW1 142 C3
Stalham Street SE16 150 C1
Stamford Street SE1 148 C4
Stanford Road W8 146 A3
Stanford Street SW1 148 A2
Stanhope Gardens SW7 146 B2
Stanhope Gate W1 147 E4
Hertford Street
Stanhope Mews East SW7 146 B2
Stanhope Mews South SW7 146 B2
Stanhope Mews West SW7 146 B2
Stanhope Place W2 146 B2
Stanhope Street NW1 143 F4
Stanhope Terrace W2 142 C1
Stannary Place SE11 149 D1
Stannary Street SE11 149 D1
Stanworth Street SE1 150 B1
Staple Inn Buildings WC1 144 C2
Staple Street SE1 149 F3
Staples Close SE16 151 E2
Star Place E1 150 B3
Star Street W2 142 C2
Star Yard WC2 144 C2
Starcross Street NW1 144 A3
Station Acces Road EC2 145 F2
Stave Yard Road SE16 151 E2
Stead Street SE17 149 E2
Stedham Place WC1 144 B2
New Oxford Street
Steedman Street SE17 149 E2
Steel's Lane E1 151 D3
Steelyard Passage EC4 145 E1
Steers Way SE16 151 E1
Stephen Mews W1 144 A2
Gresse Street
Stephen Street W1 144 A2
Stephen's Row EC4 145 F1
Walbrook
Stephenson Way NW1 144 A3
Stepney Causeway E1 151 D3
Stepney Green E1 151 D4
Stepney High Street E1 151 E4
Stepney Way E1 150 C4
Sterling Street SW7 147 D3
Montpelier Place
Sterry Street SE1 149 F3
Stevedore Street E1 150 C2
Stevens Street SE1 150 A1
Steward Street E1 150 A4
Stewart's Grove SW3 146 C2
Stillington Street SW1 148 A2
Stockholm Way E1 150 B2
Vaughan Way
Stocks Place E14 151 F3
Stone Buildings WC2 144 C2
Chancery Lane
Stone Hall Gardens W8 146 A3
Stone Hall Place W8 146 A3
Stone Hall Gardens
Stone Stairs E1 151 E3
Stonecutter Street EC4 145 D2
Stones End Street SE1 149 E3
Stoney Lane E1 150 A4
Stoney Street SE1 149 F4
Stopford Road SE17 149 E1
Store Street WC1 144 A2
Storey's Gate SW1 148 B3
Stork's Road SE16 150 C1
Stoughton Close SE11 148 C2
Stourcliffe Street W1 143 D2
Strand WC2 144 B1
Stratford Avenue W8 146 A3
Stratford Place W1 143 E2
Stratford Road W8 146 A2
Strathearn Place W2 142 C2
Hyde Park Square
Strathmore Gardens W8 146 A4
Palace Gardens Terrace
Stratton Street W1 147 F4
Streatham Street WC1 144 B2
Dyott Street
Strutton Ground SW1 148 A3
Strype Street E1 150 A4
Stukeley Street WC2 144 B2
Sturge Street SE1 149 E3
Sturgeon Road SE17 149 E1
Sturt Street N1 145 E4
Stutfield Street E1 150 B3
Sudeley Street N1 145 D4
Sudrey Street SE1 149 E3
Suffolk Lane EC4 145 F1

Suffolk Place SW1 ...... 144 B1
Suffolk Street
Suffolk Street SW1 ...... 144 B1
Sugar Quay Walk EC3 ...... 150 A3
Sullivan Road SE1 ...... 149 D2
Summercourt Road E1 ...... 151 D4
Summers Street EC1 ...... 145 D3
Back Hill
Sumner Place SW7 ...... 146 C2
Sumner Place Mews SW7 ...... 146 C2
Sumner Street SE1 ...... 149 E4
Sun Street EC2 ...... 145 F3
Sun Street Passage EC2 ...... 145 F2
Sun Walk E1 ...... 150 B3
Sunderland Terrace W2 ...... 142 A2
Sunningdale Gardens W8 ...... 146 A2
Stratford Road
Surrenale Road W9 ...... 142 A3
Surrey Quays Road SE16 ...... 151 D1
Surrey Row SE1 ...... 149 D4
Surrey Square SE17 ...... 149 F2
Surrey Street WC2 ...... 144 C1
Surrey Water Road SE16 ...... 151 E2
Sussex Gardens W2 ...... 142 C1
Sussex Place NW1 ...... 143 D4
Sussex Place W2 ...... 142 C2
Sussex Square W2 ...... 142 C1
Sussex Street SW1 ...... 147 F1
Sutherland Avenue W9 ...... 142 A3
Sutherland Row SW1 ...... 147 F1
Sutherland Street
Sutherland Square SE17 ...... 149 E1
Sutherland Street SW1 ...... 147 F1
Sutherland Walk SE17 ...... 149 E1
Sutton Row W1 ...... 144 B2
Swallow Street W1 ...... 144 A1
Swan Mead SE1 ...... 149 F3
Swan Road SE16 ...... 151 D2
Swan Street SE1 ...... 149 E3
Swan Walk SW3 ...... 147 D1
Sweden Gate SE16 ...... 151 E1
Swedenborg Gardens E1 ...... 150 C3
Sweeney Crescent SE1 ...... 150 B1
Swinton Street WC1 ...... 144 C4
Swiss Court WC2 ...... 144 B1
Leicester Square
Sycamore Street EC1 ...... 145 E3
Old Street
Sydney Close SW3 ...... 146 C2
Sydney Mews SW3 ...... 146 C2
Sydney Street SW3 ...... 146 C2
Symons Street SW3 ...... 147 D2

T

Tabard Street SE1 ...... 149 F3
Tabernacle Street EC2 ...... 145 F3
Tachbrook Street SW1 ...... 148 A2
Tailworth Street E1 ...... 150 B4
Chicksand Street
Talbot Square W2 ...... 142 C2
Talbot Street SE1 ...... 149 F4
Tallis Street EC4 ...... 145 D1
Tameraire Street SE16 ...... 151 D2
Tamworth Street SW6 ...... 145 A1
Tankerton Street WC1 ...... 144 B4
Cromer Street
Tanner Street SE1 ...... 150 A1
Taplow Street N1 ...... 145 E4
Tarbert Walk E1 ...... 151 D3
Tarling Street E1 ...... 150 C3
Tarver Road SE17 ...... 149 E1
Tatum Street SE17 ...... 149 F2
Taunton Mews NW1 ...... 143 D3
Balcombe Street
Taunton Place NW1 ...... 143 D3
Tavistock Place WC1 ...... 144 B3
Tavistock Square WC1 ...... 144 B3
Tavistock Street WC2 ...... 144 B1
Taviton Street WC1 ...... 144 A3
Tavy Close SE11 ...... 149 D2
Teak Close SE16 ...... 151 E1
Tedworth Square SW3 ...... 147 D1
Telegraph Street EC2 ...... 145 F2
Temple Avenue EC4 ...... 145 D1
Temple Lane EC4 ...... 145 D1
Temple Place WC2 ...... 144 C1
Templeton Place SW5 ...... 145 D1
Tench Street E1 ...... 150 C2
Tenison Court W1 ...... 143 F2
Regent Street
Tenison Way SE1 ...... 148 C4
Tennis Street SE1 ...... 149 F3
Tenter Ground E1 ...... 150 A4
White's Row
Tenterden Street W1 ...... 143 F2
Terminus Place SW1 ...... 147 F3
Thackeray Street W8 ...... 146 A3
Thame Road SE16 ...... 151 E2
Thames Link SE16 ...... 151 D2
Thanet Street WC1 ...... 144 B4
Thavies Inn EC4 ...... 145 D2
Thayer Street W1 ...... 143 E2
The Boltons SW10 ...... 146 B1
The Broad Walk NW1 ...... 143 E4
The Broad Walk W8 ...... 146 B4
The Cut SE1 ...... 149 D4
The Dial Walk W8 ...... 146 B4
The Economist Plaza SW1 ...... 148 A4
Bury Street
The Flower Walk SW7 ...... 146 B3
The Grange SE1 ...... 150 A1
The Highway E1 & E14 ...... 150 C2
The Limes W2 ...... 142 A1
The Little Boltons SW10 & SW5 ...... 146 B1
The Mall SW1 ...... 148 A4
The Mitre E14 ...... 151 F3
The Piazza WC2 ...... 144 B1
The Vale SW3 ...... 146 C1
Theed Street SE1 ...... 149 D4
Theobald Street SE1 ...... 149 F2
New Kent Road
Theobold's Road WC1 ...... 144 C3
Theseus Walk N1 ...... 145 E4
Rocliffe Street
Thirleby Road SE1 ...... 148 A3
Thistle Grove SW10 ...... 146 B1
Thomas Doyle Street SE1 ...... 149 D3
Thomas More Street E1 ...... 150 B2
Thomas Place W8 ...... 146 A3
St Mary's Place
Thomas Road E14 ...... 151 F4
Thoresby Street N1 ...... 145 E4
Thorney Street SW1 ...... 148 B2
Thorngate Road W9 ...... 142 A3

Thornton Place W1 ...... 143 D3
Thrale Street SE1 ...... 149 E4
Thrawl Street E1 ...... 150 B4
Threadneedle Street EC2 ...... 145 F2
Three Colt Street E14 ...... 151 F3
Three Cranes Walk EC4 ...... 145 E1
Three Kings Yard W1 ...... 143 E1
Three Oak Lane SE1 ...... 150 A2
Thrush Street SE17 ...... 149 E1
Thurland Road SE16 ...... 150 B1
Thurloe Close SW7 ...... 146 C2
Thurloe Place SW7 ...... 146 C2
Thurloe Place Mews SW7 ...... 146 C2
Thurloe Square SW7 ...... 146 C2
Thurloe Street SW7 ...... 146 C2
Thurlow Street SE17 ...... 149 F2
Tillman Street E1 ...... 150 C3
Tilney Street W1 ...... 147 E4
Timber Street EC1 ...... 145 E3
Timberland Road E1 ...... 150 C3
Timberpond Road SE16 ...... 151 E2
Tinsley Road E1 ...... 151 D4
Tinworth Street SE11 ...... 148 B2
Titchborne Row W2 ...... 142 C2
Tite Street SW3 ...... 147 D1
Tiverton Street SE1 ...... 149 E3
Tivoli Court SE16 ...... 151 F2
Tokenhouse Yard EC2 ...... 145 F2
Tolmers Square NW1 ...... 144 A3
Tonbridge Street WC1 ...... 144 B4
Took's Court EC4 ...... 144 C2
Tooley Street SE1 ...... 150 A2
Topham Street EC1 ...... 145 D3
Tor Gardens W8 ...... 146 A4
Torquay Street W2 ...... 142 A2
Torrens Street EC1 ...... 145 D4
Torrington Place E1 ...... 150 C1
Torrington Place WC1 ...... 144 A3
Tothill Street SW1 ...... 148 A3
Tottenham Court Road W1 ...... 144 A3
Tottenham Street W1 ...... 144 A3
Toulmin Street SE1 ...... 149 E3
Toussaint Walk SE16 ...... 150 B1
Tower Bridge E1 & SE1 ...... 150 A2
Tower Bridge Approach E1 ...... 150 B2
Tower Bridge Road SE1 ...... 150 A1
Tower Court WC2 ...... 144 B1
Monmouth Street
Tower Hill EC3 ...... 150 A3
Tower Hill Terrace EC3 ...... 150 A3
Gloucester Close
Tower Street WC2 ...... 144 B1
Townley Street SE1 ...... 149 E2
Townsend Street SE17 ...... 149 F2
Toynbee Street E1 ...... 150 B4
Tracey Street SE11 ...... 148 C2
Trafalgar Gardens E1 ...... 151 E4
Trafalgar Gardens W8 ...... 146 A3
South End Row
Trafalgar Square WC2 ...... 144 B1
Tranley Street SE17 ...... 149 F1
Tranton Road SE16 ...... 150 C1
Trebeck Street W1 ...... 147 E4
Curzon Street
Trebovir Road SW5 ...... 146 A2
Tregunter Road SW10 ...... 146 B1
Tresham Crescent NW8 ...... 142 C4
Treveris Street SE1 ...... 149 D4
Bear Lane
Trevor Place SW7 ...... 147 D3
Trevor Square SW7 ...... 147 D3
Trevor Street SW7 ...... 147 D3
Trinidad Street E14 ...... 151 F3
Trinity Church Square SE1 ...... 149 E3
Trinity Place EC3 ...... 150 A3
Trinity Square
Trinity Square EC3 ...... 150 A3
Trinity Street SE1 ...... 149 E3
Trio Place SE1 ...... 149 E3
Triton Square NW1 ...... 143 F3
Troon Street E1 ...... 151 E4
Trumans Street SE16 ...... 150 C1
Trump Street EC2 ...... 145 E2
Tryon Street SW3 ...... 147 D2
Tudor Street EC4 ...... 145 D1
Tufton Street SW1 ...... 148 B3
Tunley Green E14 ...... 151 F4
Tunnel Road SE16 ...... 151 D2
Turk's Row SW3 ...... 147 E1
Turner Street E1 ...... 150 C4
Turnmill Street EC1 ...... 145 D3
Turpentine Lane SW1 ...... 147 F1
Turquand Street SE17 ...... 149 E2
Twine Court E1 ...... 150 C3
Twyford Place WC2 ...... 144 C2
Kingsway
Tyers Gate SE1 ...... 149 F3
Tyers Street SE11 ...... 148 C1
Tyers Terrace SE11 ...... 148 C1
Tyne Street E1 ...... 150 B4
Tysoe Street EC1 ...... 145 D4

U

Udall Street SW1 ...... 148 A2
Ufford Street SE1 ...... 149 D3
Ulster Place NW1 ...... 143 E3
Umberston Street E1 ...... 150 C4
Undershaft EC3 ...... 145 F2
Underwood Row N1 ...... 145 E4
Shepherdess Walk
Underwood Street N1 ...... 145 E4
Union Street SE1 ...... 149 D4
University Street WC1 ...... 144 A3
Upbrook Mews W2 ...... 142 B2
Upper Belgrave Street SW1 ...... 147 E3
Upper Berkeley Street W1 ...... 143 D1
Upper Brook Street W1 ...... 143 E1
Upper Cheyne Row SW3 ...... 146 C1
Upper Grosvenor Street W1 ...... 143 E1
Upper Ground SE1 ...... 145 D1
Upper Harley Street NW1 ...... 143 E3
Upper James Street W1 ...... 144 A1
Upper John Street W1 ...... 144 A1
Upper Marsh SE1 ...... 148 C3
Upper Montagu Street W1 ...... 143 D3
Upper St Martin's Lane WC2 ...... 144 B1
Upper Tachbrook Street SW1 ...... 148 A2
Upper Thames Street EC4 ...... 145 E1
Upper Wimpole Street W1 ...... 143 E3
Upper Woburn Place WC1 ...... 144 B3

V

Vale Close W9 ...... 142 B4
Valentine Place SE1 ...... 149 D3
Valentine Row SE1 ...... 149 D3
Vandon Passage SW1 ...... 148 A3
Vandon Street SW1 ...... 148 A3
Vandy Street EC2 ...... 145 F3
Vane Street SW1 ...... 148 A2
Varden Street E1 ...... 150 C4
Varndell Street NW1 ...... 143 F4
Vauban Street SE16 ...... 150 B1
Vaughan Street SE16 ...... 151 F1
Vaughan Way E1 ...... 150 B2
Vauxhall Bridge SW1 & SE1 ...... 148 B2
Vauxhall Bridge Road SW1 ...... 147 F2
Vauxhall Grove SW8 ...... 148 B1
Vauxhall Street SE11 ...... 148 C1
Vauxhall Walk SE11 ...... 148 C2
Venables Street NW8 ...... 142 C3
Vere Street W1 ...... 143 E2
Vernon Place WC1 ...... 144 B2
Vernon Rise WC1 ...... 144 C4
Vernon Square WC1 ...... 144 C4
Penton Rise
Vernon Street W14 ...... 144 C4
Verulam Street WC1 ...... 144 C3
Vestry Street N1 ...... 145 F4
Vicarage Court W8 ...... 146 A4
Vicarage Gardens W8 ...... 146 A4
Vicarage Gate W8 ...... 146 A4
Victoria Avenue EC2 ...... 150 A4
Victoria Embankment SW1, WC2 & EC4 ...... 144 C1
Victoria Grove W8 ...... 146 B3
Victoria Road W8 ...... 146 B3
Victoria Street SW1 ...... 147 F3
Victory Place SE17 ...... 149 F2
Victory Place E14 ...... 151 E3
Victory Way SE16 ...... 151 E1
Vigo Street W1 ...... 144 A1
Villa Street SE17 ...... 149 F1
Villiers Street WC2 ...... 144 B1
Vince Street EC1 ...... 145 F4
Vincent Close SE16 ...... 151 E1
Vincent Square SW1 ...... 148 A2
Vincent Street SW1 ...... 148 A2
Vine Court E1 ...... 150 C4
Vine Lane SE1 ...... 150 A2
Vine Street EC3 ...... 150 A3
Vine Street W1 ...... 144 A1
Vine Street Bridge EC1 ...... 145 D3
Farringdon Lane
Vinegar Street E1 ...... 150 C2
Vinegar Yard SE1 ...... 149 F4
St Thomas Street
Vineyard Walk EC1 ...... 145 D3
Pine Street
Vintner's Place EC4 ...... 145 E1
Violet Hill NW8 ...... 142 B4
Virgil Place W1 ...... 143 D2
Seymour Place
Virgil Street SE1 ...... 148 C3
Virginia Street E1 ...... 150 B3
Viscount Street EC1 ...... 145 E3

W

Wadding Street SE17 ...... 149 E2
Waithman Street EC4 ...... 145 D2
Pilgrim Street
Wakefield Mews WC1 ...... 144 B4
Wakefield Street
Wakefield Street WC1 ...... 144 B4
Wakeling Street E14 ...... 151 E3
Wakley Street EC1 ...... 145 D4
Walbrook EC4 ...... 145 F1
Walburgh Street E1 ...... 150 C3
Walcorde Avenue SE17 ...... 149 E2
Walcot Square SE11 ...... 149 D2
Walden Street E1 ...... 150 C4
Waley Street E1 ...... 151 E4
Wallgrave Road SW5 ...... 146 A2
Wallwood Street E14 ...... 151 F4
Walmer Street W1 ...... 143 D3
Seymour Place
Walnut Tree Walk SE11 ...... 148 C2
Walpole Street SW3 ...... 147 D2
Walter Terrace E1 ...... 151 E4
Walton Place SW3 ...... 147 D3
Walton Street SW3 ...... 147 D3
Walton's Mews W1 ...... 143 D2
Walworth Place SE17 ...... 149 E1
Walworth Road SE1 & SE17 ...... 149 E2
Wansey Street SE17 ...... 149 E2
Wapping Dock Street E1 ...... 150 C2
Wapping High Street E1 ...... 150 B2
Wapping Lane E1 ...... 150 C3
Wapping Walk E1 ...... 150 C3
Wapping Wall E1 ...... 151 D2
Wardour Street W1 ...... 144 A2
Warner Street EC1 ...... 144 C3
Warren Street W1 ...... 143 F3
Warrington Crescent W9 ...... 142 B3
Warrington Gardens W9 ...... 142 B3
Warwick Avenue W9 ...... 142 A3
Warwick Court WC1 ...... 144 C2
Warwick Crescent W2 ...... 142 B3
Warwick House Street SW1 ...... 148 B4
Warwick Lane EC4 ...... 145 E2
Warwick Passage EC4 ...... 145 D2
Warwick Square
Warwick Place W9 ...... 142 B3
Warwick Row SW1 ...... 147 F3
Warwick Square SW1 ...... 148 A2
Warwick Square EC4 ...... 145 D2
Warwick Street W1 ...... 144 A1
Warwick Way SW1 ...... 147 F2
Water Lane EC3 ...... 150 A3
Watergate EC4 ...... 145 D2
New Bridge Street
Watergate Walk WC2 ...... 144 B1
Villiers Street
Waterloo Bridge WC2 & SE1 ...... 144 C1
Waterloo Road SE1 ...... 148 A4
Waterman Way E1 ...... 150 C2
Waterman's Walk EC4 ...... 145 F1
Waterside Close SE16 ...... 150 B1
Watling Street EC4 ...... 145 E2
Watney Market E1 ...... 150 C4
Watney Street E1 ...... 150 C3

Watson's Street SE8 ...... 150 C2
Watts Way SW7 ...... 146 C3
Waveney Close E1 ...... 150 B2
Waverton Street W1 ...... 147 E4
Weavers Lane SE1 ...... 150 A2
Webb Street SE1 ...... 149 F3
Webber Row SE1 ...... 149 D3
Webber Street SE1 ...... 149 D3
Webster Road SE16 ...... 150 C1
Weighouse Street W1 ...... 143 E1
Welbeck Street W1 ...... 143 E2
Welbeck Way W1 ...... 143 E2
Well Court EC4 ...... 145 E1
Queen Street
Welland Mews E1 ...... 150 C1
Wellclose Square E1 ...... 150 B3
Wellclose Street E1 ...... 150 C3
The Highway
Weller Street SE1 ...... 149 E3
Wellesley Street E1 ...... 151 D4
Wellesley Terrace N1 ...... 145 E4
Wellington Place NW8 ...... 142 C4
Wellington Road NW8 ...... 142 C4
Wellington Square SW3 ...... 147 D1
Wellington Street WC2 ...... 144 C1
Wells Mews W1 ...... 144 A2
Wells Square WC1 ...... 144 C4
Wells Street W1 ...... 143 F2
Wendover SE17 ...... 149 F1
Wenlock Road N1 ...... 145 E4
Wenlock Street N1 ...... 145 E4
Wentworth Market E1 ...... 150 B4
Wentworth Street
Wentworth Street E1 ...... 150 B4
Werrington Street NW1 ...... 144 A4
Wesley Close SE17 ...... 149 D2
Wesley Street W1 ...... 143 E2
Weymouth Street
West Arbour Street E1 ...... 151 D4
West Central Street WC1 ...... 144 B2
West Eaton Place SW1 ...... 147 E3
West Gardens E1 ...... 150 C3
West Halkin Street SW1 ...... 147 E3
West India Dock Road E14 ...... 151 F3
West Lane SE16 ...... 150 C1
West Mews SW1 ...... 147 F2
Warwick Way
West Poultry Avenue EC1 ...... 145 D2
West Smithfield
West Road SW4 ...... 147 D1
West Smithfield EC1 ...... 145 D2
West Square SE11 ...... 149 D2
West Street WC2 ...... 144 B1
West Tenter Street E1 ...... 150 B3
Westbourne Crescent W2 ...... 142 B2
Westbourne Gardens W2 ...... 142 A2
Westbourne Grove W2 & W11 ...... 142 A2
Westbourne Grove Terrace W2 ...... 142 A2
Westbourne Park Road W2 & W11 ...... 142 A1
Westbourne Park Villas W2 ...... 142 A1
Westbourne Terrace W2 ...... 142 B2
Westbourne Terrace Mews W2 ...... 142 B2
Westbourne Terrace Road W2 ...... 142 B2
Westcott Road SE17 ...... 149 D1
Western Place SE16 ...... 151 D2
Westgate Terrace SW10 ...... 146 A1
Westland Place N1 ...... 145 F4
Westminster Bridge SW1 & SE1 ...... 148 B3
Westminster Bridge Road SE1 ...... 148 B3
Westmoreland Place SW1 ...... 147 F1
Westmoreland Road SE17 ...... 149 E1
Westmoreland Street W1 ...... 143 E2
Westmoreland Terrace SW1 ...... 147 F1
Weston Rise WC1 ...... 144 C4
Weston Street SE1 ...... 149 F3
Westport Street E1 ...... 151 E4
Westway W12 ...... 142 B2
Wetherby Gardens SW5 ...... 146 B2
Wetherby Mews SW5 ...... 146 A2
Earls Court Road
Wetherby Place SW7 ...... 146 B2
Weymouth Mews W1 ...... 143 F2
Weymouth Street W1 ...... 143 E2
Wharf Road N1 ...... 145 E4
Wharfedale Street SW10 ...... 146 A1
Wharton Street WC1 ...... 144 C4
Wheatley Street W1 ...... 143 E2
Marylebone Street
Whetstone Park WC2 ...... 144 C2
Whidborne Street WC1 ...... 144 B4
Whiskin Street EC1 ...... 145 D4
Whitcomb Street WC2 ...... 144 A1
White Church Lane E1 ...... 150 B4
White Hart Street SE11 ...... 149 D2
White Horse Lane E1 ...... 151 E4
White Horse Mews SE1 ...... 149 D3
White Horse Road E1 ...... 151 E3
White Horse Street W1 ...... 147 F4
White Kennet Street E1 ...... 150 A4
White Lion Hill EC4 ...... 145 E1
White's Grounds SE1 ...... 150 A1
White's Row E1 ...... 150 A4
Whitechapel High Street E1 ...... 150 B4
Whitechapel Road E1 ...... 150 B4
Whitecross Place EC2 ...... 145 F3
Whitecross Street EC1 ...... 145 E3
Whitefriars Street EC4 ...... 145 D2
Whitehall SW1 ...... 148 B4
Whitehall Court SW1 ...... 148 B4
Whitehall Place SW1 ...... 148 B4
Whitehaven Street NW8 ...... 142 C3
Whitehead's Grove SW3 ...... 147 D2
Whitfield Place W1 ...... 144 A3
Whitfield Street
Whittlesey Street SE1 ...... 149 D4
Whitgift Street SE11 ...... 148 C2
Whittaker Street SW1 ...... 147 E2
Whittington Avenue EC3 ...... 145 F2
Leadenhall Street
Whittlesey Street SE1 ...... 149 D4
Wickham Street SE11 ...... 148 C1
Wicklow Street WC1 ...... 144 C4
Widegate Street E1 ...... 150 A4
Middlesex Street
Widley Road W9 ...... 142 A4
Wigmore Place W1 ...... 143 E2
Wigmore Street W1 ...... 143 E2
Wilbraham Place SW1 ...... 147 E2
Wilcox Place SW1 ...... 148 A3
Wild Court WC2 ...... 144 C2
Wild Street WC2 ...... 144 B2
Wild's Rents SE1 ...... 149 F3
Wilfred Street SW1 ...... 147 F3
Wilkes Street E1 ...... 150 B4
William IV Street WC2 ...... 144 B1
William Mews SW1 ...... 147 E3
William Road NW1 ...... 143 F4
William Square SE16 ...... 151 E3
William Street SW1 ...... 147 D3

Willoughby Street WC1 ...... 144 B2
Streatham Street
Willow Place SW1 ...... 148 A2
Willow Street EC2 ...... 145 F3
Wilmington Square WC1 ...... 145 D4
Wilmington Street WC1 ...... 145 D4
Wilson Grove SE16 ...... 150 C1
Wilson Street EC2 ...... 145 F2
Wilson's Place E14 ...... 151 F3
Wilton Crescent SW1 ...... 147 E3
Wilton Mews SW1 ...... 147 E3
Wilton Place SW1 ...... 147 E3
Wilton Road SW1 ...... 147 F2
Wilton Row SW1 ...... 147 E3
Wilton Street SW1 ...... 147 E3
Wilton Terrace SW1 ...... 147 E3
Wimpole Mews W1 ...... 143 E2
Wimpole Street W1 ...... 143 E2
Winchester Close SE17 ...... 149 D2
Winchester Square SE1 ...... 149 F4
Winchester Walk
Winchester Street SW1 ...... 147 F1
Winchester Walk SE1 ...... 149 F4
Wincott Street SE11 ...... 149 D2
Windmill Row SE11 ...... 149 D1
Windmill Street W1 ...... 144 A2
Windmill Walk SE1 ...... 149 D4
Windrose Close SE16 ...... 151 D2
Windsor Terrace N1 ...... 145 E4
Wine Close E1 ...... 150 C2
Wine Office Court EC4 ...... 145 D2
Winnett Street W1 ...... 144 A1
Rupert Street
Winsland Mews W2 ...... 142 C2
Winsland Street W2 ...... 142 C2
Winsley Street W1 ...... 144 A2
Winterton Place SW10 ...... 146 B1
Woburn Place WC1 ...... 144 B3
Woburn Square WC1 ...... 144 B3
Woburn Walk WC1 ...... 144 B3
Upper Woburn Place
Wolfe Crescent SE16 ...... 151 D1
Wolseley Street SE1 ...... 150 B1
Wood Street EC2 ...... 145 E2
Wood's Mews W1 ...... 143 E1
Wood's Place SE1 ...... 150 A1
Woodbridge Street EC1 ...... 145 D3
Woodchester Square W2 ...... 142 A3
Woodfall Street SW3 ...... 147 D1
Woodland Crescent SE16 ...... 151 D1
Woodstock Mews W1 ...... 143 E2
Westmoreland Street
Woodstock Street W1 ...... 143 F2
Woolaston Close SE1 ...... 149 E2
Wooster Street SE17 ...... 149 F1
Wooster Place SE1 ...... 149 F2
Wootton Street SE1 ...... 149 D4
Worgan Street SE11 ...... 148 C2
Wormwood Street EC2 ...... 145 F2
Worship Street EC2 ...... 145 F3
Wren Street WC1 ...... 144 C3
Wright's Lane W8 ...... 146 A3
Wyatt Close SE16 ...... 151 F1
Wybert Street NW1 ...... 143 F3
Laxton Place
Wyclif Street EC1 ...... 145 D4
Wymering Road W9 ...... 142 A4
Wyndham Mews W1 ...... 143 D2
Wyndham Place W1 ...... 143 D2
Wyndham Street W1 ...... 143 D2
Wyndham Yard W1 ...... 143 D2
Wynnstay Gardens W8 ...... 146 A3
Wynyard Place SE11 ...... 148 C1
Wynyatt Street EC1 ...... 145 D4
Wythburn Place W1 ...... 143 D2

Y

Yardley Street WC1 ...... 144 C4
Yarmouth Place W1 ...... 147 E4
Yeoman's Row SW3 ...... 147 D3
York Buildings WC2 ...... 144 B1
York Gate NW1 ...... 143 E3
York House Place W8 ...... 146 A4
York Road SE1 ...... 148 C3
York Square E14 ...... 151 E4
York Street W1 ...... 143 D3
York Terrace East NW1 ...... 143 E3
York Terrace West NW1 ...... 143 E3
Yorkshire Road E14 ...... 151 E3
Young Street W8 ...... 146 A3

Z

Zoar Street SE1 ...... 149 E4

index to place names

Place names are listed alphabetically. Each place name is followed by its County, County Borough or Council Area name, the page number and the reference to the square in which the name is found.

100 places of interest are indexed in red.

Airports are indexed in blue.

159

Scotland

Aber C	**Aberdeen City**
Abers	**Aberdeenshire**
Angus	**Angus**
Ag & B	**Argyll & Bute**
Border	**Borders (Scottish)**
C Edin	**City of Edinburgh**
C Glas	**City of Glasgow**
Clacks	**Clackmannanshire**
D & G	**Dumfries & Galloway**
Dund C	**Dundee City**
E Ayrs	**East Ayrshire**
E Duns	**East Dunbartonshire**
E Loth	**East Lothian**
E Rens	**East Renfrewshire**
Falk	**Falkirk**
Fife	**Fife**
Highld	**Highland**
Inver	**Inverclyde**
Mdloth	**Midlothian**
Moray	**Moray**
N Ayrs	**North Ayrshire**
N Lans	**North Lanarkshire**
Ork	**Orkney Islands**
P & K	**Perth & Kinross**
Rens	**Renfrewshire**
Shet	**Shetland Islands**
S Ayrs	**South Ayrshire**
S Lans	**South Lanarkshire**
Stirlg	**Stirling**
W Isls	**Western Isles**
W Duns	**West Dunbartonshire**
W Loth	**West Lothian**

Wales

Blae G	**Blaenau Gwent**
Brdgnd	**Bridgend**
Caerph	**Caerphilly**
Cardif	**Cardiff**
Carmth	**Carmarthenshire**
Cerdgn	**Ceredigion**
Conwy	**Conwy**
Denbgs	**Denbighshire**
Flints	**Flintshire**
Gwynd	**Gwynedd**
IOA	**Isle of Anglesey**
Myr Td	**Merthyr Tydfil**
Mons	**Monmouthshire**
Neath	**Neath Port Talbot**
Newpt	**Newport**
Pembks	**Pembrokeshire**
Powys	**Powys**
Rhondd	**Rhondda Cynon Taff**
Swans	**Swansea**
Torfn	**Torfaen**
V Glam	**Vale of Glamorgan**
Wrexhm	**Wrexham**

The Channel Islands & Isle of Man

Guern	**Guernsey**
Jersey	**Jersey**
IOM	**Isle of Man**

England

Beds	**Bedfordshire**
Berks	**Berkshire**
Bristl	**Bristol**
Bucks	**Buckinghamshire**
Cambs	**Cambridgeshire**
Ches	**Cheshire**
Cnwll	**Cornwall**
Cumb	**Cumbria**
Derbys	**Derbyshire**
Devon	**Devon**
Dorset	**Dorset**
Dur	**Durham**
E R Yk	**East Riding of Yorkshire**
E Susx	**East Sussex**
Essex	**Essex**
Gloucs	**Gloucestershire**
Gt Lon	**Greater London**
Gt Man	**Greater Manchester**
Hants	**Hampshire**
Herefs	**Herefordshire**
Herts	**Hertfordshire**
IOW	**Isle of Wight**
IOS	**Isles of Scilly**
Kent	**Kent**
Lancs	**Lancashire**
Leics	**Leicestershire**
Lincs	**Lincolnshire**
Mersyd	**Merseyside**
Norfk	**Norfolk**
N York	**North Yorkshire**
Nhants	**Northamptonshire**
Nthumb	**Northumberland**
Notts	**Nottinghamshire**
Oxon	**Oxfordshire**
Rutlnd	**Rutland**
Shrops	**Shropshire**
Somset	**Somerset**
S York	**South Yorkshire**
Staffs	**Staffordshire**
Suffk	**Suffolk**
Surrey	**Surrey**
T & W	**Tyne & Wear**
Warwks	**Warwickshire**
W Mids	**West Midlands**
W Susx	**West Sussex**
W York	**West Yorkshire**
Wilts	**Wiltshire**
Worcs	**Worcestershire**

A'Chill Arileod

A

A'Chill Highld 96 B3
Ab Kettleby Leics 41 H5
Abbas Combe Somset 17 H2
Abberley Worcs 39 G3
Abberley Common Worcs 39 G3
Abberton Essex 34 D1
Abberton Worcs 30 B5
Abbess Roding Essex 22 B6
Abbey Dore Herefs 28 B5
Abbey Green Staffs 50 B3
Abbey St Bathans Border 87 G2
Abbey Town Cumb 71 E4
Abbey Village Lancs 57 F5
Abbey Wood Gt Lon 21 G3
Abbeydale S York 50 D5
Abbeystead Lancs 63 E2
Abbot's Salford Warwks 30 C5
Abbotrule Border 80 C2
Abbots Bickington Devon 14 D2
Abbots Bromley Staffs 40 C5
Abbots Deuglie P & K 92 D1
Abbots Langley Herts 20 D5
Abbots Leigh Somset 17 F6
Abbots Morton Worcs 30 B5
Abbots Ripton Cambs 32 D6
Abbots Worthy Hants 9 G6
Abbotsbury Dorset 7 G4
Abbotsham Devon 14 D4
Abbotskerswell Devon 6 A3
Abbotsley Cambs 32 D4
Abbott Street Dorset 8 C3
Abbotts Ann Hants 19 E1
Abdon Shrops 39 F4
Aber-nant Rhondd 27 F3
Aberaeron Cerdgn 36 D3
Aberaman Rhondd 27 F3
Aberangell Gwynd 47 G3
Aberarder Highld 99 E5
Aberargie P & K 92 D1
Aberarth Cerdgn 36 D3
Aberavon Neath 26 D2
Abercairny P & K 92 B2
Abercanaid Myr Td 27 F3
Abercarn Caerph 27 G2
Abercastle Pembks 24 C5
Abercegir Powys 47 G2
Aberchalder Lodge Highld 98 B3
Aberchirder Abers 102 C4
Abercraf Powys 26 D4
Abercregan Neath 26 D2
Abercwmboi Rhondd 27 F3
Abercych Pembks 36 B1
Abercynon Rhondd 27 F2
Aberdalgie P & K 92 D2
Aberdare Rhondd 27 F3
Aberdaron Gwynd 46 B4
Aberdeen Aber C 95 H6
Aberdeen Airport Aber C 103 E1
Aberdour Fife 86 C4
Aberdulais Neath 26 D3
Aberdyfi Gwynd 47 E1
Aberedw Powys 38 B1
Abereiddy Pembks 24 C5
Abererch Gwynd 46 D5
Aberfan Myr Td 27 F3
Aberfeldy P & K 92 B4
Aberffraw IOA 54 C3
Aberford W York 59 E4
Aberfoyle Stirlg 85 E5
Abergavenny Mons 28 B4
Abergele Conwy 55 G4
Abergorlech Carmth 26 B5
Abergwesyn Powys 37 G2
Abergwili Carmth 25 H4
Abergwynfi Neath 27 E2
Abergwyngregyn Gwynd 55 E3
Abergynolwyn Gwynd 47 F2
Aberkenfig Brdgnd 27 E1
Aberlady E Loth 87 E4
Aberlemno Angus 93 G4
Aberllefenni Powys 47 F3
Aberllynfi Powys 27 G6
Aberlour Moray 101 E4
Abermule Powys 38 B5
Abernant Carmth 25 G5
Abernethy P & K 92 D1
Abernyte P & K 93 E3
Aberporth Cerdgn 36 B2
Abersoch Gwynd 46 C4
Abersychan Torfn 28 A3
Aberthin V Glam 16 B6
Abertillery Blae G 27 G3
Abertridwr Caerph 27 G2
Abertridwr Powys 48 A2
Aberuthven P & K 92 C1
Aberystwyth Cerdgn 37 E5
Abingdon Oxon 19 G6
Abinger Surrey 10 D6
Abinger Hammer Surrey 10 D6
Abington Nhants 32 A4
Abington S Lans 78 C5
Abington Pigotts Cambs 33 E3
Ablington Gloucs 30 C1
Abney Derbys 50 D4
Aboyne Abers 95 E5
Abram Gt Man 57 F3
Abriachan Highld 98 D6
Abridge Essex 21 G5
Abson Gloucs 17 H6
Abthorpe Nhants 31 G4
Aby Lincs 53 F3
Acaster Malbis N York 59 G4
Acaster Selby N York 59 F4
Accrington Lancs 57 G5
Acha Ag & B 88 C4
Acha Mor W Isls 111 d6
Achahoish Ag & B 83 F3
Achalader P & K 92 D4
Achaleven Ag & B 90 B2
Achanalt Highld 106 B2
Achandunie Highld 107 E3
Achany Highld 107 E5
Acharacle Highld 89 G5
Acharn Highld 89 G4
Acharn P & K 92 A4
Achavanich Highld 110 C3
Achduart Highld 105 H6
Achfary Highld 108 C3
Achiltibuie Highld 105 H6
Achinhoan Ag & B 75 F3
Achintee Highld 97 G6
Achintraid Highld 97 F6
Achmelvich Highld 108 A2
Achmore Highld 97 F5
Achmore W Isls 111 d6
Achnacarnin Highld 108 A3
Achnacarry Highld 98 A2
Achnacloich Highld 96 D3
Achnaconeran Highld 98 C4
Achnacroish Ag & B 90 A3
Achnadrish Lodge Ag & B 89 E4
Achnafauld P & K 92 B3
Achnagarron Highld 107 F3
Achnaha Highld 89 E5
Achnahaird Highld 108 A1
Achnairn Highld 109 E1
Achnalea Highld 90 A5
Achnamara Ag & B 83 F4
Achnasheen Highld 106 B2
Achnashellach Station Highld 105 H1
Achnastank Moray 101 E3
Achosnich Highld 89 E5
Achranich Highld 89 G4
Achreamie Highld 110 A5
Achriabhach Highld 90 C5
Achriesgill Highld 108 C4
Achtoty Highld 109 F5
Achurch Nhants 42 C1
Achvaich Highld 107 F5
Ackergill Highld 110 D4
Acklam N York 66 B5
Acklam N York 60 B6
Ackleton Shrops 39 G5
Acklington Nthumb 73 F6
Ackton W York 59 E2
Ackworth Moor Top W York 59 E2
Acle Norfk 45 G3
Acock's Green W Mids 40 C2
Acol Kent 23 G2
Acomb N York 59 F5
Acomb Nthumb 72 D3
Aconbury Herefs 28 C5
Acton Ches 49 F4
Acton Gt Lon 21 E3
Acton Staffs 49 G3
Acton Suffk 34 C3
Acton Worcs 39 H3
Acton Beauchamp Herefs 39 F1
Acton Bridge Ches 49 F6
Acton Burnell Shrops 39 E6
Acton Green Herefs 39 F1
Acton Park Wrexhm 48 D4
Acton Round Shrops 39 F5
Acton Scott Shrops 39 E5
Acton Trussell Staffs 40 B5
Acton Turville Gloucs 18 A4
Adbaston Staffs 49 G2
Adber Dorset 17 G1
Adbolton Notts 51 G1
Adderbury Oxon 31 F3
Adderley Shrops 49 F3
Addiewell W Loth 86 A2
Addingham W York 58 C5
Addington Bucks 31 H3
Addington Kent 22 B2
Addiscombe Gt Lon 21 F2
Addlestone Surrey 20 D2
Addlethorpe Lincs 53 G2
Adeyfield Herts 20 D6
Adfa Powys 38 B6
Adforton Herefs 38 D3
Adisham Kent 23 G1
Adlestrop Gloucs 30 D3
Adlingfleet E R Yk 60 C2
Adlington Lancs 57 F4
Admaston Shrops 49 F1
Admaston Staffs 40 B5
Admington Warwks 30 D4
Adsborough Somset 16 D2
Adscombe Somset 16 D3
Adstock Bucks 31 H3
Adversane W Susx 10 D4
Advie Highld 100 D3
Adwick Le Street S York 59 F1
Adwick upon Dearne S York 51 F6
Ae D & G 78 D2
Ae Bridgend D & G 78 D2
Affleck Abers 102 B3
Affpuddle Dorset 8 A3
Affric Lodge Highld 98 A4
Afon-wen Flints 48 B6
Agglethorpe N York 65 E2
Aigburth Mersyd 56 D2
Aike E R Yk 60 D4
Aiketgate Cumb 71 G4
Aikton Cumb 71 F4
Ailsworth Cambs 42 D2
Ainderby Quernhow N York 65 G2
Ainderby Steeple N York 65 G3
Aingers Green Essex 35 E1
Ainsdale Mersyd 56 C4
Ainstable Cumb 71 H4
Ainthorpe N York 66 D4
Ainville W Loth 86 B2
Aird Ag & B 83 F5
Aird D & G 68 C3
Aird W Isls 111 e6
Aird a Mhulaidh W Isls 111 c5
Aird Asaig W Isls 111 c5
Aird Dhubh Highld 97 E6
Aird of Kinloch Ag & B 89 F2
Aird of Sleat Highld 96 D2
Aird Uig W Isls 111 c6
Airdeny Ag & B 90 B2
Airdrie N Lans 85 F2
Airdriehill N Lans 85 F2
Airds Bay Ag & B 90 B2
Airds of Kells D & G 69 G4
Airidh a bhruaich W Isls 111 c5
Airieland D & G 70 B5
Airlie Angus 93 E4
Airmyn E R Yk 60 B3
Airntully P & K 92 D3
Airor Highld 97 E3
Airth Falk 85 H4
Airton N York 58 A5
Aisby Lincs 52 B4
Aisby Lincs 42 C5
Aish Devon 5 G3
Aish Devon 6 A2
Aisholt Somset 16 D3
Aiskew N York 65 F2
Aislaby Dur 65 G4
Aislaby N York 67 E4
Aislaby N York 66 D2
Aisthorpe Lincs 52 B3
Aith Shet 111 l2
Akeld Nthumb 81 E3
Akeley Bucks 31 G4
Akenham Suffk 35 E3
Albaston Devon 5 E4
Alberbury Shrops 48 D1
Albourne W Susx 11 E4
Albrighton Shrops 49 E2
Albrighton Shrops 39 G6
Alburgh Norfk 45 F1
Albury Herts 33 F2
Albury Surrey 10 D6
Albury Heath Surrey 10 D6
Alcaig Highld 107 E2
Alcaston Shrops 39 E4
Alcester Warwks 30 C5
Alciston E Susx 11 G3
Alconbury Cambs 32 D6
Alconbury Weston Cambs 32 D6
Aldborough N York 59 E6
Aldborough Norfk 45 E5
Aldbourne Wilts 19 E4
Aldbrough E R Yk 61 F4
Aldbrough St John N York 65 F4
Aldbury Herts 20 C6
Aldcliffe Lancs 63 E2
Aldclune P & K 92 B5
Aldeburgh Suffk 35 G4
Aldeby Norfk 45 G2
Aldenham Herts 21 E5
Alderbury Wilts 8 D6
Alderford Norfk 45 E4
Alderholt Dorset 8 D4
Alderley Gloucs 29 E2
Alderley Edge Ches 57 H1
Aldermaston Berks 19 G3
Alderminster Warwks 30 D5
Aldershot Hants 20 B1
Alderton Gloucs 30 B3
Alderton Nhants 31 H4
Alderton Suffk 35 F3
Alderton Wilts 18 B5
Alderwasley Derbys 50 D2
Aldfield N York 58 D6
Aldford Ches 48 D5
Aldgate Rutlnd 42 C3
Aldham Essex 34 C2
Aldham Suffk 34 D3
Aldingbourne W Susx 10 C3
Aldingham Cumb 62 C3
Aldington Kent 13 E5
Aldington Worcs 30 C4
Aldington Corner Kent 13 E5
Aldivalloch Moray 101 F2
Aldochlay Ag & B 84 C4
Aldreth Cambs 33 F5
Aldridge W Mids 40 B3
Aldringham Suffk 35 G4
Aldsworth Gloucs 30 C1
Aldunie Moray 101 F2
Aldwark Derbys 50 D3
Aldwark N York 59 F6
Aldwick W Susx 10 C2
Aldwincle Nhants 32 C6
Aldworth Berks 19 G4
Alexandria W Duns 84 D3
Aley Somset 16 D3
Alfington Devon 6 C5
Alfold Surrey 10 D5
Alfold Crossways Surrey 10 D5
Alford Abers 102 B1
Alford Lincs 53 F3
Alford Somset 17 G2
Alfreton Derbys 51 E2
Alfrick Worcs 39 G2
Alfrick Pound Worcs 39 G2
Alfriston E Susx 11 G2
Algarkirk Lincs 43 E5
Alhampton Somset 17 G3
Alkborough Lincs 60 C2
Alkham Kent 13 G6
Alkmonton Derbys 50 C1
All Cannings Wilts 18 C3
All Saints South Elmham Suffk 35 F6
All Stretton Shrops 39 E5
Allaleigh Devon 5 H2
Allanaquoich Abers 94 A5
Allanbank N Lans 85 G2
Allanton Border 81 E5
Allanton N Lans 85 G2
Allanton S Lans 85 F1
Allaston Gloucs 28 D3
Allbrook Hants 9 F5
Allen End Warwks 40 C3
Allen's Green Herts 33 F1
Allendale Nthumb 72 C2
Allenheads Nthumb 72 C2
Allensmore Herefs 28 C6
Allenton Derbys 41 E6
Aller Devon 15 G3
Aller Somset 17 E2
Allerby Cumb 70 D3
Allercombe Devon 6 C5
Allerford Somset 16 A4
Allerston N York 67 E2
Allerthorpe E R Yk 60 B4
Allerton Highld 107 F3
Allerton Mersyd 56 D2
Allerton W York 58 C3
Allerton Bywater W York 59 E3
Allerton Mauleverer N York 59 E5
Allesley W Mids 40 D2
Allestree Derbys 51 E1
Allexton Leics 42 A2
Allgreave Ches 50 B3
Allhallows Kent 22 D3
Alligin Shuas Highld 105 F2
Allington Dorset 7 F5
Allington Lincs 42 B5
Allington Wilts 18 B4
Allington Wilts 18 C3
Allington Wilts 18 D1
Allithwaite Cumb 62 D4
Alloa Clacks 85 G5
Allonby Cumb 70 D3
Alloway S Ayrs 76 C3
Allowenshay Somset 17 E1
Alltchaorunn Highld 90 D4
Alltwalis Carmth 25 H5
Alltwen Neath 26 D3
Alltyblaca Cerdgn 36 D2
Allweston Dorset 17 G1
Almeley Herefs 38 D1
Almholme S York 59 G1
Almington Staffs 49 G3
Almondbank P & K 92 C2
Almondbury W York 58 C2
Almondsbury Gloucs 28 D1
Alne N York 59 F6
Alness Highld 107 F3
Alnham Nthumb 81 F1
Alnmouth Nthumb 81 G1
Alnwick Nthumb 81 G2
Alperton Gt Lon 21 E4
Alphamstone Essex 34 C2
Alpheton Suffk 34 C4
Alphington Devon 6 B4
Alport Derbys 50 D3
Alpraham Ches 49 F5
Alresford Essex 34 D1
Alrewas Staffs 40 C4
Alsager Ches 49 G5
Alsop en le Dale Derbys 50 C2
Alston Cumb 72 B2
Alston Devon 7 E5
Alston Sutton Somset 17 E4
Alstone Gloucs 29 G5
Alstonefield Staffs 50 C2
Alswear Devon 15 F3
Altandhu Highld 108 A1
Altarnun Cnwll 4 C5
Altass Highld 106 D5
Altcreich Ag & B 89 G3
Altgaltraig Ag & B 83 H3
Althorne Essex 22 D5
Althorpe Lincs 60 C1
Altnabreac Station Highld 110 A4
Altnacraig Ag & B 90 A2
Altnaharra Highld 109 E3
Alton Derbys 51 E3
Alton Hants 10 A5
Alton Staffs 50 C1
Alton Barnes Wilts 18 D3
Alton Pancras Dorset 7 H5
Alton Priors Wilts 18 D3
Alton Towers Staffs 50 C1
Altrincham Gt Man 57 G2
Altskeith Hotel Stirlg 84 D5
Alva Clacks 85 G5
Alvah Abers 102 C5
Alvanley Ches 49 E6
Alvaston Derbys 41 E6
Alvechurch Worcs 40 B1
Alvecote Warwks 40 D4
Alvediston Wilts 8 C5
Alveley Shrops 39 G4
Alverdiscott Devon 15 E3
Alverstoke Hants 9 G3
Alverstone IOW 9 G2
Alverthorpe W York 58 D2
Alverton Notts 42 A6
Alves Moray 100 D5
Alvescot Oxon 30 D1
Alveston Gloucs 28 D2
Alveston Warwks 30 D5
Alvingham Lincs 53 E4
Alvington Gloucs 28 D3
Alwalton Cambs 42 D2
Alwinton Nthumb 81 E1
Alwoodley W York 58 D4
Alyth P & K 93 E4
Ambergate Derbys 51 E2
Amberley Gloucs 29 F3
Amberley W Susx 10 D3
Amble Nthumb 81 H1
Amblecote W Mids 40 A2
Ambler Thorn W York 58 C3
Ambleside Cumb 62 D6
Ambleston Pembks 24 D5
Ambrosden Oxon 31 G2
Amcotts Lincs 60 C2
Amersham Bucks 20 C5
Amesbury Wilts 18 D1
Amhuinnsuidhe W Isls 111 c5
Amisfield Town D & G 78 D1
Amlwch IOA 54 C5
Ammanford Carmth 26 C4
Amotherby N York 66 D1
Ampfield Hants 9 F5
Ampleforth N York 66 C2
Ampney Crucis Gloucs 18 C6
Ampney St Mary Gloucs 18 D6
Ampney St Peter Gloucs 18 C6
Amport Hants 19 E1
Ampthill Beds 32 C3
Ampton Suffk 34 C5
Amroth Pembks 25 E3
Amulree P & K 92 B3
Amwell Herts 21 E6
An T-ob W Isls 111 c4
Anaheilt Highld 89 H5
Ancaster Lincs 42 C6
Ancroft Nthumb 81 F4
Ancrum Border 80 C3
Anderby Lincs 53 G3
Andover Hants 19 F2
Andoversford Gloucs 30 B2
Andreas IOM 116 c5
Anerley Gt Lon 21 F2
Anfield Mersyd 56 D2
Angarrack Cnwll 2 C3
Angelbank Shrops 39 F3
Angersleigh Somset 16 D1
Angle Pembks 24 C3
Angmering W Susx 10 D3
Angram N York 59 F4
Ankerville Highld 107 G3
Anlaby E R Yk 60 D3
Anmer Norfk 44 B5
Anmore Hants 9 H4
Anna Valley Hants 19 F1
Annan D & G 71 E5
Annat Highld 105 G2
Annathill N Lans 85 F3
Annbank S Ayrs 76 D4
Anne Hathaway's Cottage Warwks 30 C5
Annesley Notts 51 F2
Annesley Woodhouse Notts 51 F2
Annfield Plain Dur 73 F2
Anniesland C Glas 85 E3
Ansdell Lancs 56 D5
Ansford Somset 17 G2
Ansley Warwks 40 D3
Anslow Staffs 40 D5
Anslow Gate Staffs 40 D5
Anstey Herts 33 F2
Anstey Leics 41 F4
Anstruther Fife 87 F6
Ansty W Susx 11 F4
Ansty Warwks 41 E2
Ansty Wilts 8 C5
Anthorn Cumb 71 E5
Antingham Norfk 45 F5
Anton's Gowt Lincs 43 E6
Antony Cnwll 5 E3
Antrobus Ches 57 F1
Anwick Lincs 52 D1
Anwoth D & G 69 G3
Aperfield Gt Lon 21 G2
Apethorpe Nhants 42 C2
Apley Lincs 52 D3
Apperknowle Derbys 51 E4
Apperley Gloucs 29 F5
Appin Ag & B 90 B3
Appleby Lincs 60 D2
Appleby Magna Leics 40 D4
Appleby Parva Leics 40 D4
Appleby-in-Westmorland Cumb 64 B5
Applecross Highld 97 E6
Appledore Devon 14 D4
Appledore Devon 16 C1
Appledore Kent 13 E5
Appleford Oxon 19 G5
Applegarth Town D & G 78 D1
Appleshaw Hants 19 E2
Appleton Ches 57 E2
Appleton Ches 57 F1
Appleton Oxon 19 F6
Appleton Roebuck N York 59 F4
Appleton Thorn Ches 57 F1
Appleton Wiske N York 65 G4
Appleton-le-Moors N York 66 D2
Appleton-le-Street N York 66 D1
Appletreehall Border 80 B2
Appletreewick N York 58 B5
Appley Somset 16 C2
Appley Bridge Lancs 57 E3
Apse Heath IOW 9 G2
Apsley End Beds 32 D2
Apuldram W Susx 10 B2
Arabella Highld 107 G3
Arbirlot Angus 93 H3
Arboll Highld 107 G4
Arborfield Berks 20 B2
Arborfield Cross Berks 20 B2
Arbroath Angus 93 H3
Arbuthnott Abers 95 G4
Archddu Carmth 25 H3
Archdeacon Newton Dur 65 F5
Archencarroch W Duns 84 D4
Archiestown Moray 101 E4
Archirondel Jersey 7 c2
Arclid Green Ches 49 G5
Ardanaiseig Hotel Ag & B 90 C2
Ardaneaskan Highld 97 F5
Ardarroch Highld 97 F6
Ardbeg Ag & B 74 C5
Ardbeg Ag & B 84 A2
Ardbeg Ag & B 84 B4
Ardcharnich Highld 106 B4
Ardchiavaig Ag & B 89 E1
Ardchonnel Ag & B 83 G6
Ardchullarie More Stirlg 85 E6
Arddarroch Ag & B 84 B5
Ardechive Highld 98 A2
Ardeer N Ayrs 76 C5
Ardeley Herts 33 E2
Ardelve Highld 97 F5
Arden Ag & B 84 C4
Ardens Grafton Warwks 30 C5
Ardentallen Ag & B 90 A2
Ardentinny Ag & B 84 B4
Ardentraive Ag & B 83 H3
Ardeonaig Hotel Stirlg 91 G3
Ardersier Highld 107 G2
Ardessie Highld 105 H4
Ardfern Ag & B 83 F5
Ardgay Highld 107 E5
Ardgour Highld 90 B5
Ardgowan Inver 84 B3
Ardhallow Ag & B 84 B3
Ardhasig W Isls 111 c5
Ardheslaig Highld 105 F2
Ardindrean Highld 106 B4
Ardingly W Susx 11 F5
Ardington Oxon 19 F5
Ardlamont Ag & B 83 G2
Ardleigh Essex 34 D2
Ardleigh Heath Essex 34 D2
Ardler P & K 93 E3
Ardley Oxon 31 F3
Ardlui Ag & B 91 E1
Ardlussa Ag & B 83 E4
Ardmaddy Ag & B 90 C3
Ardmair Highld 106 A5
Ardmaleish Ag & B 84 A3
Ardminish Ag & B 75 E5
Ardmolich Highld 89 G6
Ardmore Ag & B 84 C3
Ardmore Highld 107 F4
Ardnadam Ag & B 84 B3
Ardnagrask Highld 106 D1
Ardnarff Highld 97 F5
Ardnastang Highld 89 H5
Ardno Ag & B 84 B6
Ardochy Lodge Hotel Highld 98 A3
Ardpatrick Ag & B 83 F2
Ardrishaig Ag & B 83 F4
Ardross Highld 107 E3
Ardrossan N Ayrs 76 B5
Ardsley East W York 58 D3
Ardslignish Highld 89 F5
Ardtalla Ag & B 82 D1
Ardtoe Highld 89 F5
Arduaine Ag & B 83 F6
Ardullie Highld 107 E2
Ardvasar Highld 96 D3
Ardvorlich P & K 91 G2
Ardvourlie W Isls 111 c5
Ardwell D & G 68 C2
Ardwick Gt Man 57 H2
Areley Kings Worcs 39 G3
Arevegaig Highld 89 G5
Arford Hants 10 B5
Argoed Caerph 27 G3
Aribruach W Isls 111 c5
Aridhglas Ag & B 88 D2
Arileod Ag & B 88 C4

160

Place	County	Page	Grid
Arinagour	Ag & B	88	C4
Ariogan	Ag & B	90	A2
Arisaig	Highld	97	E1
Arisaig House	Highld	97	E1
Arkendale	N York	59	E6
Arkesden	Essex	33	F2
Arkholme	Lancs	63	F3
Arkleton	D & G	79	G2
Arkley	Gt Lon	21	E5
Arksey	S York	59	F1
Arkwright Town	Derbys	51	E4
Arle	Gloucs	29	G5
Arlecdon	Cumb	70	D2
Arlesey	Beds	32	D2
Arleston	Shrops	49	F1
Arley	Ches	57	F1
Arley	Warwks	40	D3
Arlingham	Gloucs	29	E4
Arlington	Devon	15	E5
Arlington	E Susx	12	A3
Armadale	Highld	109	G5
Armadale	Highld	96	D3
Armadale	W Loth	85	H3
Armaside	Cumb	71	E2
Armathwaite	Cumb	71	H4
Arminghall	Norfk	45	F3
Armitage	Staffs	40	C5
Armley	W York	58	D3
Armston	Nhants	42	C1
Armthorpe	S York	59	G1
Arnabost	Ag & B	88	C5
Arncliffe	N York	64	D1
Arncroach	Fife	87	E6
Arndilly House	Moray	101	K4
Arne	Dorset	8	C2
Arnesby	Leics	41	G3
Arngask	P & K	92	D1
Arnisdale	Highld	97	F3
Arnish	Highld	104	D1
Arniston	Mdloth	86	D2
Arnol	W Isls	111	d7
Arnold	E R Yk	61	E4
Arnold	Notts	51	G2
Arnprior	Stirlg	85	E5
Arnside	Cumb	63	E4
Aros	Ag & B	89	F3
Arrad Foot	Cumb	62	C4
Arram	E R Yk	60	D4
Arrathorne	N York	65	F3
Arreton	IOW	9	G2
Arrina	Highld	105	F2
Arrington	Cambs	33	E4
Arrochar	Ag & B	84	C5
Arrow	Warwks	30	C5
Arscott	Shrops	38	D6
Artafallie	Highld	107	E1
Arthington	W York	58	D4
Arthingworth	Nhants	41	H2
Arthrath	Abers	103	E3
Artrochie	Abers	103	F3
Arundel	W Susx	10	D3
Asby	Cumb	70	D2
Ascog	Ag & B	84	A2
Ascot	Berks	20	C2
Ascott-under-Wychwood	Oxon	30	D2
Asenby	N York	65	G1
Asfordby	Leics	41	G5
Asfordby Hill	Leics	41	H5
Asgarby	Lincs	42	D6
Asgarby	Lincs	53	E2
Ash	Kent	22	B2
Ash	Kent	23	G2
Ash	Somset	17	F1
Ash	Surrey	20	C1
Ash Green	Surrey	20	C1
Ash Green	Warwks	41	E2
Ash Magna	Shrops	49	E3
Ash Mill	Devon	15	G3
Ash Parva	Shrops	49	F3
Ash Priors	Somset	16	C2
Ash Street	Suffk	34	D3
Ash Thomas	Devon	6	B6
Ash Vale	Surrey	20	C1
Ashampstead	Berks	19	G4
Ashbocking	Suffk	35	E4
Ashbocking Green	Suffk	35	E4
Ashbourne	Derbys	50	C2
Ashbrittle	Somset	16	C1
Ashburton	Devon	5	G4
Ashbury	Devon	15	E1
Ashbury	Oxon	19	E5
Ashby	Lincs	52	B6
Ashby by Partney	Lincs	53	F2
Ashby cum Fenby	Lincs	53	E5
Ashby de la Launde	Lincs	52	C1
Ashby Folville	Leics	41	G4
Ashby Magna	Leics	41	F2
Ashby Parva	Leics	41	F2
Ashby Puerorum	Lincs	53	E3
Ashby St Ledgers	Nhants	31	F6
Ashby St Mary	Norfk	45	F2
Ashby-de-la-Zouch	Leics	41	E5
Ashchurch	Gloucs	29	G5
Ashcombe	Devon	6	B4
Ashcombe	Somset	17	E5
Ashcott	Somset	17	F3
Ashdon	Essex	33	G3
Ashe	Hants	19	G2
Asheldham	Essex	23	E5
Ashen	Essex	34	B3
Ashendon	Bucks	31	G2
Asheridge	Bucks	20	C5
Ashfield	Stirlg	85	G5
Ashfield	Suffk	35	E5
Ashfield Green	Suffk	35	F5
Ashford	Devon	15	E4
Ashford	Devon	5	G2
Ashford	Kent	13	E6
Ashford	Surrey	20	D3
Ashford Bowdler	Shrops	39	E3
Ashford Carbonel	Shrops	39	E3
Ashford Hill	Hants	19	G3
Ashford in the Water	Derbys	50	D4
Ashgill	S Lans	77	G6
Ashill	Devon	6	C6
Ashill	Norfk	44	C3
Ashill	Somset	17	E1
Ashington	Essex	22	D4
Ashington	Nthumb	73	F5
Ashington	Somset	17	G1
Ashington	W Susx	11	E3
Ashkirk	Border	79	G5
Ashleworth	Gloucs	29	F5
Ashleworth Quay	Gloucs	29	F5
Ashley	Cambs	34	A4
Ashley	Ches	57	G1
Ashley	Devon	15	F2
Ashley	Gloucs	29	G2
Ashley	Hants	9	F6
Ashley	Hants	9	E3
Ashley	Kent	13	G6
Ashley	Nhants	42	A1
Ashley	Staffs	49	G3
Ashley	Wilts	18	A3
Ashley Green	Bucks	20	C5
Ashmansworth	Hants	19	F3
Ashmansworthy	Devon	14	C3
Ashmore	Dorset	8	B5
Ashmore Green	Berks	19	G4
Ashorne	Warwks	30	D5
Ashover	Derbys	51	E3
Ashow	Warwks	40	D1
Ashperton	Herefs	28	D6
Ashprington	Devon	5	H3
Ashreigney	Devon	15	F2
Ashtead	Surrey	21	E2
Ashton	Ches	49	E6
Ashton	Cnwll	2	C2
Ashton	Devon	6	A4
Ashton	Herefs	39	E3
Ashton	Inver	84	B3
Ashton	Nhants	31	H5
Ashton	Nhants	42	C1
Ashton Common	Wilts	18	B3
Ashton Keynes	Wilts	18	C6
Ashton under Hill	Worcs	30	B4
Ashton-in-Makerfield	Gt Man	57	F3
Ashton-under-Lyne	Gt Man	50	B6
Ashurst	Hants	9	E4
Ashurst	Kent	11	G5
Ashurst	W Susx	11	E4
Ashurstwood	W Susx	11	G5
Ashwater	Devon	5	E6
Ashwell	Herts	33	E3
Ashwell	Rutlnd	42	B3
Ashwell End	Herts	33	E3
Ashwellthorpe	Norfk	45	E2
Ashwick	Somset	17	G4
Ashwicken	Norfk	44	A4
Askam in Furness	Cumb	62	C4
Askern	S York	59	F2
Askerswell	Dorset	7	F5
Askett	Bucks	20	B5
Askham	Cumb	71	H2
Askham	Notts	51	H4
Askham Bryan	N York	59	F4
Askham Richard	N York	59	F4
Asknish	Ag & B	83	G4
Askrigg	N York	64	D3
Askwith	N York	58	C4
Aslackby	Lincs	42	C5
Aslacton	Norfk	45	E1
Aslockton	Notts	51	H1
Aspatria	Cumb	71	E3
Aspenden	Herts	33	E2
Aspley Guise	Beds	32	B2
Aspley Heath	Beds	32	B2
Aspull	Gt Man	57	F3
Asselby	E R Yk	60	B3
Assington	Suffk	34	C3
Assington Green	Suffk	34	B4
Astbury	Ches	49	H5
Astcote	Nhants	31	G5
Asterby	Lincs	53	E3
Asterley	Shrops	38	D6
Asterton	Shrops	38	D5
Asthall	Oxon	30	D2
Asthall Leigh	Oxon	30	D2
Astle	Highld	107	F5
Astley	Gt Man	57	F3
Astley	Shrops	49	E2
Astley	Warwks	40	D2
Astley	Worcs	39	G3
Astley Abbots	Shrops	39	G5
Astley Bridge	Gt Man	57	G4
Astley Cross	Worcs	39	G3
Aston	Berks	20	B4
Aston	Ches	57	E1
Aston	Ches	49	F4
Aston	Derbys	50	C5
Aston	Flints	48	C5
Aston	Herefs	39	E3
Aston	Herts	33	E1
Aston	Oxon	31	E1
Aston	S York	51	F5
Aston	Shrops	49	E2
Aston	Shrops	49	F1
Aston	Shrops	39	G5
Aston	Staffs	49	G3
Aston	Staffs	40	A5
Aston	Staffs	40	A6
Aston Abbotts	Bucks	32	B1
Aston Botterell	Shrops	39	F4
Aston Cantlow	Warwks	30	C5
Aston Clinton	Bucks	20	C6
Aston Crews	Herefs	29	E5
Aston End	Herts	33	E1
Aston Fields	Worcs	40	B1
Aston Flamville	Leics	41	F3
Aston Ingham	Herefs	29	E5
Aston le Walls	Nhants	31	F5
Aston Magna	Gloucs	30	D3
Aston Munslow	Shrops	39	E4
Aston on Clun	Shrops	38	D4
Aston Pigott	Shrops	38	D6
Aston Rogers	Shrops	38	D6
Aston Rowant	Oxon	20	A5
Aston Somerville	Worcs	30	B4
Aston Subedge	Gloucs	30	C4
Aston Tirrold	Oxon	19	G5
Aston Upthorpe	Oxon	19	G5
Aston-Eyre	Shrops	39	F5
Aston-upon-Trent	Derbys	41	E6
Astwood	Bucks	32	B3
Astwood	Worcs	30	B6
Astwood Bank	Worcs	30	B6
Aswarby	Lincs	42	C5
Aswardby	Lincs	53	F2
Atcham	Shrops	39	E6
Athelhampton	Dorset	8	A3
Athelington	Suffk	35	E5
Athelney	Somset	17	E2
Athelstaneford	E Loth	87	E4
Atherington	Devon	15	E3
Atherstone	Warwks	40	D3
Atherstone on Stour	Warwks	30	D5
Atherton	Gt Man	57	F3
Atlow	Derbys	50	D2
Attadale	Highld	97	G5
Atterby	Lincs	52	C4
Attercliffe	S York	51	E5
Atterton	Leics	41	E3
Attleborough	Norfk	44	D2
Attleborough	Warwks	41	E3
Attlebridge	Norfk	45	E4
Attleton Green	Suffk	34	B4
Atwick	E R Yk	61	E5
Atworth	Wilts	18	B3
Aubourn	Lincs	52	B2
Auchedly	Abers	103	E3
Auchenblae	Abers	95	F4
Auchenbowie	Stirlg	85	G4
Auchencairn	D & G	70	B4
Auchencairn	D & G	78	C1
Auchencairn	N Ayrs	75	H4
Auchencrow	Border	87	H2
Auchendinny	Mdloth	86	C2
Auchengray	S Lans	86	A2
Auchenhalrig	Moray	101	F5
Auchenheath	S Lans	77	G5
Auchenhessnane	D & G	77	G1
Auchenlochan	Ag & B	83	G3
Auchenmade	N Ayrs	76	C6
Auchenmalg	D & G	68	D3
Auchentiber	N Ayrs	76	C6
Auchentroig	Stirlg	85	E5
Auchindrean	Highld	106	B4
Auchininna	Abers	102	C4
Auchinleck	E Ayrs	77	E3
Auchinloch	N Lans	85	F3
Auchinstarry	N Lans	85	F3
Auchintore	Highld	90	C6
Auchiries	Abers	103	F3
Auchlee	Abers	95	G5
Auchleven	Abers	102	C2
Auchlochan	S Lans	77	G5
Auchlossan	Abers	95	E6
Auchlyne	Stirlg	91	F2
Auchmillan	E Ayrs	77	E4
Auchmithie	Angus	93	H4
Auchmuirbridge	Fife	86	C5
Auchnacree	Angus	94	D3
Auchnagatt	Abers	103	E3
Auchnarrow	Moray	101	E2
Auchnotteroch	D & G	68	B3
Auchroisk	Moray	101	F4
Auchterarder	P & K	92	C1
Auchteraw	Highld	98	C3
Auchterblair	Highld	99	G4
Auchtercairn	Highld	105	F3
Auchterderran	Fife	86	C5
Auchterhouse	Angus	93	F3
Auchterless	Abers	102	C3
Auchtermuchty	Fife	93	E1
Auchterneed	Highld	106	D2
Auchtertool	Fife	86	C5
Auchtertyre	Highld	97	F5
Auchtubh	Stirlg	91	G1
Auckengill	Highld	110	D5
Auckley	S York	51	G6
Audenshaw	Gt Man	50	A6
Audlem	Ches	49	F4
Audley	Staffs	49	G4
Audley End	Essex	33	G3
Audley End	Essex	33	G3
Audley End	Essex	34	C4
Aughertree	Cumb	71	F3
Aughton	E R Yk	60	B4
Aughton	Lancs	56	D3
Aughton	Lancs	63	E3
Aughton	S York	51	F5
Aughton	Wilts	19	E2
Aughton Park	Lancs	56	D3
Auldearn	Highld	100	C5
Aulden	Herefs	39	E2
Auldgirth	D & G	78	C2
Auldhouse	S Lans	77	E6
Ault a' chruinn	Highld	97	G4
Ault Hucknall	Derbys	51	F3
Aultbea	Highld	105	G4
Aultgrishin	Highld	105	F4
Aultguish Inn	Highld	106	C3
Aultmore	Moray	101	F4
Aultnagoire	Highld	98	D5
Aultnamain Inn	Highld	107	F4
Aunsby	Lincs	42	C5
Aust	Gloucs	28	D2
Austerfield	S York	51	G6
Austrey	Warwks	40	D4
Austwick	N York	63	G3
Authorpe	Lincs	53	F3
Avebury	Wilts	18	D4
Aveley	Essex	22	B3
Avening	Gloucs	29	F3
Averham	Notts	51	H2
Aveton Gifford	Devon	5	G2
Aviemore	Highld	99	G4
Avington	Berks	19	F3
Avoch	Highld	107	F2
Avon	Dorset	8	D3
Avon Dassett	Warwks	31	E5
Avonbridge	Falk	85	H3
Avonmouth	Bristl	28	C1
Avonwick	Devon	5	G3
Awbridge	Hants	9	E5
Awliscombe	Devon	6	C5
Awre	Gloucs	29	E3
Awsworth	Notts	51	F1
Axbridge	Somset	17	F4
Axford	Hants	19	H1
Axford	Wilts	19	E4
Axminster	Devon	6	D5
Axmouth	Devon	6	D4
Aycliffe	Dur	65	F5
Aydon	Nthumb	72	D3
Aylburton	Gloucs	28	D3
Aylesbeare	Devon	6	B5
Aylesbury	Bucks	20	B6
Aylesby	Lincs	52	D5
Aylesford	Kent	22	C2
Aylesham	Kent	23	G1
Aylestone	Leics	41	F3
Aylmerton	Norfk	45	E5
Aylsham	Norfk	45	E4
Aylton	Herefs	28	D6
Aylworth	Gloucs	30	C2
Aymestrey	Herefs	38	D3
Aynho	Nhants	31	F3
Ayot St Lawrence	Herts	32	D1
Ayr	S Ayrs	76	C3
Aysgarth	N York	64	D2
Ayshford	Devon	16	C1
Ayside	Cumb	62	D4
Ayston	Rutlnd	42	B2
Aythorpe Roding	Essex	22	B6
Ayton	Border	81	E5
Azerley	N York	65	F1

B

Place	County	Page	Grid
Babbacombe	Devon	6	B2
Babbs Green	Herts	33	F1
Babcary	Somset	17	G2
Babington	Somset	17	H4
Babraham	Cambs	33	G4
Babworth	Notts	51	G4
Back of Keppoch	Highld	97	E1
Backaland	Ork	111	h3
Backfolds	Abers	103	F4
Backford	Ches	48	D6
Backies	Highld	107	G5
Backlass	Highld	110	C4
Backwell	Somset	17	F5
Baconsthorpe	Norfk	45	E5
Bacton	Herefs	28	B5
Bacton	Norfk	45	F5
Bacton	Suffk	34	D5
Bacup	Lancs	57	H5
Badachro	Highld	105	F3
Badbury	Wilts	18	D4
Badby	Nhants	31	F5
Badcall	Highld	108	B3
Badcall	Highld	108	C4
Badcaul	Highld	105	H5
Baddeley Clinton	Warwks	40	D1
Baddesley Ensor	Warwks	40	D3
Baddidarroch	Highld	108	B2
Baddinsgill	Border	86	B2
Badenscoth	Abers	102	C3
Badenyon	Abers	101	F2
Badger	Shrops	39	G5
Badgeworth	Gloucs	29	F4
Badgworth	Somset	17	E4
Badicaul	Highld	97	E5
Badingham	Suffk	35	F5
Badlesmere	Kent	23	E1
Badlieu	Border	78	D4
Badlipster	Highld	110	C4
Badluarach	Highld	105	G5
Badninish	Highld	107	F5
Badrallach	Highld	105	H5
Badsey	Worcs	30	C4
Badshot Lea	Surrey	10	B6
Badsworth	W York	59	F2
Badwell Ash	Suffk	34	D5
Bag Enderby	Lincs	53	E3
Bagber	Dorset	17	H1
Bagby	N York	66	B2
Bagh a Chaisteil	W Isls	111	a1
Bagh a Tuath	W Isls	111	a1
Bagillt	Flints	48	C6
Baginton	Warwks	41	E1
Baglan	Neath	26	D2
Bagley	Shrops	48	D2
Bagley	Somset	17	F3
Bagmore	Hants	19	H2
Bagnall	Staffs	50	A2
Bagot	Shrops	39	F3
Bagshot	Surrey	20	C2
Bagstone	Gloucs	29	E2
Bagworth	Leics	41	E4
Bagwy Llydiart	Herefs	28	C5
Baildon	W York	58	C4
Baildon Green	W York	58	C4
Baile a Mhanaich	W Isls	111	b3
Baile Ailein	W Isls	111	d6
Baile Mor	Ag & B	88	D2
Baillieston	C Glas	85	F2
Bainbridge	N York	64	D2
Bainshole	Abers	102	B3
Bainton	Cambs	42	C3
Bainton	E R Yk	60	D5
Baintown	Fife	86	D6
Bairnkine	Border	80	C2
Bakewell	Derbys	50	D3
Bala	Gwynd	47	H5
Balallan	W Isls	111	d6
Balbeg	Highld	98	C5
Balbeggie	P & K	92	D2
Balblair	Highld	106	D1
Balblair	Highld	107	F3
Balby	S York	51	F6
Balcary	D & G	70	B4
Balchraggan	Highld	98	D6
Balchreick	Highld	108	B5
Balcombe	W Susx	11	F5
Balcomie Links	Fife	87	F6
Baldersby	N York	65	G2
Baldersby St James	N York	65	G1
Balderstone	Lancs	57	F5
Balderton	Notts	52	A1
Baldinnie	Fife	93	F1
Baldinnies	P & K	92	C1
Baldock	Herts	33	E2
Baldovie	Dund C	93	F3
Baldrine	IOM	116	c3
Baldslow	E Susx	12	C3
Bale	Norfk	44	D5
Baledgarno	P & K	93	E2
Balemartine	Ag & B	88	B3
Balerno	C Edin	86	B3
Balfarg	Fife	86	C6
Balfield	Angus	95	E3
Balfour	Ork	111	h2
Balfron	Stirlg	85	E4
Balgaveny	Abers	102	C3
Balgavies	Angus	93	G4
Balgonar	Fife	86	A5
Balgowan	D & G	68	C2
Balgowan	Highld	99	E2
Balgown	Highld	104	C3
Balgracie	D & G	68	B3
Balgray	Angus	93	F3
Balgray	S Lans	78	C5
Balham	Gt Lon	21	F3
Balhary	P & K	93	E4
Balholmie	P & K	92	D3
Baligill	Highld	109	G5
Balintore	Angus	93	E3
Balintore	Highld	107	G3
Balintraid	Highld	107	F3
Balivanich	W Isls	111	b3
Balk	N York	66	B2
Balkeerie	Angus	93	E4
Balkholme	E R Yk	60	B3
Ballachulish	Highld	90	C4
Ballanlay	Ag & B	83	H2
Ballantrae	S Ayrs	68	C5
Ballasalla	IOM	116	b2
Ballater	Abers	94	C5
Ballaugh	IOM	116	c4
Ballchraggan	Highld	107	F3
Ballencrieff	E Loth	87	E4
Ballevullin	Ag & B	88	A3
Ballidon	Derbys	50	D2
Balliekine	N Ayrs	75	G4
Balliemore	Ag & B	84	A5
Balligmorrie	S Ayrs	68	D6
Ballimore	Ag & B	83	G4
Ballimore	Stirlg	91	F1
Ballindalloch	Moray	101	E3
Ballindean	P & K	93	E2
Ballinger Common	Bucks	20	C5
Ballingham	Herefs	28	D5
Ballingry	Fife	86	C5
Ballinluig	P & K	92	C4
Ballinshoe	Angus	93	F4
Ballintuim	P & K	92	D4
Balloch	Highld	107	F1
Balloch	N Lans	85	F3
Balloch	P & K	92	B2
Balloch	S Ayrs	76	C1
Balloch	W Duns	84	D4
Ballogie	Abers	95	E5
Balls Cross	W Susx	10	C4
Balls Green	E Susx	11	G5
Ballygown	Ag & B	89	E3
Ballygrant	Ag & B	82	C2
Ballyhaugh	Ag & B	88	C4
Ballymenoch	Ag & B	84	C4
Ballymichael	N Ayrs	75	G4
Balmacara	Highld	97	F5
Balmaclellan	D & G	69	G5
Balmae	D & G	69	G2
Balmaha	Stirlg	84	D4
Balmalcolm	Fife	86	D6
Balmangan	D & G	69	G2
Balmedie	Abers	103	E2
Balmerino	Fife	93	F2
Balmoral Castle Grounds	Abers	94	B5
Balmore	E Duns	85	E3
Balmuchy	Highld	107	G4
Balmuir	Angus	93	G4
Balmule	Fife	86	C4
Balmullo	Fife	93	F2
Balnacoil Lodge	Highld	109	G1
Balnacra	Highld	105	G1
Balnacroft	Abers	94	C5
Balnafoich	Highld	99	E6
Balnaguard	P & K	92	C4
Balnahard	Ag & B	89	E2
Balnahard	Ag & B	82	C5
Balnain	Highld	98	C5
Balnakeil	Highld	108	D5
Balnapaling	Highld	107	G3
Balquharn	P & K	92	C3
Balquhidder	Stirlg	91	F1
Balsall Common	W Mids	40	D1
Balsall Heath	W Mids	40	C2
Balscote	Oxon	31	E4
Balsham	Cambs	33	G4
Baltasound	Shet	111	m4
Baltasound Airport	Shet	111	m4
Baltersan	D & G	69	E4
Baltonsborough	Somset	17	F3
Balvarran	P & K	94	A2
Balvicar	Ag & B	89	H1
Balvraid	Highld	97	F4
Balvraid	Highld	99	F5
Bamber Bridge	Lancs	57	E5
Bamber's Green	Essex	33	G1
Bamburgh	Nthumb	81	G3
Bamburgh Castle	Nthumb	81	G3
Bamff	P & K	93	E4
Bamford	Derbys	50	D5
Bampton	Cumb	71	H1
Bampton	Devon	16	B2
Bampton	Oxon	30	D1
Bampton Grange	Cumb	71	H1
Banavie	Highld	90	C6
Banbury	Oxon	31	F4
Bancffosfelen	Carmth	26	B4
Banchory	Abers	95	F5
Banchory-Devenick	Abers	95	G6
Bancycapel	Carmth	25	G4
Bancyfelin	Carmth	25	G4
Bandirran	P & K	93	E2
Banff	Abers	102	C5
Bangor	Gwynd	54	D3
Bangor-is-y-coed	Wrexhm	48	D4
Bangors	Cnwll	14	B1
Banham	Norfk	44	D1
Bank	Hants	9	E4
Bankend	D & G	70	D6
Bankfoot	P & K	92	C3
Bankglen	E Ayrs	77	E3
Bankhead	Aber C	103	E1
Bankhead	S Lans	86	A1
Bannister Green	Essex	34	A1
Bannockburn	Stirlg	85	G4
Banstead	Surrey	21	E2
Bantham	Devon	5	G2
Banton	N Lans	85	F3
Banwell	Somset	17	E5
Bapchild	Kent	22	D2
Bapton	Wilts	18	C1
Bar Hill	Cambs	33	F5
Barabhas	W Isls	111	d7
Barassie	S Ayrs	76	C4
Barbaraville	Highld	107	F3
Barbieston	S Ayrs	76	D3
Barbon	Cumb	63	F4
Barbrook	Devon	15	F5
Barby	Nhants	41	F1
Barcaldine	Ag & B	90	B3
Barcheston	Warwks	30	D4
Barcombe	E Susx	11	G3
Barcombe Cross	E Susx	11	G4
Barden	N York	65	E3
Barden Park	Kent	12	B6

Place	Page	Grid
Bardfield End Green Essex	33	H2
Bardfield Saling Essex	34	A2
Bardney Lincs	52	D2
Bardon Leics	41	E4
Bardon Mill Nthumb	72	C3
Bardowie E Duns	85	E3
Bardrainney Inver	84	C3
Bardsea Cumb	62	C3
Bardsey W York	59	E4
Bardwell Suffk	34	C5
Bare Lancs	63	E3
Barewood Herefs	38	D2
Barfad D & G	69	E4
Barford Norfk	45	E3
Barford Warwks	30	D6
Barford St John Oxon	31	E3
Barford St Martin Wilts	8	C6
Barford St Michael Oxon	31	E3
Barfrestone Kent	23	G1
Bargeddie N Lans	85	F2
Bargoed Caerph	27	G3
Bargrennan D & G	69	E5
Barham Cambs	32	D6
Barham Kent	23	G1
Barham Suffk	35	E4
Barholm Lincs	42	C3
Barkby Leics	41	G4
Barkby Thorpe Leics	41	G4
Barkestone-le-Vale Leics	41	H6
Barkham Berks	20	B2
Barking Gt Lon	21	G4
Barking Suffk	34	D4
Barking Tye Suffk	34	D4
Barkingside Gt Lon	21	G4
Barkisland W York	58	B2
Barkla Shop Cnwll	2	D4
Barkston Lincs	42	B6
Barkston Ash N York	59	F3
Barkway Herts	33	F2
Barlanark C Glas	85	F2
Barlaston Staffs	50	A1
Barlavington W Susx	10	C4
Barlborough Derbys	51	F4
Barlby N York	59	G3
Barlestone Leics	41	E4
Barley Herts	33	F3
Barley Lancs	57	G6
Barleythorpe Rutlnd	42	B3
Barling Essex	22	D4
Barlings Lincs	52	C3
Barlochan D & G	70	B5
Barlow Derbys	51	E4
Barlow N York	59	G3
Barlow T & W	73	E3
Barmby Moor E R Yk	60	B5
Barmby on the Marsh E R Yk	59	G3
Barmollack Ag & B	75	F5
Barmouth Gwynd	47	E3
Barmpton Dur	65	G5
Barmston E R Yk	61	G5
Barnacarry Ag & B	83	H5
Barnack Cambs	42	C3
Barnard Castle Dur	65	E5
Barnard Gate Oxon	31	E1
Barnardiston Suffk	34	A3
Barnbarroch D & G	70	B5
Barnburgh S York	59	F1
Barnby Suffk	45	G1
Barnby Dun S York	59	G1
Barnby in the Willows Notts	52	B1
Barnby Moor Notts	51	G5
Barncorkrie D & G	68	C1
Barnes Gt Lon	21	E3
Barnes Street Kent	12	B6
Barnet Gt Lon	21	E5
Barnetby le Wold Lincs	52	C6
Barney Norfk	44	D5
Barnham Suffk	34	C6
Barnham W Susx	10	C3
Barnham Broom Norfk	44	D3
Barnhead Angus	93	H5
Barnhill Dund C	93	G3
Barnhill Moray	100	D5
Barnhills D & G	68	B4
Barningham Dur	65	E4
Barningham Suffk	34	C6
Barnoldby le Beck Lincs	52	D5
Barnoldswick Lancs	63	H1
Barns Green W Susx	10	D4
Barnsley Gloucs	30	C1
Barnsley S York	59	E1
Barnstaple Devon	15	E4
Barnston Essex	33	H1
Barnston Mersyd	56	C1
Barnstone Notts	41	H6
Barnt Green Worcs	40	B1
Barnton C Edin	86	C3
Barnton Ches	49	F6
Barnwell All Saints Nhants	42	C1
Barnwell St Andrew Nhants	42	C1
Barnwood Gloucs	29	F4
Barr S Ayrs	76	C1
Barra Airport W Isls	111	a2
Barrachan D & G	69	E3
Barrapoll Ag & B	88	A3
Barrasford Nthumb	72	D4
Barrhead E Rens	84	D2
Barrhill S Ayrs	68	D5
Barrington Cambs	33	F4
Barrington Somset	17	E1
Barripper Cnwll	2	C3
Barrmill N Ayrs	84	C1
Barrnacarry Bay Ag & B	89	H1
Barrock Highld	110	C6
Barrow Gloucs	29	F5
Barrow Lancs	57	G6
Barrow Rutlnd	42	B3
Barrow Somset	17	H2
Barrow Suffk	34	B5
Barrow Burn Nthumb	81	E1
Barrow Gurney Somset	17	F5
Barrow Haven Lincs	60	D2
Barrow Island Cumb	62	C3
Barrow upon Soar Leics	41	F5
Barrow upon Trent Derbys	41	E6
Barrow-in-Furness Cumb	62	C3
Barrow-upon-Humber Lincs	60	D2
Barrowby Lincs	42	B5
Barrowden Rutlnd	42	B2
Barrowford Lancs	57	H6
Barry Angus	93	G3
Barry V Glam	16	C5
Barsby Leics	41	G4
Barsham Suffk	45	G1
Barston W Mids	40	D2
Bartestree Herefs	28	D6
Barthol Chapel Abers	102	D3
Bartholomew Green Essex	34	B1
Barthomley Ches	49	G4
Bartley Hants	9	E4
Bartley Green W Mids	40	B2
Bartlow Cambs	33	G3
Barton Cambs	33	F4
Barton Ches	49	E4
Barton Devon	6	B3
Barton Gloucs	30	C3
Barton Lancs	56	D3
Barton Lancs	57	E6
Barton N York	65	F4
Barton Oxon	31	F1
Barton Bendish Norfk	44	A3
Barton End Gloucs	29	F3
Barton Hartshorn Bucks	31	G3
Barton in Fabis Notts	41	F6
Barton in the Beans Leics	41	E4
Barton Mills Suffk	34	B5
Barton Seagrave Nhants	32	B6
Barton St David Somset	17	F2
Barton Stacey Hants	19	F1
Barton Town Devon	15	F5
Barton Waterside Lincs	60	D2
Barton-le-Clay Beds	32	C2
Barton-le-Street N York	66	D1
Barton-le-Willows N York	60	B6
Barton-on-Sea Hants	9	E3
Barton-on-the-Heath Warwks	30	D3
Barton-under-Needwood Staffs	40	C5
Barton-upon-Humber Lincs	60	D2
Barvas W Isls	111	d7
Barway Cambs	33	G6
Barwell Leics	41	E3
Barwick Devon	15	E2
Barwick Somset	17	F1
Barwick in Elmet W York	59	E4
Baschurch Shrops	48	D2
Bascote Warwks	31	E6
Bashall Eaves Lancs	63	F1
Basildon Essex	22	C4
Basingstoke Hants	19	H2
Baslow Derbys	50	D4
Bason Bridge Somset	17	E3
Bassaleg Newpt	28	B2
Bassendean Border	80	C4
Bassenthwaite Cumb	71	E3
Bassett Hants	9	F5
Bassingbourn Cambs	33	E3
Bassingham Lincs	52	B2
Bassingthorpe Lincs	42	B4
Bassus Green Herts	33	E2
Baston Lincs	42	D3
Bastwick Norfk	45	G4
Batchworth Herts	20	D4
Batcombe Dorset	7	G5
Batcombe Somset	17	H3
Batford Herts	21	E6
Bath Somset	17	H5
Bathampton Somset	18	A3
Bathealton Somset	16	C2
Batheaston Somset	18	A3
Bathford Somset	18	A3
Bathgate W Loth	86	A3
Bathley Notts	51	H3
Bathpool Cnwll	4	D4
Bathpool Somset	16	D2
Bathville W Loth	85	H2
Bathway Somset	17	G4
Batley W York	58	D3
Batsford Gloucs	30	C3
Battersby N York	66	C4
Battersea Gt Lon	21	F3
Battisford Tye Suffk	34	D4
Battle E Susx	12	C3
Battle Powys	27	F5
Battle of Britain Memorial Flight Lincs	52	D1
Battledykes Angus	93	F4
Battlesbridge Essex	22	C4
Battleton Somset	16	B2
Baughton Worcs	29	F6
Baughurst Hants	19	G3
Baulds Abers	95	E5
Baulking Oxon	19	E5
Baumber Lincs	52	D3
Baunton Gloucs	30	B1
Baverstock Wilts	8	C6
Bawburgh Norfk	45	E3
Bawdeswell Norfk	44	D4
Bawdrip Somset	17	E3
Bawdsey Suffk	35	F3
Bawtry S York	51	G5
Baxenden Lancs	57	G5
Baxterley Warwks	40	D3
Bay Highld	104	B2
Baybridge Hants	9	G5
Baycliff Cumb	62	C3
Baydon Wilts	19	E4
Bayford Herts	21	F6
Bayford Somset	17	H2
Bayhead W Isls	111	a4
Baylham Suffk	34	D4
Baysham Herefs	28	D5
Bayston Hill Shrops	39	E6
Baythorne End Essex	34	B3
Bayton Worcs	39	F3
Bayworth Oxon	19	G6
Beachampton Bucks	31	H4
Beachamwell Norfk	44	B3
Beacon Devon	6	D6
Beacon End Essex	34	C1
Beacon's Bottom Bucks	20	B5
Beaconsfield Bucks	20	C4
Beadlam N York	66	C2
Beadlow Beds	32	C3
Beadnell Nthumb	81	G3
Beaford Devon	15	E3
Beal Nthumb	81	F4
Bealsmill Cnwll	4	D4
Beaminster Dorset	7	F5
Beamish Dur	73	F2
Beamsley N York	58	C5
Beanacre Wilts	18	B3
Beanley Nthumb	81	F2
Beardon Devon	5	E5
Beare Devon	6	B5
Beare Green Surrey	11	E6
Bearley Warwks	30	C5
Bearpark Dur	73	F1
Bearsden W Duns	85	E3
Bearsted Kent	22	C1
Bearstone Shrops	49	G3
Bearwood Dorset	8	C3
Bearwood W Mids	40	B2
Beattock D & G	78	D3
Beauchamp Roding Essex	22	B6
Beaufort Blae G	27	G4
Beaulieu Hants	9	F3
Beaulieu House Hants	9	F4
Beauly Highld	107	E1
Beaumaris IOA	54	D4
Beaumont Cumb	71	F5
Beaumont Essex	35	E2
Beaumont Jersey	7	b1
Beausale Warwks	40	D1
Beauworth Hants	9	G5
Beaver Green Kent	13	E6
Beaworthy Devon	14	D1
Beazley End Essex	34	B2
Bebington Mersyd	56	D1
Beccles Suffk	45	G1
Becconsall Lancs	57	E5
Beck Row Suffk	34	A6
Beck Side Cumb	62	C4
Beckbury Shrops	39	G6
Beckenham Gt Lon	21	F2
Beckering Lincs	52	D3
Beckermet Cumb	62	A6
Beckfoot Cumb	70	D4
Beckford Worcs	29	G6
Beckhampton Wilts	18	D3
Beckingham Lincs	52	B1
Beckingham Notts	51	H5
Beckington Somset	18	A2
Beckjay Shrops	38	D4
Beckley E Susx	12	D4
Beckley Oxon	31	F2
Beckton Gt Lon	21	G3
Beckwithshaw N York	58	D5
Becontree Gt Lon	21	G4
Becquet Vincent Jersey	7	b2
Bedale N York	65	F2
Bedchester Dorset	8	B5
Beddau Rhondd	27	F2
Beddgelert Gwynd	54	D1
Beddingham E Susx	11	G3
Beddington Gt Lon	21	F2
Beddington Corner Gt Lon	21	F2
Bedfield Suffk	35	E5
Bedford Beds	32	C4
Bedhampton Hants	10	A3
Bedingfield Suffk	35	E5
Bedingfield Street Suffk	35	E5
Bedlam N York	58	D6
Bedlam Lane Kent	12	D6
Bedlington Nthumb	73	F4
Bedlinog Myr Td	27	F3
Bedminster Bristl	17	G6
Bedminster Down Bristl	17	G5
Bedmond Herts	20	D5
Bednall Staffs	40	B5
Bedrule Border	80	C2
Bedstone Shrops	38	D3
Bedwas Caerph	27	G2
Bedwellty Caerph	27	G3
Bedworth Warwks	41	E2
Beeby Leics	41	G4
Beech Hants	10	A5
Beech Staffs	49	H3
Beech Hill Berks	20	A2
Beechingstoke Wilts	18	D3
Beedon Berks	19	G4
Beedon Hill Berks	19	G4
Beeford E R Yk	61	E5
Beeley Derbys	50	D3
Beelsby Lincs	52	D5
Beenham Berks	19	G3
Beer Devon	6	D4
Beer Somset	17	E2
Beer Hackett Dorset	7	G6
Beercrocombe Somset	17	E1
Beesands Devon	5	H1
Beesby Lincs	53	F3
Beeson Devon	5	H1
Beeston Beds	32	D3
Beeston Ches	49	E5
Beeston Norfk	44	C3
Beeston Notts	51	F1
Beeston N York	58	D3
Beeston Regis Norfk	45	E6
Beeswing D & G	70	C6
Beetham Cumb	63	E4
Beetham Somset	6	D6
Beetley Norfk	44	C4
Begbroke Oxon	31	F2
Begelly Pembks	25	E3
Beguildy Powys	38	C4
Beighton Norfk	45	G3
Beighton S York	51	E5
Beighton Hill Derbys	50	D2
Bein Inn P & K	92	D1
Beith N Ayrs	84	C1
Bekesbourne Kent	23	F1
Belaugh Norfk	45	F4
Belbroughton Worcs	40	A1
Belchalwell Dorset	8	A4
Belchalwell Street Dorset	8	A4
Belchamp Otten Essex	34	B3
Belchamp St Paul Essex	34	B3
Belchamp Walter Essex	34	B3
Belchford Lincs	53	E3
Belford Nthumb	81	F3
Belgrave Leics	41	G4
Belhelvie Abers	87	F1
Belhelvie Abers	103	E2
Belhinnie Abers	101	G2
Bell Busk N York	58	A5
Bell End Worcs	40	B1
Bell o' th' Hill Ches	49	E4
Bellabeg Abers	101	F1
Bellanoch Ag & B	83	F4
Bellaty Angus	93	E5
Belle Vue Cumb	71	F5
Belle Vue W York	59	E2
Belleau Lincs	53	F3
Bellerby N York	65	E3
Bellfield S Lans	78	B6
Bellfield S Lans	78	C4
Bellingdon Bucks	20	C5
Bellingham Nthumb	72	C5
Belloch Ag & B	75	E4
Bellochantuy Ag & B	75	E4
Bells Yew Green E Susx	12	B5
Bellshill N Lans	85	F2
Bellside N Lans	85	G2
Bellsquarry W Loth	86	B3
Belluton Somset	17	G5
Belmont Gt Lon	21	E2
Belmont Lancs	57	F4
Belmont S Ayrs	76	C3
Belmont Shet	111	m4
Belnacraig Abers	101	F1
Belper Derbys	51	E2
Belper Lane End Derbys	51	E2
Belsay Nthumb	73	E4
Belses Border	80	B3
Belsford Devon	5	G3
Belsize Herts	20	D5
Belstead Suffk	35	E3
Belstone Devon	5	F6
Belthorn Lancs	57	G5
Beltinge Kent	23	F2
Beltingham Nthumb	72	C3
Beltoft Lincs	52	A5
Belton Leics	41	E5
Belton Lincs	52	A5
Belton Lincs	42	B5
Belton Norfk	45	G2
Belton Rutlnd	42	A2
Belvedere Gt Lon	21	G3
Belvoir Leics	42	A5
Belvoir Castle Leics	42	A5
Bembridge IOW	9	H2
Bemerton Wilts	8	D6
Bempton E R Yk	67	G1
Benacre Suffk	45	H1
Benbecula Airport W Isls	111	b3
Benbuie D & G	77	F1
Benderloch Ag & B	90	B3
Benenden Kent	12	C5
Benfieldside Dur	73	E2
Bengeworth Worcs	30	B4
Benhall Green Suffk	35	G4
Benhall Street Suffk	35	F4
Benholm Abers	95	G3
Beningbrough N York	59	F5
Benington Herts	33	E1
Benington Lincs	43	F6
Benllech IOA	54	D4
Benmore Ag & B	84	B4
Bennacott Cnwll	4	D6
Bennan N Ayrs	75	H3
Benniworth Lincs	52	D3
Benover Kent	12	C6
Benson Oxon	19	H5
Benthoul Aber C	95	G6
Bentley E R Yk	60	D3
Bentley Hants	10	B6
Bentley S York	59	F1
Bentley Suffk	35	E3
Bentley Warwks	40	D3
Benton Devon	15	F4
Bentpath D & G	79	F2
Bentwichen Devon	15	H4
Bentworth Hants	19	H1
Benvie Angus	93	E3
Benville Dorset	7	F5
Benwick Cambs	43	E1
Beoley Worcs	40	C1
Beoraidbeg Highld	97	G3
Bepton W Susx	10	B4
Berden Essex	33	F2
Bere Alston Devon	5	E4
Bere Ferrers Devon	5	E3
Bere Regis Dorset	8	B3
Berea Pembks	24	C5
Bergh Apton Norfk	45	F2
Berinsfield Oxon	19	G6
Berkeley Gloucs	29	E3
Berkhamsted Herts	20	C6
Berkley Somset	18	A2
Berkswell W Mids	40	D2
Bermondsey Gt Lon	21	F3
Bernera Highld	97	F4
Bernice Ag & B	84	B4
Bernisdale Highld	104	C1
Berrick Prior Oxon	19	H6
Berrick Salome Oxon	19	H5
Berriedale Highld	110	B2
Berrier Cumb	71	G2
Berriew Powys	38	C6
Berrington Shrops	39	E6
Berrington Worcs	39	F3
Berrington Green Worcs	39	F3
Berrow Somset	16	D4
Berrow Green Worcs	39	G2
Berry Pomeroy Devon	5	H3
Berryhillock Moray	101	G4
Berryhillock Moray	101	G5
Berrynarbor Devon	15	E5
Bersham Wrexhm	48	C4
Berwick E Susx	11	G3
Berwick Bassett Wilts	18	D4
Berwick Hill Nthumb	73	F4
Berwick St James Wilts	18	C1
Berwick St John Wilts	8	B5
Berwick St Leonard Wilts	8	B6
Berwick-upon-Tweed Nthumb	81	F5
Bescaby Leics	42	A4
Bescar Cumb	56	D4
Besford Worcs	30	A4
Bessacarr S York	51	G6
Bessels Leigh Oxon	19	F6
Bessingby E R Yk	61	F6
Bessingham Norfk	45	E5
Besthorpe Norfk	44	D2
Besthorpe Notts	52	B2
Beswick E R Yk	60	D4
Betchworth Surrey	21	E1
Beth Chatto Garden Essex	34	D1
Bethel Gwynd	54	C3
Bethel IOA	54	C3
Bethersden Kent	12	D5
Bethesda Gwynd	55	E3
Bethesda Pembks	25	E4
Bethlehem Carmth	26	C5
Bethnal Green Gt Lon	21	F4
Betley Staffs	49	G4
Betsham Kent	22	B3
Betteshanger Kent	23	G1
Bettiscombe Dorset	7	E5
Bettisfield Wrexhm	49	E3
Bettws Newpt	28	B2
Bettws Bledrws Cerdgn	37	E2
Bettws Cedewain Powys	38	B5
Bettws Evan Cerdgn	36	C2
Bettws-Newydd Mons	28	B3
Bettyhill Highld	109	F5
Betws Brdgnd	27	E2
Betws Gwerfil Goch Denbgs	48	A4
Betws-y-coed Conwy	55	F2
Betws-yn-Rhos Conwy	55	G5
Beulah Cerdgn	36	C2
Beulah Powys	37	H2
Bevercotes Notts	51	G4
Beverley E R Yk	60	D4
Beverstone Gloucs	29	F2
Bewcastle Cumb	71	H6
Bewdley Worcs	39	G3
Bewerley N York	58	C6
Bewholme E R Yk	61	E5
Bexhill E Susx	12	C3
Bexley Gt Lon	21	G3
Bexleyheath Gt Lon	21	G3
Bexwell Norfk	43	H2
Beyton Suffk	34	C5
Beyton Green Suffk	34	C5
Bhaltos W Isls	111	c6
Bhatarsaigh W Isls	111	a1
Bibury Gloucs	30	C1
Bicester Oxon	31	G2
Bickenhill W Mids	40	C2
Bicker Lincs	42	D5
Bickerstaffe Lancs	57	E4
Bickerton N York	59	E5
Bickford Staffs	40	A4
Bickington Devon	5	H4
Bickington Devon	15	E4
Bickleigh Devon	6	B6
Bickleigh Devon	5	F3
Bickley Gt Lon	21	G2
Bickley N York	67	E3
Bickley Moss Ches	49	E4
Bicknacre Essex	22	C5
Bicknoller Somset	16	C3
Bicknor Kent	22	D2
Bicton Shrops	49	E1
Bicton Shrops	38	C4
Bidborough Kent	12	B6
Biddenden Kent	12	D5
Biddenham Beds	32	C4
Biddestone Wilts	18	B4
Biddisham Somset	17	E4
Biddlesden Bucks	31	G4
Biddulph Staffs	50	A3
Biddulph Moor Staffs	50	A3
Bideford Devon	14	D4
Bidford-on-Avon Warwks	30	C5
Bielby E R Yk	60	B4
Bieldside Aber C	95	G6
Bierley IOW	9	G2
Bierton Bucks	20	B6
Big Balcraig D & G	69	E2
Big Carlae D & G	77	F2
Big Pit Blaenavon Torfn	27	G3
Big Sand Highld	105	F4
Bigbury Devon	5	G2
Bigbury-on-Sea Devon	5	G2
Bigby Lincs	52	C5
Biggar S Lans	78	D6
Biggin Derbys	50	D2
Biggin Derbys	50	C3
Biggin N York	59	F3
Biggin Hill Gt Lon	21	G2
Biggin Hill Airport Gt Lon	21	G2
Biggleswade Beds	32	D3
Bigholms D & G	79	F1
Bighouse Highld	109	H5
Bighton Hants	9	H6
Biglands Cumb	71	F4
Bignor W Susx	10	C3
Bigrigg Cumb	70	D1
Bilborough Notts	51	F1
Bilbrook Somset	16	B3
Bilbrough N York	59	F4
Bilbster Highld	110	C4
Bildershaw Dur	65	F5
Bildeston Suffk	34	C4
Billericay Essex	22	B4
Billesdon Leics	41	H3
Billesley Warwks	30	C5
Billingborough Lincs	42	D5
Billinge Mersyd	57	E3
Billingford Norfk	44	D4
Billingford Norfk	35	E6
Billingham Dur	66	B5
Billinghay Lincs	52	D1
Billingley S York	59	E1
Billingshurst W Susx	10	D4
Billingsley Shrops	39	G4
Billington Beds	32	B1
Billington Lancs	57	G6
Billockby Norfk	45	G3
Billy Row Dur	73	F1
Bilsborrow Lancs	57	E6
Bilsby Lincs	53	F3
Bilsham W Susx	10	C2
Bilsington Kent	13	E5
Bilsthorpe Notts	51	G3
Bilston Mdloth	86	C3
Bilston W Mids	40	B3
Bilstone Leics	41	E4
Bilton E R Yk	61	E3
Bilton N York	59	E5
Bilton N York	58	D5
Bilton Warwks	41	F1
Binbrook Lincs	52	D4
Bincombe Dorset	7	G4
Binegar Somset	17	G4
Binfield Berks	20	B3
Binfield Heath Oxon	20	B3
Bingfield Nthumb	72	D4
Bingham Notts	51	H1
Bingham's Melcombe Dorset	8	A3
Bingley W York	58	C4
Binham Norfk	44	D5
Binley Hants	19	F2
Binley W Mids	41	E2
Binnegar Dorset	8	B2
Binniehill Falk	85	G3
Binns Farm Moray	101	F5
Binscombe Surrey	10	C5
Binstead IOW	9	G3
Binsted Hants	10	B6
Binsted W Susx	10	C3
Binton Warwks	30	C5
Bintree Norfk	44	D4
Birch Essex	34	C1

Birch Cross *Staffs* 40 C6
Birch Green *Essex* 34 C1
Birch Vale *Derbys* 50 B5
Birch Wood *Somset* 16 D1
Bircham Newton *Norfk* 44 B5
Bircham Tofts *Norfk* 44 B5
Birchanger *Essex* 33 G1
Bircher *Herefs* 39 E3
Birchgrove *Cardif* 27 G1
Birchgrove *E Susx* 11 G5
Birchgrove *Swans* 26 C3
Birchington *Kent* 23 G2
Birchley Heath *Warwks* 40 D3
Birchover *Derbys* 50 D3
Birchwood *Ches* 57 F2
Bircotes *Notts* 51 G5
Birdbrook *Essex* 34 A3
Birdforth *N York* 66 B1
Birdham *W Susx* 10 B2
Birdingbury *Warwks* 31 E6
Birdlip *Gloucs* 29 G4
Birds Edge *W York* 58 D1
Birds Green *Essex* 22 B6
Birdsall *N York* 60 C6
Birdsgreen *Shrops* 39 G4
Birdsmoorgate *Dorset* 7 E5
Birgham *Border* 80 D4
Birichin *Highld* 107 F5
Birkby *N York* 65 G3
Birkdale *Mersyd* 56 D4
Birkenbog *Abers* 102 B5
Birkenhead *Mersyd* 56 D2
Birkenhills *Abers* 102 C4
Birkenshaw *W York* 58 D3
Birkhall *Abers* 94 C5
Birkhill *Angus* 93 F3
Birkhill *D & G* 79 E4
Birkin *N York* 59 F3
Birley *Herefs* 39 E2
Birley Carr *S York* 51 E5
Birling *Kent* 22 B2
Birlingham *Worcs* 30 B4
Birmingham *W Mids* 40 C2
Birmingham Airport *W Mids* 40 C2
Birnam *P & K* 92 C3
Birness *Abers* 103 E3
Birse *Abers* 95 E5
Birsemore *Abers* 95 E5
Birstall *Leics* 41 G4
Birstall *W York* 58 D3
Birstwith *N York* 58 D5
Birtley *Herefs* 38 D3
Birtley *Nthumb* 72 C4
Birtley *T & W* 73 F2
Birts Street *Worcs* 29 E6
Bisbrooke *Rutlnd* 42 B2
Biscathorpe *Lincs* 52 D4
Bish Mill *Devon* 15 F3
Bisham *Berks* 20 B4
Bishampton *Worcs* 30 B5
Bishop Auckland *Dur* 65 F6
Bishop Burton *E R Yk* 60 D4
Bishop Middleham *Dur* 65 G6
Bishop Monkton *N York* 59 E6
Bishop Norton *Lincs* 52 C4
Bishop Sutton *Somset* 17 G5
Bishop Thornton *N York* 58 D6
Bishop Wilton *E R Yk* 60 B5
Bishop's Castle *Shrops* 38 D5
Bishop's Caundle *Dorset* 17 H1
Bishop's Cleeve *Gloucs* 29 G5
Bishop's Frome *Herefs* 39 F1
Bishop's Green *Essex* 33 H1
Bishop's Itchington *Warwks* 31 E5
Bishop's Norton *Gloucs* 29 F5
Bishop's Nympton *Devon* 15 G3
Bishop's Offley *Staffs* 49 G2
Bishop's Stortford *Herts* 33 F1
Bishop's Sutton *Hants* 9 H6
Bishop's Tachbrook *Warwks* 30 D6
Bishop's Tawton *Devon* 15 E4
Bishop's Waltham *Hants* 9 G5
Bishop's Wood *Staffs* 49 H1
Bishopbriggs *Lincs* 52 C4
Bishopbriggs *E Duns* 85 E3
Bishopmill *Moray* 101 E5
Bishops Cannings *Wilts* 18 C3
Bishops Hull *Somset* 16 D2
Bishops Lydeard *Somset* 16 D2
Bishopsbourne *Kent* 23 F1
Bishopsteignton *Devon* 6 A3
Bishopstoke *Hants* 9 F5
Bishopston *Swans* 26 B2
Bishopstone *Bucks* 20 B6
Bishopstone *E Susx* 11 G2
Bishopstone *Herefs* 38 D1
Bishopstone *Kent* 23 G2
Bishopstone *Wilts* 8 C5
Bishopstone *Wilts* 19 E5
Bishopstrow *Wilts* 18 B1
Bishopswood *Somset* 6 D6
Bishopsworth *Bristl* 17 G5
Bishopthorpe *N York* 59 G4
Bishopton *Dur* 65 G5
Bishopton *Rens* 84 D3
Bishton *Newpt* 28 B2
Bishton *Staffs* 40 B5
Bisley *Gloucs* 29 F3
Bisley *Surrey* 20 C2
Bissoe *Cnwll* 2 D3
Bisterne *Hants* 8 D3
Bitchfield *Lincs* 42 C5
Bittadon *Devon* 15 E5
Bittaford *Devon* 5 G3
Bitterley *Shrops* 39 E4
Bitterne *Hants* 9 F4
Bitteswell *Leics* 41 F2
Bitton *Gloucs* 17 G5
Bix *Oxon* 20 A4
Blaby *Leics* 41 F3
Black Bourton *Oxon* 30 D1
Black Callerton *T & W* 73 F3
Black Corries *Highld* 91 E4
Black Crofts *Ag & B* 90 B3
Black Dog *Devon* 15 G2
Black Notley *Essex* 34 B1
Black Pill *Swans* 26 C2
Black Street *Suffk* 45 H1
Black Torrington *Devon* 14 D2
Blackadder *Border* 80 D5
Blackawton *Devon* 5 H2
Blackborough *Devon* 6 C6
Blackborough End *Norfk* 43 H3
Blackboys *E Susx* 11 H4

Blackbrook *Derbys* 51 E2
Blackbrook *Staffs* 49 G3
Blackburn *Abers* 102 D1
Blackburn *Lancs* 57 F5
Blackburn *W Loth* 86 A3
Blackcraig *E Ayrs* 77 E2
Blackdog *Abers* 103 E1
Blackdown *Dorset* 7 E5
Blackenall Heath *W Mids* 40 B3
Blacker Hill *S York* 51 E6
Blackfen *Gt Lon* 21 G3
Blackfield *Hants* 9 F3
Blackford *P & K* 85 G6
Blackford *Somset* 17 E4
Blackford *Somset* 17 G2
Blackfordby *Leics* 41 E5
Blackhall *C Edin* 86 C3
Blackhall Colliery *Dur* 73 H1
Blackhaugh *Border* 79 G6
Blackheath *Gt Lon* 21 F3
Blackheath *Suffk* 35 G6
Blackheath *Surrey* 10 D6
Blackheath *W Mids* 40 B2
Blackhill *Abers* 103 F3
Blackhill *Abers* 103 F5
Blackhill *Abers* 103 F4
Blackhill *Dur* 73 E2
Blackhill of Clackriach *Abers* 103 E4
Blackhorse *Devon* 6 B5
Blacklaw *D & G* 78 D3
Blackley *Gt Man* 57 H3
Blacklunans *P & K* 94 B2
Blackmarstone *Herefs* 28 C6
Blackmill *Brgnd* 27 E2
Blackmoor *Hants* 10 B5
Blackmoor *Somset* 17 F5
Blackmoorfoot *W York* 58 C2
Blackmore *Essex* 22 B5
Blackmore End *Essex* 34 B2
Blackness *Falk* 86 B4
Blacknest *Hants* 10 B6
Blacko *Lancs* 57 H6
Blackpool *Devon* 6 A1
Blackpool *Lancs* 56 C6
Blackpool Airport *Lancs* 56 D5
Blackridge *W Loth* 85 G2
Blackrod *Gt Man* 57 F4
Blacksboat *Moray* 101 E3
Blackshaw *D & G* 70 D5
Blackshaw Head *W York* 58 B3
Blacksnape *Lancs* 57 G4
Blackstone *W Susx* 11 E4
Blackthorn *Oxon* 31 G2
Blackthorpe *Suffk* 34 C5
Blacktoft *E R Yk* 60 C3
Blacktop *Aber C* 95 G6
Blackwall *Derbys* 50 D2
Blackwater *Cnwll* 2 D4
Blackwater *Hants* 20 B2
Blackwater *IOW* 9 G2
Blackwater *Somset* 16 D1
Blackwaterfoot *N Ayrs* 75 G4
Blackwell *Cumb* 71 G4
Blackwell *Derbys* 50 C4
Blackwell *Derbys* 51 E3
Blackwell *Derbys* 30 D4
Blackwell *Warwks* 30 D4
Blackwell *Worcs* 40 B1
Blackwood *Caerph* 27 G3
Blackwood *D & G* 78 C2
Blackwood *S Lans* 77 G5
Blacon *Ches* 48 D6
Bladnoch *D & G* 69 E3
Bladon *Oxon* 31 E2
Blaen-y-Coed *Carmth* 25 G5
Blaen-y-cwm *Rhondd* 27 E3
Blaenannerch *Cerdgn* 36 B2
Blaenau Ffestiniog *Gwynd* 47 F5
Blaenavon *Torfn* 27 H3
Blaenffos *Pembks* 25 F6
Blaengarw *Brdgnd* 27 E2
Blaengwrach *Neath* 27 E3
Blaengwynfi *Neath* 27 E2
Blaenpennal *Cerdgn* 37 E3
Blaenplwyf *Cerdgn* 37 E4
Blaenporth *Cerdgn* 36 B2
Blaenrhondda *Rhondd* 27 E3
Blaenwaun *Carmth* 25 F5
Blagdon *Devon* 6 A2
Blagdon *Somset* 16 D1
Blagdon *Somset* 17 F5
Blagdon Hill *Somset* 16 D1
Blaich *Highld* 90 C6
Blain *Highld* 89 G5
Blaina *Blae G* 27 G3
Blair Atholl *P & K* 92 B5
Blair Drummond *Stirlg* 85 F5
Blair's Ferry *Ag & B* 83 G3
Blairgowrie *P & K* 92 D4
Blairhall *Fife* 86 A5
Blairingone *P & K* 86 A5
Blairlogie *Stirlg* 85 G5
Blairmore *Ag & B* 84 B4
Blairmore *Highld* 108 B5
Blairnamarrow *Moray* 101 E1
Blaisdon *Gloucs* 29 E4
Blake End *Essex* 34 A1
Blakebrook *Worcs* 39 G4
Blakedown *Worcs* 39 H4
Blakemere *Ches* 49 E6
Blakemere *Herefs* 28 B6
Blakeney *Gloucs* 29 E3
Blakeney *Norfk* 44 D6
Blakenhall *Ches* 49 G4
Blakenhall *W Mids* 40 A3
Blakesley *Nhants* 31 G5
Blanchland *Nthumb* 72 D2
Bland Hill *N York* 58 D5
Blandford Forum *Dorset* 8 B4
Blandford St Mary *Dorset* 8 B4
Blanefield *Stirlg* 85 E3
Blankney *Lincs* 52 C2
Blantyre *S Lans* 85 F2
Blar a' Chaorainn *Highld* 90 C5
Blargie *Highld* 98 D2
Blarmachfoldach *Highld* 90 C5
Blaston *Leics* 42 A2
Blatherwycke *Nhants* 42 B2
Blawith *Cumb* 62 C4
Blawquhairn *D & G* 69 G5
Blaxhall *Suffk* 35 F4
Blaxton *S York* 51 G6
Blaydon *T & W* 73 F3
Bleadney *Somset* 17 F3
Bleadon *Somset* 17 E4
Blean *Kent* 23 F2

Bleasby *Notts* 51 H2
Bleasdale *Lancs* 63 F1
Blebocraigs *Fife* 93 F1
Bleddfa *Powys* 38 C3
Bledington *Gloucs* 30 D2
Bledlow *Bucks* 20 B5
Bledlow Ridge *Bucks* 20 B5
Blegbie *E Loth* 87 E2
Blencarn *Cumb* 64 A6
Blencogo *Cumb* 71 E4
Blendworth *Hants* 10 A3
Blennerhasset *Cumb* 71 E3
Bletchingdon *Oxon* 31 F2
Bletchingley *Surrey* 21 F1
Bletchley *Bucks* 32 B2
Bletchley *Shrops* 49 F3
Bletherston *Pembks* 25 E4
Bletsoe *Beds* 32 C4
Blewbury *Oxon* 19 G5
Blickling *Norfk* 45 E5
Blidworth *Notts* 51 G2
Blidworth Bottoms *Notts* 51 G2
Blindcrake *Cumb* 71 E3
Blindley Heath *Surrey* 11 F6
Blisland *Cnwll* 4 B4
Bliss Gate *Worcs* 39 G3
Blissford *Hants* 8 D4
Blisworth *Nhants* 31 H5
Blithbury *Staffs* 40 C5
Blo Norton *Norfk* 34 D6
Blockley *Gloucs* 30 C3
Blofield *Norfk* 45 F3
Bloomfield *Border* 80 B3
Blore *Staffs* 49 G3
Blore *Staffs* 50 C2
Bloxham *Oxon* 31 E3
Bloxholm *Lincs* 52 C1
Bloxwich *W Mids* 40 B3
Bloxworth *Dorset* 8 B3
Blubberhouses *N York* 58 C5
Blue Anchor *Somset* 16 B3
Blue Bell Hill *Kent* 22 C2
Blue John Cavern *Derbys* 50 C5
Blundellsands *Mersyd* 56 C3
Blundeston *Suffk* 45 H2
Blunham *Beds* 32 D4
Blunsdon St Andrew *Wilts* 18 D5
Bluntington *Worcs* 40 A1
Bluntisham *Cambs* 33 E6
Blyborough *Lincs* 52 B4
Blyford *Suffk* 35 G6
Blymhill *Staffs* 49 G1
Blyth *Notts* 51 G5
Blyth *Nthumb* 73 G4
Blyth Bridge *Border* 86 B1
Blythburgh *Suffk* 35 G6
Blythe *Border* 80 B5
Blyton *Lincs* 52 B4
Bo'ness *Falk* 86 A4
Boarhills *Fife* 93 G1
Boarhunt *Hants* 9 G4
Boarstall *Bucks* 31 G2
Boat of Garten *Highld* 99 G4
Boath *Highld* 107 E3
Bobbing *Kent* 22 D2
Bobbington *Staffs* 39 G5
Bocking *Essex* 34 B1
Bocking Churchstreet *Essex* 34 B2
Boddam *Abers* 103 F4
Boddam *Shet* 111 I1
Boddington *Gloucs* 29 F5
Bodedern *IOA* 54 B4
Bodelwyddan *Denbgs* 55 H4
Bodenham *Herefs* 39 E1
Bodenham *Wilts* 8 D5
Bodenham Moor *Herefs* 39 E1
Bodewryd *IOA* 54 C5
Bodfari *Denbgs* 48 B6
Bodffordd *IOA* 54 C4
Bodfuan *Gwynd* 46 C5
Bodham *Norfk* 45 E5
Bodiam *E Susx* 12 C4
Bodiam Castle *E Susx* 12 C4
Bodicote *Oxon* 31 F4
Bodinnick *Cnwll* 4 C2
Bodle Street Green *E Susx* 12 B3
Bodmin *Cnwll* 3 G5
Bodnant Garden *Conwy* 55 F3
Bodsham Green *Kent* 13 F6
Bodwen *Cnwll* 3 F5
Bogallan *Highld* 107 E1
Bogbrae *Abers* 103 F3
Boghall *Mdloth* 86 C3
Boghall *W Loth* 86 A3
Boghead *S Lans* 77 G5
Boghead Farm *Moray* 101 F5
Bogmoor *Moray* 101 F5
Bogmuir *Abers* 95 E3
Bogniebrae *Abers* 102 B4
Bognor Regis *W Susx* 10 C2
Bogroy *Highld* 99 G5
Bogue *D & G* 69 G5
Bohortha *Cnwll* 3 E3
Bohuntine *Highld* 98 B1
Bolam *Dur* 65 F5
Bolberry *Devon* 5 G1
Boldmere *W Mids* 40 C3
Boldre *Hants* 9 E3
Boldron *Dur* 65 E4
Bole *Notts* 52 A4
Bolehill *Derbys* 50 D2
Bolham *Devon* 16 B1
Bolham Water *Devon* 6 C6
Bolingey *Cnwll* 2 D4
Bollington *Ches* 50 B4
Bolney *W Susx* 11 F4
Bolnhurst *Beds* 32 C4
Bolshan *Angus* 93 H4
Bolsover *Derbys* 51 F4
Bolsterstone *S York* 50 D6
Boltby *N York* 66 B2
Boltenstone *Abers* 101 F1
Bolton *Cumb* 64 A5
Bolton *E Loth* 87 E1
Bolton *E R Yk* 60 B5
Bolton *Gt Man* 57 G3
Bolton *Nthumb* 81 F2
Bolton Abbey *N York* 58 C5
Bolton by Bowland *Lancs* 63 G1
Bolton le Sands *Lancs* 63 E3
Bolton Low Houses *Cumb* 71 E4
Bolton Percy *N York* 59 F4
Bolton Upon Dearne *S York* 51 F6
Bolton-on-Swale *N York* 65 F3

Boltonfellend *Cumb* 71 G6
Boltongate *Cumb* 71 E3
Bolventor *Cnwll* 4 C4
Bomere Heath *Shrops* 49 E2
Bonar Bridge *Highld* 107 E5
Bonawe *Ag & B* 90 B2
Bonby *Lincs* 60 D2
Boncath *Pembks* 25 F6
Bonchester Bridge *Border* 80 B2
Bondleigh *Devon* 15 F2
Bonds *Lancs* 63 E1
Bonhill *W Duns* 84 D3
Boningale *Shrops* 39 G6
Bonjedward *Border* 80 C2
Bonkle *N Lans* 85 G2
Bonnington *Angus* 93 G3
Bonnington *Kent* 13 E5
Bonnybank *Fife* 86 D6
Bonnybridge *Falk* 85 G3
Bonnykelly *Abers* 102 D4
Bonnyrigg *Mdloth* 86 D3
Bonnyton *Angus* 93 F3
Bonsall *Derbys* 50 D3
Bonshaw Tower *D & G* 71 E6
Bont-Dolgadfan *Powys* 47 G2
Bontnewydd *Cerdgn* 37 E3
Bontnewydd *Gwynd* 54 D2
Bontuchel *Denbgs* 48 B5
Bonvilston *V Glam* 16 C6
Boode *Devon* 15 E4
Boohay *Devon* 6 A1
Booker *Bucks* 20 B4
Booley *Shrops* 49 E2
Boon *Border* 80 B4
Boosbeck *N York* 66 C5
Boose's Green *Essex* 34 C2
Boot *Cumb* 62 B5
Booth *E R Yk* 60 B3
Booth *W York* 58 B3
Boothby Graffoe *Lincs* 52 C2
Boothby Pagnell *Lincs* 42 B5
Boothstown *Gt Man* 57 G3
Bootle *Cumb* 62 B4
Bootle *Mersyd* 56 D2
Boraston *Shrops* 39 F3
Bordeaux *Guern* 6 c2
Borden *Kent* 22 D2
Bordon *Hants* 10 B5
Boreham *Essex* 22 C6
Boreham *Wilts* 18 B1
Boreham Street *E Susx* 12 B3
Borehamwood *Herts* 21 E5
Boreland *D & G* 79 E2
Boreraig *Highld* 104 A2
Borgh *W Isls* 111 d7
Borgh *W Isls* 111 a1
Borgie *Highld* 109 F5
Borgue *D & G* 69 G2
Borgue *Highld* 110 B2
Borley *Essex* 34 C3
Borneskitaig *Highld* 104 C3
Borness *D & G* 69 G2
Borough Green *Kent* 22 B1
Boroughbridge *N York* 59 E6
Borrowash *Derbys* 41 E6
Borrowby *N York* 65 H2
Borrowstoun *Falk* 86 A4
Borstal *Kent* 22 C2
Borth *Cerdgn* 37 E5
Borth-y-Gest *Gwynd* 47 E5
Borthwickbrae *Border* 79 G4
Borthwickshiels *Border* 79 G4
Borve *Highld* 104 C1
Borve *W Isls* 111 d7
Borve *W Isls* 111 a1
Borve *W Isls* 111 c5
Borwick *Lancs* 63 E3
Bosbury *Herefs* 39 F1
Boscastle *Cnwll* 4 B5
Boscombe *Dorset* 8 D3
Boscombe *Wilts* 18 D1
Bosham *W Susx* 10 B3
Bosherston *Pembks* 24 D2
Bosley *Ches* 50 A3
Bosoughan *Cnwll* 3 E5
Bossall *N York* 60 B5
Bossiney *Cnwll* 4 B5
Bossingham *Kent* 13 F6
Bossington *Somset* 16 A4
Bostock Green *Ches* 49 F6
Boston *Lincs* 43 E6
Boston Spa *W York* 59 E4
Boswinger *Cnwll* 3 F3
Botallack *Cnwll* 2 A3
Botanic Gardens *C Glas* 93 G1
Botany Bay *Gt Lon* 21 F5
Botesdale *Suffk* 34 D6
Bothal *Nthumb* 73 F5
Bothampstead *Berks* 19 G4
Bothamsall *Notts* 51 G4
Bothel *Cumb* 71 E3
Bothenhampton *Dorset* 7 F4
Bothwell *S Lans* 85 F2
Botley *Bucks* 20 C5
Botley *Hants* 9 G4
Botley *Oxon* 31 F1
Botolph Claydon *Bucks* 31 H3
Botolphs *W Susx* 11 E3
Bottesford *Leics* 42 A5
Bottesford *Lincs* 52 B5
Bottisham *Cambs* 33 G4
Bottomcraig *Fife* 93 F2
Bottoms *W York* 58 A2
Botusfleming *Cnwll* 5 E4
Botwnnog *Gwynd* 46 B4
Bough Beech *Kent* 11 G6
Boughrood *Powys* 27 G6
Boughton *Nhants* 31 H6
Boughton *Norfk* 44 A2
Boughton *Notts* 51 G3
Boughton Aluph *Kent* 13 E6
Boughton Green *Kent* 22 C1
Boughton Malherbe *Kent* 22 D1
Boughton Monchelsea *Kent* 22 C1
Boughton Street *Kent* 23 E2
Bouldon *Shrops* 39 E4
Boulmer *Nthumb* 81 H2
Boultham *Lincs* 52 B2
Bourn *Cambs* 33 E4
Bourne *Lincs* 42 C4
Bourne End *Beds* 32 B3
Bourne End *Bucks* 20 C4
Bourne End *Herts* 20 D5
Bournebridge *Essex* 21 G4

Bournebrook *W Mids* 40 B2
Bournemouth *Dorset* 8 D3
Bournemouth Airport *Dorset* 8 D3
Bournes Green *Essex* 22 D4
Bournheath *Worcs* 40 B1
Bournville *W Mids* 40 B2
Bourton *Dorset* 8 A6
Bourton *Oxon* 19 E5
Bourton *Shrops* 39 F5
Bourton *Wilts* 18 C3
Bourton on Dunsmore *Warwks* 41 E1
Bourton-on-the-Hill *Gloucs* 30 C3
Bourton-on-the-Water *Gloucs* 30 C2
Bousd *Ag & B* 88 D5
Bouth *Cumb* 62 D4
Bouthwaite *N York* 65 E1
Bovain *Stirlg* 91 F2
Boveridge *Dorset* 8 C5
Bovey Tracey *Devon* 5 H4
Bovingdon *Herts* 20 D5
Bovington Tank Museum *Dorset* 8 B2
Bow *Devon* 15 F2
Bow *Gt Lon* 21 F4
Bow *Ork* 111 h1
Bow Brickhill *Bucks* 32 B2
Bow of Fife *Fife* 93 E1
Bow Street *Cerdgn* 37 E5
Bowbridge *Gloucs* 29 F3
Bowburn *Dur* 73 G1
Bowcombe *IOW* 9 F2
Bowd *Devon* 6 C4
Bowden *Border* 80 B3
Bowden Hill *Wilts* 18 B3
Bowdon *Gt Man* 57 G2
Bower *Highld* 110 C5
Bower's Row *W York* 59 E3
Bowerchalke *Wilts* 8 C5
Bowermadden *Highld* 110 C5
Bowers *Staffs* 49 G3
Bowers Gifford *Essex* 22 C4
Bowershall *Fife* 86 B5
Bowes *Dur* 64 D4
Bowgreave *Lancs* 63 E1
Bowhouse *D & G* 70 D5
Bowland *Border* 79 G6
Bowley *Herefs* 39 E2
Bowlhead Green *Surrey* 10 C5
Bowling *W Duns* 84 D3
Bowling *W York* 58 C3
Bowmanstead *Cumb* 62 C5
Bowmore *Ag & B* 82 B2
Bowness-on-Solway *Cumb* 71 E5
Bowness-on-Windermere *Cumb* 62 D5
Bowriefauld *Angus* 93 G4
Bowsden *Nthumb* 81 F4
Box *Gloucs* 29 F3
Box *Wilts* 18 B3
Boxford *Berks* 19 F4
Boxford *Suffk* 34 C3
Boxgrove *W Susx* 10 C3
Boxley *Kent* 22 C2
Boxmoor *Herts* 20 D5
Boxted *Essex* 34 D2
Boxted *Suffk* 34 B4
Boxted Cross *Essex* 34 D2
Boxted Heath *Essex* 34 D2
Boxworth *Cambs* 33 E5
Boyden Gate *Kent* 23 G2
Boylestone *Derbys* 40 C6
Boyndie *Abers* 102 C5
Boyndlie *Abers* 103 E5
Boynton *E R Yk* 61 E6
Boysack *Angus* 93 H4
Boyton *Cnwll* 4 D6
Boyton *Suffk* 35 G3
Boyton *Wilts* 18 B1
Boyton Cross *Essex* 22 B6
Boyton End *Suffk* 34 B3
Bozeat *Nhants* 32 B4
Brabourne *Kent* 13 F6
Brabourne Lees *Kent* 13 F5
Brabstermire *Highld* 110 D6
Bracadale *Highld* 96 B6
Braceborough *Lincs* 42 C3
Bracebridge Heath *Lincs* 52 C2
Bracebridge Low Fields *Lincs* 52 B2
Braceby *Lincs* 42 C5
Bracewell *Lancs* 63 H1
Brackenfield *Derbys* 51 E3
Brackenhirst *N Lans* 85 F3
Brackletter *Highld* 98 A1
Brackley *Nhants* 31 G4
Bracknell *Berks* 20 C2
Braco *P & K* 85 G6
Bracobrae *Moray* 101 G4
Bracora *Highld* 97 E2
Bracorina *Highld* 97 E2
Bradbourne *Derbys* 50 D2
Bradbury *Dur* 65 G6
Bradden *Nhants* 31 G4
Bradenham *Bucks* 20 B5
Bradenstoke *Wilts* 18 C4
Bradfield *Berks* 19 G4
Bradfield *Devon* 6 C6
Bradfield *Essex* 35 E2
Bradfield *Norfk* 45 F5
Bradfield *S York* 50 D5
Bradfield Combust *Suffk* 34 C4
Bradfield Green *Ches* 49 F5
Bradfield Heath *Essex* 35 E2
Bradfield St Clare *Suffk* 34 C4
Bradfield St George *Suffk* 34 C4
Bradford *Devon* 14 D2
Bradford *W York* 58 C3
Bradford Abbas *Dorset* 17 G1
Bradford Leigh *Wilts* 18 B3
Bradford Peverell *Dorset* 7 G5
Bradford-on-Avon *Wilts* 18 B3
Bradford-on-Tone *Somset* 16 D2
Bradiford *Devon* 15 E4
Brading *IOW* 9 H2
Bradley *Derbys* 50 D2
Bradley *Hants* 19 H1
Bradley *Lincs* 53 E5
Bradley *Staffs* 49 H1
Bradley *W Mids* 40 B3
Bradley *Worcs* 30 B6
Bradley Green *Worcs* 30 B6
Bradley in the Moors *Staffs* 50 B1
Bradley Stoke *Gloucs* 28 D1
Bradmore *Notts* 41 G6
Bradninch *Devon* 6 B5
Bradnop *Staffs* 50 B2

Bradpole Dorset 7 F5
Bradshaw W York 58 C3
Bradstone Devon 4 D5
Bradwall Green Ches 49 G5
Bradwell Bucks 32 A3
Bradwell Derbys 50 C4
Bradwell Essex 34 B1
Bradwell Norfk 45 H3
Bradwell Waterside Essex 23 E6
Bradwell-on-Sea Essex 23 E5
Bradworthy Devon 14 C3
Brae Highld 107 F2
Brae Shet 111 I3
Brae Roy Lodge Highld 98 B2
Braeface Falk 85 G3
Braehead Angus 95 F2
Braehead D & G 69 E3
Braehead S Lans 77 H6
Braemar Abers 94 B5
Braemore Highld 110 B2
Braemore Highld 106 B4
Braes of Coul Angus 93 E5
Braes of Enzie Moray 101 F5
Braeside Inver 84 B3
Braeswick Ork 111 j3
Braevallich Ag & B 83 G6
Brafferton Dur 65 G5
Brafferton N York 66 A1
Brafield-on-the-Green Nhants 32 A4
Bragar W Isls 111 d7
Bragbury End Herts 33 E1
Braidwood S Lans 77 G6
Brailsford Derbys 50 D1
Braintree Essex 34 B1
Braiseworth Suffk 35 E5
Braishfield Hants 9 F5
Braithwaite Cumb 71 E2
Braithwell S York 51 F6
Bramber W Susx 11 E3
Bramcote Warwks 41 E2
Bramdean Hants 9 H6
Bramerton Norfk 45 F3
Bramfield Herts 21 F6
Bramfield Suffk 35 G5
Bramford Suffk 35 E3
Bramhall Gt Man 50 A5
Bramham W York 59 E4
Bramhope W York 58 D4
Bramley Hants 19 H3
Bramley S York 51 F5
Bramley Surrey 10 D6
Bramley W York 58 D3
Bramley Corner Hants 19 H3
Bramling Kent 23 G1
Brampford Speke Devon 6 B5
Brampton Cambs 32 D5
Brampton Cumb 71 H5
Brampton Cumb 64 B5
Brampton Lincs 52 A3
Brampton Norfk 45 E4
Brampton S York 51 E6
Brampton Suffk 35 G6
Brampton Abbotts Herefs 28 D5
Brampton Ash Nhants 42 A1
Brampton Bryan Herefs 38 D3
Brampton-en-le-Morthen S York 51 F3
Bramshall Staffs 40 B6
Bramshaw Hants 9 E5
Bramshott Hants 10 B5
Bramwell Somset 17 F2
Bran End Essex 33 H2
Branault Highld 89 F5
Brancaster Norfk 44 B6
Brancaster Staithe Norfk 44 B6
Brancepeth Dur 73 F1
Branchill Moray 100 D4
Branderburgh Moray 101 E6
Brandesburton E R Yk 61 E4
Brandeston Suffk 35 F4
Brandiston Norfk 45 E4
Brandon Dur 73 F1
Brandon Lincs 42 B6
Brandon Suffk 44 B1
Brandon Warwks 41 E1
Brandon Parva Norfk 44 D3
Brandsby N York 66 C1
Brandy Wharf Lincs 52 C5
Branksome Dorset 8 C3
Branksome Park Dorset 8 C3
Bransbury Hants 19 F1
Bransby Lincs 52 B3
Branscombe Devon 6 D4
Bransford Worcs 39 G2
Bransgore Hants 8 D3
Bransholme E R Yk 61 E3
Bransley Shrops 39 F3
Branston Leics 42 A5
Branston Lincs 52 C2
Branston Staffs 40 D5
Branston Booths Lincs 52 C2
Branstone IOW 9 G2
Brant Broughton Lincs 52 B1
Brantham Suffk 35 E2
Branthwaite Cumb 70 D2
Branthwaite Cumb 71 F3
Brantingham E R Yk 60 D3
Branton Nthumb 81 F2
Branton S York 51 G6
Branton Green N York 59 E6
Branxton Nthumb 81 E4
Brassington Derbys 50 D2
Brasted Kent 21 G1
Brasted Chart Kent 21 G1
Brathens Abers 95 F5
Bratoft Lincs 53 F2
Brattleby Lincs 52 B3
Bratton Wilts 18 B2
Bratton Clovelly Devon 5 E6
Bratton Fleming Devon 15 F4
Bratton Seymour Somset 17 G2
Braughing Herts 33 F2
Braunston Nhants 31 F6
Braunston Rutlnd 42 A3
Braunstone Leics 41 F4
Braunton Devon 14 D4
Brawby N York 66 D1
Brawl Highld 109 G5
Bray Berks 20 C3
Bray Shop Cnwll 4 D4
Braybrooke Nhants 41 H2
Brayford Devon 15 F4
Braythorn N York 58 D5
Brayton N York 59 G3
Braywick Berks 20 C3

Breachwood Green Herts 32 D1
Breadsall Derbys 51 E1
Breadstone Gloucs 29 E3
Breage Cnwll 2 C2
Breakachy Highld 106 D1
Brealangwell Lodge Highld 106 D5
Bream Gloucs 28 D3
Breamore Hants 8 D5
Brean Somset 16 D4
Breanais W Isls 111 b6
Brearton N York 58 D5
Breascleit W Isls 111 c6
Breasclete W Isls 111 c6
Breaston Derbys 41 F6
Brechfa Carmth 26 B5
Brechin Angus 95 E2
Breckles Norfk 44 C2
Breconside D & G 78 B2
Brecon Powys 27 F5
Bredbury Gt Man 50 A5
Brede E Susx 12 D4
Bredenbury Herefs 39 F2
Bredfield Suffk 35 F4
Bredgar Kent 22 D2
Bredhurst Kent 22 C2
Bredon Worcs 29 G6
Bredon's Hardwick Worcs 29 F6
Bredon's Norton Worcs 29 G6
Bredwardine Herefs 38 D1
Breedon on the Hill Leics 41 E5
Breich W Loth 85 H2
Breightmet Gt Man 57 G3
Breighton E R Yk 60 B3
Breinton Herefs 28 C6
Bremhill Wilts 18 C4
Brenchley Kent 12 B6
Brendon Devon 15 G5
Brenfield Ag & B 83 F4
Brenish W Isls 111 b6
Brent Eleigh Suffk 34 C3
Brent Knoll Somset 17 E4
Brent Mill Devon 5 G3
Brent Pelham Herts 33 F2
Brentford Gt Lon 21 E3
Brentingby Leics 42 A4
Brentwood Essex 22 B4
Brenzett Kent 13 E4
Brenzett Green Kent 13 E5
Brereton Staffs 40 B5
Brereton Green Ches 49 G5
Bressingham Norfk 34 D6
Bretby Derbys 40 D5
Bretford Warwks 41 E1
Bretforton Worcs 30 C4
Bretherton Lancs 57 E4
Brettabister Shet 111 I2
Brettenham Norfk 44 C1
Brettenham Suffk 34 C4
Bretton Flints 48 D5
Brewood Staffs 40 A4
Briantspuddle Dorset 8 A3
Brick Houses S York 50 D4
Brickendon Herts 21 F6
Bricket Wood Herts 20 D5
Bricklehampton Worcs 29 G6
Bride IOM 116 d5
Bridekirk Cumb 71 E3
Bridestowe Devon 5 F5
Brideswell Abers 102 B3
Bridford Devon 5 H5
Bridge Cnwll 2 D4
Bridge Kent 23 F1
Bridge Hewick N York 65 G1
Bridge of Alford Abers 102 B2
Bridge of Allan Stirlg 85 G5
Bridge of Avon Moray 101 E3
Bridge of Avon Moray 100 D2
Bridge of Balgie P & K 91 G3
Bridge of Brewlands Angus 94 B2
Bridge of Brown Highld 100 D2
Bridge of Cally P & K 92 D4
Bridge of Canny Abers 95 E5
Bridge of Craigisla Angus 93 E4
Bridge of Dee D & G 70 B5
Bridge of Don Aber C 103 E1
Bridge of Dulsie Highld 100 C3
Bridge of Dye Abers 95 E4
Bridge of Earn P & K 92 D1
Bridge of Ericht P & K 91 F4
Bridge of Feugh Abers 95 F5
Bridge of Forss Highld 110 A5
Bridge of Gairn Abers 94 C5
Bridge of Gaur P & K 91 F4
Bridge of Marnoch Abers 102 B4
Bridge of Orchy Ag & B 91 E3
Bridge of Tilt P & K 92 B5
Bridge of Tynet Moray 101 F5
Bridge of Walls Shet 111 k2
Bridge of Weir Rens 84 D2
Bridge Sollers Herefs 28 C6
Bridge Street Suffk 34 C4
Bridge Trafford Ches 49 E6
Bridgehampton Somset 17 G2
Bridgehill Dur 73 E2
Bridgemary Hants 9 G4
Bridgend Abers 101 G3
Bridgend Ag & B 82 C2
Bridgend Angus 95 E3
Bridgend Brdgnd 27 E1
Bridgend D & G 78 D3
Bridgend Fife 93 F1
Bridgend Moray 101 F3
Bridgend P & K 92 D2
Bridgend W Loth 86 B3
Bridgend of Lintrathen Angus 93 E4
Bridgerule Devon 14 C2
Bridgetown Somset 16 B2
Bridgham Norfk 44 C1
Bridgnorth Shrops 39 G5
Bridgtown Staffs 40 B4
Bridgwater Somset 16 D3
Bridlington E R Yk 61 E6
Bridport Dorset 7 F5
Bridstow Herefs 28 D5
Brierfield Lancs 57 H6
Brierley Gloucs 28 D3
Brierley W York 59 E1
Brierley Hill W Mids 40 A2
Brigg Lincs 52 C5
Briggate Norfk 45 F4
Briggswath N York 67 E4
Brigham Cumb 70 D2

Brigham E R Yk 61 E5
Brighouse W York 58 C2
Brighstone IOW 9 F2
Brighthampton Oxon 31 E1
Brightley Devon 15 E1
Brightling E Susx 12 B4
Brightlingsea Essex 34 D1
Brighton E Susx 11 F3
Brighton le Sands Mersyd 56 C3
Brightons Falk 85 H3
Brightwalton Berks 19 F4
Brightwell Suffk 35 F3
Brightwell Baldwin Oxon 19 H6
Brightwell Upperton Oxon 19 H6
Brightwell-cum-Sotwell Oxon 19 G5
Brignall Dur 65 E4
Brigsley Lincs 53 E5
Brigsteer Cumb 63 E5
Brigstock Nhants 42 B1
Brill Bucks 31 G2
Brill Cnwll 2 D2
Brilley Herefs 38 C1
Brimfield Herefs 39 E3
Brimfield Cross Herefs 39 E3
Brimington Derbys 51 E4
Brimley Devon 5 H4
Brimpsfield Gloucs 29 G4
Brimpton Berks 19 G3
Brimscombe Gloucs 29 F3
Brimstage Mersyd 56 C1
Brincliffe S York 51 E5
Brind E R Yk 60 B3
Brindister Shet 111 k2
Brindle Lancs 57 F5
Brineton Staffs 49 G1
Bringhurst Leics 42 A2
Brington Cambs 32 C6
Briningham Norfk 44 D5
Brinkhill Lincs 53 F3
Brinkley Cambs 33 H4
Brinklow Warwks 41 E2
Brinkworth Wilts 18 C5
Brinscall Lancs 57 F4
Brinsley Notts 51 F2
Brinsworth S York 51 E5
Brinton Norfk 44 D5
Brinyan Ork 111 h2
Brisley Norfk 44 C4
Brislington Bristl 17 G5
Brissenden Green Kent 12 D5
Briston Norfk 44 D5
Britford Wilts 8 D6
Brithdir Caerph 27 G3
Brithdir Gwynd 47 F3
British Legion Village Kent 22 C1
Briton Ferry Neath 26 D2
Britwell Salome Oxon 19 H5
Brixham Devon 6 B2
Brixton Devon 5 F2
Brixton Gt Lon 21 F3
Brixton Deverill Wilts 18 B1
Brixworth Nhants 41 H1
Brize Norton Oxon 30 D1
Broad Alley Worcs 30 A6
Broad Blunsdon Wilts 18 D5
Broad Campden Gloucs 30 C4
Broad Carr W York 58 C2
Broad Chalke Wilts 8 C5
Broad Green Essex 34 C1
Broad Green Worcs 39 G2
Broad Haven Pembks 24 C4
Broad Hinton Wilts 18 D4
Broad Laying Hants 19 F3
Broad Marston Worcs 30 C4
Broad Oak E Susx 12 D4
Broad Oak E Susx 12 B4
Broad Oak Herefs 28 C4
Broad Oak Kent 23 F2
Broad Oak Mersyd 57 E2
Broad Street E Susx 12 D4
Broad Street Kent 22 D1
Broad Street Kent 22 C6
Broad Town Wilts 18 D4
Broad's Green Essex 22 C6
Broadbottom Gt Man 50 B5
Broadbridge W Susx 10 B3
Broadbridge Heath W Susx 11 E5
Broadclyst Devon 6 B5
Broadfield Inver 84 C3
Broadford Highld 96 A4
Broadford Bridge W Susx 10 D4
Broadgairhill Border 79 E4
Broadhaugh Border 81 E5
Broadheath Gt Man 57 G2
Broadhembury Devon 6 C6
Broadhempston Devon 5 H3
Broadland Row E Susx 12 D4
Broadley Moray 101 F5
Broadmayne Dorset 7 H4
Broadmoor Pembks 25 E3
Broadoak Dorset 7 F5
Broadstairs Kent 23 H2
Broadstone Dorset 8 C3
Broadstone Shrops 39 E5
Broadwas Worcs 39 G2
Broadwater Herts 33 E1
Broadwater W Susx 11 E3
Broadwaters Worcs 39 H4
Broadway Pembks 24 C4
Broadway Somset 17 E1
Broadway Worcs 30 C4
Broadwell Gloucs 30 D3
Broadwell Oxon 30 D1
Broadwell Warwks 31 F6
Broadwindsor Dorset 7 F5
Broadwoodkelly Devon 15 E2
Broadwoodwidger Devon 5 E5
Brochel Highld 104 D1
Brockamin Worcs 39 G2
Brockbridge Hants 9 H5
Brockdish Norfk 35 E6
Brockenhurst Hants 9 E3
Brocketsbrae S Lans 78 B6
Brockford Street Suffk 35 E5
Brockhall Nhants 31 G6
Brockham Surrey 21 E1
Brockhampton Gloucs 30 B2
Brockhampton Hants 10 A3
Brockhampton Herefs 28 D5
Brockholes W York 58 C1
Brocklesby Lincs 61 E1

Brockley Somset 17 F5
Brockley Suffk 34 B5
Brockley Green Suffk 34 B3
Brockley Green Suffk 34 B4
Brockton Shrops 38 D6
Brockton Shrops 38 D4
Brockton Shrops 39 F5
Brockton Staffs 49 G3
Brockweir Gloucs 28 D3
Brockworth Gloucs 29 F4
Brocton Staffs 40 B5
Brodick N Ayrs 75 H4
Brodie Moray 100 C5
Brodsworth S York 59 F1
Brogaig Highld 104 C3
Broken Cross Ches 50 A4
Brokenborough Wilts 18 B5
Brokerswood Wilts 18 B2
Bromborough Mersyd 56 D1
Brome Suffk 35 E6
Brome Street Suffk 35 E6
Bromeswell Suffk 35 F4
Bromfield Cumb 71 E4
Bromfield Shrops 39 E4
Bromham Beds 32 C4
Bromham Wilts 18 C3
Bromley Gt Lon 21 G2
Bromley Shrops 39 G5
Brompton Kent 22 C2
Brompton N York 65 G3
Brompton N York 67 E2
Brompton Ralph Somset 16 C2
Brompton Regis Somset 16 B2
Brompton-on-Swale N York 65 F3
Bromsberrow Gloucs 29 E5
Bromsberrow Heath Gloucs 29 E5
Bromsgrove Worcs 40 B1
Bromyard Herefs 39 F2
Bronant Cerdgn 37 E3
Brongest Cerdgn 36 C3
Bronington Wrexhm 49 E3
Bronllys Powys 27 G6
Bronwydd Carmth 25 G5
Bronygarth Shrops 48 C3
Brook Hants 9 E5
Brook IOW 9 F2
Brook Kent 13 E6
Brook Surrey 10 C5
Brook Hill Hants 9 E4
Brook Street Essex 22 B4
Brook Street Kent 12 D5
Brook Street Suffk 34 B3
Brooke Norfk 45 F2
Brooke Rutlnd 42 B3
Brookfield Rens 84 D2
Brookhampton Somset 17 G2
Brookhouse Lancs 63 E3
Brookhouse S York 51 F5
Brookhouse Green Ches 49 G5
Brookhouses Derbys 50 B5
Brookland Kent 13 E4
Brooklands Gt Man 57 G2
Brookmans Park Herts 21 E5
Brookthorpe Gloucs 29 F4
Brookwood Surrey 20 C1
Broom Beds 32 D3
Broom N York 73 F1
Broom S York 51 E5
Broom Wilts 30 C5
Broom Hill Notts 51 F2
Broom Hill S York 51 E6
Broom Street Kent 23 E2
Broome Norfk 45 F2
Broome Shrops 38 D4
Broome Worcs 40 A2
Broomedge Ches 57 G2
Broomfield Essex 22 C6
Broomfield Kent 22 D1
Broomfield Kent 23 F2
Broomfield Somset 16 D2
Broomfleet E R Yk 60 C3
Broomhaugh Nthumb 72 D3
Broomhill Nthumb 73 F6
Brora Highld 107 G6
Broseley Shrops 39 F6
Brotherlee Dur 72 D1
Brotherton N York 59 F3
Brotton N York 66 C5
Broubster Highld 110 A5
Brough Cumb 64 C4
Brough E R Yk 60 C3
Brough Highld 110 C6
Brough Notts 52 A2
Brough Shet 111 I3
Brough Lodge Shet 111 m4
Brough Sowerby Cumb 64 C4
Broughall Shrops 49 E3
Broughton Border 78 D6
Broughton Bucks 32 B3
Broughton Cambs 33 E6
Broughton Flints 48 D5
Broughton Gt Man 57 G3
Broughton Hants 9 E6
Broughton Lancs 57 F6
Broughton Lincs 52 B6
Broughton N York 66 D1
Broughton N York 58 B5
Broughton Nhants 32 A6
Broughton Oxon 31 E4
Broughton Staffs 49 G3
Broughton V Glam 16 B5
Broughton Astley Leics 41 F3
Broughton Gifford Wilts 18 B3
Broughton Green Worcs 30 B6
Broughton Hackett Worcs 30 A5
Broughton Mains D & G 69 E2
Broughton Mills Cumb 62 C5
Broughton Moor Cumb 70 D3
Broughton Poggs Oxon 30 D1
Broughton-in-Furness Cumb 62 C4
Broughty Ferry Dund C 93 G2
Brown Candover Hants 19 G1
Brown Edge Staffs 50 A2
Brownhill Abers 102 D3
Brownhills Fife 93 G1
Brownhills W Mids 40 B4
Browninghill Green Hants 19 G3
Browns Hill Gloucs 29 F3
Brownsham Devon 14 C3
Brownston Devon 5 G2
Broxa N York 67 E3
Broxbourne Herts 21 F5
Broxburn E Loth 87 G4
Broxburn W Loth 86 B3

Broxted Essex 33 G2
Broxwood Herefs 38 D2
Bruan Highld 110 D3
Bruar P & K 92 B5
Brucefield Highld 107 H4
Bruchag Ag & B 84 A2
Bruichladdich Ag & B 82 B2
Bruisyard Suffk 35 F5
Bruisyard Street Suffk 35 F5
Brumby Lincs 52 B6
Brund Staffs 50 C3
Brundall Norfk 45 F3
Brundish Suffk 35 F5
Brundish Street Suffk 35 F5
Brunthwaite W York 58 B4
Bruntingthorpe Leics 41 G2
Brunton Fife 93 E2
Brunton Nthumb 81 G3
Brunton Wilts 19 E2
Brushford Somset 16 B2
Brushford Barton Devon 15 F2
Bruton Somset 17 G3
Bryan's Green Worcs 30 A6
Bryanston Dorset 8 B4
Brydekirk D & G 71 E6
Brympton Somset 17 F1
Bryn Neath 26 D2
Bryn Gates Lancs 57 F3
Bryn Saith Marchog Denbgs 48 B4
Bryn-coch Neath 26 D3
Bryn-Henllan Pembks 24 D6
Bryn-mawr Gwynd 46 B4
Bryn-y-Maen Conwy 55 F4
Brynaman Carmth 26 C4
Brynberian Pembks 25 E6
Bryncir Gwynd 46 D5
Bryncroes Gwynd 46 B4
Bryncrug Gwynd 47 E2
Bryneglwys Denbgs 48 B4
Brynford Flints 48 B6
Bryngwran IOA 54 B4
Bryngwyn Mons 28 B3
Bryngwyn Powys 38 C1
Brynhoffnant Cerdgn 36 C2
Brynmawr Blae G 27 G4
Brynmenyn Brdgnd 27 E2
Brynmill Swans 26 C2
Brynna Rhondd 27 F1
Brynrefail Gwynd 54 D3
Brynsadler Rhondd 27 F1
Brynsiencyn IOA 54 C3
Bualintur Highld 96 C4
Bubbenhall Warwks 41 E1
Bubwith E R Yk 60 B3
Buchanan Smithy Stirlg 84 D4
Buchanhaven Abers 103 F4
Buchanty P & K 92 B2
Buchany Stirlg 85 F5
Buchlyvie Stirlg 85 E5
Buck's Cross Devon 14 C3
Buck's Mills Devon 14 C3
Buckabank Cumb 71 F4
Buckden Cambs 32 D5
Buckden N York 64 D1
Buckenham Norfk 45 F3
Buckerell Devon 6 C5
Buckfast Devon 5 G4
Buckfastleigh Devon 5 G3
Buckhaven Fife 86 D5
Buckholm Border 79 H5
Buckholt Mons 28 C4
Buckhorn Weston Dorset 17 H2
Buckhurst Hill Essex 21 G4
Buckie Moray 101 F5
Buckingham Bucks 31 G3
Buckland Bucks 20 C6
Buckland Devon 5 G2
Buckland Gloucs 30 C3
Buckland Herts 33 E2
Buckland Kent 13 G6
Buckland Oxon 19 E6
Buckland Surrey 21 E1
Buckland Brewer Devon 14 D3
Buckland Common Bucks 20 C5
Buckland Dinham Somset 17 H4
Buckland Filleigh Devon 14 D2
Buckland in the Moor Devon 5 G4
Buckland Monachorum Devon 5 E3
Buckland Newton Dorset 7 G6
Buckland Ripers Dorset 7 G4
Buckland St Mary Somset 16 D1
Buckland-Tout-Saints Devon 5 G2
Bucklebury Berks 19 G4
Bucklers Hard Hants 9 F3
Bucklesham Suffk 35 F3
Buckley Flints 48 C5
Bucklow Hill Ches 57 G1
Buckminster Leics 42 B4
Bucknall Lincs 52 D2
Bucknall Staffs 50 A2
Bucknell Oxon 31 F3
Bucknell Shrops 38 D3
Buckpool Moray 101 F5
Bucks Green W Susx 10 D5
Bucks Horn Oak Hants 10 B6
Bucksburn Aber C 103 E1
Buckton E R Yk 67 G1
Buckton Nthumb 81 F4
Buckworth Cambs 32 D6
Budby Notts 51 G4
Budd's Titson Cnwll 14 C2
Buddon Angus 93 G3
Bude Cnwll 14 B2
Budge's Shop Cnwll 4 D3
Budleigh Salterton Devon 6 C4
Budock Water Cnwll 2 D2
Buerton Ches 49 F4
Bugbrooke Nhants 31 G5
Bugle Cnwll 3 F5
Bugley Dorset 8 A5
Bugthorpe E R Yk 60 B5
Buildwas Shrops 39 F6
Builth Wells Powys 38 A1
Bulbridge Wilts 8 D6
Buldoo Highld 110 A5
Bulford Wilts 18 D1
Bulkeley Ches 49 E4
Bulkington Warwks 41 E2
Bulkington Wilts 18 B3
Bulkworthy Devon 14 D3
Bullbrook Berks 20 C2
Bullington Hants 19 F1
Bullington Lincs 52 C3
Bulmer Essex 34 B3
Bulmer N York 60 B6

164

Bulmer Tye *Essex* 34 B3
Bulphan *Essex* 22 B4
Bulwark *Abers* 103 E4
Bulwell *Notts* 51 F1
Bulwick *Nhants* 42 B2
Bumble's Green *Essex* 21 G5
Bunacaimb *Highld* 97 E1
Bunarkaig *Highld* 98 A2
Bunbury *Ches* 49 E5
Bunchrew *Highld* 107 E1
Bundalloch *Highld* 97 F5
Bunessan *Ag & B* 89 E1
Bungay *Suffk* 45 F1
Bunnahabhain *Ag & B* 82 C3
Bunny *Notts* 41 G6
Buntait *Highld* 98 C5
Buntingford *Herts* 33 E2
Bunwell *Norfk* 45 E2
Bunwell Street *Norfk* 45 E2
Burbage *Leics* 41 E3
Burbage *Wilts* 19 E3
Burchett's Green *Berks* 20 B3
Burcombe *Wilts* 8 C6
Burcott *Bucks* 32 B1
Bures *Essex* 34 C2
Burford *Oxon* 30 D2
Burford *Shrops* 39 F3
Burg *Ag & B* 89 E3
Burgates *Hants* 10 B5
Burgess Hill *W Susx* 11 F4
Burgh *Suffk* 35 E4
Burgh by Sands *Cumb* 71 F5
Burgh Castle *Norfk* 45 G3
Burgh Heath *Surrey* 21 E2
Burgh le Marsh *Lincs* 53 G2
Burgh next Aylsham *Norfk* 45 E4
Burgh on Bain *Lincs* 52 D4
Burgh St Margaret *Norfk* 45 G3
Burgh St Peter *Norfk* 45 G2
Burghclere *Hants* 19 F3
Burghead *Moray* 100 D6
Burghfield *Berks* 19 H3
Burghfield Common *Berks* 19 H3
Burghill *Herefs* 39 E1
Burghwallis *S York* 59 F2
Burham *Kent* 22 C2
Buriton *Hants* 10 B4
Burland *Ches* 49 F4
Burlawn *Cnwll* 3 F6
Burleigh *Berks* 20 C2
Burleigh *Gloucs* 29 F3
Burlescombe *Devon* 16 C1
Burleston *Dorset* 8 A3
Burley *Hants* 8 D4
Burley *Rutlnd* 42 B3
Burley Gate *Herefs* 39 F1
Burley in Wharfedale *W York* 58 C4
Burley Street *Hants* 8 D4
Burley Wood Head *W York* 58 C4
Burleydam *Ches* 49 F3
Burlingham Green *Norfk* 45 F3
Burlton *Shrops* 49 E2
Burmarsh *Kent* 13 F5
Burmington *Warwks* 30 D4
Burn *N York* 59 G3
Burn of Cambus *Stirlg* 85 F5
Burnage *Gt Man* 57 H2
Burnaston *Derbys* 40 D6
Burnbrae *N Lans* 85 G2
Burnby *E R Yk* 60 C4
Burneside *Cumb* 63 E5
Burneston *N York* 65 G2
Burnett *Somset* 17 G5
Burnfoot *Border* 79 G4
Burnfoot *Border* 80 B2
Burnfoot *D & G* 78 C2
Burnfoot *D & G* 79 F2
Burnfoot *D & G* 79 G2
Burnfoot *P & K* 86 A6
Burnham *Bucks* 20 C3
Burnham Deepdale *Norfk* 44 B6
Burnham Green *Herts* 33 E1
Burnham Market *Norfk* 44 B6
Burnham Norton *Norfk* 44 B6
Burnham Overy *Norfk* 44 B6
Burnham Overy Staithe *Norfk* 44 B6
Burnham Thorpe *Norfk* 44 C6
Burnham-on-Crouch *Essex* 23 E5
Burnham-on-Sea *Somset* 17 E4
Burnhaven *Abers* 103 F4
Burnhead *D & G* 78 C2
Burnhervie *Abers* 102 C2
Burnhill Green *Staffs* 39 G5
Burnhope *Dur* 73 F2
Burnhouse *N Ayrs* 76 D6
Burniston *N York* 67 F3
Burnley *Lancs* 57 H5
Burnmoor *Dur* 73 G2
Burnmouth *Border* 81 E5
Burnopfield *Dur* 73 F2
Burnsall *N York* 58 B6
Burnside *Angus* 93 G4
Burnside *Angus* 93 F5
Burnside *Fife* 86 B6
Burnside *Moray* 101 E6
Burnside *W Loth* 86 B3
Burnside of Duntrune *Angus* 93 F3
Burnt Yates *N York* 58 D6
Burntisland *Fife* 86 C4
Burntwood *Staffs* 40 B4
Burnworthy *Somset* 16 D1
Burpham *Surrey* 20 D1
Burpham *W Susx* 10 D3
Burradon *Nthumb* 81 E1
Burrafirth *Shet* 111 m4
Burravoe *Shet* 111 I3
Burrells *Cumb* 64 B5
Burrelton *P & K* 92 D3
Burridge *Devon* 7 E6
Burridge *Hants* 9 G4
Burrill *N York* 65 F2
Burringham *Lincs* 52 A6
Burrington *Devon* 15 F4
Burrington *Herefs* 38 D3
Burrington *Somset* 17 F5
Burrough Green *Cambs* 33 H4
Burrough on the Hill *Leics* 41 H4
Burrow *Lancs* 63 F3
Burrow *Somset* 16 B3
Burrow Bridge *Somset* 17 E2
Burrowhill *Surrey* 20 C2
Burry Port *Carmth* 25 H3
Burrygreen *Swans* 26 A2
Burscough *Lancs* 56 D4

Burscough Bridge *Lancs* 57 E4
Bursea *E R Yk* 60 B3
Bursledon *Hants* 9 G4
Burslem *Staffs* 49 H4
Burstall *Suffk* 34 D3
Burstock *Dorset* 7 C5
Burston *Norfk* 45 E1
Burstow *Surrey* 11 F6
Burstwick *E R Yk* 61 F3
Bursersett *N York* 64 C2
Burthorpe Green *Suffk* 34 B5
Burtoft *Lincs* 43 E5
Burton *Ches* 48 D6
Burton *Ches* 49 E5
Burton *Dorset* 8 C3
Burton *Lincs* 52 B3
Burton *Pembks* 24 D3
Burton *Somset* 16 D3
Burton *Somset* 18 A4
Burton Agnes *E R Yk* 61 E6
Burton Bradstock *Dorset* 7 F4
Burton Coggles *Lincs* 42 C4
Burton Constable Hall *E R Yk* 61 E3
Burton End *Essex* 33 G1
Burton Fleming *E R Yk* 67 F1
Burton Hastings *Warwks* 41 E2
Burton in Lonsdale *N York* 63 F3
Burton Joyce *Notts* 51 G1
Burton Latimer *Nhants* 32 B6
Burton Lazars *Leics* 41 H5
Burton Leonard *N York* 59 E6
Burton on the Wolds *Leics* 41 G5
Burton Overy *Leics* 41 G3
Burton Pedwardine *Lincs* 42 D6
Burton Pidsea *E R Yk* 61 F3
Burton Salmon *N York* 59 F3
Burton upon Stather *Lincs* 60 C2
Burton upon Trent *Staffs* 40 D5
Burton's Green *Essex* 34 B2
Burton-in-Kendal *Cumb* 63 E3
Burtonwood *Ches* 57 E2
Burwardsley *Ches* 49 E5
Burwarton *Shrops* 39 F4
Burwash *E Susx* 12 B4
Burwash Common *E Susx* 12 B4
Burwash Weald *E Susx* 12 B4
Burwell *Cambs* 33 G5
Burwell *Lincs* 53 E3
Burwen *IOA* 54 C5
Burwick *Ork* 111 h1
Bury *Cambs* 43 E1
Bury *Gt Man* 57 G4
Bury *Somset* 16 B2
Bury *W Susx* 10 D3
Bury St Edmunds *Suffk* 34 C5
Burythorpe *N York* 60 B6
Busby *E Rens* 85 E2
Buscot *Wilts* 19 E6
Bush *Abers* 95 F3
Bush Bank *Herefs* 39 E2
Bush Hill Park *Gt Lon* 21 F5
Bushbury *W Mids* 40 A3
Bushey *Herts* 21 E5
Bushey Heath *Herts* 21 E4
Bushley *Worcs* 29 F6
Bushton *Wilts* 18 C4
Bussex *Somset* 17 E3
Butcombe *Somset* 17 F5
Butleigh *Somset* 17 F2
Butleigh Wootton *Somset* 17 F3
Butlers Marston *Warwks* 30 D5
Butley *Suffk* 35 G4
Buttercrambe *N York* 60 B5
Butterdean *Border* 87 G3
Butterknowle *Dur* 65 E5
Butterleigh *Devon* 6 B6
Buttermere *Cumb* 71 E1
Buttershaw *W York* 58 C3
Butterstone *P & K* 92 C4
Butterton *Staffs* 49 G3
Butterton *Staffs* 50 C2
Butterwick *Lincs* 43 F6
Butterwick *N York* 66 D1
Butterwick *N York* 67 F1
Buttington *Powys* 38 C6
Buttonoak *Shrops* 39 G4
Buxhall *Suffk* 34 D4
Buxted *E Susx* 11 G4
Buxton *Derbys* 50 B4
Buxton *Norfk* 45 E4
Buxton Heath *Norfk* 45 E4
Bwlch *Powys* 27 G5
Bwlch-y-cibau *Powys* 48 B1
Bwlch-y-ffridd *Powys* 38 B5
Bwlch-y-groes *Pembks* 25 F6
Bwlch-y-sarnau *Powys* 38 A3
Bwlchgwyn *Wrexhm* 48 C4
Bwlchllan *Cerdgn* 37 E3
Bwlchtocyn *Gwynd* 46 C4
Byers Green *Dur* 65 F6
Byfield *Nhants* 31 F5
Byfleet *Surrey* 20 D2
Byford *Herefs* 38 D1
Byker *T & W* 73 F3
Bylchau *Conwy* 55 G3
Byley *Ches* 49 G6
Byrewalls *Border* 80 C4
Byrness *Nthumb* 72 B6
Bystock *Devon* 6 B4
Bythorn *Cambs* 32 C6
Byton *Herefs* 38 D3
Bywell *Nthumb* 73 E3
Byworth *W Susx* 10 C4

C

Cabourne *Lincs* 52 D5
Cabrach *Ag & B* 82 D2
Cabrach *Moray* 101 F2
Cabus *Lancs* 63 E1
Cabvie Lodge *Highld* 106 B3
Cadbury *Devon* 6 B6
Cadder *E Duns* 85 E3
Caddington *Beds* 32 C1
Caddonfoot *Border* 79 G6
Cade Street *E Susx* 12 B4
Cadeby *Leics* 41 E3

Cadeby *S York* 51 F6
Cadeleigh *Devon* 6 B6
Cadgwith *Cnwll* 2 D1
Cadham *Fife* 86 C6
Cadishead *Gt Man* 57 G2
Cadle *Swans* 26 C2
Cadley *Lancs* 57 E5
Cadley *Wilts* 18 D3
Cadley *Wilts* 19 E2
Cadmore End *Bucks* 20 B4
Cadnam *Hants* 9 E4
Cadney *Lincs* 52 C5
Cadoxton *V Glam* 16 C5
Cadoxton Juxta-Neath *Neath* 26 D3
Caeathro *Gwynd* 54 D3
Caenby *Lincs* 52 C4
Caeo *Carmth* 37 F1
Caer Farchell *Pembks* 24 C5
Caerau *Brdgnd* 27 E2
Caerau *Cardif* 16 C6
Caergeiliog *IOA* 54 B4
Caergwrle *Flints* 48 C5
Caerlanrig *Border* 79 G3
Caerleon *Newpt* 28 B2
Caernarfon *Gwynd* 54 C3
Caernarfon Airport *Gwynd* 54 C2
Caernarfon Castle *Gwynd* 54 C3
Caerphilly *Caerph* 27 G2
Caersws *Powys* 38 A5
Caerwedros *Cerdgn* 36 C2
Caerwent *Mons* 28 C2
Caerwys *Flints* 48 B6
Cairinis *W Isls* 111 b3
Cairnbaan *Ag & B* 83 F4
Cairnbulg *Abers* 103 F5
Cairncross *Border* 81 E6
Cairncurran *Inver* 84 C3
Cairndow *Ag & B* 84 B6
Cairneyhill *Fife* 86 B4
Cairnfield House *Moray* 101 F5
Cairngarroch *D & G* 68 C3
Cairngrassie *Abers* 95 G5
Cairnie *Abers* 101 G4
Cairnorrie *Abers* 102 D3
Cairnryan *D & G* 68 C4
Cairnty *Moray* 101 F4
Caister-on-Sea *Norfk* 45 H3
Caistor *Lincs* 52 D5
Caistor St Edmund *Norfk* 45 E3
Calanais *W Isls* 111 c6
Calbourne *IOW* 9 F2
Calcot *Flints* 48 B6
Calcot *Gloucs* 30 C1
Calcot Row *Berks* 19 H4
Calcots *Moray* 101 E5
Caldbeck *Cumb* 71 F3
Caldecote *Cambs* 42 D1
Caldecote *Cambs* 33 E4
Caldecote *Herts* 33 E3
Caldecote Highfields *Cambs* 33 E4
Caldecott *Nhants* 32 C5
Caldecott *Oxon* 19 G6
Caldecott *Rutlnd* 42 B2
Calder Bridge *Cumb* 62 A6
Calder Grove *W York* 58 D2
Calder Vale *Lancs* 63 E1
Calderbank *N Lans* 85 F2
Caldercruix *N Lans* 85 G2
Caldermill *S Lans* 77 F5
Calderwood *S Lans* 85 F1
Caldicot *Mons* 28 C2
Caldwell *N York* 65 F4
Calfsound *Ork* 111 h3
Calgary *Ag & B* 89 E4
Califer *Moray* 100 D5
California *Falk* 85 H3
California *Norfk* 45 H3
Calke *Derbys* 41 E5
Callakille *Highld* 105 E2
Callander *Stirlg* 85 E6
Callanish *W Isls* 111 c6
Callestick *Cnwll* 2 D4
Calligarry *Highld* 96 D3
Callington *Cnwll* 4 D4
Callow *Herefs* 28 C6
Callow End *Worcs* 39 H1
Callow Hill *Wilts* 18 C5
Calmore *Hants* 9 E4
Calmsden *Gloucs* 30 B1
Calne *Wilts* 18 C4
Calshot *Hants* 9 G3
Calstock *Cnwll* 5 E4
Calstone Wellington *Wilts* 18 C3
Calthorpe *Norfk* 45 E5
Calthorpe Street *Norfk* 45 G4
Calthwaite *Cumb* 71 G3
Calton *N York* 58 A5
Calton *Staffs* 50 C2
Calveley *Ches* 49 F5
Calver *Derbys* 50 D4
Calverhall *Shrops* 49 F3
Calverleigh *Devon* 16 B1
Calverton *Bucks* 32 A3
Calverton *Notts* 51 G2
Calvine *P & K* 92 A5
Calvo *Cumb* 71 E4
Calzeat *Border* 78 D6
Cam *Gloucs* 29 E3
Camas Luinie *Highld* 97 G5
Camasachoirce *Highld* 89 H5
Camasine *Highld* 89 G5
Camastianavaig *Highld* 96 C6
Camault Muir *Highld* 98 D6
Camber *E Susx* 13 E4
Camberley *Surrey* 20 C2
Camberwell *Gt Lon* 21 F3
Camblesforth *N York* 59 G3
Cambo *Nthumb* 72 D5
Camborne *Cnwll* 2 C3
Cambourne *Cambs* 33 E4
Cambridge *Cambs* 33 H4
Cambridge *Gloucs* 29 E3
Cambridge Airport *Cambs* 33 F4
Cambrose *Cnwll* 2 D4
Cambus *Clacks* 85 G5
Cambus o' May *Abers* 94 D5
Cambusavie Platform *Highld* 107 F5
Cambusbarron *Stirlg* 85 G4
Cambuskenneth *Stirlg* 85 G5
Cambuslang *S Lans* 85 F2
Cambuswallace *S Lans* 78 D6
Camden Town *Gt Lon* 21 F4
Cameley *Somset* 17 G4
Camelford *Cnwll* 4 B5

Camelon *Falk* 85 G4
Camer's Green *Worcs* 29 E6
Camerory *Highld* 100 C3
Camerton *Cumb* 70 D3
Camerton *Somset* 17 G4
Camghouran *P & K* 91 G4
Camieston *Border* 80 B3
Cammachmore *Abers* 95 G5
Cammeringham *Lincs* 52 B3
Camore *Highld* 107 G5
Campbeltown *Ag & B* 75 E3
Campbeltown Airport *Ag & B* 75 E3
Cample *D & G* 78 C2
Campmuir *Angus* 93 E3
Camps *W Loth* 86 B3
Camps End *Cambs* 33 G3
Campsall *S York* 59 F2
Campsea Ash *Suffk* 35 F4
Campton *Beds* 32 D3
Camptown *Border* 80 C2
Camrose *Pembks* 24 D4
Camserney *P & K* 92 B4
Camusnagaul *Highld* 105 H4
Camusnagaul *Highld* 90 C6
Camusteel *Highld* 97 E6
Camusterrach *Highld* 97 E6
Canada *Hants* 9 E5
Candacraig *Abers* 94 C5
Candlesby *Lincs* 53 F2
Candyburn *Border* 78 D6
Cane End *Oxon* 20 A3
Canewdon *Essex* 22 D4
Canford Cliffs *Dorset* 8 C2
Canford Heath *Dorset* 8 C3
Canford Magna *Dorset* 8 C3
Canisbay *Highld* 110 D6
Canley *W Mids* 40 D1
Cann *Dorset* 8 B5
Cannich *Highld* 98 B5
Canning Town *Gt Lon* 21 G3
Cannington *Somset* 16 D3
Cannock *Staffs* 40 B4
Cannon Bridge *Herefs* 28 C6
Canon Frome *Herefs* 39 F1
Canon Pyon *Herefs* 39 E1
Canonbie *D & G* 71 G6
Canons Ashby *Nhants* 31 F5
Canonstown *Cnwll* 2 B3
Canterbury *Kent* 23 F1
Canterbury Cathedral *Kent* 23 F2
Cantley *Norfk* 45 G3
Canton *Cardif* 16 C6
Cantraywood *Highld* 107 G1
Cantsfield *Lancs* 63 F3
Canvey Island *Essex* 22 C4
Canwick *Lincs* 52 C2
Canworthy Water *Cnwll* 4 C6
Caol *Highld* 90 C6
Caolas Scalpaigh *W Isls* 111 c5
Caoles *Ag & B* 88 B4
Caonich *Highld* 97 H2
Capel *Kent* 12 B6
Capel *Surrey* 11 E6
Capel Bangor *Cerdgn* 37 E4
Capel Coch *IOA* 54 C4
Capel Curig *Conwy* 55 E2
Capel Dewi *Carmth* 26 B4
Capel Dewi *Cerdgn* 36 D1
Capel Garmon *Conwy* 55 F2
Capel Hendre *Carmth* 26 C4
Capel le Ferne *Kent* 13 G5
Capel Mawr *IOA* 54 C3
Capel Seion *Cerdgn* 37 E4
Capel St Andrew *Suffk* 35 G3
Capel St Mary *Suffk* 34 D3
Capel-Dewi *Cerdgn* 37 E5
Capelulo *Conwy* 55 F4
Capenhurst *Ches* 48 D6
Capheaton *Nthumb* 73 E4
Caplaw *E Rens* 84 D2
Cappercleuch *Border* 79 E5
Capton *Devon* 5 H2
Caputh *P & K* 92 D3
Car Colston *Notts* 51 H1
Carbeth Inn *Stirlg* 85 E3
Carbis Bay *Cnwll* 2 B3
Carbost *Highld* 96 B5
Carbost *Highld* 104 C1
Carbrook *S York* 51 E5
Carbrooke *Norfk* 44 C2
Carcroft *S York* 59 F1
Cardenden *Fife* 86 C5
Cardhu *Moray* 101 E4
Cardiff *Cardif* 16 D6
Cardiff Airport *V Glam* 16 C5
Cardigan *Cerdgn* 36 B2
Cardington *Beds* 32 C3
Cardington *Shrops* 39 E5
Cardinham *Cnwll* 4 B4
Cardrain *D & G* 68 C1
Cardrona *Border* 79 F6
Cardross *Ag & B* 84 C3
Cardryne *D & G* 68 C1
Cardurnock *Cumb* 71 E5
Careby *Lincs* 42 C4
Careston *Angus* 95 E2
Carew *Pembks* 24 D3
Carew Cheriton *Pembks* 24 D3
Carew Newton *Pembks* 24 D3
Carey *Herefs* 28 D5
Carfin *N Lans* 85 G2
Carfraemill *Border* 80 B5
Cargate Green *Norfk* 45 G3
Cargen *D & G* 70 C6
Cargenbridge *D & G* 70 C6
Cargill *P & K* 92 D3
Cargo *Cumb* 71 F5
Cargreen *Cnwll* 5 E3
Carham *Nthumb* 80 D4
Carhampton *Somset* 16 B3
Carharrack *Cnwll* 2 D3
Carie *P & K* 91 G4
Carinish *W Isls* 111 b3
Carisbrooke *IOW* 9 G2
Cark *Cumb* 62 D4
Carkeel *Cnwll* 5 E3
Carlabhagh *W Isls* 111 c6
Carlbury *Dur* 65 F5
Carlby *Lincs* 42 C3
Carlcroft *Nthumb* 80 D1
Carleen *Cnwll* 2 C2
Carleton *N York* 58 B4

Carleton Forehoe *Norfk* 44 D3
Carleton Rode *Norfk* 44 D2
Carleton St Peter *Norfk* 45 F2
Carlincraig *Abers* 102 C4
Carlingcott *Somset* 17 H4
Carlisle *Cumb* 71 G5
Carlisle Airport *Cumb* 71 G5
Carloway *W Isls* 111 c6
Carlton *Beds* 32 B4
Carlton *Cambs* 33 H4
Carlton *Dur* 65 G5
Carlton *Leics* 41 E4
Carlton *N York* 65 E2
Carlton *N York* 66 C2
Carlton *N York* 59 G2
Carlton *Notts* 51 G1
Carlton *S York* 59 E1
Carlton *Suffk* 35 G5
Carlton *W York* 59 E3
Carlton Colville *Suffk* 45 H1
Carlton Curlieu *Leics* 41 G3
Carlton Green *Cambs* 33 H4
Carlton Husthwaite *N York* 66 B1
Carlton in Lindrick *Notts* 51 G5
Carlton Miniott *N York* 65 G2
Carlton Scroop *Lincs* 42 B6
Carlton-in-Cleveland *N York* 66 B4
Carlton-le-Moorland *Lincs* 52 B2
Carlton-on-Trent *Notts* 52 A2
Carluke *S Lans* 77 G6
Carmacoup *S Lans* 77 G4
Carmarthen *Carmth* 25 G4
Carmel *Carmth* 26 B4
Carmel *Gwynd* 54 D2
Carmichael *S Lans* 78 C6
Carmunnock *C Glas* 85 E2
Carmyle *C Glas* 85 F2
Carmyllie *Angus* 93 G3
Carn Brea *Cnwll* 2 D3
Carn-gorm *Highld* 97 G4
Carnaby *E R Yk* 61 E6
Carnbee *Fife* 87 E6
Carnbo *P & K* 86 B6
Carnbrogie *Abers* 102 D2
Carndu *Highld* 97 F5
Carnduff *S Lans* 77 F5
Carnell *E Ayrs* 76 D4
Carnforth *Lancs* 63 E3
Carnhell Green *Cnwll* 2 C3
Carnie *Abers* 95 G6
Carnkie *Cnwll* 2 D3
Carno *Powys* 47 H1
Carnoch *Highld* 97 F2
Carnock *Fife* 86 B5
Carn Downs *Cnwll* 3 E3
Carnousie *Abers* 102 C4
Carnoustie *Angus* 93 G3
Carnwath *S Lans* 86 A1
Carol Green *W Mids* 40 D1
Carperby *N York* 64 D2
Carr Gate *W York* 58 D3
Carr Shield *Nthumb* 72 C2
Carradale *Ag & B* 75 F4
Carrbridge *Highld* 99 G5
Carrefour *Jersey* 7 b2
Carreglefn *IOA* 54 C5
Carrhouse *Lincs* 60 B1
Carrick *Ag & B* 83 G4
Carrick Castle *Ag & B* 84 B5
Carriden *Falk* 86 A4
Carrington *Gt Man* 57 G2
Carrington *Mdloth* 86 D2
Carrog *Denbgs* 48 B4
Carron *Falk* 85 G4
Carron *Moray* 101 E3
Carron Bridge *Stirlg* 85 F4
Carronbridge *D & G* 78 C3
Carronshore *Falk* 85 G4
Carruth House *Inver* 84 C2
Carrutherstown *D & G* 70 D6
Carrville *Dur* 73 G1
Carsaig *Ag & B* 89 F1
Carseriggan *D & G* 69 E4
Carsethorn *D & G* 70 D5
Carshalton *Gt Lon* 21 F2
Carsington *Derbys* 50 D2
Carskey *Ag & B* 75 E2
Carsluith *D & G* 69 F3
Carsphairn *D & G* 77 E1
Carstairs *S Lans* 77 H5
Carstairs Junction *S Lans* 77 H5
Carterton *Oxon* 30 D1
Carthew *Cnwll* 3 F4
Carthorpe *N York* 65 G2
Cartland *S Lans* 77 G5
Cartmel *Cumb* 62 D4
Carway *Carmth* 26 B3
Cashe's Green *Gloucs* 29 F3
Cassington *Oxon* 31 F1
Cassop Colliery *Dur* 73 G1
Casterton *Lancs* 63 F4
Castle Acre *Norfk* 44 B3
Castle Ashby *Nhants* 32 B4
Castle Bolton *N York* 65 E3
Castle Bromwich *W Mids* 40 C2
Castle Bytham *Lincs* 42 C4
Castle Caereinion *Powys* 38 B6
Castle Camps *Cambs* 33 G3
Castle Carrock *Cumb* 71 H4
Castle Cary *Somset* 17 G2
Castle Combe *Wilts* 18 B4
Castle Donington *Leics* 41 E5
Castle Douglas *D & G* 70 B5
Castle Eaton *Wilts* 18 D6
Castle Eden *Dur* 73 H1
Castle Frome *Herefs* 39 F1
Castle Gresley *Derbys* 40 D5
Castle Hedingham *Essex* 34 B2
Castle Hill *Suffk* 35 E3
Castle Kennedy *D & G* 68 C3
Castle Lachlan *Ag & B* 83 H5
Castle O'er *D & G* 79 F2
Castle Pulverbatch *Shrops* 38 D6
Castle Rising *Norfk* 43 H4
Castle Stuart *Highld* 107 F1
Castlebay *W Isls* 111 a1
Castlebythe *Pembks* 24 D5
Castlecary *Falk* 85 G3
Castleford *W York* 59 E3
Castlehill *Border* 79 E6
Castlehill *Highld* 110 C5
Castlehill *W Duns* 84 D3

Castlemartin Pembks ... 24 C3
Castlemilk C Glas ... 85 E2
Castlemorton Worcs ... 29 F6
Castlerigg Cumb ... 71 F2
Castleside Dur ... 73 E2
Castlethorpe Bucks ... 32 A3
Castleton Border ... 79 H2
Castleton Derbys ... 50 C5
Castleton Gt Man ... 58 A1
Castleton N York ... 66 C4
Castleton Newpt ... 27 H1
Castletown Highld ... 110 C5
Castletown IOM ... 116 b2
Castletown T & W ... 73 G3
Castley N York ... 58 D4
Caston Norfk ... 44 C2
Castor Cambs ... 42 D2
Cat's Ash Newpt ... 28 B2
Catacol N Ayrs ... 75 G5
Catcliffe S York ... 51 E5
Catcomb Wilts ... 18 C4
Catcott Somset ... 17 E3
Catcott Burtle Somset ... 17 E3
Catel Guern ... 6 b1
Caterham Surrey ... 21 F1
Catfield Norfk ... 45 G4
Catfirth Shet ... 111 I2
Catford Gt Lon ... 21 F3
Catforth Lancs ... 57 E6
Cathcart C Glas ... 85 E2
Cathedine Powys ... 27 G5
Catherington Hants ... 10 A3
Catherston Leweston Dorset ... 7 E5
Catisfield Hants ... 9 G4
Catlodge Highld ... 99 E2
Catmere End Essex ... 33 F3
Catmore Berks ... 19 F4
Caton Lancs ... 63 E3
Caton Green Lancs ... 63 E3
Catrine E Ayrs ... 77 E4
Catsfield E Susx ... 12 C3
Catsgore Somset ... 17 F2
Catshill Worcs ... 40 B1
Cattadale Ag & B ... 75 E2
Cattal N York ... 59 E5
Cattawade Suffk ... 34 D2
Catterall Lancs ... 57 E6
Catterick N York ... 65 F3
Catterick Bridge N York ... 65 F3
Catterlen Cumb ... 71 G3
Catterline Abers ... 95 G4
Catterton N York ... 59 F4
Catteshall Surrey ... 10 C6
Catthorpe Leics ... 41 F2
Cattistock Dorset ... 7 G5
Catton Cumb ... 72 C3
Catton N York ... 65 G1
Catton Norfk ... 45 E3
Catwick E R Yk ... 61 E4
Catworth Cambs ... 32 C5
Caudle Green Gloucs ... 29 G4
Caulcott Oxon ... 31 F3
Cauldcots Angus ... 93 H4
Cauldhame Stirlg ... 85 E5
Cauldmill Border ... 80 B2
Cauldon Staffs ... 50 C2
Cauldwell Derbys ... 40 D5
Caulkerbush D & G ... 70 C5
Caulside D & G ... 79 G1
Caundle Marsh Dorset ... 17 G1
Caunton Notts ... 51 H3
Causeway End D & G ... 69 E3
Causeway End Essex ... 34 A1
Causewayend S Lans ... 78 D6
Causewayhead Stirlg ... 85 G5
Causey Park Bridge Nthumb ... 73 F6
Causeyend Abers ... 103 E2
Cavendish Suffk ... 34 B3
Cavenham Suffk ... 34 B5
Caversfield Oxon ... 31 F3
Caversham Berks ... 20 A3
Caverswall Staffs ... 50 B1
Caverton Mill Border ... 80 D3
Cawdor Highld ... 100 B4
Cawood N York ... 59 F4
Cawsand Cnwll ... 5 E2
Cawston Norfk ... 45 E4
Cawthorne S York ... 58 D1
Caxton Cambs ... 33 E4
Caynham Shrops ... 39 E3
Caythorpe Lincs ... 42 B6
Caythorpe Notts ... 51 G2
Cayton N York ... 67 F2
Ceann a Bhaigh W Isls ... 111 a4
Ceannacroc Lodge Highld ... 98 B4
Cearsiadar W Isls ... 111 d6
Cefn Newpt ... 28 B2
Cefn Cribwr Brdgnd ... 27 E1
Cefn-brith Conwy ... 55 G2
Cefn-mawr Wrexhm ... 48 C3
Cefn-y-pant Carmth ... 25 F5
Cefngorwydd Powys ... 37 G2
Cellardyke Fife ... 87 F6
Cellarhead Staffs ... 50 B2
Cemaes IOA ... 54 C5
Cemmaes Powys ... 47 G2
Cemmaes Road Powys ... 47 G2
Cenarth Cerdgn ... 36 C1
Ceres Fife ... 93 F1
Cerne Abbas Dorset ... 7 G5
Cerney Wick Gloucs ... 18 C6
Cerrigceinwen IOA ... 54 C4
Cerrigydrudion Conwy ... 55 G1
Ceunant Gwynd ... 54 D3
Chaceley Gloucs ... 29 F5
Chacewater Cnwll ... 2 D4
Chackmore Bucks ... 31 G3
Chacombe Nhants ... 31 F4
Chadbury Worcs ... 30 B4
Chadderton Gt Man ... 58 A1
Chaddesden Derbys ... 51 E1
Chaddesley Corbett Worcs ... 40 A1
Chaddlehanger Devon ... 5 E4
Chaddleworth Berks ... 19 F4
Chadlington Oxon ... 31 E2
Chadshunt Warwks ... 31 E5
Chadwell Leics ... 42 A4
Chadwell Heath Gt Lon ... 21 G4
Chadwell St Mary Essex ... 22 B3
Chadwick Worcs ... 39 H3
Chadwick End W Mids ... 40 D1
Chaffcombe Somset ... 7 E6
Chagford Devon ... 5 G5
Chailey E Susx ... 11 G3

Chainhurst Kent ... 12 C6
Chaldon Surrey ... 21 F1
Chale IOW ... 9 G1
Chale Green IOW ... 9 G2
Chalfont Common Bucks ... 20 D4
Chalfont St Giles Bucks ... 20 C4
Chalfont St Peter Bucks ... 20 D4
Chalford Gloucs ... 29 F3
Chalford Wilts ... 18 B2
Chalgrove Oxon ... 19 H6
Chalk Kent ... 22 B3
Chalkwell Kent ... 22 D2
Challaborough Devon ... 5 F5
Challacombe Devon ... 15 F5
Challoch D & G ... 69 E4
Challock Kent ... 23 E1
Chalton Beds ... 32 C2
Chalton Hants ... 10 A4
Chalvey Berks ... 20 C3
Chalvington E Susx ... 11 G3
Chandler's Cross Herts ... 20 D5
Chandler's Ford Hants ... 9 F5
Chantry Somset ... 17 H4
Chantry Suffk ... 35 E3
Chapel Fife ... 86 C5
Chapel Allerton Somset ... 17 E4
Chapel Allerton W York ... 58 D4
Chapel Amble Cnwll ... 3 F6
Chapel Brampton Nhants ... 31 H6
Chapel Chorlton Staffs ... 49 G3
Chapel Green Warwks ... 31 F5
Chapel Haddlesey N York ... 59 F3
Chapel Hill Abers ... 103 F3
Chapel Hill Lincs ... 52 D1
Chapel Hill Mons ... 28 D3
Chapel Hill N York ... 59 E4
Chapel Lawn Shrops ... 38 D4
Chapel le Dale N York ... 64 B1
Chapel Leigh Somset ... 16 C2
Chapel of Garioch Abers ... 102 C2
Chapel Rossan D & G ... 68 C2
Chapel Row Berks ... 19 G4
Chapel St Leonards Lincs ... 53 G3
Chapel Stile Cumb ... 62 D6
Chapel-en-le-Frith Derbys ... 50 B4
Chapelend Way Essex ... 34 A3
Chapelhall N Lans ... 85 G2
Chapelhope Border ... 79 E4
Chapelknowe D & G ... 71 F6
Chapelton Angus ... 93 H4
Chapelton Devon ... 15 E4
Chapelton S Lans ... 77 F6
Chapeltown Lancs ... 57 G4
Chapeltown Moray ... 101 E2
Chapeltown S York ... 51 E6
Chapmans Well Devon ... 4 D6
Chapmanslade Wilts ... 18 B2
Chapmore End Herts ... 33 E1
Chappel Essex ... 34 C2
Chard Somset ... 7 E6
Chard Junction Somset ... 7 E6
Chardleigh Green Somset ... 7 E6
Chardstock Devon ... 7 E6
Charfield Gloucs ... 29 E2
Charing Kent ... 23 E1
Charingworth Gloucs ... 30 D4
Charlbury Oxon ... 31 E2
Charlcombe Somset ... 17 H5
Charlcutt Wilts ... 18 C4
Charlecote Warwks ... 30 D5
Charles Devon ... 15 F4
Charles Tye Suffk ... 34 D4
Charleston Angus ... 93 F4
Charlestown Aber C ... 95 H6
Charlestown Cnwll ... 3 F4
Charlestown Fife ... 86 B4
Charlestown Gt Man ... 57 G3
Charlestown Highld ... 105 F3
Charlestown Highld ... 107 E1
Charlestown W York ... 58 B3
Charlestown W York ... 58 C4
Charlesworth Derbys ... 50 B5
Charlinch Somset ... 16 D3
Charlottetown Fife ... 93 E1
Charlton Gt Lon ... 21 G3
Charlton Nhants ... 31 F3
Charlton Nthumb ... 72 C5
Charlton Oxon ... 19 F5
Charlton Shrops ... 49 F1
Charlton Somset ... 16 D2
Charlton Somset ... 17 G4
Charlton W Susx ... 10 C3
Charlton Wilts ... 8 B5
Charlton Wilts ... 18 C5
Charlton Wilts ... 18 D2
Charlton Worcs ... 30 B4
Charlton Abbots Gloucs ... 30 B3
Charlton Adam Somset ... 17 F2
Charlton Horethorne Somset ... 17 G2
Charlton Kings Gloucs ... 29 G4
Charlton Mackrell Somset ... 17 F2
Charlton Marshall Dorset ... 8 B4
Charlton Musgrove Somset ... 17 H2
Charlton on the Hill Dorset ... 8 B4
Charlton-all-Saints Wilts ... 8 D5
Charlton-on-Otmoor Oxon ... 31 F2
Charlwood Hants ... 10 A5
Charlwood Surrey ... 11 E6
Charminster Dorset ... 7 G5
Charmouth Dorset ... 7 E5
Charndon Bucks ... 31 G3
Charney Bassett Oxon ... 19 F6
Charnock Richard Lancs ... 57 E4
Charsfield Suffk ... 35 F4
Chart Sutton Kent ... 22 C1
Charter Alley Hants ... 19 G3
Charterhall Border ... 80 D4
Charterhouse Somset ... 17 F4
Chartershall Stirlg ... 85 G4
Chartham Kent ... 23 F1
Chartham Hatch Kent ... 23 F1
Chartridge Bucks ... 20 C5
Charwelton Nhants ... 31 F5
Chasetown Staffs ... 40 C4
Chastleton Oxon ... 30 D3
Chasty Devon ... 14 C2
Chatburn Lancs ... 63 G1
Chatcull Staffs ... 49 G3
Chatham Kent ... 22 C2
Chatham Green Essex ... 22 C6
Chathill Nthumb ... 81 G3
Chatsworth House Derbys ... 50 D4
Chattenden Kent ... 22 C3
Chatteris Cambs ... 43 F1
Chatterton Lancs ... 57 G2
Chattisham Suffk ... 34 D3

Chatto Border ... 80 D2
Chatton Nthumb ... 81 F3
Chawleigh Devon ... 15 F2
Chawston Beds ... 32 C4
Chawton Hants ... 10 A5
Cheadle Gt Man ... 57 H2
Cheadle Staffs ... 50 B1
Cheadle Hulme Gt Man ... 57 H2
Cheam Gt Lon ... 21 E2
Chearsley Bucks ... 31 H1
Chebsey Staffs ... 49 H2
Checkendon Oxon ... 19 H5
Checkley Ches ... 49 G4
Checkley Staffs ... 50 B1
Chedburgh Suffk ... 34 B4
Cheddar Somset ... 17 F4
Cheddington Bucks ... 32 B1
Cheddleton Staffs ... 50 B2
Cheddon Fitzpaine Somset ... 16 D2
Chedgrave Norfk ... 45 F2
Chedington Dorset ... 7 F6
Chediston Suffk ... 35 F6
Chedworth Gloucs ... 30 B2
Chedzoy Somset ... 17 E3
Cheetham Hill Gt Man ... 57 H3
Cheetwood Gt Man ... 57 G3
Cheldon Devon ... 15 F2
Chelford Ches ... 49 G6
Chellaston Derbys ... 41 E6
Chellington Beds ... 32 B4
Chelmarsh Shrops ... 39 G4
Chelmondiston Suffk ... 35 E3
Chelmorton Derbys ... 50 C4
Chelmsford Essex ... 22 C5
Chelmsley Wood W Mids ... 40 C2
Chelsea Gt Lon ... 21 F3
Chelsfield Gt Lon ... 21 G2
Chelsworth Suffk ... 34 D3
Cheltenham Gloucs ... 29 G5
Chelveston Nhants ... 32 C5
Chelvey Somset ... 17 F5
Chelwood Somset ... 17 G5
Chelwood Gate E Susx ... 11 G5
Chelworth Lower Green Wilts ... 18 D5
Chelworth Upper Green Wilts ... 18 C5
Cheney Longville Shrops ... 38 D4
Chenies Bucks ... 20 D5
Chepstow Mons ... 28 D2
Cherhill Wilts ... 18 C4
Cherington Gloucs ... 29 F3
Cherington Warwks ... 30 D4
Cheriton Hants ... 9 G6
Cheriton Kent ... 13 F5
Cheriton Swans ... 26 A2
Cheriton Bishop Devon ... 5 G6
Cheriton Fitzpaine Devon ... 15 G2
Cheriton or Stackpole Elidor
   Pembks ... 24 D3
Cherrington Shrops ... 49 F2
Cherry Burton E R Yk ... 60 D4
Cherry Hinton Cambs ... 33 F4
Cherry Orchard Worcs ... 39 H2
Cherry Willingham Lincs ... 52 C3
Chertsey Surrey ... 20 D2
Cheselbourne Dorset ... 8 A3
Chesham Bucks ... 20 C5
Chesham Gt Man ... 57 G4
Chesham Bois Bucks ... 20 C5
Cheshunt Herts ... 21 F5
Cheslyn Hay Staffs ... 40 B4
Chessetts Wood Warwks ... 40 C1
Chessington World of Adventure
   Gt Lon ... 21 E2
Chester Ches ... 48 D5
Chester Cathedral Ches ... 48 D5
Chester Moor Dur ... 73 F2
Chester Zoo Ches ... 48 D6
Chester-le-Street Dur ... 73 F2
Chesterblade Somset ... 17 G3
Chesterfield Derbys ... 51 E4
Chesterfield Staffs ... 40 C4
Chesterhill Mdloth ... 86 D3
Chesters Border ... 80 C2
Chesters Border ... 80 C1
Chesterton Cambs ... 42 D2
Chesterton Cambs ... 33 F4
Chesterton Gloucs ... 18 C6
Chesterton Oxon ... 31 F2
Chesterton Shrops ... 39 G5
Chesterton Green Warwks ... 31 E5
Chesterwood Nthumb ... 72 C3
Chestfield Kent ... 23 F2
Cheston Devon ... 5 G3
Cheswardine Shrops ... 49 G2
Cheswick Nthumb ... 81 F4
Chetnole Dorset ... 7 G6
Chettisham Cambs ... 43 G1
Chettle Dorset ... 8 B4
Chetton Shrops ... 39 F5
Chetwode Bucks ... 31 G3
Chetwynd Shrops ... 49 G2
Chetwynd Aston Shrops ... 49 G1
Cheveley Cambs ... 34 A4
Chevening Kent ... 21 G1
Chevington Suffk ... 34 B4
Chevithorne Devon ... 16 B1
Chew Magna Somset ... 17 G5
Chew Stoke Somset ... 17 F5
Chewton Keynsham Somset ... 17 G5
Chewton Mendip Somset ... 17 G4
Chicheley Bucks ... 32 B3
Chichester W Susx ... 10 B3
Chickerell Dorset ... 7 G4
Chicklade Wilts ... 8 B6
Chidden Hants ... 9 H5
Chiddingfold Surrey ... 10 C5
Chiddingly E Susx ... 12 A3
Chiddingstone Kent ... 11 G6
Chiddingstone Causeway Kent ... 11 H6
Chideock Dorset ... 7 E5
Chidham W Susx ... 10 B3
Chidswell W York ... 58 D2
Chieveley Berks ... 19 F4
Chignall Smealy Essex ... 22 B6
Chignall St James Essex ... 22 B6
Chigwell Essex ... 21 G4
Chigwell Row Essex ... 21 G4
Chilbolton Hants ... 19 F1
Chilcomb Hants ... 9 G6
Chilcombe Dorset ... 7 F4
Chilcompton Somset ... 17 G4
Chilcote Leics ... 40 D4
Child Okeford Dorset ... 8 B4
Child's Ercall Shrops ... 49 F2

Childer Thornton Ches ... 56 D1
Childrey Oxon ... 19 F5
Childswickham Worcs ... 30 C4
Childwall Mersyd ... 56 D2
Chilfrome Dorset ... 7 G5
Chilgrove W Susx ... 10 B3
Chilham Kent ... 23 E1
Chillaton Devon ... 5 E5
Chillenden Kent ... 23 G1
Chillerton IOW ... 9 G2
Chillesford Suffk ... 35 G4
Chillingham Nthumb ... 81 F3
Chillington Devon ... 5 H2
Chillington Somset ... 7 E6
Chilmark Wilts ... 8 C6
Chilmington Green Kent ... 13 E5
Chilson Oxon ... 30 D2
Chilsworthy Cnwll ... 5 E4
Chilsworthy Devon ... 14 C2
Chilthorne Domer Somset ... 17 F1
Chilton Bucks ... 31 G2
Chilton Dur ... 65 F6
Chilton Oxon ... 19 G5
Chilton Candover Hants ... 19 G1
Chilton Cantelo Somset ... 17 G2
Chilton Foliat Wilts ... 19 E4
Chilton Polden Somset ... 17 E3
Chilton Street Suffk ... 34 B3
Chilton Trinity Somset ... 16 D3
Chilwell Notts ... 41 F6
Chilworth Hants ... 9 F5
Chilworth Surrey ... 10 D6
Chimney Oxon ... 19 F6
Chineham Hants ... 19 H2
Chingford Gt Lon ... 21 F4
Chinley Derbys ... 50 B5
Chinnor Oxon ... 20 B5
Chipnall Shrops ... 49 G3
Chippenham Cambs ... 33 H5
Chippenham Wilts ... 18 B4
Chipperfield Herts ... 20 D5
Chipping Herts ... 33 E2
Chipping Lancs ... 63 F1
Chipping Campden Gloucs ... 30 C4
Chipping Norton Oxon ... 30 D3
Chipping Ongar Essex ... 22 A5
Chipping Sodbury Gloucs ... 29 E1
Chipping Warden Nhants ... 31 F4
Chipstable Somset ... 16 C2
Chipstead Kent ... 21 G1
Chipstead Surrey ... 21 F1
Chirbury Shrops ... 38 C5
Chirk Wrexhm ... 48 C3
Chirnside Border ... 81 E5
Chirnsidebridge Border ... 80 D5
Chirton Wilts ... 18 C3
Chisbury Wilts ... 19 E3
Chiselborough Somset ... 17 F1
Chiseldon Wilts ... 18 D4
Chiselhampton Oxon ... 19 G6
Chisholme Border ... 79 G4
Chislehurst Gt Lon ... 21 G2
Chislet Kent ... 23 G2
Chisley W York ... 58 B3
Chiswick Gt Lon ... 21 E3
Chisworth Derbys ... 50 B5
Chithurst W Susx ... 10 B4
Chittering Cambs ... 33 F5
Chitterne Wilts ... 18 C1
Chittlehamholt Devon ... 15 F3
Chittlehampton Devon ... 15 F3
Chittlehampton Devon ... 15 F2
Chittoe Wilts ... 18 C3
Chivelstone Devon ... 5 H1
Chivenor Devon ... 15 E4
Chlenry D & G ... 68 C4
Chobham Surrey ... 20 C2
Cholderton Wilts ... 19 E1
Cholesbury Bucks ... 20 C5
Chollerton Nthumb ... 72 D4
Cholsey Oxon ... 19 G5
Cholstrey Herefs ... 39 E2
Chop Gate N York ... 66 B3
Choppington Nthumb ... 73 F5
Chopwell T & W ... 73 E3
Chorley Ches ... 49 E4
Chorley Lancs ... 57 F4
Chorley Shrops ... 39 F4
Chorleywood Herts ... 20 D5
Chorleywood West Herts ... 20 D5
Chorlton Ches ... 49 G4
Chorlton Lane Ches ... 49 E4
Chorlton-cum-Hardy Gt Man ... 57 G3
Choulton Shrops ... 38 D4
Chowley Ches ... 49 E5
Chrishall Essex ... 33 F3
Chrisswell Inver ... 84 B3
Christchurch Cambs ... 43 F2
Christchurch Dorset ... 8 D3
Christchurch Mons ... 28 B2
Christian Malford Wilts ... 18 C4
Christleton Ches ... 49 E5
Christon Somset ... 17 E4
Christon Bank Nthumb ... 81 G2
Christow Devon ... 5 H5
Chudleigh Devon ... 6 A4
Chudleigh Knighton Devon ... 6 A3
Chulmleigh Devon ... 15 F3
Church Lancs ... 57 G5
Church Aston Shrops ... 49 G1
Church Brampton Nhants ... 31 H6
Church Broughton Derbys ... 40 D6
Church Crookham Hants ... 20 B1
Church Eaton Staffs ... 49 H1
Church End Beds ... 32 D3
Church End Essex ... 34 B2
Church End Gt Lon ... 21 E4
Church End Hants ... 19 H2
Church Enstone Oxon ... 31 E3
Church Fenton N York ... 59 F4
Church Green Devon ... 6 D5
Church Hanborough Oxon ... 31 E2
Church Hill Ches ... 49 F5
Church Houses N York ... 66 C3
Church Knowle Dorset ... 8 B2
Church Langton Leics ... 41 H3
Church Lawford Warwks ... 41 F1
Church Lawton Staffs ... 49 G5
Church Leigh Staffs ... 40 B6
Church Lench Worcs ... 30 B5
Church Mayfield Staffs ... 50 C1
Church Minshull Ches ... 49 F5
Church Norton W Susx ... 10 C2
Church Preen Shrops ... 39 E5
Church Pulverbatch Shrops ... 38 D6

Church Stowe Nhants ... 31 G5
Church Street Kent ... 22 C3
Church Stretton Shrops ... 39 E5
Church Village Rhondd ... 27 F2
Church Warsop Notts ... 51 F3
Churcham Gloucs ... 29 E4
Churchdown Gloucs ... 29 F4
Churchend Essex ... 23 E4
Churchfield W Mids ... 40 B3
Churchill Devon ... 6 D5
Churchill Oxon ... 30 D3
Churchill Somset ... 17 F5
Churchill Worcs ... 39 H4
Churchill Worcs ... 30 A5
Churchinford Somset ... 6 D6
Churchover Warwks ... 41 F2
Churchstanton Somset ... 16 D1
Churchstoke Powys ... 38 C5
Churchstow Devon ... 5 G2
Churchtown Derbys ... 50 D3
Churchtown Lancs ... 63 E1
Churston Ferrers Devon ... 6 A2
Churt Surrey ... 10 B5
Churton Ches ... 48 D5
Churwell W York ... 58 D3
Chwilog Gwynd ... 46 D5
Chyandour Cnwll ... 2 B2
Chysauster Cnwll ... 2 B3
Cilcain Flints ... 48 B5
Cilcennin Cerdgn ... 36 D3
Cilfrew Neath ... 26 D3
Cilfynydd Rhondd ... 27 F2
Cilgerran Pembks ... 36 B1
Cilmaengwyn Neath ... 26 D3
Cilmery Powys ... 38 A1
Cilsan Carmth ... 26 C5
Ciltalgarth Gwynd ... 47 G5
Cilycwm Carmth ... 37 F1
Cimla Neath ... 26 D2
Cinderford Gloucs ... 28 D4
Cippenham Berks ... 20 C3
Cirencester Gloucs ... 18 C6
City Gt Lon ... 21 F3
City Airport Gt Lon ... 21 G3
Clabhach Ag & B ... 88 C4
Clachaig Ag & B ... 84 A4
Clachan Ag & B ... 89 H1
Clachan Ag & B ... 90 A3
Clachan Ag & B ... 83 F2
Clachan Highld ... 96 D5
Clachan Mor Ag & B ... 88 B4
Clachan na Luib W Isls ... 111 b4
Clachan of Campsie E Duns ... 85 E3
Clachan-a-Luib W Isls ... 111 b4
Clachan-Seil Ag & B ... 89 H1
Clachaneasy D & G ... 69 E5
Clachnaharry Highld ... 107 E1
Clachtoll Highld ... 108 A2
Clackavoid P & K ... 94 B3
Clackmannan Clacks ... 85 H4
Clackmarras Moray ... 101 E5
Clacton-on-Sea Essex ... 23 F6
Cladich Ag & B ... 90 C1
Cladswell Worcs ... 30 B5
Claggan Highld ... 89 G4
Claigan Highld ... 104 B2
Clandown Somset ... 17 G4
Clanfield Hants ... 10 A4
Clanfield Oxon ... 19 E6
Clanville Hants ... 19 E1
Clanville Somset ... 17 G2
Claonaig Ag & B ... 83 G2
Clapgate Herts ... 33 F2
Clapham Beds ... 32 C4
Clapham Gt Lon ... 21 F3
Clapham N York ... 63 G3
Clapham W Susx ... 10 D3
Clapton Somset ... 7 E6
Clapton Somset ... 17 G4
Clapton-in-Gordano Somset ... 17 F6
Clapton-on-the-Hill Gloucs ... 30 C2
Claravale T & W ... 73 E3
Clarbeston Pembks ... 25 E4
Clarbeston Road Pembks ... 24 D4
Clarborough Notts ... 51 H5
Clare Suffk ... 34 B3
Clarebrand D & G ... 70 B5
Clarencefield D & G ... 70 D6
Clarewood Nthumb ... 72 D4
Clarilaw Border ... 80 B2
Clarkston E Rens ... 85 E2
Clashmore Highld ... 108 A2
Clashmore Highld ... 107 F4
Clashnessie Highld ... 108 A2
Clashnoir Moray ... 101 E2
Clathy P & K ... 92 C2
Clathymore P & K ... 92 C2
Clatt Abers ... 102 B2
Clatter Powys ... 38 A5
Clatworthy Somset ... 16 C2
Claughton Lancs ... 57 E6
Claughton Lancs ... 63 E3
Claughton Mersyd ... 56 C2
Claverdon Warwks ... 30 D6
Claverham Somset ... 17 F5
Clavering Essex ... 33 F2
Claverley Shrops ... 39 G5
Claverton Somset ... 18 A3
Clawdd-coch V Glam ... 27 F1
Clawdd-newydd Denbgs ... 48 B4
Clawton Devon ... 14 C1
Claxby Lincs ... 52 D4
Claxton N York ... 59 G5
Claxton Norfk ... 45 F2
Clay Coton Nhants ... 41 G1
Clay Cross Derbys ... 51 E3
Claybrooke Magna Leics ... 41 F2
Claydon Oxon ... 31 F5
Claydon Suffk ... 35 E4
Claygate D & G ... 79 G1
Claygate Kent ... 12 C6
Claygate Surrey ... 21 E2
Clayhall Gt Lon ... 21 G4
Clayhanger Devon ... 16 B2
Clayhidon Devon ... 16 C1
Clayhill E Susx ... 12 D4
Clayock Highld ... 110 B5
Claypits Gloucs ... 29 E4
Claypole Lincs ... 42 B6
Clayton S York ... 59 F1
Clayton W Susx ... 11 F3
Clayton W York ... 58 C3
Clayton West W York ... 58 D1
Clayton-le-Moors Lancs ... 57 G5
Clayton-le-Woods Lancs ... 57 E5

Clayworth *Notts* 51 H5
Cleadale *Highld* 96 C1
Cleadon *T & W* 73 G3
Clearbrook *Devon* 5 F3
Clearwell *Gloucs* 28 D3
Cleasby *N York* 65 F4
Cleat *Ork* 111 h1
Cleatlam *Dur* 65 E5
Cleator *Cumb* 70 D1
Cleator Moor *Cumb* 70 D1
Cleckheaton *W York* 58 C3
Clee St Margaret *Shrops* 39 E4
Cleehill *Shrops* 39 F3
Cleekhimin *N Lans* 85 F2
Cleethorpes *Lincs* 53 E6
Cleeton St Mary *Shrops* 39 F4
Cleeve *Oxon* 19 H4
Cleeve *Somset* 17 F5
Cleeve Hill *Gloucs* 29 G5
Cleeve Prior *Worcs* 30 C5
Cleghornie *E Loth* 87 F4
Clehonger *Herefs* 28 C6
Cleish *P & K* 86 B5
Cleland *N Lans* 85 G2
Clenamacrie *Ag & B* 90 B2
Clenchwarton *Norfk* 43 G4
Clenerty *Abers* 102 D5
Clent *Worcs* 40 A2
Cleobury Mortimer *Shrops* 39 F3
Cleobury North *Shrops* 39 F4
Cleongart *Ag & B* 75 E4
Clephanton *Highld* 107 G1
Clerkhill *D & G* 79 F3
Cleuch-head *D & G* 78 B3
Clevancy *Wilts* 18 C4
Clevedon *Somset* 17 E6
Cleveleys *Lancs* 56 D6
Cleverton *Wilts* 18 C5
Clewer *Somset* 17 F4
Cley next the Sea *Norfk* 44 D6
Cliburn *Cumb* 64 A5
Cliddesden *Hants* 19 H2
Cliff End *E Susx* 12 D3
Cliffe *Dur* 65 F4
Cliffe *Kent* 22 C3
Cliffe *N York* 59 G3
Cliffe Woods *Kent* 22 C3
Clifford *Herefs* 38 C1
Clifford *W York* 59 E4
Clifford Chambers *Warwks* 30 D5
Clifford's Mesne *Gloucs* 29 E5
Clifton *Beds* 32 D3
Clifton *Bristl* 17 G6
Clifton *Cumb* 71 H2
Clifton *Derbys* 50 C1
Clifton *Lancs* 57 E5
Clifton *N York* 58 C4
Clifton *N York* 59 G5
Clifton *Notts* 41 F6
Clifton *S York* 51 F6
Clifton *W York* 58 C2
Clifton *Worcs* 39 H1
Clifton Campville *Staffs* 40 D4
Clifton Hampden *Oxon* 19 G6
Clifton Reynes *Bucks* 32 B4
Clifton upon Dunsmore *Warwks* 41 F1
Clifton upon Teme *Worcs* 39 G2
Cliftonville *Kent* 23 H3
Climping *W Susx* 10 C2
Clink *Somset* 18 A2
Clint *N York* 58 D5
Clint Green *Norfk* 44 D3
Clinterty *Aber C* 102 D1
Clintmains *Border* 80 C3
Clippesby *Norfk* 45 G3
Clipsham *Rutlnd* 42 B4
Clipston *Nhants* 41 H2
Clipston *Notts* 41 G6
Clipstone *Beds* 32 B2
Clipstone *Notts* 51 G3
Clitheroe *Lancs* 57 G6
Clive *Shrops* 49 E2
Clixby *Lincs* 52 C5
Cloatley *Wilts* 29 G2
Clocaenog *Denbgs* 48 B4
Clochan *Moray* 101 F5
Clochtow *Angus* 93 G4
Clodock *Herefs* 28 B5
Clola *Abers* 103 E4
Clophill *Beds* 32 C3
Clopton *Nhants* 32 C6
Clopton *Suffk* 35 E4
Clopton Corner *Suffk* 35 E4
Clos du Valle *Guern* 6 c2
Closeburn *D & G* 78 D2
Closeburnmill *D & G* 78 C2
Closworth *Somset* 7 G6
Clothall *Herts* 33 E2
Clotton *Ches* 49 E5
Clough Foot *W York* 58 A2
Clough Head *W York* 58 C2
Cloughton *N York* 67 F3
Clousta *Shet* 111 k2
Clova *Angus* 94 C3
Clovelly *Devon* 14 C3
Clovenfords *Border* 79 G6
Clovulin *Highld* 90 B5
Clow Bridge *Lancs* 57 G5
Clowne *Derbys* 51 F4
Clows Top *Worcs* 39 G3
Cluanie Inn *Highld* 97 H3
Cluanie Lodge *Highld* 97 H3
Clugston *D & G* 69 E3
Clun *Shrops* 38 C4
Clunas *Highld* 100 B4
Clunbury *Shrops* 38 D4
Clune *Highld* 99 F5
Clunes *Highld* 98 A2
Clungunford *Shrops* 38 D4
Clunie *Abers* 102 C4
Clunie *P & K* 92 D4
Clunton *Shrops* 38 D4
Cluny *Fife* 86 C5
Clutton *Ches* 49 E4
Clutton *Somset* 17 G5
Clutton Hill *Somset* 17 G5
Clydach *Mons* 27 G1
Clydach *Swans* 26 C3
Clydach Vale *Rhondd* 27 E2
Clydebank *W Duns* 84 D3
Clyffe Pypard *Wilts* 18 C4
Clynder *Ag & B* 84 B4
Clynderwen *Carmth* 25 E4

Clyne *Neath* 26 D3
Clynnog-fawr *Gwynd* 54 C2
Clyro *Powys* 38 C1
Clyst Honiton *Devon* 6 B5
Clyst Hydon *Devon* 6 B5
Clyst St George *Devon* 6 B4
Clyst St Lawrence *Devon* 6 B5
Clyst St Mary *Devon* 6 B4
Cnoc *W Isls* 111 d6
Cnwch Coch *Cerdgn* 37 F4
Coad's Green *Cnwll* 4 D4
Coalburn *S Lans* 78 B6
Coalburns *T & W* 73 E3
Coaley *Gloucs* 29 E3
Coalhill *Essex* 22 C5
Coalpit Heath *Gloucs* 29 E1
Coalport *Shrops* 39 F6
Coalsnaughton *Clacks* 85 H5
Coaltown of Balgonie *Fife* 86 D5
Coaltown of Wemyss *Fife* 86 D5
Coalville *Leics* 41 E4
Coanwood *Nthumb* 72 B3
Coat *Somset* 17 F1
Coatbridge *N Lans* 85 F2
Coatdyke *N Lans* 85 F2
Coate *Wilts* 18 C3
Coate *Wilts* 18 D5
Coates *Cambs* 43 E2
Coates *Gloucs* 29 G3
Coates *Lincs* 52 B4
Coates *W Susx* 10 C4
Cobbaton *Devon* 15 E4
Coberley *Gloucs* 29 G4
Cobham *Kent* 22 B2
Cobham *Surrey* 20 D2
Cobnash *Herefs* 39 E2
Cobo *Guern* 6 b2
Coburby *Abers* 103 E5
Cock Bridge *Abers* 101 E1
Cock Clarks *Essex* 22 C5
Cock Green *Essex* 34 A1
Cock Marling *E Susx* 12 D4
Cockayne Hatley *Beds* 33 E4
Cockburnspath *Border* 87 G3
Cockenzie and Port Seton *E Loth* 86 D3
Cockerham *Lancs* 63 E2
Cockermouth *Cumb* 71 E2
Cockernhoe Green *Herts* 32 D1
Cockett *Swans* 26 C2
Cockfield *Dur* 65 E5
Cockfield *Suffk* 34 C4
Cockfosters *Gt Lon* 21 F5
Cocking *W Susx* 10 C4
Cocking Causeway *W Susx* 10 C4
Cockington *Devon* 6 A2
Cocklake *Somset* 17 F4
Cockle Park *Nthumb* 73 F5
Cockley Cley *Norfk* 44 B3
Cockpole Green *Berks* 20 B3
Cockshutt *Shrops* 48 D2
Cockthorpe *Norfk* 44 D6
Cockwood *Devon* 6 B4
Cockyard *Derbys* 50 B4
Coddenham *Suffk* 35 E4
Coddington *Herefs* 29 E6
Coddington *Notts* 52 A1
Codford St Mary *Wilts* 18 C1
Codford St Peter *Wilts* 18 C1
Codicote *Herts* 32 D1
Codmore Hill *W Susx* 10 D4
Codnor *Derbys* 51 E2
Codrington *Gloucs* 29 E1
Codsall *Staffs* 39 H6
Codsall Wood *Staffs* 39 H6
Coed Talon *Flints* 48 C5
Coed-y-paen *Mons* 28 B3
Coedana *IOA* 54 C4
Coedpoeth *Wrexhm* 48 C4
Coffinswell *Devon* 6 A3
Cofton *Devon* 6 B4
Cofton Hackett *Worcs* 40 B1
Cogan *V Glam* 16 D6
Cogenhoe *Nhants* 32 A4
Coggeshall *Essex* 34 C1
Coignafearn *Highld* 99 F4
Coilacriech *Abers* 94 C5
Coilantogle *Stirlg* 85 E6
Coillore *Highld* 96 B5
Coiltry *Highld* 98 C3
Coity *Brdgnd* 27 E1
Col *W Isls* 111 d6
Colaboll *Highld* 107 E6
Colan *Cnwll* 3 E6
Colaton Raleigh *Devon* 6 C4
Colbost *Highld* 104 A1
Colburn *N York* 65 F3
Colby *Cumb* 64 B5
Colby *IOM* 116 b2
Colby *Norfk* 45 E5
Colchester *Essex* 34 D2
Cold Ash *Berks* 19 G4
Cold Ashby *Nhants* 41 G1
Cold Ashton *Gloucs* 17 H6
Cold Aston *Gloucs* 30 C2
Cold Brayfield *Bucks* 32 B4
Cold Hanworth *Lincs* 52 C4
Cold Higham *Nhants* 31 G5
Cold Kirby *N York* 66 B2
Cold Norton *Essex* 22 D5
Cold Overton *Leics* 42 A3
Coldbackie *Highld* 109 F5
Coldean *E Susx* 11 F3
Coldeast *Devon* 5 H4
Colden *W York* 58 B3
Colden Common *Hants* 9 G5
Coldfair Green *Suffk* 35 G4
Coldharbour *Surrey* 11 E5
Coldingham *Border* 81 E6
Coldmeece *Staffs* 49 H3
Coldred *Kent* 13 G6
Coldridge *Devon* 15 F2
Coldstream *Border* 80 D4
Coldwaltham *W Susx* 10 D4
Coldwell *Herefs* 28 C6
Coldwells *Abers* 103 E3
Cole *Somset* 17 G2
Colebatch *Shrops* 38 D4
Colebrook *Devon* 6 B6
Colebrooke *Devon* 15 G1
Coleby *Lincs* 60 C2
Coleby *Lincs* 52 B2
Coleford *Devon* 15 G1
Coleford *Gloucs* 28 D4
Coleford *Somset* 17 G4

Coleford Water *Somset* 16 C3
Colegate End *Norfk* 45 E1
Colehill *Dorset* 8 C3
Coleman's Hatch *E Susx* 11 G5
Colemere *Shrops* 48 D3
Colemore *Hants* 10 A5
Colenden *P & K* 92 D2
Colerne *Wilts* 18 A4
Colesbourne *Gloucs* 30 B2
Coleshill *Bucks* 20 C5
Coleshill *Oxon* 19 E5
Coleshill *Warwks* 40 D2
Coley *Somset* 17 G4
Colgate *W Susx* 11 E5
Colinsburgh *Fife* 87 E6
Colinton *C Edin* 86 C3
Colintraive *Ag & B* 83 H3
Colkirk *Norfk* 44 C4
Collace *P & K* 93 E3
Collafirth *Shet* 111 I3
Collaton *Devon* 5 G1
Collaton St Mary *Devon* 6 A2
College of Roseisle *Moray* 100 D5
College Town *Berks* 20 B2
Collessie *Fife* 93 E1
Collier Row *Gt Lon* 21 G4
Collier Street *Kent* 12 C6
Collier's End *Herts* 33 F1
Collieston *Abers* 103 F2
Collin *D & G* 70 D6
Collingbourne Ducis *Wilts* 19 E2
Collingbourne Kingston *Wilts* 19 E2
Collingham *Notts* 52 A2
Collingham *W York* 59 E4
Collington *Herefs* 39 F2
Collingtree *Nhants* 31 H5
Collins Green *Ches* 57 E2
Colliston *Angus* 93 H4
Colliton *Devon* 6 C6
Collyweston *Nhants* 42 C2
Colmonell *S Ayrs* 68 C6
Colmworth *Beds* 32 C4
Coln Rogers *Gloucs* 30 C1
Coln St Aldwyns *Gloucs* 30 C1
Coln St Dennis *Gloucs* 30 C1
Colnbrook *Berks* 20 D3
Colne *Cambs* 33 F6
Colne *Lancs* 58 A4
Colne Engaine *Essex* 34 C2
Colney *Norfk* 45 E3
Colney Heath *Herts* 21 E5
Colpy *Abers* 102 C3
Colquhar *Border* 79 F6
Colsterworth *Lincs* 42 B4
Colston Bassett *Notts* 41 G6
Colt's Hill *Kent* 12 B6
Coltfield *Moray* 100 D5
Coltishall *Norfk* 45 F4
Colton *Cumb* 62 D4
Colton *N York* 59 F4
Colton *Norfk* 44 D3
Colton *Staffs* 40 B5
Colton *W York* 59 E3
Colvend *D & G* 70 C4
Colwall *Herefs* 29 E6
Colwell *Nthumb* 72 D4
Colwich *Staffs* 40 B5
Colwinston *V Glam* 16 B6
Colworth *W Susx* 10 C2
Colwyn Bay *Conwy* 55 F4
Colyford *Devon* 6 D5
Colyton *Devon* 6 D5
Combe *Berks* 19 F3
Combe *Oxon* 31 F2
Combe Down *Somset* 18 A3
Combe Fishacre *Devon* 6 A2
Combe Florey *Somset* 16 C2
Combe Hay *Somset* 17 H5
Combe Martin *Devon* 15 E5
Combe Raleigh *Devon* 6 C5
Combe St Nicholas *Somset* 7 E6
Combeinteignhead *Devon* 6 A3
Comberbach *Ches* 57 F1
Comberford *Staffs* 40 C4
Comberton *Cambs* 33 F4
Comberton *Herefs* 39 E3
Combrook *Warwks* 30 D5
Combs *Derbys* 50 B4
Combs *Suffk* 34 D4
Combs Ford *Suffk* 34 D4
Combwich *Somset* 16 D3
Comers *Abers* 95 F6
Comhampton *Worcs* 39 H3
Commercial *Pembks* 25 E4
Commins Coch *Powys* 47 G2
Common Moor *Cnwll* 4 C4
Commondale *N York* 66 C4
Compstall *Gt Man* 50 B5
Compstonend *D & G* 69 G3
Compton *Berks* 19 G4
Compton *Devon* 6 A2
Compton *Hants* 9 F5
Compton *Staffs* 39 G4
Compton *Surrey* 10 C6
Compton *W Susx* 10 B3
Compton *Wilts* 18 D2
Compton Abbas *Dorset* 8 B5
Compton Abdale *Gloucs* 30 B2
Compton Bassett *Wilts* 18 C4
Compton Beauchamp *Oxon* 19 E5
Compton Bishop *Somset* 17 E4
Compton Chamberlayne *Wilts* 8 C6
Compton Dando *Somset* 17 G5
Compton Dundon *Somset* 17 F2
Compton Durville *Somset* 17 E1
Compton Greenfield *Gloucs* 28 D1
Compton Martin *Somset* 17 F4
Compton Pauncefoot *Somset* 17 G2
Compton Valence *Dorset* 7 G5
Comrie *Fife* 86 A5
Comrie *P & K* 92 A2
Conaglen House *Highld* 90 C5
Conchra *Highld* 97 F5
Concraigie *P & K* 92 D4
Conderton *Worcs* 29 G6
Condicote *Gloucs* 30 C3
Condorrat *N Lans* 85 E3
Condover *Shrops* 39 E6
Coney Weston *Suffk* 34 C6
Coneyhurst Common *W Susx* 10 D4
Coneysthorpe *N York* 66 D1
Congdon's Shop *Cnwll* 4 D4
Congerstone *Leics* 41 E4

Congham *Norfk* 44 A4
Congleton *Ches* 49 H5
Congresbury *Somset* 17 F5
Conheath *D & G* 70 D6
Conicavel *Moray* 100 C4
Coningsby *Lincs* 52 D1
Conington *Cambs* 42 D1
Conington *Cambs* 33 E5
Conisbrough *S York* 51 F6
Conisholme *Lincs* 53 F1
Coniston *Cumb* 62 C5
Coniston *E R Yk* 61 E3
Coniston Cold *N York* 58 A5
Conistone *N York* 58 B6
Connah's Quay *Flints* 48 C6
Connel *Ag & B* 90 B2
Connel Park *E Ayrs* 77 E3
Connor Downs *Cnwll* 2 C3
Conon Bridge *Highld* 107 E2
Cononley *N York* 58 B4
Consall *Staffs* 50 B2
Consett *Dur* 73 E2
Constable Burton *N York* 65 F3
Constantine *Cnwll* 2 D2
Contin *Highld* 106 D2
Conwy *Conwy* 55 F4
Conyer's Green *Suffk* 34 C5
Cooden *E Susx* 12 C3
Cook's Green *Essex* 35 E1
Cookbury *Devon* 14 D2
Cookham *Berks* 20 C4
Cookham Dean *Berks* 20 B4
Cookham Rise *Berks* 20 C4
Cookhill *Warwks* 30 B5
Cookley *Suffk* 35 F6
Cookley *Worcs* 39 H4
Cookley Green *Oxon* 20 A4
Cookney *Abers* 95 G5
Cooks Green *Suffk* 34 D4
Cooksmill Green *Essex* 22 B5
Coolham *W Susx* 10 D4
Cooling *Kent* 22 C3
Coombe *Devon* 6 B3
Coombe *Devon* 6 C5
Coombe *Gloucs* 29 E2
Coombe *Hants* 9 H5
Coombe Bissett *Wilts* 8 D5
Coombe Cellars *Devon* 6 A3
Coombe End *Somset* 16 B2
Coombe Hill *Gloucs* 29 F5
Coombe Keynes *Dorset* 8 B2
Coombe Pafford *Devon* 6 B2
Coombes *W Susx* 10 D3
Coombes-Moor *Herefs* 38 D2
Cooperhill *Moray* 100 C4
Coopersale Common *Essex* 21 G5
Coopersale Street *Essex* 21 G5
Cop Street *Kent* 23 G2
Copdock *Suffk* 35 E3
Copford Green *Essex* 34 C1
Copgrove *N York* 59 E6
Copister *Shet* 111 I3
Cople *Beds* 32 C3
Copley *Dur* 65 E5
Copmanthorpe *N York* 59 F4
Copmere End *Staffs* 49 G2
Copp *Lancs* 56 D6
Coppathorne *Cnwll* 14 B1
Coppenhall *Staffs* 40 A5
Copperhouse *Cnwll* 2 C3
Coppingford *Cambs* 32 D6
Copplestone *Devon* 15 G2
Coppull *Lancs* 57 E4
Copsale *W Susx* 11 E4
Copster Green *Lancs* 57 F5
Copston Magna *Warwks* 41 F2
Copt Hewick *N York* 65 G1
Copt Oak *Leics* 41 F4
Copthorne *W Susx* 11 F5
Copythorne *Hants* 9 E4
Corbets Tey *Gt Lon* 22 B4
Corbridge *Nthumb* 72 D3
Corby *Nhants* 42 B1
Corby Glen *Lincs* 42 C4
Cordon *N Ayrs* 75 H4
Coreley *Shrops* 39 F3
Corfe *Somset* 16 D1
Corfe Castle *Dorset* 8 C2
Corfe Mullen *Dorset* 8 C3
Corfton *Shrops* 39 E4
Corgarff *Abers* 94 C6
Corhampton *Hants* 9 H5
Corley *Warwks* 40 D2
Corley Ash *Warwks* 40 D2
Corley Moor *Warwks* 40 C2
Cormuir *Angus* 94 C3
Cornard Tye *Suffk* 34 C3
Cornforth *Dur* 65 G6
Cornhill *Abers* 102 B4
Cornhill-on-Tweed *Nthumb* 81 E4
Cornholme *W York* 58 A3
Cornoigmore *Ag & B* 88 D3
Cornsay *Dur* 73 E1
Cornsay Colliery *Dur* 73 E1
Corntown *Highld* 107 E2
Corntown *V Glam* 27 E1
Cornwell *Oxon* 30 D3
Cornwood *Devon* 5 F3
Cornworthy *Devon* 5 H3
Corpach *Highld* 90 C6
Corpusty *Norfk* 45 E5
Corran *Highld* 90 C5
Corran *Highld* 90 B5
Corrie *D & G* 79 E2
Corrie *N Ayrs* 75 H5
Corriecravie *N Ayrs* 75 G3
Corriegills *N Ayrs* 75 H4
Corriegour Lodge Hotel *Highld* 98 B2
Corriemoille *Highld* 106 C2
Corrimony *Highld* 98 C5
Corringham *Essex* 22 C4
Corringham *Lincs* 52 B4
Corris *Gwynd* 47 F2
Corris Uchaf *Gwynd* 47 F2
Corrow *Ag & B* 84 B5
Corry *Highld* 96 D4
Corscombe *Devon* 15 F1
Corscombe *Dorset* 7 F6
Corse Lawn *Gloucs* 29 F5
Corsindae *Abers* 102 C1
Corsley *Wilts* 18 B2
Corsley Heath *Wilts* 18 A2
Corsock *D & G* 78 B1

Corston *Somset* 17 H5
Corston *Wilts* 18 B5
Corstorphine *C Edin* 86 C3
Cortachy *Angus* 94 C2
Corton *Suffk* 45 H2
Corton *Wilts* 18 B1
Corton Denham *Somset* 17 G2
Coruanan Lodge *Highld* 90 C5
Corwen *Denbgs* 48 B4
Coryton *Devon* 5 E4
Coryton *Essex* 22 C4
Cosby *Leics* 41 F3
Coseley *W Mids* 40 B3
Cosgrove *Nhants* 32 A3
Cosham *Hants* 9 H4
Cosheston *Pembks* 24 D3
Coshieville *P & K* 92 A4
Cossall *Notts* 51 F1
Cossington *Leics* 41 G4
Cossington *Somset* 17 E3
Costessey *Norfk* 45 E3
Costock *Notts* 41 F5
Coston *Leics* 42 A4
Coston *Norfk* 44 D3
Cote *Oxon* 19 F6
Cotebrook *Ches* 49 F5
Cotehill *Cumb* 71 G4
Cotes *Leics* 41 F5
Cotesbach *Leics* 41 F2
Cotgrave *Notts* 41 G6
Cothal *Abers* 102 D1
Cotham *Notts* 42 A6
Cotherstone *Dur* 64 D5
Cothill *Oxon* 19 F6
Cotleigh *Devon* 6 D5
Cotmanhay *Derbys* 51 F1
Coton *Cambs* 33 F4
Coton *Nhants* 41 G1
Coton *Staffs* 49 G2
Coton Clanford *Staffs* 49 H2
Coton Hill *Shrops* 49 E1
Coton in the Elms *Derbys* 40 D5
Cott *Devon* 5 H3
Cottam *Lancs* 57 E5
Cottam *Notts* 52 A3
Cottenham *Cambs* 33 F5
Cottered *Herts* 33 E2
Cotterstock *Nhants* 42 C1
Cottesbrooke *Nhants* 41 G1
Cottesmore *Rutlnd* 42 B3
Cottingham *E R Yk* 60 D3
Cottingham *Nhants* 42 A1
Cottingley *W York* 58 C4
Cottisford *Oxon* 31 G3
Cotton *Suffk* 34 D5
Cottown *Abers* 101 G2
Cottown *Abers* 102 D1
Cottown of Gight *Abers* 102 D3
Cotts *Devon* 5 E3
Coughton *Warwks* 30 C5
Coulaghailtop *Ag & B* 83 G2
Coulags *Highld* 97 G6
Coull *Abers* 94 D6
Coulport *Ag & B* 84 B4
Coulsdon *Gt Lon* 21 F2
Coulston *Wilts* 18 B2
Coulter *S Lans* 78 D5
Coulton *N York* 66 C1
Coultra *Fife* 93 F2
Cound *Shrops* 39 E6
Coundon *Dur* 65 F6
Countersett *N York* 64 D2
Countess Wear *Devon* 6 B4
Countesthorpe *Leics* 41 G3
Countisbury *Devon* 15 F5
Coupar Angus *P & K* 93 E3
Coupland *Nthumb* 81 E3
Cour *Ag & B* 75 F5
Courance *D & G* 78 D2
Court Henry *Carmth* 26 B5
Courteachan *Highld* 97 F2
Courteenhall *Nhants* 31 H5
Courtsend *Essex* 23 E4
Courtway *Somset* 16 D3
Cousland *Mdloth* 86 D3
Cousley Wood *E Susx* 12 B5
Cove *Ag & B* 84 B4
Cove *Border* 87 G3
Cove *Devon* 16 B1
Cove *Hants* 20 B1
Cove *Highld* 105 F5
Cove Bay *Aber C* 95 H6
Covehithe *Suffk* 35 H6
Coven *Staffs* 40 A4
Coveney *Cambs* 33 F6
Covenham St Bartholomew *Lincs* 53 E4
Covenham St Mary *Lincs* 53 E4
Coventry *W Mids* 41 E2
Coventry Airport *Warwks* 41 E1
Coverack *Cnwll* 2 D1
Coverack Bridges *Cnwll* 2 D2
Coverham *N York* 65 E2
Covington *Cambs* 32 C5
Covington *S Lans* 78 C6
Cow Honeybourne *Worcs* 30 C5
Cowan Bridge *Lancs* 63 F3
Cowbeech *E Susx* 12 B3
Cowbit *Lincs* 43 E4
Cowbridge *V Glam* 16 B6
Cowden *Kent* 11 G5
Cowdenbeath *Fife* 86 B5
Cowers Lane *Derbys* 50 D2
Cowes *IOW* 9 G3
Cowesby *N York* 66 B2
Cowfold *W Susx* 11 E4
Cowhill *Gloucs* 28 D2
Cowie *Stirlg* 85 F5
Cowley *Devon* 6 A5
Cowley *Gloucs* 29 G4
Cowley *Gt Lon* 20 D3
Cowley *Oxon* 31 F1
Cowling *Lancs* 57 F4
Cowling *N York* 58 B4
Cowling *N York* 65 F2
Cowlinge *Suffk* 34 A4
Cowpen *Nthumb* 73 G4
Cowplain *Hants* 10 A3
Cowshill *Dur* 72 C1
Cowslip Green *Somset* 17 F5
Cowthorpe *N York* 59 E5
Coxbank *Ches* 49 F3
Coxbench *Derbys* 51 E1
Coxford *Cnwll* 14 B1
Coxford *Norfk* 44 C5

167

Coxheath Kent ... 22 C1
Coxhoe Dur ... 65 G6
Coxley Somset ... 17 F3
Coxley Wick Somset ... 17 F3
Coxtie Green Essex ... 22 B5
Coxwold N York ... 66 B1
Coychurch Brdgnd ... 27 E1
Coylton S Ayrs ... 76 D3
Coylumbridge Highld ... 99 G4
Coytrahen Brdgnd ... 27 E2
Crabbs Cross Worcs ... 30 B6
Crabtree W Susx ... 11 E4
Crackenthorpe Cumb ... 64 B5
Crackington Haven Cnwll ... 14 B1
Cracklebank Shrops ... 49 G1
Cracoe N York ... 58 B5
Craddock Devon ... 6 C6
Cradley Herefs ... 39 G1
Cradley W Mids ... 40 B2
Cradley Heath W Mids ... 40 B2
Cradoc Powys ... 27 F5
Crafthole Cnwll ... 4 D2
Crafton Bucks ... 32 B1
Cragg Vale W York ... 58 B2
Craggan Highld ... 100 C2
Craghead Dur ... 73 F2
Crai Powys ... 27 E5
Craibstone Moray ... 101 G5
Craichie Angus ... 93 G4
Craig Angus ... 95 F2
Craig Highld ... 105 H1
Craig Llangiwg Neath ... 26 D3
Craigbank E Ayrs ... 77 E3
Craigburn Border ... 86 C2
Craigcleuch D & G ... 79 F2
Craigdam Abers ... 102 D3
Craigdhu Ag & B ... 83 F6
Craigearn Abers ... 102 C1
Craigellachie Moray ... 101 E4
Craigend P & K ... 92 D2
Craigend Rens ... 84 D3
Craigendoran Ag & B ... 84 C4
Craighlaw D & G ... 69 E4
Craighouse Ag & B ... 82 D2
Craigie P & K ... 92 D3
Craigie S Ayrs ... 76 D4
Craigiefold Abers ... 103 E5
Craigley D & G ... 70 B5
Craiglockhart C Edin ... 86 C3
Craiglug Moray ... 101 F5
Craigmillar C Edin ... 86 D3
Craigneston D & G ... 78 B2
Craigneuk N Lans ... 85 G2
Craigneuk N Lans ... 85 G2
Craignure Ag & B ... 89 G3
Craigo Angus ... 95 F3
Craigrothie Fife ... 93 F1
Craigruie Stirlg ... 91 F1
Craigton Aber C ... 95 G6
Craigton Angus ... 93 G3
Craigton E Rens ... 84 D1
Craigton of Airlie Angus ... 93 E4
Crail Fife ... 87 F6
Crailing Border ... 80 C3
Craiselound Lincs ... 51 H6
Crakehall N York ... 65 F2
Crakemarsh Staffs ... 50 D1
Crambe N York ... 60 B6
Cramlington Nthumb ... 73 F4
Cramond C Edin ... 86 C3
Cramond Bridge C Edin ... 86 C3
Cranage Ches ... 49 G6
Cranberry Staffs ... 49 G3
Cranborne Dorset ... 8 C4
Cranbrook Kent ... 12 C5
Cranfield Beds ... 32 B3
Cranford Gt Lon ... 20 D3
Cranford St Andrew Nhants ... 32 B6
Cranford St John Nhants ... 32 B6
Cranham Gloucs ... 29 F4
Crank Mersyd ... 57 E3
Cranleigh Surrey ... 10 D5
Cranmore Somset ... 17 G3
Cranoe Leics ... 41 H3
Cransford Suffk ... 35 F5
Cranshaws Border ... 87 G2
Crantock Cnwll ... 2 D5
Cranwell Lincs ... 52 C1
Cranwich Norfk ... 44 B2
Cranworth Norfk ... 44 D3
Craobh Haven Ag & B ... 83 F6
Crarae Ag & B ... 83 H5
Crask Inn Highld ... 109 E2
Crask of Aigas Highld ... 98 C6
Craster Nthumb ... 81 H2
Cratfield Suffk ... 35 F6
Crathes Abers ... 95 F5
Crathes Castle Abers ... 95 F5
Crathie Abers ... 94 C5
Crathie Highld ... 98 D2
Crathorne N York ... 66 A4
Craven Arms Shrops ... 38 D4
Crawcrook T & W ... 73 E3
Crawford S Lans ... 78 C4
Crawfordjohn S Lans ... 78 C5
Crawick D & G ... 77 G3
Crawley Hants ... 9 F6
Crawley Oxon ... 31 E2
Crawley W Susx ... 11 F5
Crawley Down W Susx ... 11 F5
Crawshawbooth Lancs ... 57 G5
Crawton Abers ... 95 G4
Cray N York ... 64 D2
Crayford Gt Lon ... 21 G3
Crayke N York ... 66 B1
Crays Hill Essex ... 22 C4
Craze Lowman Devon ... 16 B1
Creacombe Devon ... 15 G3
Creagan Inn Ag & B ... 90 B3
Creagorry W Isls ... 111 b3
Creaguaineach Lodge Highld ... 91 E5
Creaton Nhants ... 41 G1
Creca D & G ... 71 G6
Credenhill Herefs ... 39 E1
Crediton Devon ... 15 G1
Creebank D & G ... 69 E5
Creebridge D & G ... 69 E4
Creech Heathfield Somset ... 16 D2
Creech St Michael Somset ... 16 D2
Creed Cnwll ... 3 F4
Creekmouth Gt Lon ... 21 G3
Creeting St Mary Suffk ... 34 D4
Creeton Lincs ... 42 C4
Creetown D & G ... 69 F3

Cregneash IOM ... 116 a2
Creich Fife ... 93 E2
Creigiau Cardif ... 27 F1
Cremyll Cnwll ... 5 E2
Cressage Shrops ... 39 F6
Cressbrook Derbys ... 50 C4
Cresselly Pembks ... 25 E3
Cressex Bucks ... 20 B4
Cressing Essex ... 34 B1
Cresswell Nthumb ... 73 G5
Cresswell Pembks ... 25 E3
Cresswell Staffs ... 50 B1
Creswell Derbys ... 51 F4
Cretingham Suffk ... 35 E4
Cretshengan Ag & B ... 83 E2
Crew Green Powys ... 48 D1
Crewe Ches ... 48 D4
Crewe Ches ... 49 G5
Crewe Green Ches ... 49 G4
Crewkerne Somset ... 7 F6
Crewton Derbys ... 41 E6
Crianlarich Stirlg ... 91 E2
Cribyn Cerdgn ... 36 D2
Criccieth Gwynd ... 46 D5
Crich Derbys ... 51 E2
Crichton Mdloth ... 86 D2
Crick Nhants ... 41 G1
Crickadarn Powys ... 27 F6
Cricket St Thomas Somset ... 7 E6
Crickheath Shrops ... 48 C6
Crickhowell Powys ... 27 G4
Cricklade Wilts ... 18 D5
Cricklewood Gt Lon ... 21 E4
Cridling Stubbs N York ... 59 F2
Crieff P & K ... 92 B2
Criggion Powys ... 48 C1
Crigglestone W York ... 58 D2
Crimond Abers ... 103 F5
Crimplesham Norfk ... 43 H3
Crimscote Warwks ... 30 D4
Crinaglack Highld ... 98 C6
Crinan Ag & B ... 83 F5
Crindledyke N Lans ... 85 G2
Cringleford Norfk ... 45 E3
Crinow Pembks ... 25 E4
Croachy Highld ... 99 E5
Crochmore House D & G ... 78 C1
Crockenhill Kent ... 21 G2
Crocker End Oxon ... 20 A4
Crockernwell Devon ... 5 G6
Crockerton Wilts ... 18 B1
Crocketford D & G ... 70 B6
Crockham Hill Kent ... 21 G1
Croes-goch Pembks ... 24 C5
Croes-lan Cerdgn ... 36 C2
Croeserw Neath ... 27 E2
Croesor Gwynd ... 47 E5
Croesyceiliog Carmth ... 25 G4
Croesyceiliog Torfn ... 28 B2
Croft Ches ... 57 F2
Croft Leics ... 41 F3
Croft Lincs ... 53 G2
Croft-on-Tees Dur ... 65 F4
Croftamie Stirlg ... 84 D4
Crofton W York ... 59 E2
Crofts D & G ... 70 B5
Crofts Moray ... 101 E4
Crofts of Dipple Moray ... 101 F5
Crofts of Savoch Abers ... 103 F5
Crofty Swans ... 26 B2
Croggan Ag & B ... 89 G2
Croglin Cumb ... 71 H4
Croik Highld ... 106 D5
Cromarty Highld ... 107 G3
Crombie Fife ... 86 B4
Cromdale Highld ... 100 D2
Cromer Herts ... 33 E2
Cromer Norfk ... 45 E6
Cromford Derbys ... 50 D2
Cromhall Gloucs ... 29 E2
Cromor W Isls ... 111 d6
Crompton Fold Gt Man ...
Cromwell Notts ... 52 A2
Cronberry E Ayrs ... 77 E4
Crondall Hants ... 10 B6
Cronton Mersyd ... 57 E2
Crook Cumb ... 63 E5
Crook Dur ... 65 F6
Crook Inn Border ... 78 D5
Crook of Devon P & K ... 86 B5
Crooked Holme Cumb ... 71 H5
Crookedholm E Ayrs ... 76 D5
Crookes S York ... 51 E5
Crookham Berks ... 19 G3
Crookham Nthumb ... 81 E4
Crookham Village Hants ... 20 B1
Crooklands Cumb ... 63 E4
Cropredy Oxon ... 31 F4
Cropston Leics ... 41 F4
Cropthorne Worcs ... 30 B4
Cropton N York ... 66 D2
Cropwell Bishop Notts ... 41 G6
Cropwell Butler Notts ... 51 G1
Cros W Isls ... 111 e7
Crosbie N Ayrs ... 76 B6
Crosbost W Isls ... 111 d6
Crosby Cumb ... 70 D3
Crosby IOM ... 116 b3
Crosby Lincs ... 60 C2
Crosby Mersyd ... 56 D3
Crosby Garret Cumb ... 63 G6
Crosby Ravensworth Cumb ... 64 A4
Croscombe Somset ... 17 G3
Cross Somset ... 17 E4
Cross Ash Mons ... 28 C4
Cross Flatts W York ... 58 C4
Cross Gates W York ... 59 E3
Cross Green Suffk ... 34 B4
Cross Green Suffk ... 34 C4
Cross Green Suffk ... 34 D4
Cross Hands Carmth ... 26 B4
Cross Houses Shrops ... 39 E6
Cross in Hand E Susx ... 12 B4
Cross Inn Cerdgn ... 36 C3
Cross Keys Ag & B ... 84 C4
Cross Lane IOW ... 9 G2
Cross Lane Head Shrops ... 39 G5
Cross o' th' hands Derbys ... 50 D2
Cross of Jackston Abers ... 102 D3
Cross Street Suffk ... 35 E6
Cross Town Ches ... 57 G1
Cross-at-Hand Kent ... 12 C6
Crossaig Ag & B ... 75 F5
Crossapoll Ag & B ... 88 B3
Crosscanonby Cumb ... 70 D3
Crossdale Street Norfk ... 45 E5

Crossford Fife ... 86 B4
Crossford S Lans ... 77 G5
Crossgatehall E Loth ... 86 D3
Crossgates E Ayrs ... 76 C5
Crossgates Fife ... 86 B4
Crossgill Lancs ... 63 E2
Crosshands E Ayrs ... 76 D4
Crosshill Fife ... 86 C5
Crosshill S Ayrs ... 76 C2
Crosshouse E Ayrs ... 76 D5
Crosskeys Caerph ... 27 G2
Crosskirk Highld ... 110 A6
Crosslands Cumb ... 62 D5
Crosslee Rens ... 84 D2
Crossmichael D & G ... 70 B5
Crossroads Abers ... 95 E6
Crossroads Abers ... 95 F5
Crosston Angus ... 93 G4
Crossway Green Worcs ... 39 H3
Crossways Dorset ... 8 A2
Crosswell Pembks ... 25 E6
Crosthwaite Cumb ... 62 D5
Croston Lancs ... 57 E4
Crostwick Norfk ... 45 F3
Crouch End Gt Lon ... 21 F4
Crouch Hill Dorset ... 7 H6
Croucheston Wilts ... 8 C5
Croughton Nhants ... 31 F3
Crovie Abers ... 102 D5
Crow Edge S York ... 58 C1
Crow Hill Herefs ... 28 D5
Crowan Cnwll ... 2 C3
Crowborough E Susx ... 11 G5
Crowcombe Somset ... 16 C3
Crowdecote Derbys ... 50 C3
Crowell Oxon ... 20 B5
Crowfield Suffk ... 35 E4
Crowhill E Loth ... 87 G3
Crowhurst E Susx ... 12 C3
Crowhurst Surrey ... 11 F6
Crowland Lincs ... 43 E3
Crowland Suffk ... 34 D5
Crowlas Cnwll ... 2 B3
Crowle Lincs ... 60 B2
Crowle Worcs ... 30 A5
Crowle Green Worcs ... 30 A5
Crowmarsh Gifford Oxon ... 19 H5
Crown Corner Suffk ... 35 F5
Crownhill Devon ... 5 E3
Crownthorpe Norfk ... 44 D2
Crowntown Cnwll ... 2 C2
Crows-an-Wra Cnwll ... 2 A2
Crowthorne Berks ... 20 B2
Crowton Ches ... 49 F6
Croxdale Dur ... 73 F1
Croxden Staffs ... 50 C1
Croxley Green Herts ... 20 D5
Croxton Cambs ... 33 E4
Croxton Lincs ... 61 E2
Croxton Norfk ... 44 D5
Croxton Norfk ... 44 C1
Croxton Staffs ... 49 G3
Croxton Kerrial Leics ... 42 A5
Croy Highld ... 107 G1
Croy N Lans ... 85 F3
Croyde Devon ... 14 D5
Croydon Cambs ... 33 E4
Croydon Gt Lon ... 21 F2
Crubenmore Highld ... 99 E2
Cruckmeole Shrops ... 38 D6
Cruckton Shrops ... 48 D1
Cruden Bay Abers ... 103 F3
Crudgington Shrops ... 49 F1
Crudwell Wilts ... 29 G2
Crumlin Caerph ... 27 G3
Crumplehorn Cnwll ... 4 C2
Crumpsall Gt Man ... 57 H3
Crundale Kent ... 13 E6
Crunwear Pembks ... 25 F4
Crux Easton Hants ... 19 F2
Crwbin Carmth ... 26 B4
Cryers Hill Bucks ... 20 C5
Crymmych Pembks ... 25 F6
Crynant Neath ... 26 D3
Crystal Palace Gt Lon ... 21 F3
Cuaig Highld ... 105 E2
Cuan Ferry Village Ag & B ... 89 G1
Cubbington Warwks ... 31 E6
Cubert Cnwll ... 2 D5
Cublington Bucks ... 32 A1
Cublington Herefs ... 28 C6
Cuckfield W Susx ... 11 F4
Cucklington Somset ... 17 H2
Cuckney Notts ... 51 F4
Cuddesdon Oxon ... 31 G1
Cuddington Bucks ... 31 H1
Cuddington Ches ... 49 F6
Cuddington Heath Ches ... 49 E4
Cudham Gt Lon ... 21 G2
Cudliptown Devon ... 5 F5
Cudnell Dorset ... 8 C3
Cudworth S York ... 59 E1
Cudworth Somset ... 7 E6
Cuffley Herts ... 21 F5
Cuil Highld ... 90 B4
Culbokie Highld ... 107 F2
Culburnie Highld ... 98 D6
Culcabock Highld ... 107 F1
Culcharry Highld ... 100 B4
Culcheth Ches ... 57 F2
Culdrain Abers ... 101 G3
Culduie Highld ... 97 E6
Culford Suffk ... 34 B5
Culgaith Cumb ... 64 A6
Culham Oxon ... 19 G6
Culkein Highld ... 108 A3
Culkein Drumbeg Highld ... 108 B3
Culkerton Gloucs ... 29 G2
Cullen Moray ... 101 G6
Cullercoats T & W ... 73 G4
Cullerlie Abers ... 95 F6
Cullicudden Highld ... 107 F2
Cullingworth W York ... 58 C4
Cullipool House Ag & B ... 83 F6
Cullivoe Shet ... 111 I4
Culloden Highld ... 107 F1
Cullompton Devon ... 6 B6
Culm Davy Devon ... 16 C1
Culmington Shrops ... 39 E4
Culmstock Devon ... 16 C1
Culnacraig Highld ... 106 A6
Culnaightrie D & G ... 70 B4
Culnaknock Highld ... 104 D2
Culrain Highld ... 107 E5

Culross Fife ... 86 A4
Culroy S Ayrs ... 76 C3
Culsalmond Abers ... 102 C3
Culscadden D & G ... 69 F3
Culshabbin D & G ... 69 E3
Culswick Shet ... 111 k2
Cultercullen Abers ... 103 E2
Cults Aber C ... 95 G6
Culverstone Green Kent ... 22 B2
Culverthorpe Lincs ... 42 C5
Culworth Nhants ... 31 F4
Culzean Castle S Ayrs ... 76 B3
Cumbernauld N Lans ... 85 F3
Cumbernauld Village N Lans ... 85 F3
Cumberworth Lincs ... 53 G3
Cuminestown Abers ... 102 D4
Cumledge Border ... 80 D5
Cummersdale Cumb ... 71 G4
Cummertrees D & G ... 71 E5
Cummingston Moray ... 100 D6
Cumnock E Ayrs ... 77 E3
Cumnor Oxon ... 31 F1
Cumrew Cumb ... 71 H4
Cumrue D & G ... 78 D2
Cumwhinton Cumb ... 71 G4
Cumwhitton Cumb ... 71 H4
Cundall N York ... 65 H1
Cunninghamhead N Ayrs ... 76 C5
Cupar Fife ... 93 F1
Cupar Muir Fife ... 93 F1
Curbar Derbys ... 50 D4
Curbridge Hants ... 9 G4
Curbridge Oxon ... 31 E1
Curdridge Hants ... 9 G4
Curdworth Warwks ... 40 C3
Curland Somset ... 16 D1
Curridge Berks ... 19 G3
Currie C Edin ... 86 C3
Curry Mallet Somset ... 17 E2
Curry Rivel Somset ... 17 E2
Curtisden Green Kent ... 12 C5
Curtisknowle Devon ... 5 G2
Cury Cnwll ... 2 D2
Cushnie Abers ... 102 B1
Cutcloy D & G ... 69 F1
Cutcombe Somset ... 16 B3
Cuthill Highld ... 107 F4
Cutnall Green Worcs ... 39 H3
Cutsdean Gloucs ... 30 C3
Cutthorpe Derbys ... 51 E4
Cuxham Oxon ... 19 H6
Cuxton Kent ... 22 C2
Cuxwold Lincs ... 52 D5
Cwm Denbgs ... 56 B1
Cwm Crawnon Powys ... 27 G4
Cwm Llinau Powys ... 47 G2
Cwm-cou Cerdgn ... 36 C1
Cwm-y-glo Carmth ... 26 B4
Cwm-y-glo Gwynd ... 54 D3
Cwmafan Neath ... 26 D2
Cwmaman Rhondd ... 27 F3
Cwmbach Carmth ... 25 F5
Cwmbach Powys ... 27 G6
Cwmbach Rhondd ... 27 F3
Cwmbach Llechrhyd Powys ... 38 A2
Cwmbran Torfn ... 28 B2
Cwmcarn Caerph ... 27 G2
Cwmcarvan Mons ... 28 C3
Cwmdare Rhondd ... 27 F3
Cwmdu Powys ... 27 G5
Cwmdu Swans ... 26 C2
Cwmduad Carmth ... 25 G5
Cwmfelin Brdgnd ... 27 E2
Cwmfelin Myr Td ... 27 F3
Cwmfelin Boeth Carmth ... 25 F4
Cwmfelinfach Caerph ... 27 G2
Cwmffrwd Carmth ... 25 G4
Cwmgiedd Powys ... 26 D4
Cwmgorse Carmth ... 26 C4
Cwmgwili Carmth ... 26 B4
Cwmhiraeth Carmth ... 25 G6
Cwmllynfell Neath ... 26 D4
Cwmmawr Carmth ... 26 B4
Cwmparc Rhondd ... 27 E2
Cwmpengraig Carmth ... 25 G6
Cwmsychbant Cerdgn ... 36 D2
Cwmtillery Blae G ... 27 G3
Cwmystwyth Cerdgn ... 37 G4
Cwrt-newydd Cerdgn ... 36 D2
Cylibebyll Neath ... 26 D3
Cymer Neath ... 27 E2
Cymmer Rhondd ... 27 F2
Cynghordy Carmth ... 37 G1
Cynonville Neath ... 26 D2
Cynwyd Denbgs ... 48 B3
Cynwyl Elfed Carmth ... 25 G5

Daccombe Devon ... 6 A3
Dacre Cumb ... 71 G2
Dacre N York ... 58 C5
Dacre Banks N York ... 58 D6
Daddry Shield Dur ... 72 C1
Dadford Bucks ... 31 G4
Dadlington Leics ... 41 E3
Dagenham Gt Lon ... 21 G4
Daglingworth Gloucs ... 30 B1
Dagnall Bucks ... 32 C1
Dailly S Ayrs ... 76 C2
Dairsie Fife ... 93 F1
Dalabrog W Isls ... 111 a2
Dalavich Ag & B ... 83 G6
Dalbeattie D & G ... 70 B5
Dalby IOM ... 116 b3
Dalby N York ... 66 C1
Dalcapon P & K ... 92 C4
Dalchalm Highld ... 107 H6
Dalchreichart Highld ... 98 B4
Dalchruin P & K ... 91 H1
Dalcrue P & K ... 92 C2
Daldersie Abers ... ???
Dale Derbys ... 51 E1
Dale Pembks ... 24 C3
Dalgarven N Ayrs ... 76 C5
Dalgety Bay Fife ... 86 C4
Dalgig E Ayrs ... 77 E3
Dalginross P & K ... 92 A2
Dalguise P & K ... 92 C4

Dalhalvaig Highld ... 109 H4
Dalham Suffk ... 34 B5
Daliburgh W Isls ... 111 a2
Dalkeith Mdloth ... 86 D3
Dallas Moray ... 100 D4
Dallinghoo Suffk ... 35 F4
Dallington E Susx ... 12 B4
Dallington Nhants ... 31 H6
Dalmally Ag & B ... 90 D2
Dalmary Stirlg ... 85 E5
Dalmellington E Ayrs ... 76 D2
Dalmeny C Edin ... 86 B4
Dalmigavie Highld ... 99 F4
Dalmigavie Lodge Highld ... 99 F5
Dalmore Highld ... 107 F3
Dalmuir W Duns ... 84 D3
Dalnabreck Highld ... 89 G5
Dalnacardoch P & K ... 91 H5
Dalnahaitnach Highld ... 99 G4
Dalnaspidal P & K ... 91 G6
Dalnawillan Lodge Highld ... 110 A3
Daloist P & K ... 92 A5
Dalqueich P & K ... 86 B6
Dalreavoch Lodge Highld ... 107 F6
Dalry N Ayrs ... 76 C6
Dalrymple E Ayrs ... 76 C3
Dalserf S Lans ... 77 G6
Dalsmeran Ag & B ... 75 E2
Dalston Cumb ... 71 F4
Dalston Gt Lon ... 21 F4
Dalswinton D & G ... 78 C2
Dalton D & G ... 70 D6
Dalton Lancs ... 57 E6
Dalton N York ... 65 E4
Dalton N York ... 66 A1
Dalton Nthumb ... 73 E4
Dalton Piercy Dur ... 66 B6
Dalton-in-Furness Cumb ... 62 C3
Dalton-le-Dale Dur ... 73 G2
Dalton-on-Tees N York ... 65 G4
Dalveen P & K ... 78 C3
Dalveich Stirlg ... 91 G2
Dalwhinnie Highld ... 99 E1
Dalwood Devon ... 6 D5
Damerham Hants ... 8 D5
Damgate Norfk ... 45 G3
Danbury Essex ... 22 C5
Danby N York ... 66 D4
Danby Wiske N York ... 65 G3
Dandaleith Moray ... 101 E4
Danderhall Mdloth ... 86 D3
Dane End Herts ... 33 E1
Dane Hills Leics ... 41 F4
Dane Street Kent ... 23 E1
Danebridge Ches ... 50 B3
Danehill E Susx ... 11 G4
Danshillock Abers ... 102 C5
Danskine E Loth ... 87 F3
Darenth Kent ... 22 B3
Daresbury Ches ... 57 F1
Darfield S York ... 59 E1
Dargate Kent ... 23 F2
Darite Cnwll ... 4 D4
Darlaston W Mids ... 40 B3
Darlaston Green W Mids ... 40 B3
Darley N York ... 58 D5
Darley Abbey Derbys ... 51 E1
Darley Bridge Derbys ... 50 D3
Darley Dale Derbys ... 50 D3
Darley Green Warwks ... 40 C1
Darley Head N York ... 58 D5
Darleyhall Herts ... 32 D1
Darlingscott Warwks ... 30 D4
Darlington Dur ... 65 F4
Darliston Notts ... 51 H4
Darnick Border ... 80 B3
Darowen Powys ... 47 G2
Darra Abers ... 102 C4
Darracott Devon ... 14 C3
Darracott Devon ... 14 D5
Darras Hall Nthumb ... 73 E4
Darrington W York ... 59 F2
Darsham Suffk ... 35 G5
Darshill Somset ... 17 G3
Dartford Kent ... 22 A3
Dartington Devon ... 5 H3
Dartmouth Devon ... 6 A1
Darton S York ... 58 D1
Darvel E Ayrs ... 77 E5
Darwen Lancs ... 57 F5
Datchet Berks ... 20 C3
Datchworth Herts ... 33 E1
Daubhill Gt Man ... 57 F3
Dauntsey Wilts ... 18 C5
Dava Highld ... 100 C3
Davenham Ches ... 49 F6
Daventry Nhants ... 31 F6
Davidson's Mains C Edin ... 86 C3
Davidstow Cnwll ... 4 C5
Davington D & G ... 79 E3
Davington Hill Kent ... 23 E2
Daviot Abers ... 102 D2
Daviot Highld ... 99 E6
Daviot House Highld ... 99 E6
Davoch of Grange Moray ... 101 G4
Dawesgreen Surrey ... 11 E6
Dawley Shrops ... 39 F6
Dawlish Devon ... 6 B3
Dawlish Warren Devon ... 6 B3
Dawn Conwy ... 55 F3
Daybrook Notts ... 51 F1
Daylesford Gloucs ... 30 D3
Deal Kent ... 23 H1
Dean Cumb ... 70 D2
Dean Devon ... 15 F5
Dean Devon ... 5 G3
Dean Hants ... 9 F6
Dean Hants ... 9 G5
Dean Oxon ... 31 E2
Dean Somset ... 17 G3
Dean Bottom Kent ... 22 B2
Dean Court Oxon ... 31 F1
Dean Prior Devon ... 5 G3
Deanburnhaugh Border ... 79 G4
Deancombe Devon ... 5 G3
Deane Gt Man ... 57 F3
Deane Hants ... 19 G2
Deanhead W York ... 58 B2
Deanland Dorset ... 8 C5
Deanraw Nthumb ... 72 C3
Deans W Loth ... 86 A3
Deanscales Cumb ... 70 D2
Deanshanger Nhants ... 31 H4
Deanshaugh Moray ... 101 F4

D

Deanston *Stirlg*	85	F5
Dearham *Cumb*	70	D3
Debach *Suffk*	35	F4
Debden *Essex*	33	G2
Debden *Essex*	21	G5
Debenham *Suffk*	35	E5
Deblin's Green *Worcs*	39	G1
Dechmont *W Loth*	86	B3
Dechmont Road *W Loth*	86	A3
Deddington *Oxon*	31	F3
Dedham *Essex*	34	D2
Dedworth *Berks*	20	C3
Deene *Nhants*	42	B2
Deenethorpe *Nhants*	42	B2
Deepcar *S York*	50	D6
Deeping Gate *Lincs*	42	D3
Deeping St James *Lincs*	42	D3
Deeping St Nicholas *Lincs*	42	D3
Deerhurst *Gloucs*	29	F5
Defford *Worcs*	30	A4
Defynnog *Powys*	27	E5
Deganwy *Conwy*	55	F4
Degnish *Ag & B*	83	F6
Deighton *N York*	65	G3
Deighton *N York*	59	G4
Deiniolen *Gwynd*	54	D3
Delabole *Cnwll*	4	B5
Delamere *Ches*	49	E6
Delfrigs *Abers*	103	E2
Dell Quay *W Susx*	10	B2
Delliefure *Highld*	100	D3
Delnashaugh Inn *Moray*	101	E3
Delny *Highld*	107	F3
Delves *Dur*	73	E2
Delvine *P & K*	92	D3
Dembleby *Lincs*	42	C5
Den of Lindores *Fife*	93	E1
Denaby *S York*	51	F6
Denbigh *Denbgs*	48	B5
Denbrae *Fife*	93	F1
Denbury *Devon*	5	H4
Denby *Derbys*	51	E2
Denby Dale *W York*	58	D1
Denchworth *Oxon*	19	F5
Dendron *Cumb*	62	C3
Denfield *P & K*	92	C1
Denford *Nhants*	32	C6
Dengie *Essex*	23	E5
Denham *Bucks*	20	D4
Denham *Suffk*	34	B4
Denham *Suffk*	35	E6
Denham Green *Bucks*	20	D4
Denhead *Abers*	103	E4
Denhead *Fife*	93	G1
Denhead of Gray *Dund C*	93	F3
Denholm *Border*	80	B2
Denholme *W York*	58	C3
Denmead *Hants*	9	H4
Denmore *Aber C*	103	E1
Dennington *Suffk*	35	F5
Denny *Falk*	85	G4
Dennyloanhead *Falk*	85	G3
Denside *Abers*	95	G5
Densole *Kent*	13	G6
Denston *Suffk*	34	B4
Denstone *Staffs*	50	C1
Denstroude *Kent*	23	F2
Dent *Cumb*	63	G4
Denton *Cambs*	42	D1
Denton *Dur*	65	F5
Denton *E Susx*	11	G2
Denton *Gt Man*	50	A6
Denton *Kent*	13	G6
Denton *Lincs*	42	B5
Denton *N York*	58	C5
Denton *Nhants*	32	A4
Denton *Norfk*	45	F1
Denver *Norfk*	43	G2
Denwick *Nthumb*	81	G2
Deopham *Norfk*	44	D2
Deopham Green *Norfk*	44	D2
Deptford *Gt Lon*	21	F3
Deptford *Wilts*	18	C1
Derby *Derbys*	41	E6
Derby *Devon*	15	E4
Derbyhaven *IOM*	116	b2
Derculich *P & K*	92	B4
Dereham *Norfk*	44	D3
Deri *Caerph*	27	G3
Derringstone *Kent*	23	F1
Derrington *Staffs*	40	A5
Derry Hill *Wilts*	18	C4
Derrythorpe *Lincs*	52	A4
Dersingham *Norfk*	44	A5
Dervaig *Ag & B*	89	E4
Derwen *Denbgs*	48	B4
Derwenlas *Powys*	47	F2
Desborough *Nhants*	42	A1
Desford *Leics*	41	F4
Deskford *Moray*	101	H3
Detling *Kent*	22	C2
Devauden *Mons*	28	C3
Devil's Bridge *Cerdgn*	37	F4
Devizes *Wilts*	18	C3
Devonport *Devon*	5	E3
Devonside *Clacks*	85	H5
Devoran *Cnwll*	2	D3
Dewarton *Mdloth*	86	D2
Dewlish *Dorset*	8	A3
Dewsbury *W York*	58	D2
Deytheur *Powys*	48	C1
Dial Post *W Susx*	11	E4
Dibden *Hants*	9	F4
Dibden Purlieu *Hants*	9	F4
Dickleburgh *Norfk*	45	E6
Didbrook *Gloucs*	30	B3
Didcot *Oxon*	19	G5
Didcot Railway Centre *Oxon*	19	G5
Diddington *Cambs*	32	D5
Diddlebury *Shrops*	39	E4
Didling *W Susx*	10	B4
Didmarton *Gloucs*	18	A5
Didsbury *Gt Man*	57	H2
Digby *Lincs*	52	C1
Digg *Highld*	104	C3
Diggle *Gt Man*	58	B1
Digmoor *Lancs*	57	E3
Dihewyd *Cerdgn*	36	D2
Dilham *Norfk*	45	F4
Dilhorne *Staffs*	50	B1
Dillington *Cambs*	32	D5
Dilston *Nthumb*	72	D3
Dilton *Wilts*	18	B2
Dilton Marsh *Wilts*	18	B2
Dilwyn *Herefs*	38	D2
Dinas *Gwynd*	46	C5
Dinas *Pembks*	24	D6
Dinas Powys *V Glam*	16	C6
Dinas-Mawddwy *Gwynd*	47	G3
Dinder *Somset*	17	G3
Dinedor *Herefs*	28	D6
Dingestow *Mons*	28	C4
Dingle *Mersyd*	56	D2
Dingley *Nhants*	41	H2
Dingwall *Highld*	107	E2
Dinnet *Abers*	94	D5
Dinnington *S York*	51	F5
Dinnington *Somset*	17	E1
Dinnington *T & W*	73	F4
Dinorwic *Gwynd*	54	D3
Dinton *Bucks*	31	H1
Dinton *Wilts*	8	C6
Dinwoodie *D & G*	78	D2
Dinworthy *Devon*	14	C3
Dipford *Somset*	16	D2
Dippen *Ag & B*	75	F4
Dippen *N Ayrs*	75	H3
Dippertown *Devon*	5	E5
Dipple *Moray*	101	F5
Dipple *S Ayrs*	76	B2
Diptford *Devon*	5	G3
Dipton *Dur*	73	E2
Dirleton *E Loth*	87	E4
Dirt Pot *Nthumb*	72	C2
Diseworth *Leics*	41	F5
Dishforth *N York*	65	G1
Disley *Ches*	50	B5
Diss *Norfk*	35	E6
Distington *Cumb*	70	D2
Ditchampton *Wilts*	8	D6
Ditchburn *Nthumb*	81	G2
Ditcheat *Somset*	17	G3
Ditchingham *Norfk*	45	F1
Ditchling *E Susx*	11	F3
Ditherington *Shrops*	49	E1
Ditteridge *Wilts*	18	A4
Dittisham *Devon*	6	A2
Ditton *Ches*	57	E2
Ditton *Kent*	22	C2
Ditton Green *Cambs*	33	H4
Ditton Priors *Shrops*	39	F5
Dixton *Gloucs*	29	G5
Dixton *Mons*	28	C4
Dobcross *Gt Man*	58	B1
Dobwalls *Cnwll*	4	C3
Doccombe *Devon*	5	H5
Dochgarroch *Highld*	99	E6
Docker *Lancs*	63	F3
Docking *Norfk*	44	B5
Docklow *Herefs*	39	E2
Dockray *Cumb*	71	G2
Dod's Leigh *Staffs*	40	B6
Dodd's Green *Ches*	49	F4
Doddinghurst *Essex*	22	B5
Doddington *Cambs*	43	F1
Doddington *Kent*	22	D1
Doddington *Lincs*	52	B2
Doddington *Nthumb*	81	F3
Doddington *Shrops*	39	F4
Doddiscombsleigh *Devon*	6	A4
Dodford *Nhants*	31	G5
Dodford *Worcs*	40	B1
Dodington *Gloucs*	29	E1
Dodington *Somset*	16	D3
Dodleston *Ches*	48	D5
Dodworth *S York*	58	D1
Dodworth *Lincs*	52	D1
Dogdyke *Lincs*	52	D1
Dogmersfield *Hants*	20	B1
Dolanog *Powys*	48	B1
Dolau *Powys*	38	B4
Dolbenmaen *Gwynd*	46	D5
Dolfach *Powys*	47	G2
Dolfor *Powys*	38	B4
Dolgarrog *Conwy*	55	F3
Dolgellau *Gwynd*	47	F3
Doll *Highld*	107	G6
Dollar *Clacks*	85	H5
Dollarfield *Clacks*	85	H5
Dolphin *Flints*	48	C6
Dolphinholme *Lancs*	63	E2
Dolphinton *S Lans*	86	B1
Dolton *Devon*	15	E2
Dolwen *Conwy*	55	G4
Dolwyddelan *Conwy*	55	G2
Dolygaig *Powys*	48	C2
Doncaster *S York*	59	F1
Donhead St Andrew *Wilts*	8	B5
Donhead St Mary *Wilts*	8	B5
Donibristle *Fife*	86	C4
Doniford *Somset*	16	C3
Donington *Lincs*	42	D5
Donington on Bain *Lincs*	52	D3
Donisthorpe *Leics*	40	D4
Donnington *Berks*	19	F3
Donnington *Gloucs*	30	C3
Donnington *Shrops*	39	F6
Donnington *Shrops*	49	G1
Donnington *W Susx*	10	B2
Donyatt *Somset*	17	E1
Doonfoot *S Ayrs*	76	C3
Doonholm *S Ayrs*	76	C3
Dorback Lodge *Highld*	100	D1
Dorchester *Dorset*	7	H4
Dorchester *Oxon*	19	G6
Dordon *Warwks*	40	D3
Dore *S York*	50	D4
Dores *Highld*	98	D5
Dorking *Surrey*	21	E1
Dormans Land *Surrey*	11	G6
Dormington *Herefs*	28	D6
Dormston *Worcs*	30	B5
Dorney *Bucks*	20	C3
Dornie *Highld*	97	F4
Dornock *D & G*	71	E5
Dorrington *Lincs*	52	C1
Dorrington *Shrops*	39	E6
Dorrington *Shrops*	49	G3
Dorsington *Warwks*	30	C5
Dorstone *Herefs*	28	B6
Dorton *Bucks*	31	G2
Douglas *IOM*	116	c2
Douglas *S Lans*	78	B5
Douglas and Angus *Dund C*	93	F3
Douglas Castle *S Lans*	78	B5
Douglas Pier *Ag & B*	84	B5
Douglas Water *S Lans*	78	C6
Douglas West *S Lans*	78	B5
Douglastown *Angus*	93	F4
Doulting *Somset*	17	G3
Dounby *Ork*	111	g2
Doune *Highld*	106	D5
Doune *Stirlg*	85	F5
Dounepark *S Ayrs*	76	B1
Dounie *Highld*	107	E5
Dousland *Devon*	5	F4
Dove Holes *Derbys*	50	C4
Dovenby *Cumb*	70	D3
Dover *Kent*	13	G6
Dover Castle *Kent*	13	G6
Dovercourt *Essex*	35	F2
Doverdale *Worcs*	39	H3
Doveridge *Derbys*	40	C6
Doversgreen *Surrey*	11	E6
Dowally *Myr Td*	92	C4
Dowdeswell *Gloucs*	30	B2
Dowlais *Myr Td*	27	F3
Dowland *Devon*	15	E2
Dowlish Wake *Somset*	7	E6
Down Ampney *Gloucs*	18	D6
Down Hatherley *Gloucs*	29	F5
Down St Mary *Devon*	15	F2
Down Thomas *Devon*	5	E2
Downderry *Cnwll*	4	D2
Downe *Gt Lon*	21	G2
Downend *Essex*	28	D1
Downend *Gloucs*	29	F3
Downgate *Cnwll*	4	D4
Downgate *Cnwll*	4	D4
Downham *Essex*	22	C5
Downham *Gt Lon*	21	F3
Downham *Lancs*	63	G1
Downham Market *Norfk*	43	G2
Downhead *Somset*	17	G2
Downhead *Somset*	17	H3
Downhill *P & K*	92	D2
Downholme *N York*	65	E3
Downies *Abers*	95	H5
Downley *Bucks*	20	B5
Downton *Hants*	9	E3
Downton *Wilts*	8	D5
Downton on the Rock *Herefs*	38	D3
Dowsby *Lincs*	42	D5
Doynton *Gloucs*	17	H6
Draethen *Caerph*	27	G2
Draffan *S Lans*	77	G5
Drakeholes *Notts*	51	G5
Drakemyre *N Ayrs*	76	C6
Drakes Broughton *Worcs*	30	A5
Draughton *N York*	58	B5
Draughton *Nhants*	41	H1
Drax *N York*	59	G3
Draycote *Warwks*	41	E1
Draycott *Derbys*	41	E6
Draycott *Gloucs*	30	C3
Draycott *Somset*	17	F4
Draycott in the Clay *Staffs*	40	C6
Draycott in the Moors *Staffs*	50	B1
Drayton *Hants*	9	H4
Drayton *Leics*	42	A2
Drayton *Norfk*	45	E3
Drayton *Oxon*	31	E4
Drayton *Oxon*	19	G6
Drayton *Somset*	17	E2
Drayton *Worcs*	40	A1
Drayton Bassett *Staffs*	40	D3
Drayton Beauchamp *Bucks*	20	C6
Drayton Manor Park *Staffs*	40	D3
Drayton Parslow *Bucks*	32	A2
Drayton St Leonard *Oxon*	19	G6
Dreen Hill *Pembks*	24	D4
Drefach *Carmth*	25	G6
Drefach *Carmth*	26	B4
Drefach *Cerdgn*	36	D2
Dreghorn *N Ayrs*	76	C5
Drellingore *Kent*	13	G6
Drem *E Loth*	87	E4
Drewsteignton *Devon*	5	G5
Driby *Lincs*	53	F3
Driffield *E R Yk*	60	D5
Driffield *Gloucs*	18	C6
Drift *Cnwll*	2	B2
Drigg *Cumb*	62	B5
Dundee Airport *Dund C*	93	F2
Drighlington *W York*	58	D3
Drimnin *Highld*	89	F4
Drimpton *Dorset*	7	E6
Drimsallie *Highld*	90	B6
Dringhouses *N York*	59	G5
Drinkstone *Suffk*	34	C4
Drinkstone Green *Suffk*	34	C4
Droitton *Staffs*	40	B5
Droitwich *Worcs*	30	A6
Dron *P & K*	92	D1
Dronfield *Derbys*	51	E4
Drongan *E Ayrs*	76	D3
Dronley *Angus*	93	F3
Droop *Dorset*	7	H6
Droxford *Hants*	9	H5
Droylsden *Gt Man*	50	A6
Druid *Denbgs*	48	A4
Druidston *Pembks*	24	C4
Druimachoish *Highld*	90	C3
Druimarbin *Highld*	90	C5
Druimdrishaig *Ag & B*	83	F3
Druimindarroch *Highld*	97	E1
Drum *Ag & B*	83	G3
Drum *P & K*	86	B5
Drumalbin *S Lans*	78	C6
Drumbeg *Highld*	108	B3
Drumblade *Abers*	102	B3
Drumbreddon *D & G*	68	C2
Drumbuie *Highld*	97	E5
Drumburgh *Cumb*	71	F5
Drumburn *D & G*	70	C4
Drumchapel *C Glas*	85	E4
Drumchastle *P & K*	91	H4
Drumclog *S Lans*	77	F5
Drumeldrie *Fife*	87	E6
Drumelzier *Border*	79	E5
Drumfearn *Highld*	97	E4
Drumfrennie *Abers*	95	F5
Drumguish *Highld*	99	F3
Drumhead *Abers*	95	E5
Drumin *Moray*	101	E3
Drumjohn *D & G*	77	E2
Drumlamford *S Ayrs*	68	D5
Drumlasie *Abers*	95	E6
Drumleaning *Cumb*	71	F4
Drumlemble *Ag & B*	75	E3
Drumlithie *Abers*	95	G4
Drummoddie *D & G*	69	E2
Drummore *D & G*	68	C2
Drummuir *Moray*	101	F4
Drumnadrochit *Highld*	98	D5
Drumnagorrach *Moray*	102	B4
Drumpark *D & G*	78	C1
Drumrunie Lodge *Highld*	106	B6
Drumshang *S Ayrs*	76	C3
Drumuie *Highld*	104	C1
Drumuillie *Highld*	99	G5
Drumvaich *Stirlg*	85	F5
Drunzie *P & K*	86	B6
Dry Doddington *Lincs*	42	B6
Dry Drayton *Cambs*	33	F5
Drybeck *Cumb*	64	B4
Drybridge *Moray*	101	G5
Drybridge *N Ayrs*	76	C5
Drybrook *Gloucs*	28	D4
Dryburgh *Border*	80	B3
Drym *Cnwll*	2	C3
Drymen *Stirlg*	84	D4
Drymuir *Abers*	103	E4
Drynoch *Highld*	96	C5
Dubford *Abers*	102	D5
Duchally *Highld*	108	D1
Ducklington *Oxon*	31	E1
Duddenhoe End *Essex*	33	F2
Duddingston *C Edin*	86	C3
Duddington *Nhants*	42	C2
Duddlestone *Somset*	16	D1
Duddlewick *Shrops*	39	F4
Duddo *Nthumb*	81	E4
Duddon *Ches*	49	E5
Dudleston *Shrops*	48	D3
Dudley *T & W*	73	F4
Dudley *W Mids*	40	B3
Dudley Port *W Mids*	40	B3
Dudsbury *Dorset*	8	C3
Duffield *Derbys*	51	E1
Duffryn *Neath*	26	D2
Dufftown *Moray*	101	F3
Duffus *Moray*	101	E6
Dufton *Cumb*	64	B5
Duggleby *N York*	60	C6
Duirinish *Highld*	97	F5
Duisdalemore *Highld*	97	E3
Duisky *Highld*	90	B6
Duke Street *Suffk*	34	D3
Dukinfield *Gt Man*	50	B6
Dulcote *Somset*	17	G3
Dulford *Devon*	6	C6
Dull *P & K*	92	A4
Dullatur *N Lans*	85	F3
Dullingham *Cambs*	33	H4
Dullingham Ley *Cambs*	33	H4
Dulnain Bridge *Highld*	99	G5
Duloe *Beds*	32	D4
Duloe *Cnwll*	4	C3
Dulverton *Somset*	16	B2
Dulwich *Gt Lon*	21	F3
Dumbarton *W Duns*	84	D3
Dumbleton *Gloucs*	30	B3
Dumfries *D & G*	70	C6
Dumgoyne *Stirlg*	85	E4
Dummer *Hants*	19	G2
Dumpton *Kent*	23	H2
Dun *Angus*	95	F2
Dunalastair *P & K*	91	H4
Dunan *Ag & B*	84	B3
Dunan *Highld*	96	D4
Dunaverty *Ag & B*	75	E2
Dunball *Somset*	17	E3
Dunbar *E Loth*	87	F4
Dunbeath *Highld*	110	B2
Dunbeg *Ag & B*	90	A2
Dunblane *Stirlg*	85	G5
Dunbog *Fife*	93	E1
Duncanston *Highld*	107	E2
Duncanstone *Abers*	102	B2
Dunchideock *Devon*	6	A4
Dunchurch *Warwks*	41	F1
Duncow *D & G*	78	C1
Duncrievie *P & K*	86	B6
Duncton *W Susx*	10	C4
Dundee *Dund C*	93	F2
Dundon *Somset*	17	F2
Dundonald *S Ayrs*	76	C4
Dundonnell *Highld*	106	A4
Dundraw *Cumb*	71	E4
Dundreggan *Highld*	98	B4
Dundrennan *D & G*	70	B4
Dundry *Somset*	17	G5
Dunecht *Abers*	102	D1
Dunfermline *Fife*	86	B4
Dunfield *Gloucs*	18	D6
Dungavel *S Lans*	77	F5
Dunham *Notts*	52	A3
Dunham Town *Gt Man*	57	G2
Dunham Woodhouses *Gt Man*	57	G2
Dunham-on-the-Hill *Ches*	49	E6
Dunhampton *Worcs*	39	H3
Dunholme *Lincs*	52	C3
Dunino *Fife*	93	G1
Dunipace *Falk*	85	G4
Dunk's Green *Kent*	22	B1
Dunkeld *P & K*	92	C3
Dunkerton *Somset*	17	H5
Dunkeswell *Devon*	6	C6
Dunkeswick *W York*	58	D4
Dunkirk *Gloucs*	18	A5
Dunkirk *Kent*	23	F2
Dunlappie *Angus*	95	E3
Dunley *Hants*	19	G3
Dunlop *E Ayrs*	76	D6
Dunmaglass *Highld*	98	D4
Dunmore *Falk*	85	G4
Dunnet *Highld*	110	C6
Dunnichen *Angus*	93	G4
Dunning *P & K*	92	C1
Dunnington *E R Yk*	61	E5
Dunnington *N York*	59	G5
Dunnington *Warwks*	30	C5
Dunnockshaw *Lancs*	57	G5
Dunoon *Ag & B*	84	B3
Dunragit *D & G*	68	C3
Duns *Border*	80	D5
Duns Tew *Oxon*	31	F3
Dunsby *Lincs*	42	C4
Dunscore *D & G*	78	C1
Dunsdale *N York*	66	C5
Dunsden Green *Oxon*	20	A3
Dunsdon *Devon*	14	C2
Dunsfold *Surrey*	10	D5
Dunsford *Devon*	5	H5
Dunshalt *Fife*	93	E1
Dunshillock *Abers*	103	E4
Dunsill *Notts*	51	F3
Dunsley *N York*	67	E4
Dunsley *Staffs*	39	H4
Dunsmore *Bucks*	20	B5
Dunsop Bridge *Lancs*	63	F1
Dunstable *Beds*	32	C1
Dunstall *Staffs*	40	C5
Dunstan *Nthumb*	81	H2
Dunster *Somset*	16	B3
Dunston *Lincs*	52	C2
Dunston *Norfk*	45	E2
Dunston *Staffs*	40	A5
Dunston *T & W*	73	F2
Dunstone *Devon*	5	F2
Dunstone *Devon*	5	G4
Dunswell *E R Yk*	61	E3
Dunsyre *S Lans*	86	B1
Dunterton *Devon*	4	D5
Duntisbourne Abbots *Gloucs*	29	G3
Duntisbourne Rouse *Gloucs*	29	G3
Duntish *Dorset*	7	H6
Duntocher *W Duns*	84	D3
Dunton *Beds*	33	E3
Dunton *Bucks*	32	A1
Dunton *Norfk*	44	C5
Dunton Bassett *Leics*	41	F3
Dunton Green *Kent*	21	G1
Duntulm *Highld*	104	C3
Dunure *S Ayrs*	76	C3
Dunvant *Swans*	26	B2
Dunvegan *Highld*	104	B1
Dunwich *Suffk*	35	G5
Durgan *Cnwll*	2	D2
Durham *Dur*	73	F1
Durham Cathedral *Dur*	73	F1
Durisdeer *D & G*	78	C3
Durisdeermill *D & G*	78	C3
Durleigh *Somset*	16	D3
Durley *Hants*	9	G5
Durley *Wilts*	19	E3
Durley Street *Hants*	9	G5
Durlock *Kent*	23	G2
Durlock *Kent*	23	G2
Durmgley *Angus*	93	F4
Durness *Highld*	108	D5
Duror *Highld*	90	B4
Durran *Ag & B*	83	G6
Durrington *W Susx*	10	D3
Durrington *Wilts*	18	D2
Durris *Abers*	95	F5
Dursley *Gloucs*	29	E3
Dursley Cross *Gloucs*	29	E4
Durston *Somset*	16	D2
Durweston *Dorset*	8	B4
Duston *Nhants*	31	H6
Dutlhil *Highld*	99	G5
Dutton *Ches*	57	F1
Duxford *Cambs*	33	F3
Duxford *Oxon*	19	F6
Duxford Aircraft Museum *Cambs*	33	F3
Dwygyfylchi *Conwy*	55	E4
Dwyran *IOA*	54	C3
Dyce *Aber C*	103	E1
Dyffryn Ardudwy *Gwynd*	47	E4
Dyffryn Cellwen *Neath*	27	E4
Dyke *Lincs*	42	C4
Dyke *Moray*	100	C5
Dykehead *Angus*	93	E4
Dykehead *Angus*	94	C2
Dykehead *N Lans*	85	G2
Dykehead *Stirlg*	85	E5
Dykelands *Abers*	95	F3
Dykends *Angus*	93	G5
Dykeside *Abers*	102	C4
Dymchurch *Kent*	13	F5
Dymock *Gloucs*	29	E5
Dyrham *Gloucs*	17	H6
Dysart *Fife*	86	D5
Dyserth *Denbgs*	56	B1

E

Eagland Hill *Lancs*	62	D1
Eagle *Lincs*	52	B2
Eaglescliffe *Dur*	65	H4
Eaglesfield *Cumb*	70	D2
Eaglesfield *D & G*	71	E6
Eaglesham *E Rens*	85	E1
Eagley *Gt Man*	57	G4
Eakring *Notts*	51	G3
Ealand *Lincs*	60	B2
Ealing *Gt Lon*	21	E3
Eals *Nthumb*	72	B2
Eamont Bridge *Cumb*	71	H2
Earby *Lancs*	58	A4
Eardington *Shrops*	39	G5
Eardisland *Herefs*	38	D2
Eardisley *Herefs*	38	C1
Eardiston *Shrops*	48	D2
Eardiston *Worcs*	39	F3
Earith *Cambs*	33	F6
Earl Shilton *Leics*	41	F3
Earl Soham *Suffk*	35	E5
Earl Sterndale *Derbys*	50	C3
Earl's Croome *Worcs*	29	F6
Earlestown *Mersyd*	57	F2
Earley *Berks*	20	B3
Earlish *Highld*	104	C2
Earls Barton *Nhants*	32	B5
Earls Colne *Essex*	34	C2
Earls Common *Worcs*	30	A5
Earls Wood *W Mids*	40	D1
Earlsferry *Fife*	87	E5
Earlsfield *Gt Lon*	21	E3
Earlsford *Abers*	102	D3
Earlsheaton *W York*	58	D2
Earlston *Border*	80	B4
Earlston *E Ayrs*	76	D5
Earlswood *Surrey*	21	F1
Earlswood *Warwks*	40	C1
Earnley *W Susx*	10	B2
Earsdon *Nthumb*	73	F5

Earsdon T & W ... 73 G4
Earsham Norfk ... 45 F1
Eartham W Susx ... 10 C3
Easby N York ... 66 C4
Easdale Ag & B ... 89 G1
Easebourne W Susx ... 10 C4
Easenhall Warwks ... 41 F2
Eashing Surrey ... 10 C6
Easington Bucks ... 31 G1
Easington Dur ... 73 G1
Easington E R Yk ... 61 G2
Easington N York ... 66 D5
Easington Colliery Dur ... 73 H1
Easingwold N York ... 66 B1
Eassie and Nevay Angus ... 93 F4
East Aberthaw V Glam ... 16 B5
East Allington Devon ... 5 G3
East Anstey Devon ... 15 G4
East Ashey IOW ... 9 G2
East Ashling W Susx ... 10 B3
East Ayton N York ... 67 F2
East Barkwith Lincs ... 52 D3
East Barming Kent ... 22 C1
East Barnby N York ... 66 D4
East Barnet Gt Lon ... 21 F5
East Barns E Loth ... 87 G3
East Barsham Norfk ... 44 C5
East Beckham Norfk ... 45 E5
East Bedfont Gt Lon ... 20 D3
East Bergholt Suffk ... 34 D2
East Bilney Norfk ... 44 C4
East Blatchington E Susx ... 11 G2
East Boldon T & W ... 73 G3
East Boldre Hants ... 9 F3
East Bradenham Norfk ... 44 C3
East Brent Somset ... 17 E4
East Bridgford Notts ... 51 G1
East Buckland Devon ... 15 F4
East Budleigh Devon ... 6 C4
East Butterwick Lincs ... 52 A5
East Calder W Loth ... 86 B3
East Carleton Norfk ... 45 E2
East Carlton Nhants ... 42 A1
East Carlton W York ... 58 D4
East Chaldon (Chaldon Herring) Dorset ... 8 A2
East Challow Oxon ... 19 F5
East Charleton Devon ... 5 G2
East Chelborough Dorset ... 7 F6
East Chiltington E Susx ... 11 F3
East Chinnock Somset ... 17 F1
East Chisenbury Wilts ... 18 D2
East Clandon Surrey ... 20 D1
East Claydon Bucks ... 31 H3
East Coker Somset ... 7 F6
East Combe Somset ... 16 C2
East Compton Somset ... 17 G3
East Cornworthy Devon ... 6 A2
East Cottingwith E R Yk ... 60 B4
East Cowes IOW ... 9 G3
East Cowick E R Yk ... 59 G2
East Cowton N York ... 65 G4
East Cranmore Somset ... 17 G3
East Creech Dorset ... 8 B2
East Dean E Susx ... 12 B2
East Dean Gloucs ... 28 D4
East Dean Hants ... 9 E5
East Dean W Susx ... 10 C3
East Down Devon ... 15 E5
East Drayton Notts ... 51 H4
East Dulwich Gt Lon ... 21 F3
East Dundry Somset ... 17 G5
East Ella E R Yk ... 60 D3
East End Hants ... 19 F3
East End Hants ... 9 F3
East End Kent ... 12 D5
East End Oxon ... 31 E2
East End Somset ... 17 G4
East Everleigh Wilts ... 18 D2
East Farleigh Kent ... 22 C1
East Farndon Nhants ... 41 H2
East Ferry Lincs ... 52 A5
East Fortune E Loth ... 87 E4
East Garston Berks ... 19 F4
East Goscote Leics ... 41 G4
East Grafton Wilts ... 19 E3
East Grimstead Wilts ... 9 E6
East Grinstead W Susx ... 11 G5
East Guldeford E Susx ... 12 D4
East Haddon Nhants ... 31 G6
East Hagbourne Oxon ... 19 G5
East Halton Lincs ... 61 E2
East Ham Gt Lon ... 21 G4
East Hanney Oxon ... 19 F5
East Hanningfield Essex ... 22 C5
East Hardwick W York ... 59 F2
East Harling Norfk ... 44 D1
East Harlsey N York ... 65 H3
East Harnham Wilts ... 8 D6
East Harptree Somset ... 17 G4
East Hartburn Dur ... 65 H5
East Harting W Susx ... 10 B4
East Hatch Wilts ... 8 B6
East Hatley Cambs ... 33 E4
East Hauxwell N York ... 65 F3
East Haven Angus ... 93 G3
East Heckington Lincs ... 42 D6
East Hedleyhope Dur ... 73 E1
East Helmsdale Highld ... 110 A1
East Hendred Oxon ... 19 F5
East Heslerton N York ... 67 E1
East Hoathly E Susx ... 11 H4
East Holme Dorset ... 8 B2
East Horrington Somset ... 17 G4
East Horsley Surrey ... 20 D1
East Howe Dorset ... 8 C3
East Huntspill Somset ... 17 E3
East Ilsley Berks ... 19 G4
East Keal Lincs ... 53 F2
East Kennett Wilts ... 18 D3
East Keswick W York ... 59 E4
East Kilbride S Lans ... 85 E1
East Kirkby Lincs ... 53 E2
East Knighton Dorset ... 8 A2
East Knoyle Wilts ... 8 B6
East Lambrook Somset ... 17 F1
East Langdon Kent ... 13 G6
East Langton Leics ... 41 H3
East Laroch Highld ... 90 C4
East Lavant W Susx ... 10 B3
East Lavington W Susx ... 10 C4
East Layton N York ... 65 F4
East Leake Notts ... 41 F5
East Leigh Devon ... 15 F2

East Leigh Devon ... 5 G3
East Lexham Norfk ... 44 C4
East Linton E Loth ... 87 F4
East Lockinge Oxon ... 19 F5
East Lound Lincs ... 52 A5
East Lulworth Dorset ... 8 B2
East Lutton N York ... 60 D6
East Lydford Somset ... 17 G2
East Malling Kent ... 22 C1
East Marden W Susx ... 10 B3
East Markham Notts ... 51 H4
East Martin Hants ... 8 C5
East Marton N York ... 58 A5
East Meon Hants ... 10 A4
East Mersea Essex ... 23 E6
East Midlands Airport Leics ... 41 E5
East Molesey Surrey ... 21 E2
East Morden Dorset ... 8 B3
East Morton D & G ... 78 C3
East Morton W York ... 58 C4
East Ness N York ... 66 C2
East Norton Leics ... 42 A2
East Ogwell Devon ... 5 H4
East Orchard Dorset ... 8 B5
East Peckham Kent ... 12 B6
East Pennar Pembks ... 24 D3
East Pennard Somset ... 17 G3
East Perry Cambs ... 32 D5
East Portlemouth Devon ... 5 G1
East Prawle Devon ... 5 H1
East Preston W Susx ... 10 D2
East Pulham Dorset ... 7 H6
East Putford Devon ... 14 D3
East Quantoxhead Somset ... 16 C3
East Rainton T & W ... 73 G2
East Ravendale Lincs ... 52 D5
East Raynham Norfk ... 44 C4
East Rigton W York ... 59 E4
East Rounton N York ... 65 H4
East Rudham Norfk ... 44 B4
East Runton Norfk ... 45 E6
East Ruston Norfk ... 45 F4
East Saltoun E Loth ... 87 E3
East Sheen Gt Lon ... 21 E3
East Shefford Berks ... 19 F4
East Stockwith Lincs ... 52 A4
East Stoke Dorset ... 8 B2
East Stoke Notts ... 51 H2
East Stour Dorset ... 8 A5
East Stourmouth Kent ... 23 G2
East Stowford Devon ... 15 F4
East Stratton Hants ... 19 G1
East Studdal Kent ... 23 G1
East Thirston Nthumb ... 73 F6
East Tilbury Essex ... 22 B3
East Tisted Hants ... 10 A5
East Torrington Lincs ... 52 D4
East Tuddenham Norfk ... 44 D3
East Tytherley Hants ... 9 E6
East Tytherton Wilts ... 18 C4
East Village Devon ... 15 G2
East Wall Shrops ... 39 E5
East Walton Norfk ... 44 B4
East Water Somset ... 17 F4
East Week Devon ... 5 G6
East Wellow Hants ... 9 E5
East Wemyss Fife ... 86 D5
East Whitburn W Loth ... 85 H2
East Wickham Gt Lon ... 21 G3
East Williamston Pembks ... 25 E3
East Winch Norfk ... 44 A4
East Winterslow Wilts ... 9 E6
East Wittering W Susx ... 10 B2
East Witton N York ... 65 E2
East Woodburn Nthumb ... 72 D5
East Woodhay Hants ... 19 F3
East Worldham Hants ... 10 B5
East Wretham Norfk ... 44 C1
East Youlstone Devon ... 14 C3
East-the-Water Devon ... 14 D4
Eastbourne Dur ... 65 G4
Eastbourne E Susx ... 12 B2
Eastbridge Suffk ... 35 G5
Eastburn W York ... 58 B4
Eastbury Berks ... 19 E4
Eastbury Herts ... 20 D4
Eastby N York ... 58 B5
Eastchurch Kent ... 23 E3
Eastcombe Gloucs ... 29 F5
Eastcote Gt Lon ... 20 D4
Eastcote Nhants ... 31 G5
Eastcote W Mids ... 40 D2
Eastcott Wilts ... 18 C2
Eastcourt Wilts ... 29 G2
Eastcourt Wilts ... 19 E3
Eastend Essex ... 22 D4
Eastend S Lans ... 78 C6
Easter Balmoral Abers ... 94 C5
Easter Compton Gloucs ... 28 D1
Easter Dalziel Highld ... 107 F1
Easter Howgate Mdloth ... 86 C2
Easter Kinkell Highld ... 107 E2
Easter Moniack Highld ... 98 D6
Easter Ord Abers ... 95 G6
Easter Pitkierie Fife ... 87 F6
Easter Skeld Shet ... 111 I2
Easter Softlaw Border ... 80 D3
Easter Suddie Highld ... 107 F2
Eastergate W Susx ... 10 C3
Easterhouse C Glas ... 85 F2
Eastern Green W Mids ... 40 D2
Easterton Wilts ... 18 C2
Eastfield N Lans ... 85 G2
Eastfield N York ... 67 F2
Eastgate Dur ... 72 D1
Eastgate Norfk ... 45 E4
Easthampstead Berks ... 20 B2
Easthampton Herefs ... 38 D2
Easthope Shrops ... 39 E5
Eastington Devon ... 15 F2
Eastington Gloucs ... 30 C2
Eastington Gloucs ... 29 E3
Eastlands D & G ... 70 B6
Eastleach Martin Gloucs ... 30 D1
Eastleach Turville Gloucs ... 30 D1
Eastleigh Devon ... 14 D4
Eastleigh Hants ... 9 F5
Eastling Kent ... 23 E1
Eastney Hants ... 9 H3
Eastnor Herefs ... 29 E6
Eastoft Lincs ... 60 B2
Easton Cambs ... 32 D5

Easton Cumb ... 71 F5
Easton Devon ... 5 G5
Easton Dorset ... 7 H3
Easton Hants ... 9 G6
Easton Lincs ... 42 B4
Easton Norfk ... 45 E3
Easton Somset ... 17 F4
Easton Suffk ... 35 F4
Easton Wilts ... 18 B4
Easton Grey Wilts ... 18 B5
Easton Maudit Nhants ... 32 B4
Easton on the Hill Nhants ... 42 C3
Easton Royal Wilts ... 18 D3
Easton-in-Gordano Somset ... 17 F6
Eastrea Cambs ... 43 E2
Eastriggs D & G ... 71 F5
Eastrington E R Yk ... 60 B3
Eastrop Wilts ... 18 D5
Eastry Kent ... 23 G1
Eastville Bristl ... 17 G6
Eastville Lincs ... 53 F1
Eastwell Leics ... 41 H6
Eastwick Herts ... 21 G6
Eastwood Essex ... 22 D4
Eastwood Notts ... 51 F2
Eastwood W York ... 58 B3
Eaton Ches ... 49 F5
Eaton Ches ... 49 H5
Eaton Leics ... 42 A5
Eaton Norfk ... 45 E3
Eaton Notts ... 51 G4
Eaton Oxon ... 31 E1
Eaton Shrops ... 39 E5
Eaton Bray Beds ... 32 B1
Eaton Constantine Shrops ... 39 F6
Eaton Green Beds ... 32 B1
Eaton Hastings Oxon ... 19 E6
Eaton Mascott Shrops ... 39 E6
Eaton Socon Cambs ... 32 D4
Eaton upon Tern Shrops ... 49 F2
Ebberston N York ... 67 E2
Ebbesborne Wake Wilts ... 8 C5
Ebbw Vale Blae G ... 27 G4
Ebchester Dur ... 73 E2
Ebford Devon ... 6 B4
Ebley Gloucs ... 29 F3
Ebnal Ches ... 49 E4
Ebrington Gloucs ... 30 C4
Ecchinswell Hants ... 19 G3
Ecclaw Border ... 87 G3
Ecclefechan D & G ... 71 E6
Eccles Border ... 80 D4
Eccles Gt Man ... 57 G3
Eccles Kent ... 22 C2
Eccles Road Norfk ... 44 D1
Ecclesall S York ... 50 D5
Ecclesfield S York ... 51 E5
Eccleshall Staffs ... 49 G2
Eccleshill W York ... 58 C3
Ecclesmachan W Loth ... 86 B3
Eccleston Ches ... 48 D5
Eccleston Lancs ... 57 E4
Eccleston Mersyd ... 57 E2
Echt Abers ... 95 F6
Eckford Border ... 80 C3
Eckington Derbys ... 51 E4
Eckington Worcs ... 29 G6
Ecton Nhants ... 32 A5
Edale Derbys ... 50 C5
Edburton W Susx ... 11 E3
Edderton Highld ... 107 F4
Eddleston Border ... 86 C1
Eddlewood S Lans ... 85 F1
Eden Park Gt Lon ... 21 F2
Edenbridge Kent ... 11 G6
Edenfield Lancs ... 57 G4
Edenhall Cumb ... 71 H3
Edenham Lincs ... 42 C4
Edensor Derbys ... 50 D4
Edentaggart Ag & B ... 84 C5
Edenthorpe S York ... 59 G1
Edern Gwynd ... 46 C5
Edgarley Somset ... 17 G3
Edgbaston W Mids ... 40 B2
Edgcott Bucks ... 31 G2
Edgcott Somset ... 15 G5
Edge Gloucs ... 29 F4
Edge Shrops ... 38 D6
Edgefield Norfk ... 44 D5
Edgefield Green Norfk ... 44 D5
Edgerton W York ... 58 C2
Edgeworth Gloucs ... 29 G3
Edgmond Shrops ... 49 G2
Edgton Shrops ... 38 D4
Edgware Gt Lon ... 21 E4
Edgworth Lancs ... 57 G4
Edinbane Highld ... 104 B1
Edinburgh C Edin ... 86 C3
Edinburgh Airport C Edin ... 86 B3
Edinburgh Castle C Edin ... 86 C3
Edinburgh Zoo C Edin ... 86 C3
Edingale Staffs ... 40 D4
Edingham D & G ... 70 B5
Edingley Notts ... 51 G2
Edingthorpe Norfk ... 45 F5
Edingthorpe Green Norfk ... 45 F5
Edington Border ... 81 E5
Edington Nthumb ... 73 E5
Edington Somset ... 17 E3
Edington Wilts ... 18 B2
Edington Burtle Somset ... 17 E3
Edingworth Somset ... 17 E4
Edith Weston Rutlnd ... 42 B3
Edithmead Somset ... 17 E4
Edlesborough Bucks ... 32 B1
Edlington Lincs ... 52 D3
Edmondsham Dorset ... 8 C4
Edmondsley Dur ... 73 F2
Edmondthorpe Leics ... 42 B4
Edmonton Gt Lon ... 21 F4
Edmundbyers Dur ... 72 D2
Ednam Border ... 80 D4
Edradynate P & K ... 92 B4
Edrom Border ... 80 D5
Edstaston Shrops ... 49 E3
Edstone Warwks ... 30 C6
Edwalton Notts ... 41 G6
Edwinstowe Notts ... 51 G3
Edworth Beds ... 32 D3
Edwyn Ralph Herefs ... 39 F2
Edzell Angus ... 95 E3
Efail Isaf Rhondd ... 27 F1

Efail-fach Neath ... 26 D2
Efailnewydd Gwynd ... 46 C5
Efailwen Carmth ... 25 E5
Efenechtyd Denbgs ... 48 B5
Effgill D & G ... 79 F2
Effingham Surrey ... 20 D1
Efford Devon ... 15 H1
Egerton Gt Man ... 57 G3
Egerton Kent ... 12 D6
Eggborough N York ... 59 G3
Eggbuckland Devon ... 5 E3
Eggesford Devon ... 15 F2
Eggington Beds ... 32 B2
Egginton Derbys ... 40 D6
Egglescliffe Dur ... 65 G4
Eggleston Dur ... 64 D5
Egham Surrey ... 20 D3
Egleton Rutlnd ... 42 B3
Eglingham Nthumb ... 81 F2
Egloshayle Cnwll ... 3 F6
Egloskerry Cnwll ... 4 D5
Eglwys Cross Wrexhm ... 49 E3
Eglwysbach Conwy ... 55 F3
Eglwyswrw Pembks ... 25 E6
Egmanton Notts ... 51 H3
Egremont Cumb ... 70 D1
Egremont Mersyd ... 56 D2
Egton N York ... 66 D4
Egton Bridge N York ... 66 D4
Eight Ash Green Essex ... 34 C2
Eilanreach Highld ... 97 F4
Elan Village Powys ... 37 H3
Elberton Gloucs ... 28 D2
Elburton Devon ... 5 F2
Elcombe Wilts ... 18 D4
Eldersfield Worcs ... 29 F6
Elderslie Rens ... 84 D2
Eldon Dur ... 65 F6
Eldwick W York ... 58 C4
Elfhill Abers ... 95 G4
Elford Staffs ... 40 C4
Elgin Moray ... 101 E5
Elgol Highld ... 96 D4
Elham Kent ... 13 F6
Elie Fife ... 87 E5
Elilaw Nthumb ... 81 E2
Elim IOA ... 54 C4
Eling Hants ... 9 F4
Elishaw Nthumb ... 72 C5
Elkesley Notts ... 51 G4
Elkstone Gloucs ... 29 G4
Ella Abers ... 102 C5
Ellacombe Devon ... 6 B2
Ellanbeich Ag & B ... 89 G1
Elland W York ... 58 C2
Ellary Ag & B ... 83 F3
Ellastone Staffs ... 50 C1
Ellel Lancs ... 63 E2
Ellemford Border ... 87 G2
Ellen's Green Surrey ... 10 D5
Ellenhall Staffs ... 49 H2
Ellerbeck N York ... 66 A3
Ellerby N York ... 66 D4
Ellerdine Heath Shrops ... 49 F2
Elleric Ag & B ... 90 C4
Ellerker E R Yk ... 60 C3
Ellerton E R Yk ... 60 B4
Ellerton N York ... 65 F3
Ellesborough Bucks ... 20 B5
Ellesmere Shrops ... 48 D3
Ellesmere Port Ches ... 56 D1
Ellingham Norfk ... 45 F2
Ellingham Nthumb ... 81 G3
Ellingstring N York ... 65 F2
Ellington Cambs ... 32 D5
Ellington Nthumb ... 73 F5
Elliots Green Somset ... 18 A2
Ellisfield Hants ... 19 H2
Ellishader Highld ... 104 D3
Ellistown Leics ... 41 E4
Ellon Abers ... 103 E3
Ellonby Cumb ... 71 G3
Elloughton E R Yk ... 60 D3
Ellwood Gloucs ... 28 D3
Elm Cambs ... 43 F3
Elm Park Gt Lon ... 21 H4
Elmbridge Worcs ... 30 A6
Elmdon Essex ... 33 F3
Elmdon W Mids ... 40 C2
Elmers End Gt Lon ... 21 F2
Elmesthorpe Leics ... 41 F3
Elmhurst Staffs ... 40 C4
Elmley Castle Worcs ... 29 G6
Elmley Lovett Worcs ... 39 H3
Elmore Gloucs ... 29 E4
Elmore Back Gloucs ... 29 E4
Elmsett Suffk ... 34 D3
Elmstead Market Essex ... 34 D2
Elmsted Court Kent ... 13 F6
Elmstone Kent ... 23 G2
Elmstone Hardwicke Gloucs ... 29 F5
Elmswell E R Yk ... 60 D5
Elmswell Suffk ... 34 D5
Elmton Derbys ... 51 F4
Elphin Highld ... 108 C1
Elphinstone E Loth ... 86 D3
Elrick Abers ... 95 G6
Elrig D & G ... 69 E2
Elrington Nthumb ... 72 C3
Elsdon Nthumb ... 72 D5
Elsecar S York ... 51 E5
Elsenham Essex ... 33 G2
Elsfield Oxon ... 31 F1
Elsham Lincs ... 60 D2
Elsick House Abers ... 95 G5
Elsing Norfk ... 44 D4
Elslack N York ... 58 A5
Elson Hants ... 9 G3
Elsrickle S Lans ... 86 B1
Elstead Surrey ... 10 C5
Elsted W Susx ... 10 B4
Elsthorpe Lincs ... 42 C4
Elston Notts ... 51 H2
Elstone Devon ... 15 F3
Elstow Beds ... 32 C3
Elstree Herts ... 21 E5
Elstronwick E R Yk ... 61 F3
Elswick Lancs ... 56 D6
Elswick T & W ... 73 F3
Elsworth Cambs ... 33 E5
Elterwater Cumb ... 62 D6
Eltham Gt Lon ... 21 G3
Eltisley Cambs ... 33 E4
Elton Cambs ... 42 C2
Elton Ches ... 49 E6
Elton Derbys ... 50 D3
Elton Dur ... 65 G4
Elton Herefs ... 39 E3
Elton Notts ... 51 H1

Eltringham Nthumb ... 73 E3
Elvanfoot S Lans ... 78 C4
Elvaston Derbys ... 41 E6
Elveden Suffk ... 34 B6
Elvetham Heath Hants ... 20 B1
Elvingston E Loth ... 87 E3
Elvington Kent ... 23 G1
Elvington N York ... 60 B4
Elwick Dur ... 66 B6
Elworth Ches ... 49 G5
Elworthy Somset ... 16 C3
Ely Cambs ... 33 G6
Ely Cardif ... 16 C6
Emberton Bucks ... 32 B4
Embleton Cumb ... 71 E3
Embleton Nthumb ... 81 G2
Embo Highld ... 107 G5
Embo Street Highld ... 107 G5
Emborough Somset ... 17 G4
Embsay N York ... 58 B5
Emery Down Hants ... 9 E4
Emley W York ... 58 D2
Emmington Oxon ... 20 B5
Emneth Cambs ... 43 F3
Emneth Hungate Norfk ... 43 G3
Empingham Rutlnd ... 42 B3
Empshott Hants ... 10 B5
Emsworth Hants ... 10 B3
Enborne Berks ... 19 F3
Enborne Row Hants ... 19 F3
Enderby Leics ... 41 F3
Endmoor Cumb ... 63 E4
Endon Staffs ... 50 A2
Endon Bank Staffs ... 50 A2
Enfield Gt Lon ... 21 F5
Enfield Lock Gt Lon ... 21 F5
Enfield Wash Gt Lon ... 21 F5
Enford Wilts ... 18 D2
Engine Common Gloucs ... 29 E1
Englefield Berks ... 19 H4
Englefield Green Surrey ... 20 C3
English Bicknor Gloucs ... 28 D4
English Frankton Shrops ... 49 E2
Englishcombe Somset ... 17 H5
Enham-Alamein Hants ... 19 F2
Enmore Somset ... 16 D3
Enmore Green Dorset ... 8 B5
Ennerdale Bridge Cumb ... 70 D1
Enochdhu P & K ... 92 C5
Ensay Ag & B ... 88 D4
Ensbury Dorset ... 8 C3
Ensdon Shrops ... 48 D1
Ensis Devon ... 15 E4
Enstone Oxon ... 31 E3
Enterkinfoot D & G ... 78 C3
Enville Staffs ... 39 G4
Eolaigearraidh W Isls ... 111 a2
Epney Gloucs ... 29 E4
Epperstone Notts ... 51 G2
Epping Essex ... 21 G5
Epping Green Essex ... 21 G5
Epping Upland Essex ... 21 G5
Eppleby N York ... 65 F4
Epsom Surrey ... 21 E2
Epwell Oxon ... 31 E4
Epworth Lincs ... 52 A5
Erbistock Wrexhm ... 48 D3
Erdington W Mids ... 40 C3
Eridge Green E Susx ... 12 A5
Erines Ag & B ... 83 G3
Eriska Ag & B ... 90 B3
Eriswell Suffk ... 34 B6
Erith Gt Lon ... 21 G3
Erlestoke Wilts ... 18 C2
Ermington Devon ... 5 F2
Erpingham Norfk ... 45 E5
Errogie Highld ... 98 D4
Errol P & K ... 93 E2
Erskine Rens ... 84 D3
Ervie D & G ... 68 B4
Erwarton Suffk ... 35 E2
Erwood Powys ... 38 B1
Eryholme N York ... 65 G4
Eryrys Denbgs ... 48 C5
Escomb Dur ... 65 F6
Escrick N York ... 59 G4
Esgairgeiliog Powys ... 47 G2
Esh Dur ... 73 F1
Esh Winning Dur ... 73 F1
Esher Surrey ... 21 E2
Eshott Nthumb ... 73 F6
Eskadale Highld ... 98 C6
Eskbank Mdloth ... 86 D3
Eskdale Green Cumb ... 62 B5
Eskdalemuir D & G ... 79 F3
Esprick Lancs ... 56 D6
Essendine Rutlnd ... 42 C3
Essendon Herts ... 21 F6
Essich Highld ... 99 E6
Essington Staffs ... 40 B4
Esslemont Abers ... 103 E3
Eston N York ... 66 B5
Etal Nthumb ... 81 E4
Etchilhampton Wilts ... 18 C3
Etchingham E Susx ... 12 C4
Etchinghill Kent ... 13 F5
Etchinghill Staffs ... 40 B5
Eton Berks ... 20 C3
Eton Wick Berks ... 20 C3
Etruria Staffs ... 49 H4
Etteridge Highld ... 99 E2
Ettersgill Dur ... 64 C6
Ettiley Heath Ches ... 49 G5
Ettingshall W Mids ... 40 A3
Ettington Warwks ... 30 D5
Etton Cambs ... 42 D3
Etton E R Yk ... 60 D4
Ettrick Border ... 79 F4
Ettrickbridge Border ... 79 G5
Ettrickhill Border ... 79 F4
Etwall Derbys ... 40 D6
Euston Suffk ... 34 C6
Euxton Lancs ... 57 E4
Evanton Highld ... 107 E3
Evedon Lincs ... 42 C6
Evelix Highld ... 107 F5
Evenjobb Powys ... 38 C2
Evenley Oxon ... 31 G3
Evenlode Gloucs ... 30 D3
Evenwood Dur ... 65 F5
Everingham E R Yk ... 60 B4
Everleigh Wilts ... 18 D2
Eversholt Beds ... 32 C2
Evershot Dorset ... 7 G6

Eversley Hants ... 20 B2
Eversley Cross Hants ... 20 B2
Everthorpe E R Yk ... 60 C3
Everton Beds ... 32 D4
Everton Hants ... 9 E3
Everton Notts ... 51 G5
Evertown D & G ... 71 F6
Evesbatch Herefs ... 39 F1
Evesham Worcs ... 30 B4
Evington Leics ... 41 G4
Ewden Village S York ... 50 D6
Ewell Surrey ... 21 E2
Ewell Minnis Kent ... 13 G6
Ewelme Oxon ... 19 H5
Ewen Gloucs ... 18 C6
Ewenny V Glam ... 27 E1
Ewerby Lincs ... 42 D6
Ewesley Nthumb ... 73 E5
Ewhurst Surrey ... 10 D5
Ewhurst Green E Susx ... 12 C4
Ewhurst Green Surrey ... 10 D5
Ewloe Flints ... 48 C5
Eworthy Devon ... 5 E6
Ewshot Hants ... 20 B1
Ewyas Harold Herefs ... 28 B5
Exbourne Devon ... 15 E2
Exbury Hants ... 9 F3
Exebridge Somset ... 16 B2
Exelby N York ... 65 G2
Exeter Devon ... 6 B5
Exeter Airport Devon ... 6 B5
Exford Somset ... 15 G4
Exfordsgreen Shrops ... 39 E6
Exhall Warwks ... 30 C5
Exhall Warwks ... 41 E2
Exlade Street Oxon ... 19 H5
Exminster Devon ... 6 B4
Exmouth Devon ... 6 B4
Exning Suffk ... 33 G5
Exted Kent ... 13 F6
Exton Devon ... 6 B4
Exton Hants ... 9 H5
Exton Rutlnd ... 42 B3
Exton Somset ... 16 B2
Exwick Devon ... 6 A5
Eyam Derbys ... 50 D4
Eydon Nhants ... 31 F5
Eye Cambs ... 42 D2
Eye Herefs ... 39 E3
Eye Suffk ... 35 E5
Eyemouth Border ... 81 E6
Eyeworth Beds ... 33 E3
Eyhorne Street Kent ... 22 D1
Eyke Suffk ... 35 F4
Eynesbury Cambs ... 32 D4
Eynsford Kent ... 22 A2
Eynsham Oxon ... 31 E1
Eype Dorset ... 7 F4
Eyre Highld ... 104 C2
Eythorne Kent ... 23 G1
Eyton Herefs ... 39 E2
Eyton Shrops ... 48 D2
Eyton Shrops ... 38 D4
Eyton on Severn Shrops ... 39 F6
Eyton upon the Weald Moors
　Shrops ... 49 F1

F

Faccombe Hants ... 19 F3
Faceby N York ... 66 B3
Fachwen Powys ... 48 A1
Faddiley Ches ... 49 F4
Fadmoor N York ... 66 C2
Faerdre Swans ... 26 C3
Faifley W Duns ... 84 D3
Failand Somset ... 17 F6
Failford S Ayrs ... 76 D4
Failsworth Gt Man ... 50 A6
Fair Oak Hants ... 9 G5
Fair Oak Green Hants ... 19 H3
Fairbourne Gwynd ... 47 E3
Fairburn N York ... 59 F3
Fairfield Derbys ... 50 C4
Fairfield Worcs ... 40 B1
Fairford Gloucs ... 18 D6
Fairgirth D & G ... 70 C5
Fairhaven Lancs ... 56 D5
Fairlie N Ayrs ... 84 B1
Fairlight E Susx ... 12 D3
Fairmile Devon ... 6 C5
Fairmile Surrey ... 20 D2
Fairnilee Border ... 79 G5
Fairoak Shrops ... 49 G3
Fairseat Kent ... 22 B2
Fairstead Essex ... 34 B1
Fairwarp E Susx ... 11 G4
Fairwater Cardif ... 27 G1
Fairy Cross Devon ... 14 D3
Fakenham Norfk ... 44 C5
Fakenham Magna Suffk ... 34 C6
Fala Mdloth ... 87 E2
Fala Dam Mdloth ... 87 E2
Faldingworth Lincs ... 52 C4
Faldouet Jersey ... 7 c1
Falfield Gloucs ... 29 E2
Falkenham Suffk ... 35 F3
Falkirk Falk ... 85 G3
Falkland Fife ... 86 C6
Fallin Stirlg ... 85 G4
Falloden Nthumb ... 81 G2
Fallowfield Gt Man ... 57 H2
Fallowfield Nthumb ... 72 D3
Falls of Blarghour Ag & B ... 83 H6
Falmer E Susx ... 11 F3
Falmouth Cnwll ... 3 E3
Falnash Border ... 79 G3
Falsgrave N York ... 67 F2
Falstone Nthumb ... 72 B5
Fanagmore Highld ... 108 B4
Fancott Beds ... 32 C2
Fanellan Highld ... 98 D6
Fangdale Beck N York ... 66 B3
Fangfoss E R Yk ... 60 B5
Fanmore Ag & B ... 89 E3
Fannich Lodge Highld ... 106 B3
Fans Border ... 80 C4
Far Bletchley Bucks ... 32 B2

Far Cotton Nhants ... 31 H5
Far End Cumb ... 62 C5
Far Green Gloucs ... 29 E3
Far Moor Gt Man ... 57 E3
Far Oakridge Gloucs ... 29 G3
Far Sawrey Cumb ... 62 D5
Far Thorpe Lincs ... 53 E3
Farcet Cambs ... 42 D2
Fareham Hants ... 9 G4
Farewell Staffs ... 40 C4
Farforth Lincs ... 53 E3
Faringdon Oxon ... 19 E6
Farington Lancs ... 57 E5
Farkhill P & K ... 92 C3
Farlam Cumb ... 71 H5
Farleigh Somset ... 17 F5
Farleigh Surrey ... 21 F2
Farleigh Hungerford Somset ... 18 A3
Farleigh Wallop Hants ... 19 H2
Farlesthorpe Lincs ... 53 F3
Farleton Cumb ... 63 E4
Farleton Lancs ... 63 F3
Farley Staffs ... 50 C1
Farley Wilts ... 9 E6
Farley Green Suffk ... 34 B4
Farley Green Surrey ... 10 D6
Farley Hill Berks ... 20 B2
Farleys End Gloucs ... 29 E4
Farlington Hants ... 10 A3
Farlington N York ... 59 G6
Farlow Shrops ... 39 F4
Farmborough Somset ... 17 G5
Farmcote Gloucs ... 30 B3
Farmers Carmth ... 37 E2
Farmington Gloucs ... 30 C2
Farmoor Oxon ... 31 F1
Farmtown Moray ... 101 G4
Farnah Green Derbys ... 19 F5
Farnborough Gt Lon ... 21 G2
Farnborough Hants ... 20 C1
Farnborough Warwks ... 31 E5
Farnborough Park Hants ... 20 C1
Farnborough Street Hants ... 20 C1
Farncombe Surrey ... 10 C6
Farndish Beds ... 32 B5
Farndon Ches ... 48 D4
Farndon Notts ... 51 H2
Farnell Angus ... 93 H4
Farnham Dorset ... 8 C5
Farnham Essex ... 33 F1
Farnham N York ... 59 E5
Farnham Suffk ... 35 F4
Farnham Surrey ... 10 B6
Farnham Common Bucks ... 20 C4
Farnham Royal Bucks ... 20 C4
Farningham Kent ... 22 A2
Farnley N York ... 58 D4
Farnley N York ... 58 D3
Farnley Tyas W York ... 58 C2
Farnsfield Notts ... 51 G2
Farnworth Ches ... 57 E2
Farnworth Gt Man ... 57 G3
Farr Highld ... 109 F5
Farr Highld ... 99 E5
Farr Highld ... 99 F3
Farraline Highld ... 98 D4
Farringdon Devon ... 6 B4
Farrington Gurney Somset ... 17 G4
Farthinghoe Nhants ... 31 F4
Farthingstone Nhants ... 31 G5
Fartown W York ... 58 C2
Fartown W York ... 58 D3
Farway Street Devon ... 6 D5
Fasnacloich Ag & B ... 90 B4
Fasnakyle Highld ... 98 B5
Fassfern Highld ... 90 B6
Fatfield T & W ... 73 G2
Fauldhouse W Loth ... 85 H2
Faulkbourne Essex ... 34 B1
Faulkland Somset ... 17 H4
Fauls Shrops ... 49 F3
Faversham Kent ... 23 E2
Fawdington N York ... 66 A1
Fawdon T & W ... 73 F3
Fawkham Green Kent ... 22 B2
Fawler Oxon ... 31 E2
Fawley Berks ... 19 F4
Fawley Bucks ... 20 B4
Fawley Hants ... 9 F4
Faxfleet E R Yk ... 60 C3
Faygate W Susx ... 11 E5
Fazakerley Mersyd ... 56 D2
Fazeley Staffs ... 40 D3
Fearby N York ... 65 F2
Fearn Highld ... 107 G4
Fearnan P & K ... 91 H3
Fearnbeg Highld ... 105 F2
Fearnmore Highld ... 105 E2
Fearnoch Ag & B ... 83 G3
Featherstone Staffs ... 40 B4
Featherstone W York ... 59 E2
Feckenham Worcs ... 30 B6
Feering Essex ... 34 C1
Feetham N York ... 64 D3
Felbridge Surrey ... 11 F5
Felbrigg Norfk ... 45 E5
Felcourt Surrey ... 11 F6
Felin gwm Isaf Carmth ... 26 B5
Felin gwm Uchaf Carmth ... 26 B5
Felindre Carmth ... 26 B4
Felindre Carmth ... 25 G6
Felindre Powys ... 38 B4
Felindre Swans ... 26 C3
Felindre Farchog Pembks ... 36 A1
Felixkirk N York ... 66 B2
Felixstowe Suffk ... 35 F2
Felling T & W ... 73 F3
Felmersham Beds ... 32 C4
Felmingham Norfk ... 45 E5
Felpham W Susx ... 10 C2
Felsham Suffk ... 34 C4
Felsted Essex ... 34 A1
Feltham Gt Lon ... 20 D3
Felthamhill Gt Lon ... 20 D3
Felthorpe Norfk ... 45 E4
Felton Herefs ... 39 F1
Felton Nthumb ... 73 F6
Felton Somset ... 17 F5
Felton Butler Shrops ... 48 D1
Feltwell Norfk ... 44 A1
Fen Ditton Cambs ... 33 F4
Fen Drayton Cambs ... 33 E5
Fen Street Norfk ... 44 D2

Fence Lancs ... 57 G6
Fence S York ... 51 E5
Fencote N York ... 65 F3
Fencott Oxon ... 31 F2
Fendike Corner Lincs ... 53 F2
Feniscowles Lancs ... 57 F5
Feniton Devon ... 6 C5
Fenn Green Shrops ... 39 G4
Fenn Street Kent ... 22 C3
Fenny Bentley Derbys ... 50 C2
Fenny Bridges Devon ... 6 C5
Fenny Compton Warwks ... 31 E5
Fenny Drayton Leics ... 41 E3
Fenstanton Cambs ... 33 E5
Fenton Cambs ... 33 E6
Fenton Cumb ... 71 H5
Fenton Lincs ... 52 A3
Fenton Lincs ... 52 B1
Fenton Notts ... 52 A4
Fenton Nthumb ... 81 E3
Fenton S Lincs ... 50 A1
Fenton Barns E Loth ... 87 E4
Fenwick E York ... 76 D5
Fenwick Nthumb ... 81 F4
Fenwick Nthumb ... 73 E4
Fenwick S York ... 59 G2
Feock Cnwll ... 3 E3
Feolin Ferry Ag & B ... 82 C3
Feriniquarrie Highld ... 104 A1
Fermain Bay Guern ... 6 c1
Fern Angus ... 94 D2
Ferndale Rhondd ... 27 F2
Ferndown Dorset ... 8 C3
Ferness Moray ... 100 C4
Ferney Green Cumb ... 19 E5
Fernhill Heath Worcs ... 39 H2
Fernhurst W Susx ... 10 C5
Fernie Fife ... 93 E1
Fernie gar S Lans ... 85 F1
Fernilea Highld ... 96 B5
Fernilee Derbys ... 50 B4
Ferrensby N York ... 59 E5
Ferrindonald Highld ... 97 E3
Ferring W Susx ... 10 D2
Ferry Point Highld ... 107 F4
Ferryden Angus ... 95 F2
Ferryhill Dur ... 65 F6
Ferryside Carmth ... 25 G4
Ferrytown Highld ... 107 F4
Fersfield Norfk ... 44 D1
Fersit Highld ... 91 E6
Feshiebridge Highld ... 99 F3
Fetcham Surrey ... 21 E1
Fetterangus Abers ... 103 E4
Fettercairn Abers ... 95 E3
Fewston N York ... 58 D5
Ffair Rhos Cerdgn ... 37 F3
Ffairfach Carmth ... 26 C4
Ffaldybrenin Carmth ... 36 D2
Ffawyddog Powys ... 27 H4
Ffestiniog Gwynd ... 47 F5
Ffestiniog Railway Gwynd ... 47 E5
Fforest Carmth ... 26 B3
Fforest Fach Swans ... 26 C2
Ffostrasol Cerdgn ... 36 C2
Ffrith Flints ... 48 C5
Ffynnongroyw Flints ... 56 B1
Fiag Lodge Highld ... 108 D2
Fickleshole Surrey ... 21 F2
Fiddington Gloucs ... 29 G5
Fiddington Somset ... 16 D3
Fiddleford Dorset ... 8 A4
Fiddlers Green Cnwll ... 3 E4
Field Staffs ... 40 B6
Field Broughton Cumb ... 62 D4
Field Dalling Norfk ... 44 D5
Field Head Leics ... 41 F4
Fife Keith Moray ... 101 F4
Fifehead Magdalen Dorset ... 8 A5
Fifehead Neville Dorset ... 8 A4
Fifehead St Quintin Dorset ... 8 A4
Fifield Berks ... 20 C3
Fifield Oxon ... 30 D2
Figheldean Wilts ... 18 D2
Filby Norfk ... 45 G3
Filey N York ... 67 G2
Filgrave Bucks ... 32 B3
Filkins Oxon ... 30 D1
Filleigh Devon ... 15 F4
Filleigh Devon ... 15 F2
Fillingham Lincs ... 52 B4
Fillongley Warwks ... 40 D2
Filton Gloucs ... 28 D1
Fimber E R Yk ... 60 C5
Finavon Angus ... 93 G5
Fincham Norfk ... 44 A3
Finchampstead Berks ... 20 B2
Fincharn Ag & B ... 83 G5
Finchdean Hants ... 10 A3
Finchingfield Essex ... 34 A2
Finchley Gt Lon ... 21 F4
Findern Derbys ... 40 D6
Findhorn Moray ... 100 D5
Findhorn Bridge Highld ... 99 F5
Findo Gask P & K ... 92 C2
Findochty Moray ... 101 G6
Findon Abers ... 95 H5
Findon W Susx ... 10 D3
Findon Mains Highld ... 107 E2
Findrack House Abers ... 95 E6
Finedon Nhants ... 32 B5
Fingal Street Suffk ... 35 E5
Fingask P & K ... 92 D2
Fingest Bucks ... 20 B4
Finghall N York ... 65 F2
Fingland D & G ... 77 F3
Finglesham Kent ... 23 G1
Fingringhoe Essex ... 34 D1
Finlarig Stirlg ... 91 G2
Finmere Oxon ... 31 G3
Finnart P & K ... 91 F4
Finningham Suffk ... 34 D5
Finningley S York ... 51 G6
Finsbay W Isls ... 111 c4
Finstall Worcs ... 40 B1
Finsthwaite Cumb ... 62 D4
Finstock Oxon ... 31 E2
Finstown Ork ... 111 h2
Fintry Abers ... 102 D5
Fintry Stirlg ... 85 E4
Finzean Abers ... 95 E5
Fionnphort Ag & B ... 88 D2
Fionnsbhagh W Isls ... 111 c4
Fir Tree Dur ... 65 E6
Firbank Cumb ... 63 F5

Firbeck S York ... 51 F5
Firby N York ... 65 F2
Firby N York ... 60 B6
Firsby Lincs ... 53 F2
Firsby Lincs ... 53 F2
Fishbourne IOW ... 9 G3
Fishbourne W Susx ... 10 B3
Fishbourne Roman Palace W Susx ... 10 B3
Fishburn Dur ... 65 G6
Fishcross Clacks ... 85 G5
Fisher's Pond Hants ... 9 G5
Fisherford Abers ... 102 C3
Fisherrow E Loth ... 86 D3
Fisherton Highld ... 107 F1
Fisherton S Ayrs ... 76 C3
Fisherton de la Mere Wilts ... 18 C1
Fishguard Pembks ... 24 D6
Fishlake S York ... 59 G2
Fishnish Pier Ag & B ... 89 G3
Fishponds Bristl ... 17 G6
Fishtoft Lincs ... 43 E6
Fishtoft Drove Lincs ... 43 E6
Fiskavaig Highld ... 96 B5
Fiskerton Lincs ... 52 C3
Fiskerton Notts ... 51 H2
Fittleton Wilts ... 18 D2
Fittleworth W Susx ... 10 D4
Fitz Shrops ... 49 E1
Fitzhead Somset ... 16 C2
Fitzwilliam W York ... 59 E2
Five Ash Down E Susx ... 11 G4
Five Ashes E Susx ... 12 A4
Five Oak Green Kent ... 12 B6
Five Oaks Jersey ... 7 c1
Five Oaks W Susx ... 10 D5
Fivehead Somset ... 17 E2
Fivelanes Cnwll ... 4 C5
Flackwell Heath Bucks ... 20 C4
Fladbury Worcs ... 30 B4
Fladdabister Shet ... 111 I2
Flagg Derbys ... 50 C3
Flamborough E R Yk ... 67 H1
Flamingo Land Theme Park N York ... 66 D2
Flamstead Herts ... 20 D6
Flansham W Susx ... 10 C2
Flanshaw W York ... 58 D2
Flasby N York ... 58 B5
Flasby Staffs ... 50 B3
Flashader Highld ... 104 B2
Flaunden Herts ... 20 b5
Flawborough Notts ... 42 A6
Flawith N York ... 59 F6
Flax Bourton Somset ... 17 F5
Flaxby N York ... 59 E5
Flaxley Gloucs ... 29 E4
Flaxpool Somset ... 16 C3
Flaxton N York ... 59 G6
Fleckney Leics ... 41 G3
Flecknoe Warwks ... 31 F6
Fledborough Notts ... 52 A3
Fleet Dorset ... 7 G4
Fleet Hants ... 20 B1
Fleet Lincs ... 43 F4
Fleet Hargate Lincs ... 43 F4
Fleetwood Lancs ... 56 C5
Flemington S Lans ... 85 F2
Flempton Suffk ... 34 B5
Fletchertown Cumb ... 71 E3
Fletching E Susx ... 11 G4
Flexbury Cnwll ... 14 B2
Flexford Surrey ... 20 C1
Flimby Cumb ... 70 D3
Flimwell E Susx ... 12 C5
Flint Flints ... 48 C6
Flintham Notts ... 51 H2
Flinton E R Yk ... 61 F3
Flitcham Norfk ... 44 B4
Flitton Beds ... 32 C2
Flitwick Beds ... 32 C2
Flixborough Lincs ... 60 C2
Flixborough Stather Lincs ... 60 C2
Flixton Gt Man ... 57 G2
Flixton N York ... 67 F2
Flixton Suffk ... 45 F1
Flockton W York ... 58 D2
Flockton Green W York ... 58 D2
Flodigarry Highld ... 104 C3
Flookburgh Cumb ... 62 D3
Flordon Norfk ... 45 E2
Flore Nhants ... 31 G5
Flowton Suffk ... 34 D3
Flushing Cnwll ... 3 E3
Fluxton Devon ... 6 C5
Flyford Flavell Worcs ... 30 B5
Fobbing Essex ... 22 C4
Fochabers Moray ... 101 F5
Fockerby Lincs ... 60 C2
Foddington Somset ... 17 G2
Foel Powys ... 48 A1
Foggathorpe E R Yk ... 60 B4
Fogo Border ... 80 D5
Fogwatt Moray ... 101 E5
Foindle Highld ... 108 B4
Folda Angus ... 94 B3
Fole Staffs ... 50 B1
Foleshill W Mids ... 41 E2
Folke Dorset ... 17 G1
Folkestone Kent ... 13 G5
Folkingham Lincs ... 42 C5
Folkington E Susx ... 12 B3
Folksworth Cambs ... 42 D1
Folkton N York ... 67 F2
Folla Rule Abers ... 102 C3
Follifoot N York ... 59 E5
Folly Gate Devon ... 15 E1
Fonthill Bishop Wilts ... 8 B6
Fonthill Gifford Wilts ... 8 B6
Fontmell Magna Dorset ... 8 B5
Fontmell Parva Dorset ... 8 B4
Fontwell W Susx ... 10 C3
Foolow Derbys ... 50 C4
Forbestown Abers ... 101 F1
Forcett N York ... 65 F4
Ford Ag & B ... 83 G5
Ford Bucks ... 31 H1
Ford Derbys ... 51 E4
Ford Devon ... 14 D3
Ford Nthumb ... 81 E4
Ford Somset ... 16 C2
Ford Staffs ... 50 C2
Ford W Susx ... 10 C3
Ford Wilts ... 18 B4

Ford End Essex ... 34 A1
Ford Street Somset ... 16 C1
Fordcombe Kent ... 11 H5
Fordell Fife ... 86 B4
Forden Powys ... 38 C6
Forder Green Devon ... 5 H4
Fordham Cambs ... 33 H5
Fordham Essex ... 34 C2
Fordham Norfk ... 43 G2
Fordingbridge Hants ... 8 D4
Fordon E R Yk ... 67 F1
Fordoun Abers ... 95 F4
Fordstreet Essex ... 34 C2
Fordwich Kent ... 23 F2
Fordyce Abers ... 102 B5
Forebridge Staffs ... 40 A5
Forest Guern ... 6 b1
Forest Becks Lancs ... 63 G1
Forest Chapel Ches ... 50 B4
Forest Gate Gt Lon ... 21 G4
Forest Green Surrey ... 10 D6
Forest Hall T & W ... 73 F4
Forest Hill Gt Lon ... 21 F3
Forest Hill Oxon ... 31 G1
Forest Lane Head N York ... 59 E5
Forest Lodge Ag & B ... 90 D3
Forest Mill Clacks ... 85 H5
Forest Row E Susx ... 11 G5
Forestside W Susx ... 10 B3
Forfar Angus ... 93 F4
Forgandenny P & K ... 92 D1
Forge Hammer Torfn ... 28 B2
Forgie Moray ... 101 F5
Forgieside Moray ... 101 F4
Forgue Abers ... 102 B4
Formby Mersyd ... 56 C3
Forncett End Norfk ... 45 E2
Forncett St Mary Norfk ... 45 E2
Forncett St Peter Norfk ... 45 E2
Fornham All Saints Suffk ... 34 B5
Fornham St Martin Suffk ... 34 C5
Forres Moray ... 100 C5
Forsbrook Staffs ... 50 B1
Forse Highld ... 110 C3
Forse House Highld ... 110 C3
Forsinard Highld ... 109 H3
Fort Augustus Highld ... 98 C3
Fort Hommet Guern ... 6 b2
Fort le Marchant Guern ... 6 c2
Fort William Highld ... 90 C6
Forteviot P & K ... 92 C1
Forth S Lans ... 85 H1
Forthampton Gloucs ... 29 F5
Fortingall P & K ... 91 H4
Fortnighty Highld ... 100 C4
Forton Hants ... 19 F1
Forton Lancs ... 63 E1
Forton Shrops ... 48 D1
Forton Somset ... 7 E6
Forton Staffs ... 49 G2
Fortrie Abers ... 102 C4
Fortrose Highld ... 107 F2
Fortuneswell Dorset ... 7 G3
Forty Hill Gt Lon ... 21 F5
Fosbury Wilts ... 19 E3
Foscot Oxon ... 30 D2
Fosdyke Lincs ... 43 E5
Foss P & K ... 92 A5
Fossebridge Gloucs ... 30 C1
Foster Street Essex ... 21 G6
Foston Derbys ... 40 C6
Foston Leics ... 41 G3
Foston Lincs ... 42 B6
Foston N York ... 59 G6
Foston on the Wolds E R Yk ... 61 E5
Fotherby Lincs ... 53 E4
Fotheringhay Nhants ... 42 C2
Foul End Warwks ... 40 D3
Foulden Border ... 81 E5
Foulridge Lancs ... 58 A4
Foulsham Norfk ... 44 D4
Fountainhall Border ... 87 E1
Four Ashes Suffk ... 34 D5
Four Cabots Guern ... 6 b1
Four Crosses Powys ... 48 C2
Four Elms Kent ... 11 G6
Four Forks Somset ... 16 D3
Four Gotes Cambs ... 43 F4
Four Lanes Cnwll ... 2 D3
Four Marks Hants ... 9 H6
Four Mile Bridge IOA ... 54 B4
Four Oaks W Mids ... 40 D2
Four Roads Carmth ... 25 H3
Four Throws Kent ... 12 C5
Fourpenny Highld ... 107 G5
Fourstones Nthumb ... 72 C3
Fovant Wilts ... 8 C6
Foveran Abers ... 103 E2
Fowey Cnwll ... 4 B2
Fowlhall Kent ... 12 C6
Fowlis Angus ... 93 E3
Fowlis Wester P & K ... 92 B2
Fowlmere Cambs ... 33 F3
Fownhope Herefs ... 28 D5
Foxbar Rens ... 84 D2
Foxcote Somset ... 17 H4
Foxdale IOM ... 116 b3
Foxearth Essex ... 34 B3
Foxfield Cumb ... 62 C4
Foxhole Cnwll ... 3 F4
Foxholes N York ... 67 F1
Foxley Norfk ... 44 D4
Foxt Staffs ... 50 B2
Foxton Cambs ... 33 F3
Foxton Leics ... 41 G2
Foxton N York ... 65 H3
Foxwood Shrops ... 39 F4
Foy Herefs ... 28 D5
Foyers Highld ... 98 D4
Foynesfield Highld ... 100 B4
Fraddon Cnwll ... 3 F5
Fradley Staffs ... 40 C4
Fradswell Staffs ... 40 B6
Fraisthorpe E R Yk ... 61 E6
Framfield E Susx ... 11 G4
Framingham Earl Norfk ... 45 F2
Framingham Pigot Norfk ... 45 F2
Framlingham Suffk ... 35 F5
Frampton Dorset ... 7 G5
Frampton Lincs ... 43 E5
Frampton Cotterell Gloucs ... 29 E1
Frampton Mansell Gloucs ... 29 G3
Frampton on Severn Gloucs ... 29 E3

G

Framsden Suffk ... 35 E4
Framwellgate Moor Dur ... 73 F1
Frances Green Lancs ... 57 F6
Franche Worcs ... 39 G4
Frankby Mersyd ... 56 C2
Frankley Worcs ... 40 B2
Frankton Warwks ... 41 E1
Frant E Susx ... 12 B5
Fraserburgh Abers ... 103 E6
Frating Essex ... 34 D1
Frating Green Essex ... 34 D1
Fratton Hants ... 9 H3
Freathy Cnwll ... 5 E2
Freckenham Suffk ... 33 H5
Freckleton Lancs ... 56 D5
Freeby Leics ... 42 A4
Freefolk Hants ... 19 G2
Freeland Oxon ... 31 E2
Freethorpe Norfk ... 45 G3
Freethorpe Common Norfk ... 45 G3
Freiston Lincs ... 43 F6
Fremington Devon ... 15 E4
Fremington N York ... 65 E3
Frenich P & K ... 92 B5
Frensham Surrey ... 10 B6
Freshfield Mersyd ... 56 C3
Freshford Somset ... 18 A3
Freshwater IOW ... 9 E2
Fressingfield Suffk ... 35 F6
Freston Suffk ... 35 E3
Freswick Highld ... 110 D5
Fretherne Gloucs ... 29 E4
Frettenham Norfk ... 45 E4
Freuchie Fife ... 86 C6
Freystrop Pembks ... 24 D4
Friday Bridge Cambs ... 43 F3
Friday Street Suffk ... 35 G4
Fridaythorpe E R Yk ... 60 C5
Friern Barnet Gt Lon ... 21 F4
Friesland Bay Ag & B ... 88 C4
Friesthorpe Lincs ... 52 C4
Frieston Lincs ... 42 B6
Frieth Bucks ... 20 B4
Frilford Oxon ... 19 F6
Frilsham Berks ... 19 G4
Frimley Surrey ... 20 C2
Frindsbury Kent ... 22 C2
Fring Norfk ... 44 B5
Fringford Oxon ... 31 G3
Frinsted Kent ... 22 D1
Frinton-on-Sea Essex ... 35 E1
Friockheim Angus ... 93 H4
Frisby on the Wreake Leics ... 41 G5
Friskney Lincs ... 53 F1
Friston E Susx ... 12 A2
Friston Suffk ... 35 G4
Fritchley Derbys ... 51 E2
Fritham Hants ... 9 E4
Frithelstock Devon ... 14 D3
Frithelstock Stone Devon ... 14 D3
Frithville Lincs ... 53 E1
Frittenden Kent ... 12 C6
Frittiscombe Devon ... 5 H2
Fritton Norfk ... 45 G2
Fritton Norfk ... 45 E2
Fritwell Oxon ... 31 F3
Frizinghall W York ... 58 C3
Frizington Cumb ... 70 D1
Frocester Gloucs ... 29 E3
Frodesley Shrops ... 39 E6
Frodsham Ches ... 57 E1
Frog End Cambs ... 33 F3
Frog Pool Worcs ... 39 G3
Frogden Border ... 80 D3
Froggatt Derbys ... 50 D4
Froghall Staffs ... 50 B2
Frogmore Devon ... 5 G2
Frognall Lincs ... 42 D3
Frogwell Cnwll ... 4 D4
Frolesworth Leics ... 41 F3
Frome Somset ... 18 A2
Frome St Quintin Dorset ... 7 G5
Fromes Hill Herefs ... 39 F1
Fron Isaf Wrexhm ... 48 C3
Fron-goch Gwynd ... 47 G5
Froncysyllte Denbgs ... 48 C3
Frosterley Dur ... 72 D1
Froxfield Wilts ... 19 E3
Froxfield Green Hants ... 10 A4
Fryern Hill Hants ... 9 F5
Fryerning Essex ... 22 B5
Fuinary Highld ... 89 F3
Fulbeck Lincs ... 52 B1
Fulbourn Cambs ... 33 G4
Fulbrook Oxon ... 30 D2
Fulflood Hants ... 9 F6
Fulford N York ... 59 G5
Fulford Somset ... 16 D2
Fulford Staffs ... 50 B1
Fulham Gt Lon ... 21 E3
Fulking W Susx ... 11 E3
Full Sutton E R Yk ... 60 B5
Fullarton N Ayrs ... 76 C5
Fuller Street Essex ... 34 B1
Fullerton Hants ... 19 F1
Fulletby Lincs ... 53 E3
Fullready Warwks ... 30 D4
Fullwood E Ayrs ... 76 D6
Fulmer Bucks ... 20 C4
Fulmodeston Norfk ... 44 D5
Fulnetby Lincs ... 52 C3
Fulney Lincs ... 43 E4
Fulstow Lincs ... 53 E5
Fulwell Oxon ... 31 E2
Fulwood Lancs ... 57 E5
Fulwood S York ... 50 D5
Fundenhall Norfk ... 45 E2
Funtington W Susx ... 10 B3
Funtullich P & K ... 92 A2
Furley Devon ... 6 D6
Furnace Ag & B ... 83 H5
Furnace Carmth ... 26 B3
Furness Vale Derbys ... 50 B5
Furneux Pelham Herts ... 33 F2
Furzley Hants ... 9 E5
Fyfield Essex ... 22 B5
Fyfield Hants ... 19 E2
Fyfield Oxon ... 19 F6
Fyfield Wilts ... 18 D3
Fyfield Wilts ... 18 D3
Fylingthorpe N York ... 67 G4
Fyning W Susx ... 10 B4
Fyvie Abers ... 102 D3

Gabroc Hill E Ayrs ... 76 D6
Gaddesby Leics ... 41 G4
Gaddesden Row Herts ... 20 D6
Gadgirth S Ayrs ... 76 D4
Gaer-llwyd Mons ... 28 C2
Gaerwen IOA ... 54 C3
Gailes N Ayrs ... 76 C5
Gailey Staffs ... 40 A4
Gainsborough Lincs ... 52 A4
Gainsford End Essex ... 34 B2
Gairloch Highld ... 105 F3
Gairlochy Highld ... 98 A1
Gairneybridge P & K ... 86 B5
Gaisby W York ... 58 C4
Gaitsgill Cumb ... 71 G4
Galashiels Border ... 80 B3
Galgate Lancs ... 63 E2
Galhampton Somset ... 17 G2
Gallanach Ag & B ... 90 A2
Gallatown Fife ... 86 D5
Galleywood Essex ... 22 C5
Gallovie Highld ... 98 D2
Gallowfauld Angus ... 93 F3
Gallowhill P & K ... 92 D3
Galltair Highld ... 97 F4
Galmpton Devon ... 5 G1
Galmpton Devon ... 6 A2
Galphay N York ... 65 F1
Galston E Ayrs ... 76 D5
Galton Dorset ... 8 A2
Gamblesby Cumb ... 72 A1
Gamlingay Cambs ... 33 E4
Gamlingay Great Heath Beds ... 32 D4
Gamrie Abers ... 102 D5
Gamston Notts ... 51 G4
Gamston Notts ... 51 G1
Ganavan Bay Ag & B ... 90 A2
Ganllwyd Gwynd ... 47 F4
Gannachy Angus ... 95 E3
Ganstead E R Yk ... 61 E3
Ganthorpe N York ... 66 C1
Ganton N York ... 67 F1
Garbity Moray ... 101 F4
Garboldisham Norfk ... 34 D6
Garchory Abers ... 101 F1
Garden Village Derbys ... 50 D6
Gardeners Green Berks ... 20 B2
Garderhouse Shet ... 111 I2
Gare Hill Somset ... 18 A1
Garelochhead Ag & B ... 84 B4
Garford Oxon ... 19 F6
Garforth W York ... 59 F3
Gargrave N York ... 58 A5
Gargunnock Stirlg ... 85 F5
Garlic Street Norfk ... 45 E1
Garlieston D & G ... 69 F2
Garlinge Kent ... 23 G2
Garlinge Green Kent ... 23 F1
Garlogie Abers ... 95 F6
Garmond Abers ... 102 D4
Garmouth Moray ... 101 F5
Garmston Shrops ... 39 F6
Garn-Dolbenmaen Gwynd ... 46 D5
Garnkirk N Lans ... 85 F3
Garrabost W Isls ... 111 e6
Garrallan E Ayrs ... 77 E3
Garras Cnwll ... 2 D4
Garreg Gwynd ... 47 E5
Garrigill Cumb ... 72 B1
Garroch D & G ... 69 G5
Garrochtrie D & G ... 68 C2
Garrochty Ag & B ... 84 A1
Garros Highld ... 104 D2
Garsdale Head Cumb ... 64 C3
Garsdon Wilts ... 18 C5
Garshall Green Staffs ... 40 B6
Garsington Oxon ... 19 G6
Garstang Lancs ... 63 E1
Garston Herts ... 20 D5
Garston Mersyd ... 56 D1
Gartachossan Ag & B ... 82 C2
Gartcosh N Lans ... 85 F2
Garth Denbgs ... 48 C3
Garth Powys ... 37 H2
Garth Penrhyncoch Cerdgn ... 37 E5
Garth Row Cumb ... 63 E5
Garthamlock C Glas ... 85 F2
Garthmyl Powys ... 38 C5
Garthorpe Leics ... 42 A4
Garthorpe Lincs ... 60 C2
Gartly Abers ... 102 B3
Gartmore Stirlg ... 85 E5
Gartness N Lans ... 85 G2
Gartness Stirlg ... 84 D4
Gartocharn W Duns ... 84 C4
Garton E R Yk ... 61 F3
Garton-on-the-Wolds E R Yk ... 60 D5
Gartymore Highld ... 110 A1
Garvald E Loth ... 87 F3
Garvan Highld ... 90 B6
Garvard Ag & B ... 82 C4
Garve Highld ... 106 D2
Garvestone Norfk ... 44 D3
Garvock Inver ... 84 C3
Garway Herefs ... 28 C5
Garway Common Herefs ... 28 C5
Garyvard W Isls ... 111 d6
Gasper Wilts ... 8 A6
Gastard Wilts ... 18 B3
Gasthorpe Norfk ... 34 C6
Gaston Green Essex ... 33 G1
Gatcombe IOW ... 9 G2
Gate Burton Lincs ... 52 A3
Gate Helmsley N York ... 59 G5
Gateforth N York ... 59 F3
Gatehead E Ayrs ... 76 D5
Gatehouse Nthumb ... 72 C5
Gatehouse of Fleet D & G ... 69 G3
Gateley Norfk ... 44 C4
Gatenby N York ... 65 G2
Gateshaw Border ... 80 D2
Gateshead T & W ... 73 F3
Gateside Angus ... 93 F4
Gateside E Rens ... 84 D2
Gateside Fife ... 86 C6
Gateside N Ayrs ... 84 C1
Gateslack D & G ... 78 C3

Gatley Gt Man ... 57 H2
Gattonside Border ... 80 B3
Gatwick Airport W Susx ... 11 F6
Gaulby Leics ... 41 G3
Gauldry Fife ... 93 F2
Gauldswell P & K ... 93 E4
Gautby Lincs ... 52 D3
Gavinton Border ... 80 D5
Gawcott Bucks ... 31 G3
Gawsworth Ches ... 50 A4
Gawthrop Cumb ... 63 F4
Gawthwaite Cumb ... 62 C4
Gaydon Warwks ... 31 E5
Gayhurst Bucks ... 32 B3
Gayle N York ... 64 C2
Gayles N York ... 65 E4
Gayton Nhants ... 31 G5
Gayton Norfk ... 44 B4
Gayton Staffs ... 40 B6
Gayton le Marsh Lincs ... 53 F4
Gayton Thorpe Norfk ... 44 B4
Gaywood Norfk ... 43 H4
Gazeley Suffk ... 34 B5
Gearraidh Bhaird W Isls ... 111 d6
Geary Highld ... 104 B2
Gedding Suffk ... 34 C4
Geddinge Kent ... 13 G6
Geddington Nhants ... 42 B1
Gedling Notts ... 51 G1
Gedney Lincs ... 43 F4
Gedney Broadgate Lincs ... 43 F4
Gedney Drove End Lincs ... 43 F5
Gedney Dyke Lincs ... 43 F4
Gedney Hill Lincs ... 43 E3
Geeston Rutlnd ... 42 C3
Geldeston Norfk ... 45 G2
Gelli Rhondd ... 27 F3
Gelligaer Caerph ... 27 G2
Gellilydan Gwynd ... 47 F5
Gellinudd Neath ... 26 D3
Gellyburn P & K ... 92 D3
Gellywen Carmth ... 25 F5
Gelston D & G ... 70 B5
Gelston Lincs ... 42 B6
Gembling E R Yk ... 61 E5
Gentleshaw Staffs ... 40 B4
George Green Bucks ... 20 C3
George Nympton Devon ... 15 F3
Georgefield D & G ... 79 F2
Georgeham Devon ... 14 D5
Georth Ork ... 111 h2
Germansweek Devon ... 5 E6
Gerrans Cnwll ... 3 E3
Gerrards Cross Bucks ... 20 D4
Gerrick N York ... 66 D4
Gestingthorpe Essex ... 34 B3
Geuffordd Powys ... 48 C1
Gidea Park Gt Lon ... 21 H4
Giffnock E Rens ... 85 E2
Gifford E Loth ... 87 E3
Giffordtown Fife ... 93 E1
Giggleswick N York ... 63 G2
Gilberdyke E R Yk ... 60 C3
Gilchriston E Loth ... 87 E3
Gilcrux Cumb ... 70 D3
Gildersome W York ... 58 D3
Gildingwells S York ... 51 F5
Gilesgate Moor Dur ... 73 G1
Gileston V Glam ... 16 B5
Gilfach Caerph ... 27 G3
Gilfach Goch Brdgnd ... 27 E2
Gilfachrheda Cerdgn ... 36 D3
Gilgarran Cumb ... 70 D2
Gillamoor N York ... 66 C2
Gillesbie D & G ... 79 E2
Gilling East N York ... 66 C1
Gilling West N York ... 65 F4
Gillingham Dorset ... 8 A5
Gillingham Kent ... 22 C2
Gillingham Norfk ... 45 G2
Gillock Highld ... 110 C5
Gills Highld ... 110 D6
Gilmanscleuch Border ... 79 F4
Gilmerton C Edin ... 86 C3
Gilmerton P & K ... 92 B2
Gilmonby Dur ... 64 D4
Gilmorton Leics ... 41 F2
Gilsland Nthumb ... 72 A3
Gilson Warwks ... 40 D2
Gilstead W York ... 58 C3
Gilston Mdloth ... 87 E2
Gilwern Mons ... 27 H4
Gimingham Norfk ... 45 F5
Gipsey Bridge Lincs ... 53 E1
Girdle Toll N Ayrs ... 76 C5
Girlsta Shet ... 111 I2
Girsby N York ... 65 G4
Girthon D & G ... 69 G3
Girton Cambs ... 33 F5
Girton Notts ... 52 A2
Girvan S Ayrs ... 76 B2
Gisburn Lancs ... 63 G1
Gisleham Suffk ... 45 H1
Gislingham Suffk ... 34 D5
Gissing Norfk ... 45 E1
Gittisham Devon ... 6 C5
Gladestry Powys ... 38 C2
Gladsmuir E Loth ... 87 E3
Glais Swans ... 26 C3
Glaisdale N York ... 66 D4
Glamis Angus ... 93 F4
Glan-y-don Flints ... 56 B1
Glanaman Carmth ... 26 C4
Glandford Norfk ... 44 D6
Glandwr Pembks ... 25 F5
Glandy Cross Carmth ... 25 F5
Glandyfi Cerdgn ... 47 F1
Glanllynfi Brdgnd ... 27 E2
Glanrhyd Pembks ... 25 E5
Glanton Nthumb ... 81 F2
Glanvilles Wootton Dorset ... 7 G6
Glapthorn Nhants ... 42 C1
Glapwell Derbys ... 51 F3
Glasbury Powys ... 27 G6
Glascoed Powys ... 38 B2
Glascote Staffs ... 40 D4
Glascwm Powys ... 38 B2
Glasfryn Conwy ... 55 G2
Glasgow C Glas ... 85 E2
Glasgow Airport C Glas ... 84 D2
Glasgow Science Centre C Glas ... 85 E2
Glasinfryn Gwynd ... 54 D3
Glasnacardoch Bay Highld ... 97 G2
Glasnakille Highld ... 96 D3
Glasserton D & G ... 69 E2
Glassford S Lans ... 77 F6
Glasshouse Gloucs ... 29 E4
Glasshouses N York ... 58 C6

Glasson Cumb ... 71 F5
Glasson Lancs ... 63 E2
Glassonby Cumb ... 72 A1
Glasterlaw Angus ... 93 H4
Glaston Rutlnd ... 42 B2
Glastonbury Somset ... 17 F3
Glatton Cambs ... 42 D1
Glazebrook Ches ... 57 F2
Glazebury Ches ... 57 F2
Glazeley Shrops ... 39 G4
Gleaston Cumb ... 62 C3
Glebe Highld ... 98 D4
Gledhow W York ... 58 D4
Gledpark D & G ... 69 G3
Gledrid Shrops ... 48 C5
Glemsford Suffk ... 34 B3
Glen Auldyn IOM ... 116 c4
Glen Clunie Lodge Abers ... 94 B4
Glen Maye IOM ... 116 b3
Glen Nevis House Highld ... 90 C6
Glen Parva Leics ... 41 F3
Glen Trool Lodge D & G ... 69 E5
Glenallachie Highld ... 101 E3
Glenancross Highld ... 97 E3
Glenaros House Ag & B ... 89 F3
Glenbarr Ag & B ... 75 E4
Glenbarry Abers ... 102 B5
Glenbeg Highld ... 89 F5
Glenbeg Highld ... 100 C2
Glenbervie Abers ... 95 F4
Glenboig N Lans ... 85 F3
Glenborrodale Highld ... 89 F5
Glenbranter Ag & B ... 84 A5
Glenbreck Border ... 78 D4
Glenbrittle House Highld ... 96 C4
Glenbuck E Ayrs ... 77 F4
Glencally Angus ... 94 C3
Glencaple D & G ... 70 D6
Glencarron Lodge Highld ... 105 H1
Glencarse P & K ... 92 D2
Glenceitlein Highld ... 90 C4
Glencoe Highld ... 90 C4
Glencothe Border ... 78 D5
Glencraig Fife ... 86 C5
Glencrosh D & G ... 78 B2
Glendale Highld ... 104 A1
Glendaruel Ag & B ... 83 H4
Glendevon P & K ... 86 A6
Glendoe Lodge Highld ... 98 C3
Glendoick P & K ... 93 E2
Glenduckie Fife ... 93 E1
Gleneagles P & K ... 85 H6
Gleneagles Hotel P & K ... 85 H6
Glenegedale Ag & B ... 74 B5
Glenelg Highld ... 97 F4
Glenernie Moray ... 100 C4
Glenfarg P & K ... 92 D1
Glenfeshie Lodge Highld ... 99 F2
Glenfield Leics ... 41 F4
Glenfinnan Highld ... 97 F1
Glenfintaig Lodge Highld ... 98 B2
Glenfoot P & K ... 92 D1
Glenfyne Lodge Ag & B ... 90 D1
Glengarnock N Ayrs ... 84 C1
Glengolly Highld ... 110 B5
Glengorm Castle Ag & B ... 89 E4
Glengrasco Highld ... 96 C6
Glenholm Border ... 78 D5
Glenhoul D & G ... 69 G6
Glenisla Angus ... 94 B2
Glenkin Ag & B ... 84 B3
Glenkindie Abers ... 101 G1
Glenlivet Moray ... 101 E2
Glenlochar D & G ... 70 B5
Glenlomond P & K ... 86 C6
Glenluce D & G ... 68 D3
Glenmassen Ag & B ... 84 A4
Glenmavis N Lans ... 85 F2
Glenmore Highld ... 96 C6
Glenmore Lodge Highld ... 99 G3
Glenquiech Angus ... 94 D2
Glenralloch Ag & B ... 83 F3
Glenridding Cumb ... 71 G1
Glenrothes Fife ... 86 C5
Glenshee P & K ... 92 C3
Glenshera Lodge Highld ... 98 D2
Glenstriven Ag & B ... 84 A3
Glentham Lincs ... 52 C4
Glentromie Lodge Highld ... 99 F2
Glentrool Village D & G ... 69 E5
Glentruim House Highld ... 99 E2
Glentworth Lincs ... 52 B4
Glenuig Highld ... 89 G6
Glenure Ag & B ... 90 C4
Glenvarragill Highld ... 96 C6
Glenwhilly D & G ... 68 C4
Glespin S Lans ... 78 B5
Glewstone Herefs ... 28 D5
Glinton Cambs ... 42 D3
Glooston Leics ... 41 H3
Glossop Derbys ... 50 B5
Gloster Hill Nthumb ... 81 H1
Gloucester Gloucs ... 29 F4
Gloucestershire Airport Gloucs ... 29 F4
Glusburn N York ... 58 B4
Glutt Lodge Highld ... 110 A3
Gluvian Cnwll ... 3 E5
Glympton Oxon ... 31 E2
Glyn Ceiriog Wrexhm ... 48 C3
Glyn-Neath Neath ... 27 E3
Glynarthen Cerdgn ... 36 C2
Glyncorrwg Neath ... 27 E3
Glynde E Susx ... 11 G3
Glyndyfrdwy Denbgs ... 48 B3
Glyntawe Powys ... 26 D4
Glyntea Carmth ... 25 G6
Gnosall Staffs ... 49 G2
Gnosall Heath Staffs ... 49 G2
Goadby Leics ... 41 H3
Goadby Marwood Leics ... 41 H5
Goatacre Wilts ... 18 C4
Goatfield Ag & B ... 83 H5
Goathill Dorset ... 17 G1
Goathland N York ... 67 E3
Goathurst Somset ... 16 D3
Gobowen Shrops ... 48 C3
Godalming Surrey ... 10 C6
Goddard's Green Kent ... 12 D5
Godmanchester Cambs ... 33 E5
Godmanstone Dorset ... 7 G5
Godmersham Kent ... 23 E1
Godney Somset ... 17 F3
Godolphin Cross Cnwll ... 2 C4
Godre'r-graig Neath ... 26 D3

Godshill IOW ... 9 G2
Godstone Surrey ... 21 F1
Goetre Mons ... 28 B3
Goff's Oak Herts ... 21 F5
Gofilon Mons ... 28 A4
Gogar C Edin ... 86 C3
Goginan Cerdgn ... 37 F5
Golan Gwynd ... 46 D5
Golant Cnwll ... 4 B3
Golberdon Cnwll ... 4 D4
Golborne Gt Man ... 57 F3
Golcar W York ... 58 C2
Goldcliff Newpt ... 28 B1
Golden Green Kent ... 12 B6
Golden Pot Hants ... 10 A6
Golders Green Gt Lon ... 21 E4
Goldhanger Essex ... 22 D6
Goldington Beds ... 32 C4
Goldsborough N York ... 67 E4
Goldsborough N York ... 59 E5
Goldsithney Cnwll ... 2 C2
Goldsworth Park Surrey ... 20 C2
Goldthorpe S York ... 59 F1
Goldworthy Devon ... 14 D3
Gollanfield Highld ... 107 G2
Golspie Highld ... 107 G5
Gomeldon Wilts ... 8 D6
Gomshall Surrey ... 10 D6
Gonalston Notts ... 51 G2
Gonfirth Shet ... 111 I3
Good Easter Essex ... 22 B6
Gooderstone Norfk ... 44 B2
Goodleigh Devon ... 15 E4
Goodmanham E R Yk ... 60 C4
Goodmayes Gt Lon ... 21 G4
Goodnestone Kent ... 23 E2
Goodnestone Kent ... 23 G1
Goodrich Herefs ... 28 D4
Goodrich Castle Herefs ... 28 D4
Goodrington Devon ... 6 A2
Goodshaw Fold Lancs ... 57 G5
Goodwick Pembks ... 24 D6
Goodworth Clatford Hants ... 19 F1
Goole E R Yk ... 60 B2
Goom's Hill Worcs ... 30 B5
Goonbell Cnwll ... 2 D4
Goonhavern Cnwll ... 2 D4
Goonvrea Cnwll ... 2 D4
Goose Green Essex ... 35 E2
Goose Green Essex ... 35 E2
Goose Green Gloucs ... 17 G6
Goosecruives Abers ... 95 F4
Gooseford Devon ... 5 G6
Goosey Oxon ... 19 F5
Goosnargh Lancs ... 57 E6
Goostrey Ches ... 49 G6
Gordon Border ... 80 C4
Gordon Arms Hotel Border ... 79 F5
Gordonstown Abers ... 102 B5
Gordonstown Abers ... 102 C3
Gorebridge Mdloth ... 86 D2
Gorefield Cambs ... 43 F3
Gores Wilts ... 18 D3
Gorey Jersey ... 7 c1
Goring Oxon ... 19 G4
Goring-by-Sea W Susx ... 10 D2
Gorleston on Sea Norfk ... 45 H3
Gorrachie Abers ... 102 C5
Gorran Cnwll ... 3 F3
Gorran Haven Cnwll ... 3 F3
Gorse Hill Wilts ... 18 D5
Gorsedd Flints ... 56 B1
Gorseinon Swans ... 26 B3
Gorsgoch Cerdgn ... 36 D2
Gorslas Carmth ... 26 B4
Gorsley Gloucs ... 29 E5
Gorsley Common Gloucs ... 29 E5
Gorstan Highld ... 106 C2
Gorstello Ches ... 48 D5
Gorsty Hill Staffs ... 40 C6
Gorten Ag & B ... 89 G2
Gorthleck Highld ... 98 D4
Gorton Gt Man ... 50 A6
Gosbeck Suffk ... 35 E4
Gosberton Lincs ... 43 E5
Gosfield Essex ... 34 B2
Gosforth Cumb ... 62 B6
Gosforth T & W ... 73 F3
Gospel End Staffs ... 40 A3
Gosport Hants ... 9 H3
Gossington Gloucs ... 29 E3
Gotham Notts ... 41 F6
Gotherington Gloucs ... 29 G5
Gotton Somset ... 16 D2
Goudhurst Kent ... 12 C5
Goulceby Lincs ... 53 E3
Gourdas Abers ... 102 D3
Gourdie Angus ... 93 F3
Gourdon Abers ... 95 G3
Gourock Inver ... 84 B3
Govan C Glas ... 85 E2
Goveton Devon ... 5 G2
Gowdall E R Yk ... 59 G2
Gower Highld ... 106 D2
Gowerton Swans ... 26 B2
Gowkhall Fife ... 86 B4
Gowthorpe E R Yk ... 60 B5
Goxhill E R Yk ... 61 E4
Goxhill Lincs ... 61 E2
Grabhair W Isls ... 111 d5
Graffham W Susx ... 10 C4
Grafham Cambs ... 32 D5
Grafham Surrey ... 10 D6
Grafton N York ... 59 E6
Grafton Oxon ... 19 E6
Grafton Shrops ... 48 D2
Grafton Worcs ... 29 G6
Grafton Flyford Worcs ... 30 B5
Grafton Regis Nhants ... 31 H4
Grafton Underwood Nhants ... 32 B6
Grafty Green Kent ... 12 D6
Graig Conwy ... 55 F3
Graig-fechan Denbgs ... 48 B4
Grain Kent ... 22 D3
Grainsby Lincs ... 53 E5
Grainthorpe Lincs ... 53 F5
Grampound Cnwll ... 3 F4
Grampound Road Cnwll ... 3 E4
Gramsdal W Isls ... 111 b3
Gramsdale W Isls ... 111 b3
Granborough Bucks ... 31 H3
Granby Notts ... 41 H6
Grand Chemins Jersey ... 7 c1
Grand Prix Collection Leics ... 41 E5
Grandborough Warwks ... 31 F6

Grandes Rocques Guern 6 b2
Grandtully P & K 92 B4
Grange Cumb 71 F1
Grange Kent 22 C2
Grange P & K 93 E2
Grange Crossroads Moray 101 G5
Grange Hall Moray 100 D5
Grange Hill Gt Lon 21 G4
Grange Moor W York 58 D2
Grange of Lindores Fife 93 E1
Grange Villa Dur 73 F2
Grange-over-Sands Cumb 62 D4
Grangehall S Lans 78 C6
Grangemill Derbys 50 D3
Grangemouth Falk 85 H4
Grangepans Falk 86 A4
Grangetown Cardif 66 B5
Grangetown T & W 73 G2
Gransmoor E R Yk 61 E5
Granston Pembks 24 C6
Grantchester Cambs 33 F4
Grantham Lincs 42 B5
Granton C Edin 86 C4
Grantown-on-Spey Highld 100 C2
Grantshouse Border 87 G3
Grasby Lincs 52 C5
Grasmere Cumb 62 D6
Grasscroft Gt Man 58 B1
Grassendale Mersyd 56 D2
Grassington N York 58 B6
Grassmoor Derbys 51 E3
Grassthorpe Notts 52 A2
Grateley Hants 19 E1
Graveley Cambs 33 E5
Graveley Herts 32 D2
Graveney Kent 23 E2
Gravesend Kent 22 B3
Gravir W Isls 111 d5
Grayingham Lincs 52 B5
Grayrigg Cumb 63 F5
Grays Essex 22 B3
Grayshott Hants 10 C5
Grayswood Surrey 10 C5
Greasbrough S York 51 E6
Greasby Mersyd 56 C2
Greasley Notts 51 F2
Great Abington Cambs 33 G3
Great Addington Nhants 32 B6
Great Alne Warwks 30 C5
Great Altcar Lancs 56 D3
Great Amwell Herts 21 F6
Great Asby Cumb 64 B4
Great Ayton N York 66 B4
Great Baddow Essex 22 C5
Great Badminton Gloucs 18 A5
Great Bardfield Essex 34 A2
Great Barford Beds 32 D4
Great Barrington Gloucs 30 D2
Great Barrow Ches 49 E6
Great Barton Suffk 34 C5
Great Barugh N York 66 D2
Great Bavington Nthumb 72 D4
Great Bealings Suffk 35 E3
Great Bedwyn Wilts 19 E3
Great Bentley Essex 35 E1
Great Billing Nhants 32 A5
Great Bircham Norfk 44 B5
Great Blakenham Suffk 35 E4
Great Blencow Cumb 71 G3
Great Bolas Shrops 49 F2
Great Bookham Surrey 21 E1
Great Bosullow Cnwll 2 B3
Great Bourton Oxon 31 F4
Great Bowden Leics 41 H2
Great Bradley Suffk 34 A4
Great Braxted Essex 22 D6
Great Bricett Suffk 34 D4
Great Brickhill Bucks 32 B2
Great Bridgeford Staffs 40 A5
Great Brington Nhants 31 G6
Great Bromley Essex 34 D2
Great Broughton Cumb 70 D3
Great Broughton N York 66 B4
Great Budworth Ches 57 F1
Great Burdon Dur 65 G5
Great Burstead Essex 22 B4
Great Busby N York 66 B4
Great Carlton Lincs 53 F4
Great Casterton Rutlnd 42 C3
Great Chalfield Wilts 18 B3
Great Chart Kent 13 E6
Great Chatwell Staffs 49 G1
Great Chesterford Essex 33 G3
Great Cheverell Wilts 18 C2
Great Chishill Cambs 33 F3
Great Clacton Essex 35 E1
Great Clifton Cumb 70 D2
Great Coates Lincs 61 F1
Great Comberton Worcs 29 G6
Great Corby Cumb 71 G4
Great Cornard Suffk 34 C3
Great Cowden E R Yk 61 F4
Great Coxwell Oxon 19 E5
Great Cransley Nhants 32 A6
Great Cressingham Norfk 44 C2
Great Crosthwaite Cumb 71 F2
Great Cubley Derbys 50 C1
Great Dalby Leics 41 H4
Great Doddington Nhants 32 B5
Great Dunham Norfk 44 C3
Great Dunmow Essex 33 H1
Great Durnford Wilts 18 D1
Great Easton Essex 33 G2
Great Easton Leics 42 B2
Great Eccleston Lancs 56 D6
Great Ellingham Norfk 44 D2
Great Elm Somset 17 H4
Great Englebourne Devon 5 H3
Great Everdon Nhants 31 G5
Great Eversden Cambs 33 E4
Great Finborough Suffk 34 D4
Great Fransham Norfk 44 C3
Great Gaddesden Herts 20 D6
Great Gidding Cambs 42 D1
Great Givendale E R Yk 60 C5
Great Glemham Suffk 35 F5
Great Glen Leics 41 G3
Great Gonerby Lincs 42 B5
Great Gransden Cambs 33 E4
Great Green Cambs 33 E3
Great Green Suffk 34 C5
Great Green Suffk 34 C5
Great Habton N York 66 D1
Great Hale Lincs 42 D6

Great Hallingbury Essex 33 G1
Great Harrowden Nhants 32 B5
Great Harwood Lancs 57 G5
Great Haseley Oxon 19 H6
Great Hatfield E R Yk 61 E4
Great Haywood Staffs 40 B5
Great Heck N York 59 G2
Great Henny Essex 34 C3
Great Hinton Wilts 18 B3
Great Hockham Norfk 44 C2
Great Holland Essex 35 E1
Great Horkesley Essex 34 C2
Great Hormead Herts 33 F2
Great Horton W York 58 C3
Great Horwood Bucks 31 H3
Great Houghton Nhants 32 A4
Great Houghton S York 59 E1
Great Hucklow Derbys 50 C4
Great Kelk E R Yk 61 E5
Great Kimble Bucks 20 B5
Great Kingshill Bucks 20 C5
Great Langdale Cumb 62 C6
Great Langton N York 65 G3
Great Leighs Essex 34 B1
Great Limber Lincs 52 D6
Great Linford Bucks 32 B3
Great Livermere Suffk 34 C5
Great Longstone Derbys 50 D4
Great Lumley Dur 73 G2
Great Malvern Worcs 39 G1
Great Maplestead Essex 34 B2
Great Marton Lancs 56 D6
Great Massingham Norfk 44 B4
Great Milton Oxon 31 G1
Great Missenden Bucks 20 C5
Great Mitton Lancs 57 G6
Great Mongeham Kent 23 H1
Great Moulton Norfk 45 E1
Great Musgrave Cumb 64 B4
Great Ness Shrops 48 D2
Great Oak Mons 28 B4
Great Oakley Essex 35 E2
Great Oakley Nhants 42 B1
Great Offley Herts 32 D2
Great Ormside Cumb 64 B5
Great Orton Cumb 71 F4
Great Ouseburn N York 59 E6
Great Oxendon Nhants 41 H2
Great Oxney Green Essex 22 B5
Great Plumpton Lancs 56 D5
Great Plumstead Norfk 45 F3
Great Ponton Lincs 42 B5
Great Preston W York 59 E3
Great Raveley Cambs 33 E6
Great Rissington Gloucs 30 D2
Great Rollright Oxon 31 E3
Great Ryburgh Norfk 44 C4
Great Ryle Nthumb 81 F2
Great Ryton Shrops 39 E6
Great Saling Essex 34 A2
Great Salkeld Cumb 71 H3
Great Sampford Essex 33 H2
Great Saughall Ches 48 D6
Great Shefford Berks 19 F4
Great Shelford Cambs 33 F4
Great Smeaton N York 65 G4
Great Snoring Norfk 44 C5
Great Somerford Wilts 18 C5
Great Soudley Shrops 49 G2
Great Stainton Dur 65 G5
Great Stambridge Essex 22 D4
Great Staughton Cambs 32 D5
Great Steeping Lincs 53 F2
Great Stoke Bristl 28 D1
Great Strickland Cumb 71 H2
Great Stukeley Cambs 32 D6
Great Sturton Lincs 52 D3
Great Swinburne Nthumb 72 D4
Great Tew Oxon 31 E3
Great Tey Essex 34 C2
Great Torrington Devon 15 E3
Great Tosson Nthumb 72 D6
Great Totham Essex 22 D6
Great Totham Essex 22 D6
Great Urswick Cumb 62 C3
Great Wakering Essex 22 D4
Great Waldingfield Suffk 34 C3
Great Walsingham Norfk 44 C5
Great Waltham Essex 22 C6
Great Warley Essex 22 B4
Great Washbourne Gloucs 29 G6
Great Weeke Devon 5 G5
Great Weldon Nhants 42 B1
Great Wenham Suffk 34 D3
Great Whittington Nthumb 72 D4
Great Wigborough Essex 23 E6
Great Wilbraham Cambs 33 G4
Great Wishford Wilts 8 C6
Great Witcombe Gloucs 29 F4
Great Witley Worcs 39 G3
Great Wolford Warwks 30 D3
Great Wratting Essex 34 A3
Great Wymondley Herts 32 D2
Great Wyrley Staffs 40 B4
Great Yarmouth Norfk 45 H3
Great Yeldham Essex 34 B3
Greatford Lincs 42 C3
Greatgate Staffs 50 B1
Greatham Dur 66 B5
Greatham Hants 10 B5
Greatham W Susx 10 D4
Greatstone-on-Sea Kent 13 F4
Greatworth Nhants 31 F4
Green End Herts 33 E1
Green End Herts 33 E2
Green Hammerton N York 59 F5
Green Heath Staffs 40 B4
Green Ore Somset 17 G4
Green Quarter Cumb 63 E6
Green Street Herts 33 F1
Green Street Herts 21 E5
Green Street Green Kent 22 B3
Green Tye Herts 33 F1
Greenburn W Loth 85 H2
Greenfield Ag & B 84 B4
Greenfield Beds 32 C2
Greenfield Flints 56 C1
Greenfield Gt Man 58 B1
Greenfield Highld 98 A3
Greenfield Gt Lon 21 E3
Greengairs N Lans 85 G3
Greengates W York 58 D4
Greenhalgh Lancs 56 D6

Greenham Somset 16 C1
Greenhaugh Nthumb 72 C5
Greenhill D & G 78 D1
Greenhill Falk 85 G3
Greenhill Kent 23 F2
Greenhill S Lans 78 C5
Greenhithe Kent 22 B3
Greenholm E Ayrs 77 E5
Greenhouse Border 80 B2
Greenhow Hill N York 58 C6
Greenland Highld 110 C5
Greenland S York 51 E5
Greenlaw Border 80 C4
Greenlea D & G 70 D6
Greenloaning P & K 85 G6
Greenmount Gt Man 57 G4
Greenock Inver 84 C3
Greenodd Cumb 62 D4
Greens Norton Nhants 31 G5
Greenshields S Lans 86 A1
Greenside T & W 73 E3
Greenside W York 58 C2
Greenstead Essex 34 D2
Greenstead Green Essex 34 B2
Greenway Somset 17 E2
Greenwich Gt Lon 21 F3
Greet Gloucs 30 B3
Greete Shrops 39 F3
Greetham Lincs 53 E3
Greetham Rutlnd 42 B3
Greetland W York 58 C2
Greinton Somset 17 E3
Grenaby IOM 116 b2
Grendon Nhants 32 B4
Grendon Warwks 40 D3
Grendon Underwood Bucks 31 G2
Grenoside S York 51 E5
Greosabhagh W Isls 111 c5
Gresford Wrexhm 48 D4
Gresham Norfk 45 E5
Greshornish House Hotel Highld 104 B2
Gressenhall Norfk 44 C3
Gressenhall Green Norfk 44 C3
Gressingham Lancs 63 E3
Greta Bridge Dur 65 E4
Gretna D & G 71 F5
Gretna Green D & G 71 F6
Gretton Gloucs 30 B3
Gretton Nhants 42 B2
Gretton Shrops 39 E5
Grewelthorpe N York 65 F1
Greyrigg D & G 78 D2
Greys Green Oxon 20 A4
Greysouthen Cumb 70 D2
Greystoke Cumb 71 G3
Greystone Angus 93 G3
Greywell Hants 20 A1
Griff Warwks 41 E2
Griffithstown Torfn 28 B3
Grimeford Village Lancs 57 F4
Grimesthorpe S York 51 E5
Grimethorpe S York 59 E1
Grimley Worcs 39 H2
Grimmet S Ayrs 76 C3
Grimoldby Lincs 53 F4
Grimpo Shrops 48 D2
Grimsargh Lancs 57 F5
Grimsby Lincs 61 F1
Grimscote Nhants 31 G5
Grimscott Cnwll 14 C2
Grimshader W Isls 111 d6
Grimsthorpe Lincs 42 C4
Grimston Leics 41 G5
Grimston Norfk 44 B4
Grimstone Dorset 7 G5
Grimstone End Suffk 34 C5
Grindale E R Yk 67 G1
Grindleford Derbys 50 D4
Grindleton Lancs 63 G1
Grindley Brook Shrops 49 E3
Grindlow Derbys 50 C4
Grindon Staffs 50 C2
Grindon T & W 73 G2
Gringley on the Hill Notts 51 H5
Grinsdale Cumb 71 F5
Grinshill Shrops 49 E2
Grinton N York 65 E3
Griomaisiader W Isls 111 d6
Griomsaigh W Isls 111 b3
Grishipoll Ag & B 88 C4
Griston Norfk 44 C2
Gritley Ork 111 h2
Grittenham Wilts 18 C5
Grittleton Wilts 18 B4
Grizebeck Cumb 62 C4
Grizedale Cumb 62 D5
Groby Leics 41 F4
Groes Conwy 55 H3
Groes-faen Rhondd 27 F1
Groes-Wen Caerph 27 G2
Grogarry W Isls 111 a3
Grogport Ag & B 75 F5
Groigearraidh W Isls 111 a3
Gronant Flints 56 B1
Groombridge E Susx 11 H5
Grosebay W Isls 111 c5
Grosmont Mons 28 C5
Grosmont N York 67 E4
Groton Suffk 34 C3
Grouville Jersey 7 c1
Grove Notts 51 H4
Grove Oxon 19 F5
Grove Park Gt Lon 21 G3
Grovesend Swans 26 B3
Gruinard Highld 105 G5
Gruinart Ag & B 82 B2
Gruline Ag & B 89 F3
Grula Highld 96 B5
Grundisburgh Suffk 35 E4
Gruting Shet 111 k2
Gualachulain Highld 90 C3
Guardbridge Fife 93 F1
Guarlford Worcs 39 G1
Guay P & K 92 C4
Guernsey Airport Guern 6 b1
Guestling Green E Susx 12 D5
Guestling Thorn E Susx 12 D4
Guestwick Norfk 44 D4
Guide Lancs 57 G5
Guide Post Nthumb 73 F5
Guilden Morden Cambs 33 E3
Guilden Sutton Ches 49 E6

Guildford Surrey 20 C1
Guildtown P & K 92 D3
Guilsborough Nhants 41 G1
Guilsfield Powys 48 C1
Guiltreehill S Ayrs 76 C3
Guineaford Devon 15 E4
Guisborough N York 66 C5
Guiseley W York 58 D4
Guist Norfk 44 D4
Guiting Power Gloucs 30 C3
Gullane E Loth 87 E4
Gulval Cnwll 2 B2
Gulworthy Devon 5 E4
Gumfreston Pembks 25 E3
Gumley Leics 41 G2
Gun Hill E Susx 12 B3
Gunby Lincs 42 B4
Gunby Lincs 53 F2
Gundleton Hants 9 H6
Gunn Devon 15 F4
Gunnerside N York 64 D3
Gunnerton Nthumb 72 D4
Gunness Lincs 60 C1
Gunnislake Cnwll 5 E4
Gunnista Shet 111 I2
Gunthorpe Lincs 52 A5
Gunthorpe Norfk 44 D5
Gunthorpe Notts 51 G1
Gunwalloe Cnwll 2 C2
Gurnard IOW 9 G3
Gurnos Powys 26 D3
Gurney Slade Somset 17 G4
Gurnos Powys 26 D3
Gussage All Saints Dorset 8 C4
Gussage St Andrew Dorset 8 C4
Gussage St Michael Dorset 8 C4
Guston Kent 13 G6
Gutcher Shet 111 I4
Guthrie Angus 93 G3
Guyhirn Cambs 43 F3
Guyzance Nthumb 81 G1
Gwaenysgor Flints 56 B1
Gwalchmai IOA 54 C4
Gwaun-Cae-Gurwen Carmth 26 C4
Gweek Cnwll 2 D2
Gwenddwr Powys 38 B1
Gwennap Cnwll 2 D3
Gwernaffield Flints 48 C5
Gwernesney Mons 28 C3
Gwernogle Carmth 26 B5
Gwernymynydd Flints 48 C5
Gwespyr Flints 56 B1
Gwinear Cnwll 2 C3
Gwithian Cnwll 2 C3
Gwyddelwern Denbgs 48 B4
Gwyddgrug Carmth 26 B6
Gwytherin Conwy 55 G3

H

Habberley Shrops 38 D6
Habberley Worcs 39 G4
Habergham Lancs 57 G5
Habertoft Lincs 53 G2
Habrough Lincs 61 E2
Hacconby Lincs 42 C4
Haceby Lincs 42 C5
Hacheston Suffk 35 F4
Hackbridge Gt Lon 21 F2
Hackenthorpe S York 51 F4
Hackford Norfk 44 D2
Hackforth N York 65 F3
Hackland Ork 111 h2
Hackleton Nhants 32 A4
Hacklinge Kent 23 H1
Hackness N York 67 F2
Hackney Gt Lon 21 F4
Hackthorn Lincs 52 C3
Hackthorpe Cumb 71 H2
Hadden Border 80 D3
Haddenham Bucks 20 A6
Haddenham Cambs 33 F6
Haddington E Loth 87 E3
Haddington Lincs 52 B2
Haddiscoe Norfk 45 G2
Haddo Abers 102 D3
Haddon Cambs 42 D2
Hadfield Derbys 50 B6
Hadham Ford Herts 33 F1
Hadleigh Essex 22 C4
Hadleigh Suffk 34 D3
Hadley Worcs 39 H3
Hadley End Staffs 40 C5
Hadley Wood Gt Lon 21 F5
Hadlow Kent 22 B1
Hadlow Down E Susx 11 H4
Hadnall Shrops 49 E2
Hadstock Essex 33 G3
Hadzor Worcs 30 A6
Haggerston Nthumb 81 F4
Haggs Falk 85 G3
Hagley Herefs 28 D6
Hagley Worcs 40 A2
Hagworthingham Lincs 53 E2
Hail Weston Cambs 32 D5
Haile Cumb 62 A6
Hailey Oxon 31 E2
Hailsham E Susx 12 B3
Hainault Gt Lon 21 G4
Hainford Norfk 45 E4
Hainton Lincs 52 D4
Haisthorpe E R Yk 61 E6
Hakin Pembks 24 C3
Halam Notts 51 G2
Halbeath Fife 86 B4
Halberton Devon 16 B1
Halcro Highld 110 C5
Hale Ches 57 E1
Hale Cumb 63 E4
Hale Gt Man 57 G2
Hale Hants 8 D5
Hale Surrey 10 B6
Hale Green E Susx 12 A3
Hale Street Kent 22 B1
Hales Norfk 45 G2
Hales Staffs 49 G3
Hales Place Kent 23 F2
Halesowen W Mids 40 B2
Halesworth Suffk 35 G6
Halewood Mersyd 57 E2

Halford Devon 5 H4
Halford Warwks 30 D4
Halfpenny Green Staffs 39 G5
Halfway House Shrops 48 D1
Halfway Houses Kent 22 D3
Halifax W York 58 C3
Halkirk Highld 110 B5
Halkyn Flints 48 C6
Hall E Rens 84 D1
Hall Dunnerdale Cumb 62 C5
Hall Glen Falk 85 G3
Hall Green W Mids 40 C2
Hall's Green Herts 33 E2
Halland E Susx 11 G4
Hallaton Leics 42 A2
Hallatrow Somset 17 G4
Hallbankgate Cumb 72 A3
Hallen Gloucs 28 D1
Hallgarth Dur 73 G1
Hallin Highld 104 B2
Halling Kent 22 C2
Hallington Lincs 53 E4
Hallington Nthumb 72 D4
Halloughton Notts 51 G2
Hallow Worcs 39 G2
Hallsands Devon 5 H1
Hallyne Border 79 E6
Halmore Gloucs 29 E3
Halnaker W Susx 10 C3
Halsall Lancs 56 D4
Halse Nhants 31 F4
Halse Somset 16 C2
Halsetown Cnwll 2 B3
Halsham E R Yk 61 F3
Halstead Essex 34 B2
Halstead Kent 21 G2
Halstead Leics 41 H4
Halstock Dorset 7 F6
Halsway Somset 16 C3
Haltham Lincs 53 E2
Halton Bucks 20 C6
Halton Lancs 63 E3
Halton Nthumb 72 D3
Halton W York 59 E3
Halton Wrexhm 48 C3
Halton East N York 58 B5
Halton Gill N York 64 C1
Halton Holegate Lincs 53 F2
Halton Lea Gate Nthumb 72 B3
Halton Shields Nthumb 72 D3
Halton West N York 63 H2
Haltwhistle Nthumb 72 B3
Halvergate Norfk 45 G3
Halwell Devon 5 H2
Halwill Devon 14 D1
Halwill Junction Devon 14 D1
Ham Devon 6 D5
Ham Gloucs 29 E3
Ham Gt Lon 21 E3
Ham Kent 23 G1
Ham Somset 16 D2
Ham Wilts 19 E3
Ham Green Worcs 30 B6
Ham Street Somset 17 F3
Hamble-le-Rice Hants 9 G4
Hambleden Bucks 20 B4
Hambledon Hants 9 H5
Hambledon Surrey 10 C5
Hambleton Lancs 56 D6
Hambleton N York 59 F3
Hambridge Somset 17 E2
Hambrook W Susx 10 B3
Hameringham Lincs 53 E2
Hamerton Cambs 32 D6
Hamilton S Lans 85 F1
Hamlet Dorset 7 G6
Hammersmith Gt Lon 21 E3
Hammerwich Staffs 40 C4
Hammoon Dorset 8 A4
Hamnavoe Shet 111 I2
Hamnavoe Shet 111 I3
Hampden Park E Susx 12 B2
Hampden Row Bucks 20 B5
Hampnett Gloucs 30 C2
Hampole S York 59 F1
Hampreston Dorset 8 C3
Hampstead Gt Lon 21 F4
Hampstead Norrey's Berks 19 G4
Hampsthwaite N York 58 D5
Hampton Gt Lon 21 E2
Hampton Kent 23 F2
Hampton Shrops 39 G4
Hampton Worcs 18 D5
Hampton Worcs 30 B4
Hampton Bishop Herefs 28 D6
Hampton Court Palace & Gardens Gt Lon 21 E2
Hampton Heath Ches 49 E4
Hampton in Arden W Mids 40 D2
Hampton Lovett Worcs 30 A6
Hampton Lucy Warwks 30 D5
Hampton Poyle Oxon 31 F2
Hampton Wick Gt Lon 21 E2
Hamptworth Wilts 9 E5
Hamsey E Susx 11 G3
Hamstall Ridware Staffs 40 C5
Hamstead Marshall Berks 19 F3
Hamsterley Dur 73 F2
Hamsterley Dur 65 E6
Hamstreet Kent 13 E5
Hamworthy Dorset 8 C3
Hanbury Staffs 40 C6
Hanbury Worcs 30 B6
Hanchurch Staffs 49 H3
Hand and Pen Devon 6 C5
Handbridge Ches 48 D5
Handcross W Susx 11 F5
Handforth Ches 57 H1
Handley Ches 49 E5
Handley Derbys 51 E3
Handsworth S York 51 E5
Handsworth W Mids 40 B2
Hanging Houghton Nhants 41 H1
Hanging Langford Wilts 18 C1
Hangleton E Susx 11 F3
Hanham Gloucs 17 G6
Hankelow Ches 49 F4
Hankerton Wilts 29 G2
Hanley Staffs 50 A2
Hanley Castle Worcs 29 F6
Hanley Child Worcs 39 F3
Hanley Swan Worcs 39 G1
Hanley William Worcs 39 F3

Hanlith N York 58 A6
Hanmer Wrexhm 49 E3
Hannaford Devon 15 E4
Hannington Hants 19 G2
Hannington Nhants 32 A5
Hannington Wilts 18 D5
Hannington Wick Wilts 18 D6
Hanslope Bucks 32 A3
Hanthorpe Lincs 42 C4
Hanwell Gt Lon 21 E3
Hanwell Oxon 31 E4
Hanwood Shrops 49 E1
Hanworth Gt Lon 20 D3
Hanworth Norfk 45 E5
Happendon S Lans 78 C5
Happisburgh Norfk 45 G5
Happisburgh Common Norfk 45 G5
Hapsford Ches 49 E6
Hapton Lancs 57 G5
Hapton Norfk 45 E2
Harberton Devon 5 H3
Harbertonford Devon 5 H3
Harbledown Kent 23 F2
Harborne W Mids 40 B2
Harborough Magna Warwks 41 F2
Harbottle Nthumb 81 E1
Harbourneford Devon 5 G3
Harbury Warwks 31 E5
Harby Leics 41 H6
Harby Notts 52 B3
Harcombe Devon 6 A4
Harcombe Devon 6 C4
Harcombe Bottom Devon 7 E5
Harden W York 58 C4
Hardgate Abers 95 G6
Hardgate D & G 70 B5
Hardgate W Duns 84 D3
Hardham W Susx 10 D4
Hardingham Norfk 44 D3
Hardingstone Nhants 31 H5
Hardington Somset 17 H4
Hardington Mandeville Somset 7 F6
Hardington Marsh Somset 7 F6
Hardington Moor Somset 7 F6
Hardisworthy Devon 14 C3
Hardley Hants 9 F4
Hardley Street Norfk 45 G2
Hardraw N York 64 C3
Hardstoft Derbys 51 E3
Hardway Hants 9 H3
Hardway Somset 17 H3
Hardwick Bucks 32 A1
Hardwick Cambs 33 F4
Hardwick Nhants 32 B5
Hardwick Norfk 45 E1
Hardwick Oxon 31 E1
Hardwick Oxon 31 F3
Hardwicke Gloucs 29 F4
Hardwicke Gloucs 29 F5
Hardy's Green Essex 34 C1
Hare Croft W York 58 C3
Hare Green Essex 34 D2
Hare Hatch Berks 20 B3
Hare Street Essex 21 G6
Hare Street Herts 33 F2
Hareby Lincs 53 E2
Harefield Gt Lon 20 D4
Harehill Derbys 40 C6
Harehills W York 59 E3
Harelaw Border 80 B2
Harelaw D & G 79 G1
Harescombe Gloucs 29 F4
Haresfield Gloucs 29 F4
Harestock Hants 9 F6
Harewood W York 58 D4
Harewood End Herefs 28 C5
Harford Devon 5 F3
Hargrave Ches 49 E5
Hargrave Nhants 32 C5
Hargrave Green Suffk 34 B4
Harkstead Suffk 35 E2
Harlaston Staffs 40 D4
Harlaxton Lincs 42 B5
Harle Syke Lancs 57 H6
Harlech Gwynd 47 E4
Harlescott Shrops 49 E1
Harlesden Gt Lon 21 E4
Harlesthorpe Derbys 51 F4
Harleston Devon 5 H2
Harleston Norfk 45 F1
Harleston Suffk 34 D4
Harlestone Nhants 31 G6
Harley S York 51 E6
Harley Shrops 39 F6
Harlington Beds 32 C2
Harlington Gt Lon 20 D3
Harlington S York 51 F6
Harlosh Highld 96 B6
Harlow Essex 21 G6
Harlow Hill Nthumb 73 E3
Harlthorpe E R Yk 60 B4
Harlton Cambs 33 F4
Harlyn Bay Cnwll 3 E6
Harman's Cross Dorset 8 C2
Harmby N York 65 E2
Harmer Green Herts 33 E1
Harmer Hill Shrops 49 E2
Harmston Lincs 52 B2
Harnage Shrops 39 E6
Harnhill Gloucs 18 C6
Harold Hill Gt Lon 21 H4
Harold Wood Gt Lon 22 A4
Haroldston West Pembks 24 C4
Haroldswick Shet 111 m4
Harome N York 66 C2
Harpenden Herts 21 E6
Harpford Devon 6 C4
Harpham E R Yk 61 E6
Harpley Norfk 44 B4
Harpley Worcs 39 F2
Harpole Nhants 31 G6
Harpsdale Highld 110 B4
Harpswell Lincs 52 B4
Harpurhey Gt Man 57 H3
Harraby Cumb 71 G4
Harracott Devon 15 E4
Harrapool Highld 97 E4
Harrietfield P & K 92 C2
Harrietsham Kent 22 D1
Harringay Gt Lon 21 F4
Harrington Cumb 70 D2
Harrington Lincs 53 F3
Harrington Nhants 41 H2
Harringworth Nhants 42 B2

Harrogate N York 58 D5
Harrold Beds 32 B4
Harrow Gt Lon 21 E4
Harrow Green Suffk 34 C4
Harrow on the Hill Gt Lon 21 E4
Harrow Weald Gt Lon 21 E4
Harrowbarrow Cnwll 5 E4
Harston Cambs 33 F4
Harston Leics 42 A5
Harswell E R Yk 60 C4
Hart Dur 66 B6
Hartburn Nthumb 73 E5
Hartest Suffk 34 B4
Hartfield E Susx 11 G5
Hartford Cambs 33 E5
Hartford Ches 49 F6
Hartford End Essex 34 A1
Hartfordbridge Hants 20 B2
Harthill N York 65 F4
Harthill Ches 49 E5
Harthill N Lans 85 H2
Harthill S York 51 F4
Hartington Derbys 50 C3
Hartland Devon 14 C3
Hartland Quay Devon 14 B3
Hartlebury Worcs 39 H3
Hartlepool Dur 66 B6
Hartley Cumb 64 C4
Hartley Kent 22 B2
Hartley Kent 12 C5
Hartley Wespall Hants 20 A2
Hartley Wintney Hants 20 B1
Hartlip Kent 22 D2
Harton N York 60 B6
Harton T & W 73 G3
Hartpury Gloucs 29 F5
Hartshead W York 58 C2
Hartshill Staffs 49 H4
Hartshill Warwks 41 E3
Hartshorne Derbys 41 E5
Hartside Nthumb 81 E2
Hartwell Nhants 32 A4
Hartwith N York 58 D6
Hartwood N Lans 85 G2
Hartwoodmyres Border 79 G5
Harvel Kent 22 B2
Harvington Worcs 39 H3
Harvington Worcs 30 B5
Harwell Notts 51 G5
Harwell Oxon 19 G5
Harwich Essex 35 F2
Harwood Dale N York 67 F3
Harworth Notts 51 G5
Hasbury W Mids 40 B2
Hascombe Surrey 10 D5
Haselbech Nhants 41 G1
Haselbury Plucknett Somset 7 F6
Haseley Warwks 30 D6
Haselor Warwks 30 C5
Hasfield Gloucs 29 F5
Haskayne Lancs 56 D3
Hasketon Suffk 35 F4
Haslemere Surrey 10 C5
Haslingden Lancs 57 G5
Haslingfield Cambs 33 F4
Haslington Ches 49 G5
Hassingham Norfk 45 G3
Hassocks W Susx 11 F3
Hassop Derbys 50 D4
Haster Highld 110 D4
Hastingleigh Kent 13 F6
Hastings E Susx 12 D3
Hastingwood Essex 21 G6
Hastoe Herts 20 C6
Haswell Dur 73 G1
Haswell Plough Dur 73 G1
Hatch Beauchamp Somset 17 E1
Hatch End Gt Lon 21 E4
Hatchmere Ches 49 E6
Hatcliffe Lincs 52 D5
Hatfield Herefs 39 F2
Hatfield Herts 21 E6
Hatfield S York 59 G1
Hatfield Broad Oak Essex 33 G1
Hatfield Heath Essex 21 H6
Hatfield Peverel Essex 22 C6
Hatfield Woodhouse S York 59 G1
Hatford Oxon 19 E6
Hatherden Hants 19 E2
Hatherleigh Devon 15 E2
Hathern Leics 41 F5
Hatherop Gloucs 30 C1
Hathersage Derbys 50 D4
Hathersage Booths Derbys 50 D4
Hatherton Ches 49 F4
Hatherton Staffs 40 B4
Hatley St George Cambs 33 E4
Hatt Cnwll 5 E3
Hattersley Gt Man 50 B6
Hatton Abers 103 F3
Hatton Angus 93 G3
Hatton Ches 57 F1
Hatton Derbys 40 D6
Hatton Gt Lon 20 D3
Hatton Lincs 52 D3
Hatton Shrops 39 E5
Hatton Warwks 30 D6
Hatton of Fintray Abers 102 D1
Haugh Ayrs 76 D4
Haugh of Glass Moray 101 F3
Haugh of Urr D & G 70 B5
Haugham Lincs 53 E3
Haughhead Inn E Duns 85 E3
Haughley Suffk 34 D5
Haughley Green Suffk 34 D5
Haughton Shrops 48 D2
Haughton Shrops 39 G6
Haughton Staffs 49 H2
Haughton le Skerne Dur 65 G6
Haughton Moss Ches 49 F5
Haultwick Herts 33 E1
Haunton Staffs 40 D4
Hautes Croix Jersey 7 b2
Hauxley Nthumb 73 F6
Hauxton Cambs 33 F4
Havant Hants 10 A3
Havenstreet IOW 9 G3
Havercroft W York 59 E2
Haverfordwest Pembks 24 D4
Haverhill Suffk 33 H3
Haverigg Cumb 62 B4
Havering-atte-Bower Essex 21 G4
Haversham Bucks 32 A3

Haverthwaite Cumb 62 D4
Havyat Somset 17 F5
Hawarden Flints 48 D5
Hawbush Green Essex 34 B1
Hawe's Green Norfk 45 F2
Hawen Cerdgn 36 C2
Hawes N York 64 C2
Hawford Worcs 39 H2
Hawick Border 80 B2
Hawkchurch Devon 7 E5
Hawkedon Suffk 34 B4
Hawkeridge Wilts 18 B2
Hawkesbury Gloucs 18 A5
Hawkesbury Upton Gloucs 18 A5
Hawkhurst Kent 12 C5
Hawkinge Kent 13 G5
Hawkley Hants 10 B5
Hawkridge Somset 15 G4
Hawkshead Cumb 62 D5
Hawkshead Hill Cumb 62 D5
Hawksland S Lans 78 B6
Hawkspur Green Essex 33 H2
Hawkstone Shrops 49 F2
Hawkswick N York 64 D1
Hawksworth Notts 51 H1
Hawksworth W York 58 C4
Hawkwell Essex 22 D4
Hawley Hants 20 B2
Hawling Gloucs 30 C2
Hawnby N York 66 B2
Haworth W York 58 B4
Hawstead Suffk 34 C4
Hawthorn Dur 73 H1
Hawthorn Hill Lincs 52 D1
Hawton Notts 52 A1
Haxby N York 59 G5
Haxey Lincs 51 H6
Hay Street Herts 33 F2
Hay-on-Wye Powys 27 G6
Haydock Mersyd 57 E2
Haydon Bridge Nthumb 72 C3
Haydon Wick Wilts 18 D5
Hayes Gt Lon 20 D3
Hayes Gt Lon 21 G2
Hayes End Gt Lon 20 D3
Hayfield Ag & B 90 C2
Hayfield Derbys 50 B5
Hayhillock Angus 93 G3
Hayle Cnwll 2 C3
Hayley Green W Mids 40 B2
Hayne Devon 16 B1
Hayne Devon 5 G5
Haynes (Church End) Beds 32 C3
Haynes (Northwood End) Beds 32 C3
Haynes (Silver End) Beds 32 C3
Haynes (West End) Beds 32 C3
Hayscastle Pembks 24 C5
Hayscastle Cross Pembks 24 C5
Hayton Cumb 70 D3
Hayton Cumb 71 H5
Hayton E R Yk 60 C4
Hayton Notts 51 H5
Haytor Vale Devon 5 G4
Haytown Devon 14 D3
Haywards Heath W Susx 11 F4
Haywood S York 59 G2
Hazel Grove Gt Man 50 A5
Hazelbank S Lans 77 G5
Hazelbury Bryan Dorset 7 H6
Hazeleigh Essex 22 D5
Hazelton Walls Fife 93 F2
Hazelwood Derbys 51 E2
Hazlemere Bucks 20 C5
Hazlerigg T & W 73 F4
Hazleton Gloucs 30 C2
Heacham Norfk 44 A5
Headbourne Worthy Hants 9 G6
Headcorn Kent 12 D6
Headingley W York 58 D3
Headington Oxon 31 F1
Headlam Dur 65 F5
Headland Dur 66 B6
Headlesscross N Lans 85 H2
Headley Hants 19 G3
Headley Hants 10 B5
Headley Surrey 21 E1
Headon Notts 51 H4
Heads S Lans 77 F6
Heads Nook Cumb 71 G4
Heage Derbys 51 E2
Healaugh N York 64 D3
Healaugh N York 59 F4
Heald Green Gt Man 57 H2
Heale Somset 16 D1
Heale Somset 17 E2
Healey N York 65 F2
Healeyfield Dur 73 E2
Healing Lincs 61 F1
Heamoor Cnwll 2 B2
Heanor Derbys 51 E2
Heanton Punchardon Devon 15 E4
Heapham Lincs 52 B4
Heasley Mill Devon 15 F4
Heast Highld 96 D4
Heath Derbys 51 E3
Heath W York 59 E2
Heath and Reach Beds 32 B2
Heath End Surrey 10 B6
Heath Green Worcs 40 C1
Heath Hall D & G 78 D1
Heath Hayes & Wimblebury Staffs 40 B4
Heath Hill Shrops 49 G1
Heath Town W Mids 40 A3
Heathcote Derbys 50 C3
Heather Leics 41 E4
Heathfield E Susx 12 B4
Heathfield Somset 16 C2
Heathrow Airport Gt Lon 20 D3
Heathton Shrops 39 G5
Heatley Gt Man 57 G2
Heatley Staffs 40 C5
Heaton Staffs 50 B3
Heaton T & W 73 F3
Heaton W York 58 C3
Heaton's Bridge Lancs 56 D1
Heaverham Kent 22 B2
Heavitree Devon 6 B5
Hebburn T & W 73 G3
Hebden N York 58 B6
Hebden Bridge W York 58 B3
Hebing End Herts 33 E1
Hebron Carmth 25 F5
Hebron Nthumb 73 F5
Heckfield Hants 20 A2

Heckfield Green Suffk 35 E6
Heckfordbridge Essex 34 C1
Heckington Lincs 42 D6
Heckmondwike W York 58 C3
Heddington Wilts 18 C3
Heddon-on-the-Wall Nthumb 73 E3
Hedenham Norfk 45 F2
Hedge End Hants 9 G4
Hedgerley Bucks 20 C4
Hedging Somset 17 E2
Hedley on the Hill Nthumb 73 E3
Hednesford Staffs 40 B4
Hedon E R Yk 61 E3
Hedsor Bucks 20 C4
Heglibister Shet 111 I2
Heighington Dur 65 F5
Heighington Lincs 52 C2
Heightington Worcs 39 G3
Heiton Border 80 C3
Hele Devon 15 E5
Hele Devon 6 B5
Hele Somset 16 D2
Helensburgh Ag & B 84 C4
Helenton S Ayrs 76 D4
Helford Cnwll 2 D2
Helford Passage Cnwll 2 D2
Helhoughton Norfk 44 C4
Helions Bumpstead Essex 33 H3
Helland Cnwll 3 G6
Hellescott Cnwll 4 D5
Hellesdon Norfk 45 E3
Hellidon Nhants 31 F5
Hellifield N York 63 H2
Hellingly E Susx 12 B3
Helm Nthumb 73 F6
Helmdon Nhants 31 G4
Helme W York 58 C2
Helmingham Suffk 35 E4
Helmsdale Highld 110 A1
Helmshore Lancs 57 G4
Helmsley N York 66 C2
Helperby N York 59 E6
Helperthorpe N York 67 E1
Helpringham Lincs 42 D5
Helpston Cambs 42 D3
Helsby Ches 49 E6
Helston Cnwll 2 C2
Helstone Cnwll 4 B5
Helton Cumb 71 H2
Hemblington Norfk 45 F3
Hemel Hempstead Herts 20 D6
Hemerdon Devon 5 F3
Hemingbrough N York 59 G3
Hemingby Lincs 53 E3
Hemingford Abbots Cambs 33 E5
Hemingford Grey Cambs 33 E5
Hemingstone Suffk 35 E4
Hemington Nhants 42 C1
Hemington Somset 17 H4
Hemley Suffk 35 F3
Hemlington N York 66 B4
Hempnall Norfk 45 F2
Hempnall Green Norfk 45 F2
Hempriggs Moray 100 D5
Hempstead Essex 33 H3
Hempstead Norfk 44 D5
Hempstead Norfk 45 G4
Hempton Norfk 44 C5
Hempton Oxon 31 E3
Hemsby Norfk 45 G4
Hemswell Lincs 52 B4
Hemswell Cliff Lincs 52 B4
Hemsworth W York 59 E2
Hemyock Devon 16 C1
Henderside Park Border 80 D3
Hendon Gt Lon 21 E4
Hendon T & W 73 G2
Hendy Carmth 26 B3
Henfield W Susx 11 E4
Hengoed Caerph 27 G2
Hengoed Powys 38 C2
Hengrave Suffk 34 B5
Henham Essex 33 G2
Heniarth Powys 38 B6
Henlade Somset 16 D2
Henley Dorset 7 H6
Henley Somset 17 F2
Henley Suffk 35 E4
Henley W Susx 10 C4
Henley's Down E Susx 12 C3
Henley-in-Arden Warwks 30 C6
Henley-on-Thames Oxon 20 B4
Henllan Cerdgn 36 C1
Henllan Denbgs 55 H3
Henllys Torfn 28 A2
Henlow Beds 32 D3
Hennock Devon 5 H5
Henny Street Essex 34 C3
Henry's Moat (Castell Hendre) Pembks 24 D5
Henryd Conwy 55 F4
Hensall N York 59 G2
Henshaw Nthumb 72 B3
Hensingham Cumb 70 D1
Henstead Suffk 45 G1
Hensting Hants 9 G5
Henstridge Somset 17 H1
Henstridge Ash Somset 17 H1
Henton Oxon 20 B5
Henton Somset 17 F3
Henwick Worcs 39 H2
Henwood Cnwll 4 D4
Heol-y-Cyw Brdgnd 27 E1
Hepple Nthumb 72 D6
Hepscott Nthumb 73 F5
Heptonstall W York 58 B3
Hepworth Suffk 34 D6
Hepworth W York 58 C1
Herbrandston Pembks 24 C3
Hereford Herefs 28 C6
Hereson Kent 23 H2
Heribusta Highld 104 C3
Heriot Border 86 D2
Hermiston C Edin 86 C3
Hermitage Berks 19 G4
Hermitage Border 79 G2
Hermitage Dorset 7 G6
Hermon Pembks 25 F5
Herne Kent 23 F2
Herne Bay Kent 23 F2
Herne Hill Gt Lon 21 F3
Herne Pound Kent 22 B1
Herner Devon 15 E4

Hernhill Kent 23 E2
Herodsfoot Cnwll 4 C3
Heronsford S Ayrs 68 C5
Herriard Hants 19 H2
Herringfleet Suffk 45 G2
Herringswell Suffk 34 B5
Herringthorpe S York 51 E5
Herrington T & W 73 G2
Hersden Kent 23 F2
Hersham Surrey 20 D2
Herstmonceux E Susx 12 B3
Herston Ork 111 h1
Hertford Herts 21 F6
Hertford Heath Herts 21 F6
Hertingfordbury Herts 21 F6
Hesket Newmarket Cumb 71 F3
Hesketh Bank Lancs 57 E5
Hesketh Lane Lancs 57 F6
Hesleden Dur 73 H1
Heslington N York 59 G5
Hessay N York 59 F5
Hessenford Cnwll 4 D3
Hessett Suffk 34 C5
Hessle E R Yk 60 D3
Hessle W York 59 E2
Heston Gt Lon 20 D3
Hestwall Ork 111 g2
Heswall Mersyd 56 C1
Hethe Oxon 31 G3
Hethersett Norfk 45 E3
Hethersgill Cumb 71 G5
Hethpool Nthumb 81 E3
Hett Dur 73 F1
Hetton N York 58 B5
Hetton-le-Hole T & W 73 G2
Heugh Nthumb 73 E4
Heugh Head Border 87 H2
Heughhead Abers 101 F1
Heveningham Suffk 35 F5
Hever Kent 11 G6
Heversham Cumb 63 E4
Hevingham Norfk 45 E4
Hewas Water Cnwll 3 F4
Hewelsfield Gloucs 28 D3
Hewish Somset 7 E6
Hewood Dorset 7 E5
Hexham Nthumb 72 D3
Hextable Kent 21 G3
Hexthorpe S York 51 F6
Hexton Herts 32 C2
Hexworthy Cnwll 4 D5
Hexworthy Devon 5 G4
Heybridge Essex 22 D6
Heybridge Essex 22 B5
Heybrook Bay Devon 5 E2
Heydon Cambs 33 F3
Heydon Norfk 45 E4
Heydour Lincs 42 C5
Heylipoll Ag & B 88 A3
Heylor Shet 111 k3
Heysham Lancs 62 D2
Heyshott W Susx 10 C4
Heytesbury Wilts 18 B1
Heythrop Oxon 31 E3
Heywood Gt Man 57 H4
Heywood Wilts 18 B2
Hibaldstow Lincs 52 B5
Hickleton S York 59 F1
Hickling Norfk 45 G4
Hickling Notts 41 G6
Hickling Green Norfk 45 G4
Hickstead W Susx 11 F4
Hidcote Bartrim Gloucs 30 C4
Hidcote Boyce Gloucs 30 C4
High Ackworth W York 59 E2
High Ardwell D & G 68 C2
High Auldgirth D & G 78 C2
High Bankhill Cumb 71 H3
High Beach Essex 21 G5
High Bentham N York 63 F3
High Bickington Devon 15 E3
High Biggins Cumb 63 F4
High Blantyre S Lans 85 F2
High Bonnybridge Falk 85 G3
High Bray Devon 15 F4
High Brooms Kent 12 B6
High Casterton Cumb 63 F4
High Catton E R Yk 60 B5
High Coniscliffe Dur 65 F4
High Crosby Cumb 71 G5
High Cross E Ayrs 76 D5
High Cross Hants 10 A4
High Cross Herts 33 E1
High Cross Warwks 30 D6
High Drummore D & G 68 C1
High Easter Essex 22 B6
High Ellington N York 65 F2
High Ercall Shrops 49 F1
High Etherley Dur 65 F6
High Garrett Essex 34 B2
High Grantley N York 65 F1
High Green Norfk 45 E3
High Green Norfk 45 E1
High Green S York 51 E6
High Green Worcs 39 H1
High Halden Kent 12 D5
High Halstow Kent 22 C3
High Ham Somset 17 E2
High Harrogate N York 58 D5
High Hatton Shrops 49 F2
High Hawsker N York 67 E4
High Hesket Cumb 71 G4
High Hoyland S York 58 D1
High Hurstwood E Susx 11 G4
High Hutton N York 60 B6
High Ireby Cumb 71 E3
High Kilburn N York 66 B2
High Lands Dur 65 E5
High Lane Gt Man 50 B5
High Lanes Cnwll 2 C3
High Legh Ches 57 F1
High Leven N York 66 B4
High Littleton Somset 17 G4
High Lorton Cumb 71 E2
High Marnham Notts 52 A2
High Melton S York 51 F6
High Mickley Nthumb 73 E3
High Newport T & W 73 G2
High Newton Cumb 62 D4
High Nibthwaite Cumb 62 C5
High Offley Staffs 49 G2
High Ongar Essex 22 B5
High Onn Staffs 49 G1
High Park Corner Essex 34 D1

High Pennyvenie E Ayrs ... 76 D2
High Roding Essex ... 33 G1
High Salvington W Susx ... 10 D3
High Spen T & W ... 73 E3
High Street Cnwll ... 3 F4
High Street Suffk ... 35 G4
High Toynton Lincs ... 53 E2
High Trewhitt Nthumb ... 81 F1
High Urpeth Dur ... 73 F2
High Valleyfield Fife ... 86 A4
High Wray Cumb ... 62 D5
High Wych Herts ... 21 G6
High Wycombe Bucks ... 20 B4
Higham Derbys ... 51 E3
Higham Kent ... 12 B6
Higham Kent ... 22 C3
Higham Lancs ... 57 G6
Higham S York ... 58 D1
Higham Suffk ... 34 B5
Higham Suffk ... 34 D2
Higham Dykes Nthumb ... 73 E4
Higham Ferrers Nhants ... 32 B5
Higham Gobion Beds ... 32 C2
Higham Hill Gt Lon ... 21 F4
Higham on the Hill Leics ... 41 E3
Highampton Devon ... 14 D2
Highams Park Gt Lon ... 21 F4
Highbridge Somset ... 17 E4
Highbrook W Susx ... 11 F5
Highburton W York ... 58 C2
Highbury Gt Lon ... 21 F4
Highbury Somset ... 17 H4
Highclere Hants ... 19 F3
Highcliffe Dorset ... 8 D3
Higher Ansty Dorset ... 8 A4
Higher Bartle Lancs ... 57 E5
Higher Bockhampton Dorset ... 7 H5
Higher Brixham Devon ... 6 B2
Higher Chillington Somset ... 7 E6
Higher Combe Somset ... 16 A2
Higher Gabwell Devon ... 6 B3
Higher Heysham Lancs ... 62 D2
Higher Irlam Gt Man ... 57 G2
Higher Kinnerton Flints ... 48 D5
Higher Muddiford Devon ... 15 E4
Higher Penwortham Lancs ... 57 E5
Higher Town Cnwll ... 3 E4
Higher Town Cnwll ... 3 F5
Higher Town IOS ... 2 b2
Higher Walton Ches ... 57 F2
Higher Walton Lancs ... 57 F5
Higher Wambrook Somset ... 6 D6
Higher Waterston Dorset ... 7 H5
Higher Wheelton Lancs ... 57 F5
Higher Whitley Ches ... 57 F1
Higher Wraxall Dorset ... 7 G5
Higher Wych Ches ... 49 E4
Highfield N Ayrs ... 76 C6
Highfield T & W ... 73 E3
Highgate Gt Lon ... 21 F4
Highland Wildlife Park Highld ... 99 F3
Highlane S York ... 51 E5
Highleadon Gloucs ... 29 E5
Highleigh W Susx ... 10 B2
Highley Shrops ... 39 G4
Highmoor Oxon ... 20 A4
Highmoor Cross Oxon ... 20 A4
Highnam Gloucs ... 29 E4
Highsted Kent ... 22 D2
Highstreet Kent ... 23 F2
Highstreet Green Essex ... 34 B2
Highstreet Green Surrey ... 10 C5
Hightae D & G ... 78 D1
Hightown Mersyd ... 56 C3
Hightown Green Suffk ... 34 C4
Highweek Devon ... 6 A3
Highwood Hill Gt Lon ... 21 E4
Highworth Wilts ... 18 D5
Hilborough Norfk ... 44 B2
Hilden Park Kent ... 12 B6
Hildenborough Kent ... 12 B6
Hildersham Cambs ... 33 G3
Hilderstone Staffs ... 40 B6
Hilderthorpe E R Yk ... 61 E6
Hilfield Dorset ... 7 G6
Hilgay Norfk ... 43 G2
Hill Gloucs ... 28 D2
Hill Warwks ... 31 F6
Hill Brow Hants ... 10 B4
Hill Chorlton Staffs ... 49 G3
Hill Common Somset ... 16 C2
Hill Dyke Lincs ... 43 E6
Hill End Fife ... 86 B5
Hill End Gloucs ... 29 F6
Hill Green Kent ... 22 D2
Hill Head Hants ... 9 G4
Hill of Beath Fife ... 86 B5
Hill of Fearn Highld ... 107 G4
Hill of Tarvit Mansion House Fife ... 93 F1
Hill Ridware Staffs ... 40 C5
Hill Side W York ... 58 C2
Hill Top W York ... 59 E2
Hillam N York ... 59 F3
Hillbutts Dorset ... 8 C3
Hillclifflane Derbys ... 50 D2
Hillcott Wilts ... 18 D3
Hillend Fife ... 86 B4
Hillend Mdloth ... 86 C3
Hillend N Lans ... 85 G2
Hillesden Bucks ... 31 G3
Hillesley Gloucs ... 29 E2
Hillfarrance Somset ... 16 C2
Hillhead S Lans ... 78 C6
Hillhead of Cocklaw Abers ... 103 F4
Hillhead of Durno Abers ... 102 C2
Hilliclay Highld ... 110 B5
Hillingdon Gt Lon ... 20 D4
Hillington C Glas ... 85 E2
Hillington Norfk ... 44 B4
Hillmorton Warwks ... 41 F1
Hillowton D & G ... 70 B5
Hills Town Derbys ... 51 F4
Hillside Abers ... 95 H5
Hillside Angus ... 95 F2
Hillstreet Hants ... 9 E5
Hillswick Shet ... 111 k3
Hilltown Devon ... 5 F5
Hilltown E Loth ... 86 D3
Hillwell Shet ... 111 I1
Hilmarton Wilts ... 18 C4
Hilperton Wilts ... 18 B3
Hilsea Hants ... 9 H4
Hilston E R Yk ... 61 F3
Hilton Border ... 81 E5

Hilton Cambs ... 33 E5
Hilton Cumb ... 64 B5
Hilton Derbys ... 40 D6
Hilton Dorset ... 8 A4
Hilton Dur ... 65 F5
Hilton Highld ... 107 G3
Hilton N York ... 66 B4
Hilton Shrops ... 39 G5
Himbleton Worcs ... 30 B5
Himley Staffs ... 40 A3
Hincaster Cumb ... 63 E4
Hinchley Wood Surrey ... 21 E2
Hinckley Leics ... 41 E3
Hinderclay Suffk ... 34 D6
Hinderwell N York ... 66 D5
Hindhead Surrey ... 10 C5
Hindley Gt Man ... 57 F3
Hindlip Worcs ... 39 H2
Hindolveston Norfk ... 44 D5
Hindon Wilts ... 8 B6
Hindringham Norfk ... 44 D5
Hingham Norfk ... 44 D2
Hinstock Shrops ... 49 F2
Hintlesham Suffk ... 34 D3
Hinton Gloucs ... 17 H6
Hinton Herefs ... 28 B6
Hinton Shrops ... 38 D6
Hinton Ampner Hants ... 9 G6
Hinton Blewett Somset ... 17 G4
Hinton Charterhouse Somset ... 18 A3
Hinton Martell Dorset ... 8 C4
Hinton on the Green Worcs ... 30 B4
Hinton Parva Wilts ... 19 E5
Hinton St George Somset ... 7 E6
Hinton St Mary Dorset ... 8 A5
Hinton Waldrist Oxon ... 19 F6
Hinton-in-the-Hedges Nhants ... 31 F4
Hints Staffs ... 40 C4
Hinwick Beds ... 32 B4
Hinxhill Kent ... 13 E6
Hinxton Cambs ... 33 F3
Hinxworth Herts ... 32 D3
Hipperholme W York ... 58 C3
Hipswell N York ... 65 F3
Hirn Abers ... 95 F6
Hirnant Powys ... 48 A2
Hirst Nthumb ... 73 F5
Hirst Courtney N York ... 59 G3
Hirwaun Rhondd ... 27 E3
Hiscott Devon ... 15 E3
Histon Cambs ... 33 F5
Hitcham Suffk ... 34 D4
Hitcham Causeway Suffk ... 34 D4
Hitcham Street Suffk ... 34 D4
Hitchin Herts ... 32 D2
Hither Green Gt Lon ... 21 F3
Hittisleigh Devon ... 5 G6
Hive E R Yk ... 60 C3
Hixon Staffs ... 40 B5
Hoaden Kent ... 23 G2
Hoar Cross Staffs ... 40 C5
Hoarwithy Herefs ... 28 D5
Hoath Kent ... 23 F2
Hobarris Shrops ... 38 C4
Hobkirk Border ... 80 B1
Hobson Dur ... 73 F2
Hoby Leics ... 41 G5
Hockering Norfk ... 44 D3
Hockerton Notts ... 51 H2
Hockley Essex ... 22 D4
Hockley Heath W Mids ... 40 C1
Hockliffe Beds ... 32 B2
Hockwold cum Wilton Norfk ... 44 B1
Hockworthy Devon ... 16 B1
Hoddesdon Herts ... 21 F6
Hoddlesden Lancs ... 57 G5
Hoddom Cross D & G ... 71 E6
Hoddom Mains D & G ... 71 E6
Hodgeston Pembks ... 24 D3
Hodnet Shrops ... 49 F2
Hodsall Street Kent ... 22 B2
Hodsock Notts ... 51 G5
Hodson Wilts ... 18 D4
Hodthorpe Derbys ... 51 F4
Hoe Norfk ... 44 D4
Hogben's Hill Kent ... 23 E1
Hoggeston Bucks ... 32 A2
Hoggrill's End Warwks ... 40 D3
Hoghton Lancs ... 57 F5
Hognaston Derbys ... 50 D2
Hogsthorpe Lincs ... 53 G3
Holbeach Lincs ... 43 E4
Holbeach Drove Lincs ... 43 E3
Holbeach Hurn Lincs ... 43 F4
Holbeach St Johns Lincs ... 43 E4
Holbeach St Mark's Lincs ... 43 F5
Holbeach St Matthew Lincs ... 43 F5
Holbeck Notts ... 51 F4
Holberrow Green Worcs ... 30 B5
Holbeton Devon ... 5 F2
Holborn Gt Lon ... 21 F3
Holbrook Derbys ... 51 E1
Holbrook Suffk ... 35 E2
Holbury Hants ... 9 F4
Holcombe Devon ... 6 B3
Holcombe Somset ... 17 G4
Holcombe Rogus Devon ... 16 C1
Holcot Nhants ... 32 A5
Holden Lancs ... 63 G1
Holdenby Nhants ... 31 G6
Holder's Green Essex ... 33 H2
Holdgate Shrops ... 39 E5
Holdingham Lincs ... 42 C6
Holditch Dorset ... 7 E5
Hole Devon ... 14 D2
Holford Somset ... 16 C3
Holgate N York ... 59 G5
Holker Cumb ... 62 D4
Holkham Norfk ... 44 C6
Holkham Hall Norfk ... 44 C6
Hollacombe Devon ... 14 D2
Holland Fen Lincs ... 52 D1
Holland-on-Sea Essex ... 35 E1
Hollandstoun Ork ... 111 j3
Hollee D & G ... 71 F6
Hollesley Suffk ... 35 F3
Hollicombe Devon ... 6 A2
Hollingbourne Kent ... 22 D1
Hollingbury E Susx ... 11 F3
Hollingdon Bucks ... 32 B2
Hollington Derbys ... 50 D1
Hollington Staffs ... 50 B1
Hollingworth Gt Man ... 50 B6
Hollins Green Ches ... 57 F2

Hollinsclough Staffs ... 50 C3
Hollocombe Devon ... 15 F2
Holloway Derbys ... 51 E2
Holloway Gt Lon ... 21 F4
Hollowell Nhants ... 41 G1
Hollowmoor Heath Ches ... 49 E6
Hollows D & G ... 79 G1
Holly Green Worcs ... 29 F6
Hollybush Caerph ... 27 G3
Hollybush E Ayrs ... 76 D3
Hollybush Herefs ... 29 E6
Hollym E R Yk ... 61 G3
Holmbridge W York ... 58 C1
Holmbury St Mary Surrey ... 10 D6
Holmbush Cnwll ... 3 F4
Holmcroft Staffs ... 40 A5
Holme Cambs ... 42 D1
Holme Cumb ... 63 E4
Holme Notts ... 52 A2
Holme N York ... 65 G2
Holme W York ... 58 C1
Holme Chapel Lancs ... 57 H5
Holme Green N York ... 59 F4
Holme Hale Norfk ... 44 C3
Holme Lacy Herefs ... 28 D6
Holme Marsh Herefs ... 38 D2
Holme next the Sea Norfk ... 44 A6
Holme on the Wolds E R Yk ... 60 D4
Holme Pierrepont Notts ... 51 G1
Holme St Cuthbert Cumb ... 70 D4
Holme upon Spalding Moor
    E R Yk ... 60 B4
Holmer Herefs ... 28 C6
Holmer Green Bucks ... 20 C5
Holmes Chapel Ches ... 49 G5
Holmesfield Derbys ... 50 D4
Holmeswood Lancs ... 56 D4
Holmethorpe Surrey ... 21 F1
Holmewood Derbys ... 51 E3
Holmfirth W York ... 58 C1
Holmhead E Ayrs ... 77 E3
Holmpton E R Yk ... 61 G2
Holmrook Cumb ... 62 B5
Holmside Dur ... 73 F2
Holne Devon ... 5 G4
Holnest Dorset ... 7 G6
Holnicote Somset ... 16 B4
Holsworthy Devon ... 14 C2
Holsworthy Beacon Devon ... 14 D2
Holt Dorset ... 8 C4
Holt Norfk ... 44 D5
Holt Wilts ... 18 B3
Holt Worcs ... 39 G2
Holt Wrexhm ... 48 D4
Holt End Worcs ... 40 C1
Holt Heath Worcs ... 39 G2
Holtby N York ... 59 G5
Holton Oxon ... 31 G1
Holton Somset ... 17 G2
Holton Suffk ... 35 G6
Holton cum Beckering Lincs ... 52 D3
Holton le Clay Lincs ... 53 E5
Holton le Moor Lincs ... 52 C5
Holton St Mary Suffk ... 34 D3
Holwell Dorset ... 7 H6
Holwell Herts ... 32 D2
Holwell Leics ... 41 H5
Holwell Oxon ... 30 D1
Holwick Dur ... 64 D5
Holworth Dorset ... 7 H4
Holy Island Nthumb ... 81 G4
Holybourne Hants ... 10 A6
Holyhead IOA ... 54 B4
Holymoorside Derbys ... 51 E3
Holyport Berks ... 20 C3
Holystone Nthumb ... 72 D6
Holytown N Lans ... 85 F2
Holywell Cambs ... 33 E5
Holywell Cnwll ... 2 D5
Holywell Dorset ... 7 G6
Holywell Flints ... 48 C6
Holywell Green W York ... 58 C2
Holywell Lake Somset ... 16 C1
Holywell Row Suffk ... 34 A6
Holywood D & G ... 78 C1
Holywood Village D & G ... 78 C1
Homer Shrops ... 39 F6
Homer Green Mersyd ... 56 D3
Homersfield Suffk ... 45 F1
Homington Wilts ... 8 D5
Honey Tye Suffk ... 34 C2
Honeybourne Worcs ... 30 C4
Honeychurch Devon ... 15 F2
Honeystreet Wilts ... 18 D3
Honiley Warwks ... 40 D1
Honing Norfk ... 45 F4
Honingham Norfk ... 44 D3
Honington Lincs ... 42 B6
Honington Suffk ... 34 C6
Honington Warwks ... 30 D4
Honiton Devon ... 6 C5
Honley W York ... 58 C2
Hoo Green Ches ... 57 G1
Hoo St Werburgh Kent ... 22 C3
Hooe Devon ... 5 E2
Hooe E Susx ... 12 C3
Hoohill Lancs ... 56 D6
Hook E R Yk ... 60 B3
Hook Hants ... 20 A1
Hook Kent ... 22 B3
Hook Pembks ... 24 D4
Hook Surrey ... 21 E2
Hook Wilts ... 18 C5
Hook Green Kent ... 12 B5
Hook Norton Oxon ... 31 E3
Hooke Dorset ... 7 F5
Hookway Devon ... 15 G1
Hooton Levitt S York ... 51 F5
Hooton Pagnell S York ... 59 F1
Hooton Roberts S York ... 51 F5
Hope Derbys ... 50 C5
Hope Devon ... 5 G1
Hope Flints ... 48 C5
Hope Shrops ... 39 F3
Hope Staffs ... 50 C2
Hope Bowdler Shrops ... 39 E5
Hope Mansell Herefs ... 28 D4
Hope under Dinmore Herefs ... 39 E2
Hopehouse Border ... 79 F4
Hopeman Moray ... 100 D6
Hopesay Shrops ... 38 D4
Hopperton N York ... 59 G5
Hopstone Shrops ... 39 G5
Hopton Derbys ... 50 D2

Hopton Staffs ... 40 B5
Hopton Suffk ... 34 D6
Hopton Cangeford Shrops ... 39 E4
Hopton Castle Shrops ... 38 D4
Hopton on Sea Norfk ... 45 H2
Hopton Wafers Shrops ... 39 F4
Hoptonheath Shrops ... 38 D4
Hopwas Staffs ... 40 C4
Hopwood Worcs ... 40 B1
Horam E Susx ... 12 B4
Horbling Lincs ... 42 D5
Horbury W York ... 58 D2
Horden Dur ... 73 H1
Hordle Hants ... 9 E3
Hordley Shrops ... 48 D3
Horfield Bristl ... 17 G6
Horham Suffk ... 35 E5
Horkesley Heath Essex ... 34 D2
Horkstow Lincs ... 60 D2
Horley Oxon ... 31 E4
Horley Surrey ... 11 F6
Hornblotton Green Somset ... 17 G2
Hornby Lancs ... 63 F3
Hornby N York ... 65 G4
Hornby N York ... 65 F3
Horncastle Lincs ... 53 E2
Hornchurch Gt Lon ... 21 H4
Horncliffe Nthumb ... 81 E5
Horndean Border ... 81 E5
Horndean Hants ... 10 A3
Horndon Devon ... 5 F5
Horndon on the Hill Essex ... 22 B4
Horne Surrey ... 11 F6
Horner Somset ... 16 A3
Horning Norfk ... 45 F4
Horninghold Leics ... 42 A2
Horninglow Staffs ... 40 D5
Horningsea Cambs ... 33 F5
Horningsham Wilts ... 18 A1
Horningtoft Norfk ... 44 C4
Horns Cross Devon ... 14 D3
Hornsea E R Yk ... 61 E4
Hornsey Gt Lon ... 21 F4
Hornton Oxon ... 31 E4
Horra Shet ... 111 I4
Horrabridge Devon ... 5 E4
Horridge Devon ... 5 G4
Horringer Suffk ... 34 B5
Horrocksford Lancs ... 63 G1
Horsebridge E Susx ... 12 B3
Horsebridge Hants ... 9 F6
Horsebridge Shrops ... 38 D6
Horseheath Cambs ... 33 G3
Horsehouse N York ... 65 E2
Horsell Surrey ... 20 C2
Horseman's Green Wrexhm ... 49 E3
Horsey Norfk ... 45 G4
Horsey Somset ... 17 E3
Horsford Norfk ... 45 E4
Horsforth W York ... 58 D4
Horsham W Susx ... 11 E5
Horsham St Faith Norfk ... 45 E3
Horsington Lincs ... 52 D2
Horsington Somset ... 17 H2
Horsley Derbys ... 51 E1
Horsley Gloucs ... 29 F3
Horsley Nthumb ... 72 C6
Horsley Nthumb ... 73 E3
Horsley Woodhouse Derbys ... 51 E1
Horsleycross Street Essex ... 35 E2
Horsleyhill Border ... 80 B2
Horspath Oxon ... 31 F1
Horstead Norfk ... 45 E4
Horsted Keynes W Susx ... 11 F4
Horton Bucks ... 32 B1
Horton Dorset ... 8 C4
Horton Gloucs ... 18 A5
Horton Lancs ... 63 H1
Horton Nhants ... 32 A4
Horton Shrops ... 49 F1
Horton Somset ... 17 E1
Horton Staffs ... 50 B3
Horton Swans ... 26 B2
Horton Wilts ... 18 C3
Horton Green Ches ... 49 E4
Horton in Ribblesdale N York ... 64 C1
Horton Kirby Kent ... 22 B2
Horton-cum-Studley Oxon ... 31 G2
Horwich Gt Man ... 57 F4
Horwood Devon ... 15 E4
Hoscote Border ... 79 G4
Hose Leics ... 41 H6
Hosh P & K ... 92 B2
Hoswick Shet ... 111 I1
Hotham E R Yk ... 60 C3
Hothfield Kent ... 13 E6
Hoton Leics ... 41 F5
Hott Nthumb ... 72 C5
Hough Ches ... 49 G4
Hough Green Ches ... 57 E2
Hough-on-the-Hill Lincs ... 42 B6
Hougham Lincs ... 42 B6
Houghton Cambs ... 33 E5
Houghton Hants ... 9 E6
Houghton Pembks ... 24 D3
Houghton W Susx ... 10 D3
Houghton Conquest Beds ... 32 C3
Houghton Green E Susx ... 12 D4
Houghton le Spring T & W ... 73 G2
Houghton on the Hill Leics ... 41 G4
Houghton Regis Beds ... 32 C1
Houghton St Giles Norfk ... 44 C5
Hound Green Hants ... 20 A2
Houndslow Border ... 80 C4
Houndwood Border ... 87 H2
Hounslow Gt Lon ... 21 E3
Hounslow Green Essex ... 33 H1
Househill Highld ... 100 B5
Houses Hill W York ... 58 D2
Housesteads Roman Fort Nthumb ... 72 C3
Housieside Abers ... 103 E2
Houston Rens ... 84 D2
Houstry Highld ... 110 B3
Houton Ork ... 111 g2
Hove E Susx ... 11 F3
Hoveringham Notts ... 51 G2
Hoveton Norfk ... 45 F4
Hovingham N York ... 66 C1
How Caple Herefs ... 28 D5
How Mill Cumb ... 71 H5

Howden E R Yk ... 60 B3
Howden-le-Wear Dur ... 65 F6
Howe Highld ... 110 C5
Howe N York ... 65 G2
Howe Norfk ... 45 F2
Howe Green Essex ... 22 C5
Howe of Teuchar Abers ... 102 D4
Howe Street Essex ... 22 C6
Howe Street Essex ... 34 A2
Howegreen Essex ... 22 D5
Howell Lincs ... 42 D6
Howes D & G ... 71 E5
Howey Powys ... 38 B2
Howgate Mdloth ... 86 C2
Howick Nthumb ... 81 H2
Howle Dur ... 65 E5
Howle Shrops ... 49 F2
Howle Hill Herefs ... 28 D4
Howlett End Essex ... 33 G2
Howley Somset ... 6 D6
Howmore W Isls ... 111 a3
Hownam Border ... 80 D2
Howsham Lincs ... 52 C5
Howsham N York ... 60 B6
Howtel Nthumb ... 81 E3
Howwood Rens ... 84 D2
Hoxne Suffk ... 35 E6
Hoylake Mersyd ... 56 C2
Hoyland Nether S York ... 51 E6
Hoyland Swaine S York ... 58 D1
Hubberston Pembks ... 24 C3
Huby N York ... 58 D4
Huby N York ... 59 F6
Hucclecote Gloucs ... 29 F4
Hucking Kent ... 22 D2
Hucknall Notts ... 51 F2
Huddersfield W York ... 58 C2
Huddington Worcs ... 30 B5
Hudswell N York ... 65 E3
Huggate E R Yk ... 60 C5
Hugh Town IOS ... 2 b2
Hughenden Valley Bucks ... 20 B5
Hughley Shrops ... 39 E5
Huish Devon ... 15 E2
Huish Wilts ... 18 D3
Huish Champflower Somset ... 16 C2
Huish Episcopi Somset ... 17 F2
Hulcott Bucks ... 32 B1
Hulham Devon ... 6 B4
Hull E R Yk ... 61 E3
Hulland Derbys ... 50 D2
Hulland Ward Derbys ... 50 D2
Hullavington Wilts ... 18 B5
Hullbridge Essex ... 22 C5
Hulme Ches ... 57 F2
Hulme Gt Man ... 57 H1
Hulme Staffs ... 50 B2
Hulme End Staffs ... 50 C3
Hulme Walfield Ches ... 49 H5
Hulver Street Suffk ... 45 G1
Hulverstone IOW ... 9 F2
Humber Devon ... 5 H5
Humberside Airport Lincs ... 61 E1
Humberston Lincs ... 53 E5
Humberstone Leics ... 41 G4
Humbie E Loth ... 87 E2
Humbleton E R Yk ... 61 F3
Humby Lincs ... 42 C5
Hume Border ... 80 C4
Humshaugh Nthumb ... 72 D4
Huna Highld ... 110 D6
Huncote Leics ... 41 F3
Hundalee Border ... 80 C2
Hunderthwaite Dur ... 64 D5
Hundleby Lincs ... 53 F2
Hundleton Pembks ... 24 D3
Hundon Suffk ... 34 B3
Hundred End Lancs ... 56 D5
Hundred House Powys ... 38 B2
Hungarton Leics ... 41 G4
Hungerford Berks ... 19 E3
Hungerford Somset ... 16 C3
Hungerford Newtown Berks ... 19 F4
Hungerstone Herefs ... 28 C6
Hunmanby N York ... 67 G1
Hunningham Warwks ... 31 E6
Hunsdon Herts ... 21 G6
Hunsingore N York ... 59 E5
Hunslet W York ... 59 E3
Hunsonby Cumb ... 64 A6
Hunstanton Norfk ... 43 H5
Hunstanworth Dur ... 72 D2
Hunsterson Ches ... 49 F4
Hunston Suffk ... 34 C5
Hunston W Susx ... 10 B2
Hunstrete Somset ... 17 G5
Hunsworth W York ... 58 C3
Hunter's Quay Ag & B ... 84 B3
Huntham Somset ... 17 E2
Hunthill Lodge Angus ... 94 D3
Huntingdon Cambs ... 33 E5
Huntingfield Suffk ... 35 F6
Huntington Ches ... 48 D5
Huntington E Loth ... 87 E3
Huntington Herefs ... 38 C2
Huntington N York ... 59 G5
Huntington Staffs ... 40 B4
Huntley Gloucs ... 29 E4
Huntly Abers ... 102 B3
Hunton Hants ... 19 G1
Hunton Kent ... 22 C1
Hunton N York ... 65 F3
Huntscott Somset ... 16 B3
Huntsham Devon ... 16 B1
Huntshaw Devon ... 15 E3
Huntspill Somset ... 17 E3
Huntstile Somset ... 16 D2
Huntworth Somset ... 17 E3
Hunwick Dur ... 65 F6
Hunworth Norfk ... 44 D5
Hurdcott Wilts ... 8 D6
Hurdsfield Ches ... 50 A4
Hurley Berks ... 20 B4
Hurley Warwks ... 40 D3
Hurley Common Warwks ... 40 D3
Hurlford E Ayrs ... 76 D5
Hurn Dorset ... 8 D3
Hursley Hants ... 9 F5
Hurst Berks ... 20 B3
Hurst Green E Susx ... 12 C4
Hurst Green Essex ... 34 D1
Hurst Green Lancs ... 57 F6
Hurst Green Surrey ... 21 G1
Hurstbourne Priors Hants ... 19 F2
Hurstbourne Tarrant Hants ... 19 F2

175

Hurstpierpoint *W Susx* ... 11 F4
Hurstwood *Lancs* ... 57 H5
Hurtiso *Ork* ... 111 b2
Hurworth Place *Dur* ... 65 G4
Hurworth-on-Tees *Dur* ... 65 G4
Husbands Bosworth *Leics* ... 41 G2
Husborne Crawley *Beds* ... 32 B2
Husthwaite *N York* ... 66 B1
Huthwaite *Notts* ... 51 F3
Huttoft *Lincs* ... 53 G3
Hutton *Border* ... 81 E5
Hutton *E R Yk* ... 60 D6
Hutton *Essex* ... 22 B5
Hutton *Lancs* ... 57 E5
Hutton *Somset* ... 17 E5
Hutton Bonville *N York* ... 65 G3
Hutton Buscel *N York* ... 67 F2
Hutton Conyers *N York* ... 65 G1
Hutton Cranswick *E R Yk* ... 60 D5
Hutton End *Cumb* ... 71 G3
Hutton Henry *Dur* ... 65 H6
Hutton Lowcross *N York* ... 66 C4
Hutton Magna *Dur* ... 65 E4
Hutton Roof *Cumb* ... 71 F3
Hutton Roof *Cumb* ... 63 E4
Hutton Rudby *N York* ... 66 B4
Hutton Sessay *N York* ... 66 B1
Hutton Wandesley *N York* ... 59 F5
Hutton-le-Hole *N York* ... 66 D2
Huxham *Devon* ... 6 B5
Huxley *Ches* ... 49 E5
Huyton *Mersyd* ... 57 E2
Hycemoor *Cumb* ... 62 B5
Hyde *Gt Man* ... 50 B6
Hyde Heath *Bucks* ... 20 C5
Hyde Lea *Staffs* ... 40 A5
Hyndford Bridge *S Lans* ... 78 C6
Hynish *Ag & B* ... 88 B3
Hyssington *Powys* ... 38 C5
Hythe *Hants* ... 9 F4
Hythe *Kent* ... 13 F5
Hythe End *Berks* ... 20 D3

I

Ibberton *Dorset* ... 8 A4
Ible *Derbys* ... 50 D2
Ibsley *Hants* ... 8 D4
Ibstock *Leics* ... 41 E4
Ibstone *Bucks* ... 20 B4
Ibthorpe *Hants* ... 19 F2
Iburndale *N York* ... 67 E4
Ibworth *Hants* ... 19 G2
Ickburgh *Norfk* ... 44 B2
Ickenham *Gt Lon* ... 20 D4
Ickford *Bucks* ... 31 G1
Ickham *Kent* ... 23 G2
Ickleford *Herts* ... 32 D2
Icklesham *E Susx* ... 12 D4
Ickleton *Cambs* ... 33 F3
Icklingham *Suffk* ... 34 B5
Ickornshaw *N York* ... 58 B4
Ickwell Green *Beds* ... 32 D3
Ickworth *Suffk* ... 34 B5
Icomb *Gloucs* ... 30 D2
Idbury *Oxon* ... 30 D2
Iddesleigh *Devon* ... 15 E2
Ide *Devon* ... 6 A4
Ide Hill *Kent* ... 21 G1
Ideford *Devon* ... 6 A3
Iden *E Susx* ... 12 D4
Iden Green *Kent* ... 12 C5
Iden Green *Kent* ... 12 C5
Idle *W York* ... 58 C4
Idless *Cnwll* ... 3 E4
Idlicote *Warwks* ... 30 D4
Idmiston *Wilts* ... 18 D1
Idridgehay *Derbys* ... 50 D2
Idrigill *Highld* ... 104 C2
Idstone *Oxon* ... 19 E5
Iffley *Oxon* ... 31 F1
Ifield *W Susx* ... 11 E5
Iford *Dorset* ... 8 D3
Iford *E Susx* ... 11 G3
Ifton *Mons* ... 28 C2
Ightfield *Shrops* ... 49 F3
Ightham *Kent* ... 22 B1
Iken *Suffk* ... 35 G4
Ilam *Staffs* ... 50 C2
Ilchester *Somset* ... 17 F2
Ilderton *Nthumb* ... 81 F2
Ilford *Gt Lon* ... 21 G4
Ilford *Somset* ... 17 E1
Ilfracombe *Devon* ... 15 E5
Ilkeston *Derbys* ... 51 F1
Ilketshall St Andrew *Suffk* ... 45 G1
Ilketshall St Margaret *Suffk* ... 45 F1
Ilkley *W York* ... 58 C4
Illand *Cnwll* ... 4 D4
Illey *W Mids* ... 40 B2
Illogan *Cnwll* ... 2 D3
Illston on the Hill *Leics* ... 41 G3
Ilmer *Bucks* ... 20 B5
Ilmington *Warwks* ... 30 D4
Ilminster *Somset* ... 17 E1
Ilsington *Devon* ... 5 H4
Ilston *Swans* ... 26 B2
Ilton *N York* ... 65 F1
Ilton *Somset* ... 17 E1
Imachar *N Ayrs* ... 75 G5
Immingham *Lincs* ... 61 E2
Immingham Dock *Lincs* ... 61 E2
Ince *Ches* ... 57 E1
Ince Blundell *Mersyd* ... 56 D3
Ince-in-Makerfield *Gt Man* ... 57 F3
Inchbae Lodge Hotel *Highld* ... 106 D3
Inchbare *Angus* ... 95 E3
Inchberry *Moray* ... 101 F5
Inchinnan *Rens* ... 84 D3
Inchlaggan *Highld* ... 98 A3
Inchmichael *P & K* ... 93 E2
Inchnacardoch Hotel *Highld* ... 98 C4
Inchture *P & K* ... 93 E2
Inchvuilt *Highld* ... 98 B6
Inchyra *P & K* ... 92 D2
Indian Queens *Cnwll* ... 3 E5
Ingatestone *Essex* ... 22 B5
Ingbirchworth *S York* ... 58 D1

Ingestre *Staffs* ... 40 B5
Ingham *Lincs* ... 52 B4
Ingham *Norfk* ... 45 G4
Ingham *Suffk* ... 34 C5
Ingham Corner *Norfk* ... 45 G4
Ingleby *Derbys* ... 41 E5
Ingleby Arncliffe *N York* ... 66 B3
Ingleby Barwick *N York* ... 66 B4
Ingleby Greenhow *N York* ... 66 C4
Ingleigh Green *Devon* ... 15 E2
Inglesbatch *Somset* ... 17 H5
Inglesham *Wilts* ... 18 D6
Ingleston *D & G* ... 70 C5
Ingleton *Dur* ... 65 F5
Ingleton *N York* ... 63 F3
Inglewhite *Lancs* ... 57 E6
Ingoe *Nthumb* ... 73 E4
Ingoldisthorpe *Norfk* ... 44 A5
Ingoldmells *Lincs* ... 53 G2
Ingoldsby *Lincs* ... 42 C5
Ingram *Nthumb* ... 81 F2
Ingrave *Essex* ... 22 B4
Ingrow *W York* ... 58 B4
Ingst *Gloucs* ... 28 D2
Ingthorpe *Lincs* ... 42 C3
Ingworth *Norfk* ... 45 E5
Inkberrow *Worcs* ... 30 B5
Inkhorn *Abers* ... 103 E3
Inkpen *Berks* ... 19 F3
Inkstack *Highld* ... 110 C6
Innellan *Ag & B* ... 84 B3
Innerleithen *Border* ... 79 F6
Innerleven *Fife* ... 86 D5
Innermessan *D & G* ... 68 C4
Innerwick *E Loth* ... 87 G3
Innsmill *Moray* ... 101 E5
Insch *Abers* ... 102 C2
Insh *Highld* ... 99 F3
Inskip *Lancs* ... 57 E6
Instow *Devon* ... 14 D4
Intake *S York* ... 51 E5
Inver *Abers* ... 94 B5
Inver *Highld* ... 107 G4
Inver *P & K* ... 92 C3
Inver-boyndie *Abers* ... 102 C5
Inverailort *Highld* ... 97 E1
Inveralligin *Highld* ... 105 F2
Inverallochy *Abers* ... 103 F5
Inveran *Highld* ... 107 E5
Inveraray *Ag & B* ... 84 A6
Inverarish *Highld* ... 96 D5
Inverarity *Angus* ... 93 F4
Inverarnan *Stirlg* ... 91 E1
Inverasdale *Highld* ... 105 F4
Inveravon *Falk* ... 85 H3
Inverawe *Ag & B* ... 90 B2
Inverbeg *Ag & B* ... 84 C5
Inverbervie *Abers* ... 95 G3
Inverbroom *Highld* ... 106 B4
Invercreran House Hotel *Ag & B* ... 90 B3
Inverdruie *Highld* ... 99 G4
Inveresk *E Loth* ... 86 D3
Inveresragan *Ag & B* ... 90 B3
Inverey *Abers* ... 94 A5
Inverfarigaig *Highld* ... 98 D5
Inverfolla *Ag & B* ... 90 B3
Invergarry *Highld* ... 98 B3
Invergeldie *P & K* ... 91 H2
Invergloy *Highld* ... 98 B2
Invergordon *Highld* ... 107 F3
Invergowrie *P & K* ... 93 F2
Inverguseran *Highld* ... 97 E3
Inverhadden *P & K* ... 91 G4
Inverherive Hotel *Stirlg* ... 91 E2
Inverie *Highld* ... 97 E2
Inverinan *Ag & B* ... 90 B1
Inverinate *Highld* ... 97 G4
Inverkeilor *Angus* ... 93 H4
Inverkeithing *Fife* ... 86 B4
Inverkeithny *Abers* ... 102 C4
Inverkip *Inver* ... 84 B3
Inverkirkaig *Highld* ... 108 A2
Inverlael *Highld* ... 106 B4
Inverlair *Highld* ... 98 B1
Inverliever Lodge *Ag & B* ... 83 G6
Inverlochy *Ag & B* ... 90 D2
Invermark *Angus* ... 94 D4
Invermarkie *Abers* ... 101 F3
Invermoriston *Highld* ... 98 C4
Invernaver *Highld* ... 107 F1
Inverness *Highld* ... 107 F1
Inverness Dalcross Airport *Highld* ... 107 F1
Invernoaden *Ag & B* ... 84 B5
Inveroran Hotel *Ag & B* ... 90 D3
Inverquharity *Angus* ... 93 F5
Inverquhomery *Abers* ... 103 F4
Inverroy *Highld* ... 98 B1
Inversanda *Highld* ... 90 B5
Invershiel *Highld* ... 97 G4
Invershin *Highld* ... 107 E5
Invershore *Highld* ... 110 C3
Inversnaid Hotel *Stirlg* ... 84 C6
Inverugie *Abers* ... 103 F4
Inveruglas *Ag & B* ... 84 C6
Inveruglass *Highld* ... 99 F3
Inverurie *Abers* ... 102 D2
Inwardleigh *Devon* ... 15 E1
Inworth *Essex* ... 34 C1
Iochdar *W Isls* ... 111 a3
Iping *W Susx* ... 10 B4
Ipplepen *Devon* ... 5 H3
Ipsden *Oxon* ... 19 H5
Ipstones *Staffs* ... 50 B2
Ipswich *Suffk* ... 35 E3
Irby *Mersyd* ... 56 C1
Irby in the Marsh *Lincs* ... 53 F2
Irby upon Humber *Lincs* ... 52 D5
Irchester *Nhants* ... 32 B5
Ireby *Cumb* ... 71 E3
Ireby *Lancs* ... 63 F3
Ireland *Beds* ... 32 D3
Ireleth *Cumb* ... 62 C4
Ireshopeburn *Dur* ... 72 C1
Ireton Wood *Derbys* ... 50 D2
Irlam *Gt Man* ... 57 G2
Irnham *Lincs* ... 42 C4
Iron Acton *Gloucs* ... 29 E1
Iron Bridge Museum *Shrops* ... 39 F6
Ironbridge *Shrops* ... 39 F6
Ironmacannie *D & G* ... 69 G5
Ironville *Derbys* ... 51 E2
Irstead *Norfk* ... 45 F4
Irthington *Cumb* ... 71 G5
Irthlingborough *Nhants* ... 32 B5

Irton *N York* ... 67 F2
Irvine *N Ayrs* ... 76 C5
Isauld *Highld* ... 110 A5
Isbister *Shet* ... 111 I4
Isfield *E Susx* ... 11 G4
Isham *Nhants* ... 32 B5
Isington *Hants* ... 10 B6
Islay Airport *Ag & B* ... 74 B5
Isle Abbotts *Somset* ... 17 E1
Isle Brewers *Somset* ... 17 E1
Isle of Dogs *Gt Lon* ... 21 F3
Isle of Man Ronaldsway Airport *IOM* ... 116 b2
Isle of Whithorn *D & G* ... 69 F2
Isleham *Cambs* ... 33 H6
Isleornsay *Highld* ... 97 E3
Isles of Scilly St Mary's Airport *IOS* ... 2 b2
Islesteps *D & G* ... 70 C6
Islet Village *Guern* ... 6 c2
Isleworth *Gt Lon* ... 21 E3
Isley Walton *Leics* ... 41 E5
Islibhig *W Isls* ... 111 b6
Islington *Gt Lon* ... 21 F4
Islip *Nhants* ... 32 C6
Islip *Oxon* ... 31 F2
Islivig *W Isls* ... 111 b6
Isombridge *Shrops* ... 49 F1
Itchen Abbas *Hants* ... 9 G6
Itchen Stoke *Hants* ... 9 G6
Itchingfield *W Susx* ... 11 E5
Itteringham *Norfk* ... 45 E5
Itton *Devon* ... 15 F1
Itton *Mons* ... 28 C2
Ivegill *Cumb* ... 71 G4
Iver *Bucks* ... 20 D3
Iver Heath *Bucks* ... 20 D4
Iveston *Dur* ... 73 E2
Ivinghoe *Bucks* ... 32 B1
Ivinghoe Aston *Bucks* ... 32 B1
Ivington *Herefs* ... 39 E2
Ivington Green *Herefs* ... 39 E2
Ivy Hatch *Kent* ... 22 B1
Ivybridge *Devon* ... 5 F3
Ivychurch *Kent* ... 13 E4
Iwade *Kent* ... 22 D2
Iwerne Courtney or Shroton *Dorset* ... 8 B4
Iwerne Minster *Dorset* ... 8 B4
Ixworth *Suffk* ... 34 C5
Ixworth Thorpe *Suffk* ... 34 C5

J

Jack-in-the-Green *Devon* ... 6 B5
Jackton *S Lans* ... 85 E1
Jacobstow *Cnwll* ... 4 C6
Jacobstowe *Devon* ... 15 E2
Jameston *Pembks* ... 25 E3
Jamestown *Highld* ... 106 D2
Jamestown *W Duns* ... 84 D4
Janets-town *Highld* ... 110 D4
Janetstown *Highld* ... 110 C3
Jardine Hall *D & G* ... 78 D2
Jarrow *T & W* ... 73 G3
Jasper's Green *Essex* ... 34 B2
Jawcraig *Falk* ... 85 G3
Jaywick *Essex* ... 23 F6
Jedburgh *Border* ... 80 C2
Jeffreyston *Pembks* ... 25 E3
Jemimaville *Highld* ... 107 F3
Jerbourg *Guern* ... 6 c1
Jersey Airport *Jersey* ... 7 a1
Jesmond *T & W* ... 73 F3
Jevington *E Susx* ... 12 B2
Jockey End *Herts* ... 20 D6
John o' Groats *Highld* ... 110 D6
Johnby *Cumb* ... 71 G3
Johnshaven *Abers* ... 95 G3
Johnston *Pembks* ... 24 D4
Johnstone *D & G* ... 79 F3
Johnstone *Rens* ... 84 D2
Johnstonebridge *D & G* ... 78 D2
Johnstown *Carmth* ... 25 G4
Johnstown *Wrexhm* ... 48 C4
Joppa *C Edin* ... 86 D3
Joppa *Cerdgn* ... 37 E3
Joppa *S Ayrs* ... 76 D3
Jordanston *Pembks* ... 24 D5
Joyden's Wood *Kent* ... 21 G3
Juniper *Nthumb* ... 72 D3
Juniper Green *C Edin* ... 86 C3
Jurby *IOM* ... 116 c5

K

Kaber *Cumb* ... 64 C4
Kaimend *S Lans* ... 86 A1
Kames *Ag & B* ... 83 G3
Kames *E Ayrs* ... 77 F4
Kea *Cnwll* ... 3 E3
Keadby *Lincs* ... 60 C2
Keal Cotes *Lincs* ... 53 E2
Kearsley *Bolton* ... 57 G3
Kearsley *Nthumb* ... 72 D4
Kearsney *Kent* ... 13 G6
Kearstwick *Cumb* ... 63 F4
Kedington *Suffk* ... 34 A3
Kedleston *Derbys* ... 50 D1
Keelby *Lincs* ... 61 E1
Keele *Staffs* ... 49 G4
Keelham *W York* ... 58 C3
Keeston *Pembks* ... 24 C4
Keevil *Wilts* ... 18 B3
Kegworth *Leics* ... 41 F5
Kehelland *Cnwll* ... 2 C3
Keig *Abers* ... 102 B2
Keighley *W York* ... 58 B4
Keilarsbrae *Clacks* ... 85 G5
Keillour *P & K* ... 92 C2
Keiloch *Abers* ... 94 B5
Keils *Ag & B* ... 82 D3
Keinton Mandeville *Somset* ... 17 F2
Keir Mill *D & G* ... 78 D3

Keisley *Cumb* ... 64 B5
Keiss *Highld* ... 110 D5
Keith *Moray* ... 101 G4
Keithick *P & K* ... 93 E2
Keithock *Angus* ... 95 E3
Keithtown *Highld* ... 106 D2
Kelbrook *Lancs* ... 58 A4
Kelburn *N Ayrs* ... 84 B2
Kelby *Lincs* ... 42 C6
Keld *N York* ... 64 C3
Kelfield *N York* ... 59 G4
Kelham *Notts* ... 51 H2
Kelhead *D & G* ... 71 E6
Kellamergh *Lancs* ... 56 D5
Kellas *Angus* ... 93 F3
Kellas *Moray* ... 101 E4
Kellaton *Devon* ... 5 H1
Kelling *Norfk* ... 44 D6
Kellington *N York* ... 59 F3
Kelloe *Dur* ... 73 G1
Kelloholm *D & G* ... 77 F3
Kelly *Devon* ... 5 E5
Kelmarsh *Nhants* ... 41 H2
Kelmscot *Oxon* ... 19 E6
Kelsale *Suffk* ... 35 G5
Kelsall *Ches* ... 49 E6
Kelshall *Herts* ... 33 E2
Kelsick *Cumb* ... 71 E4
Kelso *Border* ... 80 D3
Kelstedge *Derbys* ... 51 E3
Kelstern *Lincs* ... 53 E4
Kelston *Somset* ... 17 H5
Keltneyburn *P & K* ... 92 A4
Kelton *D & G* ... 70 D6
Kelty *Fife* ... 86 B5
Kelvedon *Essex* ... 34 C1
Kelvedon Hatch *Essex* ... 22 B5
Kelynack *Cnwll* ... 2 A2
Kemback *Fife* ... 93 F1
Kemberton *Shrops* ... 39 G6
Kemble *Gloucs* ... 29 G3
Kemerton *Worcs* ... 29 G6
Kemeys Commander *Mons* ... 28 B3
Kemnay *Abers* ... 102 C1
Kemp Town *E Susx* ... 11 F3
Kempley *Gloucs* ... 29 E5
Kempley Green *Gloucs* ... 29 E5
Kempsey *Worcs* ... 39 H1
Kempsford *Gloucs* ... 18 D6
Kempshott *Hants* ... 19 G2
Kempston *Beds* ... 32 C3
Kempton *Shrops* ... 38 D4
Kemsing *Kent* ... 22 A2
Kenardington *Kent* ... 13 E5
Kenchester *Herefs* ... 38 D1
Kencot *Oxon* ... 30 D1
Kendal *Cumb* ... 63 E5
Kenfig *Brdgnd* ... 26 D1
Kenilworth *Warwks* ... 40 D1
Kenley *Gt Lon* ... 21 F2
Kenley *Shrops* ... 39 E5
Kenmore *Highld* ... 105 F2
Kenmore *P & K* ... 92 A4
Kenn *Devon* ... 6 B4
Kenn *Somset* ... 17 E5
Kennacraig *Ag & B* ... 83 F2
Kennerleigh *Devon* ... 15 G2
Kennessee Green *Mersyd* ... 56 D3
Kennet *Clacks* ... 85 H4
Kennethmont *Abers* ... 102 B2
Kennett *Cambs* ... 34 A5
Kennford *Devon* ... 6 B4
Kenninghall *Norfk* ... 44 D1
Kennington *Kent* ... 13 E6
Kennington *Oxon* ... 19 G6
Kennoway *Fife* ... 86 D6
Kenny *Somset* ... 17 E1
Kennyhill *Suffk* ... 33 H6
Kennythorpe *N York* ... 60 B6
Kenovay *Ag & B* ... 88 B3
Kensaleyre *Highld* ... 104 C1
Kensington *Gt Lon* ... 21 E3
Kensworth *Beds* ... 32 C1
Kensworth Common *Beds* ... 32 C1
Kent's Green *Gloucs* ... 29 E5
Kent's Oak *Hants* ... 9 E5
Kentallen *Highld* ... 90 B4
Kentchurch *Herefs* ... 28 C5
Kentford *Suffk* ... 34 A5
Kentisbeare *Devon* ... 6 C6
Kentisbury *Devon* ... 15 F5
Kentish Town *Gt Lon* ... 21 F4
Kentmere *Cumb* ... 63 E6
Kenton *Devon* ... 6 B4
Kenton *Gt Lon* ... 21 E4
Kenton *Suffk* ... 35 E5
Kenton *T & W* ... 73 F3
Kentra *Highld* ... 89 G5
Kenwyn *Cnwll* ... 3 E4
Keoldale *Highld* ... 108 D5
Keppoch *Highld* ... 97 F4
Kepwick *N York* ... 66 B3
Keresley *W Mids* ... 40 D2
Kerris *Cnwll* ... 2 B2
Kerry *Powys* ... 38 B5
Kerrycroy *Ag & B* ... 84 A2
Kersall *Notts* ... 51 H3
Kersbrook *Devon* ... 6 C4
Kersey *Suffk* ... 34 D3
Kershader *W Isls* ... 111 d6
Kerswell *Devon* ... 6 C6
Kerswell Green *Worcs* ... 39 H1
Kesgrave *Suffk* ... 35 E3
Kessingland *Suffk* ... 45 H1
Kestle *Cnwll* ... 3 F4
Kestle Mill *Cnwll* ... 3 E5
Keston *Gt Lon* ... 21 G2
Keswick *Cumb* ... 71 F2
Keswick *Norfk* ... 45 E3
Ketsby *Lincs* ... 53 F3
Kettering *Nhants* ... 32 B6
Ketteringham *Norfk* ... 45 E2
Kettins *Angus* ... 93 E3
Kettlebaston *Suffk* ... 34 C4
Kettlebridge *Fife* ... 86 D6
Kettleburgh *Suffk* ... 35 F4
Kettleholm *D & G* ... 79 E1
Kettleshulme *Ches* ... 50 B4
Kettlesing *N York* ... 58 D5
Kettlesing Bottom *N York* ... 58 D5
Kettlestone *Norfk* ... 44 C5
Kettlethorpe *Lincs* ... 52 B3
Kettletoft *Ork* ... 111 j3
Kettlewell *N York* ... 64 D1

Ketton *Rutlnd* ... 42 C3
Kew *Gt Lon* ... 21 E3
Kew Gardens *Gt Lon* ... 21 E3
Kewstoke *Somset* ... 17 E5
Kexby *Lincs* ... 52 B4
Kexby *N York* ... 60 B5
Key Green *Ches* ... 50 A3
Keyham *Leics* ... 41 G4
Keyhaven *Hants* ... 9 E3
Keyingham *E R Yk* ... 61 F3
Keymer *W Susx* ... 11 F3
Keynsham *Somset* ... 17 G5
Keysoe *Beds* ... 32 C5
Keysoe Row *Beds* ... 32 C4
Keyston *Cambs* ... 32 C6
Keyworth *Notts* ... 41 G6
Kibblesworth *T & W* ... 73 F2
Kibworth Beauchamp *Leics* ... 41 G3
Kibworth Harcourt *Leics* ... 41 G3
Kidbrooke *Gt Lon* ... 21 G3
Kidderminster *Worcs* ... 39 H4
Kidlington *Oxon* ... 31 F2
Kidmore End *Oxon* ... 20 A3
Kidsdale *D & G* ... 69 F2
Kidsgrove *Staffs* ... 49 H4
Kidwelly *Carmth* ... 25 G3
Kiel Crofts *Ag & B* ... 90 B3
Kielder *Nthumb* ... 72 A5
Kiells *Ag & B* ... 82 C3
Kilbarchan *Rens* ... 84 D2
Kilbeg *Highld* ... 97 E3
Kilberry *Ag & B* ... 83 E2
Kilbirnie *N Ayrs* ... 84 C1
Kilbride *Ag & B* ... 90 A2
Kilbride *Ag & B* ... 83 F3
Kilbride *Ag & B* ... 83 H2
Kilbuiack *Moray* ... 100 D5
Kilburn *Derbys* ... 51 E2
Kilburn *Gt Lon* ... 21 E4
Kilburn *N York* ... 66 B2
Kilby *Leics* ... 41 G3
Kilchamaig *Ag & B* ... 83 F2
Kilchattan *Ag & B* ... 82 C5
Kilchattan *Ag & B* ... 84 A1
Kilcheran *Ag & B* ... 89 H3
Kilchoan *Highld* ... 89 E5
Kilchoman *Ag & B* ... 82 B2
Kilchrenan *Ag & B* ... 90 C2
Kilconquhar *Fife* ... 87 E6
Kilcot *Gloucs* ... 29 E5
Kilcoy *Highld* ... 107 E1
Kilcreggan *Ag & B* ... 84 B4
Kildale *N York* ... 66 C4
Kildalloig *Ag & B* ... 75 F3
Kildary *Highld* ... 107 F3
Kildavaig *Ag & B* ... 83 H2
Kildavanan *Ag & B* ... 83 H2
Kildonan *Highld* ... 109 H2
Kildonan *N Ayrs* ... 75 H3
Kildonan Lodge *Highld* ... 109 H2
Kildonnan *Highld* ... 96 C1
Kildrochet House *D & G* ... 68 C3
Kildrummy *Abers* ... 101 G2
Kildwick *N York* ... 58 B4
Kilfinan *Ag & B* ... 83 G3
Kilfinnan *Highld* ... 98 B2
Kilgetty *Pembks* ... 25 E3
Kilgwrrwg Common *Mons* ... 28 C3
Kilham *E R Yk* ... 60 D6
Kilkenneth *Ag & B* ... 88 A3
Kilkenzie *Ag & B* ... 75 E3
Kilkhampton *Cnwll* ... 14 C2
Killamarsh *Derbys* ... 51 F4
Killay *Swans* ... 26 C2
Killearn *Stirlg* ... 85 E4
Killen *Highld* ... 107 F2
Killerby *Dur* ... 65 F5
Killerton *Devon* ... 6 B5
Killichonan *P & K* ... 91 F4
Killiechronan *Ag & B* ... 89 F3
Killiecrankie *P & K* ... 92 B5
Killilan *Highld* ... 97 G5
Killin *Stirlg* ... 91 G2
Killinghall *N York* ... 58 D5
Killington *Cumb* ... 63 F4
Killingworth *T & W* ... 73 F4
Killochyett *Border* ... 87 E1
Kilmacolm *Inver* ... 84 C3
Kilmahog *Stirlg* ... 85 E6
Kilmahumaig *Ag & B* ... 83 F5
Kilmaluag *Highld* ... 104 C3
Kilmany *Fife* ... 93 F2
Kilmarnock *E Ayrs* ... 76 D5
Kilmartin *Ag & B* ... 83 F5
Kilmaurs *E Ayrs* ... 76 D5
Kilmelford *Ag & B* ... 83 F6
Kilmersdon *Somset* ... 17 H4
Kilmeston *Hants* ... 9 G5
Kilmichael *Ag & B* ... 75 E3
Kilmichael Glassary *Ag & B* ... 83 G5
Kilmichael of Inverlussa *Ag & B* ... 83 F4
Kilmington *Devon* ... 6 D5
Kilmington *Wilts* ... 18 A1
Kilmington Common *Wilts* ... 8 A6
Kilmington Street *Wilts* ... 8 A6
Kilmorack *Highld* ... 106 D1
Kilmore *Ag & B* ... 90 A2
Kilmore *Highld* ... 97 E3
Kilmory *Ag & B* ... 83 E3
Kilmory *Highld* ... 89 F5
Kilmory *N Ayrs* ... 75 G3
Kilmuir *Highld* ... 104 B1
Kilmuir *Highld* ... 104 C3
Kilmuir *Highld* ... 107 F1
Kilmuir *Highld* ... 107 F3
Kilmun *Ag & B* ... 84 B4
Kiln Pit Hill *Nthumb* ... 73 E2
Kilnave *Ag & B* ... 82 B3
Kilncadzow *S Lans* ... 77 G6
Kilndown *Kent* ... 12 C5
Kilninver *Ag & B* ... 89 H1
Kilnsea *E R Yk* ... 61 G2
Kilnsey *N York* ... 58 B6
Kilnwick *E R Yk* ... 60 D5
Kiloran *Ag & B* ... 82 C5
Kilpatrick *N Ayrs* ... 75 G3
Kilpeck *Herefs* ... 28 C5
Kilpin *E R Yk* ... 60 B3
Kilrenny *Fife* ... 87 F6
Kilsby *Nhants* ... 41 F1
Kilspindie *P & K* ... 93 E2
Kilstay *D & G* ... 68 C2
Kilsyth *N Lans* ... 85 F3

Kiltarlity *Highld* 98 D6
Kilton *N York* 66 C5
Kilton Thorpe *N York* 66 C5
Kilvaxter *Highld* 104 C3
Kilve *Somset* 16 C3
Kilvington *Notts* 42 A6
Kilwinning *N Ayrs* 76 C5
Kimberley *Norfk* 44 D3
Kimberley *Notts* 51 F1
Kimberworth *S York* 51 E5
Kimblesworth *Dur* 73 F2
Kimbolton *Cambs* 32 C5
Kimbolton *Herefs* 39 E2
Kimcote *Leics* 41 G2
Kimmeridge *Dorset* 8 B2
Kimpton *Hants* 19 E2
Kimpton *Herts* 32 D1
Kinbrace *Highld* 109 H3
Kinbuck *Stirlg* 85 G5
Kincaple *Fife* 93 G1
Kincardine *Fife* 85 H4
Kincardine *Highld* 107 E4
Kincardine O'Neil *Abers* 95 E5
Kinclaven *P & K* 92 D3
Kincorth *Aber C* 95 H6
Kincorth House *Moray* 100 C5
Kincraig *Highld* 99 F3
Kincraigie *P & K* 92 C4
Kindallachan *P & K* 92 C4
Kinerarach *Ag & B* 75 E6
Kineton *Gloucs* 30 C3
Kineton *Warwks* 31 E5
Kinfauns *P & K* 92 D2
Kinfold *S Ayrs* 76 C5
King Arthur's Labyrinth *Gwynd* 47 F2
King's Bromley *Staffs* 40 C5
King's Cliffe *Nhants* 42 C2
King's Coughton *Warwks* 30 C5
King's Heath *W Mids* 40 C2
King's Lynn *Norfk* 43 G4
King's Mills *Guern* 6 b1
King's Norton *Leics* 41 G3
King's Norton *W Mids* 40 B2
King's Nympton *Devon* 15 F3
King's Pyon *Herefs* 38 D1
King's Somborne *Hants* 9 F6
King's Stag *Dorset* 7 H6
King's Stanley *Gloucs* 29 F3
King's Sutton *Oxon* 31 F4
King's Walden *Herts* 32 D1
Kingarth *Ag & B* 84 A2
Kingcausie *Abers* 95 G5
Kingcoed *Mons* 28 C3
Kingerby *Lincs* 52 C4
Kingford *Devon* 14 C2
Kingham *Oxon* 30 D3
Kingholm Quay *D & G* 70 C6
Kinghorn *Fife* 86 C4
Kinglassie *Fife* 86 C5
Kingoldrum *Angus* 93 F4
Kingoodie *P & K* 93 F2
Kings Caple *Herefs* 28 D5
Kings Hill *Kent* 22 B1
Kings House Hotel *Highld* 90 D4
Kings Langley *Herts* 20 D5
Kings Meaburn *Cumb* 64 A5
Kings Muir *Border* 79 F6
Kings Newnham *Warwks* 41 F1
Kings Ripton *Cambs* 33 E6
Kings Weston *Bristl* 28 D1
Kings Worthy *Hants* 9 G6
Kingsand *Cnwll* 5 E2
Kingsbarns *Fife* 93 H1
Kingsbridge *Devon* 5 G2
Kingsbridge *Somset* 16 B3
Kingsburgh *Highld* 104 C2
Kingsbury *Gt Lon* 21 E4
Kingsbury *Warwks* 40 D3
Kingsbury Episcopi *Somset* 17 F1
Kingsclere *Hants* 19 G3
Kingscote *Gloucs* 29 F2
Kingscott *Devon* 15 E3
Kingscross *N Ayrs* 75 H4
Kingsdon *Somset* 17 F2
Kingsdown *Kent* 13 H6
Kingsdown *Wilts* 18 A3
Kingsdown *Wilts* 18 D5
Kingseat *Fife* 86 B5
Kingsey *Bucks* 20 B5
Kingsfold *W Susx* 11 E5
Kingsford *Aber C* 95 G6
Kingsford *E Ayrs* 76 D6
Kingsgate *Kent* 23 H3
Kingshall Street *Suffk* 34 C5
Kingsheanton *Devon* 15 E4
Kingshouse Hotel *Stirlg* 91 G1
Kingskerswell *Devon* 6 A3
Kingskettle *Fife* 86 D6
Kingsland *Herefs* 39 E2
Kingsland *IOA* 54 B4
Kingsley *Ches* 49 E6
Kingsley *Hants* 10 B5
Kingsley *Staffs* 50 B2
Kingsley Green *W Susx* 10 C5
Kingsley Park *Nhants* 31 H6
Kingsmuir *Angus* 93 G4
Kingsmuir *Fife* 87 E6
Kingsnorth *Kent* 13 E5
Kingsteignton *Devon* 6 A3
Kingsthorne *Herefs* 28 C5
Kingsthorpe *Nhants* 31 H6
Kingston *Cambs* 33 E4
Kingston *Cnwll* 4 D4
Kingston *Devon* 5 F2
Kingston *Dorset* 7 H6
Kingston *Dorset* 8 C2
Kingston *E Loth* 87 E4
Kingston *IOW* 9 G2
Kingston *Kent* 23 F1
Kingston Bagpuize *Oxon* 19 F6
Kingston Blount *Oxon* 20 A5
Kingston Deverill *Wilts* 18 B1
Kingston Lisle *Oxon* 19 E5
Kingston near Lewes *E Susx* 11 G3
Kingston on Soar *Notts* 41 F6
Kingston on Spey *Moray* 101 F5
Kingston Russell *Dorset* 7 G4
Kingston Seymour *Somset* 17 E5
Kingston St Mary *Somset* 16 D2
Kingston upon Thames *Gt Lon* 21 E2
Kingstone *Herefs* 28 C6
Kingstone *Somset* 17 E1
Kingstone *Staffs* 40 B6
Kingswear *Devon* 6 A1

Kingswells *Aber C* 95 G6
Kingswinford *W Mids* 40 A2
Kingswood *Bucks* 31 G2
Kingswood *Gloucs* 17 G6
Kingswood *Gloucs* 29 E2
Kingswood *Somset* 16 C3
Kingswood *Surrey* 21 E1
Kingswood *Warwks* 40 C1
Kingswood Common *Staffs* 39 H6
Kingthorpe *Lincs* 52 D3
Kington *Gloucs* 28 D2
Kington *Herefs* 38 C2
Kington *Worcs* 30 B5
Kington Langley *Wilts* 18 B4
Kington Magna *Dorset* 8 A5
Kington St Michael *Wilts* 18 B4
Kingussie *Highld* 99 F3
Kingweston *Somset* 17 F2
Kinharrachie *Abers* 103 E3
Kinharvie *D & G* 70 C5
Kinkell Bridge *P & K* 92 B1
Kinknockie *Abers* 103 F3
Kinleith *C Edin* 86 C3
Kinlet *Shrops* 39 G4
Kinloch *Highld* 108 D3
Kinloch *Highld* 109 E4
Kinloch *Highld* 96 C2
Kinloch *P & K* 92 D4
Kinloch *P & K* 93 E4
Kinloch Hourn *Highld* 97 G3
Kinloch Rannoch *P & K* 91 G4
Kinlochard *Stirlg* 84 D5
Kinlochbervie *Highld* 108 C5
Kinlocheil *Highld* 90 B6
Kinlochewe *Highld* 105 H2
Kinlochlaggan *Highld* 98 D2
Kinlochleven *Highld* 90 D5
Kinlochmoidart *Highld* 89 G6
Kinlochnanuagh *Highld* 97 E1
Kinloss *Moray* 100 D5
Kinmel Bay *Conwy* 55 G4
Kinmuck *Abers* 102 D2
Kinmundy *Abers* 103 E2
Kinnabus *Ag & B* 74 B5
Kinnadie *Abers* 103 E4
Kinnaird *P & K* 92 C5
Kinnaird Castle *Angus* 93 H5
Kinneddar *Moray* 101 E6
Kinneff *Abers* 95 G4
Kinnelhead *D & G* 78 D3
Kinnell *Angus* 93 H4
Kinnerley *Shrops* 48 D2
Kinnersley *Herefs* 38 D1
Kinnersley *Worcs* 39 H1
Kinnerton *Powys* 38 C2
Kinnesswood *P & K* 86 C6
Kinninvie *Dur* 65 E5
Kinnordy *Angus* 93 F4
Kinoulton *Notts* 41 G6
Kinross *P & K* 86 B6
Kinrossie *P & K* 92 D3
Kinsham *Herefs* 38 D3
Kinsham *Worcs* 29 G6
Kinsley *W York* 59 E2
Kinson *Dorset* 8 C3
Kintbury *Berks* 19 F3
Kintessack *Moray* 100 C5
Kintillo *P & K* 92 D1
Kinton *Herefs* 38 D3
Kinton *Shrops* 48 D2
Kintore *Abers* 102 D1
Kintour *Ag & B* 74 C5
Kintra *Ag & B* 88 D2
Kintraw *Ag & B* 83 F5
Kinveachy *Highld* 99 G4
Kinver *Staffs* 39 H4
Kippax *W York* 59 E3
Kippen *Stirlg* 85 F5
Kippford or Scaur *D & G* 70 B4
Kipping's Cross *Kent* 12 B5
Kirbister *Ork* 111 h2
Kirburd *Border* 86 B1
Kirby Bedon *Norfk* 45 F3
Kirby Bellars *Leics* 41 H5
Kirby Cane *Norfk* 45 G2
Kirby Cross *Essex* 35 E1
Kirby Fields *Leics* 41 F4
Kirby Grindalythe *N York* 60 C6
Kirby Hill *N York* 65 E4
Kirby Hill *N York* 59 E6
Kirby Knowle *N York* 66 B2
Kirby le Soken *Essex* 35 E1
Kirby Misperton *N York* 66 D2
Kirby Muxloe *Leics* 41 F4
Kirby Row *Norfk* 45 G2
Kirby Sigston *N York* 65 G3
Kirby Underdale *E R Yk* 60 B5
Kirby Wiske *N York* 65 G2
Kirconnel *D & G* 70 C6
Kirdford *W Susx* 10 D4
Kirk *Highld* 110 C5
Kirk Bramwith *S York* 59 G2
Kirk Deighton *N York* 59 E5
Kirk Ella *E R Yk* 60 D3
Kirk Hallam *Derbys* 51 F1
Kirk Hammerton *N York* 59 F5
Kirk Ireton *Derbys* 50 D2
Kirk Langley *Derbys* 50 D1
Kirk Merrington *Dur* 65 F6
Kirk Michael *IOM* 116 b4
Kirk of Shotts *N Lans* 85 G2
Kirk Sandall *S York* 59 G1
Kirk Smeaton *N York* 59 F2
Kirk Yetholm *Border* 80 D3
Kirkabister *Shet* 111 l2
Kirkandrews *D & G* 69 G2
Kirkandrews upon Eden *Cumb* 71 F5
Kirkbampton *Cumb* 71 F5
Kirkbean *D & G* 70 C5
Kirkbride *Cumb* 71 E5
Kirkbuddo *Angus* 93 G3
Kirkburn *Border* 79 F6
Kirkburn *E R Yk* 60 D5
Kirkburton *W York* 58 D2
Kirkby *Lincs* 52 C4
Kirkby *Mersyd* 56 D3
Kirkby *N York* 66 B4
Kirkby Fleetham *N York* 65 F3
Kirkby Green *Lincs* 52 C1
Kirkby in Ashfield *Notts* 51 F2
Kirkby la Thorpe *Lincs* 42 C6
Kirkby Lonsdale *Cumb* 63 F4
Kirkby Malham *N York* 58 A5
Kirkby Mallory *Leics* 41 F3

Kirkby Malzeard *N York* 65 F1
Kirkby on Bain *Lincs* 53 E2
Kirkby Overblow *N York* 59 E5
Kirkby Stephen *Cumb* 64 C4
Kirkby Thore *Cumb* 64 A5
Kirkby Underwood *Lincs* 42 C4
Kirkby Wharf *N York* 59 F4
Kirkby-in-Furness *Cumb* 62 C4
Kirkbymoorside *N York* 66 C2
Kirkcaldy *Fife* 86 C5
Kirkcambeck *Cumb* 71 H6
Kirkchrist *D & G* 69 G3
Kirkcolm *D & G* 68 B4
Kirkconnel *D & G* 77 F3
Kirkconnell *D & G* 69 G3
Kirkcowan *D & G* 69 E3
Kirkcudbright *D & G* 69 G3
Kirkdale *Mersyd* 56 D2
Kirkfieldbank *S Lans* 77 G5
Kirkgunzeon *D & G* 70 C5
Kirkham *Lancs* 56 D5
Kirkham *N York* 60 B6
Kirkhamgate *W York* 58 D2
Kirkharle *Nthumb* 72 D5
Kirkhaugh *Nthumb* 72 B2
Kirkheaton *Nthumb* 72 D4
Kirkheaton *W York* 58 C2
Kirkhill *Highld* 107 E1
Kirkhope *S Lans* 78 C3
Kirkibost *Highld* 96 D4
Kirkinch *P & K* 93 E4
Kirkinner *D & G* 69 E3
Kirkintilloch *E Duns* 85 F3
Kirkland *Cumb* 70 D1
Kirkland *D & G* 77 F3
Kirkland *D & G* 78 B2
Kirkland *D & G* 78 D2
Kirkleatham *N York* 66 C5
Kirklevington *N York* 66 A4
Kirkley *Suffk* 45 H2
Kirklington *N York* 65 G2
Kirklington *Notts* 51 G3
Kirklinton *Cumb* 71 G5
Kirkliston *C Edin* 86 B3
Kirkmabreck *D & G* 69 F3
Kirkmaiden *D & G* 68 C2
Kirkmichael *P & K* 92 C3
Kirkmichael *S Ayrs* 76 C2
Kirkmuirhill *S Lans* 77 G5
Kirknewton *Nthumb* 81 E3
Kirknewton *W Loth* 86 B3
Kirkney *Abers* 101 G3
Kirkoswald *Cumb* 71 H3
Kirkoswald *S Ayrs* 76 B2
Kirkpatrick *D & G* 78 C2
Kirkpatrick *IOM* 116 b3
Kirkpatrick Durham *D & G* 70 B6
Kirkpatrick-Fleming *D & G* 71 F6
Kirksanton *Cumb* 62 B4
Kirkstall *W York* 58 D3
Kirkstead *Lincs* 52 D2
Kirkstile *Abers* 102 B3
Kirkstile *D & G* 79 F2
Kirkstyle *Highld* 110 D6
Kirkthorpe *W York* 59 E2
Kirkton *Abers* 102 C2
Kirkton *Abers* 102 D4
Kirkton *D & G* 78 C1
Kirkton *Fife* 93 F2
Kirkton *Highld* 97 F5
Kirkton *Highld* 97 G6
Kirkton *P & K* 92 C1
Kirkton Manor *Border* 79 E6
Kirkton of Airlie *Angus* 93 E4
Kirkton of Auchterhouse *Angus* 93 F3
Kirkton of Barevan *Highld* 107 G1
Kirkton of Collace *P & K* 92 D3
Kirkton of Glenbuchat *Abers* 101 F1
Kirkton of Logie Buchan *Abers* 103 E3
Kirkton of Menmuir *Angus* 95 E3
Kirkton of Monikie *Angus* 93 G3
Kirkton of Rayne *Abers* 102 C3
Kirkton of Skene *Abers* 95 G6
Kirkton of Strathmartine *Angus* 93 F3
Kirkton of Tealing *Angus* 93 F3
Kirktown *Abers* 103 E5
Kirktown *Abers* 103 F4
Kirktown of Bourtie *Abers* 102 D2
Kirktown of Fetteresso *Abers* 95 G4
Kirktown of Mortlach *Moray* 101 F3
Kirktown of Slains *Abers* 103 F2
Kirkwall *Ork* 111 h2
Kirkwall Airport *Ork* 111 h2
Kirkwhelpington *Nthumb* 72 D5
Kirmington *Lincs* 61 E1
Kirmond le Mire *Lincs* 52 D4
Kirn *Ag & B* 84 B3
Kirriemuir *Angus* 93 F4
Kirstead Green *Norfk* 45 F2
Kirtlebridge *D & G* 71 E6
Kirtling *Cambs* 34 A4
Kirtling Green *Suffk* 34 A4
Kirtlington *Oxon* 31 F2
Kirtomy *Highld* 109 G5
Kirton *Abers* 102 B1
Kirton *Lincs* 43 E5
Kirton *Notts* 51 G3
Kirton *Suffk* 35 F3
Kirton in Lindsey *Lincs* 52 B3
Kirtonhill *W Duns* 84 D3
Kirwaugh *D & G* 69 E3
Kishorn *Highld* 97 F6
Kislingbury *Nhants* 31 G5
Kittisford *Somset* 16 C2
Kittybrewster *Aber C* 95 H6
Kivernoll *Herefs* 28 C5
Knaith *Lincs* 52 A4
Knap Corner *Dorset* 8 A5
Knaphill *Surrey* 20 C2
Knaplock *Somset* 15 G4
Knapp *Somset* 17 E2
Knapton *N York* 59 F5
Knapton *N York* 67 E1
Knapton *Norfk* 45 E5
Knapwell *Cambs* 33 E5
Knaresborough *N York* 59 E5
Knarsdale *Nthumb* 72 B2
Knaven *Abers* 103 E4
Knayton *N York* 66 A2
Knebworth *Herts* 33 E1
Knedlington *E R Yk* 60 B3
Kneesall *Notts* 51 G3
Kneesworth *Cambs* 33 E3
Kneeton *Notts* 51 G2

Knelston *Swans* 26 B2
Knenhall *Staffs* 50 A1
Knightcote *Warwks* 31 E5
Knightley *Staffs* 49 G2
Knighton *Dorset* 7 G6
Knighton *Leics* 41 G3
Knighton *Powys* 38 C3
Knighton *Somset* 16 D3
Knighton *Staffs* 49 G3
Knighton *Staffs* 49 G2
Knighton on Teme *Worcs* 39 F3
Knightwick *Worcs* 39 G2
Knill *Herefs* 38 C2
Knipton *Leics* 42 A5
Kniveton *Derbys* 50 D2
Knock *Cumb* 64 B5
Knock *Highld* 97 E3
Knock *Moray* 102 B4
Knock *W Isls* 111 d6
Knock Castle *N Ayrs* 84 B2
Knockally *Highld* 110 B2
Knockan *Highld* 106 B6
Knockando *Moray* 101 E3
Knockbain *Highld* 98 D6
Knockbain *Highld* 107 E2
Knockdee *Highld* 110 B5
Knockdown *Wilts* 18 B5
Knockeen *S Ayrs* 76 C1
Knockenkelly *N Ayrs* 75 H3
Knockentiber *E Ayrs* 76 D5
Knockholt *Kent* 21 G2
Knockholt Pound *Kent* 21 G2
Knockin *Shrops* 48 D2
Knockinlaw *E Ayrs* 76 D5
Knocknain *D & G* 68 B4
Knocksheen *D & G* 69 G5
Knockvennie Smithy *D & G* 70 B6
Knodishall *Suffk* 35 G5
Knole *Somset* 17 F2
Knolls Green *Ches* 57 G1
Knolton *Wrexhm* 48 D3
Knook *Wilts* 18 B1
Knossington *Leics* 42 A3
Knott End-on-Sea *Lancs* 62 D1
Knotting *Beds* 32 C5
Knotting Green *Beds* 32 C5
Knottingley *W York* 59 F2
Knotty Ash *Mersyd* 56 D2
Knotty Green *Bucks* 20 C3
Knowbury *Shrops* 39 F3
Knowe *D & G* 69 E4
Knowehead *D & G* 69 G6
Knoweside *S Ayrs* 76 C3
Knowl Hill *Berks* 20 B3
Knowle *Bristl* 17 G5
Knowle *Devon* 15 E4
Knowle *Devon* 15 G2
Knowle *Devon* 6 B6
Knowle *Devon* 6 C4
Knowle *Shrops* 39 F3
Knowle *Somset* 16 B3
Knowle *W Mids* 40 C1
Knowle Green *Lancs* 57 F6
Knowle St Giles *Somset* 7 E6
Knowlefield *Cumb* 71 G5
Knowsley *Mersyd* 56 D2
Knowsley Safari Park *Mersyd* 57 E2
Knowstone *Devon* 15 G3
Knox Bridge *Kent* 12 C6
Knucklas *Powys* 38 C3
Knuston *Nhants* 32 B5
Knutsford *Ches* 57 G1
Krumlin *W York* 58 B2
Kuggar *Cnwll* 2 D1
Kyle of Lochalsh *Highld* 97 E5
Kyleakin *Highld* 97 E5
Kylerhea *Highld* 97 F4
Kyles Scalpay *W Isls* 111 c5
Kylesku *Highld* 108 C3
Kylesmorar *Highld* 97 F2
Kylestrome *Highld* 108 C3
Kynnersley *Shrops* 49 F1
Kyrewood *Worcs* 39 F3

L

L'Ancresse *Guern* 6 c2
L'Eree *Guern* 6 a1
L'Etacq *Jersey* 7 a2
La Bellieuse *Guern* 6 b1
La Fontenelle *Guern* 6 c1
La Fosse *Guern* 6 b1
La Greve *Guern* 6 c2
La Greve de Lecq *Jersey* 7 a2
La Hougue Bie *Jersey* 7 c1
La Houguette *Guern* 6 b1
La Passee *Guern* 6 b2
La Pulente *Jersey* 7 a1
La Rocque *Jersey* 7 c1
La Rousaillerie *Guern* 6 b2
La Villette *Guern* 6 b1
Lacadal *W Isls* 111 d6
Lacasaigh *W Isls* 111 d6
Laceby *Lincs* 52 D5
Lacey Green *Bucks* 20 B5
Lach Dennis *Ches* 49 G6
Lackford *Suffk* 34 B5
Lackford Green *Suffk* 34 B5
Lacock *Wilts* 18 B3
Ladbroke *Warwks* 31 E5
Laddingford *Kent* 12 C6
Ladock *Cnwll* 3 E4
Lady Hall *Cumb* 62 C4
Lady Village *Ork* 111 j3
Ladybank *Fife* 86 D6
Ladygill *S Lans* 78 C5
Ladykirk *Border* 81 E4
Ladywood *W Mids* 40 B2
Ladywood *Worcs* 39 H2
Lag *D & G* 78 C2
Laga *Highld* 89 G5
Lagavulin *Ag & B* 74 C5
Lagg *N Ayrs* 75 G3
Laggan *Highld* 98 B2
Laggan *Highld* 99 E2
Laid *Highld* 108 D5
Laide *Highld* 105 G5
Laig *Highld* 96 C1
Laigh Clunch *E Ayrs* 76 D6
Laigh Fenwick *E Ayrs* 76 D5

Laigh Glenmuir *E Ayrs* 77 E3
Laighstonehall *S Lans* 85 F1
Laindon *Essex* 22 B4
Lairg *Highld* 107 D6
Laisterdyke *W York* 58 C3
Lake *Dorset* 8 C3
Lake *IOW* 9 G2
Lake *Wilts* 18 D1
Lakenheath *Suffk* 44 A1
Lakesend *Norfk* 43 G2
Laleston *Brdgnd* 27 E1
Lamancha *Border* 86 C2
Lamarsh *Essex* 34 C2
Lamas *Norfk* 45 F4
Lambden *Border* 80 D4
Lamberhurst *Kent* 12 B5
Lamberhurst Down *Kent* 12 B5
Lamberton *Border* 81 E5
Lambeth *Gt Lon* 21 F3
Lambfair Green *Suffk* 34 A4
Lambley *Notts* 51 G2
Lambley *Nthumb* 72 B3
Lambourn *Berks* 19 E4
Lambourne End *Essex* 21 G4
Lambs Green *W Susx* 11 E5
Lamellion *Cnwll* 4 C3
Lamerton *Devon* 5 E4
Lamesley *T & W* 73 F3
Lamington *S Lans* 78 C5
Lamlash *N Ayrs* 75 H4
Lamonby *Cumb* 71 G3
Lamorna *Cnwll* 2 B2
Lamorran *Cnwll* 3 E3
Lampeter *Cerdgn* 37 E2
Lampeter Velfrey *Pembks* 25 E4
Lamphey *Pembks* 24 D3
Lamplugh *Cumb* 70 D2
Lamport *Nhants* 41 H1
Lamyatt *Somset* 17 G3
Lanark *S Lans* 77 G5
Lancaster *Lancs* 63 E2
Lanchester *Dur* 73 F2
Lancing *W Susx* 11 E3
Land's End Airport *Cnwll* 2 A2
Land-hallow *Highld* 110 C3
Landbeach *Cambs* 33 F5
Landcross *Devon* 14 D3
Landerberry *Abers* 95 F6
Landford *Wilts* 9 E5
Landimore *Swans* 26 B2
Landkey *Devon* 15 E4
Landkey Town *Devon* 15 E4
Landore *Swans* 26 C2
Landrake *Cnwll* 4 D3
Landscove *Devon* 5 H4
Landulph *Cnwll* 5 E3
Lane *Cnwll* 3 E5
Lane End *Bucks* 20 B4
Lane End *Wilts* 18 A2
Lane End Waberthwaite *Cumb* 62 B5
Lane Ends *Derbys* 40 D6
Lane Head *Dur* 65 E4
Laneast *Cnwll* 4 C5
Laneham *Notts* 52 A3
Lanehead *Dur* 72 C1
Langaller *Somset* 16 D2
Langar *Notts* 41 H6
Langbank *Rens* 84 C3
Langbar *N York* 58 C5
Langcliffe *N York* 63 G3
Langdale End *N York* 67 E3
Langdown *Hants* 9 F4
Langdyke *Fife* 86 D6
Langenhoe *Essex* 34 D1
Langford *Beds* 32 D3
Langford *Devon* 6 B5
Langford *Essex* 22 D6
Langford *Notts* 52 A2
Langford *Oxon* 30 D1
Langford Budville *Somset* 16 C2
Langford End *Beds* 32 D4
Langham *Essex* 34 D2
Langham *Norfk* 44 D6
Langham *Rutlnd* 42 A3
Langham *Suffk* 34 C5
Langho *Lancs* 57 G5
Langholm *D & G* 79 F1
Langlee *Border* 80 B3
Langley *Berks* 20 D3
Langley *Hants* 9 F3
Langley *Herts* 32 D1
Langley *Kent* 22 C1
Langley *Nthumb* 72 C3
Langley *Somset* 16 C2
Langley *W Susx* 10 B5
Langley *Warwks* 30 C6
Langley Burrell *Wilts* 18 B4
Langley Green *Essex* 34 C1
Langley Marsh *Somset* 16 C2
Langley Park *Dur* 73 F1
Langley Street *Norfk* 45 G2
Langley Upper Green *Essex* 33 F2
Langney *E Susx* 12 B2
Langold *Notts* 51 G5
Langore *Cnwll* 4 D5
Langport *Somset* 17 E2
Langrick *Lincs* 43 E6
Langridge *Somset* 17 H5
Langrigg *Cumb* 71 E4
Langrish *Hants* 10 A4
Langsett *S York* 50 D6
Langside *P & K* 92 A1
Langthorne *N York* 65 F3
Langthorpe *N York* 59 E6
Langthwaite *N York* 64 D3
Langtoft *E R Yk* 60 D6
Langtoft *Lincs* 42 D3
Langton *Dur* 65 F5
Langton *Lincs* 52 D2
Langton *Lincs* 53 F2
Langton *N York* 60 B6
Langton by Wragby *Lincs* 52 D3
Langton Green *Kent* 12 A5
Langton Herring *Dorset* 7 G4
Langton Matravers *Dorset* 8 C2
Langtree *Devon* 14 D3
Langwathby *Cumb* 71 H3
Langwell House *Highld* 110 B2
Langworth *Lincs* 52 C3
Lanhydrock House & Gardens *Cnwll* 3 F5
Lanivet *Cnwll* 3 F5
Lank *Cnwll* 3 G6
Lanlivery *Cnwll* 3 G5

177

Lanner Cnwll ... 2 D3
Lanreath Cnwll ... 4 C3
Lansallos Cnwll ... 4 C2
Lanteglos Cnwll ... 4 B5
Lanteglos Highway Cnwll ... 4 C2
Lanton Border ... 80 C2
Lanton Nthumb ... 81 E3
Lapford Devon ... 15 F2
Laphroaig Ag & B ... 74 C5
Lapley Staffs ... 49 H1
Lapworth Warwks ... 40 C1
Larachbeg Highld ... 89 G4
Larbert Falk ... 85 G4
Largie Abers ... 102 B3
Largiemore Ag & B ... 83 G4
Largoward Fife ... 87 E6
Largs N Ayrs ... 84 B2
Largybeg N Ayrs ... 75 H3
Largymore N Ayrs ... 75 H3
Larkfield Inver ... 84 B3
Larkfield Kent ... 22 C2
Larkhall S Lans ... 77 F6
Larkhill Wilts ... 18 D1
Larling Norfk ... 44 D1
Lartington Dur ... 64 D5
Lasham Hants ... 10 A6
Lask Edge Staffs ... 50 A2
Lassodie Fife ... 86 B5
Lasswade Mdloth ... 86 D3
Lastingham N York ... 66 D2
Latchingdon Essex ... 22 D5
Latchley Cnwll ... 5 E4
Latebrook Staffs ... 49 H4
Lathbury Bucks ... 32 B3
Latheron Highld ... 110 C3
Latheronwheel Highld ... 110 C3
Lathones Fife ... 87 E6
Latimer Bucks ... 20 D5
Latteridge Gloucs ... 29 E2
Lattiford Somset ... 17 H2
Latton Wilts ... 18 D6
Lauder Border ... 80 B4
Laugharne Carmth ... 25 F4
Laughterton Lincs ... 52 A3
Laughton E Susx ... 11 G3
Laughton Leics ... 41 G2
Laughton Lincs ... 52 A5
Laughton Lincs ... 42 C5
Laughton-en-le-Morthen S York ... 51 F5
Launcells Cnwll ... 14 C2
Launceston Cnwll ... 4 D5
Launton Oxon ... 31 G2
Laurencekirk Abers ... 95 F3
Laurieston D & G ... 69 G4
Laurieston Falk ... 85 H3
Lavendon Bucks ... 32 B4
Lavenham Suffk ... 34 C3
Lavernock V Glam ... 16 D5
Laversdale Cumb ... 71 G5
Laverstock Wilts ... 8 D6
Laverstoke Hants ... 19 G2
Laverton Gloucs ... 30 C3
Laverton N York ... 65 F1
Laverton Somset ... 18 A2
Lavister Wrexhm ... 48 D5
Law S Lans ... 85 G1
Law Hill S Lans ... 85 G1
Lawers P & K ... 91 H3
Lawford Essex ... 34 D2
Lawford Somset ... 16 C3
Lawgrove P & K ... 92 D2
Lawhitton Cnwll ... 4 D5
Lawkland N York ... 63 G3
Lawrenny Pembks ... 24 D3
Lawshall Suffk ... 34 C4
Laxay W Isls ... 111 d6
Laxdale W Isls ... 111 d6
Laxey IOM ... 116 c4
Laxfield Suffk ... 35 F5
Laxford Bridge Highld ... 108 C4
Laxo Shet ... 111 I3
Laxton E R Yk ... 60 B3
Laxton Nhants ... 42 B2
Laxton Notts ... 51 H3
Laycock W York ... 58 B4
Layer Breton Essex ... 34 C1
Layer Marney Essex ... 34 C1
Layer-de-la-Haye Essex ... 34 C1
Layham Suffk ... 34 D3
Laymore Dorset ... 7 E3
Laytham E R Yk ... 60 B4
Laythes Cumb ... 71 E5
Lazonby Cumb ... 71 H3
Le Bigard Guern ... 6 b1
Le Bourg Guern ... 6 b1
Le Bourg Jersey ... 7 c1
Le Gron Guern ... 6 b1
Le Haguais Jersey ... 7 c1
Le Hocq Jersey ... 7 c1
Le Villocq Guern ... 6 b2
Lea Derbys ... 51 E3
Lea Herefs ... 28 D5
Lea Lincs ... 52 A4
Lea Shrops ... 38 D5
Lea Wilts ... 18 C5
Lea Marston Warwks ... 40 D3
Leachkin Highld ... 107 E1
Leadburn Mdloth ... 86 C2
Leaden Roding Essex ... 22 B6
Leadenham Lincs ... 52 B1
Leadgate Dur ... 73 E2
Leadhills S Lans ... 78 C4
Leafield Oxon ... 30 D2
Leagrave Beds ... 32 C1
Leake Common Side Lincs ... 53 F1
Lealholm N York ... 66 D4
Lealt Highld ... 104 D2
Leamington Hastings Warwks ... 31 E6
Leamington Spa Warwks ... 30 D6
Leasgill Cumb ... 63 E4
Leasingham Lincs ... 42 C6
Leasingthorne Dur ... 65 F6
Leatherhead Surrey ... 21 E1
Leathley N York ... 58 C5
Leaton Shrops ... 49 E2
Leaveland Kent ... 23 E1
Leavenheath Suffk ... 34 C3
Leavening N York ... 60 B6
Leaves Green Gt Lon ... 21 G2
Lebberston N York ... 67 F2
Lechlade Gloucs ... 18 D6
Lecht Gruinart Ag & B ... 82 B3
Leck Lancs ... 63 F4
Leckbuie P & K ... 91 H3

Leckford Hants ... 19 F1
Leckhampstead Berks ... 19 F4
Leckhampstead Bucks ... 31 H4
Leckhampstead Thicket Berks ... 19 F4
Leckhampton Gloucs ... 29 G4
Leckmelm Highld ... 106 B5
Leconfield E R Yk ... 60 D4
Ledaig Ag & B ... 90 B3
Ledburn Bucks ... 32 B1
Ledbury Herefs ... 29 E6
Ledgemoor Herefs ... 38 D1
Ledmore Junction Highld ... 108 C1
Ledsham W York ... 59 F3
Ledston W York ... 59 E3
Ledwell Oxon ... 31 E3
Lee Devon ... 14 D5
Lee Gt Lon ... 21 F3
Lee Brockhurst Shrops ... 49 E2
Lee Chapel Essex ... 22 C4
Lee Clump Bucks ... 20 C5
Lee Mill Devon ... 5 F3
Lee-on-the-Solent Hants ... 9 G3
Leebotwood Shrops ... 39 E5
Leece Cumb ... 62 C3
Leeds Kent ... 22 D1
Leeds W York ... 58 D3
Leeds Bradford Airport W York ... 58 D4
Leeds Castle Kent ... 22 D1
Leedstown Cnwll ... 2 C3
Leek Staffs ... 50 B2
Leek Wootton Warwks ... 30 D6
Leeming N York ... 65 G2
Leeming Bar N York ... 65 F2
Lees Derbys ... 50 D1
Lees Gt Man ... 58 B1
Lees Green Derbys ... 50 D1
Leesthorpe Leics ... 42 A3
Leeswood Flints ... 48 C5
Leetown P & K ... 93 E2
Leftwich Ches ... 49 F6
Legbourne Lincs ... 53 F4
Legburn Lincs ... 53 F4
Legerwood Border ... 80 B4
Legoland Berks ... 20 C3
Legsby Lincs ... 52 D4
Leicester Leics ... 41 G4
Leicester Forest East Leics ... 41 F4
Leigh Dorset ... 7 G6
Leigh Gloucs ... 29 F5
Leigh Gt Man ... 57 F3
Leigh Kent ... 12 A6
Leigh Surrey ... 11 E6
Leigh Wilts ... 18 C5
Leigh Worcs ... 39 G2
Leigh Beck Essex ... 22 C4
Leigh Delamere Wilts ... 18 B4
Leigh Green Kent ... 12 D5
Leigh Knoweglass S Lans ... 77 E6
Leigh Park Dorset ... 8 C3
Leigh Sinton Worcs ... 39 G1
Leigh upon Mendip Somset ... 17 H4
Leigh Woods Somset ... 17 G6
Leigh-on-Sea Essex ... 22 D4
Leighterton Gloucs ... 29 F2
Leighton Powys ... 38 C6
Leighton Shrops ... 39 F6
Leighton Bromswold Cambs ... 32 D6
Leighton Buzzard Beds ... 32 B2
Leinthall Earls Herefs ... 39 E3
Leinthall Starkes Herefs ... 38 D3
Leintwardine Herefs ... 38 D3
Leire Leics ... 41 F2
Leiston Suffk ... 35 G5
Leitfie P & K ... 93 E4
Leith C Edin ... 86 C3
Leitholm Border ... 80 D4
Lelant Cnwll ... 2 C3
Lelley E R Yk ... 61 F3
Lem Hill Worcs ... 39 G3
Lempitlaw Border ... 80 D3
Lemreway W Isls ... 111 d5
Lemsford Herts ... 21 E6
Lenchwick Worcs ... 30 B4
Lendalfoot S Ayrs ... 68 C6
Lendrum Terrace Abers ... 103 F3
Lenham Kent ... 22 D1
Lenham Heath Kent ... 22 D1
Lenie Highld ... 98 D5
Lennel Border ... 80 D4
Lennox Plunton D & G ... 69 G3
Lennoxtown E Duns ... 85 E3
Lenton Lincs ... 42 C5
Lenwade Norfk ... 44 D4
Lenzie E Duns ... 85 E3
Leochel-Cushnie Abers ... 102 B1
Leominster Herefs ... 39 E2
Leonard Stanley Gloucs ... 29 F3
Leoville Jersey ... 7 a2
Lephin Highld ... 104 A1
Leppington N York ... 60 B6
Lepton W York ... 58 D2
Lerryn Cnwll ... 4 C3
Lerwick Shet ... 111 I2
Les Arquets Guern ... 6 b1
Les Hubits Guern ... 6 b1
Les Lohiers Guern ... 6 b1
Les Murchez Guern ... 6 b1
Les Nicolles Guern ... 6 b1
Les Quartiers Guern ... 6 b1
Les Quennevais Jersey ... 7 a1
Les Sages Guern ... 6 b1
Les Villets Guern ... 6 b1
Lesbury Nthumb ... 81 G2
Leslie Abers ... 102 B2
Leslie Fife ... 86 C6
Lesmahagow S Lans ... 78 B6
Lesnewth Cnwll ... 4 C5
Lessingham Norfk ... 45 G4
Lessonhall Cumb ... 71 E4
Leswalt D & G ... 68 B4
Letchmore Heath Herts ... 21 E5
Letchworth Herts ... 32 D2
Letcombe Bassett Oxon ... 19 F5
Letcombe Regis Oxon ... 19 F5
Letham Angus ... 93 G4
Letham Border ... 80 C1
Letham Falk ... 85 G4
Letham Fife ... 93 E1
Letham Grange Angus ... 93 H4
Lethendy P & K ... 92 D3
Lethenty Abers ... 102 B2
Lethenty Abers ... 102 D3
Letheringham Suffk ... 35 F4
Letheringsett Norfk ... 44 D5

Letterewe Highld ... 105 G3
Letterfearn Highld ... 97 F4
Letterfinlay Lodge Hotel Highld ... 98 B2
Lettermorar Highld ... 97 E2
Letters Highld ... 106 B4
Lettershaw S Lans ... 78 C4
Letterston Pembks ... 24 D5
Lettoch Highld ... 99 H4
Lettoch Highld ... 100 D3
Letton Herefs ... 38 D1
Letty Green Herts ... 21 F6
Letwell S York ... 51 F5
Leuchars Fife ... 93 F2
Leumrabhagh W Isls ... 111 d5
Leurbost W Isls ... 111 d6
Level's Green Essex ... 33 F1
Leven E R Yk ... 61 E4
Leven Fife ... 86 D5
Levens Cumb ... 63 E4
Levens Green Herts ... 33 E1
Levenshulme Gt Man ... 57 H2
Levenwick Shet ... 111 I1
Leverburgh W Isls ... 111 c4
Leverington Cambs ... 43 F3
Leverstock Green Herts ... 20 D5
Leverton Lincs ... 43 F6
Levington Suffk ... 35 E3
Levisham N York ... 67 E3
Lew Oxon ... 31 E1
Lewannick Cnwll ... 4 D5
Lewdown Devon ... 5 E5
Lewes E Susx ... 11 G3
Leweston Pembks ... 24 D5
Lewisham Gt Lon ... 21 F3
Lewiston Highld ... 98 D5
Lewknor Oxon ... 20 A5
Lewson Street Kent ... 23 E2
Lewtrenchard Devon ... 5 E5
Lexden Essex ... 34 C2
Lexworthy Somset ... 16 D3
Ley Hill Bucks ... 20 C5
Leybourne Kent ... 22 B2
Leyburn N York ... 65 E2
Leygreen Herts ... 32 D2
Leyland Lancs ... 57 E5
Leylodge Abers ... 102 D1
Leys Abers ... 103 E4
Leys Abers ... 93 E3
Leys of Cossans Angus ... 93 F4
Leysdown-on-Sea Kent ... 23 E3
Leysmill Angus ... 93 H4
Leysters Herefs ... 39 E3
Leyton Gt Lon ... 21 F4
Leytonstone Gt Lon ... 21 G4
Lezant Cnwll ... 4 D5
Lezayre IOM ... 116 c4
Lhanbryde Moray ... 101 F3
Libanus Powys ... 27 F5
Libberton S Lans ... 78 D6
Liberton C Edin ... 86 C3
Lichfield Staffs ... 40 C4
Lickey Worcs ... 40 B1
Lickey End Worcs ... 40 B1
Lickfold W Susx ... 10 C4
Liddesdale Highld ... 89 H5
Liddington Wilts ... 18 D4
Lidgate Suffk ... 34 B4
Lidlington Beds ... 32 C3
Liff Angus ... 93 F3
Lifford W Mids ... 40 B2
Lifton Devon ... 5 E5
Liftondown Devon ... 4 D5
Lighthorne Warwks ... 31 E5
Lighthorne Heath Warwks ... 31 E5
Lightwater Surrey ... 20 C2
Lilbourne Nhants ... 41 F1
Lilleshall Shrops ... 49 G1
Lilley Herts ... 32 D2
Lilliesleaf Border ... 80 B3
Lillingstone Dayrell Bucks ... 31 G4
Lillingstone Lovell Bucks ... 31 G4
Lillington Dorset ... 7 G6
Lilliput Dorset ... 8 C2
Lilstock Somset ... 16 C3
Limbury Beds ... 32 C1
Lime Street Worcs ... 29 F5
Limekilnburn S Lans ... 77 F6
Limekilns Fife ... 86 B4
Limerigg Falk ... 85 G3
Limerstone IOW ... 9 F2
Limington Somset ... 17 F2
Limmerhaugh E Ayrs ... 77 K4
Limpley Stoke Wilts ... 18 A3
Limpsfield Surrey ... 21 G1
Limpsfield Chart Surrey ... 21 G1
Linby Notts ... 51 F2
Linchmere W Susx ... 10 B5
Lincludem D & G ... 78 C1
Lincoln Lincs ... 52 B3
Lincomb Worcs ... 39 G3
Lindal in Furness Cumb ... 62 C3
Lindale Cumb ... 62 D4
Lindfield W Susx ... 11 F4
Lindford Hants ... 10 B5
Lindley W York ... 58 C2
Lindley Green N York ... 58 C5
Lindridge Worcs ... 39 F3
Lindsell Essex ... 33 H2
Lindsey Suffk ... 34 D3
Lindsey Tye Suffk ... 34 D3
Lingdale N York ... 66 C5
Lingen Herefs ... 38 D3
Lingfield Surrey ... 11 F6
Lingwood Norfk ... 45 F3
Linicro Highld ... 104 C3
Linkend Worcs ... 29 F5
Linkenholt Hants ... 19 F3
Linkinhorne Cnwll ... 4 D4
Linktown Fife ... 86 C5
Linkwood Moray ... 101 F3
Linley Shrops ... 38 D5
Linley Green Herefs ... 39 F2
Linleygreen Shrops ... 39 F5
Linlithgow W Loth ... 86 A4
Linsidemore Highld ... 107 E5
Linslade Beds ... 32 B2
Linstead Parva Suffk ... 35 F6
Linstock Cumb ... 71 G5
Linthurst Worcs ... 40 B1
Linthwaite W York ... 58 C2
Lintlaw Border ... 87 H2
Lintmill Moray ... 101 G5

Linton Border ... 80 D3
Linton Cambs ... 33 G3
Linton Derbys ... 40 D5
Linton Herefs ... 28 D5
Linton Kent ... 22 C1
Linton N York ... 58 B6
Linton W York ... 59 E4
Linton Hill Gloucs ... 29 E5
Linton-on-Ouse N York ... 59 F5
Linwood Lincs ... 52 D4
Linwood Rens ... 84 D2
Lionacleit W Isls ... 111 b3
Lional W Isls ... 111 e7
Liphook Hants ... 10 B5
Liscard Mersyd ... 56 C2
Liscombe Somset ... 15 G4
Liskeard Cnwll ... 4 C3
Liss Hants ... 10 B4
Lissett E R Yk ... 61 E5
Lissington Lincs ... 52 D4
Lisvane Cardif ... 27 G1
Liswerry Newpt ... 28 B2
Litcham Norfk ... 44 C4
Litchborough Nhants ... 31 G5
Litchfield Hants ... 19 F2
Litherland Mersyd ... 56 D3
Litlington Cambs ... 33 E3
Litlington E Susx ... 11 H2
Little Abington Cambs ... 33 G3
Little Addington Nhants ... 32 B5
Little Airies D & G ... 69 E2
Little Alne Warwks ... 30 C6
Little Altcar Mersyd ... 56 C3
Little Amwell Herts ... 21 F6
Little Asby Cumb ... 63 F6
Little Aston Staffs ... 40 C3
Little Ayton N York ... 66 B4
Little Baddow Essex ... 22 C6
Little Badminton Gloucs ... 18 A5
Little Bampton Cumb ... 71 F4
Little Bardfield Essex ... 33 H2
Little Barford Beds ... 32 D4
Little Barningham Norfk ... 45 E5
Little Barrington Gloucs ... 30 D2
Little Barrow Ches ... 49 E6
Little Bavington Nthumb ... 72 D4
Little Bedwyn Wilts ... 19 E3
Little Bentley Essex ... 35 E2
Little Berkhamsted Herts ... 21 F6
Little Billing Nhants ... 32 A5
Little Billington Beds ... 32 B1
Little Birch Herefs ... 28 D5
Little Blakenham Suffk ... 34 D3
Little Blencow Cumb ... 71 G3
Little Bognor W Susx ... 10 D4
Little Bolehill Derbys ... 50 D2
Little Bookham Surrey ... 20 D1
Little Bourton Oxon ... 31 F4
Little Bradley Suffk ... 34 A4
Little Braxted Essex ... 22 D6
Little Brechin Angus ... 95 E2
Little Brickhill Bucks ... 32 B2
Little Brington Nhants ... 31 G6
Little Bromley Essex ... 34 D2
Little Budworth Ches ... 49 F5
Little Burstead Essex ... 22 B4
Little Bytham Lincs ... 42 C4
Little Carlton Lincs ... 53 F4
Little Casterton Rutlnd ... 42 C3
Little Cawthorpe Lincs ... 53 E4
Little Chalfont Bucks ... 20 C5
Little Chart Kent ... 12 D6
Little Chesterford Essex ... 33 G3
Little Cheverell Wilts ... 18 C2
Little Chishill Cambs ... 33 F3
Little Clacton Essex ... 35 E1
Little Clifton Cumb ... 70 D2
Little Comberton Worcs ... 30 B4
Little Common E Susx ... 12 C3
Little Compton Warwks ... 30 D3
Little Cornard Suffk ... 34 C3
Little Cowarne Herefs ... 39 F1
Little Coxwell Oxon ... 19 E5
Little Crakehall N York ... 65 F2
Little Cressingham Norfk ... 44 C2
Little Crosby Mersyd ... 56 D3
Little Cubley Derbys ... 50 C1
Little Dalby Leics ... 41 H4
Little Dens Abers ... 103 F4
Little Dewchurch Herefs ... 28 C5
Little Ditton Cambs ... 33 H4
Little Downham Cambs ... 43 G1
Little Driffield E R Yk ... 60 D5
Little Dunham Norfk ... 44 C4
Little Dunkeld P & K ... 92 C3
Little Dunmow Essex ... 33 H1
Little Durnford Wilts ... 8 D6
Little Easton Essex ... 33 G1
Little Eaton Derbys ... 51 E1
Little Ellingham Norfk ... 44 D2
Little Everdon Nhants ... 31 G5
Little Eversden Cambs ... 33 F4
Little Faringdon Oxon ... 19 E6
Little Fencote N York ... 65 F3
Little Fenton N York ... 59 F3
Little Fransham Norfk ... 44 C3
Little Gaddesden Herts ... 20 C6
Little Glemham Suffk ... 35 F4
Little Gorsley Herefs ... 29 E5
Little Gransden Cambs ... 33 E4
Little Green Somset ... 17 H4
Little Grimsby Lincs ... 53 E4
Little Hadham Herts ... 33 F1
Little Hale Lincs ... 42 D6
Little Hallam Derbys ... 51 F1
Little Hallingbury Essex ... 33 G1
Little Harrowden Nhants ... 32 A5
Little Haseley Oxon ... 19 H6
Little Haven Pembks ... 24 C4
Little Hay Staffs ... 40 C3
Little Haywood Staffs ... 40 B5
Little Heath W Mids ... 41 E1
Little Hereford Herefs ... 39 E3
Little Horkesley Essex ... 34 C2
Little Hormead Herts ... 33 F2
Little Horsted E Susx ... 11 G4
Little Horton W York ... 58 C3
Little Horwood Bucks ... 32 A2
Little Houghton Nhants ... 32 A4
Little Houghton S York ... 59 E1
Little Hucklow Derbys ... 50 C4
Little Hutton N York ... 66 B1

Little Irchester Nhants ... 32 B5
Little Keyford Somset ... 18 A2
Little Kimble Bucks ... 20 B5
Little Kineton Warwks ... 31 E5
Little Kingshill Bucks ... 20 C5
Little Knox D & G ... 70 B5
Little Langdale Cumb ... 62 D6
Little Langford Wilts ... 18 C1
Little Lashbrook Devon ... 14 D2
Little Leigh Ches ... 49 F6
Little Leighs Essex ... 34 B1
Little Lever Gt Man ... 57 G3
Little Linford Bucks ... 32 A3
Little Load Somset ... 17 F2
Little London E Susx ... 12 A4
Little London Essex ... 33 F2
Little London Hants ... 19 F2
Little London Hants ... 19 H3
Little Longstone Derbys ... 50 C4
Little Malvern Worcs ... 29 E6
Little Maplestead Essex ... 34 B2
Little Marcle Herefs ... 29 E6
Little Marlow Bucks ... 20 C4
Little Massingham Norfk ... 44 B4
Little Melton Norfk ... 45 E3
Little Mill Mons ... 28 B3
Little Milton Oxon ... 19 H6
Little Missenden Bucks ... 20 C5
Little Musgrave Cumb ... 64 B4
Little Ness Shrops ... 48 D2
Little Newcastle Pembks ... 24 D5
Little Newsham Dur ... 65 E5
Little Norton Somset ... 17 F1
Little Oakley Essex ... 35 E2
Little Oakley Nhants ... 42 B1
Little Onn Staffs ... 49 H1
Little Orton Cumb ... 71 F4
Little Packington Warwks ... 40 D2
Little Paxton Cambs ... 32 D5
Little Petherick Cnwll ... 3 E6
Little Plumstead Norfk ... 45 F3
Little Ponton Lincs ... 42 B5
Little Preston Nhants ... 31 G5
Little Raveley Cambs ... 33 E6
Little Reedness E R Yk ... 60 B2
Little Ribston N York ... 59 E5
Little Rissington Gloucs ... 30 C2
Little Rollright Oxon ... 30 D3
Little Ryburgh Norfk ... 44 C4
Little Salkeld Cumb ... 71 H3
Little Sampford Essex ... 33 H2
Little Saughall Ches ... 48 D6
Little Saxham Suffk ... 34 B5
Little Scatwell Highld ... 106 C2
Little Sessay N York ... 66 B1
Little Shelford Cambs ... 33 F4
Little Silver Devon ... 15 G1
Little Singleton Lancs ... 56 D6
Little Skipwith N York ... 59 G4
Little Smeaton N York ... 59 F2
Little Snoring Norfk ... 44 C5
Little Sodbury Gloucs ... 18 A5
Little Somborne Hants ... 9 F4
Little Somerford Wilts ... 18 C5
Little Soudley Shrops ... 49 G2
Little Stainton Dur ... 65 G5
Little Stanney Ches ... 48 D6
Little Staughton Beds ... 32 C5
Little Steeping Lincs ... 53 F2
Little Stonham Suffk ... 35 E4
Little Stretton Leics ... 41 G3
Little Stretton Shrops ... 39 E5
Little Strickland Cumb ... 71 H2
Little Stukeley Cambs ... 32 D6
Little Sugnall Staffs ... 49 G3
Little Swinburne Nthumb ... 72 D4
Little Sypland D & G ... 70 A4
Little Tew Oxon ... 31 E3
Little Tey Essex ... 34 C1
Little Thetford Cambs ... 33 G6
Little Thorpe Dur ... 73 H1
Little Thurlow Green Suffk ... 34 A4
Little Thurrock Essex ... 22 B3
Little Torrington Devon ... 15 E3
Little Town Lancs ... 57 F6
Little Urswick Cumb ... 62 C3
Little Wakering Essex ... 22 D4
Little Walden Essex ... 33 G3
Little Waldingfield Suffk ... 34 C3
Little Walsingham Norfk ... 44 C5
Little Waltham Essex ... 22 C6
Little Washbourne Gloucs ... 29 G5
Little Weighton E R Yk ... 60 D3
Little Weldon Nhants ... 42 B1
Little Wenham Suffk ... 34 D3
Little Wenlock Shrops ... 39 F6
Little Weston Somset ... 17 G2
Little Whitefield IOW ... 9 G2
Little Wilbraham Cambs ... 33 G4
Little Witcombe Gloucs ... 29 F4
Little Witley Worcs ... 39 G3
Little Wittenham Oxon ... 19 G5
Little Wolford Warwks ... 30 D3
Little Woodcote Surrey ... 21 F2
Little Wratting Suffk ... 34 A3
Little Wymington Beds ... 32 B5
Little Wymondley Herts ... 32 D2
Little Wyrley Staffs ... 40 B4
Little Yeldham Essex ... 34 B3
Littleborough Gt Man ... 58 B2
Littleborough Notts ... 52 A4
Littlebourne Kent ... 23 G1
Littlebredy Dorset ... 7 G4
Littleburn Highld ... 107 E2
Littlebury Essex ... 33 G3
Littlebury Green Essex ... 33 G3
Littledean Gloucs ... 29 E4
Littleham Devon ... 14 D3
Littleham Devon ... 6 B4
Littlehampton W Susx ... 10 D2
Littlehaven W Susx ... 11 E5
Littlehempston Devon ... 5 H3
Littlemill Abers ... 94 C5
Littlemill Highld ... 100 C4
Littlemore Oxon ... 31 F1
Littleover Derbys ... 41 E6
Littleport Cambs ... 43 G1
Littlestone-on-Sea Kent ... 13 F4
Littlethorpe Leics ... 41 F3
Littlethorpe N York ... 59 E6
Littleton Angus ... 93 F4
Littleton Ches ... 48 D5
Littleton D & G ... 69 G3
Littleton Hants ... 9 F6

Littleton Somset 17 F2
Littleton Surrey 20 D2
Littleton Drew Wilts 18 B4
Littleton Pannell Wilts 18 C2
Littleton-on-Severn Gloucs 28 D2
Littletown Dur 73 G1
Littlewick Green Berks 20 B3
Littleworth Oxon 19 E6
Littleworth Staffs 40 B5
Littleworth Worcs 30 A5
Littley Green Essex 34 A1
Litton Derbys 50 C4
Litton N York 64 D1
Litton Somset 17 G4
Litton Cheney Dorset 7 F4
Liurbost W Isls 111 d6
Liverpool Mersyd 56 D2
Liverpool Airport Mersyd 56 D1
Liversedge W York 58 D2
Liverton Devon 5 H4
Liverton N York 66 D5
Livingston W Loth 86 B3
Livingston Village W Loth 86 B3
Lixton Devon 5 G2
Lixwm Flints 48 B6
Lizard Cnwll 2 D1
Llanaelhaearn Gwynd 46 C5
Llanafan Cerdgn 37 F4
Llanallgo IOA 54 D4
Llanarmon Dyffryn Ceiriog Wrexhm 48 B3
Llanarmon-yn-Ial Denbgs 48 C5
Llanarth Cerdgn 36 D3
Llanarth Mons 28 B4
Llanarthne Carmth 26 B4
Llanasa Flints 56 B1
Llanbadarn Fawr Cerdgn 37 E5
Llanbadarn Fynydd Powys 38 B4
Llanbadoc Mons 28 B3
Llanbeder Newpt 28 B2
Llanbedr Gwynd 47 E4
Llanbedr Powys 27 G4
Llanbedr-Dyffryn-Clwyd Denbgs 48 B5
Llanbedr-y-Cennin Conwy 55 F3
Llanbedrgoch IOA 54 D4
Llanbedrog Gwynd 46 C4
Llanberis Gwynd 54 D2
Llanbethery V Glam 16 B5
Llanbister Powys 38 B3
Llanblethian V Glam 16 B6
Llanboidy Carmth 25 F5
Llanbradach Caerph 27 G2
Llanbrynmair Powys 47 G2
Llancadle V Glam 16 B5
Llancarfan V Glam 16 C5
Llancloudy Herefs 28 C4
Llandaff Cardif 27 G1
Llandanwg Gwynd 47 E4
Llanddaniel fab IOA 54 D3
Llanddarog Carmth 26 B4
Llanddeiniol Cerdgn 37 E4
Llanddeiniolen Gwynd 54 D3
Llandderfel Gwynd 47 H5
Llanddeusant IOA 54 B4
Llanddew Powys 27 F5
Llanddewi Swans 26 A2
Llanddewi Brefi Cerdgn 37 F2
Llanddewi Rhydderch Mons 28 B4
Llanddewi Velfrey Pembks 25 E4
Llanddewi Ystradenni Powys 38 B3
Llanddoget Conwy 55 F3
Llanddona IOA 54 D4
Llanddowror Carmth 25 F4
Llanddulas Conwy 55 G4
Llanddwywe Gwynd 47 E4
Llanddyfnan IOA 54 D4
Llandefaelog-Trer-Graig Powys 27 G5
Llandefalle Powys 27 F6
Llandegfan IOA 54 D4
Llandegla Denbgs 48 C4
Llandegley Powys 38 B2
Llandegveth Mons 28 B2
Llandeilo Carmth 26 C5
Llandeilo Graban Powys 38 B1
Llandeloy Pembks 24 C5
Llandenny Mons 28 C3
Llandevaud Newpt 28 C2
Llandevenny Mons 28 C2
Llandinam Powys 38 A4
Llandissilio Pembks 25 E4
Llandogo Mons 28 C3
Llandough V Glam 16 B6
Llandough V Glam 16 C6
Llandovery Carmth 26 D6
Llandow V Glam 16 B6
Llandre Carmth 37 F1
Llandre Cerdgn 37 E5
Llandre Isaf Pembks 25 E5
Llandrillo Denbgs 48 A3
Llandrillo-yn-Rhos Conwy 55 F4
Llandrindod Wells Powys 38 B2
Llandrinio Powys 48 C1
Llandudno Conwy 55 F4
Llandudno Junction Conwy 55 F4
Llandwrog Gwynd 46 C5
Llandulas Powys 37 G1
Llandwrog Gwynd 54 C2
Llandybie Carmth 26 C4
Llandyfaelog Carmth 25 G4
Llandyfriog Cerdgn 36 C1
Llandygai Gwynd 54 D3
Llandygwydd Cerdgn 36 B1
Llandyrnog Denbgs 48 B5
Llandyssil Powys 38 C5
Llandysul Cerdgn 36 D1
Llanedeyrn Cardif 27 G1
Llaneglwys Powys 27 F6
Llanegryn Gwynd 47 E2
Llanegwad Carmth 26 B4
Llaneilian IOA 54 C5
Llanelian-yn-Rhos Conwy 55 F4
Llanelidan Denbgs 48 B4
Llanelieu Powys 27 G5
Llanellen Mons 28 B4
Llanelli Carmth 26 B3
Llanelltyd Gwynd 47 F3
Llanelwedd Powys 38 A2
Llanenddwyn Gwynd 47 E4
Llanengan Gwynd 46 C4
Llanerchymedd IOA 54 C4
Llanerfyl Powys 48 A1
Llanfachraeth IOA 54 B4
Llanfachreth Gwynd 47 F4
Llanfaelog IOA 54 B4

Llanfaelrhys Gwynd 46 B4
Llanfaethlu IOA 54 B5
Llanfair Gwynd 47 E4
Llanfair Caereinion Powys 38 B6
Llanfair Clydogau Cerdgn 37 F2
Llanfair Dyffryn Clwyd Denbgs 48 B5
Llanfair P G IOA 54 D3
Llanfair Talhaiarn Conwy 55 G3
Llanfair Waterdine Shrops 38 C4
Llanfair-is-gaer Gwynd 54 D3
Llanfair-y-Cwmwd IOA 54 C3
Llanfair-yn-Neubwll IOA 54 B4
Llanfairfechan Conwy 55 E4
Llanfairynghornwy IOA 54 B5
Llanfallteg Carmth 25 E4
Llanfallteg West Carmth 25 E4
Llanfarian Cerdgn 37 E4
Llanfechain Powys 48 C2
Llanfechell IOA 54 C5
Llanferres Denbgs 48 C5
Llanfihangel Glyn Myfyr Conwy 55 G2
Llanfihangel Nant Bran Powys 27 E6
Llanfihangel Rhydithon Powys 38 B2
Llanfihangel Rogiet Mons 28 C2
Llanfihangel yn Nhowyn IOA 54 B4
Llanfihangel-ar-Arth Carmth 36 D1
Llanfihangel-y-Creuddyn Cerdgn 37 F4
Llanfihangel-y-traethau Gwynd 47 E5
Llanfihangel-yng-Ngwynfa Powys 48 B1
Llanfilo Powys 27 G5
Llanfoist Mons 28 B4
Llanfor Gwynd 47 H5
Llanfrechfa Torfn 28 B2
Llanfrynach Powys 27 F5
Llanfwrog Denbgs 48 B5
Llanfwrog IOA 54 B4
Llanfyllin Powys 48 B2
Llanfynydd Carmth 26 B5
Llanfynydd Flints 48 C5
Llanfyrnach Pembks 25 F5
Llangadfan Powys 48 A1
Llangadog Carmth 26 C5
Llangadwaladr IOA 54 C3
Llangaffo IOA 54 C3
Llangammarch Wells Powys 37 H2
Llangan V Glam 27 E1
Llangarron Herefs 28 C4
Llangathen Carmth 26 B5
Llangattock Powys 27 G4
Llangattock Lingoed Mons 28 B4
Llangedwyn Powys 48 C2
Llangefni IOA 54 C4
Llangeinor Brdgnd 27 E2
Llangeinwen IOA 54 C3
Llangeitho Cerdgn 37 E3
Llangeler Carmth 36 C1
Llangelynin Gwynd 47 E2
Llangendeirne Carmth 26 A4
Llangennech Carmth 26 B3
Llangennith Swans 25 G2
Llangernyw Conwy 55 G3
Llangian Gwynd 46 C4
Llangloffan Pembks 24 C5
Llanglydwen Carmth 25 F5
Llangoed IOA 54 D4
Llangollen Denbgs 48 C3
Llangolman Pembks 25 E5
Llangors Powys 27 G5
Llangower Gwynd 47 G4
Llangranog Cerdgn 36 C2
Llangristiolus IOA 54 C4
Llangrove Herefs 28 C4
Llangunllo Powys 38 C3
Llangunnor Carmth 25 G4
Llangurig Powys 37 G4
Llangwm Conwy 47 H5
Llangwm Mons 28 C3
Llangwm Pembks 24 D4
Llangwm-isaf Mons 28 C3
Llangwnnadl Gwynd 46 B4
Llangwyryfon Cerdgn 37 E4
Llangybi Cerdgn 37 E2
Llangybi Gwynd 46 D5
Llangybi Mons 28 B2
Llangynhafal Denbgs 48 B5
Llangynidr Powys 27 G4
Llangynin Carmth 25 F4
Llangynog Carmth 25 G4
Llangynog Powys 48 A2
Llangynwyd Brdgnd 27 E2
Llanhamlach Powys 27 F5
Llanharan Rhondd 27 F1
Llanharry Rhondd 27 F1
Llanhennock Mons 28 B2
Llanhilleth Blae G 27 G3
Llanidloes Powys 37 H5
Llaniestyn Gwynd 46 C4
Llanigon Powys 27 G6
Llanilar Cerdgn 37 E4
Llanilid Rhondd 27 E1
Llanina Cerdgn 36 D3
Llanishen Cardif 27 G1
Llanishen Mons 28 C3
Llanllechid Gwynd 55 E3
Llanllowell Mons 28 B3
Llanllugan Powys 38 B6
Llanllwch Carmth 25 G4
Llanllwchaiarn Powys 38 B5
Llanllwni Carmth 36 D1
Llanllyfni Gwynd 54 C2
Llanmadoc Swans 25 H2
Llanmaes V Glam 16 B5
Llanmartin Newpt 28 B2
Llanmiloe Carmth 25 F3
Llanmorlais Swans 26 B2
Llannefydd Conwy 55 G3
Llannon Carmth 26 B3
Llannor Gwynd 46 D5
Llanon Cerdgn 36 D3
Llanover Mons 28 B3
Llanpumsaint Carmth 25 G5
Llanrhaeadr-ym-Mochnant Powys 48 B2
Llanrhian Pembks 24 C5
Llanrhidian Swans 26 B2
Llanrhychwyn Conwy 55 F3
Llanrhyddlad IOA 54 B5
Llanrhystud Cerdgn 37 E4
Llanrothal Herefs 28 C4
Llanrug Gwynd 54 D3
Llanrumney Cardif 27 G1
Llanrwst Conwy 55 F3
Llansadurnen Carmth 25 F4
Llansadwrn Carmth 26 C5
Llansadwrn IOA 54 D4

Llansaint Carmth 25 G3
Llansamlet Swans 26 C3
Llansanffraid Glan Conwy Conwy 55 F4
Llansannan Conwy 55 G3
Llansantffraed Powys 27 G5
Llansantffraed-Cwmdeuddwr Powys 37 H3
Llansantffraid-in-Elvel Powys 38 A2
Llansantffraid Cerdgn 36 D3
Llansantffraid-ym-Mechain Powys 48 C2
Llansawel Carmth 26 C6
Llansilin Powys 48 C2
Llansoy Mons 28 C3
Llanspyddid Powys 27 F5
Llanstadwell Pembks 24 C4
Llansteffan Carmth 25 G4
Llantarnam Torfn 28 B2
Llanteg Pembks 25 F4
Llanthewy Skirrid Mons 28 B4
Llanthony Mons 28 B5
Llantilio Pertholey Mons 28 B4
Llantilio-Crossenny Mons 28 B4
Llantrisant Mons 28 B2
Llantrisant Rhondd 27 F1
Llantrithyd V Glam 16 C6
Llantwit Fardre Rhondd 27 F1
Llantwit Major V Glam 16 B5
Llanuwchllyn Gwynd 47 G4
Llanvaches Newpt 28 C2
Llanvair Discoed Mons 28 C2
Llanvapley Mons 28 B4
Llanvetherine Mons 28 B4
Llanvihangel Crucorney Mons 28 B4
Llanwddyn Powys 48 A2
Llanwenog Cerdgn 36 D2
Llanwern Newpt 28 B2
Llanwinio Carmth 25 F5
Llanwnda Gwynd 54 C2
Llanwnda Pembks 24 D6
Llanwnnen Cerdgn 37 E2
Llanwnog Powys 38 A5
Llanwrda Carmth 26 C5
Llanwrin Powys 47 F2
Llanwrthwl Powys 37 H3
Llanwrtyd Wells Powys 37 G2
Llanwyddelan Powys 38 B6
Llanyblodwel Shrops 48 C2
Llanybri Carmth 25 G4
Llanybydder Carmth 36 D2
Llanycefn Pembks 25 E5
Llanychaer Bridge Pembks 24 D6
Llanymawddwy Gwynd 47 G3
Llanymynech Powys 48 C2
Llanynghenedl IOA 54 B4
Llanynys Denbgs 48 B5
Llanyre Powys 38 A2
Llanystumdwy Gwynd 46 D5
Llanywern Powys 27 F5
Llawhaden Pembks 25 E4
Llawryglyn Powys 37 H5
Llay Wrexhm 48 D5
Llechrhyd Caerph 27 F3
Llechryd Cerdgn 36 B1
Lledrod Cerdgn 37 E4
Llithfaen Gwynd 46 C5
Lloc Flints 56 B1
Llowes Powys 27 G6
Llwydcoed Rhondd 27 F3
Llwydiarth Powys 48 A1
Llwyncelyn Cerdgn 36 D3
Llwyndafydd Cerdgn 36 C2
Llwyngwril Gwynd 47 E2
Llwynmawr Wrexhm 48 C3
Llwynypia Rhondd 27 F2
Llynclys Shrops 48 C2
Llynfaes IOA 54 C4
Llys-y-fran Pembks 24 D5
Llysfaen Conwy 55 G4
Llyswen Powys 27 G6
Llysworney V Glam 16 B6
Llywel Powys 27 E5
Loan Falk 85 H3
Loanhead Mdloth 86 C3
Loaningfoot D & G 70 C5
Loans S Ayrs 76 C4
Lobhillcross Devon 5 E5
Loch Baghasdail W Isls 111 b6
Loch Euphoirt W Isls 111 b4
Loch Katrine Pier Stirlg 84 D6
Loch Maree Hotel Highld 105 G3
Loch nam Madadh W Isls 111 b4
Lochailort Highld 97 G1
Lochaline Highld 89 G3
Lochans D & G 68 C3
Locharbriggs D & G 78 D1
Lochavich Ag & B 90 B1
Lochawe Ag & B 90 C2
Lochboisdale W Isls 111 b2
Lochcarron Highld 97 G6
Lochdon Ag & B 89 G2
Lochdonhead Ag & B 89 G2
Lochead Ag & B 83 F3
Lochearnhead Stirlg 91 G2
Lochee Dund C 93 F3
Locheilside Station Highld 90 B6
Lochend Highld 98 D6
Locheport W Isls 111 b4
Lochfoot D & G 70 D1
Lochgair Ag & B 83 G4
Lochgelly Fife 86 C5
Lochgilphead Ag & B 83 G4
Lochgoilhead Ag & B 84 B5
Lochieheads Fife 93 E1
Lochill Moray 101 E5
Lochindorb Lodge Highld 100 C3
Lochinver Highld 108 B2
Lochluichart Highld 106 C2
Lochmaben D & G 78 D1
Lochmaddy W Isls 111 b4
Lochore Fife 86 C5
Lochranza N Ayrs 75 G5
Lochside Abers 95 F3
Lochside D & G 78 C1
Lochside Highld 107 G1
Lochton S Ayrs 68 D5
Lochty Angus 95 E2
Lochty Fife 87 E6
Lochuisge Highld 89 H4
Lochwinnoch Rens 84 C3
Lochwood D & G 78 D2
Lockengate Cnwll 3 F5
Lockerbie D & G 79 E1
Lockeridge Wilts 18 D3

Lockerley Hants 9 E5
Locking Somset 17 E5
Locking Stumps Ches 57 F2
Lockington E R Yk 60 D4
Lockleywood Shrops 49 E2
Locksbottom Gt Lon 21 G3
Lockton N York 67 E2
Loddington Leics 42 A2
Loddington Nhants 32 A6
Loddiswell Devon 5 G2
Loddon Norfk 45 F2
Lode Cambs 33 G5
Lode Heath W Mids 40 C2
Loders Dorset 7 F5
Lodsworth W Susx 10 C4
Lofthouse N York 65 E1
Lofthouse W York 59 E3
Lofthouse Gate W York 59 E3
Loftus N York 66 D5
Logan E Ayrs 77 E3
Loganlea W Loth 86 A2
Loggerheads Staffs 49 G3
Logie Angus 95 F3
Logie Fife 93 F2
Logie Coldstone Abers 94 D6
Logie Moray 100 C4
Logie Pert Angus 95 F3
Logierait P & K 92 C4
Logierieve Abers 103 E2
Login Carmth 25 E5
Lolworth Cambs 33 F5
Lonbain Highld 105 E2
Londesborough E R Yk 60 C4
London Gt Lon 21 F3
London Apprentice Cnwll 3 G4
London Colney Herts 21 E5
Londonderry N York 65 G2
Londonthorpe Lincs 42 D5
Lonemore Highld 105 F4
Long Ashton Somset 17 F5
Long Bank Worcs 39 G3
Long Bennington Lincs 42 A6
Long Bredy Dorset 7 G4
Long Buckby Nhants 31 G6
Long Clawson Leics 41 H5
Long Compton Staffs 49 H2
Long Compton Warwks 30 D3
Long Crendon Bucks 20 A6
Long Crichel Dorset 8 C4
Long Ditton Surrey 21 E2
Long Duckmanton Derbys 51 E4
Long Eaton Derbys 41 F6
Long Green Ches 49 E6
Long Green Worcs 29 F5
Long Hanborough Oxon 31 E2
Long Itchington Warwks 31 E6
Long Lawford Warwks 41 F1
Long Load Somset 17 F2
Long Marston Herts 20 C6
Long Marston N York 59 F5
Long Marston Warwks 30 C5
Long Marton Cumb 64 B5
Long Melford Suffk 34 C3
Long Newnton Gloucs 29 F2
Long Newton E Loth 87 E3
Long Preston N York 63 H2
Long Riston E R Yk 61 E4
Long Stratton Norfk 45 E2
Long Street Bucks 32 A3
Long Sutton Hants 10 A6
Long Sutton Lincs 43 F4
Long Sutton Somset 17 F2
Long Thurlow Suffk 34 D5
Long Waste Shrops 49 F1
Long Whatton Leics 41 F5
Long Wittenham Oxon 19 G5
Longbenton T & W 73 F3
Longborough Gloucs 30 C3
Longbridge W Mids 40 B1
Longbridge Deverill Wilts 18 B1
Longburton Dorset 7 G6
Longcliffe Derbys 50 D2
Longcombe Devon 5 H3
Longcot Oxon 19 E5
Longden Shrops 38 D6
Longdon Staffs 40 C4
Longdon Worcs 29 F6
Longdon Green Staffs 40 C4
Longdon upon Tern Shrops 49 F1
Longdown Devon 6 A4
Longdowns Cnwll 2 D3
Longfield Kent 22 B2
Longford Derbys 50 D1
Longford Gloucs 29 F4
Longford Shrops 49 F3
Longford Shrops 49 G2
Longforgan P & K 93 E2
Longformacus Border 87 G2
Longframlington Nthumb 73 E6
Longham Dorset 8 C3
Longham Norfk 44 C3
Longhaven Abers 103 F3
Longhirst Nthumb 73 F5
Longhope Gloucs 29 E4
Longhope Ork 111 g1
Longhorsley Nthumb 73 E5
Longhoughton Nthumb 81 G2
Longlane Derbys 50 D1
Longleat Safari Park Wilts 18 A1
Longlevens Gloucs 29 F4
Longley W York 58 B2
Longleys P & K 93 E3
Longmanhill Abers 102 C5
Longmoor Camp Hants 10 B5
Longmorn Moray 101 E5
Longmoss Ches 50 A4
Longnewton Border 80 B3
Longnewton Dur 65 G5
Longney Gloucs 29 E4
Longniddry E Loth 87 E3
Longnor Shrops 39 E5
Longnor Staffs 50 C3
Longparish Hants 19 F2
Longridge Lancs 57 F6
Longridge W Loth 85 H2
Longriggend N Lans 85 G3
Longrock Cnwll 2 B2
Longsdon Staffs 50 B2
Longside Abers 103 F4
Longstanton Cambs 33 F5
Longstock Hants 19 F1
Longstowe Cambs 33 E4
Longstreet Wilts 18 D2

Longthorpe Cambs 42 D2
Longthwaite Cumb 71 G2
Longton Lancs 57 E5
Longton Staffs 50 A1
Longtown Cumb 71 G6
Longtown Herefs 28 B5
Longueville Jersey 7 c1
Longville in the Dale Shrops 39 E5
Longwick Bucks 20 B5
Longwitton Nthumb 73 E5
Longwood D & G 70 A5
Longworth Oxon 19 F6
Longyester E Loth 87 E3
Lonmay Abers 103 F5
Lonmore Highld 104 B1
Looe Cnwll 4 C2
Loose Kent 22 C1
Loosley Row Bucks 20 B5
Lootcherbrae Abers 102 B4
Lopen Somset 17 E1
Loppington Shrops 49 E2
Lords Wood Kent 22 C2
Lornty P & K 92 D4
Loscoe Derbys 51 E2
Lossiemouth Moray 101 E6
Lost Gardens of Heligan Cnwll 3 F4
Lostock Gralam Ches 49 F6
Lostock Green Ches 49 F6
Lostock Hall Lancs 57 E5
Lostwithiel Cnwll 4 B3
Lothbeg Highld 107 H6
Lothersdale N York 58 B4
Lothmore Highld 110 A1
Loughborough Leics 41 F5
Loughor Swans 26 B3
Loughton Bucks 32 A3
Loughton Essex 21 G5
Loughton Shrops 39 F4
Lound Lincs 42 C4
Lound Notts 51 F5
Lound Suffk 45 H2
Lount Leics 41 E5
Louth Lincs 53 E4
Love Clough Lancs 57 G5
Lovedean Hants 10 A3
Lover Wilts 8 D5
Loversall S York 51 F6
Loves Green Essex 22 B5
Loveston Pembks 25 E3
Lovington Somset 17 G2
Low Ackworth W York 59 E2
Low Barbeth D & G 68 B4
Low Bentham N York 63 F3
Low Biggins Cumb 63 F4
Low Borrowbridge Cumb 63 F5
Low Bradfield S York 50 D5
Low Bradley N York 58 B4
Low Burnham Lincs 52 A5
Low Catton E R Yk 60 B5
Low Crosby Cumb 71 G5
Low Dinsdale Dur 65 G4
Low Eggborough N York 59 F2
Low Ellington N York 65 F2
Low Fell T & W 73 F3
Low Gartachorrans Stirlg 84 D4
Low Grantley N York 65 F1
Low Ham Somset 17 F2
Low Harrogate N York 58 D5
Low Hesket Cumb 71 G4
Low Hutton N York 60 B6
Low Lorton Cumb 71 E2
Low Marnham Notts 52 A2
Low Mill N York 66 C3
Low Moorsley T & W 73 G2
Low Mowthorpe N York 60 C6
Low Newton Cumb 62 D4
Low Row Cumb 72 A3
Low Row N York 64 D3
Low Salchrie D & G 68 B4
Low Santon Lincs 60 D2
Low Tharston Norfk 45 E2
Low Torry Fife 86 A4
Low Worsall N York 65 G4
Low Wray Cumb 62 D6
Lowdham Notts 51 G2
Lower Aisholt Somset 16 D3
Lower Ansty Dorset 8 A4
Lower Apperley Gloucs 29 F5
Lower Ashton Devon 6 A4
Lower Assendon Oxon 20 B4
Lower Bartle Lancs 57 E5
Lower Basildon Berks 19 H4
Lower Beeding W Susx 11 E4
Lower Benefield Nhants 42 C1
Lower Bentley Worcs 30 B6
Lower Boddington Nhants 31 F5
Lower Bourne Surrey 10 B6
Lower Brailes Warwks 30 D4
Lower Breakish Highld 97 E4
Lower Broadheath Worcs 39 G2
Lower Brockhampton Manor Herefs 39 F2
Lower Bullingham Herefs 28 C6
Lower Burgate Hants 8 D5
Lower Caldecote Beds 32 D3
Lower Cam Gloucs 29 E3
Lower Chapel Powys 27 F6
Lower Chicksgrove Wilts 8 C6
Lower Chute Wilts 19 E2
Lower Clapton Gt Lon 21 F4
Lower Clent Worcs 40 A2
Lower Cumberworth W York 58 D1
Lower Dean Beds 32 C5
Lower Diabaig Highld 105 F2
Lower Dicker E Susx 12 A3
Lower Down Shrops 38 D4
Lower Dunsforth N York 59 E6
Lower Egleton Herefs 39 F1
Lower End Bucks 32 B3
Lower Eythorne Kent 23 G1
Lower Failand Somset 17 F6
Lower Farringdon Hants 10 A5
Lower Feltham Gt Lon 20 D3
Lower Froyle Hants 10 B6
Lower Gabwell Devon 6 B3
Lower Gledfield Highld 107 E5
Lower Godney Somset 17 F3
Lower Gravenhurst Beds 32 D2
Lower Green Kent 12 B5
Lower Green Kent 12 B6
Lower Halliford Surrey 20 D2
Lower Halstow Kent 22 D2
Lower Hamworthy Dorset 8 C3
Lower Hardres Kent 23 F1

179

Lower Hartwell *Bucks* ... 20 B6
Lower Hergest *Herefs* ... 38 C2
Lower Heyford *Oxon* ... 31 F3
Lower Irlam *Gt Man* ... 57 G2
Lower Killeyan *Ag & B* ... 74 B5
Lower Kinnerton *Ches* ... 48 D5
Lower Langford *Somset* ... 17 F5
Lower Largo *Fife* ... 86 D6
Lower Leigh *Staffs* ... 40 B6
Lower Loxhore *Devon* ... 15 E4
Lower Lydbrook *Gloucs* ... 28 D4
Lower Lye *Herefs* ... 38 D3
Lower Machen *Newpt* ... 27 G2
Lower Merridge *Somset* ... 16 D3
Lower Middleton Cheney *Nhants* ... 31 F4
Lower Moor *W Mids* ... 30 B4
Lower Morton *Gloucs* ... 28 D2
Lower Nazeing *Essex* ... 21 G5
Lower Penarth *V Glam* ... 16 D5
Lower Penn *Staffs* ... 39 H5
Lower Peover *Ches* ... 49 G6
Lower Quinton *Warwks* ... 30 C4
Lower Raydon *Suffk* ... 34 D3
Lower Roadwater *Somset* ... 16 B3
Lower Seagry *Wilts* ... 18 C4
Lower Shelton *Beds* ... 32 C3
Lower Shiplake *Oxon* ... 20 B3
Lower Shuckburgh *Warwks* ... 31 F6
Lower Slaughter *Gloucs* ... 30 C2
Lower Standen *Kent* ... 13 G5
Lower Stanton St Quintin *Wilts* ... 18 B4
Lower Stoke *Kent* ... 22 D3
Lower Stone *Gloucs* ... 29 E2
Lower Stow Bedon *Norfk* ... 44 C2
Lower Street *Norfk* ... 45 F5
Lower Street *Suffk* ... 35 E4
Lower Sundon *Beds* ... 32 C2
Lower Swanwick *Hants* ... 9 G4
Lower Swell *Gloucs* ... 30 C3
Lower Tean *Staffs* ... 50 B1
Lower Town *Devon* ... 5 G4
Lower Town *Pembks* ... 24 D6
Lower Tysoe *Warwks* ... 31 E4
Lower Upcott *Devon* ... 6 A4
Lower Upham *Hants* ... 9 G5
Lower Vexford *Somset* ... 16 C3
Lower Weare *Somset* ... 17 E4
Lower Westmancote *Worcs* ... 29 G6
Lower Whatley *Somset* ... 17 H4
Lower Whitley *Ches* ... 57 F1
Lower Wield *Hants* ... 19 H1
Lower Willingdon *E Susx* ... 12 B2
Lower Withington *Ches* ... 49 G6
Lower Woodford *Wilts* ... 8 D6
Lower Wraxhall *Dorset* ... 7 G5
Lowesby *Leics* ... 41 H4
Lowestoft *Suffk* ... 45 H2
Loweswater *Cumb* ... 71 E2
Lowfield Heath *W Susx* ... 11 F5
Lowick *Nhants* ... 32 C6
Lowick *Nthumb* ... 81 F4
Lowick Green *Cumb* ... 62 C4
Lowsonford *Warwks* ... 30 C6
Lowther *Cumb* ... 71 H2
Lowthorpe *E R Yk* ... 61 E5
Lowton *Somset* ... 16 D1
Loxbeare *Devon* ... 16 B1
Loxhill *Surrey* ... 10 D5
Loxhore *Devon* ... 15 E4
Loxley *Warwks* ... 30 D5
Loxton *Somset* ... 17 E4
Loxwood *W Susx* ... 10 D5
Loyal Lodge *Highld* ... 109 F4
Lubenham *Leics* ... 41 G2
Luccombe *Somset* ... 16 B3
Luccombe Village *IOW* ... 9 G2
Lucker *Nthumb* ... 81 G3
Luckett *Cnwll* ... 5 E4
Lucking Street *Essex* ... 34 B2
Luckington *Wilts* ... 18 B5
Luckwell Bridge *Somset* ... 16 A3
Lucton *Herefs* ... 38 D3
Ludag *W Isls* ... 111 b2
Ludborough *Lincs* ... 53 E5
Ludbrook *Devon* ... 5 G3
Ludchurch *Pembks* ... 25 E4
Luddenden *W York* ... 58 B3
Luddenden Foot *W York* ... 58 B3
Luddesdown *Kent* ... 22 B2
Luddington *Lincs* ... 60 C2
Luddington *Warwks* ... 30 C5
Luddington in the Brook *Nhants* ... 42 C1
Ludford *Lincs* ... 52 D4
Ludford *Shrops* ... 39 E3
Ludgershall *Bucks* ... 31 G2
Ludgershall *Wilts* ... 19 E2
Ludgvan *Cnwll* ... 2 B3
Ludham *Norfk* ... 45 G4
Ludlow *Shrops* ... 39 E3
Ludney *Somset* ... 7 E6
Ludwell *Wilts* ... 8 B5
Ludworth *Dur* ... 73 G1
Luffincott *Devon* ... 4 D6
Luffness *E Loth* ... 87 E4
Lugar *E Ayrs* ... 77 E3
Luggate Burn *E Loth* ... 87 F3
Luggiebank *N Lans* ... 85 F3
Lugton *E Ayrs* ... 84 D1
Lugwardine *Herefs* ... 28 D6
Luib *Highld* ... 96 D5
Lulham *Herefs* ... 28 C6
Lullington *Derbys* ... 40 D4
Lullington *Somset* ... 18 A2
Lulsgate Bottom *Somset* ... 17 F5
Lulsley *Worcs* ... 39 G2
Lumb *Lancs* ... 57 H5
Lumb *W York* ... 58 B2
Lumby *N York* ... 59 F3
Lumloch *E Duns* ... 85 E3
Lumphanan *Abers* ... 95 E6
Lumphinnans *Fife* ... 86 C5
Lumsden *Abers* ... 101 G2
Lunan *Angus* ... 95 F2
Lunanhead *Angus* ... 93 G4
Luncarty *P & K* ... 92 D2
Lund *E R Yk* ... 60 D4
Lund *N York* ... 59 G3
Lundie *Angus* ... 93 E3
Lundie *Stirlg* ... 85 F5
Lundin Links *Fife* ... 86 D6
Lundin Mill *Fife* ... 86 D6
Lunna *Shet* ... 111 I3
Lunsford *Kent* ... 22 C2
Lunsford's Cross *E Susx* ... 12 C3

Lunt *Mersyd* ... 56 D3
Luppitt *Devon* ... 6 C6
Lupridge *Devon* ... 5 G2
Lupset *W York* ... 58 D2
Lupton *Cumb* ... 63 E4
Lurgashall *W Susx* ... 10 C4
Lurley *Devon* ... 16 B1
Luscombe *Devon* ... 5 H3
Luss *Ag & B* ... 84 C5
Lusta *Highld* ... 104 B2
Lustleigh *Devon* ... 5 H5
Luston *Herefs* ... 39 E2
Luthermuir *Abers* ... 95 F3
Luthrie *Fife* ... 93 E2
Luton *Beds* ... 32 C1
Luton *Devon* ... 6 C5
Luton *Devon* ... 6 A3
Luton *Kent* ... 22 C2
Luton Airport *Beds* ... 32 D1
Lutterworth *Leics* ... 41 F2
Lutton *Devon* ... 5 F3
Lutton *Devon* ... 5 G3
Lutton *Lincs* ... 43 F4
Lutton *Nhants* ... 42 D1
Luxborough *Somset* ... 16 B3
Luxulyan *Cnwll* ... 3 F5
Lybster *Highld* ... 110 C3
Lydbury North *Shrops* ... 38 D4
Lydd *Kent* ... 13 E4
Lydd Airport *Kent* ... 13 E4
Lydden *Kent* ... 13 G6
Lydden *Kent* ... 23 H2
Lyddington *Rutlnd* ... 42 B2
Lydeard St Lawrence *Somset* ... 16 C2
Lydford *Devon* ... 5 E5
Lydford on Fosse *Somset* ... 17 G2
Lydgate *W York* ... 58 A3
Lydham *Shrops* ... 38 D5
Lydiard Millicent *Wilts* ... 18 D5
Lydiard Tregoze *Wilts* ... 18 D5
Lydiate *Mersyd* ... 56 D3
Lydiate Ash *Worcs* ... 40 B1
Lydlinch *Dorset* ... 17 H1
Lydney *Gloucs* ... 28 D3
Lydstep *Pembks* ... 25 E3
Lye *W Mids* ... 40 A2
Lye Green *E Susx* ... 11 G5
Lye Green *Warwks* ... 30 D6
Lye's Green *Wilts* ... 18 A2
Lyford *Oxon* ... 19 F6
Lymbridge Green *Kent* ... 13 F6
Lyme Regis *Dorset* ... 7 E5
Lyminge *Kent* ... 13 F6
Lymington *Hants* ... 9 E3
Lyminster *W Susx* ... 10 D3
Lymm *Ches* ... 57 F2
Lympne *Kent* ... 13 F5
Lympsham *Somset* ... 17 E4
Lympstone *Devon* ... 6 B4
Lynch Green *Norfk* ... 45 E3
Lynchat *Highld* ... 99 F3
Lyndhurst *Hants* ... 9 E4
Lyndon *Rutlnd* ... 42 B3
Lyne *Border* ... 79 E6
Lyne *Surrey* ... 20 D2
Lyne of Skene *Abers* ... 102 D1
Lyneal *Shrops* ... 49 E3
Lyneham *Oxon* ... 30 D2
Lyneham *Wilts* ... 18 C4
Lyneham Airport *Wilts* ... 18 C4
Lyness *Ork* ... 111 g1
Lyng *Norfk* ... 44 D4
Lyng *Somset* ... 17 E2
Lynmouth *Devon* ... 15 F5
Lynn of Shenval *Moray* ... 101 E3
Lynsted *Kent* ... 22 D2
Lynton *Devon* ... 15 F5
Lyon's Gate *Dorset* ... 7 G6
Lyonshall *Herefs* ... 38 D2
Lytchett Matravers *Dorset* ... 8 B3
Lytchett Minster *Dorset* ... 8 C3
Lyth *Highld* ... 110 C5
Lytham *Lancs* ... 56 D5
Lytham St Anne's *Lancs* ... 56 D5
Lythe *N York* ... 67 E4
Lythmore *Highld* ... 110 B5

M

Mabe Burnthouse *Cnwll* ... 2 D3
Mabie *D & G* ... 70 C6
Mablethorpe *Lincs* ... 53 G4
Macclesfield *Ches* ... 50 A4
Macduff *Abers* ... 102 C5
Macharioch *Ag & B* ... 75 F2
Machen *Caerph* ... 27 G2
Machrie *N Ayrs* ... 75 G4
Machrihanish *Ag & B* ... 75 E3
Machrins *Ag & B* ... 82 C5
Machynlleth *Powys* ... 47 F2
Machynys *Carmth* ... 26 B3
Mackworth *Derbys* ... 50 D1
Macmerry *E Loth* ... 87 E3
Maddaford *Devon* ... 5 F6
Madderty *P & K* ... 92 C2
Maddiston *Falk* ... 85 H3
Madehurst *W Susx* ... 10 D4
Madeley *Staffs* ... 49 G4
Madingley *Cambs* ... 33 F4
Madley *Herefs* ... 28 C6
Madresfield *Worcs* ... 39 G1
Madron *Cnwll* ... 2 B2
Maen-y-groes *Cerdgn* ... 36 C3
Maenclochog *Pembks* ... 25 E5
Maendy *V Glam* ... 16 B6
Maentwrog *Gwynd* ... 47 F5
Maer *Staffs* ... 49 G3
Maerdy *Rhondd* ... 27 E3
Maesbrook *Shrops* ... 48 C2
Maesbury *Shrops* ... 48 C2
Maesbury Marsh *Shrops* ... 48 D2
Maesllyn *Cerdgn* ... 36 C2
Maesteg *Brdgnd* ... 27 E2
Maesybont *Carmth* ... 26 B4
Maesycwmmer *Caerph* ... 27 G2
Maggieknockater *Moray* ... 101 F4
Maggots End *Essex* ... 33 F2
Magham Down *E Susx* ... 12 B3
Maghull *Mersyd* ... 56 D3
Magor *Mons* ... 28 C2

Maiden Bradley *Wilts* ... 18 A1
Maiden Head *Somset* ... 17 G5
Maiden Newton *Dorset* ... 7 G5
Maiden Wells *Pembks* ... 24 D3
Maidenbower *W Susx* ... 11 F5
Maidencombe *Devon* ... 6 B3
Maidenhayne *Devon* ... 6 D5
Maidenhead *Berks* ... 20 C3
Maidensleigh *Devon* ... 15 F3
Maidens *S Ayrs* ... 76 B2
Maidenwell *Lincs* ... 53 E3
Maidford *Nhants* ... 31 G5
Maids Moreton *Bucks* ... 31 G3
Maidstone *Kent* ... 22 C1
Maidwell *Nhants* ... 41 H1
Maindee *Newpt* ... 28 B2
Mains of Balhall *Angus* ... 94 D3
Mains of Balnakettle *Abers* ... 95 E3
Mains of Dalvey *Highld* ... 100 D3
Mains of Haulkerton *Abers* ... 95 F3
Mainsforth *Dur* ... 65 G6
Mainsriddle *D & G* ... 70 C5
Mainstone *Shrops* ... 38 C4
Maisemore *Gloucs* ... 29 F4
Makeney *Derbys* ... 51 E1
Malborough *Devon* ... 5 G1
Malden *Surrey* ... 21 E2
Maldon *Essex* ... 22 D5
Malham *N York* ... 58 A6
Mallaig *Highld* ... 97 E2
Mallaigvaig *Highld* ... 97 E2
Malleny Mills *C Edin* ... 86 C3
Malltraeth *IOA* ... 54 C3
Mallwyd *Gwynd* ... 47 G3
Malmesbury *Wilts* ... 18 B5
Malmsmead *Somset* ... 15 G5
Malpas *Ches* ... 49 E4
Malpas *Cnwll* ... 3 E3
Malpas *Newpt* ... 28 B2
Maltby *N York* ... 66 B4
Maltby *S York* ... 51 F5
Maltby le Marsh *Lincs* ... 53 F3
Malting Green *Essex* ... 34 C1
Maltman's Hill *Kent* ... 12 D6
Malton *N York* ... 66 D1
Malvern Link *Worcs* ... 39 G1
Malvern Wells *Worcs* ... 29 E6
Malzie *D & G* ... 69 F3
Mamble *Worcs* ... 39 F3
Mamhilad *Mons* ... 28 B3
Manaccan *Cnwll* ... 2 D2
Manafon *Powys* ... 38 B6
Manais *W Isls* ... 111 c5
Manaton *Devon* ... 5 G5
Manby *Lincs* ... 53 F4
Mancetter *Warwks* ... 40 D3
Manchester *Gt Man* ... 57 H3
Manchester Airport *Gt Man* ... 57 G1
Mancot *Flints* ... 48 D5
Mandally *Highld* ... 98 B3
Manderston House *Border* ... 80 D5
Manea *Cambs* ... 43 F1
Maney *W Mids* ... 40 C3
Manfield *N York* ... 65 F4
Mangotsfield *Gloucs* ... 17 G6
Manish *W Isls* ... 111 c5
Manley *Ches* ... 49 E6
Manmoel *Caerph* ... 27 G3
Mannel *Ag & B* ... 88 B3
Manning's Heath *W Susx* ... 11 E5
Manningford Bohune *Wilts* ... 18 D3
Manningford Bruce *Wilts* ... 18 D3
Manningham *W York* ... 58 C3
Mannington *Dorset* ... 8 C4
Manningtree *Essex* ... 34 D2
Mannofield *Aber C* ... 95 H6
Manor Park *Gt Lon* ... 21 G4
Manorbier *Pembks* ... 25 E3
Manorbier Newton *Pembks* ... 24 D3
Manorhill *Border* ... 80 C3
Manorowen *Pembks* ... 24 D6
Mansell Gamage *Herefs* ... 38 D1
Mansell Lacy *Herefs* ... 38 D1
Mansfield *E Ayrs* ... 77 E3
Mansfield *Notts* ... 51 F3
Mansfield Woodhouse *Notts* ... 51 F3
Manston *Dorset* ... 8 A5
Manston *N York* ... 59 E3
Manston Airport *Kent* ... 23 G2
Manswood *Dorset* ... 8 C4
Manthorpe *Lincs* ... 42 C3
Manton *Lincs* ... 52 B5
Manton *Rutlnd* ... 42 B3
Manton *Wilts* ... 18 D3
Manuden *Essex* ... 33 F2
Maperton *Somset* ... 17 G2
Maplebeck *Notts* ... 51 G3
Mapledurham *Oxon* ... 19 H4
Mapledurwell *Hants* ... 20 A1
Maplehurst *W Susx* ... 11 E4
Maplescombe *Kent* ... 22 B2
Mapleton *Derbys* ... 50 C2
Mapperley *Derbys* ... 51 E1
Mapperley Park *Notts* ... 51 F1
Mapperton *Dorset* ... 7 F5
Mappleborough Green *Warwks* ... 30 C6
Mappleton *E R Yk* ... 61 F4
Mapplewell *S York* ... 59 E1
Mappowder *Dorset* ... 7 H6
Marazanvose *Cnwll* ... 2 D4
Marazion *Cnwll* ... 2 B2
Marbury *Ches* ... 49 E4
March *Cambs* ... 43 F2
March *S Lans* ... 78 D4
Marcham *Oxon* ... 19 F6
Marchamley *Shrops* ... 49 F2
Marchington *Staffs* ... 40 C6
Marchington Woodlands *Staffs* ... 40 C6
Marchros *V Glam* ... 16 B5
Marchwiel *Wrexhm* ... 48 D4
Marchwood *Hants* ... 9 E4
Marcross *V Glam* ... 16 B5
Marden *Herefs* ... 39 E1
Marden *Kent* ... 12 C6
Marden *Wilts* ... 18 D2
Marden Thorn *Kent* ... 12 C6
Mardy *Mons* ... 28 B4
Mareham le Fen *Lincs* ... 53 E2
Mareham on the Hill *Lincs* ... 53 E2
Marehill *W Susx* ... 10 D4
Maresfield *E Susx* ... 11 G4
Marfleet *E R Yk* ... 61 E3
Marford *Wrexhm* ... 48 D5
Margam *Neath* ... 26 D2
Margaret Marsh *Dorset* ... 8 A5
Margaretting *Essex* ... 22 B5
Margaretting Tye *Essex* ... 22 B5

Margate *Kent* ... 23 H3
Margnaheglish *N Ayrs* ... 75 H4
Margrie *D & G* ... 69 G3
Margrove Park *N York* ... 66 C5
Marham *Norfk* ... 44 A3
Marhamchurch *Cnwll* ... 14 B2
Marholm *Cambs* ... 42 D2
Mariansleigh *Devon* ... 15 F3
Marine Town *Kent* ... 22 D3
Marionburgh *Abers* ... 95 F6
Marishader *Highld* ... 104 D2
Maristow *Devon* ... 5 E3
Maritime Centre *Moray* ... 76 C5
Marjoriebanks *D & G* ... 78 D1
Mark *Somset* ... 17 E4
Mark Cross *E Susx* ... 11 G3
Mark Cross *E Susx* ... 12 B5
Markby *Lincs* ... 53 F3
Market Bosworth *Leics* ... 41 E4
Market Deeping *Lincs* ... 42 D3
Market Drayton *Shrops* ... 49 F3
Market Harborough *Leics* ... 41 H2
Market Lavington *Wilts* ... 18 C2
Market Overton *Rutlnd* ... 42 B4
Market Rasen *Lincs* ... 52 D4
Market Stainton *Lincs* ... 52 D3
Market Weighton *E R Yk* ... 60 C4
Market Weston *Suffk* ... 34 D6
Markfield *Leics* ... 41 F4
Markham *Caerph* ... 27 G3
Markham Moor *Notts* ... 51 H4
Markinch *Fife* ... 86 D6
Markington *N York* ... 58 D6
Markle *E Loth* ... 87 F4
Marks Tey *Essex* ... 34 C1
Marksbury *Somset* ... 17 G5
Markyate *Herts* ... 32 C1
Marlborough *Wilts* ... 18 D3
Marlcliff *Warwks* ... 30 C5
Marldon *Devon* ... 6 A2
Marlesford *Suffk* ... 35 F4
Marlingford *Norfk* ... 45 E3
Marloes *Pembks* ... 24 C3
Marlow *Bucks* ... 20 B4
Marlow Bottom *Bucks* ... 20 B4
Marlpit Hill *Kent* ... 11 G6
Marnhull *Dorset* ... 8 A5
Marple *Gt Man* ... 50 B5
Marr *S York* ... 59 F1
Marrick *N York* ... 65 E3
Marsden *T & W* ... 73 G3
Marsden *W York* ... 58 B2
Marsh Baldon *Oxon* ... 19 G6
Marsh Chapel *Lincs* ... 53 E5
Marsh Gibbon *Bucks* ... 31 G2
Marsh Green *Devon* ... 6 C5
Marsh Green *Kent* ... 11 G6
Marsh Lane *Derbys* ... 51 E4
Marsh Street *Somset* ... 16 B3
Marshalswick *Herts* ... 21 E6
Marsham *Norfk* ... 45 E4
Marshborough *Kent* ... 23 G1
Marshbrook *Shrops* ... 38 D5
Marshfield *Gloucs* ... 18 A4
Marshfield *Newpt* ... 28 A1
Marshgate *Cnwll* ... 4 C6
Marshland St James *Norfk* ... 43 G3
Marshwood *Dorset* ... 7 E5
Marske *N York* ... 65 E3
Marske-by-the-Sea *N York* ... 66 C5
Marston *Herefs* ... 38 D2
Marston *Lincs* ... 42 B6
Marston *Oxon* ... 31 F1
Marston *Staffs* ... 40 A5
Marston *Wilts* ... 18 C2
Marston Green *W Mids* ... 40 C2
Marston Magna *Somset* ... 17 G2
Marston Meysey *Wilts* ... 18 D6
Marston Montgomery *Derbys* ... 50 C1
Marston Moretaine *Beds* ... 32 C3
Marston on Dove *Derbys* ... 40 D6
Marston St Lawrence *Nhants* ... 31 F4
Marston Trussell *Nhants* ... 41 G2
Marstow *Herefs* ... 28 D4
Marsworth *Bucks* ... 20 C6
Marten *Wilts* ... 19 E3
Marthall *Ches* ... 49 G6
Martham *Norfk* ... 45 G4
Martin *Hants* ... 8 C5
Martin *Kent* ... 13 H6
Martin *Lincs* ... 52 D2
Martin *Lincs* ... 53 E2
Martin Hussingtree *Worcs* ... 39 H2
Martinhoe *Devon* ... 15 F5
Martinstown *Dorset* ... 7 G4
Martlesham *Suffk* ... 35 F3
Martlesham Heath *Suffk* ... 35 F3
Martletwy *Pembks* ... 24 D3
Martley *Worcs* ... 39 G2
Martock *Somset* ... 17 F1
Marton *Ches* ... 49 H6
Marton *E R Yk* ... 61 E4
Marton *Lincs* ... 52 A3
Marton *N York* ... 59 E6
Marton *N York* ... 66 D2
Marton *Shrops* ... 38 C6
Marton *Warwks* ... 31 E6
Marton-le-Moor *N York* ... 65 G1
Martyr Worthy *Hants* ... 9 G6
Marwick *Ork* ... 111 g2
Marwood *Devon* ... 15 E4
Mary Tavy *Devon* ... 5 E5
Marybank *Highld* ... 106 D2
Maryburgh *Highld* ... 107 E2
Maryculter *Abers* ... 95 G5
Marygold *Border* ... 87 G2
Maryhill *Abers* ... 102 D4
Maryhill *C Glas* ... 85 E3
Marykirk *Abers* ... 95 F3
Marylebone *Gt Lon* ... 21 F3
Marylebone *Gt Man* ... 57 F3
Marypark *Moray* ... 101 E3
Maryport *Cumb* ... 70 D3
Maryport *D & G* ... 68 C1
Marystow *Devon* ... 5 E5
Maryton *Angus* ... 95 F2
Marywell *Abers* ... 95 G5
Marywell *Abers* ... 95 H5
Marywell *Angus* ... 93 H4
Masham *N York* ... 65 F2
Masongill *N York* ... 63 F3
Mastin Moor *Derbys* ... 51 F4

Matching Green *Essex* ... 21 H6
Matching Tye *Essex* ... 21 G6
Matfen *Nthumb* ... 73 E4
Matfield *Kent* ... 12 B6
Mathern *Mons* ... 28 C2
Mathon *Herefs* ... 39 G1
Mathry *Pembks* ... 24 C5
Matlask *Norfk* ... 45 E5
Matlock *Derbys* ... 50 D3
Matlock Bath *Derbys* ... 50 D3
Matson *Gloucs* ... 29 F4
Mattersey *Notts* ... 51 G5
Mattingley *Hants* ... 20 A2
Mattishall *Norfk* ... 44 D3
Mattishall Burgh *Norfk* ... 44 D3
Mauchline *E Ayrs* ... 76 D4
Maud *Abers* ... 103 H3
Maufant *Jersey* ... 7 c2
Maugersbury *Gloucs* ... 30 D3
Maughold *IOM* ... 116 d4
Mauld *Highld* ... 98 C6
Maulden *Beds* ... 32 C3
Maulds Meaburn *Cumb* ... 64 A5
Maunby *N York* ... 65 G2
Maund Bryan *Herefs* ... 39 E1
Maundown *Somset* ... 16 C2
Mautby *Norfk* ... 45 G3
Mavesyn Ridware *Staffs* ... 40 C5
Mavis Enderby *Lincs* ... 53 E2
Mawbray *Cumb* ... 70 D4
Mawdesley *Lancs* ... 57 E4
Mawdlam *Brdgnd* ... 26 D1
Mawgan *Cnwll* ... 2 D2
Mawgan Porth *Cnwll* ... 3 E5
Mawla *Cnwll* ... 2 D4
Mawnan *Cnwll* ... 2 D2
Mawnan Smith *Cnwll* ... 2 D2
Maxey *Cambs* ... 42 D3
Maxstoke *Warwks* ... 40 D2
Maxted Street *Kent* ... 13 F6
Maxton *Border* ... 80 C3
Maxton *Kent* ... 13 G6
Maxwell Town *D & G* ... 70 C6
Maxworthy *Cnwll* ... 4 D6
May Bank *Staffs* ... 49 H4
Maybole *S Ayrs* ... 76 C3
Maybury *Surrey* ... 20 D2
Mayfield *E Susx* ... 12 B4
Mayfield *Mdloth* ... 86 D3
Mayfield *Staffs* ... 50 C2
Mayford *Surrey* ... 20 C1
Maynard's Green *E Susx* ... 12 B4
Maypole Green *Norfk* ... 45 G2
Maypole Green *Suffk* ... 34 C4
Meadgate *Somset* ... 17 G4
Meadle *Bucks* ... 20 B5
Meadowfield *Dur* ... 73 F4
Meadwell *Devon* ... 5 E5
Mealrigg *Cumb* ... 71 E4
Meanwood *W York* ... 58 D4
Meare *Somset* ... 17 F3
Meare Green *Somset* ... 17 E2
Meare Green *Somset* ... 16 D2
Mearns *E Rens* ... 85 E1
Mears Ashby *Nhants* ... 32 A5
Measham *Leics* ... 41 E4
Meathop *Cumb* ... 62 D4
Meavy *Devon* ... 5 F4
Medbourne *Leics* ... 42 A2
Meden Vale *Notts* ... 51 G4
Medmenham *Berks* ... 20 B4
Medomsley *Dur* ... 73 E2
Medstead *Hants* ... 19 H1
Meerbrook *Staffs* ... 50 B3
Meesden *Herts* ... 33 F2
Meeth *Devon* ... 15 E2
Meeting House Hill *Norfk* ... 45 F4
Meidrim *Carmth* ... 25 F4
Meifod *Powys* ... 48 B1
Meigle *P & K* ... 93 E4
Meikle Carco *D & G* ... 77 G3
Meikle Earnock *S Lans* ... 85 F1
Meikle Kilmory *Ag & B* ... 83 H2
Meikle Obney *P & K* ... 92 C3
Meikle Wartle *Abers* ... 102 C3
Meikleour *P & K* ... 92 D3
Meinciau *Carmth* ... 26 A4
Meir *Staffs* ... 50 B1
Melbourn *Cambs* ... 33 F3
Melbourne *Derbys* ... 41 E5
Melbourne *E R Yk* ... 60 B4
Melbury Abbas *Dorset* ... 8 B5
Melbury Bubb *Dorset* ... 7 G6
Melbury Osmond *Dorset* ... 7 G6
Melchbourne *Beds* ... 32 C5
Melcombe Bingham *Dorset* ... 8 A4
Meldon *Devon* ... 5 F6
Meldon *Nthumb* ... 73 E5
Meldreth *Cambs* ... 33 F3
Meldrum *Stirlg* ... 85 F5
Melfort *Ag & B* ... 90 A1
Melgund Castle *Angus* ... 93 G4
Meliden *Denbgs* ... 56 B1
Melin-y-wig *Denbgs* ... 48 A4
Melkinthorpe *Cumb* ... 71 H2
Melkridge *Nthumb* ... 72 B3
Melksham *Wilts* ... 18 B3
Melling *Lancs* ... 63 F3
Melling *Mersyd* ... 56 D3
Mellis *Suffk* ... 34 D5
Mellon Charles *Highld* ... 105 F5
Mellon Udrigle *Highld* ... 105 G5
Mellor *Gt Man* ... 50 B5
Mellor *Lancs* ... 57 F5
Mellor Brook *Lancs* ... 57 F5
Mells *Somset* ... 17 H4
Melmerby *Cumb* ... 72 A1
Melmerby *N York* ... 65 E2
Melmerby *N York* ... 65 G1
Melness *Highld* ... 109 E5
Melplash *Dorset* ... 7 F5
Melrose *Border* ... 80 B3
Melsetter *Ork* ... 111 g1
Melsonby *N York* ... 65 F4
Meltham *W York* ... 58 C1
Melton *E R Yk* ... 60 D3
Melton *Suffk* ... 35 F4
Melton Constable *Norfk* ... 44 D5
Melton Mowbray *Leics* ... 41 H5
Melton Ross *Lincs* ... 60 D1
Melvaig *Highld* ... 105 F4
Melverley *Shrops* ... 48 D1
Melvich *Highld* ... 109 H5
Membury *Devon* ... 6 D5

Memsie Abers ... 103 E5
Memus Angus ... 93 F5
Menai Bridge IOA ... 54 D3
Mendham Suffk ... 45 F1
Mendlesham Suffk ... 34 D5
Mendlesham Green Suffk ... 34 D5
Menheniot Cnwll ... 4 D3
Mennock D & G ... 77 G2
Menston W York ... 58 C4
Menstrie Clacks ... 85 G5
Mentmore Bucks ... 32 B1
Meoble Highld ... 97 F1
Meole Brace Shrops ... 49 E1
Meonstoke Hants ... 9 H5
Meopham Kent ... 22 B2
Mepal Cambs ... 33 F6
Meppershall Beds ... 32 D2
Mere Ches ... 57 G1
Mere Wilts ... 8 A6
Mere Brow Lancs ... 56 D4
Mereclough Lancs ... 57 H5
Mereworth Kent ... 22 B1
Meriden W Mids ... 40 D2
Merkadale Highld ... 96 B5
Merrion Pembks ... 24 D2
Merriott Somset ... 7 F6
Merrow Surrey ... 20 D1
Merry Hill Herts ... 21 E4
Merryhill W Mids ... 40 A3
Merrymeet Cnwll ... 4 D3
Mersham Kent ... 13 E5
Merstham Surrey ... 21 F1
Merston W Susx ... 10 C2
Merstone IOW ... 9 G2
Merther Cnwll ... 3 E4
Merthyr Cynog Powys ... 27 F6
Merthyr Mawr Brdgnd ... 27 E1
Merthyr Tydfil Myr Td ... 27 F3
Merthyr Vale Myr Td ... 27 F3
Merton Devon ... 15 E2
Merton Gt Lon ... 21 E2
Merton Norfk ... 44 C2
Merton Oxon ... 31 F2
Meshaw Devon ... 15 G3
Messing Essex ... 34 C1
Messingham Lincs ... 52 B5
Metfield Suffk ... 35 F6
Metherell Cnwll ... 5 E4
Metheringham Lincs ... 52 C2
Methil Fife ... 86 D5
Methilhill Fife ... 86 D5
Methley W York ... 59 E3
Methlick Abers ... 102 D3
Methven P & K ... 92 C2
Methwold Norfk ... 44 B2
Methwold Hythe Norfk ... 44 A2
Mettingham Suffk ... 45 F1
Metton Norfk ... 45 E5
Mevagissey Cnwll ... 3 F4
Mexborough S York ... 51 F6
Mey Highld ... 110 C6
Meyllteyrn Gwynd ... 46 B4
Meysey Hampton Gloucs ... 18 D6
Miabhig W Isls ... 111 c6
Miavaig W Isls ... 111 c6
Michaelchurch Herefs ... 28 C5
Michaelchurch Escley Herefs ... 28 B5
Michaelston-le-Pit V Glam ... 16 C6
Michaelstone-y-Fedw Newpt ... 27 G1
Michaelstow Cnwll ... 4 B5
Micheldever Hants ... 19 G1
Micheldever Station Hants ... 19 G1
Michelmersh Hants ... 9 F5
Mickfield Suffk ... 35 E5
Mickle Trafford Ches ... 49 E6
Micklebring S York ... 51 F6
Mickleby N York ... 66 D4
Micklefield W York ... 59 E3
Mickleham Surrey ... 21 E1
Mickleover Derbys ... 40 D6
Mickleton Dur ... 64 D5
Mickleton Gloucs ... 30 C4
Mickletown W York ... 59 E3
Mickley N York ... 65 F1
Mickley Green Suffk ... 34 B4
Mickley Square Nthumb ... 73 E3
Mid Ardlaw Abers ... 103 E5
Mid Beltie Abers ... 95 E6
Mid Calder W Loth ... 86 B3
Mid Clyth Highld ... 110 C3
Mid Lavant W Susx ... 10 B3
Mid Mains Highld ... 98 C6
Mid Yell Shet ... 111 I4
Midbea Ork ... 111 h3
Middle Aston Oxon ... 31 F3
Middle Barton Oxon ... 31 E3
Middle Chinnock Somset ... 17 F1
Middle Claydon Bucks ... 31 H3
Middle Duntisbourne Gloucs ... 29 G3
Middle Handley Derbys ... 51 E4
Middle Kames Ag & B ... 83 G4
Middle Littleton Worcs ... 30 C4
Middle Mayfield Staffs ... 50 C2
Middle Rasen Lincs ... 52 C4
Middle Rocombe Devon ... 6 A3
Middle Stoke Kent ... 22 D3
Middle Town IOS ... 2 a1
Middle Tysoe Warwks ... 31 E4
Middle Wallop Hants ... 19 E1
Middle Winterslow Wilts ... 9 E6
Middle Woodford Wilts ... 18 D1
Middlebie D & G ... 71 E6
Middlebridge P & K ... 92 B5
Middleham N York ... 65 E2
Middlehill Wilts ... 18 A3
Middlehope Shrops ... 39 E5
Middlemarsh Dorset ... 7 G6
Middlesbrough N York ... 66 B5
Middleshaw Cumb ... 63 E5
Middlesmoor N York ... 65 E1
Middlestone Dur ... 65 F6
Middleton W York ... 58 D2
Middlethird Border ... 80 C4
Middleton Ag & B ... 88 A3
Middleton Derbys ... 50 D3
Middleton Derbys ... 50 D2
Middleton Essex ... 34 C3
Middleton Gt Man ... 57 H3
Middleton Hants ... 19 F1
Middleton Herefs ... 39 E3
Middleton N Ayrs ... 84 D1
Middleton N York ... 58 C5
Middleton N York ... 66 D2
Middleton Nhants ... 42 A1

Middleton Norfk ... 43 H4
Middleton Nthumb ... 73 E5
Middleton P & K ... 86 B6
Middleton Shrops ... 39 E4
Middleton Suffk ... 35 G5
Middleton Swans ... 25 G2
Middleton W York ... 58 D3
Middleton Warwks ... 40 C3
Middleton Moor Suffk ... 35 G5
Middleton on the Hill Herefs ... 39 E3
Middleton on the Wolds E R Yk ... 60 D5
Middleton One Row Dur ... 65 G4
Middleton Quernhow N York ... 65 G2
Middleton Scriven Shrops ... 39 F4
Middleton St George Dur ... 65 G4
Middleton Stoney Oxon ... 31 F2
Middleton Tyas N York ... 65 F4
Middleton-in-Teesdale Dur ... 64 D5
Middleton-on-Sea W Susx ... 10 C2
Middletown Powys ... 48 C1
Middlewich Ches ... 49 G5
Middlewood Cnwll ... 4 D4
Middlewood Green Suffk ... 34 D4
Middleyard E Ayrs ... 77 E4
Middlezoy Somset ... 17 E2
Midford Somset ... 18 A3
Midgham Berks ... 19 G3
Midgley W York ... 58 B3
Midgley W York ... 58 D2
Midhopestones S York ... 50 D6
Midhurst W Susx ... 10 C4
Midlem Border ... 80 B3
Midpark Ag & B ... 83 H2
Midsomer Norton Somset ... 17 G4
Midtown Highld ... 109 E5
Migvie Abers ... 94 D6
Milborne Port Somset ... 17 G1
Milborne St Andrew Dorset ... 8 A3
Milborne Wick Somset ... 17 G1
Milbourne Nthumb ... 73 E4
Milbourne Wilts ... 18 B5
Milburn Cumb ... 64 B6
Milbury Heath Gloucs ... 29 E2
Milby N York ... 59 E6
Milcombe Oxon ... 31 E3
Milden Suffk ... 34 C3
Mildenhall Suffk ... 34 A6
Mildenhall Wilts ... 18 D4
Mile Oak E Susx ... 11 E3
Mile Town Kent ... 22 D3
Mileham Norfk ... 44 C4
Miles Platting Gt Man ... 57 H3
Milesmark Fife ... 86 B4
Milfield Nthumb ... 81 E3
Milford Derbys ... 51 E2
Milford Staffs ... 40 B5
Milford Surrey ... 10 C6
Milford Haven Pembks ... 24 C3
Milford on Sea Hants ... 9 E3
Milkwall Gloucs ... 28 D3
Mill Bank W York ... 58 B2
Mill Brow Gt Man ... 50 B5
Mill End Bucks ... 20 B4
Mill End Herts ... 33 E2
Mill Green Cambs ... 33 G3
Mill Green Essex ... 22 B5
Mill Green Lincs ... 42 D4
Mill Green Suffk ... 34 C3
Mill Green Suffk ... 34 D4
Mill Green Suffk ... 35 E4
Mill Hill Gt Lon ... 21 E4
Mill Meece Staffs ... 49 H3
Mill of Drummond P & K ... 92 B1
Mill of Haldane W Duns ... 84 D4
Mill Street Suffk ... 34 D5
Millais Jersey ... 7 a2
Milland W Susx ... 10 B5
Millbreck Abers ... 103 E4
Millbrex Abers ... 102 D4
Millbridge Surrey ... 10 B6
Millbrook Beds ... 32 C3
Millbrook Cnwll ... 5 E2
Millbrook Hants ... 9 F4
Millbrook Jersey ... 7 b1
Millbuie Abers ... 102 D1
Millbuie Highld ... 107 E1
Millburn S Ayrs ... 76 D4
Millcorner E Susx ... 12 D4
Millcraig Highld ... 107 F3
Milldale Staffs ... 50 C2
Miller's Dale Derbys ... 50 C4
Millerhill Mdloth ... 86 D3
Millerston N Lans ... 85 F2
Millhalf Herefs ... 38 C1
Millheugh S Lans ... 77 F6
Millhouse Ag & B ... 83 G3
Millhouse Green S York ... 58 D1
Millhousebridge D & G ... 78 D2
Millhouses S York ... 51 E5
Millington E R Yk ... 60 C5
Millom Cumb ... 62 B4
Millport N Ayrs ... 84 B1
Millthrop Cumb ... 63 F5
Milltimber Aber C ... 95 G6
Milltown Abers ... 101 E1
Milltown Abers ... 101 G1
Milltown D & G ... 71 F6
Milltown Devon ... 15 E5
Milltown of Campfield Abers ... 95 F6
Milltown of Edinville Moray ... 101 E3
Milltown of Learney Abers ... 95 E6
Milnathort P & K ... 86 B6
Milngavie W Duns ... 85 E3
Milnrow Gt Man ... 58 A2
Milnthorpe Cumb ... 63 E4
Milovaig Highld ... 104 A1
Milson Shrops ... 39 F3
Milstead Kent ... 22 D2
Milston Wilts ... 18 D2
Milthorpe Nhants ... 31 G4
Milton Cambs ... 33 F5
Milton Cumb ... 71 H5
Milton D & G ... 68 D3
Milton D & G ... 70 B6
Milton Derbys ... 40 D5
Milton Highld ... 110 D4
Milton Highld ... 97 G6
Milton Highld ... 98 D5
Milton Highld ... 107 E1
Milton Highld ... 107 F3
Milton Inver ... 84 D3
Milton Kent ... 22 B3

Milton Moray ... 101 G5
Milton Notts ... 51 G4
Milton Oxon ... 31 F3
Milton Oxon ... 19 G5
Milton P & K ... 92 D5
Milton Pembks ... 24 D3
Milton Somset ... 17 E5
Milton Somset ... 17 F2
Milton Stirlg ... 84 D5
Milton W Duns ... 84 D3
Milton Abbas Dorset ... 8 A3
Milton Abbot Devon ... 5 E5
Milton Bridge Mdloth ... 86 C2
Milton Bryan Beds ... 32 B2
Milton Clevedon Somset ... 17 G3
Milton Combe Devon ... 5 E3
Milton Damerel Devon ... 14 D2
Milton Ernest Beds ... 32 C4
Milton Green Ches ... 49 E5
Milton Hill Oxon ... 19 F5
Milton Keynes Bucks ... 32 B3
Milton Lilbourne Wilts ... 18 D3
Milton Malsor Nhants ... 31 H5
Milton Morenish P & K ... 91 G3
Milton of Auchinhove Abers ... 95 E6
Milton of Balgonie Fife ... 86 D5
Milton of Buchanan Stirlg ... 84 D4
Milton of Campsie E Duns ... 85 F3
Milton of Leys Highld ... 99 E6
Milton of Tullich Abers ... 94 C5
Milton on Stour Dorset ... 8 A6
Milton Regis Kent ... 22 D2
Milton-under-Wychwood Oxon ... 30 D2
Milverton Somset ... 16 C2
Milverton Warwks ... 30 D6
Milwich Staffs ... 40 B6
Minard Ag & B ... 83 G5
Minchinhampton Gloucs ... 29 F3
Minehead Somset ... 16 B4
Minera Wrexhm ... 48 C4
Minety Wilts ... 18 C5
Minffordd Gwynd ... 47 E5
Mingarrypark Highld ... 89 G5
Miningsby Lincs ... 53 E2
Minions Cnwll ... 4 D4
Minishant S Ayrs ... 76 C3
Minllyn Gwynd ... 47 G3
Minnigaff D & G ... 69 E4
Minnonie Abers ... 102 D5
Minskip N York ... 59 E6
Minstead Hants ... 9 E4
Minsted W Susx ... 10 B4
Minster Kent ... 23 E3
Minster Kent ... 23 G2
Minster Lovell Oxon ... 30 D2
Minsterley Shrops ... 38 D6
Minsterworth Gloucs ... 29 E4
Minterne Magna Dorset ... 7 G6
Minting Lincs ... 52 D3
Mintlaw Abers ... 103 E4
Minto Border ... 80 B2
Minton Shrops ... 38 D5
Mirehouse Cumb ... 70 C1
Mirfield W York ... 58 D2
Miserden Gloucs ... 29 G3
Miskin Rhondd ... 27 F1
Misson Notts ... 51 G6
Misterton Leics ... 41 F2
Misterton Notts ... 51 H6
Misterton Somset ... 7 F6
Mistley Essex ... 35 E2
Mitcham Gt Lon ... 21 E2
Mitchel Troy Mons ... 28 C4
Mitcheldean Gloucs ... 29 E4
Mitchell Cnwll ... 3 E4
Mitchellslacks D & G ... 78 C2
Mitford Nthumb ... 73 F5
Mithian Cnwll ... 2 D4
Mixbury Oxon ... 31 G3
Mobberley Ches ... 57 G1
Mobberley Staffs ... 50 B1
Mochdre Powys ... 38 B5
Mochrum D & G ... 69 E2
Mockbeggar Kent ... 12 C6
Mockerkin Cumb ... 70 D2
Modbury Devon ... 5 G2
Moddershall Staffs ... 50 A1
Moelfre IOA ... 54 D5
Moelfre Powys ... 48 C2
Moffat D & G ... 78 D3
Mogerhanger Beds ... 32 D4
Moira Leics ... 40 D5
Mol-chlach Highld ... 96 C3
Molash Kent ... 23 E1
Mold Flints ... 48 C5
Moldgreen W York ... 58 C2
Molehill Green Essex ... 33 G2
Molescroft E R Yk ... 60 D4
Molesworth Cambs ... 32 C6
Molland Devon ... 15 G4
Mollington Ches ... 48 D6
Mollington Oxon ... 31 E4
Mollinsburn N Lans ... 85 F3
Mondynes Abers ... 95 F4
Monewden Suffk ... 35 F4
Moneydie P & K ... 92 C2
Moniaive D & G ... 78 B2
Monifieth Angus ... 93 G3
Monikie Angus ... 93 G3
Monimail Fife ... 93 E1
Monk Fryston N York ... 59 F3
Monk Sherborne Hants ... 19 H2
Monk Soham Suffk ... 35 E5
Monk Street Essex ... 33 G2
Monken Hadley Gt Lon ... 21 E5
Monkhide Herefs ... 39 F1
Monkhill Cumb ... 71 F5
Monkhopton Shrops ... 39 F5
Monkland Herefs ... 39 E2
Monkleigh Devon ... 14 D3
Monknash V Glam ... 16 B5
Monkokehampton Devon ... 15 E2
Monks Eleigh Suffk ... 34 C3
Monks Heath Ches ... 49 H6
Monks Horton Kent ... 13 F5
Monks Kirby Warwks ... 41 F2
Monkseaton T & W ... 73 G4
Monksilver Somset ... 16 C3
Monksthorpe Lincs ... 53 F2
Monkswood Mons ... 28 B3
Monkton Devon ... 6 D5
Monkton Kent ... 23 G2
Monkton S Ayrs ... 76 C4

Monkton T & W ... 73 G3
Monkton Combe Somset ... 18 A3
Monkton Deverill Wilts ... 18 B1
Monkton Farleigh Wilts ... 18 A3
Monkton Heathfield Somset ... 16 D2
Monkton Wyld Dorset ... 7 E5
Monkwood Hants ... 9 H6
Monmore Green W Mids ... 40 A3
Monmouth Mons ... 28 C4
Monnington on Wye Herefs ... 38 D1
Monreith D & G ... 69 E2
Mont Saint Guern ... 6 b1
Montacute Somset ... 17 F1
Montford Shrops ... 48 D1
Montford Bridge Shrops ... 48 D1
Montgarrie Abers ... 102 B2
Montgomery Powys ... 38 C5
Montgreenan N Ayrs ... 76 C5
Montrose Angus ... 95 F2
Monxton Hants ... 19 E1
Monymusk Abers ... 102 C1
Monzie P & K ... 92 B2
Moodiesburn N Lans ... 85 F3
Moonzie Fife ... 93 F1
Moor Allerton W York ... 58 D4
Moor Crichel Dorset ... 8 C4
Moor End W York ... 58 B3
Moor Monkton N York ... 59 F5
Moorby Lincs ... 53 E2
Moordown Dorset ... 8 D3
Moore Ches ... 57 F1
Moorends S York ... 59 G2
Moorgreen Notts ... 51 F2
Moorhead W York ... 58 C4
Moorhouse Cumb ... 71 F5
Moorhouse Notts ... 51 H3
Moorhouse Bank Surrey ... 21 G1
Moorlinch Somset ... 17 E3
Moorsholm N York ... 66 C4
Moorside Dorset ... 8 A5
Moorswater Cnwll ... 4 C3
Moorthorpe W York ... 59 F1
Moortown Lincs ... 52 C5
Moortown W York ... 58 D4
Morangie Highld ... 107 F4
Morar Highld ... 97 E2
Morborne Cambs ... 42 D2
Morchard Bishop Devon ... 15 G2
Morcombelake Dorset ... 7 E5
Morcott Rutlnd ... 42 B2
Morda Shrops ... 48 C2
Morden Dorset ... 8 B3
Morden Gt Lon ... 21 E2
Mordiford Herefs ... 28 D6
Mordon Dur ... 65 G5
More Shrops ... 38 D5
Morebath Devon ... 16 B2
Morebattle Border ... 80 D3
Morecambe Lancs ... 62 D3
Moredon Wilts ... 18 D5
Morefield Highld ... 106 A5
Morehall Kent ... 13 G5
Moreleigh Devon ... 5 G2
Morenish P & K ... 91 G3
Moresby Cumb ... 70 D2
Morestead Hants ... 9 G5
Moreton Dorset ... 8 A2
Moreton Essex ... 21 H5
Moreton Herefs ... 39 E3
Moreton Mersyd ... 56 C2
Moreton Oxon ... 20 A5
Moreton Corbet Shrops ... 49 E2
Moreton Jeffries Herefs ... 39 F1
Moreton Morrell Warwks ... 30 D5
Moreton on Lugg Herefs ... 39 E1
Moreton Pinkney Nhants ... 31 F5
Moreton Say Shrops ... 49 F3
Moreton Valence Gloucs ... 29 E4
Moreton-in-Marsh Gloucs ... 30 D3
Moretonhampstead Devon ... 5 G5
Morfa Nefyn Gwynd ... 46 C5
Morham E Loth ... 87 E3
Morland Cumb ... 64 A5
Morley Ches ... 57 G1
Morley Derbys ... 51 E1
Morley W York ... 58 D3
Morley Green Ches ... 57 G1
Morley St Botolph Norfk ... 44 D2
Morningside C Edin ... 86 C3
Morningside N Lans ... 85 G1
Morningthorpe Norfk ... 45 E2
Morpeth Nthumb ... 73 F5
Morphie Abers ... 95 F4
Morrey Staffs ... 40 C5
Morriston Swans ... 26 C3
Morston Norfk ... 44 D6
Mortehoe Devon ... 14 D5
Morthen S York ... 51 F5
Mortimer Berks ... 19 H3
Mortimer West End Hants ... 19 H3
Mortlake Gt Lon ... 21 E3
Morton Cumb ... 71 G4
Morton Derbys ... 51 E3
Morton Lincs ... 52 A4
Morton Lincs ... 42 C4
Morton Notts ... 51 H2
Morton Shrops ... 48 C2
Morton on the Hill Norfk ... 45 E4
Morton-on-Swale N York ... 65 G3
Morvah Cnwll ... 2 A3
Morval Cnwll ... 4 D3
Morvich Highld ... 97 G4
Morville Shrops ... 39 F5
Morwellham Quay Devon ... 5 E4
Morwenstow Cnwll ... 14 B3
Mosborough S York ... 51 E4
Moscow E Ayrs ... 76 D5
Mosedale Cumb ... 71 F2
Moseley W Mids ... 40 B3
Moseley W Mids ... 40 C2
Moseley Worcs ... 39 G2
Moss Ag & B ... 88 A3
Moss S York ... 59 G2
Moss Bank Mersyd ... 57 E3
Moss Edge Lancs ... 62 D1
Moss Side Mersyd ... 56 C3
Moss-side Highld ... 100 B5
Mossat Abers ... 101 G2
Mossbank Shet ... 111 I3
Mossbay Cumb ... 70 D2
Mossblown S Ayrs ... 76 D4
Mossburnford Border ... 80 C2

Mossdale D & G ... 69 G4
Mossdale E Ayrs ... 76 D2
Mossend N Lans ... 85 F2
Mossley Gt Man ... 50 D0
Mosspaul Hotel Border ... 79 G3
Mosstodloch Moray ... 101 F5
Mossy Lea Lancs ... 57 E4
Mossyard D & G ... 69 F3
Mosterton Dorset ... 7 F6
Moston Gt Man ... 57 H3
Mostyn Flints ... 56 B1
Motcombe Dorset ... 8 B5
Mothecombe Devon ... 5 F2
Motherby Cumb ... 71 G2
Motherwell N Lans ... 85 F2
Motspur Park Gt Lon ... 21 E2
Mottingham Gt Lon ... 21 G3
Mottisfont Hants ... 9 E5
Mottistone IOW ... 9 F2
Mottram in Longdendale Gt Man ... 50 B6
Mottram St Andrew Ches ... 57 H1
Mouilpied Guern ... 6 b1
Mouldsworth Ches ... 49 E6
Moulin P & K ... 92 C5
Moulsecoomb E Susx ... 11 F3
Moulsford Oxon ... 19 G5
Moulsoe Bucks ... 32 B3
Moultavie Highld ... 107 E3
Moulton Ches ... 49 F6
Moulton Lincs ... 43 E4
Moulton N York ... 65 F4
Moulton Nhants ... 32 A5
Moulton Suffk ... 34 A5
Moulton V Glam ... 16 C5
Moulton Chapel Lincs ... 43 E4
Moulton Seas End Lincs ... 43 E4
Moulton St Mary Norfk ... 45 G3
Mount Cnwll ... 4 C4
Mount Ambrose Cnwll ... 2 D3
Mount Bures Essex ... 34 C2
Mount Hawke Cnwll ... 2 D4
Mount Lothian Mdloth ... 86 C2
Mount Pleasant Derbys ... 51 E2
Mount Pleasant Suffk ... 34 B3
Mount Tabor W York ... 58 B3
Mountain W York ... 58 C3
Mountain Ash Rhondd ... 27 F3
Mountain Cross Border ... 86 B1
Mountfield E Susx ... 12 C4
Mountgerald House Highld ... 107 E2
Mountjoy Cnwll ... 3 E5
Mountnessing Essex ... 22 B5
Mounton Mons ... 28 C2
Mountsorrel Leics ... 41 F4
Mousehill Surrey ... 10 C6
Mousehole Cnwll ... 2 B2
Mouswald D & G ... 70 D6
Mowhaugh Border ... 80 D2
Mowsley Leics ... 41 G2
Mowtie Abers ... 95 G5
Moy Highld ... 99 F5
Moy Highld ... 98 C1
Moye Highld ... 97 F4
Moylgrove Pembks ... 36 A2
Muasdale Ag & B ... 75 E5
Much Birch Herefs ... 28 C5
Much Cowarne Herefs ... 39 F1
Much Dewchurch Herefs ... 28 C5
Much Hadham Herts ... 33 F1
Much Hoole Lancs ... 57 E5
Much Marcle Herefs ... 28 D5
Much Wenlock Shrops ... 39 F5
Muchalls Abers ... 95 G5
Muchelney Somset ... 17 E2
Muchelney Ham Somset ... 17 F2
Muchlarnick Cnwll ... 4 C3
Muckleburgh Collection Norfk ... 44 D6
Mucklestone Staffs ... 49 G3
Muckton Lincs ... 53 F3
Muddiford Devon ... 15 E4
Muddles Green E Susx ... 12 A3
Mudeford Dorset ... 8 D3
Mudford Dorset ... 17 G1
Mudford Sock Somset ... 17 F1
Mugdock Stirlg ... 85 E3
Mugeary Highld ... 96 C6
Mugginton Derbys ... 50 D1
Muir of Fowlis Abers ... 102 B1
Muir of Miltonduff Moray ... 101 E5
Muir of Ord Highld ... 107 E1
Muir of Thorn P & K ... 92 C3
Muirden Abers ... 102 C4
Muirdrum Angus ... 93 G3
Muiresk Abers ... 102 C4
Muirhead Angus ... 93 F3
Muirhead Fife ... 86 C6
Muirhead N Lans ... 85 F3
Muirkirk E Ayrs ... 77 F4
Muirmill Stirlg ... 85 F4
Muirshearlich Highld ... 98 A1
Muirtack Abers ... 103 E3
Muirton P & K ... 85 H6
Muirton Mains Highld ... 106 D2
Muirton of Ardblair P & K ... 92 D3
Muker N York ... 64 D3
Mulbarton Norfk ... 45 E2
Mulben Moray ... 101 F4
Mullion Cnwll ... 2 D1
Mullion Cove Cnwll ... 2 C1
Mumby Lincs ... 53 G3
Munderfield Row Herefs ... 39 F2
Munderfield Stocks Herefs ... 39 F2
Mundesley Norfk ... 45 F5
Mundford Norfk ... 44 B2
Mundham Norfk ... 45 F2
Mundon Hill Essex ... 22 D5
Mungrisdale Cumb ... 71 F2
Munlochy Highld ... 107 E2
Munnoch N Ayrs ... 76 C6
Munsley Herefs ... 29 E6
Munslow Shrops ... 39 E4
Murchington Devon ... 5 G5
Murcott Oxon ... 31 G2
Murkle Highld ... 110 B5
Murlaggan Highld ... 97 G2
Murroes Angus ... 93 G3
Murrow Cambs ... 43 F3
Mursley Bucks ... 32 A2
Murthill Angus ... 93 G5
Murthly P & K ... 92 D3
Murton Cumb ... 64 B5
Murton Dur ... 73 G2
Murton N York ... 59 G5
Murton Nthumb ... 81 E4

Musbury Devon	6	D5
Musselburgh E Loth	86	D3
Muston Leics	42	A5
Muston N York	67	G2
Muswell Hill Gt Lon	21	F4
Mutehill D & G	69	G3
Mutford Suffk	45	G1
Muthill P & K	92	B1
Mybster Highld	110	B4
Myddfai Carmth	26	D5
Myddle Shrops	49	E2
Mydroilyn Cerdgn	36	D2
Mylor Cnwll	3	E3
Mylor Bridge Cnwll	3	E3
Mynachlog ddu Pembks	25	E5
Myndtown Shrops	38	D5
Mynydd-bach Mons	28	C2
Mynydd-Bach Swans	26	C3
Myrebird Abers	95	F5
Myredykes Border	72	A6
Mytchett Surrey	20	C1
Mytholm W York	58	B3
Mytholmroyd W York	58	B3
Myton-on-Swale N York	59	E6

N

Na Buirgh W Isls	111	c5
Naast Highld	105	F4
Naburn N York	59	G4
Nackington Kent	23	F1
Nacton Suffk	35	E3
Nafferton E R Yk	60	D5
Nailbourne Somset	16	D2
Nailsea Somset	17	F5
Nailstone Leics	41	E4
Nailsworth Gloucs	29	F3
Nairn Highld	100	B5
Nannerch Flints	48	B6
Nanpantan Leics	41	F5
Nanpean Cnwll	3	F4
Nanstallon Cnwll	3	F5
Nant Peris Gwynd	54	D2
Nant-y-moel Brdgnd	27	E2
Nanternis Cerdgn	36	C3
Nantgaredig Carmth	26	B4
Nantglyn Denbgs	55	H3
Nantmel Powys	38	A3
Nantmor Gwynd	47	E5
Nantwich Ches	49	F4
Nantyglo Blae G	27	G4
Naphill Bucks	20	B5
Napton on the Hill Warwks	31	F6
Narberth Pembks	25	E4
Narborough Leics	41	F3
Narborough Norfk	44	B3
Nasareth Gwynd	54	C2
Naseby Nhants	41	G2
Nash Bucks	32	A2
Nash Newpt	28	B1
Nash Shrops	39	F3
Nash's Green Hants	19	H2
Nassington Nhants	42	C2
Nateby Cumb	64	C4
Nateby Lancs	63	E1
National Shire Horse Centre Devon	5	F2
National Space Science Centre Leics	41	G4
Natland Cumb	63	E5
Naughton Suffk	34	D3
Naunton Gloucs	30	C2
Naunton Worcs	29	F6
Naunton Beauchamp Worcs	30	B5
Navenby Lincs	52	C2
Navestock Essex	21	H5
Navestock Side Essex	22	B5
Navidale House Hotel Highld	110	A1
Navity Highld	107	G3
Nawton N York	66	C2
Nayland Suffk	34	C2
Nazeing Essex	21	G5
Neap Shet	111	I2
Near Cotton Staffs	50	C2
Near Sawrey Cumb	62	D5
Neasden Gt Lon	21	E4
Neasham Dur	65	G4
Neath Neath	26	D3
Neatham Hants	10	B5
Neatishead Norfk	45	F4
Nebo Cerdgn	37	E3
Nebo Conwy	55	F2
Nebo Gwynd	54	C2
Nebo IOA	54	C5
Necton Norfk	44	C3
Nedd Highld	108	B3
Nedging Suffk	34	D3
Nedging Tye Suffk	34	D4
Needham Norfk	35	E6
Needham Market Suffk	34	D4
Needingworth Cambs	33	E5
Neen Savage Shrops	39	F4
Neen Sollars Shrops	39	F3
Neenton Shrops	39	F4
Nefyn Gwynd	46	C5
Neilston E Rens	84	D2
Nelson Caerph	27	F2
Nelson Lancs	57	H6
Nemphlar S Lans	77	G5
Nempnett Thrubwell Somset	17	F5
Nenthall Cumb	72	C1
Nenthorn Border	80	C4
Nercwys Flints	48	C5
Nereabolls Ag & B	82	B1
Nerston S Lans	85	F2
Nesbit Nthumb	81	E3
Nesfield N York	58	C5
Ness Botanic Gardens Ches	48	C6
Nesscliffe Shrops	48	D2
Neston Ches	56	C1
Neston Wilts	18	B3
Netchwood Shrops	39	F5
Nether Alderley Ches	49	H6
Nether Blainslie Border	80	B4
Nether Broughton Notts	41	G5
Nether Cerne Dorset	7	G5
Nether Compton Dorset	17	G1
Nether Crimond Abers	102	D2
Nether Dallachy Moray	101	F5

Nether Exe Devon	6	B5
Nether Fingland S Lans	78	C4
Nether Handwick Angus	93	F3
Nether Haugh S York	51	E6
Nether Headon Notts	51	H4
Nether Heage Derbys	51	E2
Nether Heyford Nhants	31	G5
Nether Howcleugh S Lans	78	D4
Nether Kellet Lancs	63	E3
Nether Kinmundy Abers	103	H4
Nether Langwith Notts	51	F4
Nether Moor Derbys	51	E3
Nether Padley Derbys	50	D4
Nether Poppleton N York	59	F5
Nether Silton N York	66	B3
Nether Stowey Somset	16	D3
Nether Wallop Hants	19	E1
Nether Wasdale Cumb	62	B6
Nether Westcote Gloucs	30	D2
Nether Whitacre Warwks	40	D3
Nether Whitecleuch S Lans	78	B4
Nether Winchendon Bucks	31	H2
Netheravon Wilts	18	D2
Netherbrae Abers	102	D5
Netherburn S Lans	77	G6
Netherbury Dorset	7	F5
Netherby N York	59	E4
Nethercleuch D & G	79	E2
Netherend Gloucs	28	D3
Netherfield E Susx	12	C4
Netherfield Road E Susx	12	C4
Netherhampton Wilts	8	D6
Netherhay Dorset	7	E6
Netherlaw D & G	70	B4
Netherley Abers	95	G5
Nethermill D & G	78	D2
Nethermuir Abers	103	E4
Netherplace E Rens	85	E1
Netherseal Derbys	40	D4
Netherthong W York	58	C1
Netherton Angus	93	G5
Netherton Devon	6	A3
Netherton N Lans	85	G1
Netherton Nthumb	81	E1
Netherton P & K	92	D4
Netherton Shrops	39	G4
Netherton Stirlg	85	E3
Netherton W Mids	40	B2
Netherton Worcs	58	D2
Nethertown Cumb	62	A6
Nethertown Highld	110	D6
Nethertown Staffs	40	C5
Netherurd Border	86	B1
Netherwitton Nthumb	73	E5
Nethy Bridge Highld	99	H4
Netley Hants	9	F4
Netley Marsh Hants	9	E4
Nettlebed Oxon	20	A4
Nettlebridge Somset	17	G4
Nettlecombe Dorset	7	F5
Nettleden Herts	20	D6
Nettleham Lincs	52	C3
Nettlestead Kent	22	B1
Nettlestead Green Kent	22	B1
Nettlestone IOW	9	H3
Nettlesworth Dur	73	F2
Nettleton Lincs	52	D5
Nettleton Wilts	18	A4
Netton Wilts	18	D1
Nevern Pembks	36	A1
Nevill Holt Leics	42	A2
New Abbey D & G	70	C5
New Aberdour Abers	103	E5
New Addington Gt Lon	21	F2
New Alresford Hants	9	G6
New Alyth P & K	93	E4
New Ash Green Kent	22	B2
New Balderton Notts	52	A1
New Barn Kent	22	B2
New Barnet Gt Lon	21	F5
New Bewick Nthumb	81	F2
New Bilton Warwks	41	F1
New Bolingbroke Lincs	53	E1
New Boultham Lincs	52	B3
New Bradwell Bucks	32	A3
New Brampton Derbys	51	E4
New Brancepeth Dur	73	F1
New Brighton Mersyd	56	C2
New Brinsley Derbys	51	E4
New Byth Abers	102	D4
New Costessey Norfk	45	E3
New Crofton W York	59	E2
New Cross Gt Lon	21	F3
New Cross Somset	17	E1
New Cumnock E Ayrs	77	E3
New Deer Abers	103	E4
New Denham Bucks	20	D4
New Duston Nhants	31	H6
New Earswick N York	59	G5
New Edlington S York	51	F6
New Elgin Moray	101	E5
New Ellerby E R Yk	61	E4
New Eltham Gt Lon	21	G3
New End Worcs	30	B5
New England Cambs	42	D2
New Fletton Cambs	42	D2
New Galloway D & G	69	G5
New Gilston Fife	87	E6
New Grimsby IOS	2	a2
New Hartley Nthumb	73	G4
New Haw Surrey	20	D2
New Holkham Norfk	44	C5
New Holland Lincs	61	E2
New Houghton Derbys	51	F3
New Houghton Norfk	44	B4
New Hutton Cumb	63	E5
New Inn Carmth	26	B6
New Inn Torfn	28	B3
New Invention Shrops	38	D6
New Lanark S Lans	78	C6
New Langholm D & G	79	F1
New Leake Lincs	53	F1
New Leeds Abers	103	E5
New Lodge S York	59	E1
New Longton Lancs	57	E5
New Luce D & G	68	D4
New Malden Gt Lon	21	E2
New Marske N York	66	C5
New Marston Oxon	31	F1
New Mill Abers	95	G4
New Mill Cnwll	2	B3
New Mill W York	58	C1
New Mills Cnwll	3	E4
New Mills Derbys	50	B5

New Mills Powys	38	B6
New Milton Hants	9	E3
New Mistley Essex	35	E2
New Moat Pembks	25	E5
New Ollerton Notts	51	G3
New Pitsligo Abers	103	E5
New Prestwick S Ayrs	76	C4
New Quay Cerdgn	36	C3
New Rackheath Norfk	45	F3
New Radnor Powys	38	C2
New Ridley Nthumb	73	E3
New Romney Kent	13	E4
New Rossington S York	51	G6
New Sauchie Clacks	85	G5
New Sharlston W York	59	E2
New Silksworth T & W	73	G2
New Somerby Lincs	42	B5
New Stevenston N Lans	85	F2
New Town Dorset	8	C3
New Town Dorset	8	B5
New Town Dorset	8	C5
New Town E Loth	87	E3
New Town E Susx	11	G4
New Tredegar Caerph	27	G3
New Trows S Lans	77	G5
New Walsoken Cambs	43	F3
New Waltham Lincs	53	E5
New Winton E Loth	87	E3
New York Lincs	53	E1
Newall W York	58	D4
Newark Ork	111	j3
Newark-on-Trent Notts	52	A1
Newarthill N Lans	85	G2
Newbattle Mdloth	86	D3
Newbie D & G	71	E5
Newbiggin Cumb	71	G2
Newbiggin Cumb	71	H4
Newbiggin Cumb	64	A6
Newbiggin Dur	64	D5
Newbiggin N York	64	D2
Newbiggin-by-the-Sea Nthumb	73	G5
Newbiggin-on-Lune Cumb	63	G6
Newbigging Angus	93	E3
Newbigging Angus	93	F3
Newbigging Angus	93	G3
Newbigging S Lans	86	A1
Newbold Derbys	51	E4
Newbold on Avon Warwks	41	F1
Newbold on Stour Warwks	30	D4
Newbold Pacey Warwks	30	D5
Newbold Verdon Leics	41	E4
Newborough Cambs	42	D3
Newborough IOA	54	C3
Newborough Staffs	40	C5
Newbourne Suffk	35	F3
Newbridge C Edin	86	B3
Newbridge Caerph	27	G3
Newbridge Cnwll	2	B2
Newbridge D & G	78	C1
Newbridge Hants	9	E5
Newbridge IOW	9	F2
Newbridge Green Worcs	29	F6
Newbridge on Wye Powys	38	A2
Newbrough Nthumb	72	C3
Newbuildings Devon	15	G2
Newburgh Abers	103	E5
Newburgh Abers	103	E2
Newburgh Fife	93	E1
Newburgh Lancs	57	E4
Newburgh Priory N York	66	B1
Newburn T & W	73	F3
Newbury Berks	19	F3
Newbury Somset	17	H4
Newbury Park Gt Lon	21	G4
Newby Cumb	64	A5
Newby Lancs	63	G1
Newby N York	66	B4
Newby N York	63	G3
Newby Bridge Cumb	62	D4
Newby East Cumb	71	G5
Newby West Cumb	71	F4
Newby Wiske N York	65	G2
Newcastle Mons	28	C4
Newcastle Shrops	38	C4
Newcastle Airport Nthumb	73	F4
Newcastle Emlyn Carmth	36	C1
Newcastle upon Tyne T & W	73	F3
Newcastle-under-Lyme Staffs	49	H4
Newcastleton Border	79	G2
Newchapel Pembks	36	B1
Newchapel Surrey	11	F6
Newchurch IOW	9	G2
Newchurch Kent	13	E5
Newchurch Mons	28	C3
Newchurch Powys	38	C1
Newchurch Staffs	40	C5
Newcraighall C Edin	86	D3
Newdigate Surrey	11	E6
Newell Green Berks	20	C3
Newenden Kent	12	D4
Newent Gloucs	29	E5
Newfield Dur	65	F6
Newfield Highld	107	G3
Newgale Pembks	24	C5
Newgate Street Herts	21	F5
Newhall Ches	49	F4
Newhaven E Susx	11	G2
Newholm N York	67	E4
Newhouse N Lans	85	G2
Newick E Susx	11	G4
Newington Kent	22	D2
Newington Kent	13	F5
Newington Oxon	19	H6
Newland Gloucs	28	D3
Newland N York	59	G3
Newland Somset	15	G4
Newland Worcs	39	G1
Newlandrig Mdloth	86	D2
Newlands Border	79	H2
Newlands Nthumb	73	E2
Newlands of Dundurcas Moray	101	F4
Newlyn Cnwll	2	B2
Newlyn East Cnwll	3	E4
Newmachar Abers	103	E2
Newmains N Lans	85	G2
Newman's Green Suffk	34	C3
Newmarket Suffk	33	H5
Newmarket W Isls	111	d6
Newmill Border	79	G4
Newmill Moray	101	G4
Newmill of Inshewan Angus	94	D2
Newmillerdam W York	59	E2
Newmills C Edin	86	C3

Newmills Fife	86	A4
Newmills Mons	28	C3
Newmiln P & K	92	D2
Newmilns E Ayrs	77	E5
Newney Green Essex	22	B5
Newnham Gloucs	29	E4
Newnham Hants	20	A1
Newnham Herts	33	E3
Newnham Kent	23	E1
Newnham Nhants	31	F5
Newnham Worcs	39	F3
Newport Cnwll	4	D5
Newport Devon	15	E4
Newport E R Yk	60	C3
Newport Essex	33	G2
Newport Gloucs	29	E3
Newport Highld	110	B2
Newport IOW	9	G2
Newport Newpt	28	B2
Newport Pembks	25	E6
Newport Shrops	49	G2
Newport Pagnell Bucks	32	B3
Newport-on-Tay Fife	93	F2
Newquay Cnwll	3	E5
Newquay Airport Cnwll	3	E5
Newseat Abers	102	C3
Newsham Lancs	57	E6
Newsham N York	65	E4
Newsham N York	65	G2
Newsham Nthumb	73	G4
Newsholme E R Yk	60	B3
Newstead Border	80	B3
Newstead Notts	51	F2
Newstead Nthumb	81	G3
Newtack Moray	101	G4
Newthorpe N York	59	F3
Newthorpe Notts	51	F2
Newton Ag & B	83	H5
Newton Beds	32	D3
Newton Border	80	C2
Newton Brdgnd	26	D1
Newton Cambs	43	F3
Newton Cambs	33	F4
Newton Ches	48	D6
Newton Ches	49	E5
Newton Ches	62	C3
Newton Derbys	51	E3
Newton Herefs	28	B5
Newton Herefs	39	E2
Newton Highld	107	E1
Newton Highld	107	F1
Newton Highld	107	F3
Newton Lancs	63	F1
Newton Lancs	42	C5
Newton Mdloth	86	D3
Newton Moray	100	D5
Newton Moray	101	F5
Newton Nhants	42	B1
Newton Norfk	44	B3
Newton Notts	51	G1
Newton Nthumb	73	E3
Newton S Lans	85	F2
Newton S Lans	78	C5
Newton Somset	16	C4
Newton Staffs	40	B5
Newton Suffk	34	C3
Newton W Loth	86	B4
Newton Warwks	41	F2
Newton Abbot Devon	6	A3
Newton Arlosh Cumb	71	E4
Newton Aycliffe Dur	65	F5
Newton Bewley Dur	66	B5
Newton Blossomville Bucks	32	B4
Newton Bromswold Beds	32	C5
Newton Burgoland Leics	41	E4
Newton by Toft Lincs	52	C4
Newton Ferrers Cnwll	4	D3
Newton Ferrers Devon	5	F2
Newton Ferry W Isls	111	b4
Newton Flotman Norfk	45	E2
Newton Harcourt Leics	41	G3
Newton Heath Gt Man	57	H3
Newton Kyme N York	59	F4
Newton Longville Bucks	32	B2
Newton Mearns E Rens	85	E1
Newton Morrell N York	65	F4
Newton of Balcanquhal P & K	92	D1
Newton of Balcormo Fife	87	E6
Newton on Ouse N York	59	F5
Newton on Trent Lincs	52	A3
Newton Poppleford Devon	6	C4
Newton Purcell Oxon	31	G3
Newton Regis Warwks	40	D4
Newton Reigny Cumb	71	G3
Newton Row Highld	110	D4
Newton Solney Derbys	40	D5
Newton St Cyres Devon	15	H1
Newton St Faith Norfk	45	E3
Newton St Loe Somset	17	H5
Newton St Petrock Devon	14	D2
Newton Stacey Hants	19	F1
Newton Stewart D & G	69	E4
Newton Toney Wilts	19	E1
Newton Tracey Devon	15	E4
Newton under Roseberry N York	66	B4
Newton upon Derwent E R Yk	60	B5
Newton Valence Hants	10	A5
Newton Wamphray D & G	78	D2
Newton with Scales Lancs	57	E5
Newton-by-the-Sea Nthumb	81	G3
Newton-le-Willows Mersyd	57	F2
Newton-le-Willows N York	65	F2
Newton-on-Rawcliffe N York	66	D2
Newton-on-the-Moor Nthumb	81	G1
Newtongarry Croft Abers	102	B3
Newtongrange Mdloth	86	D3
Newtonhill Abers	95	G5
Newtonloan Mdloth	86	D2
Newtonmill Angus	95	E3
Newtonmore Highld	99	E3
Newtown Ches	49	F4
Newtown Ches	49	F4
Newtown Cumb	50	A3
Newtown Cumb	70	D4
Newtown Cumb	71	G5
Newtown D & G	77	G3
Newtown Devon	6	C5
Newtown Devon	15	G3
Newtown Dorset	8	C3
Newtown Gloucs	29	E3
Newtown Gt Man	57	E3
Newtown Hants	9	H4
Newtown Herefs	39	F1
Newtown Herefs	29	E6
Newtown Highld	98	C3

Newtown IOW	9	F3
Newtown Nthumb	73	E6
Newtown Nthumb	81	F3
Newtown Powys	38	B5
Newtown Shrops	48	D2
Newtown Shrops	49	E3
Newtown Somset	6	D6
Newtown Worcs	39	H2
Newtown Linford Leics	41	F4
Newtown of Beltrees Rens	84	C2
Newtown St Boswells Border	80	B3
Newtyle Angus	93	E3
Newyork Ag & B	83	G6
Neyland Pembks	24	D3
Nicholashayne Devon	16	C1
Nicholaston Swans	26	B2
Nidd N York	58	D5
Nigg Aber C	95	H6
Nigg Highld	107	G3
Nightcott Somset	16	A2
Nine Elms Wilts	18	D5
Ninebanks Nthumb	72	C2
Nineveh Worcs	39	F3
Ninfield E Susx	12	C3
Ningwood IOW	9	F2
Nisbet Border	80	C3
Nisbet Hill Border	80	D5
Niton IOW	9	G1
Nitshill C Glas	85	E2
No Man's Heath Ches	49	E4
No Man's Heath Warwks	40	D4
Nocton Lincs	52	C2
Noke Oxon	31	F2
Nolton Pembks	24	C4
Nolton Haven Pembks	24	C4
Nomansland Devon	15	G2
Nomansland Wilts	9	E5
Noneley Shrops	49	E2
Nonington Kent	23	G1
Nook Cumb	63	E4
Norbiton Gt Lon	21	E2
Norbury Ches	49	E4
Norbury Derbys	50	C1
Norbury Gt Lon	21	F2
Norbury Shrops	38	D5
Norbury Staffs	49	G2
Norchard Worcs	39	H3
Nordelph Norfk	43	G2
Nordley Shrops	39	F5
Norham Nthumb	81	E4
Norland Town W York	58	C2
Norley Ches	49	E6
Norleywood Hants	9	F3
Norman's Green Devon	6	C5
Normanby Lincs	60	C2
Normanby Lincs	52	C4
Normanby N York	66	B5
Normanby N York	66	D2
Normanby le Wold Lincs	52	D4
Normandy Surrey	20	C1
Normanton Derbys	41	E6
Normanton Leics	42	A6
Normanton Lincs	42	B6
Normanton Notts	51	G2
Normanton W York	59	E2
Normanton le Heath Leics	41	E4
Normanton on Soar Notts	41	F5
Normanton on the Wolds Notts	41	G6
Normanton on Trent Notts	52	A2
Norney Surrey	10	C6
North Anston S York	51	F5
North Aston Oxon	31	F3
North Baddesley Hants	9	F5
North Ballachulish Highld	90	C5
North Barrow Somset	17	G2
North Barsham Norfk	44	C5
North Benfleet Essex	22	C4
North Bersted W Susx	10	C2
North Berwick E Loth	87	E4
North Boarhunt Hants	9	G4
North Bovey Devon	5	G5
North Bradley Wilts	18	B2
North Brentor Devon	5	E5
North Brewham Somset	17	H3
North Buckland Devon	14	D5
North Burlingham Norfk	45	G3
North Cadbury Somset	17	G2
North Carlton Lincs	52	B3
North Carlton Notts	51	G5
North Cave E R Yk	60	C3
North Cerney Gloucs	30	B1
North Chailey E Susx	11	G4
North Charford Hants	8	D5
North Charlton Nthumb	81	G2
North Cheam Gt Lon	21	E2
North Cheriton Somset	17	H2
North Chideock Dorset	7	E5
North Cliffe E R Yk	60	C4
North Clifton Notts	52	A3
North Cockerington Lincs	53	F4
North Connel Ag & B	90	B2
North Cornelly Brdgnd	26	D1
North Corry Highld	90	A4
North Cotes Lincs	53	E5
North Cove Suffk	45	G1
North Cowton N York	65	F4
North Crawley Bucks	32	B3
North Creake Norfk	44	C5
North Curry Somset	17	E2
North Dalton E R Yk	60	C5
North Deighton N York	59	E5
North Duffield N York	59	G4
North Duntulm Highld	104	C3
North Elham Kent	13	F6
North Elmham Norfk	44	D4
North Elmsall W York	59	F2
North End Essex	33	H1
North End Hants	8	D5
North End Hants	9	H3
North End Nhants	32	B5
North End W Susx	10	C3
North Erradale Highld	105	F4
North Evington Leics	41	G4
North Fambridge Essex	22	D5
North Ferriby E R Yk	60	D3
North Frodingham E R Yk	61	E5
North Gorley Hants	8	D4
North Green Suffk	35	F5
North Grimston N York	60	C6
North Hayling Hants	10	A2
North Hill Cnwll	4	D4
North Hillingdon Gt Lon	20	D4
North Hinksey Oxon	31	F1
North Holmwood Surrey	11	E6

North Huish Devon ... 5 G3
North Hykeham Lincs ... 52 B2
North Kelsey Lincs ... 52 C5
North Kessock Highld ... 107 F1
North Killingholme Lincs ... 61 E2
North Kilvington N York ... 65 H2
North Kilworth Leics ... 41 G2
North Kyme Lincs ... 52 D1
North Landing E R Yk ... 67 H1
North Lee Bucks ... 20 B6
North Leigh Oxon ... 31 E2
North Leverton with
   Habblesthorpe Notts ... 52 A3
North Littleton Worcs ... 30 C4
North Lopham Norfk ... 44 D1
North Luffenham Rutlnd ... 42 B2
North Marden W Susx ... 10 B4
North Marston Bucks ... 31 H2
North Middleton Mdloth ... 86 D2
North Milmain D & G ... 68 C3
North Molton Devon ... 15 F4
North Moreton Oxon ... 19 G5
North Mundham W Susx ... 10 C2
North Muskham Notts ... 52 A2
North Newbald E R Yk ... 60 C4
North Newington Oxon ... 31 E4
North Newnton Wilts ... 18 D3
North Newton Somset ... 17 E2
North Nibley Gloucs ... 29 E2
North Ormesby N York ... 66 B5
North Ormsby Lincs ... 53 E4
North Otterington N York ... 65 G2
North Owersby Lincs ... 52 C4
North Perrott Somset ... 7 F6
North Petherton Somset ... 16 D2
North Petherwin Cnwll ... 4 D5
North Pickenham Norfk ... 44 C3
North Piddle Worcs ... 30 B5
North Pool Devon ... 5 H1
North Poorton Dorset ... 7 F5
North Quarme Somset ... 16 B3
North Queensferry C Edin ... 86 B4
North Radworthy Devon ... 15 G4
North Rauceby Lincs ... 42 C6
North Reston Lincs ... 53 F4
North Rigton N York ... 58 D5
North Rode Ches ... 50 A3
North Ronaldsay Airport Ork ... 111 i1
North Runcton Norfk ... 43 H4
North Scarle Lincs ... 52 B2
North Shian Ag & B ... 90 B3
North Shields T & W ... 73 G3
North Shoebury Essex ... 22 D4
North Shore Lancs ... 56 C6
North Side Cambs ... 43 E2
North Somercotes Lincs ... 53 F5
North Stainley N York ... 65 F1
North Stifford Essex ... 22 B3
North Stoke Oxon ... 19 H5
North Stoke Somset ... 17 H5
North Stoke W Susx ... 10 D3
North Street Berks ... 19 H4
North Street Kent ... 23 E2
North Sunderland Nthumb ... 81 G3
North Tamerton Cnwll ... 14 C1
North Tawton Devon ... 15 F2
North Third Stirlg ... 85 F4
North Thoresby Lincs ... 53 E5
North Tidworth Wilts ... 19 E2
North Town Berks ... 20 C3
North Town Devon ... 15 E2
North Town Somset ... 17 G3
North Tuddenham Norfk ... 44 D3
North Walsham Norfk ... 45 F5
North Waltham Hants ... 19 G2
North Warnborough Hants ... 20 A1
North Weald Bassett Essex ... 21 G5
North Wheatley Notts ... 51 H5
North Widcombe Somset ... 17 G4
North Willingham Lincs ... 52 D4
North Wingfield Derbys ... 51 E3
North Witham Lincs ... 42 B4
North Wootton Dorset ... 17 G1
North Wootton Norfk ... 43 H4
North Wootton Somset ... 17 G3
North Wraxall Wilts ... 18 A4
Northall Bucks ... 32 B1
Northallerton N York ... 65 G3
Northam Devon ... 14 D4
Northam Hants ... 9 F4
Northampton Nhants ... 31 H6
Northampton Worcs ... 39 H3
Northaw Herts ... 21 F5
Northay Somset ... 6 D6
Northborough Cambs ... 42 D3
Northbourne Kent ... 23 G1
Northbrook Hants ... 19 G1
Northchapel W Susx ... 10 C5
Northchurch Herts ... 20 C6
Northcott Devon ... 4 D6
Northcourt Oxon ... 19 G6
Northdown Kent ... 23 H3
Northend Warwks ... 31 E5
Northenden Gt Man ... 57 G2
Northfield Aber C ... 103 E1
Northfield E R Yk ... 60 D3
Northfield W Mids ... 40 B2
Northfields Lincs ... 42 C3
Northfleet Kent ... 22 B3
Northiam E Susx ... 12 D4
Northill Beds ... 32 D3
Northington Hants ... 19 G1
Northlands Lincs ... 53 E1
Northleach Gloucs ... 30 C2
Northleigh Devon ... 6 D5
Northlew Devon ... 15 E1
Northmoor Oxon ... 31 E1
Northmuir Angus ... 93 F4
Northney Hants ... 10 A3
Northolt Gt Lon ... 21 E4
Northop Flints ... 48 C6
Northop Hall Flints ... 48 C6
Northorpe Lincs ... 52 B5
Northorpe Lincs ... 42 D5
Northowram W York ... 58 C3
Northport Dorset ... 8 B2
Northrepps Norfk ... 45 F5
Northton W Isls ... 111 b5
Northway Somset ... 16 C2
Northwich Ches ... 49 F6
Northwold Norfk ... 44 B2
Northwood Gt Lon ... 20 D4
Northwood IOW ... 9 G3

Northwood Shrops ... 49 E3
Northwood Green Gloucs ... 29 E4
Norton Dur ... 66 B5
Norton E Susx ... 11 G2
Norton Gloucs ... 29 F5
Norton N York ... 66 D1
Norton Nhants ... 31 G6
Norton Notts ... 51 F4
Norton Powys ... 38 C3
Norton S York ... 59 F2
Norton Shrops ... 39 G5
Norton Suffk ... 34 C5
Norton W Susx ... 10 C3
Norton Wilts ... 18 B5
Norton Worcs ... 39 H1
Norton Worcs ... 30 B4
Norton Bavant Wilts ... 18 B1
Norton Bridge Staffs ... 49 H2
Norton Canes Staffs ... 40 B4
Norton Canon Herefs ... 38 D1
Norton Disney Lincs ... 52 B2
Norton Fitzwarren Somset ... 16 D2
Norton Green IOW ... 9 E2
Norton Hawkfield Somset ... 17 G5
Norton Heath Essex ... 22 B5
Norton in Hales Shrops ... 49 G3
Norton Lindsey Warwks ... 30 D6
Norton Little Green Suffk ... 34 C5
Norton Malreward Somset ... 17 G5
Norton St Philip Somset ... 18 A2
Norton sub Hamdon Somset ... 17 F1
Norton Subcourse Norfk ... 45 G2
Norton Wood Herefs ... 38 D1
Norton-Juxta-Twycross Leics ... 41 E4
Norton-le-Clay N York ... 65 G1
Norwell Notts ... 51 H3
Norwell Woodhouse Notts ... 51 H3
Norwich Norfk ... 45 E3
Norwich Cathedral Norfk ... 45 E3
Norwick Shet ... 111 m4
Norwood Clacks ... 85 G5
Norwood Green Gt Lon ... 21 E3
Norwood Hill Surrey ... 11 E6
Noseley Leics ... 41 H3
Noss Mayo Devon ... 5 F2
Nosterfield N York ... 65 F2
Nostie Highld ... 97 F5
Notgrove Gloucs ... 30 C2
Nottage Brdgnd ... 26 D1
Notter Cnwll ... 4 C3
Nottingham Notts ... 51 F1
Notton W York ... 59 E2
Notton Wilts ... 18 B4
Noutard's Green Worcs ... 39 G3
Nox Shrops ... 48 D1
Nuffield Oxon ... 19 H5
Nun Monkton N York ... 59 F5
Nunburnholme E R Yk ... 60 C4
Nuneaton Warwks ... 41 E3
Nuneham Courtenay Oxon ... 19 G6
Nunhead Gt Lon ... 21 F3
Nunkeeling E R Yk ... 61 E5
Nunney Somset ... 17 H3
Nunnington N York ... 66 C2
Nunsthorpe Lincs ... 53 E6
Nunthorpe N York ... 59 G5
Nunthorpe N York ... 66 B4
Nunthorpe Village N York ... 66 B4
Nunton Wilts ... 8 D5
Nunwick N York ... 65 G1
Nursling Hants ... 9 F5
Nutbourne W Susx ... 10 B3
Nutbourne W Susx ... 10 D4
Nutfield Surrey ... 21 F1
Nuthall Notts ... 51 F1
Nuthampstead Herts ... 33 F2
Nuthurst W Susx ... 11 E4
Nutley E Susx ... 11 G4
Nybster Highld ... 110 D5
Nyetimber W Susx ... 10 C2
Nyewood W Susx ... 10 B4
Nymet Rowland Devon ... 15 F2
Nymet Tracey Devon ... 15 F1
Nympsfield Gloucs ... 29 F3
Nyton W Susx ... 10 C3

O

Oad Street Kent ... 22 D2
Oadby Leics ... 41 G3
Oak Cross Devon ... 15 E1
Oakamoor Staffs ... 50 B1
Oakbank W Loth ... 86 B3
Oakdale Caerph ... 27 G3
Oake Somset ... 16 C2
Oaken Staffs ... 39 H6
Oakenclough Lancs ... 63 E1
Oakengates Shrops ... 49 G1
Oakenshaw Dur ... 73 F1
Oakenshaw W York ... 58 C3
Oaker Side Derbys ... 50 D3
Oakford Cerdgn ... 36 D3
Oakford Devon ... 16 B1
Oakham Rutlnd ... 42 B3
Oakhanger Hants ... 10 B5
Oakhill Somset ... 17 G4
Oakington Cambs ... 33 F5
Oakle Street Gloucs ... 29 E4
Oakley Beds ... 32 C4
Oakley Bucks ... 31 G2
Oakley Fife ... 86 A5
Oakley Hants ... 19 G2
Oakley Suffk ... 35 E6
Oakridge Gloucs ... 29 F3
Oaksey Wilts ... 29 G2
Oakthorpe Leics ... 40 D4
Oakwood Derbys ... 51 E1
Oakwoodhill Surrey ... 11 E5
Oakworth W York ... 58 B4
Oare Kent ... 23 E2
Oare Somset ... 15 G5
Oare Wilts ... 18 D4
Oasby Lincs ... 42 C5
Oath Somset ... 17 E2
Oathlaw Angus ... 93 G5
Oatlands Park Surrey ... 20 D2
Oban Ag & B ... 90 A2
Obley Shrops ... 38 D4

Obney P & K ... 92 C3
Oborne Dorset ... 17 G1
Occold Suffk ... 35 E5
Occumster Highld ... 110 C3
Ochiltree E Ayrs ... 76 D3
Ockbrook Derbys ... 41 E6
Ockham Surrey ... 20 D1
Ockle Highld ... 89 F5
Ockley Surrey ... 11 E5
Ocle Pychard Herefs ... 39 F1
Odcombe Somset ... 17 F1
Odd Down Somset ... 17 H5
Oddingley Worcs ... 30 A5
Oddington Gloucs ... 30 D2
Oddington Oxon ... 31 F2
Odell Beds ... 32 B4
Odiham Hants ... 20 B1
Odsal W York ... 58 C3
Odsey Herts ... 33 E3
Odstock Wilts ... 8 D3
Odstone Leics ... 41 E4
Offchurch Warwks ... 31 E6
Offenham Worcs ... 30 B4
Offham E Susx ... 11 G3
Offham Kent ... 22 B1
Offham W Susx ... 10 D3
Offord Cluny Cambs ... 32 D5
Offord Darcy Cambs ... 32 D5
Offton Suffk ... 34 D4
Offwell Devon ... 6 D5
Ogbourne Maizey Wilts ... 18 D4
Ogbourne St Andrew Wilts ... 18 D4
Ogbourne St George Wilts ... 18 D4
Ogle Nthumb ... 73 E4
Oglet Mersyd ... 56 D1
Ogmore V Glam ... 16 A6
Ogmore Vale Brdgnd ... 27 E2
Ogmore-by-Sea V Glam ... 16 A6
Okeford Fitzpaine Dorset ... 8 A4
Okehampton Devon ... 5 F6
Old Nhants ... 32 A5
Old Aberdeen Aber C ... 95 H6
Old Alresford Hants ... 9 G6
Old Auchenbrack D & G ... 77 F1
Old Basford Notts ... 51 F1
Old Basing Hants ... 19 H2
Old Bewick Nthumb ... 81 F2
Old Bolingbroke Lincs ... 53 E2
Old Bramhope W York ... 58 D4
Old Brampton Derbys ... 51 E4
Old Bridge of Urr D & G ... 70 B5
Old Buckenham Norfk ... 44 D2
Old Burghclere Hants ... 19 F3
Old Byland N York ... 66 B2
Old Cantley S York ... 51 G6
Old Clee Lincs ... 53 E6
Old Cleeve Somset ... 16 C3
Old Clipstone Notts ... 51 G3
Old Dailly S Ayrs ... 76 B2
Old Dalby Leics ... 41 G5
Old Deer Abers ... 103 E4
Old Edlington S York ... 51 F6
Old Ellerby E R Yk ... 61 E4
Old Felixstowe Suffk ... 35 F2
Old Fletton Cambs ... 42 D2
Old Forge Herefs ... 28 D4
Old Grimsby IOS ... 2 a2
Old Hall Green Herts ... 33 F1
Old Harlow Essex ... 21 G6
Old Hunstanton Norfk ... 44 A6
Old Hurst Cambs ... 33 E6
Old Hutton Cumb ... 63 E4
Old Kea Cnwll ... 3 E3
Old Kilpatrick W Duns ... 84 D3
Old Knebworth Herts ... 32 D1
Old Langho Lancs ... 57 F6
Old Leake Lincs ... 53 F1
Old Malton N York ... 66 D1
Old Micklefield W York ... 59 E3
Old Milverton Warwks ... 30 D6
Old Newton Suffk ... 34 D5
Old Radnor Powys ... 38 C2
Old Rayne Abers ... 102 C2
Old Romney Kent ... 13 E4
Old Shoreham W Susx ... 11 E3
Old Sodbury Gloucs ... 29 E1
Old Somerby Lincs ... 42 B5
Old Stratford Nhants ... 31 H4
Old Swinford W Mids ... 40 A2
Old Thirsk N York ... 66 A2
Old Town Cumb ... 63 F4
Old Town E Susx ... 12 B2
Old Town IOS ... 2 b2
Old Trafford Gt Man ... 57 G2
Old Warden Beds ... 32 D3
Old Weston Cambs ... 32 C6
Old Wick Highld ... 110 D4
Old Windsor Berks ... 20 C3
Old Wives Lees Kent ... 23 E1
Old Woking Surrey ... 20 D1
Oldany Highld ... 108 B3
Oldberrow Warwks ... 30 C6
Oldbury Shrops ... 39 G5
Oldbury W Mids ... 40 B2
Oldbury Warwks ... 40 D3
Oldbury on the Hill Gloucs ... 18 A5
Oldbury-on-Severn Gloucs ... 28 D2
Oldcastle Mons ... 28 B5
Oldcotes Notts ... 51 G5
Oldfield Worcs ... 39 H3
Oldford Somset ... 18 A2
Oldham Gt Man ... 58 A1
Oldhamstocks E Loth ... 87 G3
Oldland S Glos ... 17 G6
Oldmeldrum Abers ... 102 D2
Oldmill Cnwll ... 4 D4
Oldmixon Somset ... 17 E4
Oldshoremore Highld ... 108 B5
Oldstead N York ... 66 B2
Oldwall Cumb ... 71 G5
Oldwalls Swans ... 26 B2
Olive Green Staffs ... 40 C5
Oliver Border ... 78 D5
Oliver's Battery Hants ... 9 F6
Ollaberry Shet ... 111 I3
Ollach Highld ... 96 C5
Ollerton Ches ... 57 G1
Ollerton Notts ... 51 G3
Ollerton Shrops ... 49 F2
Olney Bucks ... 32 B4
Olrig House Highld ... 110 C5
Olton W Mids ... 40 C2
Olveston Gloucs ... 28 D2
Ombersley Worcs ... 39 H3

Ompton Notts ... 51 G3
Onchan IOM ... 116 c3
Onecote Staffs ... 50 B2
Onibury Shrops ... 39 E4
Onich Highld ... 90 C5
Onllwyn Neath ... 26 D4
Onneley Staffs ... 49 G4
Onslow Village Surrey ... 20 C1
Onston Ches ... 49 F6
Opinan Highld ... 105 F3
Orbliston Moray ... 101 F5
Orbost Highld ... 96 A6
Orby Lincs ... 53 F2
Orchard Portman Somset ... 16 D2
Orcheston Wilts ... 18 C2
Orcop Herefs ... 28 C5
Orcop Hill Herefs ... 28 C5
Ord Abers ... 102 C5
Ordhead Abers ... 102 C1
Ordie Abers ... 94 D6
Ordiequish Moray ... 101 F5
Ordley Nthumb ... 72 D3
Ordsall Notts ... 51 G4
Ore E Susx ... 12 D3
Oreton Shrops ... 39 F4
Orford Ches ... 57 F2
Orford Suffk ... 35 G4
Organford Dorset ... 8 B3
Orlestone Kent ... 13 E5
Orleton Herefs ... 39 E3
Orleton Worcs ... 39 F3
Orlingbury Nhants ... 32 B5
Ormesby N York ... 66 B5
Ormesby St Margaret Norfk ... 45 G3
Ormesby St Michael Norfk ... 45 G3
Ormiscaig Highld ... 105 F5
Ormiston E Loth ... 86 D3
Ormsaigmore Highld ... 89 F5
Ormsary Ag & B ... 83 F3
Ormskirk Lancs ... 56 D3
Oronsay Ag & B ... 82 C4
Orphir Ork ... 111 g2
Orpington Gt Lon ... 21 G2
Orrell Gt Man ... 57 E3
Orrell Mersyd ... 56 D2
Orroland D & G ... 70 B4
Orsett Essex ... 22 B3
Orslow Staffs ... 49 G1
Orston Notts ... 51 H1
Orton Cumb ... 63 F6
Orton Nhants ... 32 A6
Orton Longueville Cambs ... 42 D2
Orton Waterville Cambs ... 42 D2
Orton-on-the-Hill Leics ... 40 D4
Orwell Cambs ... 33 E4
Osbaldeston Lancs ... 57 F5
Osbaldwick N York ... 59 G5
Osbaston Shrops ... 48 D2
Osborne House IOW ... 9 G3
Osbournby Lincs ... 42 C5
Oscroft Ches ... 49 E5
Ose Highld ... 96 B6
Osgathorpe Leics ... 41 E5
Osgodby Lincs ... 52 C4
Osgodby N York ... 59 G3
Osgodby N York ... 67 F2
Oskaig Highld ... 96 D5
Oskamull Ag & B ... 89 E3
Osmaston Derbys ... 50 D1
Osmington Dorset ... 7 H4
Osmington Mills Dorset ... 7 H4
Osmondthorpe W York ... 59 E3
Osmotherley N York ... 66 B3
Osney Oxon ... 31 F1
Ospringe Kent ... 23 E2
Ossett W York ... 58 D2
Ossington Notts ... 51 H3
Osterley Gt Lon ... 21 E3
Oswaldkirk N York ... 66 C2
Oswaldtwistle Lancs ... 57 G5
Oswestry Shrops ... 48 C2
Otford Kent ... 21 H2
Otham Kent ... 22 C1
Othery Somset ... 17 E2
Otley Suffk ... 35 E4
Otley W York ... 58 D4
Otter Ferry Ag & B ... 83 G4
Otterbourne Hants ... 9 F5
Otterburn N York ... 63 H2
Otterburn Nthumb ... 72 C5
Otterham Cnwll ... 4 C5
Otterhampton Somset ... 16 D3
Otternish W Isls ... 111 b4
Ottershaw Surrey ... 20 D2
Otterswick Shet ... 111 I3
Otterton Devon ... 6 C4
Ottery Devon ... 5 E4
Ottery St Mary Devon ... 6 C4
Ottinge Kent ... 13 F6
Ottringham E R Yk ... 61 F3
Oughterside Cumb ... 71 E3
Oughtibridge S York ... 50 D5
Oughtrington Ches ... 57 F2
Oulston N York ... 66 B1
Oulton Cumb ... 71 E4
Oulton Norfk ... 45 E5
Oulton Staffs ... 40 A6
Oulton Suffk ... 45 H2
Oulton Broad Suffk ... 45 H2
Oulton Street Norfk ... 45 E5
Oundle Nhants ... 42 C1
Ousby Cumb ... 72 A3
Ousden Suffk ... 34 B4
Ousefleet E R Yk ... 60 C2
Ouston Dur ... 73 F2
Outgate Cumb ... 62 D5
Outhgill Cumb ... 64 C3
Outlands Staffs ... 49 H5
Outlane W York ... 58 C2
Outwell Norfk ... 43 G3
Outwood Surrey ... 11 F6
Outwoods Staffs ... 49 G1
Ouzlewell Green W York ... 59 E3
Over Cambs ... 33 F5
Over Compton Dorset ... 17 G1
Over Green Warwks ... 40 C3
Over Haddon Derbys ... 50 D3
Over Kellet Lancs ... 63 E3
Over Kiddington Oxon ... 31 E2
Over Norton Oxon ... 30 D3
Over Peover Ches ... 49 G6

Over Silton N York ... 66 B3
Over Stowey Somset ... 16 D3
Over Stratton Somset ... 17 F1
Over Wallop Hants ... 19 E1
Over Whitacre Warwks ... 40 D3
Over Worton Oxon ... 31 E3
Overbury Worcs ... 29 G6
Overcombe Dorset ... 7 H4
Overleigh Somset ... 17 F3
Overpool Ches ... 56 D1
Overscaig Hotel Highld ... 108 D2
Overseal Derbys ... 40 D5
Oversland Kent ... 23 E1
Overstone Nhants ... 32 A5
Overstrand Norfk ... 45 F5
Overthorpe Nhants ... 31 F4
Overton Aber C ... 102 D1
Overton Hants ... 19 G2
Overton Lancs ... 62 D2
Overton N York ... 59 F5
Overton Shrops ... 39 E3
Overton Swans ... 26 A2
Overton W York ... 58 D2
Overton Wrexhm ... 48 D3
Overtown N Lans ... 85 G1
Oving Bucks ... 32 A1
Oving W Susx ... 10 C3
Ovingdean E Susx ... 11 F3
Ovingham Nthumb ... 73 E3
Ovington Dur ... 65 E4
Ovington Essex ... 34 B3
Ovington Hants ... 9 G6
Ovington Norfk ... 44 C2
Ovington Nthumb ... 73 E3
Ower Hants ... 9 E5
Owermoigne Dorset ... 8 A2
Owlerton S York ... 51 E5
Owlsmoor Berks ... 20 B2
Owlswick Bucks ... 20 B5
Owmby Lincs ... 52 C5
Owmby Lincs ... 52 C4
Owslebury Hants ... 9 G5
Owston Leics ... 41 H4
Owston S York ... 59 F1
Owston Ferry Lincs ... 52 A5
Owstwick E R Yk ... 61 F3
Owthorne E R Yk ... 61 G3
Owthorpe Notts ... 41 G6
Oxborough Norfk ... 44 B2
Oxcombe Lincs ... 53 E3
Oxen End Essex ... 33 H2
Oxen Park Cumb ... 62 D4
Oxenholme Cumb ... 63 E5
Oxenhope W York ... 58 B3
Oxenpill Somset ... 17 F3
Oxenton Gloucs ... 29 G5
Oxenwood Wilts ... 19 E3
Oxford Oxon ... 31 F1
Oxhey Herts ... 20 D5
Oxhill Warwks ... 30 D4
Oxley W Mids ... 40 A3
Oxley Green Essex ... 22 D6
Oxlode Cambs ... 43 F1
Oxnam Border ... 80 C2
Oxnead Norfk ... 45 E4
Oxshott Surrey ... 21 E2
Oxspring S York ... 50 D6
Oxted Surrey ... 21 F1
Oxton Border ... 80 B5
Oxton N York ... 59 F4
Oxton Notts ... 51 G2
Oxwich Swans ... 26 B2
Oxwich Green Swans ... 26 B2
Oykel Bridge Hotel Highld ... 106 C5
Oyne Abers ... 102 C2
Oystermouth Swans ... 26 C2

P

Pabail W Isls ... 111 e6
Packington Leics ... 41 E4
Padanaram Angus ... 93 F4
Padbury Bucks ... 31 H3
Paddington Gt Lon ... 21 F3
Paddlesworth Kent ... 22 B2
Paddlesworth Kent ... 13 F5
Paddock Wood Kent ... 12 B6
Padiham Lancs ... 57 G5
Padside N York ... 58 C5
Padstow Cnwll ... 3 E6
Padworth Berks ... 19 H3
Pagham W Susx ... 10 C2
Paglesham Essex ... 22 D4
Paignton Devon ... 6 A2
Pailton Warwks ... 41 F2
Painscastle Powys ... 38 B1
Painshawfield Nthumb ... 73 E3
Painsthorpe E R Yk ... 60 C5
Painswick Gloucs ... 29 F4
Painter's Forstal Kent ... 23 E2
Paisley Rens ... 84 D2
Pakefield Suffk ... 45 H1
Pakenham Suffk ... 34 C5
Paley Street Berks ... 20 C3
Palgrave Suffk ... 35 E6
Pallington Dorset ... 8 A3
Palmerston E Ayrs ... 76 D3
Palnackie D & G ... 70 B5
Palnure D & G ... 69 F4
Palterton Derbys ... 51 F3
Pamber End Hants ... 19 H3
Pamber Green Hants ... 19 H3
Pamber Heath Hants ... 19 H3
Pamington Gloucs ... 29 G5
Pamphill Dorset ... 8 C3
Pampisford Cambs ... 33 G3
Panbride Angus ... 93 G3
Pancrasweek Devon ... 14 C2
Pandy Mons ... 28 B5
Pandy Tudur Conwy ... 55 F3
Panfield Essex ... 34 B2
Pangbourne Berks ... 19 H4
Pangdean W Susx ... 11 F3
Pannal N York ... 58 D5
Pannal Ash N York ... 58 D5
Pannanich Wells Hotel Abers ... 94 D5
Pant Shrops ... 48 C2

Pant Glas Gwynd	46 D6	Pen-y-bont-fawr Powys	48 B2
Pant-ffrwyth Brdgnd	27 E1	Pen-y-bryn Pembks	36 B1
Pant-y-dwr Powys	37 H4	Pen-y-clawdd Mons	28 C3
Pant-y-mwyn Flints	48 C5	Pen-y-coedcae Rhondd	27 F2
Pantasaph Flints	48 B6	Pen-y-cwn Pembks	24 C5
Pantglas Powys	47 F2	Pen-y-felin Flints	48 B6
Panton Lincs	52 D3	Pen-y-Garnedd Powys	48 B2
Panxworth Norfk	45 F3	Pen-y-graig Gwynd	46 B4
Papa Westray Airport Ork	111 H3	Pen-y-stryt Denbgs	48 C4
Papcastle Cumb	70 D3	Penallt Mons	28 C4
Papigoe Highld	110 D4	Penally Pembks	25 E3
Papple E Loth	87 F3	Penalt Herefs	28 D5
Papplewick Notts	51 F2	Penarth V Glam	16 D6
Papworth Everard Cambs	33 E5	Penbryn Cerdgn	36 C2
Papworth St Agnes Cambs	33 E5	Pencader Carmth	25 H6
Par Cnwll	3 G4	Pencaitland E Loth	87 E3
Parbold Lancs	57 E4	Pencarnisiog IOA	54 B4
Parbrook Somset	17 G3	Pencarreg Carmth	37 E2
Parc Gwynd	47 G4	Pencelli Powys	27 F5
Parc Seymour Newpt	28 C2	Penclawdd Swans	26 B2
Pardshaw Cumb	70 D2	Pencoed Brdgnd	27 E1
Parham Suffk	35 F4	Pencombe Herefs	39 F2
Park Abers	95 G5	Pencraig Herefs	28 D4
Park D & G	78 C2	Pencraig Powys	48 A2
Park Nthumb	72 B3	Pendeen Cnwll	2 A3
Park Corner Oxon	20 A4	Penderyn Rhondd	27 E3
Park Gate Hants	9 G4	Pendine Carmth	25 F3
Park Gate W York	58 C4	Pendlebury Gt Man	57 F3
Park Royal Gt Lon	21 E3	Pendleton Lancs	57 G6
Park Street Herts	21 E5	Pendock Worcs	29 E5
Parkend Gloucs	28 D3	Pendoggett Cnwll	4 B5
Parkers Green Kent	12 B6	Pendomer Somset	7 F6
Parkgate Ches	56 C1	Pendoylan V Glam	16 C6
Parkgate D & G	78 D2	Penegoes Powys	47 F2
Parkgate Surrey	11 E6	Pengam Caerph	27 G3
Parkhall W Duns	84 D3	Pengam Cardif	27 G1
Parkham Devon	14 D3	Penge Gt Lon	21 F3
Parkhill House Abers	103 E1	Pengelly Cnwll	4 B5
Parkmill Swans	26 B2	Pengrugla Cnwll	3 F4
Parkside Dur	73 H2	Penhallow Cnwll	2 D4
Parkside N Lans	85 G2	Penhalvean Cnwll	2 D3
Parkstone Dorset	8 C3	Penhill Wilts	18 D5
Parndon Essex	21 G6	Penhow Newpt	28 C2
Parracombe Devon	15 F5	Penicuik Mdloth	86 C2
Parson Drove Cambs	43 F3	Penifiler Highld	96 C6
Parson's Heath Essex	34 D2	Peninver Ag & B	75 F3
Partick C Glas	85 E2	Penistone S York	58 D1
Partington Gt Man	57 G2	Penkill S Ayrs	76 B2
Partney Lincs	53 F2	Penkridge Staffs	40 A4
Parton Cumb	70 C2	Penlean Cnwll	14 B1
Partridge Green W Susx	11 E4	Penley Wrexhm	48 D3
Parwich Derbys	50 C2	Penllyn V Glam	16 B6
Passenham Nhants	32 A3	Penmachno Conwy	55 F2
Passfield Hants	10 B5	Penmaen Caerph	27 G3
Paston Norfk	45 F5	Penmaen Swans	26 B2
Patcham E Susx	11 F3	Penmaenmawr Conwy	55 E4
Patching W Susx	10 D3	Penmaenpool Gwynd	47 F3
Patchway Gloucs	28 D1	Penmark V Glam	16 C5
Pateley Bridge N York	58 C6	Penmorfa Gwynd	47 E5
Path of Condie P & K	92 D1	Penmynydd IOA	54 D4
Pathhead Fife	86 C5	Penn Bucks	20 C4
Pathhead Mdloth	86 D2	Penn Street Bucks	20 C5
Patna E Ayrs	76 D3	Pennal Gwynd	47 F2
Patney Wilts	18 C3	Pennan Abers	102 D5
Patrick Brompton N York	65 F3	Pennant Powys	47 G2
Patricroft Gt Man	57 G3	Pennerley Shrops	38 D5
Patrington E R Yk	61 F2	Pennington Cumb	62 C4
Patrixbourne Kent	23 F1	Pennorth Powys	27 F5
Patterdale Cumb	71 G1	Penny Bridge Cumb	62 C4
Pattingham Staffs	39 G5	Penny Hill Lincs	43 E4
Pattishall Nhants	31 G5	Pennycross Ag & B	89 F2
Pattiswick Green Essex	34 B2	Pennyghael Ag & B	89 F2
Paul Cnwll	2 B2	Pennyglen S Ayrs	76 C3
Paul's Dene Wilts	8 D6	Pennymoor Devon	15 G2
Paulerspury Bucks	31 H4	Penparc Cerdgn	36 B2
Paull E R Yk	61 E3	Penperlleni Mons	28 B3
Paulton Somset	17 G4	Penpoll Cnwll	4 C3
Pauperhaugh Nthumb	73 E6	Penponds Cnwll	2 C3
Pavenham Beds	32 C4	Penpont D & G	78 B2
Pawlett Somset	16 D3	Penrherber Cerdgn	36 C2
Paxford Gloucs	30 C4	Penrhiwceiber Rhondd	27 F3
Paxton Border	81 E5	Penrhiwllan Cerdgn	36 C1
Payhembury Devon	6 C5	Penrhos Gwynd	46 C4
Paythorne Lancs	63 G2	Penrhos Mons	28 C4
Peacehaven E Susx	11 G2	Penrhyn Bay Conwy	55 F4
Peak Forest Derbys	50 C4	Penrhyn Castle Gwynd	54 D3
Peakirk Cambs	42 D3	Penrhyndeudraeth Gwynd	47 E5
Peanmeanach Highld	89 G6	Penrice Swans	26 B2
Pease Pottage W Susx	11 F5	Penrioch N Ayrs	75 G5
Peasedown St John Somset	17 H4	Penrith Cumb	71 H2
Peaseland Green Norfk	44 D4	Penrose Cnwll	3 G6
Peasemore Berks	19 F4	Penruddock Cumb	71 G2
Peasenhall Suffk	35 F5	Penryn Cnwll	2 D3
Peaslake Surrey	10 D6	Pensarn Carmth	25 G4
Peasley Cross Mersyd	57 E2	Pensarn Conwy	55 G4
Peasmarsh E Susx	12 D4	Pensax Worcs	39 G3
Peat Inn Fife	87 E6	Penselwood Somset	17 H2
Peathill Abers	103 E5	Pensford Somset	17 G5
Peatling Magna Leics	41 G3	Pensham Worcs	30 A4
Peatling Parva Leics	41 G2	Penshaw T & W	73 G2
Pebmarsh Essex	34 C2	Penshurst Kent	11 H6
Pebworth Worcs	30 C4	Pensilva Cnwll	4 D4
Pecket Well W York	58 B3	Pentewan Cnwll	3 F4
Peckforton Ches	49 E5	Pentir Gwynd	54 D3
Peckham Gt Lon	21 F3	Pentire Cnwll	2 D5
Peckleton Leics	41 F3	Pentlow Essex	34 B3
Pedlinge Kent	13 F5	Pentney Norfk	44 B3
Pedmore W Mids	40 A2	Penton Mewsey Hants	19 E2
Pedwell Somset	17 E3	Pentonbridge Cumb	79 G1
Peebles Border	79 F6	Pentraeth IOA	54 D4
Peel IOM	116 b3	Pentre Rhondd	27 E2
Peene Kent	13 F5	Pentre Shrops	48 D1
Pegsdon Beds	32 D2	Pentre Berw IOA	54 C3
Pegswood Nthumb	73 F5	Pentre Hodrey Shrops	38 D4
Pegwell Kent	23 H2	Pentre Llanrhaeadr Denbgs	48 B5
Peinchorran Highld	96 D5	Pentre Meyrick V Glam	16 B6
Peinlich Highld	104 C2	Pentre-bach Powys	27 E5
Peldon Essex	34 D1	Pentre-celyn Denbgs	48 B4
Pelsall W Mids	40 B4	Pentre-celyn Powys	47 G2
Pelton Dur	73 F2	Pentre-chwyth Swans	26 C2
Pelynt Cnwll	4 C3	Pentre-cwrt Carmth	25 G6
Pemberton Carmth	26 B3	Pentre-Gwenlais Carmth	26 C4
Pemberton Gt Man	57 E3	Pentre-tafarn-y-fedw Conwy	55 F3
Pembrey Carmth	25 G3	Pentrebach Myr Td	27 F3
Pembridge Herefs	38 D2	Pentredwr Denbgs	48 C4
Pembroke Pembks	24 D3	Pentrefelin Gwynd	47 E5
Pembroke Dock Pembks	24 D3	Pentrefoelas Conwy	55 F2
Pembury Kent	12 B6	Pentregat Cerdgn	36 C2
Pen Rhiwfawr Neath	26 C4	Pentrich Derbys	51 E2
Pen-bont Rhydybeddau Cerdgn	37 F3	Pentridge Hill Dorset	8 C5
Pen-ffordd Pembks	25 E5	Pentwynmaur Caerph	27 G2
Pen-rhiw Pembks	36 B1	Pentyrch Cardif	27 F1
Pen-twyn Mons	28 C3	Penwithick Cnwll	3 F4
Pen-y-bont Powys	48 C2	Penybanc Carmth	26 C3

Penybont Powys	38 B3	Pirton Worcs	30 A4
Penycae Wrexhm	48 C4	Pishill Oxon	20 A4
Penyffordd Flints	48 C5	Pistyll Gwynd	46 C5
Penygraig Rhondd	27 F2	Pitagowan P & K	92 B5
Penygroes Carmth	26 B4	Pitblae Abers	103 E5
Penygroes Gwynd	54 C2	Pitcairngreen P & K	92 C2
Penysarn IOA	54 C5	Pitcalnie Highld	107 G3
Penywaun Rhondd	27 E3	Pitcaple Abers	102 C3
Penzance Cnwll	2 B2	Pitcarity Angus	94 C3
Penzance Heliport Cnwll	2 B2	Pitch Green Bucks	20 B5
Peopleton Worcs	30 B5	Pitch Place Surrey	10 C5
Peplow Shrops	49 F2	Pitchcombe Gloucs	29 F3
Perceton N Ayrs	76 C5	Pitchcott Bucks	31 H2
Percie Abers	95 E5	Pitchford Shrops	39 E6
Percyhorner Abers	103 E5	Pitchroy Moray	101 E3
Perelle Guern	6 b1	Pitcombe Somset	17 G2
Periton Somset	16 B3	Pitcox E Loth	87 F3
Perivale Gt Lon	21 E4	Pitfichie Abers	102 C1
Perkins Village Devon	6 B4	Pitglassie Abers	102 C4
Perlethorpe Notts	51 G4	Pitgrudy Highld	107 G5
Perranarworthal Cnwll	2 D3	Pitkennedy Angus	93 G4
Perranporth Cnwll	2 D4	Pitlessie Fife	86 D6
Perranuthnoe Cnwll	2 B2	Pitlochry P & K	92 B5
Perranwell Cnwll	2 D3	Pitmachie Abers	102 C2
Perranzabuloe Cnwll	2 D4	Pitmain Highld	99 F3
Perry Barr W Mids	40 C3	Pitmedden Abers	103 E2
Perry Green Wilts	18 C5	Pitmedden Garden Abers	103 E2
Pershall Staffs	49 G2	Pitmuies Angus	93 G4
Pershore Worcs	30 B4	Pitmunie Abers	102 C1
Pertenhall Beds	32 C5	Pitney Somset	17 F2
Perth P & K	92 D2	Pitroddie P & K	93 E2
Perthy Shrops	48 D3	Pitscottie Fife	93 F1
Perton Herefs	28 D6	Pitsea Essex	22 C4
Perton Staffs	39 H5	Pitsford Nhants	31 H6
Peter Tavy Devon	5 E4	Pitstone Bucks	20 C6
Peter's Green Herts	32 D1	Pittarrow Abers	95 F3
Peterborough Cambs	42 D2	Pittenweem Fife	87 E6
Peterchurch Herefs	28 B6	Pitteuchar Fife	86 C5
Peterculter Aber C	95 G6	Pittington Dur	73 G1
Peterhead Abers	103 F4	Pittodrie House Hotel Abers	102 C2
Peterlee Dur	73 H1	Pitton Wilts	8 D6
Peters Marland Devon	14 D2	Pittulie Abers	103 E6
Petersfield Hants	10 B4	Pity Me Dur	73 F2
Petersham Gt Lon	21 E3	Pixham Surrey	21 E1
Peterstone Wentlooge Newpt	28 A1	Plains N Lans	85 G2
Peterston-super-Ely V Glam	16 C6	Plaish Shrops	39 E5
Peterstow Herefs	28 D5	Plaistow Derbys	51 E2
Petham Kent	23 F1	Plaistow Gt Lon	21 G4
Petherwin Gate Cnwll	4 C5	Plaistow W Susx	10 D5
Petrockstow Devon	15 E2	Plaitford Hants	9 E5
Pett E Susx	12 D3	Plas Cymyran IOA	54 B4
Pettaugh Suffk	35 E4	Plastow Green Hants	19 G3
Petterden Angus	93 F3	Platt Kent	22 B1
Pettinain S Lans	78 C6	Plawsworth Dur	73 F2
Pettistree Suffk	35 F4	Plaxtol Kent	22 B1
Petton Devon	16 B2	Play Hatch Oxon	20 A3
Petts Wood Gt Lon	21 G2	Playden E Susx	12 D4
Pettycur Fife	86 C4	Playford Suffk	35 E3
Pettymuk Abers	103 E2	Playley Green Gloucs	29 E5
Pevensey E Susx	12 B3	Plealey Shrops	38 D6
Pewsey Wilts	18 D3	Plean Stirlg	85 G4
Phepson Worcs	30 B5	Pleasance Fife	93 E1
Philham Devon	14 C3	Pleasington Lancs	57 F5
Philiphaugh Border	79 G5	Pleasley Derbys	51 F3
Phillack Cnwll	2 C3	Pleinheaume Guern	6 b2
Philleigh Cnwll	3 E3	Plemont Jersey	7 a2
Philpstoun W Loth	86 B4	Plemstall Ches	49 E6
Phoenix Green Hants	20 B1	Pleshey Essex	22 B6
Phoines Highld	99 E2	Plockton Highld	97 F5
Pibsbury Somset	17 F2	Plowden Shrops	38 D4
Pica Cumb	70 D2	Plox Green Shrops	38 D6
Pickburn S York	59 F1	Pluckley Kent	12 D6
Pickering N York	66 D2	Pluckley Thorne Kent	12 D6
Pickford W Mids	40 D7	Plumbland Cumb	71 E3
Pickhill N York	65 G2	Plumley Ches	49 G6
Picklescott Shrops	38 D5	Plumpton Cumb	71 G3
Pickmere Ches	57 F1	Plumpton E Susx	11 F3
Pickney Somset	16 D2	Plumpton Nhants	31 G4
Pickup Bank Lancs	57 G5	Plumpton End Nhants	31 H4
Pickwell Leics	42 A3	Plumpton Green E Susx	11 F4
Pickworth Lincs	42 C3	Plumstead Gt Lon	21 G3
Pickworth Lincs	42 C5	Plumstead Norfk	45 E5
Pictillum Abers	102 C1	Plumtree Notts	41 G6
Picton Ches	48 D6	Plungar Leics	41 H6
Picton N York	65 G4	Plurenden Kent	12 D5
Piddinghoe E Susx	11 G2	Plush Dorset	7 H5
Piddington Nhants	32 A4	Plwmp Cerdgn	36 C2
Piddington Oxon	31 G2	Plymouth Devon	5 E3
Piddlehinton Dorset	7 H5	Plymouth Airport Devon	5 E3
Piddletrenthide Dorset	7 H5	Plympton Devon	5 E3
Pidley Cambs	33 E6	Plymstock Devon	5 F2
Piercebridge Dur	65 F5	Plymtree Devon	6 C5
Pierowall Ork	111 h3	Pockley N York	66 C2
Pilgrims Hatch Essex	22 B5	Pocklington E R Yk	60 B5
Pilham Lincs	52 B4	Podimore Somset	17 F2
Pill N Som	28 D2	Podington Beds	32 B5
Pillaton Cnwll	4 D3	Podmore Staffs	49 G3
Pillerton Hersey Warwks	30 D5	Pointon Lincs	42 D5
Pillerton Priors Warwks	30 D4	Pokesdown Dorset	8 D3
Pilley Hants	9 E3	Polbain Highld	105 H6
Pilley S York	51 E6	Polbathic Cnwll	4 D3
Pilling Lancs	62 D1	Polbeth W Loth	86 A2
Pilning Gloucs	28 D2	Poldark Mine Cnwll	2 D2
Pilsbury Derbys	50 C3	Polebrook Nhants	42 C1
Pilsdon Dorset	7 E5	Polegate E Susx	12 B3
Pilsley Derbys	50 D4	Polesworth Warwks	40 D3
Pilsley Derbys	51 E3	Polglass Highld	105 H6
Pilson Green Norfk	45 G3	Polgooth Cnwll	3 F4
Piltdown E Susx	11 G4	Polgown D & G	77 F2
Pilton Devon	15 E4	Poling W Susx	10 D3
Pilton Nhants	42 C1	Poling Corner W Susx	10 D3
Pilton Rutlnd	42 B2	Polkerris Cnwll	4 B2
Pilton Somset	17 G3	Pollington E R Yk	59 G2
Pimperne Dorset	8 B4	Polloch Highld	89 H5
Pin Green Herts	33 E2	Pollokshaws C Glas	85 E2
Pinchbeck Lincs	43 E4	Pollokshields C Glas	85 E2
Pinhoe Devon	6 B5	Polmassick Cnwll	3 F4
Pinley Green Warwks	30 D6	Polmont Falk	85 H3
Pinminnoch S Ayrs	76 B1	Polnish Highld	97 E1
Pinmore S Ayrs	76 B1	Polperro Cnwll	4 C2
Pinn Devon	6 C4	Polruan Cnwll	4 C2
Pinner Gt Lon	20 D4	Polstead Suffk	34 D3
Pinner Green Gt Lon	20 D4	Poltalloch Ag & B	83 F5
Pinvin Worcs	30 B5	Poltimore Devon	6 B5
Pinwherry S Ayrs	68 D6	Polton Mdloth	86 C3
Pinxton Derbys	51 F2	Polwarth Border	80 D5
Pipe and Lyde Herefs	39 E1	Polyphant Cnwll	4 C5
Pipe Gate Shrops	49 G3	Polzeath Cnwll	4 A5
Piperhill Highld	100 B4	Pomathorn Mdloth	86 C2
Pipewell Nhants	42 A1	Ponders End Gt Lon	21 F5
Pirbright Surrey	20 C1	Pondersbridge Cambs	43 E2
Pirnie Border	80 C3	Ponsanooth Cnwll	2 D3
Pirnmill N Ayrs	75 G5	Ponsworthy Devon	5 G4
Pirton Herts	32 D2		

Pont Robert Powys	48 B1
Pont-ar-gothi Carmth	26 B4
Pont-faen Powys	27 F5
Pont-Nedd-Fechan Neath	27 E3
Pont-rhyd-y-fen Neath	26 D2
Pont-y-pant Conwy	55 F2
Pontac Jersey	7 c1
Pontantwn Carmth	25 H4
Pontardawe Neath	26 C3
Pontarddulais Swans	26 B3
Pontarsais Carmth	25 H5
Pontblyddyn Flints	48 C5
Pontefract W York	59 F2
Ponteland Nthumb	73 F4
Ponterwyd Cerdgn	37 F5
Pontesbury Shrops	38 D6
Pontesford Shrops	38 D6
Pontfadog Wrexhm	48 C3
Pontfaen Pembks	24 D5
Pontgarreg Cerdgn	36 C2
Ponthenry Carmth	26 B4
Ponthir Torfn	28 B2
Ponthirwaun Cerdgn	36 B2
Pontlanfraith Caerph	27 G2
Pontlliw Swans	26 C3
Pontlyfni Gwynd	54 C2
Pontnewydd Torfn	28 B2
Pontop Dur	73 E2
Pontrhydfendigaid Cerdgn	37 F3
Pontrhydygroes Cerdgn	37 F4
Pontrilas Herefs	28 B5
Ponts Green E Susx	12 B4
Pontshaen Cerdgn	36 C2
Pontshill Herefs	28 D4
Pontsticill Powys	27 F4
Pontwelly Carmth	36 D1
Pontyates Carmth	26 B3
Pontyberem Carmth	26 B4
Pontybodkin Flints	48 C5
Pontyclun Rhondd	27 F1
Pontycymer Brdgnd	27 E2
Pontypool Torfn	28 B3
Pontypridd Rhondd	27 F2
Pontywaun Caerph	27 G2
Pool Cnwll	2 D3
Pool W York	58 D4
Pool of Muckhart Clacks	86 A5
Pool Street Essex	34 B3
Poole Dorset	8 C3
Poole Keynes Gloucs	18 C6
Poolewe Highld	105 F4
Pooley Bridge Cumb	71 G2
Poolfold Staffs	50 A3
Poolhill Gloucs	29 E5
Poplar Gt Lon	21 F3
Porchfield IOW	9 F3
Poringland Norfk	45 F2
Porkellis Cnwll	2 D3
Porlock Somset	15 H5
Porlock Weir Somset	15 G5
Port Appin Ag & B	90 B3
Port Askaig Ag & B	82 C3
Port Bannatyne Ag & B	84 A2
Port Carlisle Cumb	71 E5
Port Charlotte Ag & B	82 B2
Port Driseach Ag & B	83 H3
Port Einon Swans	26 B2
Port Ellen Ag & B	74 C5
Port Elphinstone Abers	102 D2
Port Erin IOM	116 a2
Port Gaverne Cnwll	4 B5
Port Glasgow Inver	84 C3
Port Henderson Highld	105 F3
Port Isaac Cnwll	4 B5
Port Logan D & G	68 C2
Port Mor Highld	89 E6
Port nan Giuran W Isls	111 e6
Port nan Long W Isls	111 b4
Port Nis W Isls	111 e7
Port of Menteith Stirlg	85 E5
Port of Ness W Isls	111 e7
Port Quin Cnwll	4 A5
Port Ramsay Ag & B	90 A3
Port Soderick IOM	116 c2
Port St Mary IOM	116 a2
Port Talbot Neath	26 D2
Port Wemyss Ag & B	74 A5
Port William D & G	69 E2
Port-an-Eorna Highld	97 E5
Portachoillan Ag & B	83 F2
Portavadie Ag & B	83 G3
Portbury Somset	17 F6
Portchester Hants	9 H4
Portencalzie D & G	68 B4
Portencross N Ayrs	76 B6
Portesham Dorset	7 G4
Portessie Moray	101 G5
Portfield Gate Pembks	24 D4
Portgate Devon	5 E5
Portgordon Moray	101 F5
Portgower Highld	110 A1
Porth Cnwll	3 E5
Porth Rhondd	27 F2
Porth Navas Cnwll	2 D2
Porthallow Cnwll	2 D2
Porthallow Cnwll	4 C2
Porthcawl Brdgnd	26 D1
Porthcothan Cnwll	3 E6
Porthcurno Cnwll	2 A2
Porthgain Pembks	24 C5
Porthgwarra Cnwll	2 A2
Porthkerry V Glam	16 C5
Porthleven Cnwll	2 C2
Porthmadog Gwynd	47 E5
Porthoustock Cnwll	3 E2
Porthpean Cnwll	3 F4
Porthtowan Cnwll	2 C3
Porthyrhyd Carmth	26 B4
Portincaple Ag & B	84 B5
Portinfer Jersey	7 a2
Portington E R Yk	60 B3
Portinnisherrich Ag & B	83 G6
Portinscale Cumb	71 F2
Portishead Somset	17 F6
Portknockie Moray	101 G6
Portlethen Abers	95 H5
Portling D & G	70 C4
Portloe Cnwll	3 F3
Portmahomack Highld	107 H4
Portmeirion Gwynd	47 E5
Portmellon Cnwll	3 F3
Portnacroish Ag & B	90 B4
Portnaguran W Isls	111 e6
Portnahaven Ag & B	74 A6

Portnalong Rishton

Portnalong Highld 96 B5
Portobello C Edin 86 D3
Portobello W Mids 40 B3
Porton Wilts 18 D1
Portpatrick D & G 68 B3
Portreath Cnwll 2 C4
Portree Highld 96 C6
Portscatho Cnwll 3 E3
Portsea Hants 9 H3
Portskerra Highld 109 H5
Portskewett Mons 28 C2
Portslade E Susx 11 E3
Portslade-by-Sea E Susx 11 F3
Portslogan D & G 68 B3
Portsmouth Hants 9 H3
Portsmouth W York 58 A3
Portsonachan Hotel Ag & B 90 C1
Portsoy Abers 102 B5
Portswood Hants 9 F4
Portuairk Highld 89 E5
Portway Worcs 40 C1
Portwrinkle Cnwll 4 D2
Portyerrock D & G 69 F2
Poslingford Suffk 34 B3
Posso Border 79 E5
Postbridge Devon 5 G5
Postcombe Oxon 20 A5
Postling Kent 13 F5
Postwick Norfk 45 F3
Potarch Abers 95 E5
Potsgrove Beds 32 B2
Pott Shrigley Ches 50 B4
Potten End Herts 20 D6
Potter Brompton N York 67 F1
Potter Heigham Norfk 45 G4
Potterhanworth Lincs 52 C2
Potterhanworth Booths Lincs 52 C2
Potterne Wilts 18 C3
Potterne Wick Wilts 18 C3
Potters Bar Herts 21 E5
Potters Crouch Herts 20 D5
Potters Marston Leics 41 F3
Potterspury Nhants 31 H4
Potterton Abers 103 E1
Potto N York 66 B4
Potton Beds 32 D4
Poughill Cnwll 14 B2
Poughill Devon 15 G2
Poulner Hants 8 D4
Poulshot Wilts 18 C3
Poulton Gloucs 18 D6
Poulton-le-Fylde Lancs 56 D6
Pound Green E Susx 11 G4
Pound Green Suffk 34 B4
Pound Hill W Susx 11 F5
Poundffald Swans 26 B2
Poundon Bucks 31 G3
Poundsgate Devon 5 G4
Poundstock Cnwll 14 B1
Pouton D & G 69 F2
Povey Cross Surrey 11 F6
Powburn Nthumb 81 F2
Powderham Devon 6 B4
Powerstock Dorset 7 F5
Powfoot D & G 71 E5
Powhill Cumb 71 E4
Powick Worcs 39 H2
Powmill P & K 86 A5
Poxwell Dorset 7 H4
Poyle Surrey 20 D3
Poynings W Susx 11 F3
Poyntington Dorset 17 G1
Poynton Ches 50 A5
Poynton Green Shrops 49 E2
Praa Sands Cnwll 2 C2
Pratt's Bottom Gt Lon 21 G2
Praze-an-Beeble Cnwll 2 C3
Prees Shrops 49 E3
Prees Green Shrops 49 E3
Preesall Lancs 62 D1
Pren-gwyn Cerdgn 36 D2
Prendwick Nthumb 81 F2
Prenteg Gwynd 47 E5
Prescot Mersyd 57 E2
Prescott Devon 16 C1
Presnerb Angus 94 B3
Prestatyn Denbgs 56 B1
Prestbury Ches 50 A4
Prestbury Gloucs 29 G5
Presteigne Powys 38 D3
Prestleigh Somset 17 G3
Preston Border 87 G2
Preston Devon 6 A3
Preston Devon 6 A2
Preston Dorset 7 H4
Preston E Loth 87 F4
Preston E R Yk 61 E3
Preston E Susx 11 F3
Preston Gloucs 18 C6
Preston Herts 32 D2
Preston Kent 23 E2
Preston Kent 23 G2
Preston Lancs 57 E5
Preston Nthumb 81 G3
Preston Rutlnd 42 B2
Preston Somset 16 C3
Preston Suffk 34 C4
Preston Wilts 19 E4
Preston Bagot Warwks 30 C6
Preston Bissett Bucks 31 G3
Preston Bowyer Somset 16 C2
Preston Brockhurst Shrops 49 E2
Preston Brook Ches 57 E1
Preston Candover Hants 19 H1
Preston Capes Nhants 31 F5
Preston Green Warwks 30 C6
Preston Gubbals Shrops 49 E2
Preston on Stour Warwks 30 D5
Preston on the Hill Ches 57 E1
Preston on Wye Herefs 28 B6
Preston Patrick Cumb 63 E4
Preston Plucknett Somset 17 F1
Preston upon the Weald Moors Shrops 49 F1
Preston Wynne Herefs 39 E1
Preston-under-Scar N York 65 E3
Prestonpans E Loth 86 D3
Prestwich Gt Man 57 G3
Prestwick S Ayrs 76 C4
Prestwick Airport S Ayrs 76 C4
Prestwood Bucks 20 C5
Prickwillow Cambs 33 G6
Priddy Somset 17 F4
Priest Hutton Lancs 63 E3
Priestland E Ayrs 77 E5
Priestweston Shrops 38 C5
Primrosehill Border 87 G2
Primsidemill Border 80 D3
Princes Risborough Bucks 20 B5
Princethorpe Warwks 41 E1
Princetown Devon 5 F4
Priors Hardwick Warwks 31 F5
Priors Marston Warwks 31 F5
Priors Norton Gloucs 29 F5
Priston Somset 17 H5
Prittlewell Essex 22 D4
Privett Hants 10 A4
Probus Cnwll 3 E4
Prora E Loth 87 E4
Prospect Cumb 71 E3
Prospidnick Cnwll 2 C2
Protstonhill Abers 102 D5
Prudhoe Nthumb 73 E3
Publow Somset 17 G5
Puckeridge Herts 33 F1
Puckington Somset 17 E1
Pucklechurch Gloucs 17 H6
Puddington Ches 48 D6
Puddington Devon 15 G2
Puddletown Dorset 7 H5
Pudsey W York 58 D3
Pulborough W Susx 10 D4
Pulford Ches 48 D5
Pulham Dorset 7 H6
Pulham Market Norfk 45 E1
Pulham St Mary Norfk 45 E1
Pulloxhill Beds 32 C2
Pumpherston W Loth 86 B3
Pumsaint Carmth 37 E1
Puncheston Pembks 24 D5
Puncknowle Dorset 7 F4
Punnett's Town E Susx 12 B4
Purbrook Hants 10 A3
Purfleet Essex 22 A3
Puriton Somset 17 E3
Purleigh Essex 22 D5
Purley Berks 19 H4
Purley Gt Lon 21 F2
Purse Caundle Dorset 17 H1
Purtington Somset 7 E6
Purton Gloucs 29 E3
Purton Gloucs 29 E3
Purton Wilts 18 D5
Purton Stoke Wilts 18 D5
Pury End Nhants 31 G4
Pusey Oxon 19 F6
Putley Herefs 28 D6
Putley Green Herefs 28 D6
Putloe Gloucs 29 E4
Putney Gt Lon 21 E3
Putron Village Guern 6 c1
Puttenham Surrey 10 C6
Puxley Nhants 31 H4
Puxton Somset 17 E5
Pwll Carmth 26 B3
Pwll Trap Carmth 25 F4
Pwll-glas Denbgs 48 B4
Pwll-y-glaw Neath 26 D2
Pwllgloyw Powys 27 F5
Pwllheli Gwynd 46 C5
Pwllmeyric Mons 28 C2
Pye Bridge Derbys 51 E2
Pye Corner Herts 21 G6
Pyecombe W Susx 11 F3
Pyle Brdgnd 26 D1
Pyleigh Somset 16 C2
Pylle Somset 17 G3
Pymoor Cambs 43 F1
Pymore Dorset 7 F5
Pyrford Surrey 20 D2
Pyrton Oxon 20 A5
Pytchley Nhants 32 B6
Pyworthy Devon 14 C2

Q

Quadring Lincs 42 D5
Quainton Bucks 31 H2
Quarley Hants 19 E1
Quarndon Derbys 51 E1
Quarrier's Village Inver 84 C2
Quarrington Lincs 42 C6
Quarrington Hill Dur 73 G1
Quarry Bank W Mids 40 A2
Quarrywood Moray 101 E5
Quarter N Ayrs 84 B2
Quarter S Lans 85 F1
Quatford Shrops 39 G5
Quatt Shrops 39 G4
Quebec Dur 73 F1
Quedgeley Gloucs 29 F4
Queen Adelaide Cambs 33 G6
Queen Camel Somset 17 G2
Queen Charlton Somset 17 G5
Queen Oak Dorset 8 A6
Queen Street Kent 12 B6
Queen's Bower IOW 9 G2
Queenborough Kent 22 D3
Queenhill Worcs 29 F6
Queensbury W York 58 C3
Queensferry Flints 48 D6
Queenslie C Glas 85 F2
Queenzieburn N Lans 85 F3
Quendon Essex 33 G2
Queniborough Leics 41 G4
Quenington Gloucs 30 C1
Quethiock Cnwll 4 D3
Quidenham Norfk 44 D1
Quidhampton Wilts 8 D6
Quinton Nhants 31 H5
Quintrell Downs Cnwll 3 E5
Quither Devon 5 E5
Quixwood Border 87 G2
Quoditch Devon 14 D1
Quorn Leics 41 F5
Quothquan S Lans 78 D6
Quoyburray Ork 111 h2
Quoyloo Ork 111 g2

R

Rachan Mill Border 79 E5
Rachub Gwynd 55 E3
Rackenford Devon 15 G3
Rackham W Susx 10 D3
Rackheath Norfk 45 F3
Racks D & G 70 D6
Rackwick Ork 111 g1
Radbourne Derbys 40 D6
Radcliffe Gt Man 57 G3
Radcliffe Nthumb 73 F6
Radcliffe on Trent Notts 51 G1
Radclive Bucks 31 G3
Raddery Highld 107 F2
Radernie Fife 87 E6
Radford Semele Warwks 31 E6
Radlett Herts 21 E5
Radley Oxon 19 G6
Radley Green Essex 22 B5
Radnage Bucks 20 B5
Radstock Somset 17 G4
Radstone Nhants 31 G4
Radway Warwks 31 E4
Radwell Beds 32 C4
Radwell Herts 32 D2
Radwinter Essex 33 G3
Radyr Cardif 27 G1
Rafford Moray 100 D5
Ragdale Leics 41 G5
Raglan Mons 28 C3
Ragnall Notts 52 A3
Raigbeg Highld 99 F5
Rainbow Hill Worcs 39 H2
Rainford Mersyd 57 E3
Rainham Gt Lon 21 H3
Rainham Kent 22 C2
Rainhill Mersyd 57 E2
Rainhill Stoops Mersyd 57 E2
Rainow Ches 50 B4
Rainton N York 65 G1
Rainworth Notts 51 G3
Raisthorpe N York 60 C6
Rait P & K 93 E2
Raithby Lincs 53 E4
Raithby Lincs 53 F2
Rake W Susx 10 B4
Ralia Highld 99 E2
Ramasaig Highld 96 A6
Rame Cnwll 2 D3
Rame Cnwll 5 E2
Rampisham Dorset 7 G5
Rampside Cumb 62 C3
Rampton Cambs 33 F5
Rampton Notts 52 A3
Ramsbottom Gt Man 57 G4
Ramsbury Wilts 19 E4
Ramscraigs Highld 110 B2
Ramsdean Hants 10 A4
Ramsdell Hants 19 G3
Ramsden Oxon 31 E2
Ramsden Bellhouse Essex 22 C4
Ramsey Cambs 43 E1
Ramsey Essex 35 E2
Ramsey IOM 116 d4
Ramsey Forty Foot Cambs 43 E1
Ramsey Heights Cambs 43 E1
Ramsey Island Essex 23 E5
Ramsey Mereside Cambs 43 E1
Ramsey St Mary's Cambs 43 E1
Ramsgate Kent 23 H2
Ramsgill N York 65 E1
Ramshope Nthumb 80 D1
Ramshorn Staffs 50 C2
Ramsnest Common Surrey 10 C5
Ranby Lincs 52 D3
Ranby Notts 51 G5
Rand Lincs 52 D3
Randwick Gloucs 29 F3
Ranfurly Rens 84 D2
Rangemore Staffs 40 C5
Rangeworthy Gloucs 29 E2
Rankinston E Ayrs 76 D3
Rann Lancs 57 G5
Rannoch Station P & K 91 F4
Ranscombe Somset 16 B3
Ranskill Notts 51 G5
Ranton Staffs 49 H2
Ranton Green Staffs 49 H2
Ranworth Norfk 45 F3
Raploch Stirlg 85 G5
Rapness Ork 111 h3
Rascarrel D & G 70 B4
Rashfield Ag & B 84 B4
Rashwood Worcs 30 A6
Raskelf N York 66 B1
Ratagan Highld 97 G4
Ratby Leics 41 F4
Ratcliffe Culey Leics 41 E3
Ratcliffe on Soar Notts 41 F6
Ratcliffe on the Wreake Leics 41 G4
Rathen Abers 103 E5
Rathillet Fife 93 F2
Rathmell N York 63 G2
Ratho C Edin 86 B3
Rathven Moray 101 G5
Ratley Warwks 31 E4
Ratling Kent 23 G1
Ratlinghope Shrops 38 D5
Rattar Highld 110 C6
Rattery Devon 5 G3
Rattlesden Suffk 34 C4
Ratton Village E Susx 12 B2
Rattray P & K 92 D4
Raunds Nhants 32 C5
Ravenfield S York 51 F6
Ravenglass Cumb 62 B5
Raveningham Norfk 45 G2
Ravenscar N York 67 F3
Ravenscliffe Staffs 49 H4
Ravensden Beds 32 C4
Ravenshead Notts 51 F2
Ravensthorpe Nhants 41 G1
Ravensthorpe W York 58 D2
Ravenstone Bucks 32 B4
Ravenstone Leics 41 E4
Ravenstonedale Cumb 63 G6
Ravenstruther S Lans 77 H5
Ravensworth N York 65 E4
Rawcliffe E R Yk 59 G2
Rawcliffe N York 59 F5
Rawdon W York 58 D4
Rawling Street Kent 22 D2
Rawmarsh S York 51 E6
Rawreth Essex 22 C4
Rawridge Devon 6 D6
Rawtenstall Lancs 57 G5
Raydon Suffk 34 D3
Rayleigh Essex 22 C4
Rayne Essex 34 B1
Raynes Park Gt Lon 21 E2
Reach Cambs 33 G5
Read Lancs 57 G6
Reading Berks 20 A3
Reading Street Kent 12 D5
Reading Street Kent 23 H2
Reagill Cumb 64 A5
Rearquhar Highld 107 F5
Rearsby Leics 41 G4
Reay Highld 110 A5
Reculver Kent 23 G2
Red Ball Somset 16 C1
Red Hill Dorset 8 D3
Red Hill Warwks 30 C5
Red Lodge Suffk 34 A5
Red Roses Carmth 25 F4
Red Row T & W 73 F6
Red Wharf Bay IOA 54 D4
Redberth Pembks 25 E3
Redbourn Herts 20 D6
Redbourne Lincs 52 B5
Redbrook Gloucs 28 D4
Redbrook Wrexhm 49 E3
Redbrook Street Kent 12 D5
Redburn Highld 100 C4
Redcar N York 66 C5
Redcastle D & G 70 B5
Redcastle Highld 107 E1
Redding Falk 85 H3
Reddingmuirhead Falk 85 H3
Redditch Worcs 30 B6
Rede Suffk 34 B4
Redenhall Norfk 45 F1
Redesmouth Nthumb 72 C4
Redford Abers 95 F3
Redford Angus 93 G4
Redford W Susx 10 B4
Redfordgreen Border 79 F4
Redgorton P & K 92 D2
Redgrave Suffk 34 D6
Redhill Abers 95 F6
Redhill Herts 33 E2
Redhill Somset 17 F5
Redhill Surrey 21 F1
Redisham Suffk 45 G1
Redland Bristl 17 G6
Redland Ork 111 h2
Redlingfield Suffk 35 E5
Redlingfield Green Suffk 35 E5
Redlynch Somset 17 H2
Redlynch Wilts 8 D5
Redmarley Worcs 39 G3
Redmarley D'Abitot Gloucs 29 E5
Redmarshall Dur 65 G5
Redmile Leics 42 A5
Redmire N York 65 E3
Redmyre Abers 95 F4
Rednal Shrops 48 D2
Redpath Border 80 B3
Redpoint Highld 105 E3
Redruth Cnwll 2 D3
Redstone P & K 92 D3
Redwick Gloucs 28 D2
Redwick Newpt 28 C1
Redworth Dur 65 F5
Reed Herts 33 E2
Reedham Norfk 45 G2
Reedness E R Yk 60 B2
Reepham Lincs 52 C3
Reepham Norfk 44 D4
Reeth N York 65 E3
Reeves Green W Mids 40 D1
Reiff Highld 108 A1
Reigate Surrey 21 E1
Reighton N York 67 G1
Reisque Abers 103 E2
Reiss Highld 110 D4
Relubbus Cnwll 2 C3
Relugas Moray 100 C4
Remenham Berks 20 B4
Remenham Hill Berks 20 B4
Rempstone Notts 41 F5
Rendcomb Gloucs 30 B1
Rendham Suffk 35 F5
Renfrew Rens 84 D2
Renhold Beds 32 C4
Renishaw Derbys 51 E4
Rennington Nthumb 81 G2
Renton W Duns 84 D3
Renwick Cumb 72 A1
Repps Norfk 45 G4
Repton Derbys 40 D5
Resaurie Highld 107 F1
Rescassa Cnwll 3 F3
Resipole Highld 89 G5
Reskadinnick Cnwll 2 C3
Resolis Highld 107 F3
Resolven Neath 26 D3
Rest and be thankful Ag & B 84 B6
Reston Border 87 H2
Reswallie Angus 93 G4
Retford Notts 51 G4
Rettendon Essex 22 C5
Revesby Lincs 53 E2
Rew Street IOW 9 F3
Rewe Devon 6 B5
Reydon Suffk 35 G6
Reymerston Norfk 44 D3
Reynalton Pembks 25 E3
Reynoldston Swans 26 B2
Rezare Cnwll 4 D4
Rhandirmwyn Carmth 37 F1
Rhayader Powys 37 H3
Rheindown Highld 106 D1
Rhes-y-cae Flints 48 C6
Rhewl Denbgs 48 B5
Rhewl Denbgs 48 B4
Rhicarn Highld 108 B2
Rhiconich Highld 108 C4
Rhicullen Highld 107 F3
Rhigos Rhondd 27 E3
Rhireavach Highld 105 H5
Rhives Highld 107 G5
Rhiwbina Cardif 27 G1
Rhiwderyn Newpt 28 A2
Rhiwlas Gwynd 54 D3
Rhoden Green Kent 12 B6
Rhodes Minnis Kent 13 F6
Rhodiad-y-brenin Pembks 24 B5
Rhonehouse D & G 70 B5
Rhoose V Glam 16 C5
Rhos Carmth 25 G6
Rhos Neath 26 D3
Rhos-on-Sea Conwy 55 F4
Rhos-y-gwaliau Gwynd 47 H5
Rhosbeirio IOA 54 C5
Rhoscolyn IOA 54 B4
Rhoscrowther Pembks 24 C3
Rhosesmor Flints 48 C6
Rhosgoch Powys 38 C1
Rhoshill Pembks 36 B1
Rhoshirwaun Gwynd 46 B4
Rhoslefain Gwynd 47 E2
Rhosllanerchrugog Wrexhm 48 C4
Rhosmeirch IOA 54 C4
Rhosneigr IOA 54 B3
Rhossili Swans 25 G2
Rhostryfan Gwynd 54 D2
Rhostyllen Wrexhm 48 C4
Rhosybol IOA 54 C5
Rhosymedre Wrexhm 48 C3
Rhu Ag & B 84 C4
Rhuallt Denbgs 48 B6
Rhubodach Ag & B 83 H3
Rhuddlan Denbgs 55 H4
Rhunahaorine Ag & B 75 E5
Rhyd Gwynd 47 E5
Rhyd-Ddu Gwynd 54 D2
Rhyd-uchaf Gwynd 47 G5
Rhyd-y-pennau Cerdgn 37 E5
Rhyd-y-clafdy Gwynd 46 C5
Rhyd-y-foel Conwy 55 G4
Rhyd-y-groes Gwynd 54 D3
Rhydargaeau Carmth 25 H5
Rhydcymerau Carmth 26 B6
Rhydlewis Cerdgn 36 C2
Rhydowen Cerdgn 36 D2
Rhydyfro Neath 26 C3
Rhyl Denbgs 55 H4
Rhymney Caerph 27 G3
Rhynd P & K 92 D2
Rhynie Abers 101 G2
Rhynie Highld 107 G4
Ribbesford Worcs 39 G3
Ribbleton Lancs 57 E5
Ribchester Lancs 57 F6
Riby Lincs 52 D5
Riccall N York 59 G4
Riccarton Border 79 H2
Riccarton E Ayrs 76 D5
Richards Castle Herefs 39 E3
Richmond Gt Lon 21 E3
Richmond N York 65 F3
Richmond S York 51 E5
Richmond Fort Guern 6 b1
Rickerscote Staffs 40 A5
Rickford Somset 17 F5
Rickham Devon 5 G1
Rickinghall Suffk 34 D6
Rickling Essex 33 F2
Rickling Green Essex 33 G2
Rickmansworth Herts 20 D4
Riddell Border 80 B3
Riddlecombe Devon 15 E3
Riddlesden W York 58 C4
Ridge Dorset 8 B2
Ridge Herts 21 E5
Ridge Wilts 8 B6
Ridge Lane Warwks 40 D3
Ridgehill Somset 17 F5
Ridgeway Derbys 51 E4
Ridgewell Essex 34 B3
Ridgewood E Susx 11 G4
Ridgmont Beds 32 B2
Riding Mill Nthumb 72 D3
Ridlington Norfk 45 F5
Ridlington Rutlnd 42 B2
Ridsdale Nthumb 72 D5
Rievaulx N York 66 C2
Rievaulx Abbey N York 66 C2
Rigg D & G 71 F5
Riggend N Lans 85 F3
Righoul Highld 100 B4
Rigsby Lincs 53 F3
Rigside S Lans 78 C6
Riley Green Lancs 57 F5
Rilla Mill Cnwll 4 D4
Rillington N York 67 E1
Rimington Lancs 63 G1
Rimpton Somset 17 G2
Rimswell E R Yk 61 F3
Rinaston Pembks 24 D5
Rindleford Shrops 39 G5
Ringford D & G 69 H3
Ringland Norfk 45 E3
Ringmer E Susx 11 G3
Ringmore Devon 5 G2
Ringmore Devon 6 B3
Ringorm Moray 101 E4
Ringsfield Suffk 45 G1
Ringsfield Corner Suffk 45 G1
Ringshall Bucks 20 C6
Ringshall Suffk 34 D4
Ringshall Stocks Suffk 34 D4
Ringstead Nhants 32 C6
Ringstead Norfk 44 A5
Ringwood Hants 8 D4
Ringwould Kent 13 H6
Ripe E Susx 11 G3
Ripley Derbys 51 E2
Ripley Hants 8 D3
Ripley N York 58 D5
Ripley Surrey 20 D1
Riplington Hants 9 H5
Ripon N York 65 G1
Rippingale Lincs 42 C4
Ripple Kent 23 H1
Ripple Worcs 29 F6
Ripponden W York 58 B2
Risabus Ag & B 74 B5
Risbury Herefs 39 E2
Risby Suffk 34 B5
Risca Caerph 27 G2
Rise E R Yk 61 E4
Risegate Lincs 42 D5
Riseley Beds 32 C5
Riseley Berks 20 A2
Rishangles Suffk 35 E5
Rishton Lancs 57 G5

185

Rishworth *W York*	58	B2
Risley *Ches*	57	F2
Risley *Derbys*	41	F6
Risplith *N York*	58	D6
River *Kent*	13	G6
River *W Susx*	10	C4
Riverford *Highld*	107	E2
Riverhead *Kent*	21	G1
Rivington *Lancs*	57	F4
Roade *Nhants*	31	H5
Roadmeetings *S Lans*	77	G6
Roadside *E Ayrs*	77	E3
Roadside *Highld*	110	B5
Roadwater *Somset*	16	B3
Roag *Highld*	96	B6
Roan of Craigoch *S Ayrs*	76	C2
Roast Green *Essex*	33	F2
Roath *Cardif*	27	G1
Roberton *Border*	79	G4
Roberton *S Lans*	78	C5
Robertsbridge *E Susx*	12	C4
Roberttown *W York*	58	D2
Robeston Wathen *Pembks*	25	E4
Robgill Tower *D & G*	71	F6
Robin Hood's Bay *N York*	67	E4
Roborough *Devon*	15	E3
Roborough *Devon*	5	E3
Roby *Mersyd*	56	D2
Rocester *Staffs*	50	C1
Roch *Pembks*	24	C4
Rochdale *Gt Man*	58	A2
Roche *Cnwll*	3	F5
Rochester *Kent*	22	C2
Rochester *Nthumb*	72	C6
Rochford *Essex*	22	D4
Rochford *Worcs*	39	F3
Rock *Cnwll*	3	F6
Rock *Nthumb*	81	G2
Rock *Worcs*	39	G3
Rock Ferry *Mersyd*	56	D2
Rockbeare *Devon*	6	B5
Rockbourne *Hants*	8	D5
Rockcliffe *Cumb*	71	F5
Rockcliffe *D & G*	70	B4
Rockend *Devon*	6	B2
Rockfield *Highld*	107	H4
Rockfield *Mons*	28	C4
Rockford *Devon*	15	G5
Rockhampton *Gloucs*	28	D2
Rockhill *Shrops*	38	C4
Rockingham *Nhants*	42	B2
Rockland All Saints *Norfk*	44	D2
Rockland St Mary *Norfk*	45	F3
Rockland St Peter *Norfk*	44	D2
Rockley *Notts*	51	H4
Rockley *Wilts*	18	D4
Rockville *Ag & B*	84	B4
Rockwell End *Bucks*	20	B4
Rodborough *Gloucs*	29	F3
Rodbourne *Wilts*	18	D5
Rodbourne *Wilts*	18	B5
Rodden *Dorset*	7	G4
Rode *Somset*	18	A2
Rode Heath *Ches*	49	G5
Rodel *W Isls*	111	c4
Roden *Shrops*	49	F1
Rodhuish *Somset*	16	B3
Rodington *Shrops*	49	F1
Rodington Heath *Shrops*	49	F1
Rodley *Gloucs*	29	E4
Rodmarton *Gloucs*	29	G3
Rodmell *E Susx*	11	G3
Rodmersham *Kent*	22	D2
Rodmersham Green *Kent*	22	D2
Rodney Stoke *Somset*	17	F4
Rodsley *Derbys*	50	D1
Roe Green *Herts*	21	E6
Roe Green *Herts*	33	E2
Roecliffe *N York*	59	E6
Roehampton *Gt Lon*	21	E3
Roffey *W Susx*	11	E5
Rogart *Highld*	107	F6
Rogate *W Susx*	10	B4
Rogerstone *Newpt*	28	B2
Roghadal *W Isls*	111	c4
Rogiet *Mons*	28	C2
Roke *Oxon*	19	H5
Roker *T & W*	73	G3
Rollesby *Norfk*	45	G3
Rolleston *Leics*	41	H3
Rolleston *Notts*	51	H2
Rolleston *Staffs*	40	D5
Rolston *E R Yk*	61	F4
Rolvenden *Kent*	12	D5
Rolvenden Layne *Kent*	12	D5
Romaldkirk *Dur*	64	D5
Roman Amphitheatre Caerleon *Newpt*	28	B2
Roman Baths & Pump Room *Somset*	17	H5
Romanby *N York*	65	G3
Romanno Bridge *Border*	86	B1
Romansleigh *Devon*	15	F3
Romesdal *Highld*	104	C2
Romford *Dorset*	8	C4
Romford *Gt Lon*	21	G4
Romiley *Gt Man*	50	B5
Romsey *Hants*	9	F5
Romsley *Shrops*	39	G4
Romsley *Worcs*	40	B2
Ronachan *Ag & B*	83	F1
Rookhope *Dur*	72	D1
Rookley *IOW*	9	G2
Rooks Bridge *Somset*	17	E4
Rooks Nest *Somset*	16	C2
Rookwith *N York*	65	F2
Roos *E R Yk*	61	F3
Roothams Green *Beds*	32	C4
Ropley *Hants*	9	H6
Ropley Dean *Hants*	9	H6
Ropsley *Lincs*	42	C5
Rora *Abers*	103	F4
Rorrington *Shrops*	38	C5
Rosarie *Moray*	101	F4
Rose *Cnwll*	2	D4
Rose Ash *Devon*	15	G3
Rose Green *Essex*	34	C2
Rose Green *Suffk*	34	C2
Rose Green *Suffk*	34	C3
Rose Green *W Susx*	10	C2
Rose Hill *Lancs*	57	G5
Rosebank *S Lans*	77	G6
Rosebush *Pembks*	25	E5
Rosedale Abbey *N York*	66	D3
Rosehall *Highld*	106	D6
Rosehearty *Abers*	103	E6
Roseisle *Moray*	100	D6
Roselands *E Susx*	12	B2
Rosemarket *Pembks*	24	D3
Rosemarkie *Highld*	107	F2
Rosemary Lane *Devon*	16	C1
Rosemount *P & K*	92	D3
Rosenannon *Cnwll*	3	F5
Rosewell *Mdloth*	86	C2
Roseworth *Dur*	65	H5
Rosgill *Cumb*	71	H1
Roskhill *Highld*	96	B6
Rosley *Cumb*	71	F4
Roslin *Mdloth*	86	C2
Rosliston *Derbys*	40	D5
Rosneath *Ag & B*	84	C4
Ross *D & G*	69	G2
Ross-on-Wye *Herefs*	28	D5
Rossett *Wrexhm*	48	D5
Rossett Green *N York*	58	D5
Rossington *S York*	51	G6
Rossland *Rens*	84	D3
Roster *Highld*	110	C3
Rostherne *Ches*	57	G1
Rosthwaite *Cumb*	71	F1
Roston *Derbys*	50	C1
Rosyth *Fife*	86	B4
Rothbury *Nthumb*	73	E6
Rotherby *Leics*	41	G5
Rotherfield *E Susx*	12	A5
Rotherfield Greys *Oxon*	20	A3
Rotherfield Peppard *Oxon*	20	A3
Rotherham *S York*	51	E5
Rothersthorpe *Nhants*	31	H5
Rotherwick *Hants*	20	A1
Rothes *Moray*	101	E4
Rothesay *Ag & B*	84	A2
Rothiebrisbane *Abers*	102	D3
Rothiemay *Moray*	102	B4
Rothiemurchus Lodge *Highld*	99	G3
Rothienorman *Abers*	102	C3
Rothley *Leics*	41	G4
Rothmaise *Abers*	102	C3
Rothwell *Lincs*	52	D5
Rothwell *Nhants*	32	A6
Rothwell *W York*	59	E3
Rottal Lodge *Angus*	94	C3
Rottingdean *E Susx*	11	F2
Rottington *Cumb*	70	C1
Roucan *D & G*	78	D1
Rough Common *Kent*	23	F2
Rougham *Norfk*	44	B4
Rougham Green *Suffk*	34	C5
Roughpark *Abers*	101	F1
Roughton *Lincs*	53	E2
Roughton *Norfk*	45	E5
Roughton *Shrops*	39	G5
Roundbush Green *Essex*	22	B6
Roundham *Somset*	7	E6
Roundhay *W York*	59	E4
Roundway *Wilts*	18	C3
Roundyhill *Angus*	93	F4
Rous Lench *Worcs*	30	B5
Rousdon *Devon*	6	D4
Rousham *Oxon*	31	F3
Routenburn *N Ayrs*	84	B2
Routh *E R Yk*	61	E4
Row *Cnwll*	4	B4
Row *Cumb*	63	E5
Row Green *Essex*	34	B1
Rowanburn *D & G*	79	G1
Rowardennan Hotel *Stirlg*	84	C5
Rowardennan Lodge *Stirlg*	84	C5
Rowarth *Derbys*	50	B5
Rowberrow *Somset*	17	F4
Rowde *Wilts*	18	C3
Rowen *Conwy*	55	F3
Rowfoot *Nthumb*	72	B3
Rowhedge *Essex*	34	D1
Rowington *Warwks*	40	D1
Rowland *Derbys*	50	D4
Rowland's Castle *Hants*	10	A3
Rowland's Gill *T & W*	73	F3
Rowledge *Surrey*	10	B6
Rowley *Dur*	73	E2
Rowley *E R Yk*	60	D3
Rowley Green *W Mids*	41	E2
Rowley Regis *W Mids*	40	B2
Rowlstone *Herefs*	28	B5
Rowly *Surrey*	10	D6
Rowner *Hants*	9	G3
Rowney Green *Worcs*	40	B1
Rownhams *Hants*	9	F5
Rowrah *Cumb*	70	D2
Rowsham *Bucks*	32	B1
Rowsley *Derbys*	50	D3
Rowston *Lincs*	52	C1
Rowton *Ches*	49	E5
Rowton *Shrops*	49	F2
Roxburgh *Border*	80	C3
Roxby *Lincs*	60	C2
Roxton *Beds*	32	D4
Roxwell *Essex*	22	B6
Roy Bridge *Highld*	98	B1
Royal Botanic Gardens *C Edin*	93	G1
Roydon *Essex*	21	G6
Roydon *Norfk*	44	A4
Roydon *Norfk*	34	D6
Roydon Hamlet *Essex*	21	G6
Royston *Herts*	33	E3
Royston *S York*	59	E1
Royton *Gt Man*	58	A1
Rozel *Jersey*	7	c2
Ruabon *Wrexhm*	48	C4
Ruaig *Ag & B*	88	B4
Ruan Lanihorne *Cnwll*	3	E3
Ruan Major *Cnwll*	2	D1
Ruan Minor *Cnwll*	2	D1
Ruardean *Gloucs*	28	D4
Ruardean Hill *Gloucs*	28	D4
Ruardean Woodside *Gloucs*	28	D4
Rubery *Worcs*	40	B1
Rubha Ban *W Isls*	111	b2
Ruckhall *Herefs*	28	C6
Ruckinge *Kent*	13	E5
Ruckley *Shrops*	39	E5
Rudby *N York*	66	B4
Rudchester *Nthumb*	73	E3
Ruddington *Notts*	41	F6
Rudge *Somset*	18	B2
Rudgeway *Gloucs*	28	D2
Rudgwick *W Susx*	10	D5
Rudhall *Herefs*	28	D5
Rudheath *Ches*	57	G2
Rudley Green *Essex*	22	D5
Rudloe *Wilts*	18	B4
Rudry *Caerph*	27	G2
Rudston *E R Yk*	61	E6
Rudyard *Staffs*	50	B3
Ruecastle *Border*	80	C2
Rufford *Lancs*	57	E4
Rufforth *N York*	59	F5
Rugby *Warwks*	41	F1
Rugeley *Staffs*	40	B5
Ruishton *Somset*	16	D2
Ruislip *Gt Lon*	20	D4
Rumbach *Moray*	101	F4
Rumbling Bridge *P & K*	86	A5
Rumburgh *Suffk*	35	F6
Rumford *Cnwll*	3	E6
Rumford *Falk*	85	H3
Rumney *Cardif*	27	G1
Runcorn *Ches*	57	E1
Runcton *W Susx*	10	C2
Runcton Holme *Norfk*	43	G3
Runfold *Surrey*	10	B6
Runhall *Norfk*	44	D3
Runham *Norfk*	45	G3
Runnington *Somset*	16	C2
Runswick *N York*	66	D5
Runtaleave *Angus*	94	C3
Runwell *Essex*	22	C4
Ruscombe *Berks*	20	B3
Rush Green *Essex*	23	F6
Rush Green *Gt Lon*	21	G4
Rushall *Herefs*	28	D6
Rushall *Norfk*	45	E1
Rushall *Wilts*	18	D2
Rushbrooke *Suffk*	34	C4
Rushbury *Shrops*	39	E5
Rushden *Herts*	33	E2
Rushden *Nhants*	32	B5
Rushford *Norfk*	34	C6
Rushlake Green *E Susx*	12	B4
Rushmere *Suffk*	45	G1
Rushmoor *Surrey*	10	C5
Rushock *Worcs*	40	A1
Rusholme *Gt Man*	57	H2
Rushton *Ches*	49	F5
Rushton *Nhants*	42	A1
Rushton Spencer *Staffs*	50	B3
Rushwick *Worcs*	39	G2
Rushyford *Dur*	65	F6
Ruskie *Stirlg*	85	E5
Ruskington *Lincs*	52	C1
Rusland *Cumb*	62	D4
Rusper *W Susx*	11	E5
Ruspidge *Gloucs*	29	E4
Russ Hill *Surrey*	11	E5
Russell's Water *Oxon*	20	A4
Rusthall *Kent*	12	B5
Rustington *W Susx*	10	D2
Ruston *N York*	67	E2
Ruston Parva *E R Yk*	60	D6
Ruswarp *N York*	67	E4
Rutherford *Border*	80	C3
Rutherglen *S Lans*	85	E2
Ruthernbridge *Cnwll*	3	F5
Ruthin *Denbgs*	48	B5
Ruthrieston *Aber C*	95	H6
Ruthven *Abers*	101	G4
Ruthven *Angus*	93	E4
Ruthven *Highld*	99	F3
Ruthven House *Angus*	93	E4
Ruthvoes *Cnwll*	3	E5
Ruthwell *D & G*	70	D5
Ruyton-XI-Towns *Shrops*	48	D2
Ryal *Nthumb*	72	D4
Ryall *Dorset*	7	E5
Ryall *Worcs*	29	F6
Ryarsh *Kent*	22	B2
Rydal *Cumb*	62	D6
Ryde *IOW*	9	G3
Rye *E Susx*	12	D4
Rye Foreign *E Susx*	12	D4
Rye Street *Worcs*	29	E6
Ryhall *Rutlnd*	42	C3
Ryhill *W York*	59	E2
Ryhope *T & W*	73	G2
Ryland *Lincs*	52	C3
Rylands *Notts*	41	F6
Rylstone *N York*	58	B5
Ryme Intrinseca *Dorset*	7	G6
Ryther *N York*	59	F4
Ryton *Shrops*	39	G6
Ryton *T & W*	73	E3
Ryton-on-Dunsmore *Warwks*	41	E1

S

Sabden *Lancs*	57	G6
Sacombe *Herts*	33	E1
Sacriston *Dur*	73	F2
Sadberge *Dur*	65	G5
Saddell *Ag & B*	75	F4
Saddington *Leics*	41	G3
Saddle Bow *Norfk*	43	G3
Saddlescombe *W Susx*	11	F3
Saffron Walden *Essex*	33	G3
Sageston *Pembks*	25	E3
Saham Hills *Norfk*	44	C2
Saham Toney *Norfk*	44	C2
Saighton *Ches*	49	E5
St Abbs *Border*	81	E6
St Agnes *Border*	87	F2
St Agnes *Cnwll*	2	D4
St Albans *Herts*	21	E6
St Allen *Cnwll*	3	E4
St Andrew *Guern*	6	b1
St Andrew's Major *V Glam*	16	C6
St Andrews *Fife*	93	G1
St Andrews Well *Dorset*	7	F5
St Ann's *D & G*	78	D2
St Ann's Chapel *Devon*	5	G2
St Anne's *Lancs*	56	D5
St Anthony *Cnwll*	2	D2
St Anthony's Hill *E Susx*	12	B2
St Arvans *Mons*	28	C2
St Asaph *Denbgs*	48	A6
St Athan *V Glam*	16	B5
St Aubin *Jersey*	7	b1
St Austell *Cnwll*	3	F4
St Bees *Cumb*	70	C1
St Blazey *Cnwll*	3	G4
St Boswells *Border*	80	B3
St Brelade *Jersey*	7	a1
St Brelade's Bay *Jersey*	7	a1
St Breock *Cnwll*	3	F6
St Breward *Cnwll*	4	B4
St Briavels *Gloucs*	28	D3
St Brides Major *V Glam*	16	A6
St Brides super-Ely *V Glam*	27	F1
St Brides Wentlooge *Newpt*	28	B1
St Budeaux *Devon*	5	E3
St Buryan *Cnwll*	2	B2
St Catherines *Ag & B*	84	B6
St Chloe *Gloucs*	29	F3
St Clears *Carmth*	25	F4
St Cleer *Cnwll*	4	C4
St Clement *Cnwll*	3	E3
St Clement *Jersey*	7	c1
St Clether *Cnwll*	4	C5
St Colmac *Ag & B*	83	H2
St Columb Major *Cnwll*	3	E5
St Columb Minor *Cnwll*	3	E5
St Columb Road *Cnwll*	3	E5
St Combs *Abers*	103	F5
St Cross South Elmham *Suffk*	45	F1
St Cyrus *Abers*	95	F3
St David's *P & K*	92	C2
St David's *Pembks*	24	B5
St Day *Cnwll*	2	D3
St Dennis *Cnwll*	3	F5
St Dogmaels *Cerdgn*	36	B2
St Dominick *Cnwll*	5	E4
St Donats *V Glam*	16	B5
St Endellion *Cnwll*	4	B4
St Enoder *Cnwll*	3	E5
St Erme *Cnwll*	3	E4
St Erney *Cnwll*	4	D3
St Erth *Cnwll*	2	C3
St Erth Praze *Cnwll*	2	C3
St Ervan *Cnwll*	3	E6
St Ewe *Cnwll*	3	F4
St Fagans *Cardif*	27	G1
St Fagans Welsh Life Museum *Cardif*	27	G1
St Fergus *Abers*	103	F4
St Fillans *P & K*	91	H2
St Florence *Pembks*	25	E3
St Gennys *Cnwll*	14	B1
St George *Conwy*	55	G4
St George's *V Glam*	16	C6
St Georges *Somset*	17	E5
St Germans *Cnwll*	4	D3
St Giles in the Wood *Devon*	15	E3
St Giles-on-the-Heath *Cnwll*	4	D5
St Harmon *Powys*	38	A3
St Helen Auckland *Dur*	65	F5
St Helena *Norfk*	45	E4
St Helens *IOW*	9	H2
St Helens *Mersyd*	57	E2
St Helier *Gt Lon*	21	F2
St Helier *Jersey*	7	b1
St Hilary *Cnwll*	2	C2
St Hilary *V Glam*	16	B6
St Ippollitts *Herts*	32	D2
St Ishmael's *Pembks*	24	C3
St Issey *Cnwll*	3	F6
St Ive *Cnwll*	4	D4
St Ives *Cambs*	33	E5
St Ives *Cnwll*	2	C3
St James South Elmham *Suffk*	35	F6
St James's End *Nhants*	31	H5
St John *Cnwll*	5	E2
St John *Jersey*	7	b2
St John's *IOM*	116	B3
St John's Chapel *Devon*	15	E4
St John's Chapel *Dur*	72	C1
St John's Fen End *Norfk*	43	G3
St John's Kirk *S Lans*	78	C6
St John's Town of Dalry *D & G*	69	G5
St John's Wood *Gt Lon*	21	F4
St Johns *Kent*	21	H1
St Johns *Surrey*	20	C2
St Johns *Worcs*	39	H2
St Jude's *IOM*	116	c5
St Just *Cnwll*	2	A2
St Just-in-Roseland *Cnwll*	3	E3
St Katherines *Abers*	102	D3
St Keverne *Cnwll*	2	D2
St Kew *Cnwll*	3	F6
St Kew Highway *Cnwll*	3	F6
St Keyne *Cnwll*	4	C3
St Lawrence *Essex*	23	E5
St Lawrence *IOW*	9	G1
St Lawrence *Jersey*	7	b2
St Lawrence *Kent*	23	H2
St Leonards *Bucks*	20	C5
St Leonards *Dorset*	8	D4
St Leonards *E Susx*	12	C3
St Levan *Cnwll*	2	A2
St Lythans *V Glam*	16	C6
St Mabyn *Cnwll*	3	F6
St Madoes *P & K*	92	D2
St Margaret South Elmham *Suffk*	45	F1
St Margaret's at Cliffe *Kent*	13	H6
St Margaret's Hope *Ork*	111	h1
St Margarets *Herefs*	28	B5
St Margarets *Herts*	21	F6
St Marks *IOM*	116	b3
St Martin *Cnwll*	4	D3
St Martin *Guern*	6	b1
St Martin *Jersey*	7	c2
St Martin's *P & K*	92	D2
St Martins *Shrops*	48	D3
St Mary *Jersey*	7	a2
St Mary Bourne *Hants*	19	F2
St Mary Church *V Glam*	16	B6
St Mary Cray *Gt Lon*	21	G2
St Mary in the Marsh *Kent*	13	E4
St Mary's *Ork*	111	h2
St Mary's Bay *Kent*	13	F4
St Mary's Hoo *Kent*	22	C3
St Marychurch *Devon*	6	B2
St Maughans Green *Mons*	28	C4
St Mawes *Cnwll*	3	E3
St Mawgan *Cnwll*	3	E5
St Mellion *Cnwll*	5	E3
St Mellons *Cardif*	27	G1
St Merryn *Cnwll*	3	E6
St Mewan *Cnwll*	3	F4
St Michael Caerhays *Cnwll*	3	F3
St Michael Church *Somset*	17	E2
St Michael Penkevil *Cnwll*	3	E3
St Michael South Elmham *Suffk*	45	F1
St Michael's on Wyre *Lancs*	57	E6
St Michaels *Kent*	12	D5
St Michaels *Worcs*	39	F3
St Minver *Cnwll*	3	F6
St Monans *Fife*	87	E6
St Neot *Cnwll*	4	C4
St Neots *Cambs*	32	D4
St Nicholas *Pembks*	24	C4
St Nicholas *V Glam*	16	C6
St Nicholas at Wade *Kent*	23	G2
St Ninians *Stirlg*	85	G4
St Olaves *Norfk*	45	G2
St Osyth *Essex*	23	F6
St Ouen *Jersey*	7	a2
St Owens Cross *Herefs*	28	D5
St Paul's Walden *Herts*	32	D1
St Pauls Cray *Gt Lon*	21	G2
St Peter *Jersey*	7	a2
St Peter Port *Guern*	6	c1
St Peter's *Guern*	6	b1
St Peter's *Kent*	23	H2
St Pinnock *Cnwll*	4	C3
St Quivox *S Ayrs*	76	C4
St Sampson *Guern*	6	c2
St Saviour *Guern*	6	b1
St Saviour *Jersey*	7	b1
St Stephen *Cnwll*	3	F4
St Stephen's Coombe *Cnwll*	3	F4
St Stephens *Cnwll*	4	D5
St Stephens *Cnwll*	5	E3
St Teath *Cnwll*	4	B5
St Tudy *Cnwll*	3	G6
St Twynnells *Pembks*	24	D3
St Veep *Cnwll*	4	C3
St Vigeans *Angus*	93	H3
St Wenn *Cnwll*	3	F5
St Weonards *Herefs*	28	C5
Saintbury *Gloucs*	30	C4
Salachail *Ag & B*	90	C4
Salcombe *Devon*	5	G1
Salcombe Regis *Devon*	6	C4
Salcott *Essex*	23	E6
Sale *Gt Man*	57	G2
Sale Green *Worcs*	30	A5
Saleby *Lincs*	53	F3
Salehurst *E Susx*	12	C4
Salem *Cerdgn*	37	F5
Salem *Gwynd*	54	D2
Salen *Ag & B*	89	F3
Salen *Highld*	89	G5
Salford *Beds*	32	B3
Salford *Gt Man*	57	G3
Salford *Oxon*	30	D3
Salford Priors *Warwks*	30	C5
Salfords *Surrey*	11	F6
Salhouse *Norfk*	45	F3
Saline *Fife*	86	A5
Salisbury *Wilts*	8	D6
Salisbury Cathedral *Wilts*	8	D6
Salkeld Dykes *Cumb*	71	H3
Salle *Norfk*	45	E4
Salmonby *Lincs*	53	E3
Salperton *Gloucs*	30	C2
Salsburgh *N Lans*	85	G2
Salt *Staffs*	40	B6
Saltaire *W York*	58	C4
Saltash *Cnwll*	5	E3
Saltburn *Highld*	107	F3
Saltburn-by-the-Sea *N York*	66	C5
Saltby *Leics*	42	B4
Saltcoats *N Ayrs*	76	B5
Saltdean *E Susx*	11	F2
Salterbeck *Cumb*	70	D2
Salterforth *Lancs*	58	A4
Salterton *Wilts*	18	D1
Saltfleet *Lincs*	53	F4
Saltfleetby All Saints *Lincs*	53	F4
Saltfleetby St Clement *Lincs*	53	F4
Saltfleetby St Peter *Lincs*	53	F4
Salford *Somset*	17	G5
Salthouse *Norfk*	44	D6
Saltmarshe *E R Yk*	60	B3
Saltney *Flints*	48	D5
Salton *N York*	66	D2
Saltrens *Devon*	14	D3
Saltwood *Kent*	13	F5
Salvington *W Susx*	10	D3
Salwarpe *Worcs*	39	H2
Salwayash *Dorset*	7	F5
Sambourne *Warwks*	30	B6
Sambrook *Shrops*	49	G2
Samlesbury *Lancs*	57	F5
Sampford Arundel *Somset*	16	C1
Sampford Brett *Somset*	16	C3
Sampford Courtenay *Devon*	15	F1
Sampford Moor *Somset*	16	C1
Sampford Peverell *Devon*	16	B1
Sampford Spiney *Devon*	5	F4
Samsonlane *Ork*	111	j2
Samuelston *E Loth*	87	E3
Sanaigmore *Ag & B*	82	B3
Sancreed *Cnwll*	2	B2
Sancton *E R Yk*	60	C4
Sand Hills *W York*	59	E4
Sand Hole *E R Yk*	60	C4
Sand Hutton *N York*	59	G5
Sandaig *Highld*	97	E3
Sandal Magna *W York*	59	E2
Sandavore *Highld*	96	C1
Sanday Airport *Ork*	111	j3
Sandbach *Ches*	49	G5
Sandbank *Ag & B*	84	B4
Sandbanks *Dorset*	8	C2
Sandend *Abers*	102	B5
Sanderstead *Gt Lon*	21	F2
Sandford *Cumb*	64	B5
Sandford *Devon*	15	G2
Sandford *Dorset*	8	B2
Sandford *Hants*	8	D3
Sandford *IOW*	9	G2
Sandford *S Lans*	77	F5
Sandford *Somset*	17	E5
Sandford Orcas *Dorset*	17	G1
Sandford St Martin *Oxon*	31	E3
Sandford-on-Thames *Oxon*	19	G6
Sandgate *Kent*	13	F5
Sandhaven *Abers*	103	E6
Sandhead *D & G*	68	C3
Sandhills *Oxon*	31	F1
Sandhills *Surrey*	10	C5
Sandhoe *Nthumb*	72	D3
Sandhole *Ag & B*	83	H5
Sandholme *E R Yk*	60	C3
Sandhurst *Berks*	20	B2
Sandhurst *Gloucs*	29	F5
Sandhurst *Kent*	12	C5

Sandhutton N York ... 65 G2
Sandiacre Derbys ... 51 F1
Sandilands Lincs ... 53 G3
Sandleheath Hants ... 8 D5
Sandleigh Oxon ... 19 F6
Sandley Dorset ... 8 A5
Sandness Shet ... 111 k2
Sandon Essex ... 22 C5
Sandon Herts ... 33 E2
Sandon Staffs ... 40 B6
Sandon Bank Staffs ... 40 B6
Sandown IOW ... 9 G2
Sandplace Cnwll ... 4 C3
Sandridge Herts ... 21 E6
Sandringham Norfk ... 44 A5
Sandsend N York ... 67 E4
Sandtoft Lincs ... 60 B1
Sandway Kent ... 22 D1
Sandwich Kent ... 23 G2
Sandwick W Isls ... 111 I1
Sandwick W Isls ... 111 d6
Sandwith Cumb ... 70 C1
Sandy Beds ... 32 D3
Sandy Lane Wilts ... 18 C3
Sandy Park Devon ... 5 G5
Sandyford D & G ... 79 E2
Sandygate Devon ... 6 A3
Sandygate IOM ... 116 c5
Sandyhills D & G ... 70 C4
Sandylands Lancs ... 62 D2
Sangobeg Highld ... 108 D5
Sangomore Highld ... 108 D5
Sankyn's Green Worcs ... 39 G3
Sanna Bay Highld ... 89 E5
Sanndabhaig W Isls ... 111 d6
Sanquhar D & G ... 77 G3
Santon Bridge Cumb ... 62 B6
Santon Downham Suffk ... 44 B1
Sapcote Leics ... 41 F3
Sapey Common Herefs ... 39 G3
Sapiston Suffk ... 34 C6
Sapperton Gloucs ... 29 G3
Sapperton Lincs ... 42 C5
Saracen's Head Lincs ... 43 E4
Sarclet Highld ... 110 D3
Sarisbury Hants ... 9 G4
Sarn Gwynd ... 46 B4
Sarn Powys ... 47 H2
Sarn Powys ... 38 C5
Sarnau Cerdgn ... 36 C2
Sarnau Powys ... 48 C1
Sarnesfield Herefs ... 38 D1
Saron Carmth ... 26 C4
Saron Gwynd ... 54 D3
Sarratt Herts ... 20 D5
Sarre Kent ... 23 G2
Sarsden Oxon ... 30 D2
Satley Dur ... 73 E1
Satterleigh Devon ... 15 F3
Satterthwaite Cumb ... 62 D5
Sauchen Abers ... 102 C1
Saucher P & K ... 92 D3
Sauchieburn Abers ... 95 F3
Saul Gloucs ... 29 E3
Saundby Notts ... 52 A4
Saundersfoot Pembks ... 25 E3
Saunderton Bucks ... 20 B5
Saunton Devon ... 14 D4
Sausthorpe Lincs ... 53 F2
Savile Town W York ... 58 D2
Sawbridge Warwks ... 31 F6
Sawbridgeworth Herts ... 21 G6
Sawdon N York ... 67 E2
Sawley Lancs ... 63 G1
Sawley N York ... 58 D6
Sawston Cambs ... 33 F3
Sawtry Cambs ... 42 D1
Saxby Leics ... 42 A4
Saxby Lincs ... 52 C4
Saxby All Saints Lincs ... 60 D2
Saxelbye Leics ... 41 G5
Saxham Street Suffk ... 34 D4
Saxilby Lincs ... 52 B3
Saxlingham Norfk ... 44 D5
Saxlingham Green Norfk ... 45 F2
Saxlingham Nethergate Norfk ... 45 E2
Saxlingham Thorpe Norfk ... 45 E2
Saxmundham Suffk ... 35 G5
Saxon Street Cambs ... 34 A4
Saxondale Notts ... 51 G1
Saxtead Suffk ... 35 F5
Saxtead Green Suffk ... 35 F5
Saxtead Little Green Suffk ... 35 F5
Saxthorpe Norfk ... 45 E5
Saxton N York ... 59 F4
Sayers Common W Susx ... 11 F4
Scackleton N York ... 66 C1
Scaftworth Notts ... 51 G5
Scagglethorpe N York ... 67 E1
Scalasaig Ag & B ... 82 C5
Scalby E R Yk ... 60 C3
Scalby N York ... 67 F2
Scaldwell Nhants ... 41 H1
Scaleby Cumb ... 71 G5
Scalebyhill Cumb ... 71 G5
Scales Cumb ... 71 F2
Scales Cumb ... 62 C3
Scalford Leics ... 41 H5
Scaling N York ... 66 D4
Scalloway Shet ... 111 I2
Scamblesby Lincs ... 53 E3
Scamodale Highld ... 90 A6
Scampston N York ... 67 E1
Scampton Lincs ... 52 B3
Scaniport Highld ... 99 E6
Scapegoat Hill W York ... 58 C2
Scarborough N York ... 67 F2
Scarcewater Cnwll ... 3 E4
Scarcliffe Derbys ... 51 F3
Scarcroft W York ... 59 E4
Scarfskerry Highld ... 110 C6
Scargill Dur ... 65 E4
Scarinish Ag & B ... 88 B3
Scarisbrick Lancs ... 56 D4
Scarning Norfk ... 44 C3
Scarrington Notts ... 51 H1
Scartho Lincs ... 53 E5
Scatsta Airport Shet ... 111 I3
Scawby Lincs ... 52 B5
Scawsby S York ... 59 F1
Scawthorpe S York ... 59 F1
Scawton N York ... 66 B2
Scayne's Hill W Susx ... 11 F4

Scethrog Powys ... 27 F5
Scholes Gt Man ... 57 F3
Scholes S York ... 51 E6
Scholes W York ... 58 C1
Scissett W York ... 58 D1
Scleddau Pembks ... 24 D6
Scofton Notts ... 51 G4
Scole Norfk ... 35 E6
Scone P & K ... 92 D2
Sconser Highld ... 96 C5
Scoonie Fife ... 86 D6
Scopwick Lincs ... 52 C1
Scoraig Highld ... 105 H5
Scorborough E R Yk ... 60 D4
Scorrier Cnwll ... 2
Scorton Lancs ... 63 E1
Scorton N York ... 65 F3
Scot's Gap Nthumb ... 73 E5
Scotby Cumb ... 71 G4
Scotch Corner N York ... 65 F4
Scotforth Lancs ... 63 E2
Scothern Lincs ... 52 C3
Scotland Highld ... 110 B4
Scotlandwell P & K ... 86 C6
Scotsmill Abers ... 102 B2
Scotstoun C Glas ... 85 E2
Scotswood T & W ... 73 F3
Scotter Lincs ... 52 B5
Scotterthorpe Lincs ... 52 B5
Scotton Lincs ... 52 B5
Scotton N York ... 65 F3
Scotton N York ... 59 E5
Scoulton Norfk ... 44 D2
Scourie Highld ... 108 B4
Scourie More Highld ... 108 B3
Scousburgh Shet ... 111 I1
Scrabster Highld ... 110 B6
Scraesburgh Border ... 80 C2
Scrane End Lincs ... 43 F6
Scraptoft Leics ... 41 G4
Scratby Norfk ... 45 H3
Scrayingham N York ... 60 B5
Scredington Lincs ... 42 C5
Scremby Lincs ... 53 F2
Scremerston Nthumb ... 81 F5
Screveton Notts ... 51 H1
Scriven N York ... 59 E5
Scrooby Notts ... 51 G5
Scropton Derbys ... 40 D6
Scrub Hill Lincs ... 52 D1
Scruschloch Angus ... 93 E5
Scruton N York ... 65 G3
Scullomie Highld ... 109 F5
Sculthorpe Norfk ... 44 C5
Scunthorpe Lincs ... 60 C1
Sea Palling Norfk ... 45 G4
Seaborough Dorset ... 7 G6
Seabrook Kent ... 13 F5
Seaburn T & W ... 73 G3
Seacombe Mersey ... 56 D2
Seacroft W York ... 59 E3
Seafield Highld ... 96 C6
Seafield W Loth ... 86 A3
Seaford E Susx ... 11 G2
Seaforth Mersey ... 56 D2
Seagrave Leics ... 41 G5
Seaham Dur ... 73 G2
Seahouses Nthumb ... 81 G3
Seal Kent ... 22 A1
Seale Surrey ... 10 C6
Seamer N York ... 66 B4
Seamer N York ... 67 F2
Seamill N Ayrs ... 76 B6
Searby Lincs ... 52 C5
Seascale Cumb ... 62 A5
Seathwaite Cumb ... 62 C5
Seatoller Cumb ... 71 F1
Seaton Cnwll ... 4 D3
Seaton Cumb ... 70 D3
Seaton Devon ... 6 D4
Seaton E R Yk ... 61 E4
Seaton Kent ... 23 G2
Seaton Nthumb ... 73 G4
Seaton Rutlnd ... 42 B2
Seaton Carew Dur ... 66 B6
Seaton Delaval Nthumb ... 73 G4
Seaton Ross E R Yk ... 60 B4
Seaton Sluice Nthumb ... 73 G4
Seatown Dorset ... 7 E5
Seave Green N York ... 66 B3
Seaview IOW ... 9 H3
Seaville Cumb ... 71 E4
Seavington St Mary Somset ... 17 E1
Seavington St Michael Somset ... 17 E1
Sebergham Cumb ... 71 F3
Seckington Warwks ... 40 D4
Sedbergh Cumb ... 63 F5
Sedbury Gloucs ... 28 D2
Sedbusk N York ... 64 C3
Seddington Beds ... 32 D3
Sedgeberrow Worcs ... 30 B4
Sedgebrook Lincs ... 42 B5
Sedgefield Dur ... 65 G6
Sedgeford Norfk ... 44 A5
Sedgehill Wilts ... 8 B6
Sedgley W Mids ... 40 A3
Sedgwick Cumb ... 63 E4
Sedlescombe E Susx ... 12 C4
Sedrup Bucks ... 20 B6
Seend Wilts ... 18 B3
Seend Cleeve Wilts ... 18 B3
Seer Green Bucks ... 20 C4
Seething Norfk ... 45 F2
Sefton Mersey ... 56 D3
Seighford Staffs ... 49 H2
Seion Gwynd ... 54 D3
Seisdon Staffs ... 39 H5
Selattyn Shrops ... 48 C3
Selborne Hants ... 10 B5
Selby N York ... 59 G3
Selham W Susx ... 10 C4
Selhurst Gt Lon ... 21 F2
Selkirk Border ... 79 G5
Sellack Herefs ... 28 D5
Sellafirth Shet ... 111 I4
Sellick's Green Somset ... 16 D1
Sellindge Kent ... 13 F5
Selling Kent ... 23 E1
Sells Green Wilts ... 18 B3
Selly Oak W Mids ... 40 B2
Selmeston E Susx ... 11 G3
Selsdon Gt Lon ... 21 F2
Selside N York ... 64 C1
Selsley Gloucs ... 29 F3

Selsted Kent ... 13 G6
Selston Notts ... 51 F2
Selworthy Somset ... 16 B4
Semer Suffk ... 34 D3
Semington Wilts ... 18 B3
Semley Wilts ... 8 B5
Send Surrey ... 20 D1
Senghenydd Caerph ... 27 G2
Sennen Cnwll ... 2 A2
Sennen Cove Cnwll ... 2 A2
Sennybridge Powys ... 27 E5
Sessay N York ... 66 B1
Setchey Norfk ... 43 H3
Seton Mains E Loth ... 87 E3
Settle N York ... 63 G2
Settrington N York ... 67 E1
Seven Ash Somset ... 16 C2
Seven Kings Gt Lon ... 21 G4
Seven Sisters Neath ... 26 D3
Seven Star Green Essex ... 34 C2
Seven Wells Gloucs ... 30 C3
Sevenhampton Gloucs ... 30 B2
Sevenhampton Wilts ... 18 D5
Sevenoaks Kent ... 21 H1
Sevenoaks Weald Kent ... 21 H1
Severn Beach Gloucs ... 28 D2
Severn Stoke Worcs ... 39 H1
Sevington Kent ... 13 E6
Sewards End Essex ... 33 G3
Sewardstone Essex ... 21 F4
Sewell Beds ... 32 C1
Sewerby E R Yk ... 61 F6
Seworgan Cnwll ... 2 D2
Sewstern Leics ... 42 B4
Sgiogarstaigh W Isls ... 111 e7
Shabbington Bucks ... 31 G1
Shackerstone Leics ... 41 E4
Shackleford Surrey ... 10 C6
Shader W Isls ... 111 d7
Shadforth Dur ... 73 G1
Shadingfield Suffk ... 45 G1
Shadoxhurst Kent ... 13 E5
Shadwell Norfk ... 44 C1
Shaftenhoe End Herts ... 33 F3
Shaftesbury Dorset ... 8 B5
Shafton S York ... 59 E1
Shalbourne Wilts ... 19 E3
Shalden Hants ... 10 A6
Shaldon Devon ... 6 B3
Shalfleet IOW ... 9 F2
Shalford Essex ... 34 B2
Shalford Surrey ... 10 D6
Shalford Green Essex ... 34 A2
Shalmsford Street Kent ... 23 F1
Shalstone Bucks ... 31 G4
Shamley Green Surrey ... 10 D6
Shandford Angus ... 94 D2
Shandon Ag & B ... 84 C4
Shandwick Highld ... 107 G3
Shangton Leics ... 41 H3
Shanklin IOW ... 9 G2
Shap Cumb ... 71 H1
Shapwick Dorset ... 8 B3
Shapwick Somset ... 17 E3
Shardlow Derbys ... 41 E6
Shareshill Staffs ... 40 B4
Sharlston W York ... 59 E2
Sharnbrook Beds ... 32 C4
Sharnford Leics ... 41 F3
Sharoe Green Lancs ... 57 E5
Sharow N York ... 65 G1
Sharpenhoe Beds ... 32 C2
Sharperton Nthumb ... 81 E1
Sharpness Gloucs ... 29 E3
Sharrington Norfk ... 44 D5
Shatterford Worcs ... 39 G4
Shaugh Prior Devon ... 5 F3
Shavington Ches ... 49 F4
Shaw Berks ... 19 G3
Shaw Gt Man ... 58 B1
Shaw Wilts ... 18 B3
Shaw Mills N York ... 58 D6
Shawbost W Isls ... 111 d7
Shawbury Shrops ... 49 E2
Shawell Leics ... 41 F2
Shawford Hants ... 9 F5
Shawhead D & G ... 70 C6
Shawsburn S Lans ... 77 G6
Shearington D & G ... 70 D5
Shearsby Leics ... 41 G3
Shearston Somset ... 16 D2
Shebbear Devon ... 14 D2
Shebdon Staffs ... 49 G2
Shebster Highld ... 110 A5
Sheddens E Rens ... 85 E2
Shedfield Hants ... 9 G4
Sheen Derbys ... 50 C3
Sheepscar N York ... 59 E3
Sheepscombe Gloucs ... 29 F4
Sheepstor Devon ... 5 F4
Sheepwash Devon ... 14 D2
Sheepy Magna Leics ... 41 E3
Sheepy Parva Leics ... 41 E3
Sheering Essex ... 21 G6
Sheerness Kent ... 22 D3
Sheerwater Surrey ... 20 D2
Sheet Hants ... 10 B4
Sheffield S York ... 51 E5
Sheffield City Airport S York ... 51 E5
Shefford Beds ... 32 D3
Sheigra Highld ... 108 B5
Sheinton Shrops ... 39 F6
Shelderton Shrops ... 38 D4
Sheldon Derbys ... 50 C3
Sheldon Devon ... 6 C6
Sheldon W Mids ... 40 C2
Sheldwich Kent ... 23 E1
Shelfanger Norfk ... 45 E1
Shelford Notts ... 51 G1
Shellacres Border ... 81 E4
Shelden Kent ... 23 H1
Shelley Suffk ... 34 D3
Shelley W York ... 58 D1
Shellingford Oxon ... 19 E5
Shellow Bowells Essex ... 22 B6
Shelsley Beauchamp Worcs ... 39 G2
Shelsley Walsh Worcs ... 39 G2
Shelton Beds ... 32 C5
Shelton Norfk ... 45 E1
Shelton Notts ... 42 A6
Shelton Under Harley Staffs ... 49 G3
Shelve Shrops ... 38 D5
Shelwick Herefs ... 39 E1
Shenfield Essex ... 22 B5
Shenington Oxon ... 31 E4
Shenley Herts ... 21 E5

Shenley Brook End Bucks ... 32 A2
Shenley Church End Bucks ... 32 A2
Shenmore Herefs ... 28 B6
Shennanton D & G ... 69 E4
Shenstone Staffs ... 40 C4
Shenstone Worcs ... 39 H3
Shenton Leics ... 41 E3
Shephall Herts ... 33 E1
Shepherd's Bush Gt Lon ... 21 E3
Shepherdswell Kent ... 13 G6
Shepley W York ... 58 D1
Shepperton Surrey ... 20 D2
Shepreth Cambs ... 33 F3
Shepshed Leics ... 41 F5
Shepton Beauchamp Somset ... 17 E1
Shepton Mallet Somset ... 17 G3
Shepton Montague Somset ... 17 G2
Shepway Kent ... 22 C1
Sheraton Dur ... 66 B6
Sherborne Dorset ... 17 G1
Sherborne Gloucs ... 30 C2
Sherborne Somset ... 17 G4
Sherborne St John Hants ... 19 H2
Sherbourne Warwks ... 30 D6
Sherburn Dur ... 73 G1
Sherburn N York ... 67 E1
Sherburn Hill Dur ... 73 G1
Sherburn in Elmet N York ... 59 F3
Shere Surrey ... 10 D6
Shereford Norfk ... 44 C5
Sherfield English Hants ... 9 E5
Sherfield on Loddon Hants ... 20 A2
Sherford Devon ... 5 H2
Sheriff Hutton N York ... 59 G6
Sheriffhales Shrops ... 49 G1
Sheringham Norfk ... 45 E6
Sherington Bucks ... 32 B3
Shernborne Norfk ... 44 A5
Sherrington Wilts ... 18 C1
Sherston Wilts ... 18 B5
Sherwood Notts ... 51 F1
Shettleston C Glas ... 85 F2
Shevington Gt Man ... 57 E3
Sheviock Cnwll ... 4 D3
Shibden Head W York ... 58 C3
Shide IOW ... 9 G2
Shidlaw Nthumb ... 80 D4
Shiel Bridge Highld ... 97 G4
Shieldaig Highld ... 105 F2
Shieldhill D & G ... 78 D1
Shieldhill Falk ... 85 G3
Shieldhill House Hotel S Lans ... 78 D6
Shields N Lans ... 85 G1
Shielfoot Highld ... 89 G5
Shielhill Angus ... 93 F5
Shielhill Inver ... 84 B3
Shifnal Shrops ... 39 G6
Shilbottle Nthumb ... 81 G1
Shildon Dur ... 65 F5
Shillford E Rens ... 84 D2
Shillingford Devon ... 16 B2
Shillingford Oxon ... 19 G5
Shillingford Abbot Devon ... 6 A4
Shillingford St George Devon ... 6 A4
Shillingstone Dorset ... 8 B4
Shillington Beds ... 32 D2
Shilton Oxon ... 30 D1
Shilton Warwks ... 41 E2
Shimpling Norfk ... 45 E1
Shimpling Suffk ... 34 C4
Shimpling Street Suffk ... 34 C4
Shincliffe Dur ... 73 G1
Shiney Row T & W ... 73 G2
Shinfield Berks ... 20 A2
Shinness Highld ... 109 E1
Shipbourne Kent ... 22 B1
Shipdham Norfk ... 44 C3
Shipham Somset ... 17 F4
Shiphay Devon ... 6 A2
Shiplake Oxon ... 20 B3
Shipley W Susx ... 11 E4
Shipley W York ... 58 C4
Shipley Bridge Surrey ... 11 F5
Shipmeadow Suffk ... 45 G1
Shippon Oxon ... 19 G6
Shipston on Stour Warwks ... 30 D4
Shipton Gloucs ... 30 B2
Shipton N York ... 59 F5
Shipton Shrops ... 39 E5
Shipton Bellinger Hants ... 19 E2
Shipton Gorge Dorset ... 7 F4
Shipton Green W Susx ... 10 B2
Shipton Moyne Gloucs ... 29 F2
Shipton-on-Cherwell Oxon ... 31 F2
Shipton-under-Wychwood Oxon ... 30 D2
Shiptonthorpe E R Yk ... 60 C4
Shirburn Oxon ... 20 A5
Shirdley Hill Lancs ... 56 D4
Shiregreen S York ... 51 E5
Shirehampton Bristl ... 28 D1
Shiremoor T & W ... 73 G4
Shirenewton Mons ... 28 C2
Shireoaks Notts ... 51 F4
Shirland Derbys ... 51 E3
Shirley Derbys ... 50 D1
Shirley Gt Lon ... 21 F2
Shirley Hants ... 9 F4
Shirley W Mids ... 40 C2
Shirrell Heath Hants ... 9 G4
Shirvan Ag & B ... 83 G4
Shirwell Devon ... 15 E4
Shiskine N Ayrs ... 75 G4
Shobdon Herefs ... 38 D2
Shobrooke Devon ... 15 G1
Shoby Leics ... 41 G5
Shocklach Ches ... 48 D4
Shoeburyness Essex ... 22 D4
Sholden Kent ... 23 H1
Sholing Hants ... 9 F4
Shop Cnwll ... 14 C3
Shop Cnwll ... 3 E6
Shop Street Suffk ... 35 E5
Shoreditch Gt Lon ... 21 F4
Shoreditch Somset ... 16 D2
Shoreham Kent ... 21 G2
Shoreham Airport W Susx ... 11 E3
Shoreham-by-Sea W Susx ... 11 E3
Shorley Hants ... 9 G5
Shorne Kent ... 22 C3
Shortgate E Susx ... 11 G3
Shortlanesend Cnwll ... 3 E4
Shortstown Beds ... 32 C3
Shorwell IOW ... 9 F2

Shoscombe Somset ... 17 H4
Shotesham Norfk ... 45 F2
Shotgate Essex ... 22 C4
Shotley Suffk ... 35 E2
Shotley Bridge Dur ... 73 E2
Shotley Gate Suffk ... 35 F2
Shotley Street Suffk ... 35 E2
Shottenden Kent ... 23 E1
Shottery Warwks ... 30 C5
Shotteswell Warwks ... 31 E4
Shottisham Suffk ... 35 F3
Shottle Derbys ... 50 D2
Shottlegate Derbys ... 50 D2
Shotton Dur ... 73 G1
Shotton Flints ... 48 C6
Shotts N Lans ... 85 G2
Shotwick Ches ... 48 D6
Shougle Moray ... 101 E5
Shouldham Norfk ... 44 A3
Shouldham Thorpe Norfk ... 43 H3
Shoulton Worcs ... 39 G2
Shrawardine Shrops ... 48 D1
Shrawley Worcs ... 39 G3
Shrewley Warwks ... 30 D6
Shrewsbury Shrops ... 49 E1
Shrewton Wilts ... 18 C1
Shripney W Susx ... 10 C2
Shrivenham Oxon ... 19 E5
Shropham Norfk ... 44 D2
Shucknall Herefs ... 28 D6
Shudy Camps Cambs ... 33 G3
Shurdington Gloucs ... 29 G4
Shurlock Row Berks ... 20 B3
Shurrery Highld ... 110 A5
Shurrery Lodge Highld ... 110 A5
Shurton Somset ... 16 D3
Shustoke Warwks ... 40 D3
Shut Heath Staffs ... 49 H2
Shute Devon ... 6 D5
Shutford Oxon ... 31 E4
Shuthonger Gloucs ... 29 F6
Shutlanger Nhants ... 31 H5
Shuttington Warwks ... 40 D4
Shuttlewood Derbys ... 51 F4
Shuttleworth Lancs ... 57 G4
Siabost W Isls ... 111 d7
Siadar W Isls ... 111 d7
Sibbertoft Nhants ... 41 G2
Sibford Ferris Oxon ... 31 E4
Sibford Gower Oxon ... 31 E4
Sible Hedingham Essex ... 34 B2
Sibley's Green Essex ... 33 G2
Sibsey Lincs ... 53 E1
Sibson Cambs ... 42 C2
Sibson Leics ... 41 E3
Sibster Highld ... 110 D4
Sibthorpe Notts ... 51 H4
Sibthorpe Notts ... 51 H2
Sibton Suffk ... 35 F5
Sicklesmere Suffk ... 34 C4
Sicklinghall N York ... 59 E4
Sidbury Devon ... 6 C5
Sidbury Shrops ... 39 F4
Sidcot Somset ... 17 E4
Sidcup Gt Lon ... 21 G3
Siddington Ches ... 49 H6
Siddington Gloucs ... 18 C6
Sidestrand Norfk ... 45 F5
Sidford Devon ... 6 C4
Sidlesham W Susx ... 10 B2
Sidley E Susx ... 12 C3
Sidmouth Devon ... 6 C4
Sigglesthorne E R Yk ... 61 E4
Signingstone V Glam ... 16 B6
Silchester Hants ... 19 H3
Sileby Leics ... 41 G4
Silecroft Cumb ... 62 B4
Silfield Norfk ... 45 E2
Silk Willoughby Lincs ... 42 C6
Silkstone S York ... 58 D1
Silkstone Common S York ... 58 D1
Silksworth T & W ... 73 G2
Silloth Cumb ... 70 D4
Silpho N York ... 67 F3
Silsden W York ... 58 B4
Silsoe Beds ... 32 C2
Silton Dorset ... 8 A6
Silver End Essex ... 34 B1
Silverburn Mdloth ... 86 C2
Silverdale Lancs ... 63 E3
Silverdale Staffs ... 49 G4
Silverford Abers ... 102 D5
Silverstone Nhants ... 31 G4
Silverton Devon ... 6 B5
Silvington Shrops ... 39 F4
Simonburn Nthumb ... 72 C4
Simons Burrow Devon ... 16 C1
Simonsbath Somset ... 15 G5
Simonstone Lancs ... 57 G5
Simprim Border ... 80 D4
Simpson Bucks ... 32 B2
Simpson Cross Pembks ... 24 C4
Sinclair's Hill Border ... 80 D5
Sinclairston E Ayrs ... 76 D3
Sinderby N York ... 65 G2
Sinderland Green Gt Man ... 57 G2
Sindlesham Berks ... 20 B2
Sinfin Derbys ... 41 E6
Singleton Lancs ... 56 D6
Singleton W Susx ... 10 C3
Singlewell Kent ... 22 B3
Sinnarhard Abers ... 101 G1
Sinnington N York ... 66 D2
Sinton Worcs ... 39 G2
Sinton Green Worcs ... 39 G2
Sissinghurst Kent ... 12 C5
Siston Gloucs ... 17 G6
Sithney Cnwll ... 2 C2
Sittingbourne Kent ... 22 D2
Six Ashes Staffs ... 39 G5
Six Mile Bottom Cambs ... 33 G4
Six Rues Jersey ... 7 b2
Sixhills Lincs ... 52 D4
Sixmile Cottages Kent ... 13 F6
Sixpenny Handley Dorset ... 8 C5
Sizergh Castle Cumb ... 63 E4
Skaill Ork ... 111 h2
Skares E Ayrs ... 77 E3
Skateraw Abers ... 95 G5
Skateraw E Loth ... 87 H3
Skeabost Highld ... 104 C1
Skeeby N York ... 65 F3
Skeffington Leics ... 41 H3
Skeffling E R Yk ... 61 G2

Skegby *Notts*	51 F3	Snape Street *Suffk*	35 G4
Skegby *Notts*	52 A2	Snaresbrook *Gt Lon*	21 G4
Skegness *Lincs*	53 G2	Snarestone *Leics*	41 E4
Skelbo *Highld*	107 G5	Snarford *Lincs*	52 C3
Skelbo Street *Highld*	107 G5	Snargate *Kent*	13 E5
Skelbrooke *S York*	59 F2	Snave *Kent*	13 E5
Skeldyke *Lincs*	43 E5	Sneaton *N York*	67 E4
Skellingthorpe *Lincs*	52 B3	Snelland *Lincs*	52 C3
Skellow *S York*	59 F1	Snelston *Derbys*	50 C1
Skelmanthorpe *W York*	58 D1	Snetterton *Norfk*	44 D1
Skelmersdale *Lancs*	57 E3	Snettisham *Norfk*	44 A5
Skelmorlie *N Ayrs*	84 B2	Snig's End *Gloucs*	29 E5
Skelpick *Highld*	109 F4	Snitter *Nthumb*	81 F1
Skelston *D & G*	78 B2	Snitterby *Lincs*	52 C4
Skelton *Cumb*	71 G3	Snitterfield *Warwks*	30 D5
Skelton *E R Yk*	60 B3	Snitton *Shrops*	39 E3
Skelton *N York*	66 C5	Snodland *Kent*	22 C2
Skelton *N York*	59 E6	Snowshill *Gloucs*	30 C3
Skelton *N York*	59 F5	Snowshill *Gloucs*	30 C3
Skelwith Bridge *Cumb*	62 D6	Soake *Hants*	9 H4
Skendleby *Lincs*	53 F2	Soberton *Hants*	9 H5
Skene House *Abers*	102 D1	Soberton Heath *Hants*	9 G4
Skenfrith *Mons*	28 C4	Sockburn *Dur*	65 G4
Skerne *E R Yk*	60 D5	Soham *Cambs*	33 G5
Skerray *Highld*	109 F5	Solas *W Isls*	111 b4
Skerricha *Highld*	108 C4	Soldridge *Hants*	9 H6
Skerton *Lancs*	63 E2	Sole Street *Kent*	22 B2
Sketchley *Leics*	41 E3	Sole Street *Kent*	23 F1
Sketty *Swans*	26 C2	Solihull *W Mids*	40 C2
Skewen *Neath*	26 D2	Sollers Dilwyn *Herefs*	38 D2
Skewsby *N York*	66 C1	Sollers Hope *Herefs*	28 D5
Skiall *Highld*	110 A5	Solva *Pembks*	24 C5
Skidby *E R Yk*	60 D3	Solwaybank *D & G*	79 F1
Skigersta *W Isls*	111 e7	Somerby *Leics*	41 H4
Skilgate *Somset*	16 B2	Somerby *Lincs*	52 C5
Skillington *Lincs*	42 B4	Somercotes *Derbys*	51 E2
Skinburness *Cumb*	71 E5	Somerford *Dorset*	8 D3
Skinflats *Falk*	85 H4	Somerford Keynes *Gloucs*	18 C6
Skinidin *Highld*	104 B1	Somerley *W Susx*	10 B2
Skipness *Ag & B*	83 G2	Somerleyton *Suffk*	45 G2
Skipsea *E R Yk*	61 E5	Somersal Herbert *Derbys*	40 C6
Skipton *N York*	58 B5	Somersby *Lincs*	53 E3
Skipton-on-Swale *N York*	65 G2	Somersham *Cambs*	33 E6
Skipwith *N York*	59 G4	Somersham *Suffk*	34 D3
Skirlaugh *E R Yk*	61 E4	Somerton *Oxon*	31 F3
Skirling *Border*	78 D6	Somerton *Somset*	17 F2
Skirmett *Bucks*	20 B4	Somerton *Suffk*	34 B4
Skirpenbeck *E R Yk*	60 B5	Sompting *W Susx*	11 E3
Skirwith *Cumb*	64 A6	Sonning *Berks*	20 B3
Skirza *Highld*	110 D5	Sonning Common *Oxon*	20 A3
Skulamus *Highld*	97 E4	Sopley *Hants*	8 D3
Skye Green *Essex*	34 C1	Sopworth *Wilts*	18 B5
Skye of Curr *Highld*	99 G5	Sorbie *D & G*	69 F2
Slack *W York*	58 B3	Sordale *Highld*	110 B5
Slacks of Cairnbanno *Abers*	102 D4	Sorisdale *Ag & B*	88 D5
Slad *Gloucs*	29 F3	Sorn *E Ayrs*	77 E4
Slade *Devon*	15 E5	Sortat *Highld*	110 C5
Slade *Somset*	15 G4	Sosgill *Cumb*	70 D2
Slade Green *Kent*	21 H3	Sotby *Lincs*	52 D3
Slade Hooton *S York*	51 F5	Sots Hole *Lincs*	52 D2
Slaggyford *Nthumb*	72 B2	Sotterly *Suffk*	45 G1
Slaidburn *Lancs*	63 G2	Soughton *Flints*	48 C5
Slaithwaite *W York*	58 C2	Soulbury *Bucks*	32 B2
Slaley *Nthumb*	72 D3	Soulby *Cumb*	64 B4
Slamannan *Falk*	85 G3	Souldern *Oxon*	31 F3
Slapton *Bucks*	32 B1	Souldrop *Beds*	32 C5
Slapton *Devon*	5 H2	Sound Muir *Moray*	101 F4
Slapton *Nhants*	31 G4	Soundwell *Gloucs*	17 G6
Slaugham *W Susx*	11 E4	Sourton *Devon*	5 F5
Slaughterford *Wilts*	18 B4	Soutergate *Cumb*	62 C4
Slawston *Leics*	41 H3	South Acre *Norfk*	44 B3
Sleaford *Hants*	10 B5	South Alkham *Kent*	13 G6
Sleaford *Lincs*	42 C6	South Allington *Devon*	5 H1
Sleagill *Cumb*	64 A5	South Alloa *Falk*	85 G4
Sleapford *Shrops*	49 F1	South Ambersham *W Susx*	10 C4
Sleasdairidh *Highld*	107 E5	South Anston *S York*	51 F5
Sledmere *E R Yk*	60 C6	South Ashford *Kent*	13 E6
Sleightholme *Dur*	64 D4	South Baddesley *Hants*	9 F4
Sleights *N York*	67 E4	South Bank *N York*	59 G5
Slickly *Highld*	110 C5	South Barrow *Somset*	17 G2
Sliddery *N Ayrs*	75 G3	South Beddington *Gt Lon*	21 F2
Sligachan *Highld*	96 C5	South Benfleet *Essex*	22 C4
Sligrachan *Ag & B*	84 B4	South Bersted *W Susx*	10 C2
Slimbridge *Gloucs*	29 E3	South Bramwith *S York*	59 G1
Slindon *Staffs*	49 G3	South Brent *Devon*	5 G3
Slindon *W Susx*	10 C3	South Brewham *Somset*	17 H3
Slinfold *W Susx*	10 D5	South Broomhill *Nthumb*	73 F6
Slingsby *N York*	66 C1	South Burlingham *Norfk*	45 G3
Slip End *Beds*	32 C1	South Cadbury *Somset*	17 G2
Slip End *Herts*	33 E3	South Carlton *Lincs*	52 B3
Slipton *Nhants*	32 B6	South Carlton *Notts*	51 G5
Slitting Mill *Staffs*	40 B5	South Cave *E R Yk*	60 C3
Slockavullin *Ag & B*	83 F5	South Cerney *Gloucs*	18 C6
Slogarie *D & G*	69 G4	South Chailey *E Susx*	11 G4
Sloncombe *Devon*	5 G5	South Charlton *Nthumb*	81 G2
Sloothby *Lincs*	53 F3	South Cheriton *Somset*	17 H2
Slough *Berks*	20 C3	South Church *Dur*	65 F6
Slough Green *Somset*	16 D1	South Cliffe *E R Yk*	60 C3
Slumbay *Highld*	97 F6	South Clifton *Notts*	52 A2
Slyne *Lancs*	63 E3	South Cockerington *Lincs*	53 F4
Smailholm *Border*	80 C3	South Cornelly *Brdgnd*	26 D1
Small Dole *W Susx*	11 E3	South Cove *Suffk*	35 G6
Small Heath *W Mids*	40 C2	South Creake *Norfk*	44 C5
Small Hythe *Kent*	12 D5	South Croxton *Leics*	41 G4
Smallburgh *Norfk*	45 F4	South Dalton *E R Yk*	60 D4
Smalley *Derbys*	51 E1	South Duffield *N York*	59 G3
Smallfield *Surrey*	11 F6	South Elkington *Lincs*	53 E4
Smallridge *Devon*	7 E5	South Elmsall *W York*	59 F1
Smallworth *Norfk*	34 D6	South Erradale *Highld*	105 F3
Smannell *Hants*	19 F2	South Fambridge *Essex*	22 D4
Smarden *Kent*	12 D6	South Ferriby *Lincs*	60 D2
Smarden Bell *Kent*	12 D6	South Field *E R Yk*	60 D3
Smart's Hill *Kent*	11 H6	South Gorley *Hants*	8 D4
Smearisary *Highld*	89 G6	South Gosforth *T & W*	73 F3
Smeatharpe *Devon*	6 D6	South Green *Essex*	22 B4
Smeeth *Kent*	13 E5	South Green *Kent*	22 D2
Smeeton Westerby *Leics*	41 G3	South Green *Norfk*	44 D3
Smerral *Highld*	110 B3	South Gyle *C Edin*	86 C3
Smestow *Staffs*	39 H5	South Hanningfield *Essex*	22 C5
Smethwick *W Mids*	40 B2	South Harting *W Susx*	10 B4
Smisby *Derbys*	41 E5	South Hayling *Hants*	10 A2
Smith's Green *Essex*	33 H3	South Heath *Bucks*	20 C5
Smithfield *Cumb*	71 G5	South Hetton *Dur*	73 G2
Smithstown *Highld*	105 F4	South Hiendley *W York*	59 E2
Smithton *Highld*	107 F1	South Hill *Cnwll*	4 D4
Smoo *Highld*	108 D5	South Hinksey *Oxon*	31 F1
Smythe's Green *Essex*	34 C1	South Holmwood *Surrey*	11 E6
Snade *D & G*	78 B2	South Hornchurch *Gt Lon*	21 G4
Snailbeach *Shrops*	38 D6	South Huish *Devon*	5 G1
Snailwell *Cambs*	33 H5	South Hykeham *Lincs*	52 B2
Snainton *N York*	67 E2	South Hylton *T & W*	73 G2
Snaith *E R Yk*	59 G2	South Kelsey *Lincs*	52 C5
Snape *N York*	65 F2	South Kessock *Highld*	107 F1
Snape *Suffk*	35 G4	South Killingholme *Lincs*	61 E2
South Kilvington *N York*	65 H2	Sowton *Devon*	5 E3
South Kilworth *Nhants*	41 G2	Sowton *Devon*	6 B5
South Kirkby *W York*	59 E1	Soyland Town *W York*	58 B2
South Kyme *Lincs*	52 D1	Spain's End *Essex*	33 H3
South Leigh *Oxon*	31 E1	Spalding *Lincs*	43 E4
South Leverton *Notts*	52 A3	Spaldington *E R Yk*	60 B3
South Littleton *Worcs*	30 C4	Spaldwick *Cambs*	32 D5
South Lopham *Norfk*	34 D6	Spalford *Notts*	52 A2
South Luffenham *Rutlnd*	42 B2	Spanby *Lincs*	42 C5
South Malling *E Susx*	11 G3	Sparham *Norfk*	44 D4
South Marston *Wilts*	18 D5	Spark Bridge *Cumb*	62 C4
South Merstham *Surrey*	21 F1	Sparkford *Somset*	17 G2
South Milford *N York*	59 F3	Sparkhill *W Mids*	40 C2
South Milton *Devon*	5 G2	Sparkwell *Devon*	5 F3
South Mimms *Herts*	21 E5	Sparrowpit *Derbys*	50 C4
South Molton *Devon*	15 F3	Sparrows Green *E Susx*	12 B5
South Moor *Dur*	73 F2	Sparsholt *Hants*	9 F6
South Moreton *Oxon*	19 G5	Sparsholt *Oxon*	19 F5
South Mundham *W Susx*	10 C2	Spaunton *N York*	66 D2
South Newbald *E R Yk*	60 C3	Spaxton *Somset*	16 D3
South Newington *Oxon*	31 E3	Spean Bridge *Highld*	98 B1
South Newton *Wilts*	8 D6	Spearywell *Hants*	9 E6
South Normanton *Derbys*	51 E2	Speen *Berks*	19 F3
South Norwood *Gt Lon*	21 F2	Speen *Bucks*	20 B5
South Ockendon *Essex*	22 B4	Speeton *N York*	67 G1
South Ormsby *Lincs*	53 F3	Speke *Mersyd*	56 D1
South Otterington *N York*	65 G2	Speldhurst *Kent*	12 A6
South Owersby *Lincs*	52 C4	Spellbrook *Herts*	33 F1
South Park *Surrey*	11 E6	Spen Green *Ches*	49 G5
South Perrott *Dorset*	7 F6	Spencers Wood *Berks*	20 A3
South Petherton *Somset*	17 F1	Spennithorne *N York*	65 E2
South Petherwin *Cnwll*	4 D5	Spennymoor *Dur*	65 F6
South Pickenham *Norfk*	44 C3	Spetchley *Worcs*	30 A5
South Pill *Cnwll*	5 E3	Spetisbury *Dorset*	8 B3
South Pool *Devon*	5 H1	Spexhall *Suffk*	35 G6
South Poorton *Dorset*	7 F5	Spey Bay *Moray*	101 F5
South Queensferry *C Edin*	86 B4	Speybridge *Highld*	100 D2
South Radworthy *Devon*	15 G4	Speyview *Moray*	101 F5
South Rauceby *Lincs*	42 C6	Spilsby *Lincs*	53 F2
South Raynham *Norfk*	44 C4	Spinkhill *Derbys*	51 F4
South Reston *Lincs*	53 F4	Spinningdale *Highld*	107 F5
South Runcton *Norfk*	43 H3	Spital Hill *S York*	51 G5
South Scarle *Notts*	52 A2	Spittal *E Loth*	87 E4
South Shian *Ag & B*	90 B3	Spittal *Highld*	110 B4
South Shields *T & W*	73 G3	Spittal *Nthumb*	81 F5
South Shore *Lancs*	56 C5	Spittal *Pembks*	24 D5
South Stainley *N York*	58 D6	Spittal of Glenmuick *Abers*	94 C4
South Stoke *Lincs*	42 B4	Spittal of Glenshee *P & K*	94 A3
South Stoke *Oxon*	19 G5	Spittal-on-Rule *Border*	80 B2
South Stoke *Somset*	17 H5	Spittalfield *P & K*	92 D3
South Stoke *W Susx*	10 D3	Spixworth *Norfk*	45 F3
South Street *Kent*	23 E2	Splatt *Devon*	15 E2
South Street *Kent*	23 F2	Splayne's Green *E Susx*	11 G4
South Tarbrax *S Lans*	86 A2	Splottlands *Cardif*	27 G1
South Tawton *Devon*	5 G6	Spofforth *N York*	59 E5
South Thoresby *Lincs*	53 F3	Spondon *Derbys*	41 E6
South Walsham *Norfk*	45 F3	Spooner Row *Norfk*	44 D2
South Warnborough *Hants*	10 A6	Sporle *Norfk*	44 C3
South Weald *Essex*	22 B4	Spott *E Loth*	87 F3
South Weston *Oxon*	20 A5	Spottiswoode *Border*	80 C5
South Wheatley *Cnwll*	4 C6	Spratton *Nhants*	41 H1
South Widcombe *Somset*	17 G4	Spreakley *Surrey*	10 B6
South Wigston *Leics*	41 G3	Spreyton *Devon*	15 F1
South Willesborough *Kent*	13 E6	Spriddlestone *Devon*	5 F2
South Willingham *Lincs*	52 D4	Spridlington *Lincs*	52 C4
South Wingate *Dur*	65 G6	Springburn *C Glas*	85 E3
South Wingfield *Derbys*	51 E2	Springfield *D & G*	71 F6
South Witham *Lincs*	42 B4	Springfield *Essex*	22 C6
South Woodham Ferrers *Essex*	22 C5	Springfield *Fife*	93 F1
South Wootton *Norfk*	43 H4	Springholm *D & G*	70 B6
South Wraxall *Wilts*	18 B3	Springside *N Ayrs*	76 C5
South Zeal *Devon*	5 G6	Springthorpe *Lincs*	52 B4
Southall *Gt Lon*	20 D3	Springwell *T & W*	73 F3
Southam *Gloucs*	29 H5	Sproatley *E R Yk*	61 E3
Southam *Warwks*	31 E6	Sproston Green *Ches*	49 G5
Southampton *Hants*	9 F4	Sprotbrough *S York*	51 F6
Southampton Airport *Hants*	9 F5	Sproughton *Suffk*	35 E3
Southborough *Gt Lon*	21 G2	Sprouston *Border*	80 D3
Southborough *Kent*	12 B6	Sprowston *Norfk*	45 F3
Southbourne *Dorset*	8 D3	Sproxton *Leics*	42 B4
Southbourne *W Susx*	10 B3	Sproxton *N York*	66 C2
Southburgh *Norfk*	44 D3	Spurstow *Ches*	49 E5
Southchurch *Essex*	22 D4	Spyway *Dorset*	7 F5
Southcott *Cnwll*	4 C6	Stableford *Shrops*	39 G5
Southcott *Devon*	5 F6	Stacey Bank *Derbys*	50 D5
Southcott *Devon*	5 F6	Stackhouse *N York*	63 G3
Southcourt *Bucks*	20 B6	Stackpole *Pembks*	24 D2
Southease *E Susx*	11 G3	Staddiscombe *Devon*	5 E2
Southend *Ag & B*	75 E2	Stadhampton *Oxon*	19 H6
Southend Airport *Essex*	22 D4	Stadhlaigearraidh *W Isls*	111 a3
Southend-on-Sea *Essex*	22 D4	Staffield *Cumb*	71 H3
Southerndown *V Glam*	16 A6	Staffin *Highld*	104 D3
Southerness *D & G*	70 C4	Stafford *Staffs*	40 A5
Southerton *Devon*	6 C4	Stagsden *Beds*	32 C3
Southery *Norfk*	43 G2	Stainburn *Cumb*	70 D2
Southfield *Falk*	85 G3	Stainburn *N York*	58 D5
Southfleet *Kent*	22 B3	Stainby *Lincs*	42 B4
Southgate *Gt Lon*	21 F4	Staincross *S York*	59 E1
Southgate *Swans*	26 B2	Staindrop *Dur*	65 E5
Southill *Beds*	32 D3	Staines *Surrey*	20 D3
Southington *Hants*	19 G2	Stainfield *Lincs*	52 C3
Southleigh *Devon*	6 D5	Stainforth *N York*	59 G2
Southminster *Essex*	23 E5	Stainforth *N York*	63 G3
Southmoor *Oxon*	19 F6	Staining *Lancs*	56 C6
Southmuir *Angus*	93 F4	Stainland *W York*	58 C2
Southoe *Cambs*	32 D5	Stainsacre *N York*	67 E4
Southolt *Suffk*	35 E5	Stainton *Cumb*	71 G2
Southorpe *Cambs*	42 C2	Stainton *Cumb*	63 E4
Southover *Dorset*	7 G5	Stainton *Dur*	65 E5
Southowram *W York*	58 C2	Stainton *N York*	66 B4
Southport *Mersyd*	56 D4	Stainton *S York*	51 F5
Southrepps *Norfk*	45 F5	Stainton by Langworth *Lincs*	52 C3
Southrey *Lincs*	52 D2	Stainton le Vale *Lincs*	52 D4
Southrop *Gloucs*	30 D1	Stainton with Adgarley *Cumb*	62 C3
Southrope *Hants*	19 H2	Staintondale *N York*	67 F3
Southsea *Hants*	9 H3	Stair *E Ayrs*	76 D4
Southside *Dur*	65 E5	Stair Haven *D & G*	68 D3
Southtown *Norfk*	45 H3	Stakeford *Nthumb*	73 F5
Southwaite *Cumb*	71 G4	Stakes *Hants*	10 A3
Southwark *Gt Lon*	21 F3	Stalbridge *Dorset*	17 H1
Southwater *W Susx*	11 E4	Stalbridge Weston *Dorset*	17 H1
Southwell *Notts*	51 G2	Stalham *Norfk*	45 G4
Southwick *Hants*	9 H4	Stalisfield Green *Kent*	23 E1
Southwick *Nhants*	42 C2	Stallen *Dorset*	17 G1
Southwick *T & W*	73 G3	Stallingborough *Lincs*	61 E1
Southwick *W Susx*	11 E3	Stalmine *Lancs*	62 D1
Southwick *Wilts*	18 B2	Stalybridge *Gt Man*	50 B6
Southwold *Suffk*	35 H6	Stambourne *Essex*	34 A3
Sowerby *N York*	66 A2	Stamford *Lincs*	42 C3
Sowerby *N York*	58 B2	Stamford *Nthumb*	81 G2
Sowerby Bridge *W York*	58 B2	Stamford Bridge *Ches*	49 E5
Sowerby Bridge *W York*	58 B2	Stamford Bridge *E R Yk*	60 B5
Sowood *W York*	58 C2	Stamford Hill *Gt Lon*	21 F4
		Stamfordham *Nthumb*	73 E4
		Stanbridge *Beds*	32 B1
		Stanbury *W York*	58 B4
		Stand *N Lans*	85 F3
		Standburn *Falk*	85 H3
		Standeford *Staffs*	40 A4
		Standen *Kent*	12 D5
		Standerwick *Somset*	18 A2
		Standford *Hants*	10 B5
		Standingstone *Cumb*	70 D3
		Standish *St Man*	57 E4
		Standlake *Oxon*	31 E1
		Standon *Hants*	9 F5
		Standon *Herts*	33 F1
		Standon *Staffs*	49 G3
		Stane *N Lans*	85 G2
		Stanfield *Norfk*	44 C4
		Stanford *Beds*	32 D3
		Stanford *Kent*	13 F5
		Stanford Bishop *Herefs*	39 F2
		Stanford Bridge *Worcs*	39 G3
		Stanford Dingley *Berks*	19 G4
		Stanford in the Vale *Oxon*	19 E5
		Stanford le Hope *Essex*	22 B3
		Stanford on Avon *Nhants*	41 G2
		Stanford on Soar *Notts*	41 F5
		Stanford on Teme *Worcs*	39 G3
		Stanfree *Derbys*	51 F4
		Stanghow *N York*	66 C5
		Stanground *Cambs*	42 D2
		Stanhoe *Norfk*	44 B5
		Stanhope *Border*	79 E5
		Stanhope *Dur*	72 D1
		Stanion *Nhants*	42 B1
		Stanley *Derbys*	51 E1
		Stanley *Dur*	73 F2
		Stanley *P & K*	92 D3
		Stanley *Staffs*	50 A2
		Stanley Crook *Dur*	73 F1
		Stanley Pontlarge *Gloucs*	30 B3
		Stanmer *E Susx*	11 F3
		Stanmore *Gt Lon*	21 E4
		Stanmore *Hants*	9 F6
		Stannersburn *Nthumb*	72 B5
		Stanningfield *Suffk*	34 C4
		Stannington *Nthumb*	73 F4
		Stannington *S York*	50 D5
		Stannington Station *Nthumb*	73 F4
		Stansbatch *Herefs*	38 D2
		Stansfield *Suffk*	34 B4
		Stanstead *Suffk*	34 B4
		Stanstead Abbotts *Herts*	21 F6
		Stanstead Street *Suffk*	34 B3
		Stansted *Kent*	22 B2
		Stansted Airport *Essex*	33 G1
		Stansted Mountfitchet *Essex*	33 G2
		Stanton *Gloucs*	30 C3
		Stanton *Nthumb*	73 E5
		Stanton *Staffs*	50 C2
		Stanton *Suffk*	34 C5
		Stanton by Bridge *Derbys*	41 E5
		Stanton by Dale *Derbys*	51 F1
		Stanton Drew *Somset*	17 G5
		Stanton Fitzwarren *Wilts*	18 D5
		Stanton Harcourt *Oxon*	31 E1
		Stanton in Peak *Derbys*	50 D3
		Stanton Lacy *Shrops*	39 E4
		Stanton Lees *Derbys*	50 D3
		Stanton Long *Shrops*	39 F5
		Stanton on the Wolds *Notts*	41 G6
		Stanton Prior *Somset*	17 G5
		Stanton St Bernard *Wilts*	18 D3
		Stanton St John *Oxon*	31 F1
		Stanton St Quintin *Wilts*	18 B4
		Stanton Street *Suffk*	34 C5
		Stanton under Bardon *Leics*	41 F4
		Stanton upon Hine Heath *Shrops*	49 E2
		Stanton Wick *Somset*	17 G5
		Stanway *Essex*	34 C1
		Stanway *Gloucs*	30 B3
		Stanwell *Surrey*	20 D3
		Stanwick *Nhants*	32 C5
		Stanwix *Cumb*	71 G5
		Staoinebrig *W Isls*	111 a3
		Stape *N York*	66 D3
		Stapeley *Ches*	49 F4
		Stapenhill *Staffs*	40 D5
		Staple *Kent*	23 G1
		Staple *Somset*	16 C3
		Staple Cross *Devon*	16 B1
		Staple Cross *E Susx*	12 C4
		Staple Fitzpaine *Somset*	16 D1
		Staplefield *W Susx*	11 F4
		Stapleford *Cambs*	33 F4
		Stapleford *Herts*	33 E1
		Stapleford *Leics*	42 A4
		Stapleford *Lincs*	52 B1
		Stapleford *Notts*	51 F1
		Stapleford *Wilts*	18 C1
		Stapleford Abbotts *Essex*	21 G4
		Staplegrove *Somset*	16 D2
		Staplehay *Somset*	16 D2
		Staplehurst *Kent*	12 C6
		Staplestreet *Kent*	23 E2
		Stapleton *Herefs*	38 D3
		Stapleton *Leics*	41 E3
		Stapleton *N York*	65 F4
		Stapleton *Shrops*	39 E6
		Stapleton *Somset*	17 F1
		Stapley *Somset*	16 D1
		Staploe *Beds*	32 D4
		Staplow *Herefs*	29 E6
		Star *Fife*	86 D6
		Star *Pembks*	25 F6
		Star *Somset*	17 F4
		Starbeck *N York*	59 E5
		Starbotton *N York*	64 D1
		Starcross *Devon*	6 B4
		Stareton *Warwks*	41 E1
		Starlings Green *Essex*	33 F2
		Starston *Norfk*	45 E1
		Startforth *Dur*	65 E5
		Startley *Wilts*	18 B5
		Statenborough *Kent*	23 G1
		Stathe *Somset*	17 E2
		Stathern *Leics*	41 H6
		Staughton Green *Cambs*	32 D5
		Staunton *Gloucs*	28 D4
		Staunton *Gloucs*	29 E5
		Staunton Green *Herefs*	38 D2
		Staunton in the Vale *Notts*	51 H2
		Staunton on Arrow *Herefs*	38 D2
		Staunton on Wye *Herefs*	38 D1
		Staveley *Cumb*	62 D4
		Staveley *Cumb*	63 E5

Name	Page	Grid
Staveley Derbys	51	E4
Staveley N York	59	E6
Staverton Devon	5	H3
Staverton Gloucs	29	F5
Staverton Nhants	31	F6
Staverton Wilts	18	B3
Stawell Somset	17	E3
Stawley Somset	16	C2
Staxigoe Highld	110	D4
Staxton N York	67	F2
Staynall Lancs	62	D1
Stean N York	65	E1
Steane Nhants	31	F4
Stearsby N York	66	C1
Steart Somset	16	D3
Stebbing Essex	33	H1
Stebbing Green Essex	34	A1
Stebbing Park Essex	33	H2
Stedham W Susx	10	B4
Steele Road Border	79	H2
Steelend Fife	86	A5
Steen's Bridge Herefs	39	E2
Steep Hants	10	B4
Steep Lane W York	58	B2
Steeple Essex	22	D5
Steeple Ashton Wilts	18	B2
Steeple Aston Oxon	31	F3
Steeple Bumpstead Essex	34	A3
Steeple Claydon Bucks	31	G3
Steeple Gidding Cambs	32	D6
Steeple Langford Wilts	18	C1
Steeple Morden Cambs	33	E3
Steeton W York	58	B4
Stein Highld	104	B2
Stelling Minnis Kent	13	F6
Stembridge Somset	17	E1
Stenalees Cnwll	3	F5
Stenhouse D & G	77	G1
Stenhousemuir Falk	85	G4
Stenscholl Highld	104	C3
Stenton E Loth	87	F3
Steornabhagh W Isls	111	d6
Stepaside Pembks	25	E3
Stepney Gt Lon	21	F3
Steppingley Beds	32	C2
Stepps N Lans	85	F3
Sternfield Suffk	35	G4
Stert Wilts	18	C3
Stetchworth Cambs	33	H4
Stevenage Herts	32	D2
Stevenston N Ayrs	76	C5
Steventon Hants	19	G2
Steventon Oxon	19	F5
Steventon End Essex	33	G3
Stevington Beds	32	C4
Stewartby Beds	32	C3
Stewartfield S Lans	85	E1
Stewarton E Ayrs	76	D5
Stewkley Bucks	32	B2
Stewley Somset	17	E1
Steyning W Susx	11	E3
Steynton Pembks	24	D3
Stibb Cnwll	14	B2
Stibb Cross Devon	14	D3
Stibb Green Wilts	19	E3
Stibbard Norfk	44	D5
Stibbington Cambs	42	C2
Stichill Border	80	C4
Sticker Cnwll	3	F4
Stickford Lincs	53	E2
Sticklepath Devon	5	F6
Stickling Green Essex	33	F2
Stickney Lincs	53	E1
Stiffkey Norfk	44	C6
Stilligarry W Isls	111	a3
Stillingfleet N York	59	G4
Stillington Dur	65	G5
Stillington N York	59	G6
Stilton Cambs	42	D1
Stinchcombe Gloucs	29	E3
Stinsford Dorset	7	H4
Stiperstones Shrops	38	D5
Stirling Abers	103	F4
Stirling Stirlg	85	G5
Stirtloe Cambs	32	D5
Stirton N York	58	B5
Stisted Essex	34	B2
Stithians Cnwll	2	D3
Stivichall W Mids	41	E1
Stixwould Lincs	52	D2
Stoak Ches	48	D6
Stobo Border	79	E6
Stoborough Dorset	8	B2
Stobs Castle Border	80	B1
Stobswood Nthumb	73	F6
Stock Essex	22	C5
Stock Somset	17	F5
Stock Green Worcs	30	B5
Stock Wood Worcs	30	B5
Stockbridge Hants	9	F6
Stockbriggs S Lans	77	G5
Stockbury Kent	22	D2
Stockcross Berks	19	F3
Stockerston Leics	42	A2
Stocking Herefs	28	D5
Stocking Pelham Herts	33	F2
Stockingford Warwks	41	E3
Stockland Devon	6	D6
Stockland Bristol Somset	16	D3
Stockleigh English Devon	15	G2
Stockleigh Pomeroy Devon	15	G2
Stockley Wilts	18	C3
Stocklinch Somset	17	E1
Stockport Gt Man	50	A5
Stocksbridge S York	50	D6
Stocksfield Nthumb	73	E3
Stockton Herefs	39	E2
Stockton Norfk	45	G2
Stockton Shrops	49	G1
Stockton Shrops	39	G5
Stockton Warwks	31	E6
Stockton Wilts	18	C1
Stockton Heath Ches	57	F2
Stockton on Teme Worcs	39	G3
Stockton on the Forest N York	59	G5
Stockton-on-Tees Dur	66	B5
Stockwood Bristl	17	G5
Stockwood Dorset	7	G6
Stodmarsh Kent	23	G2
Stody Norfk	44	D5
Stoer Highld	108	A2
Stoford Somset	17	G1
Stoford Wilts	8	C6
Stogumber Somset	16	C3

Name	Page	Grid
Stogursey Somset	16	D3
Stoke Devon	14	C3
Stoke Hants	19	F2
Stoke Hants	10	A2
Stoke Kent	22	D3
Stoke W Mids	41	E2
Stoke Abbott Dorset	7	F5
Stoke Albany Nhants	42	A1
Stoke Ash Suffk	35	E5
Stoke Bardolph Notts	51	G1
Stoke Bliss Worcs	39	F2
Stoke Bruerne Nhants	31	H5
Stoke by Clare Suffk	34	B3
Stoke Canon Devon	6	B5
Stoke Charity Hants	19	G1
Stoke Climsland Cnwll	4	D4
Stoke Cross Herefs	39	F1
Stoke D'Abernon Surrey	20	D2
Stoke Doyle Nhants	42	C1
Stoke Dry Rutlnd	42	B2
Stoke Edith Herefs	28	D6
Stoke Farthing Wilts	8	C5
Stoke Ferry Norfk	44	A2
Stoke Fleming Devon	6	A1
Stoke Gabriel Devon	6	A2
Stoke Gifford Gloucs	28	D1
Stoke Golding Leics	41	E3
Stoke Goldington Bucks	32	A3
Stoke Hammond Bucks	32	B2
Stoke Holy Cross Norfk	45	E2
Stoke Lacy Herefs	39	F1
Stoke Lyne Oxon	31	F3
Stoke Mandeville Bucks	20	B6
Stoke Newington Gt Lon	21	F4
Stoke Orchard Gloucs	29	F5
Stoke Poges Bucks	20	C4
Stoke Prior Herefs	39	E2
Stoke Prior Worcs	30	B6
Stoke Rivers Devon	15	F4
Stoke Row Oxon	20	A4
Stoke St Gregory Somset	17	E2
Stoke St Mary Somset	16	D2
Stoke St Michael Somset	17	G4
Stoke St Milborough Shrops	39	E4
Stoke sub Hamdon Somset	17	F1
Stoke Talmage Oxon	20	A5
Stoke Trister Somset	17	H2
Stoke upon Tern Shrops	49	F2
Stoke Wake Dorset	8	A4
Stoke-by-Nayland Suffk	34	D2
Stoke-on-Trent Staffs	50	A2
Stoke-upon-Trent Staffs	49	H4
Stokeford Dorset	8	B2
Stokeham Notts	52	A3
Stokeinteignhead Devon	6	B3
Stokenchurch Bucks	20	B5
Stokenham Devon	5	H2
Stokesay Castle Shrops	38	D4
Stokesby Norfk	45	G3
Stokesley N York	66	B4
Stolford Somset	16	D3
Ston Easton Somset	17	G4
Stondon Massey Essex	22	B5
Stone Bucks	20	B6
Stone Gloucs	29	E2
Stone Kent	12	D4
Stone S York	51	F5
Stone Staffs	40	A6
Stone Worcs	39	H3
Stone Allerton Somset	17	E4
Stone Cross Kent	23	G1
Stone Street Kent	22	B1
Stone Street Suffk	35	G6
Stonebridge Somset	17	E5
Stonebridge W Mids	40	D2
Stonebroom Derbys	51	E3
Stonecrouch Kent	12	C5
Stoneferry E R Yk	61	E3
Stonefield Castle Hotel Ag & B	83	G3
Stonegate E Susx	12	B5
Stonegrave N York	66	C1
Stonehaven Abers	95	G4
Stonehenge Wilts	18	D1
Stonehouse Ches	49	E6
Stonehouse D & G	70	B6
Stonehouse Devon	5	E2
Stonehouse Gloucs	29	F3
Stonehouse S Lans	77	F5
Stoneleigh Warwks	41	E1
Stones Green Essex	35	E2
Stonesby Leics	42	A4
Stonesfield Oxon	31	E2
Stonewells Moray	101	E5
Stoney Middleton Derbys	50	D4
Stoney Stanton Leics	41	F3
Stoney Stoke Somset	17	H2
Stoney Stratton Somset	17	G3
Stoney Stretton Shrops	48	D1
Stoneybridge W Isls	111	a3
Stoneyburn W Loth	86	A2
Stoneygate Leics	41	G3
Stoneykirk D & G	68	C3
Stoneywood Aber C	103	E1
Stoneywood Falk	85	G4
Stonham Aspal Suffk	35	E4
Stonnall Staffs	40	C4
Stonor Oxon	20	A4
Stonton Wyville Leics	41	H3
Stony Houghton Derbys	51	F3
Stony Stratford Bucks	32	A3
Stoodleigh Devon	15	F4
Stoodleigh Devon	16	B1
Stopham W Susx	10	D4
Stopsley Beds	32	C1
Stornoway W Isls	111	d6
Stornoway Airport W Isls	111	d6
Storrington W Susx	10	D3
Storwood E R Yk	60	B4
Stotfield Moray	101	E6
Stotfold Beds	32	D2
Stottesdon Shrops	39	F4
Stoughton Leics	41	G3
Stoughton Surrey	20	C1
Stoughton W Susx	10	B3
Stoul Highld	97	E2
Stoulton Worcs	30	A5
Stour Kent	22	C2
Stour Provost Dorset	8	A5
Stour Row Dorset	8	A5
Stourbridge W Mids	40	A2
Stourpaine Dorset	8	B4
Stourport-on-Severn Worcs	39	G3
Stourton Staffs	39	H4
Stourton Warwks	30	D4
Stourton Wilts	8	A6

Name	Page	Grid
Stourton Caundle Dorset	17	H1
Stove Shet	111	I1
Stoven Suffk	35	G6
Stow Border	87	E1
Stow Lincs	52	B3
Stow Bardolph Norfk	43	G3
Stow Bedon Norfk	44	C2
Stow Longa Cambs	32	D5
Stow Maries Essex	22	D5
Stow-cum-Quy Cambs	33	G4
Stow-on-the-Wold Gloucs	30	C3
Stowbridge Norfk	43	G3
Stowe Shrops	38	C3
Stowe by Chartley Staffs	40	B5
Stowell Somset	17	G2
Stowey Somset	17	G5
Stowford Devon	14	D1
Stowford Devon	15	F5
Stowford Devon	5	E5
Stowlangtoft Suffk	34	C5
Stowmarket Suffk	34	D4
Stowting Kent	13	F6
Stowting Common Kent	13	F6
Stowupland Suffk	34	D4
Straanruie Moray	99	G4
Strachan Abers	95	F5
Stradbroke Suffk	35	E5
Stradishall Suffk	34	B4
Stradsett Norfk	43	H3
Stragglethorpe Lincs	52	B1
Straiton Mdloth	86	C3
Straiton S Ayrs	76	D2
Straloch Abers	102	D2
Straloch P & K	92	C5
Stramshall Staffs	40	C6
Strang IOM	116	c3
Strangford Herefs	28	D5
Stranraer D & G	68	C3
Stratfield Mortimer Berks	19	H3
Stratfield Saye Hants	20	A2
Stratfield Turgis Hants	20	A2
Stratford Gt Lon	21	F4
Stratford St Andrew Suffk	35	F4
Stratford St Mary Suffk	34	D2
Stratford Tony Wilts	8	D5
Stratford-upon-Avon Warwks	30	D5
Strath Highld	105	F4
Strathan Highld	108	B2
Strathan Highld	109	E5
Strathaven S Lans	77	F5
Strathblane Stirlg	85	E3
Strathcanaird Highld	106	B5
Strathcarron Station Highld	97	G3
Strathcoil Ag & B	89	G2
Strathdon Abers	101	F1
Strathkinness Fife	93	F1
Strathloanhead W Loth	85	H3
Strathmashie House Highld	98	D2
Strathmiglo Fife	86	C6
Strathpeffer Highld	106	D2
Strathtay P & K	92	B4
Strathwhillan N Ayrs	75	H4
Strathy Highld	109	G5
Strathy Inn Highld	109	G5
Strathyre Stirlg	91	G1
Stratton Cnwll	14	C2
Stratton Dorset	7	G5
Stratton Gloucs	30	B1
Stratton Audley Oxon	31	G3
Stratton St Margaret Wilts	18	D5
Stratton St Michael Norfk	45	E2
Stratton Strawless Norfk	45	E4
Stratton-on-the-Fosse Somset	17	G4
Stravithie Fife	93	G1
Streat E Susx	11	F3
Streatham Gt Lon	21	F3
Streatley Beds	32	C2
Streatley Berks	19	G4
Street Devon	6	D4
Street Somset	17	F3
Street Ashton Warwks	41	F2
Street Dinas Shrops	48	D3
Street End Kent	23	F1
Street End W Susx	10	B2
Street on the Fosse Somset	17	G3
Streethay Staffs	40	C4
Streetlam N York	65	G3
Streetly End Cambs	33	H3
Strelitz P & K	92	D3
Strelley Notts	51	F1
Strensall N York	59	G5
Strensham Worcs	16	D3
Strete Devon	5	H2
Stretford Gt Man	57	G2
Strethall Essex	33	F3
Stretham Cambs	33	G6
Strettington W Susx	10	C3
Stretton Ches	57	F1
Stretton Derbys	51	E3
Stretton Rutlnd	42	B3
Stretton Staffs	40	A4
Stretton Staffs	40	D5
Stretton Grandison Herefs	39	F1
Stretton on Fosse Warwks	30	D4
Stretton Sugwas Herefs	28	C6
Stretton under Fosse Warwks	41	F2
Stretton Westwood Shrops	39	F5
Stretton-on-Dunsmore Warwks	41	E1
Strichen Abers	103	E5
Stringston Somset	16	D3
Strixton Nhants	32	B5
Stroat Gloucs	28	D3
Stromeferry Highld	97	F5
Stromness Ork	111	g2
Stronachlachar Stirlg	84	D1
Stronafian Ag & B	83	H4
Stronchrubie Highld	108	C1
Strone Ag & B	84	B4
Strone Highld	98	A1
Stronenaba Highld	98	A1
Stronmilchan Ag & B	90	C2
Stronsay Airport Ork	111	j2
Strontian Highld	89	H5
Strood Kent	22	C2
Stroud Gloucs	29	F3
Stroud Hants	10	A4
Stroud Green Essex	22	D4
Stroud Green Gloucs	29	F3
Stroxton Lincs	42	B5
Struan Highld	96	B5
Struan P & K	92	A5
Strumpshaw Norfk	45	F3

Name	Page	Grid
Strutherhill S Lans	77	F6
Struthers Fife	86	D6
Struy Highld	98	C6
Stuartfield Abers	103	E4
Stubbington Hants	9	G4
Stubbins N York	57	G4
Stubton Lincs	42	B6
Stuckton Hants	8	D4
Studham Beds	32	C1
Studholme Cumb	71	F5
Studland Dorset	8	C2
Studley Warwks	30	C6
Studley Wilts	18	C4
Studley Roger N York	65	G1
Studley Royal N York	65	F1
Stuntney Cambs	33	G6
Sturmer Essex	34	A3
Sturminster Common Dorset	8	A4
Sturminster Marshall Dorset	8	B3
Sturminster Newton Dorset	8	A4
Sturry Kent	23	F2
Sturton Lincs	52	B5
Sturton by Stow Lincs	52	B3
Sturton le Steeple Notts	52	A4
Stuston Suffk	35	E6
Stutton N York	59	F4
Stutton Suffk	35	E2
Styal Ches	57	H1
Stynie Moray	101	F5
Styrrup Notts	51	G5
Succoth Ag & B	84	C6
Suckley Worcs	39	G2
Sudborough Nhants	32	B6
Sudbourne Suffk	35	G4
Sudbrook Lincs	42	B6
Sudbrook Mons	28	C2
Sudbrooke Lincs	52	C3
Sudbury Derbys	40	C6
Sudbury Gt Lon	21	E4
Sudbury Suffk	34	C3
Suddington Worcs	39	H2
Suffield N York	67	F3
Suffield Norfk	45	E5
Sugnall Staffs	49	G3
Sugwas Pool Herefs	28	C6
Suisnish Highld	96	D4
Sulby IOM	116	c4
Sulgrave Nhants	31	F4
Sulgrave Manor Nhants	31	F4
Sulham Berks	19	H4
Sulhamstead Berks	19	H3
Sullom Shet	111	I3
Sullom Voe Shet	111	I3
Sully V Glam	16	C5
Sumburgh Airport Shet	111	I1
Summerbridge N York	58	D6
Summercourt Cnwll	3	E4
Summerfield Norfk	44	B5
Summerhouse Dur	65	F5
Summersdale W Susx	10	B3
Summerseat Gt Man	57	G4
Summertown Oxon	31	F1
Sunbury Surrey	20	D2
Sundaywell D & G	78	B1
Sunderland Ag & B	82	B2
Sunderland Cumb	71	E3
Sunderland Lancs	62	D2
Sunderland T & W	73	G2
Sunderland Bridge Dur	73	F1
Sundhope Border	79	F5
Sundon Park Beds	32	C1
Sundridge Kent	21	G1
Sunningdale Berks	20	C2
Sunninghill Surrey	20	C2
Sunningwell Oxon	19	G6
Sunniside Dur	73	E1
Sunniside T & W	73	F2
Sunnyhill Derbys	41	E6
Sunnyhurst Lancs	57	F5
Sunnylaw Stirlg	85	G5
Sunnymead Oxon	31	F1
Surbiton Gt Lon	21	E2
Surfleet Lincs	43	E4
Surlingham Norfk	45	F3
Surrex Essex	34	C1
Sustead Norfk	45	E5
Susworth Lincs	52	A5
Sutcombe Devon	14	C2
Sutcombemill Devon	14	C2
Sutterby Lincs	53	F3
Sutterton Lincs	43	E5
Sutton Beds	32	D3
Sutton Cambs	42	C2
Sutton Cambs	33	F6
Sutton Devon	5	G2
Sutton E Susx	11	G2
Sutton Gt Lon	21	E2
Sutton Kent	23	G1
Sutton N York	59	F3
Sutton Norfk	45	G4
Sutton Notts	51	H1
Sutton Shrops	39	G4
Sutton Staffs	49	G2
Sutton Suffk	35	F3
Sutton W Susx	10	C3
Sutton at Hone Kent	22	A2
Sutton Bassett Nhants	41	H2
Sutton Benger Wilts	18	B4
Sutton Bonington Notts	41	F5
Sutton Bridge Lincs	43	F4
Sutton Cheney Leics	41	E3
Sutton Coldfield W Mids	40	C3
Sutton Courtenay Oxon	19	G6
Sutton cum Lound Notts	51	G5
Sutton Grange N York	65	F1
Sutton Green Surrey	20	D1
Sutton Howgrave N York	65	G2
Sutton in Ashfield Notts	51	F3
Sutton Maddock Shrops	39	G6
Sutton Mallet Somset	17	E3
Sutton Mandeville Wilts	8	C6
Sutton Montis Somset	17	G2
Sutton on Sea Lincs	53	G3
Sutton on the Hill Derbys	40	D6
Sutton on Trent Notts	52	A2
Sutton Scotney Hants	19	F1
Sutton St Edmund Lincs	43	F3
Sutton St James Lincs	43	F4
Sutton St Nicholas Herefs	39	E1
Sutton upon Derwent E R Yk	60	B4
Sutton Valence Kent	12	C6
Sutton Veny Wilts	18	B1
Sutton Waldron Dorset	8	B5
Sutton Weaver Ches	57	E1
Sutton Wick Oxon	19	G6

Name	Page	Grid
Sutton Wick Somset	17	G5
Sutton-in-Craven N York	58	B4
Sutton-on-Hull E R Yk	61	E3
Sutton-on-the-Forest N York	59	F6
Sutton-under-Brailes Warwks	30	D4
Sutton-under-Whitestonecliffe N York	66	B2
Swaby Lincs	53	F3
Swadlincote Derbys	40	D5
Swaffham Norfk	44	B3
Swaffham Bulbeck Cambs	33	G5
Swaffham Prior Cambs	33	G5
Swafield Norfk	45	F5
Swainby N York	66	B3
Swainsthorpe Norfk	45	E2
Swainswick Somset	18	A3
Swalcliffe Oxon	31	E4
Swalecliffe Kent	23	F2
Swallow Lincs	52	D5
Swallow Beck Lincs	52	B2
Swallowcliffe Wilts	8	C5
Swallowfield Berks	20	A2
Swan Green Ches	49	G6
Swanage Dorset	8	C2
Swanbourne Bucks	32	A2
Swanland E R Yk	60	D3
Swanley Kent	21	G2
Swanley Village Kent	21	H2
Swanmore Hants	9	G5
Swannington Leics	41	E5
Swannington Norfk	45	E4
Swanpool Garden Suburb Lincs	52	B2
Swanscombe Kent	22	B3
Swansea Swans	26	C2
Swansea Airport Swans	26	B2
Swanton Abbot Norfk	45	F4
Swanton Morley Norfk	44	D4
Swanton Novers Norfk	44	D5
Swanwick Derbys	51	E2
Swanwick Hants	9	G4
Swarby Lincs	42	C5
Swardeston Norfk	45	E2
Swarkestone Derbys	41	E6
Swarland Nthumb	73	F6
Swarraton Hants	19	G1
Swavesey Cambs	33	E5
Sway Hants	9	E3
Swayfield Lincs	42	C4
Swaythling Hants	9	F5
Sweetham Devon	15	H1
Sweethaws E Susx	11	G5
Sweets Cnwll	4	C6
Sweetshouse Cnwll	3	G5
Swefling Suffk	35	F5
Swepstone Leics	41	E4
Swerford Oxon	31	E3
Swettenham Ches	49	G5
Swilland Suffk	35	E4
Swillington W York	59	E3
Swimbridge Devon	15	F4
Swimbridge Newland Devon	15	E4
Swinbrook Oxon	30	D2
Swincliffe N York	58	D5
Swinderby Lincs	52	B2
Swindon Gloucs	29	G5
Swindon Staffs	39	H5
Swindon Swindn	18	D5
Swine E R Yk	61	E3
Swinefleet E R Yk	60	B2
Swineshead Beds	32	C5
Swineshead Lincs	43	E5
Swiney Highld	110	C3
Swinford Leics	41	F2
Swingfield Minnis Kent	13	G6
Swingfield Street Kent	13	G6
Swingleton Green Suffk	34	C3
Swinhoe Nthumb	81	G3
Swinithwaite N York	65	E2
Swinscoe Staffs	50	C2
Swinside Cumb	71	E2
Swinstead Lincs	42	C4
Swinton Border	80	D4
Swinton Gt Man	57	G3
Swinton N York	65	F2
Swinton N York	66	D1
Swinton S York	51	E6
Swithland Leics	41	F4
Swordale Highld	107	E3
Swordland Highld	97	F2
Swordly Highld	109	G5
Swynnerton Staffs	49	H3
Swyre Dorset	7	F4
Sychtyn Powys	38	A4
Syde Gloucs	29	G4
Sydenham Gt Lon	21	F3
Sydenham Oxon	20	A5
Sydenham Damerel Devon	5	E4
Syderstone Norfk	44	B5
Sydling St Nicholas Dorset	7	G5
Sydmonton Hants	19	G3
Syerston Notts	51	H2
Sygun Copper Mine Gwynd	54	D2
Sykehouse S York	59	G2
Symbister Shet	111	I3
Symington S Ayrs	76	D4
Symington S Lans	78	D6
Symonds Yat Herefs	28	D4
Symondsbury Dorset	7	F5
Syre Highld	109	F3
Syreford Gloucs	30	B2
Syresham Nhants	31	G4
Syston Leics	41	G4
Syston Lincs	42	B6
Sytchampton Worcs	39	H3
Sywell Nhants	32	A5

189

T

Name	Page	Grid
Tackley Oxon	31	F2
Tacolneston Norfk	45	E2
Tadcaster N York	59	F4
Taddington Derbys	50	C4
Taddiport Gloucs	30	C3
Tadley Hants	19	G3
Tadlow Cambs	33	E3
Tadmarton Oxon	31	E4
Tadworth Surrey	21	E1

Taff's Well Cardif 27 G1
Taibach Neath 26 D2
Tain Highld 110 C5
Tain Highld 107 F4
Tairbeart W Isls 111 c5
Takeley Essex 33 G1
Takeley Street Essex 33 G1
Tal-y-bont Cerdgn 37 E5
Tal-y-bont Gwynd 55 F3
Tal-y-bont Gwynd 47 E3
Tal-y-bont Gwynd 54 D3
Tal-y-Cafn Conwy 55 F3
Tal-y-coed Mons 28 C4
Talaton Devon 6 C5
Talbenny Pembks 24 C4
Taleford Devon 6 C5
Talerddig Powys 47 H2
Talgarreg Cerdgn 36 D2
Talgarth Powys 27 G5
Talisker Highld 96 B5
Talke Staffs 49 G4
Talkin Cumb 71 H5
Talla Linnfoots Border 79 E4
Talladale Highld 105 G3
Tallaminnock S Ayrs 76 D2
Tallarn Green Wrexhm 49 E4
Tallentire Cumb 70 D3
Talley Carmth 26 C5
Tallington Lincs 42 C3
Talmine Highld 109 E5
Talog Carmth 25 G5
Talsarn Cerdgn 37 E2
Talsarnau Gwynd 47 E5
Talskiddy Cnwll 3 E5
Talwrn IOA 54 D4
Talybont-on-Usk Powys 27 G5
Talysarn Gwynd 54 D2
Tamerton Foliot Devon 5 E3
Tamworth Staffs 40 D4
Tan-y-groes Cerdgn 36 C2
Tandridge Surrey 21 F1
Tanfield Dur 73 F2
Tanfield Lea Dur 73 F2
Tangley Hants 19 E2
Tangmere W Susx 10 C3
Tangusdale W Isls 111 a1
Tankerness Ork 111 h2
Tankersley S York 51 E6
Tankerton Kent 23 F2
Tannach Highld 110 D4
Tannachie Abers 95 F4
Tannadice Angus 93 G5
Tanner's Green Worcs 40 C1
Tannington Suffk 35 F5
Tannochside N Lans 85 F2
Tansley Derbys 51 E3
Tansor Nhants 42 C1
Tantobie Dur 73 F2
Tanton N York 66 B4
Tanworth in Arden Warwks 40 C1
Taobh Tuath W Isls 111 b5
Taplow Bucks 20 C3
Tarbert Ag & B 75 E5
Tarbert Ag & B 83 G3
Tarbert W Isls 111 c5
Tarbet Ag & B 84 C5
Tarbet Highld 108 B4
Tarbet Highld 97 F2
Tarbolton S Ayrs 76 D4
Tarbrax S Lans 86 A2
Tardebigge Worcs 30 B6
Tarfside Angus 94 D4
Tarland Abers 94 D6
Tarleton Lancs 57 E4
Tarlton Gloucs 29 G3
Tarnock Somset 17 G4
Tarporley Ches 49 E5
Tarr Somset 15 G4
Tarr Somset 16 C2
Tarrant Crawford Dorset 8 B4
Tarrant Gunville Dorset 8 B4
Tarrant Hinton Dorset 8 B4
Tarrant Keyneston Dorset 8 B4
Tarrant Launceston Dorset 8 B4
Tarrant Monkton Dorset 8 B4
Tarrant Rawston Dorset 8 B4
Tarrant Rushton Dorset 8 B4
Tarring Neville E Susx 11 G3
Tarrington Herefs 28 D6
Tarskavaig Highld 96 D3
Tarves Abers 102 D3
Tarvie P & K 92 C5
Tarvin Ches 49 E5
Tasburgh Norfk 45 E2
Tatenhill Staffs 40 D5
Tathwell Lincs 53 E4
Tatsfield Surrey 21 G1
Tattenhall Ches 49 E5
Tatterford Norfk 44 C4
Tattersett Norfk 44 C5
Tattershall Lincs 52 D1
Tattershall Thorpe Lincs 52 D2
Tattingstone Suffk 35 E3
Tattingstone White Horse Suffk 35 E3
Tatworth Somset 7 E6
Tauchers Moray 101 F4
Taunton Somset 16 D2
Taverham Norfk 45 E3
Tavernspite Pembks 25 F4
Tavistock Devon 5 E4
Taw Green Devon 15 F1
Tawstock Devon 15 E4
Taxal Derbys 50 B4
Taychreggan Hotel Ag & B 90 C1
Tayinloan Ag & B 75 E5
Taynton Gloucs 29 E5
Taynton Oxon 30 D2
Tayport Fife 93 F2
Tayvallich Ag & B 83 F4
Tealby Lincs 52 D4
Team Valley T & W 73 F3
Teangue Highld 97 E3
Teanord Highld 107 E2
Tebay Cumb 63 F6
Tebworth Beds 32 C2
Tedburn St Mary Devon 5 H6
Teddington Gloucs 29 G5
Teddington Gt Lon 21 E3
Tedstone Delamere Herefs 39 F2
Tedstone Wafer Herefs 39 F2
Teesside Airport Dur 65 G3
Teeton Nhants 41 G1
Teffont Evias Wilts 8 C6

Teffont Magna Wilts 8 C6
Tegryn Pembks 25 F5
Teigh Rutlnd 42 B3
Teigngrace Devon 6 A3
Teignmouth Devon 6 B3
Teindside Border 79 G3
Telford Shrops 39 F6
Tellisford Somset 18 A2
Telscombe E Susx 11 G3
Tempar P & K 91 H4
Templand D & G 78 D2
Temple Cnwll 4 C4
Temple Mdloth 86 D2
Temple Bar Cerdgn 37 E2
Temple Cloud Somset 17 G4
Temple Ewell Kent 13 G6
Temple Grafton Warwks 30 C5
Temple Guiting Gloucs 30 C3
Temple Hirst N York 59 G3
Temple Normanton Derbys 51 E3
Temple of Fiddes Abers 95 G4
Temple Pier Highld 98 D5
Temple Sowerby Cumb 64 A5
Templecombe Somset 17 H2
Templeton Devon 15 H2
Templeton Pembks 25 E4
Templeton Dur 73 E2
Tempsford Beds 32 D4
Tenbury Wells Worcs 39 F3
Tenby Pembks 25 E3
Tendring Essex 35 E1
Tendring Green Essex 35 E2
Tendring Heath Essex 35 E2
Tenterden Kent 12 D5
Terling Essex 22 C6
Ternhill Shrops 49 F3
Terregles D & G 78 C1
Terrington N York 66 C1
Terrington St Clement Norfk 43 G4
Terrington St John Norfk 43 G3
Teston Kent 22 C1
Testwood Hants 9 F4
Tetbury Gloucs 29 F2
Tetchill Shrops 48 D3
Tetcott Devon 14 C1
Tetford Lincs 53 E3
Tetney Lincs 53 E5
Tetsworth Oxon 20 A5
Tettenhall W Mids 40 A3
Teversal Notts 51 F3
Teversham Cambs 33 F4
Teviothead Border 79 G3
Tewin Herts 21 F6
Tewkesbury Gloucs 29 F5
Teynham Kent 23 E2
Thackley W York 58 C4
Thakeham W Susx 10 D4
Thame Oxon 20 A5
Thames Ditton Surrey 21 E2
Thamesmead Gt Lon 21 G3
Thanington Kent 23 F1
Thankerton S Lans 78 C6
Tharston Norfk 45 E2
Thatcham Berks 19 G3
Thaxted Essex 33 G2
The Beeches Gloucs 18 C6
The Braes Highld 96 D5
The Brunt E Loth 87 F3
The Bungalow IOM 116 c4
The Butts Gloucs 29 F4
The City Bucks 20 B5
The Common Wilts 9 E6
The Corner Shrops 38 D4
The Den N Ayrs 76 C6
The Eden Project Cnwll 3 F4
The Forstal Kent 12 D6
The Forstal Kent 13 E5
The Green Cumb 62 B4
The Green Essex 34 B1
The Green N York 66 D4
The Hill Cumb 62 B4
The Lee Bucks 20 C5
The Lhen IOM 116 c5
The Lochs Moray 101 F5
The Moor Kent 12 C5
The Mumbles Swans 26 C2
The Murray S Lans 85 E1
The Neuk Abers 95 F5
The Reddings Gloucs 29 F4
The Ross P & K 92 A2
The Stocks Kent 12 D4
The Strand Wilts 18 B3
Theakston N York 65 G2
Thealby Lincs 60 C2
Theale Berks 19 H4
Theale Somset 17 F3
Thearne E R Yk 61 E4
Theberton Suffk 35 G5
Theddingworth Leics 41 G2
Theddlethorpe All Saints Lincs 53 F4
Theddlethorpe St Helen Lincs 53 F4
Thelnetham Suffk 34 D6
Thelveton Norfk 35 E6
Thelwall Ches 57 F2
Themelthorpe Norfk 44 D4
Thenford Nhants 31 F4
Therfield Herts 33 E3
Thetford Norfk 44 C1
Theydon Bois Essex 21 G5
Thickwood Wilts 18 B4
Thimbleby Lincs 53 E2
Thimbleby N York 66 B3
Thingwall Mersyd 56 C1
Thirkleby N York 66 B2
Thirlby N York 66 B2
Thirlestane Border 80 B4
Thirlspot Cumb 71 F1
Thirn N York 65 F2
Thirsk N York 65 H2
Thistleton Lancs 56 D6
Thistleton Rutlnd 42 B4
Thistley Green Suffk 33 H6
Thixendale N York 60 C5
Thockrington Nthumb 72 D4
Tholomas Drove Cambs 43 F3
Tholthorpe N York 59 F6
Thomastown Abers 102 B3
Thompson Norfk 44 C2
Thong Kent 22 B3
Thoralby N York 64 D2
Thoresway Lincs 52 D5
Thorganby Lincs 52 D5
Thorganby N York 59 G4
Thorgill N York 66 D3

Thorington Suffk 35 G6
Thorington Street Suffk 34 D2
Thorlby N York 58 B5
Thorley Herts 33 F1
Thorley Street IOW 9 F2
Thormanby N York 66 B1
Thornaby-on-Tees N York 66 B5
Thornage Norfk 44 D5
Thornborough Bucks 31 H3
Thornborough N York 65 G2
Thornbury Devon 14 D2
Thornbury Gloucs 28 D2
Thornbury Herefs 39 F2
Thornby Nhants 41 G1
Thorncliff Staffs 50 B3
Thorncombe Dorset 7 E5
Thorndon Suffk 35 E5
Thorndon Cross Devon 5 F6
Thorne S York 59 G2
Thorne Somset 17 F1
Thorne St Margaret Somset 16 C1
Thorner W York 59 E4
Thornes Staffs 40 C4
Thorney Cambs 43 E3
Thorney Notts 52 B3
Thorney Somset 17 E2
Thorney Hill Hants 8 D3
Thornfalcon Somset 16 D2
Thornford Dorset 17 G1
Thorngrafton Nthumb 72 C3
Thorngumbald E R Yk 61 F3
Thornham Norfk 44 B6
Thornham Magna Suffk 34 D5
Thornham Parva Suffk 35 E5
Thornhaugh Cambs 42 C2
Thornhill D & G 78 C2
Thornhill Derbys 50 D5
Thornhill Hants 9 F4
Thornhill Stirlg 85 F5
Thornhill W York 58 D2
Thornholme E R Yk 61 E6
Thornicombe Dorset 8 B4
Thornington Nthumb 81 E3
Thornley Dur 73 E1
Thornley Dur 73 G1
Thornliebank E Rens 85 E2
Thorns Suffk 34 B4
Thornsett Derbys 50 B5
Thornthwaite Cumb 71 E2
Thornthwaite N York 58 C5
Thornton Angus 93 F4
Thornton Bucks 31 H3
Thornton E R Yk 60 B4
Thornton Fife 86 C5
Thornton Lancs 56 D6
Thornton Leics 41 F4
Thornton Lincs 53 E2
Thornton N York 66 B4
Thornton Nthumb 81 E4
Thornton W York 58 C3
Thornton Curtis Lincs 61 E2
Thornton Heath Gt Lon 21 F2
Thornton Hough Mersyd 56 C1
Thornton in Lonsdale N York 63 F3
Thornton le Dale N York 67 E2
Thornton le Moor Lincs 52 C5
Thornton Rust N York 64 D2
Thornton Steward N York 65 F2
Thornton Watlass N York 65 F2
Thornton-in-Craven N York 58 A4
Thornton-le-Beans N York 65 G2
Thornton-le-Clay N York 59 G6
Thornton-le-Moor N York 65 G2
Thornton-le-Moors Ches 48 D6
Thornton-le-Street N York 65 G2
Thorntonhall S Lans 85 E1
Thorntonloch E Loth 87 G3
Thornydykes Border 80 C4
Thornythwaite Cumb 71 G2
Thoroton Notts 51 H1
Thorp Arch W York 59 E4
Thorpe Derbys 50 C2
Thorpe E R Yk 60 D4
Thorpe N York 58 B6
Thorpe Notts 51 H2
Thorpe Surrey 20 D2
Thorpe Abbotts Norfk 35 E6
Thorpe Arnold Leics 41 H5
Thorpe Audlin W York 59 F2
Thorpe Bassett N York 67 E1
Thorpe Bay Essex 22 D4
Thorpe by Water Rutlnd 42 B2
Thorpe Constantine Staffs 40 D4
Thorpe End Norfk 45 F3
Thorpe Green Essex 35 E1
Thorpe Green Suffk 34 C4
Thorpe Hesley S York 51 E6
Thorpe in Balne S York 59 G1
Thorpe in the Fallows Lincs 52 B3
Thorpe Langton Leics 41 H3
Thorpe le Street E R Yk 60 C4
Thorpe Lea Surrey 20 D3
Thorpe Malsor Nhants 32 A6
Thorpe Mandeville Nhants 31 F4
Thorpe Market Norfk 45 E5
Thorpe Morieux Suffk 34 C4
Thorpe on the Hill Lincs 52 B2
Thorpe Park Surrey 20 D2
Thorpe Salvin S York 51 F4
Thorpe Satchville Leics 41 H4
Thorpe St Andrew Norfk 45 F3
Thorpe St Peter Lincs 53 F2
Thorpe Thewles Dur 65 G5
Thorpe Tilney Lincs 52 D1
Thorpe Underwood N York 59 F5
Thorpe Waterville Nhants 32 C6
Thorpe Willoughby N York 59 F3
Thorpe-le-Soken Essex 35 E1
Thorpeness Suffk 35 G4
Thorrington Essex 34 D1
Thorverton Devon 6 B5
Thrandeston Suffk 35 E6
Thrapston Nhants 32 C6
Threapwood Ches 48 D4
Threapwood Staffs 50 B1
Threave S Ayrs 76 C2
Threave Castle D & G 70 B5
Three Bridges W Susx 11 F5
Three Chimneys Kent 12 D5
Three Cocks Powys 27 G6
Three Crosses Swans 26 B2
Three Cups Corner E Susx 12 B4
Three Leg Cross E Susx 12 B5

Three Legged Cross Dorset 8 C4
Three Mile Cross Berks 20 A2
Three Miletown W Loth 86 B3
Three Oaks E Susx 12 D3
Threekingham Lincs 42 C5
Threlkeld Cumb 71 F2
Threshfield N York 58 B6
Thrigby Norfk 45 G3
Thringstone Leics 41 E5
Thrintoft N York 65 G3
Thriplow Cambs 33 F3
Throcking Herts 33 E2
Throckley T & W 73 E3
Throckmorton Worcs 30 B5
Throop Dorset 8 D3
Thropton Nthumb 72 D6
Throughgate D & G 78 C1
Throwleigh Devon 5 G5
Throwley Forstal Kent 23 E1
Thrumpton Notts 41 F6
Thrumster Highld 110 D4
Thrunscoe Lincs 53 E6
Thrupp Gloucs 29 F3
Thrushesbush Essex 21 G6
Thrussington Leics 41 G5
Thruxton Hants 19 E2
Thruxton Herefs 28 C6
Thrybergh S York 51 F6
Thulston Derbys 41 E6
Thundersley Essex 22 C4
Thurcaston Leics 41 F4
Thurcroft S York 51 F5
Thurgarton Norfk 45 E5
Thurgarton Notts 51 G2
Thurgoland S York 50 D6
Thurlaston Leics 41 F3
Thurlaston Warwks 41 F1
Thurlbear Somset 16 D1
Thurlby Lincs 42 C4
Thurlby Lincs 53 F3
Thurleigh Beds 32 C4
Thurlestone Devon 5 G2
Thurlow Suffk 34 A4
Thurloxton Somset 16 D2
Thurlstone S York 58 D1
Thurlton Norfk 45 G2
Thurmaston Leics 41 G4
Thurnby Leics 41 G4
Thurne Norfk 45 G3
Thurnham Kent 22 C1
Thurning Nhants 42 C1
Thurning Norfk 44 D5
Thurnscoe S York 59 F1
Thursby Cumb 71 F4
Thursford Norfk 44 D5
Thursley Surrey 10 C5
Thurso Highld 110 B5
Thurstaston Mersyd 56 C1
Thurston Suffk 34 C5
Thurstonfield Cumb 71 F5
Thurstonland W York 58 C1
Thurton Norfk 45 F2
Thurvaston Derbys 50 D1
Thuxton Norfk 44 D3
Thwaite N York 64 D3
Thwaite Suffk 35 E5
Thwaite Head Cumb 62 D5
Thwaite St Mary Norfk 45 F2
Thwing E R Yk 67 F1
Tibbermore P & K 92 C2
Tibberton Gloucs 29 E5
Tibberton Shrops 49 F2
Tibberton Worcs 30 A5
Tibbie Shiels Inn Border 79 E3
Tibenham Norfk 45 E1
Tibshelf Derbys 51 E3
Tibthorpe E R Yk 60 D5
Ticehurst E Susx 12 C5
Tichborne Hants 9 G6
Tickencote Rutlnd 42 C3
Tickenham Somset 17 F6
Tickhill S York 51 G5
Ticklerton Shrops 39 E5
Ticknall Derbys 41 E5
Tickton E R Yk 60 D4
Tidcombe Wilts 19 E3
Tiddington Oxon 31 G1
Tiddington Warwks 30 D5
Tidebrook E Susx 12 B5
Tideford Cnwll 4 D3
Tidenham Gloucs 28 D2
Tideswell Derbys 50 C4
Tidmarsh Berks 19 H4
Tidmington Warwks 30 D4
Tiers Cross Pembks 24 C4
Tiffield Nhants 31 G5
Tigerton Angus 95 E3
Tigh a Ghearraidh W Isls 111 a4
Tigharry W Isls 111 a4
Tighnabruaich Ag & B 83 G3
Tigley Devon 5 G3
Tilbrook Cambs 32 C5
Tilbury Essex 22 B3
Tilbury Green Essex 34 B3
Tile Hill W Mids 40 D1
Tilehurst Berks 19 H4
Tilford Surrey 10 C6
Tilgate W Susx 11 F5
Tilham Street Somset 17 F3
Tillicoultry Clacks 85 H5
Tillietudlem S Lans 77 G5
Tillingham Essex 23 E5
Tillington Herefs 39 E1
Tillington W Susx 10 C4
Tillington Common Herefs 39 E1
Tillybirloch Abers 95 F6
Tillycairn Abers 94 D5
Tillyfourie Abers 102 C1
Tillygreig Abers 103 E2
Tillyrie P & K 86 B6
Tilmanstone Kent 23 G1
Tilney All Saints Norfk 43 G4
Tilney High End Norfk 43 G4
Tilney St Lawrence Norfk 43 G3
Tilshead Wilts 18 C2
Tilstock Shrops 49 E3
Tilston Ches 49 E4
Tilstone Fearnall Ches 49 E5
Tilsworth Beds 32 C1
Tilton on the Hill Leics 41 H4

Tiltups End Gloucs 29 F3
Timberland Lincs 52 D2
Timbersbrook Ches 50 A3
Timberscombe Somset 16 B3
Timble N York 58 C5
Timpanheck D & G 71 F6
Timperley Gt Man 57 G2
Timsbury Hants 9 F5
Timsbury Somset 17 G5
Timsgarry W Isls 111 c6
Timsgearraidh W Isls 111 c6
Timworth Suffk 34 C5
Timworth Green Suffk 34 C5
Tincleton Dorset 8 A3
Tindale Cumb 72 A3
Tindale Crescent Dur 65 F5
Tingewick Bucks 31 G3
Tingley W York 58 D3
Tingrith Beds 32 C2
Tingwall Airport Shet 111 I2
Tinhay Devon 5 E5
Tinsley S York 51 E5
Tinsley Green W Susx 11 F5
Tintagel Cnwll 4 B5
Tintagel Castle Cnwll 4 B5
Tintern Abbey Mons 28 D3
Tintern Parva Mons 28 C3
Tintinhull Somset 17 F1
Tintwistle Derbys 50 B6
Tinwald D & G 78 D1
Tinwell Rutlnd 42 C3
Tipton W Mids 40 B3
Tipton St John Devon 6 C4
Tiptree Essex 34 C1
Tiptree Heath Essex 22 D6
Tirabad Powys 37 G1
Tiree Airport Ag & B 88 B3
Tiretigan Ag & B 83 E2
Tirley Gloucs 29 F5
Tirphil Caerph 27 G3
Tirril Cumb 71 G2
Tisbury Wilts 8 B6
Tissington Derbys 50 C2
Titchberry Devon 14 C4
Titchfield Hants 9 G4
Titchmarsh Nhants 32 C6
Titchwell Norfk 44 B6
Tithby Notts 51 G1
Titley Herefs 38 D2
Titsey Surrey 21 G1
Tittensor Staffs 49 H3
Tittleshall Norfk 44 C4
Titton Worcs 39 G3
Tiverton Ches 49 E5
Tiverton Devon 6 B6
Tivetshall St Margaret Norfk 45 E1
Tivetshall St Mary Norfk 45 E1
Tivington Somset 16 B3
Tixall Staffs 40 B5
Tixover Rutlnd 42 B2
Tobermory Ag & B 89 F4
Toberonochy Ag & B 83 F6
Tobha Mor W Isls 111 a3
Tocher Abers 102 C3
Tochieneal Moray 101 G5
Tockenham Wilts 18 C4
Tockholes Lancs 57 F5
Tockington Gloucs 28 D2
Tockwith N York 59 F5
Todber Dorset 8 A5
Todburn Nthumb 73 E6
Toddington Beds 32 C2
Toddington Gloucs 30 B3
Todenham Gloucs 30 D3
Todhills Angus 93 F3
Todhills Cumb 71 F5
Todmorden W York 58 B3
Todwick S York 51 F5
Toft Cambs 33 E4
Toft Lincs 42 C4
Toft Shet 111 I3
Toft Hill Dur 65 E6
Toft Monks Norfk 45 G2
Toft next Newton Lincs 52 C4
Toftrees Norfk 44 C4
Togston Nthumb 73 F6
Tokavaig Highld 96 D3
Tokers Green Oxon 20 A3
Tolastadh W Isls 111 e7
Toll Bar S York 59 F1
Tolland Somset 16 C2
Tollard Royal Wilts 8 B5
Toller Fratrum Dorset 7 G5
Toller Porcorum Dorset 7 G5
Toller Whelme Dorset 7 F5
Tollerton N York 59 F6
Tollerton Notts 41 G6
Tollesbury Essex 23 E6
Tolleshunt D'Arcy Essex 22 D6
Tolleshunt Knights Essex 22 D6
Tolleshunt Major Essex 22 D6
Tolob Shet 111 I1
Tolpuddle Dorset 8 A3
Tolsta W Isls 111 e7
Tolworth Gt Lon 21 E2
Tomatin Highld 99 F5
Tomchrasky Highld 98 B4
Tomdoun Highld 98 A3
Tomich Highld 107 E6
Tomich Highld 98 B5
Tomich Highld 107 E1
Tomich Highld 107 F3
Tomintoul Moray 101 E2
Tomnacross Highld 98 D6
Tomnavoulin Moray 101 E2
Tonbridge Kent 12 B6
Tondu Brdgnd 27 E1
Tonedale Somset 16 C1
Tong Kent 23 E1
Tong Shrops 39 G6
Tong W York 58 D3
Tong Norton Shrops 39 G6
Tong Street W York 58 C3
Tonge Leics 41 E5
Tongham Surrey 10 C6
Tongland D & G 69 H3
Tongue Highld 109 E5
Tongwynlais Cardif 27 G1
Tonna Neath 26 D3
Tonwell Herts 33 E1
Tonypandy Rhondd 27 F2
Tonyrefail Rhondd 27 F2
Toot Baldon Oxon 19 G6
Toot Hill Essex 21 G5

Toothill Wilts 18 D5
Tooting Gt Lon 21 F3
Tooting Bec Gt Lon 21 F3
Topcliffe N York 65 G1
Topcroft Norfk 45 F2
Topcroft Street Norfk 45 F2
Toppesfield Essex 34 B3
Toprow Norfk 45 E2
Topsham Devon 6 B4
Torbeg N Ayrs 75 G4
Torboll Highld 107 F5
Torbreck Highld 99 E6
Torbryan Devon 5 H4
Torcastle Highld 90 C6
Torcross Devon 5 H2
Tore Highld 107 E2
Torinturk Ag & B 83 F2
Torksey Lincs 52 A3
Tormarton Gloucs 18 A4
Tormore N Ayrs 75 G4
Tornagrain Highld 107 F1
Tornaveen Abers 95 E6
Torness Highld 98 D5
Toronto Dur 65 F6
Torosay Castle Ag & B 89 G3
Torpenhow Cumb 71 E3
Torphichen W Loth 86 A3
Torphins Abers 95 E6
Torpoint Cnwll 5 E3
Torquay Devon 6 B2
Torquhan Border 87 E1
Torran Highld 104 D1
Torrance E Duns 85 E3
Torranyard N Ayrs 76 C5
Torridon Highld 105 G2
Torridon House Highld 105 F2
Torrin Highld 96 D4
Torrisdale Ag & B 75 F4
Torrisdale Highld 109 F5
Torrish Highld 110 A1
Torrisholme Lancs 63 E2
Torrobull Highld 107 E6
Torry Aber C 95 H6
Torryburn Fife 86 A4
Tortan Worcs 39 H3
Torteval Guern 6 a1
Torthorwald D & G 78 D1
Tortington W Susx 10 D3
Tortworth Gloucs 29 E2
Torvaig Highld 96 C6
Torver Cumb 62 C5
Torwood Falk 85 G4
Torwoodlee Border 79 G6
Torworth Notts 51 G5
Toscaig Highld 97 E5
Toseland Cambs 33 E5
Tosside N York 63 G2
Tostock Suffk 34 C5
Totaig Highld 104 A1
Tote Highld 104 C1
Tote Highld 104 D2
Totland IOW 9 E2
Totley S York 50 D4
Totnes Devon 5 H3
Toton Notts 41 F6
Totronald Ag & B 88 C4
Totscore Highld 104 C3
Tottenham Gt Lon 21 F4
Tottenhill Norfk 43 H3
Totteridge Gt Lon 21 E4
Totternhoe Beds 32 C1
Tottington Gt Man 57 G4
Totton Hants 9 F4
Toulton Somset 16 D2
Toulvaddie Highld 107 G4
Tovil Kent 22 C1
Tow Law Dur 73 E1
Toward Ag & B 84 B3
Toward Quay Ag & B 84 A2
Towcester Nhants 31 G5
Towednack Cnwll 2 B3
Towersey Oxon 20 A5
Towie Abers 101 G1
Town End Cambs 43 F2
Town End Cumb 62 C5
Town Littleworth E Susx 11 G4
Town Street Suffk 44 B1
Town Yetholm Border 80 D3
Townend W Duns 84 D3
Townhead D & G 78 D2
Townhead S York 50 C6
Townhead of Greenlaw D & G 70 B5
Townhill Fife 86 B5
Towns End Hants 19 G3
Townshend Cnwll 2 C3
Towthorpe N York 59 G5
Towton N York 59 F4
Towyn Conwy 55 G4
Toxteth Mersyd 56 D2
Toy's Hill Kent 21 G1
Toynton All Saints Lincs 53 F2
Trabboch E Ayrs 76 D3
Trabbochburn E Ayrs 76 D3
Tradespark Highld 100 B5
Traethsaith Cerdgn 36 C2
Trallong Powys 27 E5
Tramway Museum Derbys 51 E2
Tranent E Loth 86 D3
Tranmere Mersyd 56 D2
Trantelbeg Highld 109 H4
Trantlemore Highld 109 H4
Trapp Carmth 26 C4
Traprain E Loth 87 F3
Traquair Border 79 F5
Traveller's Rest Devon 15 E4
Trawden Lancs 58 A4
Trawsfynydd Gwynd 47 F5
Tre Taliesin Cerdgn 37 F5
Tre-groes Cerdgn 36 D2
Trealaw Rhondd 27 F2
Treales Lancs 56 D5
Trearddur Bay IOA 54 B4
Treaslane Highld 104 C2
Trebarwith Cnwll 4 B5
Trebetherick Cnwll 4 A4
Treborough Somset 16 B3
Trebullett Cnwll 4 D4
Treburley Cnwll 4 D4
Trecastle Powys 27 E5
Trecwn Pembks 24 D5
Trecynon Rhondd 27 F3
Tredaule Cnwll 4 C5
Tredegar Blae G 27 G3
Tredington Gloucs 29 F5

Tredington Warwks 30 D4
Tredunnock Mons 28 B2
Treen Cnwll 2 A2
Treeton S York 51 E5
Trefasser Pembks 24 C6
Trefecca Powys 27 G5
Trefeglwys Powys 37 H5
Treffgarne Pembks 24 D5
Treffgarne Owen Pembks 24 C5
Trefforest Rhondd 27 F2
Trefilan Cerdgn 37 E3
Trefin Pembks 24 C5
Trefnant Denbgs 48 A6
Trefonen Shrops 48 C2
Trefor Gwynd 46 C5
Trefrew Cnwll 4 B5
Trefriw Conwy 55 F3
Tregadillett Cnwll 4 D5
Tregare Mons 28 C6
Tregaron Cerdgn 37 F3
Tregarth Gwynd 54 D3
Tregeare Cnwll 4 C5
Tregeiriog Wrexhm 48 B3
Tregele IOA 54 C5
Tregidden Cnwll 2 D2
Treglemais Pembks 24 C5
Tregole Cnwll 14 B1
Tregonetha Cnwll 3 F5
Tregony Cnwll 3 E4
Tregoyd Powys 27 G6
Tregynon Powys 38 B5
Trehafod Rhondd 27 F2
Trehan Cnwll 5 E3
Treharris Myr Td 27 F2
Treherbert Rhondd 27 E3
Trekenner Cnwll 4 D4
Treknow Cnwll 4 B5
Trelan Cnwll 2 D3
Trelash Cnwll 4 C3
Trelassick Cnwll 3 E4
Trelawnyd Flints 56 B1
Trelech Carmth 25 F5
Treleddyd-fawr Pembks 24 B5
Trelewis Myr Td 27 F2
Trelights Cnwll 4 A5
Trelill Cnwll 4 B4
Trelissick Garden Cnwll 3 E3
Trelleck Mons 28 C3
Trelogan Flints 56 B1
Trelow Cnwll 3 E6
Trelowarren Cnwll 4 C5
Tremadog Gwynd 47 E5
Tremail Cnwll 4 C5
Tremain Cerdgn 36 B2
Tremaine Cnwll 4 C5
Tremar Cnwll 4 D4
Trematon Cnwll 5 E3
Tremeirchion Denbgs 48 B6
Trenance Cnwll 3 E5
Trenance Cnwll 3 F6
Trencreek Cnwll 14 B1
Trenear Cnwll 2 D2
Treneglos Cnwll 4 C5
Trent Dorset 17 G1
Trentishoe Devon 15 F5
Treoes V Glam 27 E1
Treorchy Rhondd 27 E3
Trequite Cnwll 3 F6
Trerhyngyll V Glam 27 F1
Trerulefoot Cnwll 4 D3
Trescowe Cnwll 2 C2
Tresean Cnwll 2 D5
Tresham Gloucs 29 F2
Tresillian Cnwll 3 E4
Treskinnick Cross Cnwll 14 B1
Tresmeer Cnwll 4 C5
Tresparrett Cnwll 4 C6
Tressait P & K 92 B5
Tresta Shet 111 I2
Tresta Shet 111 m4
Treswell Notts 52 A3
Trethevey Cnwll 4 B5
Trethewey Cnwll 2 A2
Trethurgy Cnwll 3 F4
Tretire Herefs 28 C5
Tretower Powys 27 G4
Treuddyn Flints 48 C5
Trevague Cnwll 4 C5
Trevalga Cnwll 4 B5
Trevalyn Wrexhm 48 D5
Trevarrian Cnwll 3 E5
Treveal Cnwll 2 D5
Treveighan Cnwll 4 B5
Trevellas Downs Cnwll 2 C4
Trevelmond Cnwll 4 C5
Treverva Cnwll 2 D2
Trevescan Cnwll 2 A2
Treviscoe Cnwll 3 F4
Trevone Cnwll 3 E6
Trevor Denbgs 48 C3
Trewalder Cnwll 4 B5
Trewarlett Cnwll 4 D5
Trewarmett Cnwll 4 B5
Treween Cnwll 4 C5
Trewen Cnwll 3 F6
Trewint Cnwll 4 C5
Trewithian Cnwll 3 E3
Trewoon Cnwll 3 F4
Treyford W Susx 10 B4
Triangle W York 58 B2
Trimdon Dur 65 G6
Trimdon Colliery Dur 65 G6
Trimdon Grange Dur 65 G6
Trimingham Norfk 45 F5
Trimley Suffk 35 F3
Trimsaran Carmth 26 A3
Trimstone Devon 15 E5
Trinafour P & K 91 H5
Tring Herts 20 C6
Trinity Angus 95 G2
Trinity Jersey 7 b2
Trinity Gask P & K 92 C1
Triscombe Somset 16 B3
Triscombe Somset 16 C3
Trislaig Highld 90 C6
Trispen Cnwll 3 E4
Tritlington Nthumb 73 F5
Trochry P & K 92 C3
Troedyraur Cerdgn 36 C2
Troedyrhiw Myr Td 27 F3
Trois Bois Jersey 7 b2
Troon Cnwll 2 C5
Troon S Ayrs 76 C4
Tropical World Roundhay Park
    W York 59 E4
Troston Suffk 34 C5
Trotshill Worcs 30 A5

Trottiscliffe Kent 22 B2
Trotton W Susx 10 B4
Troughend Nthumb 72 C5
Troutbeck Cumb 62 D6
Troutbeck Bridge Cumb 62 D5
Troway Derbys 51 E4
Trowbridge Wilts 18 B3
Trowell Notts 51 F1
Trowse Newton Norfk 45 F3
Trudoxhill Somset 17 H3
Trull Somset 16 D2
Trumpan Highld 104 B2
Trumpet Herefs 28 D6
Trumpington Cambs 33 F4
Trunch Norfk 45 F5
Truro Cnwll 3 E4
Truro Cathedral Cnwll 3 E4
Trusham Devon 6 A4
Trusley Derbys 40 D6
Trusthorpe Lincs 53 G4
Trysull Staffs 39 H5
Tubney Oxon 19 F6
Tuckenhay Devon 5 H3
Tuckhill Shrops 39 G4
Tuckingmill Cnwll 2 C3
Tuckingmill Wilts 8 B6
Tuckton Dorset 8 D3
Tuddenham Suffk 34 B5
Tuddenham Suffk 35 E3
Tudeley Kent 12 B6
Tudhoe Dur 65 F6
Tudweiloig Gwynd 46 B5
Tuffley Gloucs 29 F4
Tufton Hants 19 F2
Tufton Pembks 24 D5
Tugby Leics 41 H3
Tugford Shrops 39 E4
Tughall Nthumb 81 G3
Tullibody Clacks 85 G5
Tullich Highld 99 E5
Tullich Highld 107 G3
Tulliemet P & K 92 C4
Tulloch Abers 102 D3
Tulloch Stirlg 91 F1
Tulloch Station Highld 98 C1
Tullochgorm Ag & B 83 G5
Tullybeagles Lodge P & K 92 C3
Tullynessle Abers 102 B2
Tulse Hill Gt Lon 21 F3
Tumble Carmth 26 B4
Tumby Lincs 53 E2
Tumby Woodside Lincs 53 E1
Tummel Bridge P & K 92 A5
Tunbridge Wells Kent 12 B5
Tundergarth D & G 79 E1
Tunga W Isls 111 c6
Tunstall E R Yk 61 F3
Tunstall Kent 22 D2
Tunstall Lancs 63 F3
Tunstall N York 65 F3
Tunstall Norfk 45 G3
Tunstall Staffs 49 G2
Tunstall Staffs 49 H4
Tunstall Suffk 35 F4
Tunstall T & W 73 G2
Tunstead Derbys 50 C4
Tunstead Norfk 45 F4
Tunstead Milton Derbys 50 B4
Tunworth Hants 10 A6
Tur Langton Leics 41 H3
Turgis Green Hants 20 A2
Turkdean Gloucs 30 C2
Turleigh Wilts 18 A3
Turnastone Herefs 28 B6
Turnberry S Ayrs 76 B2
Turnditch Derbys 50 D2
Turner's Hill W Susx 11 F5
Turners Puddle Dorset 8 B3
Turnhouse C Edin 86 B3
Turnworth Dorset 8 A4
Turriff Abers 102 C4
Turton Bottoms Gt Man 57 G4
Turves Cambs 43 E2
Turvey Beds 32 B4
Turville Bucks 20 B4
Turweston Bucks 31 G4
Tushielaw Inn Border 79 F4
Tushingham cum Grindley Ches 49 E4
Tutbury Staffs 40 D6
Tutshill Gloucs 28 D2
Tuttington Norfk 45 E4
Tuxford Notts 51 H4
Twatt Ork 111 g2
Twatt Shet 111 I2
Twechar E Duns 85 F3
Tweedmouth Nthumb 81 F5
Tweedsmuir Border 78 D5
Twelveheads Cnwll 2 D3
Twemlow Green Ches 49 G6
Twenty Lincs 42 D4
Twerton Somset 17 H5
Twickenham Gt Lon 21 E3
Twigworth Gloucs 29 F5
Twineham W Susx 11 E4
Twinstead Essex 34 C2
Twitchen Devon 15 G4
Two Dales Derbys 50 D3
Twycross Leics 41 E4
Twycross Zoo Leics 40 D4
Twyford Berks 20 B3
Twyford Bucks 31 G3
Twyford Hants 9 G5
Twyford Leics 41 H4
Twyford Norfk 44 D4
Twynholm D & G 69 G3
Twyning Gloucs 29 F6
Twyning Green Gloucs 29 F6
Twynllanan Carmth 26 D5
Twywell Nhants 32 B6
Ty'n-dwr Denbgs 48 C3
Ty'n-y-Groes Conwy 55 F3
Ty-nant Conwy 48 A4
Tyberton Herefs 28 B6
Tycroes Carmth 26 C4
Tycrwyn Powys 48 B2
Tydd Gote Lincs 43 F4
Tydd St Giles Cambs 43 F4
Tydd St Mary Lincs 43 F4
Tye Green Essex 33 G2
Tyldesley Gt Man 57 F3
Tyler Hill Kent 23 F2
Tylorstown Rhondd 27 F2
Tyn-y-nant Rhondd 27 F2
Tyndrum Stirlg 91 E2
Tynemouth T & W 73 G3

Tyninghame E Loth 87 F4
Tynron D & G 77 G1
Tynygraig Cerdgn 37 F4
Tyringham Bucks 32 B3
Tythegston Brdgnd 27 E1
Tytherington Ches 50 A4
Tytherington Gloucs 29 E2
Tytherington Wilts 18 B1
Tytherleigh Devon 7 E5
Tytherton Lucas Wilts 18 B4
Tywardreath Cnwll 3 G4
Tywyn Gwynd 47 E2

U

Ubbeston Green Suffk 35 F5
Ubley Somset 17 F4
Uckerby N York 65 F3
Uckfield E Susx 11 G4
Uckinghall Worcs 29 F6
Uckington Gloucs 29 F5
Uckington Shrops 49 F1
Uddingston S Lans 85 F2
Uddington S Lans 78 C5
Udimore E Susx 12 D4
Udny Green Abers 103 E2
Udny Station Abers 103 E2
Uffculme Devon 16 C1
Uffington Lincs 42 C3
Uffington Oxon 19 E5
Uffington Shrops 49 E1
Ufford Cambs 42 C3
Ufford Suffk 35 F4
Ufton Warwks 31 E6
Ufton Nervet Berks 19 H3
Ugadale Ag & B 75 F4
Ugborough Devon 5 G3
Uggeshall Suffk 35 G6
Ugglebarnby N York 67 E4
Ughill Derbys 50 D5
Ugley Essex 33 G2
Ugley Green Essex 33 G2
Ugthorpe N York 66 D4
Uig Ag & B 88 C4
Uig Highld 104 A2
Uig Highld 104 C2
Uigshader Highld 104 C1
Uisken Ag & B 89 E1
Ulbster Highld 110 D3
Ulcat Row Cumb 71 G2
Ulceby Lincs 61 E2
Ulceby Lincs 53 F3
Ulceby Skitter Lincs 61 E2
Ulcombe Kent 12 D6
Uldale Cumb 71 F3
Uley Gloucs 29 E3
Ulgham Nthumb 73 F5
Ullapool Highld 106 A5
Ullenhall Warwks 30 C6
Ulleskelf N York 59 F4
Ullesthorpe Leics 41 F2
Ulley S York 51 F5
Ullingswick Herefs 39 F1
Ullinish Lodge Hotel Highld 96 B5
Ullock Cumb 70 D2
Ulpha Cumb 62 C5
Ulrome E R Yk 61 E5
Ulsta Shet 111 I3
Ulverston Cumb 62 C4
Ulwell Dorset 8 C2
Umachan Highld 105 E1
Umberleigh Devon 15 E3
Unapool Highld 108 C3
Under Burnmouth Border 79 G1
Under River Kent 22 A1
Underbarrow Cumb 63 E5
Undercliffe W York 58 C3
Underdale Shrops 49 E1
Underwood Notts 51 F2
Undy Mons 28 C2
Union Mills IOM 116 c3
Unstone Derbys 51 E4
Up Cerne Dorset 7 G3
Up Exe Devon 6 B5
Up Holland Lancs 57 E3
Up Marden W Susx 10 B3
Up Mudford Somset 17 G1
Up Nately Hants 20 A1
Up Somborne Hants 9 F6
Up Sydling Dorset 7 G3
Upavon Wilts 18 D2
Upchurch Kent 22 D2
Upcott Devon 15 G4
Upcott Somset 16 A2
Upgate Norfk 45 E4
Uphall Dorset 7 F5
Uphall W Loth 86 B3
Upham Devon 15 H2
Upham Hants 9 G5
Uphampton Herefs 38 D2
Uphampton Worcs 39 H3
Uphill Somset 17 E4
Uplawmoor E Rens 84 D1
Upleadon Gloucs 29 E5
Upleatham N York 66 C5
Uploders Dorset 7 F5
Uplowman Devon 16 B1
Uplyme Devon 7 E5
Upminster Gt Lon 22 B4
Upottery Devon 6 D6
Upper & Lower Stondon Beds 32 D2
Upper Affcot Shrops 39 E4
Upper Ardchronie Highld 107 E4
Upper Arley Worcs 39 G4
Upper Basildon Berks 19 G4
Upper Beeding W Susx 11 E3
Upper Benefield Nhants 42 C1
Upper Bentley Worcs 30 B6
Upper Bighouse Highld 109 H5
Upper Boddington Nhants 31 F5
Upper Brailes Warwks 30 D4
Upper Breakish Highld 97 E4
Upper Broadheath Worcs 39 G2
Upper Broughton Notts 41 G5
Upper Bucklebury Berks 19 G3
Upper Burgate Hants 8 D5
Upper Caldecote Beds 32 D3
Upper Catesby Nhants 31 F5

Upper Chapel Powys 27 F6
Upper Chicksgrove Wilts 8 C6
Upper Chute Wilts 19 E2
Upper Clapton Gt Lon 21 F4
Upper Clatford Hants 19 F1
Upper Coberley Gloucs 29 G4
Upper Cound Shrops 39 E6
Upper Cumberworth W York 58 D1
Upper Dallachy Moray 101 F5
Upper Deal Kent 23 H1
Upper Dean Beds 32 C5
Upper Denby W York 58 D1
Upper Dicker E Susx 12 A3
Upper Dounreay Highld 110 A5
Upper Dovercourt Essex 35 G2
Upper Drumbane Stirlg 85 F6
Upper Dunsforth N York 59 E6
Upper Eashing Surrey 10 C6
Upper Egleton Herefs 39 F1
Upper Elkstone Staffs 50 B3
Upper Ellastone Staffs 50 C1
Upper Farringdon Hants 10 A5
Upper Framilode Gloucs 29 E4
Upper Froyle Hants 10 B6
Upper Godney Somset 17 F3
Upper Gravenhurst Beds 32 D2
Upper Green Berks 19 F3
Upper Green Essex 33 G2
Upper Hale Surrey 10 B6
Upper Halliford Surrey 20 D2
Upper Hambleton Rutlnd 42 B3
Upper Harbledown Kent 23 F2
Upper Hartfield E Susx 11 G5
Upper Hatherley Gloucs 29 F4
Upper Heaton W York 58 C2
Upper Helmsley N York 59 G5
Upper Hergest Herefs 38 C2
Upper Heyford Nhants 31 G5
Upper Heyford Oxon 31 F3
Upper Hill Herefs 39 E2
Upper Hopton W York 58 D2
Upper Hulme Staffs 50 B3
Upper Inglesham Wilts 18 D6
Upper Killay Swans 26 B2
Upper Kinchrackine Ag & B 90 D2
Upper Lambourn Berks 19 E4
Upper Landywood Staffs 40 B4
Upper Langford Somset 17 F5
Upper Langwith Derbys 51 F3
Upper Largo Fife 87 E6
Upper Leigh Staffs 50 B1
Upper Longdon Staffs 40 B4
Upper Lybster Highld 110 C3
Upper Lydbrook Gloucs 28 D4
Upper Lye Herefs 38 D3
Upper Milton Worcs 39 G3
Upper Minety Wilts 18 C5
Upper Mulben Moray 101 F4
Upper Netchwood Shrops 39 F5
Upper Nobut Staffs 40 B6
Upper Norwood W Susx 10 C4
Upper Poppleton N York 59 F5
Upper Quinton Warwks 30 C4
Upper Ratley Hants 9 E5
Upper Rochford Worcs 39 F3
Upper Ruscoe D & G 69 G4
Upper Sapey Herefs 39 F3
Upper Seagry Wilts 18 B4
Upper Shelton Beds 32 C3
Upper Sheringham Norfk 45 E6
Upper Skelmorlie N Ayrs 84 B2
Upper Slaughter Gloucs 30 C2
Upper Soudley Gloucs 28 D4
Upper Standen Kent 13 G5
Upper Stepford D & G 78 C1
Upper Stoke Norfk 45 F2
Upper Stowe Nhants 31 G5
Upper Street Hants 8 D5
Upper Street Norfk 45 F4
Upper Street Norfk 45 F4
Upper Street Suffk 34 B4
Upper Street Suffk 34 D4
Upper Sundon Beds 32 C2
Upper Swell Gloucs 30 C3
Upper Tasburgh Norfk 45 E2
Upper Tean Staffs 50 B1
Upper Town Derbys 50 D3
Upper Town Herefs 39 F1
Upper Town Somset 17 F5
Upper Town Suffk 34 C5
Upper Tumble Carmth 26 B4
Upper Tysoe Warwks 31 E4
Upper Victoria Angus 93 G3
Upper Wardington Oxon 31 F4
Upper Wellingham E Susx 11 G3
Upper Weybread Suffk 35 E6
Upper Wield Hants 19 H1
Upper Winchendon Bucks 31 H2
Upper Woodford Wilts 18 D1
Upper Wraxall Wilts 18 A4
Upperby Cumb 71 G4
Upperglen Highld 104 B1
Uppermill Gt Man 58 B1
Upperthong W York 58 C1
Upperton W Susx 10 C4
Uppertown Highld 110 D6
Uppingham Rutlnd 42 B2
Uppington Shrops 49 F1
Upsall N York 66 B2
Upsettlington Border 81 E4
Upshire Essex 21 G5
Upstreet Kent 23 G2
Upton Bucks 31 H2
Upton Cambs 42 D2
Upton Cambs 32 D6
Upton Ches 48 D6
Upton Cnwll 4 D4
Upton Devon 6 C5
Upton Devon 5 G2
Upton Dorset 7 H4
Upton Dorset 8 C3
Upton Hants 19 F2
Upton Hants 9 F5
Upton Leics 41 E3
Upton Lincs 52 B4
Upton Mersyd 56 C2
Upton Norfk 45 G3
Upton Notts 51 H2
Upton Notts 51 H4
Upton Oxon 19 G5
Upton Somset 16 B2
Upton Somset 17 F2

191

Upton W York 59 F2
Upton Wilts 8 B6
Upton Bishop Herefs 28 D5
Upton Cheyney Gloucs 17 H5
Upton Cressett Shrops 39 F5
Upton Cross Cnwll 4 D4
Upton Grey Hants 10 A6
Upton Hellions Devon 15 G2
Upton Lovell Wilts 18 B1
Upton Magna Shrops 49 E1
Upton Noble Somset 17 H3
Upton Pyne Devon 6 B5
Upton Scudamore Wilts 18 B2
Upton Snodsbury Worcs 30 B5
Upton St Leonards Gloucs 29 F4
Upton upon Severn Worcs 29 F6
Upton Warren Worcs 30 A6
Upwaltham W Susx 10 C3
Upwell Norfk 43 G2
Upwick Green Herts 33 F1
Upwood Cambs 43 E1
Urchfont Wilts 18 C3
Urmston Gt Man 57 G2
Urquhart Moray 101 E5
Urra N York 66 B3
Urray Highld 106 D2
Usan Angus 95 F2
Ushaw Moor Dur 73 F1
Usk Mons 28 B3
Usselby Lincs 52 C4
Usworth T & W 73 G3
Utkinton Ches 49 E5
Utley W York 58 B4
Uton Devon 15 G1
Utterby Lincs 53 E4
Uttoxeter Staffs 40 C6
Uxbridge Gt Lon 20 D4
Uyeasound Shet 111 m4
Uzmaston Pembks 24 D4

V

Vale Guern 6 c2
Vale of Rheidol Railway Cerdgn 37 F4
Valley IOA 54 B4
Valtos Highld 104 D2
Valtos W Isls 111 c6
Vange Essex 22 C4
Vatsetter Shet 111 l4
Vatten Highld 96 B6
Vaynor Myr Td 27 F4
Vazon Bay Guern 6 b1
Velindre Powys 27 G6
Venn Ottery Devon 6 C4
Venngreen Devon 14 D2
Ventnor IOW 9 G1
Venton Devon 5 F3
Vernham Dean Hants 19 E2
Vernham Street Hants 19 F3
Verwood Dorset 8 D4
Veryan Cnwll 3 E3
Vickerstown Cumb 62 C3
Victoria Cnwll 3 F5
Vidlin Shet 111 l3
Viewfield Moray 101 E6
Viewpark N Lans 85 F2
Vigo Kent 22 B2
Ville la Bas Jersey 7 a2
Villiaze Guern 6 b1
Vines Cross E Susx 12 B4
Virginia Water Surrey 20 D2
Virginstow Devon 4 D6
Vobster Somset 17 H4
Voe Shet 111 l3
Vowchurch Herefs 28 B6

W

Wackerfield Dur 65 E5
Wacton Norfk 45 E2
Wadborough Worcs 30 A4
Waddesdon Bucks 31 H2
Waddeton Devon 6 A2
Waddingham Lincs 52 C5
Waddington Lancs 63 G1
Waddington Lincs 52 B2
Wadebridge Cnwll 3 F6
Wadeford Somset 7 E6
Wadenhoe Nhants 42 C1
Wadesmill Herts 33 E1
Wadhurst E Susx 12 B5
Wadshelf Derbys 50 D4
Wadworth S York 51 F6
Wainfleet All Saints Lincs 53 G2
Wainhouse Corner Cnwll 4 C6
Wainscott Kent 22 C3
Wainstalls W York 58 B3
Waitby Cumb 64 B4
Waithe Lincs 53 E5
Wakefield W York 59 E2
Wakerley Nhants 42 B2
Wakes Colne Essex 34 C2
Walberswick Suffk 35 G6
Walberton W Susx 10 C3
Walbutt D & G 70 B6
Walcombe Somset 17 F4
Walcot Lincs 42 C5
Walcot Shrops 49 F1
Walcot Wilts 18 D5
Walcot Green Norfk 35 E6
Walcote Leics 41 F2
Walcott Lincs 52 D1
Walcott Norfk 45 F5
Walden Stubbs N York 59 F2
Walderslade Kent 22 C2
Walderton W Susx 10 B3
Walditch Dorset 7 F5
Waldridge Dur 73 F2
Waldringfield Suffk 35 F3
Waldron E Susx 12 A4
Wales S York 51 F5
Wales Somset 17 G2
Walesby Lincs 52 D4
Walesby Notts 51 G4

Walford Herefs 38 D3
Walford Herefs 28 D4
Walford Heath Shrops 49 E2
Walgherton Ches 49 F4
Walgrave Nhants 32 A5
Walk Mill Lancs 57 H5
Walkden Gt Man 57 G3
Walker T & W 73 F3
Walker's Green Herefs 39 E1
Walkerburn Border 79 F6
Walkeringham Notts 51 H5
Walkerith Lincs 52 A4
Walkern Herts 33 E2
Walkerton Fife 86 C5
Walkford Dorset 8 D3
Walkhampton Devon 5 F4
Walkington E R Yk 60 D4
Walkley S York 51 E5
Walkwood Worcs 30 B6
Wall Nthumb 72 D3
Wall Staffs 40 C4
Wallacetown S Ayrs 76 C2
Wallacetown S Ayrs 76 C3
Wallands Park E Susx 11 G3
Wallasey Mersyd 56 C2
Wallingford Oxon 19 G5
Wallington Gt Lon 21 F2
Wallington Hants 9 G4
Wallington Herts 33 E2
Wallisdown Dorset 8 C3
Walls Shet 111 k2
Wallsend T & W 73 G3
Wallyford E Loth 86 D3
Walmer Kent 23 H1
Walmer Bridge Lancs 57 E5
Walpole Suffk 35 F6
Walpole Cross Keys Norfk 43 G4
Walpole Highway Norfk 43 G3
Walpole St Andrew Norfk 43 G4
Walpole St Peter Norfk 43 G4
Walsall W Mids 40 B3
Walsden W York 58 B2
Walsham le Willows Suffk 34 D5
Walshford N York 59 E5
Walsoken Norfk 43 F3
Walston S Lans 86 B1
Walsworth Herts 32 D2
Waltham Kent 13 F6
Waltham Lincs 53 E5
Waltham Abbey Essex 21 F5
Waltham Chase Hants 9 G5
Waltham Cross Herts 21 F5
Waltham on the Wolds Leics 42 A4
Waltham St Lawrence Berks 20 B3
Walton Bucks 32 B2
Walton Cumb 71 H5
Walton Derbys 51 E3
Walton Leics 41 G2
Walton Powys 38 C2
Walton Shrops 49 F2
Walton Somset 17 F3
Walton Suffk 35 F2
Walton W Susx 10 B3
Walton W York 59 E2
Walton W York 59 E4
Walton Cardiff Gloucs 29 F5
Walton East Pembks 24 D5
Walton on the Hill Surrey 21 E1
Walton on the Naze Essex 35 F1
Walton on the Wolds Leics 41 G5
Walton Park Somset 17 E6
Walton West Pembks 24 C4
Walton-in-Gordano Somset 17 E6
Walton-le-Dale Lancs 57 E5
Walton-on-Thames Surrey 20 D2
Walton-on-the-Hill Staffs 40 B5
Walton-on-Trent Derbys 40 D5
Walworth Dur 65 F5
Walworth Gt Lon 21 F3
Walwyn's Castle Pembks 24 C4
Wambrook Somset 6 D6
Wanborough Surrey 10 C6
Wanborough Wilts 18 D5
Wandsworth Gt Lon 21 E3
Wangford Suffk 35 G6
Wanlip Leics 41 G4
Wanlockhead D & G 78 C4
Wannock E Susx 12 B3
Wansford Cambs 42 C2
Wansford E R Yk 60 D5
Wanshurst Green Kent 12 C6
Wanstead Gt Lon 21 G4
Wanstrow Somset 17 H3
Wanswell Gloucs 29 E3
Wantage Oxon 19 F5
Wapley Gloucs 29 E1
Wappenbury Warwks 41 E1
Wappenham Nhants 31 G4
Warbleton E Susx 12 B4
Warborough Oxon 19 G5
Warboys Cambs 33 E6
Warbreck Lancs 56 D6
Warbstow Cnwll 4 C5
Warburton Gt Man 57 F2
Warcop Cumb 64 B4
Warden Nthumb 72 D3
Wardington Oxon 31 F4
Wardle Ches 49 F5
Wardle Gt Man 58 A2
Wardley Rutlnd 42 A2
Wardley T & W 73 G3
Wardlow Derbys 50 C4
Wardy Hill Cambs 33 F6
Ware Herts 21 F6
Wareham Dorset 8 B2
Warehorne Kent 13 E5
Warenford Nthumb 81 G3
Wareside Herts 21 G6
Waresley Cambs 33 E4
Warfield Berks 20 C3
Warfleet Devon 6 A1
Wargrave Berks 20 B3
Warham All Saints Norfk 44 C6
Warham St Mary Norfk 44 C6
Wark Nthumb 80 D4
Wark Nthumb 72 C4
Warkleigh Devon 15 F3
Warkton Nhants 32 B6
Warkworth Nhants 31 F4
Warkworth Nthumb 81 G1
Warlaby N York 65 G3
Warleggan Cnwll 4 C4
Warley Town W York 58 B3
Warlingham Surrey 21 F2

Warmanbie D & G 71 E6
Warmfield W York 59 E2
Warmingham Ches 49 G5
Warmington Nhants 42 C1
Warmington Warwks 31 E4
Warminster Wilts 18 B2
Warmley Gloucs 17 G6
Warmsworth S York 51 F6
Warmwell Dorset 7 H4
Warnford Hants 9 H5
Warnham W Susx 11 E5
Warningcamp W Susx 10 D3
Warninglid W Susx 11 E4
Warren Ches 50 A4
Warren Pembks 24 D3
Warren Row Berks 20 B3
Warren Street Kent 22 D1
Warrenhill S Lans 78 C6
Warrington Bucks 32 B4
Warrington Ches 57 F2
Warriston C Edin 86 C3
Warsash Hants 9 G4
Warslow Staffs 50 C3
Warsop Notts 51 F3
Warter E R Yk 60 C5
Warthermaske N York 65 F2
Warthill N York 59 G5
Wartling E Susx 12 B3
Wartnaby Leics 41 G5
Warton Lancs 56 D5
Warton Lancs 63 E3
Warton Warwks 40 D4
Warwick Cumb 71 G5
Warwick Warwks 30 D6
Warwick Castle Warwks 30 D6
Wasbister Ork 111 h3
Wasdale Head Cumb 62 C6
Washaway Cnwll 3 F6
Washbourne Devon 5 H3
Washbrook Suffk 35 E3
Washfield Devon 16 B1
Washfold N York 65 E3
Washford Somset 16 C3
Washford Pyne Devon 15 G2
Washingborough Lincs 52 C3
Washington T & W 73 G2
Washington W Susx 10 D3
Wasperton Warwks 30 D5
Wass N York 66 B2
Watchet Somset 16 C3
Watchfield Oxon 19 E5
Watchgate Cumb 63 E5
Water Devon 5 G5
Water End E R Yk 60 B4
Water End Essex 33 G3
Water Newton Cambs 42 D2
Water Orton Warwks 40 C3
Water Stratford Bucks 31 G3
Waterbeach Cambs 33 F5
Waterbeach W Susx 10 C3
Waterbeck D & G 79 F1
Watercombe Dorset 7 H4
Waterfall Staffs 50 C2
Waterfoot S Lans 85 E1
Waterford Herts 21 F6
Watergate Cnwll 4 B5
Waterhead E Ayrs 77 E3
Waterheads Border 86 C1
Waterhouses Staffs 50 C2
Wateringbury Kent 22 C1
Waterloo Highld 97 E4
Waterloo Mersyd 56 D3
Waterloo N Lans 85 G1
Waterloo P & K 92 C3
Waterloo Pembks 24 D3
Waterlooville Hants 10 A3
Watermillock Cumb 71 G2
Waterperry Oxon 31 G1
Waterrow Somset 16 C2
Waters Upton Shrops 49 F2
Watersfield W Susx 10 D4
Waterside E Ayrs 76 D2
Waterside E Ayrs 76 D5
Waterside E Duns 85 F3
Waterside E Susx 57 G5
Waterstein Highld 104 A1
Waterstock Oxon 31 G1
Waterston Pembks 24 D3
Watford Herts 20 D5
Watford Nhants 31 G6
Wath N York 58 C6
Wath N York 65 G1
Wath upon Dearne S York 51 E6
Watlington Norfk 43 G3
Watlington Oxon 20 A4
Watten Highld 110 C4
Wattisfield Suffk 34 D6
Wattisham Suffk 34 D4
Watton Dorset 7 F5
Watton E R Yk 60 D5
Watton Norfk 44 C2
Watton-at-Stone Herts 33 E1
Wattston N Lans 85 G3
Wattsville Caerph 27 G2
Waulkmill Abers 95 E5
Waunarlwydd Swans 26 C2
Waunfawr Cerdgn 37 E5
Waunfawr Gwynd 54 D2
Wavendon Bucks 32 B3
Waverbridge Cumb 71 E4
Waverton Ches 49 E5
Waverton Cumb 71 E4
Wawne E R Yk 61 E4
Waxham Norfk 45 G4
Way Village Devon 15 H2
Wayford Somset 7 E6
Waytown Dorset 7 F5
Weacombe Somset 16 C3
Weald Oxon 19 E6
Wealdstone Gt Lon 21 E4
Weardley W York 58 D4
Weare Somset 17 E4
Weare Giffard Devon 14 D3
Wearhead Dur 72 C1
Wearne Somset 17 E2
Weasenham All Saints Norfk 44 C4
Weasenham St Peter Norfk 44 C4
Weaste Gt Man 57 G3
Weaverham Ches 49 F6
Weaverthorpe N York 67 F1
Webheath Worcs 30 B6
Wedderlairs Abers 102 D3
Weddington Warwks 41 E3
Wedhampton Wilts 18 C3

Wedmore Somset 17 F4
Wednesbury W Mids 40 B3
Wednesfield W Mids 40 B3
Weedon Bucks 32 A1
Weedon Nhants 31 G5
Weedon Lois Nhants 31 G4
Weeford Staffs 40 C4
Week Somset 16 B2
Week St Mary Cnwll 14 C1
Weeke Hants 9 F6
Weekley Nhants 32 B6
Weel E R Yk 60 D4
Weeley Essex 35 E1
Weeley Heath Essex 35 E1
Weem P & K 92 B4
Weethley Warwks 30 B5
Weeting Norfk 44 B1
Weeton E R Yk 61 G2
Weeton Lancs 56 D6
Weeton N York 58 D4
Weetwood W York 58 D4
Weir Lancs 57 H5
Weir Quay Devon 5 E3
Welborne Norfk 44 D3
Welbourn Lincs 52 B1
Welburn N York 60 B6
Welbury N York 65 G3
Welby Lincs 42 B5
Welcombe Devon 14 C3
Welford Berks 19 F4
Welford Nhants 41 G2
Welford-on-Avon Warwks 30 C5
Welham Leics 41 H3
Welham Notts 51 H4
Welham Green Herts 21 E5
Well Hants 10 B6
Well Lincs 53 F3
Well N York 65 F2
Well Head Herts 32 D2
Welland Worcs 29 F6
Wellbank Angus 93 G3
Wellesbourne Warwks 30 D5
Welling Gt Lon 21 G3
Wellingborough Nhants 32 B5
Wellingham Norfk 44 C4
Wellingore Lincs 52 C1
Wellington Cumb 62 B6
Wellington Herefs 39 E1
Wellington Shrops 49 F1
Wellington Somset 16 C1
Wellington Heath Herefs 29 E6
Wellow IOW 9 F2
Wellow Notts 51 G3
Wellow Somset 17 H4
Wells Somset 17 F3
Wells-next-the-sea Norfk 44 C6
Wellstye Green Essex 33 H1
Welltree P & K 92 C2
Wellwood Fife 86 B4
Welney Norfk 43 G2
Welsh Frankton Shrops 48 D3
Welsh Newton Herefs 28 C4
Welsh St Donats V Glam 16 B6
Welshampton Shrops 48 D3
Welshpool Powys 38 C6
Welton Cumb 71 F4
Welton E R Yk 60 D3
Welton Lincs 52 C3
Welton Nhants 31 G6
Welton le Marsh Lincs 53 F2
Welton le Wold Lincs 53 E4
Welwick E R Yk 61 G2
Welwyn Herts 32 D1
Welwyn Garden City Herts 21 E6
Wem Shrops 49 E2
Wembdon Somset 16 D3
Wembley Gt Lon 21 E4
Wembury Devon 5 F2
Wembworthy Devon 15 F2
Wemyss Bay Inver 84 B3
Wendens Ambo Essex 33 G2
Wendlebury Oxon 31 F2
Wendling Norfk 44 C3
Wendover Bucks 20 B6
Wendron Cnwll 2 D2
Wendy Cambs 33 E3
Wenhaston Suffk 35 G6
Wennington Cambs 33 E6
Wennington Gt Lon 22 A3
Wennington Lancs 63 F3
Wensley Derbys 50 D3
Wensley N York 65 E2
Wentbridge W York 59 F2
Wentnor Shrops 38 D5
Wentworth Cambs 33 F6
Wentworth S York 51 E6
Wenvoe V Glam 16 C6
Weobley Herefs 38 D2
Weobley Marsh Herefs 38 D1
Wepham W Susx 10 D3
Wereham Norfk 44 A2
Werrington Cambs 42 D2
Werrington Cnwll 4 D5
Wervin Ches 48 D6
Wesham Lancs 56 D5
Wessington Derbys 51 E3
West Acre Norfk 44 B3
West Alvington Devon 5 G2
West Anstey Devon 15 G4
West Ashby Lincs 53 E3
West Ashling W Susx 10 B3
West Ashton Wilts 18 B2
West Auckland Dur 65 F5
West Ayton N York 67 F2
West Bagborough Somset 16 D2
West Bank Ches 57 E1
West Barkwith Lincs 52 D3
West Barnby N York 66 D4
West Barns E Loth 87 F4
West Barsham Norfk 44 C5
West Bay Dorset 7 F4
West Beckham Norfk 45 E5
West Bedfont Surrey 20 D3
West Bergholt Essex 34 C2
West Bexington Dorset 7 F4
West Bilney Norfk 44 A3
West Blatchington E Susx 11 F3
West Boldon T & W 73 G3
West Bowling W York 58 C3
West Brabourne Kent 13 F6
West Bradenham Norfk 44 C3
West Bradford Lancs 63 G1
West Bradley Somset 17 F3
West Bretton W York 58 D2

West Bridgford Notts 51 G1
West Bromwich W Mids 40 B3
West Buccleuch Hotel Border 79 F4
West Buckland Devon 15 F4
West Burton N York 64 D2
West Butterwick Lincs 52 A5
West Byfleet Surrey 20 D2
West Cairngaan D & G 68 C1
West Caister Norfk 45 H3
West Calder W Loth 86 A2
West Camel Somset 17 G2
West Chaldon Dorset 8 A2
West Challow Oxon 19 F5
West Charleton Devon 5 G2
West Chevington Nthumb 73 F6
West Chiltington W Susx 10 D4
West Chinnock Somset 17 F1
West Clandon Surrey 20 D1
West Cliffe Kent 13 H6
West Coker Somset 17 F1
West Compton Somset 17 G3
West Compton Abbas Dorset 7 G5
West Cottingwith N York 59 G4
West Cowick E R Yk 59 G2
West Cross Swans 26 C2
West Curthwaite Cumb 71 F4
West Dean W Susx 10 B3
West Dean Wilts 9 E5
West Deeping Lincs 42 D3
West Derby Mersyd 56 D2
West Dereham Norfk 43 H2
West Down Devon 15 E5
West Drayton Gt Lon 20 D3
West Drayton Notts 51 G4
West Dunnet Highld 110 C6
West Ella E R Yk 60 D3
West End Beds 32 C4
West End Hants 9 F4
West End Norfk 45 H3
West End Somset 17 F5
West End Surrey 20 C2
West End Wilts 8 C5
West End Green Hants 19 H3
West Farleigh Kent 22 C1
West Farndon Nhants 31 F5
West Felton Shrops 48 D2
West Firle E Susx 11 G3
West Grafton Wilts 19 E3
West Green Hants 20 B1
West Grimstead Wilts 8 D5
West Grinstead W Susx 11 E4
West Haddlesey N York 59 F3
West Haddon Nhants 41 G1
West Hagbourne Oxon 19 G5
West Hagley Worcs 40 A2
West Hallam Derbys 51 E1
West Halton Lincs 60 C2
West Ham Gt Lon 21 G4
West Handley Derbys 51 E4
West Hanney Oxon 19 F5
West Hanningfield Essex 22 C5
West Harnham Wilts 8 D6
West Harptree Somset 17 F4
West Harting W Susx 10 B4
West Hatch Somset 16 D1
West Hatch Wilts 8 B6
West Haven Angus 93 G3
West Heath W Mids 40 B1
West Helmsdale Highld 110 A1
West Hendred Oxon 19 F5
West Hesleton N York 67 E1
West Hewish Somset 17 E5
West Hill Devon 6 C5
West Hoathly W Susx 11 F5
West Holme Dorset 8 B2
West Horrington Somset 17 G4
West Horsley Surrey 20 D1
West Hougham Kent 13 G5
West Howe Dorset 8 C3
West Huntingdon P & K 92 D2
West Huntspill Somset 17 E3
West Hythe Kent 13 F5
West Ilsley Berks 19 F5
West Itchenor W Susx 10 B2
West Kennett Wilts 18 D3
West Kilbride N Ayrs 76 B6
West Kingsdown Kent 22 B2
West Kington Wilts 18 A4
West Kirby Mersyd 56 C2
West Knapton N York 67 E1
West Knighton Dorset 7 H4
West Knoyle Wilts 8 B6
West Lambrook Somset 17 E1
West Langdon Kent 13 G6
West Laroch Highld 90 C4
West Lavington W Susx 10 C4
West Lavington Wilts 18 C2
West Layton N York 65 E4
West Leake Notts 41 F5
West Leigh Devon 15 F2
West Leigh Devon 5 G3
West Leigh Somset 16 C2
West Lexham Norfk 44 B4
West Lilling N York 59 G6
West Linton Border 86 B2
West Littleton Gloucs 18 A4
West Lockinge Oxon 19 F5
West Lulworth Dorset 8 A2
West Lutton N York 60 C6
West Lydford Somset 17 G2
West Lyng Somset 17 E2
West Lynn Norfk 43 G4
West Malling Kent 22 B2
West Malvern Worcs 39 G1
West Marden W Susx 10 B3
West Markham Notts 51 H4
West Marsh Lincs 61 F1
West Marton N York 58 A5
West Melbury Dorset 8 B5
West Meon Hants 9 H5
West Mersea Essex 23 E6
West Midlands Safari Park Worcs 39 G3
West Milton Dorset 7 F5
West Minster Kent 22 D3
West Molesey Surrey 21 E2
West Monkton Somset 16 D2
West Moors Dorset 8 C4
West Morden Dorset 8 B3
West Morriston Border 80 C4
West Mudford Somset 17 G1
West Ness N York 66 C2
West Newton E R Yk 61 F4
West Newton Norfk 44 A4
West Newton Somset 16 D2

West Norwood Gt Lon 21 F3
West Ogwell Devon 5 H4
West Orchard Dorset 8 A5
West Overton Wilts 18 D3
West Parley Dorset 8 D3
West Peckham Kent 22 B1
West Pelton Dur 73 F2
West Pennard Somset 17 F3
West Pentire Cnwll 2 D5
West Perry Cambs 32 D5
West Porlock Somset 15 G5
West Pulham Dorset 7 H6
West Putford Devon 14 D3
West Quantoxhead Somset 16 C3
West Raddon Devon 15 H2
West Rainton Dur 73 G2
West Rasen Lincs 52 C4
West Raynham Norfk 44 C4
West Rounton N York 65 G4
West Row Suffk 34 A6
West Rudham Norfk 44 B4
West Runton Norfk 45 E6
West Saltoun E Loth 87 E3
West Sandford Devon 15 G2
West Sandwick Shet 111 I3
West Scrafton N York 65 E2
West Stafford Dorset 7 H4
West Stockwith Notts 52 A4
West Stoke W Susx 10 B3
West Stour Dorset 8 A5
West Stourmouth Kent 23 G2
West Stow Suffk 34 B5
West Stowell Wilts 18 D3
West Street Suffk 34 D5
West Tanfield N York 65 F2
West Taphouse Cnwll 4 C3
West Tarbert Ag & B 83 F2
West Tarring W Susx 10 D3
West Thirston Nthumb 73 F6
West Thorney W Susx 10 B2
West Thorpe Notts 41 G5
West Thurrock Essex 22 B3
West Tilbury Essex 22 B3
West Tisted Hants 9 H6
West Torrington Lincs 52 D3
West Town Hants 10 A2
West Town Somset 17 F5
West Tytherley Hants 9 E6
West Walton Norfk 43 F3
West Walton Highway Norfk 43 F3
West Wellow Hants 9 E5
West Wembury Devon 5 F2
West Wemyss Fife 86 D5
West Wickham Cambs 33 G4
West Wickham Gt Lon 21 F2
West Williamston Pembks 24 D3
West Winch Norfk 43 H4
West Winterslow Wilts 9 E6
West Wittering W Susx 10 B2
West Witton N York 65 E2
West Woodburn Nthumb 72 C5
West Woodhay Berks 19 F3
West Worldham Hants 10 B5
West Worthing W Susx 11 E2
West Wratting Essex 33 G4
West Youlstone Cnwll 14 C3
Westbere Kent 23 F2
Westborough Lincs 42 B6
Westbourne Dorset 8 C3
Westbourne W Susx 10 B3
Westbrook Berks 19 F4
Westbrook Kent 23 H3
Westbury Bucks 31 G3
Westbury Shrops 38 D6
Westbury Wilts 18 B2
Westbury Leigh Wilts 18 B2
Westbury on Severn Gloucs 29 E4
Westbury-on-Trym Bristl 28 D1
Westbury-sub-Mendip Somset 17 F4
Westby Lancs 56 D5
Westcliff-on-Sea Essex 22 D4
Westcombe Somset 17 G3
Westcote Gloucs 30 D2
Westcott Bucks 31 H2
Westcott Devon 6 B6
Westcott Surrey 11 E6
Westcourt Wilts 19 E3
Westdean E Susx 11 H2
Westdowns Cnwll 4 B5
Wester Drumashie Highld 99 E5
Wester Ochiltree W Loth 86 A3
Wester Pitkierie Fife 87 E6
Westerdale Highld 110 B4
Westerdale N York 66 C4
Westerfield Suffk 35 E3
Westergate W Susx 10 C3
Westerham Kent 21 G1
Westerhope T & W 73 F3
Westerland Devon 6 A2
Westerleigh Gloucs 29 E1
Westerton Angus 93 H4
Westfield Cumb 70 D2
Westfield E Susx 12 C3
Westfield Highld 110 B5
Westfield N Lans 85 F3
Westfield Norfk 44 D3
Westfield Somset 17 G4
Westfield W Loth 85 H3
Westfields of Rattray P & K 92 D4
Westgate Dur 72 D1
Westgate Lincs 60 B1
Westgate on Sea Kent 23 G3
Westhall Suffk 35 G6
Westham Dorset 7 G3
Westham E Susx 12 B3
Westham Somset 17 E4
Westhampnett W Susx 10 C3
Westhay Somset 17 F3
Westhide Herefs 39 F1
Westhill Abers 95 G6
Westhope Herefs 39 E1
Westhope Shrops 39 E4
Westhorpe Lincs 42 D5
Westhorpe Suffk 34 D5
Westhoughton Gt Man 57 F3
Westhouse N York 63 F3
Westhouses Derbys 51 E3
Westhumble Surrey 21 E1
Westlake Devon 5 F2
Westleigh Devon 14 D4
Westleigh Devon 16 C1
Westleton Suffk 35 G5
Westley Suffk 34 B5
Westley Waterless Cambs 33 G4

Westlington Bucks 31 H1
Westlinton Cumb 71 G5
Westmarsh Kent 23 G2
Westmeston E Susx 11 F3
Westmill Herts 33 E2
Westminster Gt Lon 21 F3
Westmuir Angus 93 F4
Westnewton Cumb 71 E4
Westoe T & W 73 G3
Weston Berks 19 F4
Weston Ches 49 G4
Weston Devon 6 C5
Weston Devon 6 C4
Weston Hants 10 A4
Weston Herts 33 E2
Weston Lincs 43 E4
Weston N York 58 C4
Weston Nhants 31 G4
Weston Notts 51 H3
Weston Shrops 39 F5
Weston Shrops 48 C2
Weston Somset 17 H5
Weston Staffs 40 B5
Weston Beggard Herefs 28 D6
Weston by Welland Nhants 41 H3
Weston Colley Hants 19 G1
Weston Colville Cambs 33 G4
Weston Corbett Hants 10 A6
Weston Coyney Staffs 50 B1
Weston Favell Nhants 32 A5
Weston Green Cambs 33 G4
Weston Heath Shrops 49 G1
Weston Jones Staffs 49 G2
Weston Longville Norfk 45 E3
Weston Lullingfields Shrops 48 D2
Weston Patrick Hants 10 A6
Weston Rhyn Shrops 48 C3
Weston Subedge Gloucs 30 C4
Weston Turville Bucks 20 B6
Weston under Penyard Herefs 28 D5
Weston under Wetherley Warwks 41 E1
Weston Underwood Bucks 32 B4
Weston Underwood Derbys 50 D1
Weston-in-Gordano Somset 17 F6
Weston-on-the-Green Oxon 31 F2
Weston-Super-Mare Somset 17 E5
Weston-under-Lizard Staffs 49 G1
Weston-under-Redcastle Shrops 49 E2
Weston-upon-Trent Derbys 41 E6
Westonbirt Gloucs 18 B5
Westoning Beds 32 C2
Westonzoyland Somset 17 E3
Westow N York 60 B6
Westport Somset 17 E1
Westquarter Falk 85 H3
Westray Airport Ork 111 h3
Westridge Green Berks 19 G4
Westrigg W Loth 85 H2
Westrop Wilts 18 D5
Westry Cambs 43 F2
Westward Cumb 71 F4
Westward Ho! Devon 14 D4
Westwell Kent 13 E6
Westwell Oxon 30 D1
Westwell Leacon Kent 13 E6
Westwick Cambs 33 F5
Westwood Devon 6 B5
Westwood Kent 23 H2
Westwood Wilts 18 A3
Westwoodside Lincs 51 H6
Wetheral Cumb 71 G4
Wetherby W York 59 E4
Wetherden Suffk 34 D5
Wetheringsett Suffk 35 E5
Wethersfield Essex 34 A2
Wetherup Street Suffk 35 E5
Wetley Rocks Staffs 50 B2
Wettenhall Ches 49 F5
Wetton Staffs 50 C2
Wetwang E R Yk 60 C5
Wetwood Staffs 49 G3
Wexcombe Wilts 19 E3
Weybourne Norfk 45 E6
Weybread Suffk 35 F6
Weybread Street Suffk 35 F6
Weybridge Surrey 20 D2
Weycroft Devon 7 E5
Weydale Highld 110 B5
Weyhill Hants 19 E2
Weymouth Dorset 7 G3
Whaddon Bucks 32 A2
Whaddon Cambs 33 E3
Whaddon Gloucs 29 F4
Whaddon Wilts 18 B3
Whaddon Wilts 8 D5
Whaley Derbys 51 F4
Whaley Bridge Derbys 50 B4
Whaley Thorns Derbys 51 F4
Whaligoe Highld 110 D3
Whalley Lancs 57 G6
Whalton Nthumb 73 E4
Whaplode Lincs 43 E4
Whaplode Drove Lincs 43 E3
Wharf Warwks 31 E5
Wharfe N York 63 G3
Wharles Lancs 57 E6
Wharncliffe Side S York 50 D6
Wharram-le-Street N York 60 C6
Wharton Herefs 39 E2
Whashton N York 65 E4
Whasset Cumb 63 E4
Whatcote Warwks 30 D4
Whateley Warwks 40 D3
Whatfield Suffk 34 D3
Whatley Somset 7 E4
Whatley Somset 17 H4
Whatlington E Susx 12 C4
Whatsole Street Kent 13 F6
Whatstandwell Derbys 51 E2
Whatton Notts 51 H1
Whauphill D & G 69 E3
Wheatacre Norfk 45 G2
Wheathampstead Herts 21 E6
Wheathill Shrops 39 F4
Wheatley Hants 10 B5
Wheatley Oxon 31 G1
Wheatley Hill Dur 73 G1
Wheatley Hills S York 59 G1
Wheaton Aston Staffs 49 H1
Wheddon Cross Somset 16 B3
Wheelock Ches 49 G5
Wheelton Lancs 57 F4
Wheldrake N York 59 G4

Whelford Gloucs 18 D6
Whelpley Hill Bucks 20 C5
Whempstead Herts 33 E1
Whenby N York 66 C1
Whepstead Suffk 34 B4
Wherstead Suffk 35 E3
Wherwell Hants 19 F1
Wheston Derbys 50 C4
Whetsted Kent 12 B6
Whetstone Leics 41 F3
Whicham Cumb 62 B4
Whichford Warwks 30 D3
Whickham T & W 73 F3
Whiddon Down Devon 5 G6
Whigstreet Angus 93 G4
Whilton Nhants 31 G6
Whimple Devon 6 C5
Whimpwell Green Norfk 45 G5
Whinburgh Norfk 44 D3
Whinnie Liggate D & G 70 A4
Whinnyfold Abers 103 F3
Whippingham IOW 9 G3
Whipsnade Beds 32 C1
Whipsnade Wild Animal Park
    Bucks 32 C1
Whipton Devon 6 B5
Whisby Lincs 52 B2
Whissendine Rutlnd 42 A3
Whissonsett Norfk 44 C4
Whistlefield Ag & B 84 B5
Whistlefield Inn Ag & B 84 B5
Whistley Green Berks 20 B3
Whiston Mersyd 57 E2
Whiston Nhants 32 B4
Whiston S York 51 E5
Whiston Staffs 40 A4
Whiston Staffs 50 B2
Whitbeck Cumb 62 B4
Whitbourne Herefs 39 G2
Whitburn T & W 73 G3
Whitburn W Loth 85 H2
Whitby N York 67 E4
Whitchester Border 87 G2
Whitchurch Bucks 32 A1
Whitchurch Cardif 27 G1
Whitchurch Devon 5 E4
Whitchurch Hants 19 F2
Whitchurch Herefs 28 D4
Whitchurch Oxon 19 H4
Whitchurch Pembks 24 C5
Whitchurch Shrops 49 E3
Whitchurch Somset 17 G5
Whitchurch Canonicorum Dorset 7 E5
Whitchurch Hill Oxon 19 H4
Whitcombe Dorset 7 H4
Whitcott Shrops 38 D5
Whitcott Keysett Shrops 38 C4
White Ball Somset 16 C1
White Chapel Lancs 57 E6
White Colne Essex 34 C2
White Cross Cnwll 2 D2
White End Worcs 29 E6
White Lackington Dorset 7 H5
White Ladies Aston Worcs 30 A5
White Notley Essex 34 B1
White Pit Lincs 53 F3
White Roding Essex 22 B6
White Stone Herefs 28 D6
White Waltham Berks 20 B3
Whiteacre Heath Warwks 40 D3
Whitebridge Highld 98 D4
Whitebrook Mons 28 D3
Whitecairns Abers 103 E2
Whitechapel Gt Lon 21 F3
Whitecliffe Gloucs 28 D4
Whitecraig E Loth 86 D3
Whitecrook D & G 68 C3
Whitecross Falk 85 H3
Whiteface Highld 107 F4
Whitefarland N Ayrs 75 G5
Whitefaulds S Ayrs 76 C3
Whitefield Gt Man 57 G3
Whitefield Somset 16 C2
Whiteford Abers 102 C2
Whitegate Ches 49 F6
Whitehall Ork 111 j2
Whitehaven Cumb 70 C1
Whitehill Hants 10 B5
Whitehills Abers 102 C5
Whitehouse Abers 102 C1
Whitehouse Ag & B 83 F2
Whitekirk E Loth 87 F4
Whitelackington Somset 17 E1
Whiteley Devon 9 G4
Whiteley Bank IOW 9 G2
Whitemire Moray 100 C4
Whitemoor Cnwll 3 F5
Whitemoor Notts 51 F1
Whiteness Shet 111 I2
Whiteparish Wilts 9 E5
Whiterashes Abers 102 D2
Whiterow Highld 110 D4
Whiterow Moray 100 C5
Whiteshill Gloucs 29 F3
Whitesmith E Susx 11 H3
Whitestaunton Somset 6 D6
Whitestone Cross Devon 6 A5
Whitewell Lancs 63 F1
Whitfield Gloucs 29 E2
Whitfield Kent 13 G6
Whitfield Nhants 31 G4
Whitfield Nthumb 72 C3
Whitford Devon 6 D5
Whitford Flints 56 B1
Whitgift E R Yk 60 C2
Whitgreave Staffs 40 A6
Whithorn D & G 69 F2
Whiting Bay N Ayrs 75 H3
Whitkirk W York 59 E3
Whitland Carmth 25 F4
Whitlaw Border 80 B2
Whitletts S Ayrs 76 C4
Whitley Berks 20 A3
Whitley N York 59 F2
Whitley S York 51 E6
Whitley Wilts 18 B3
Whitley Bay T & W 73 G4
Whitley Chapel Nthumb 72 D3
Whitley Lower W York 58 D2
Whitminster Gloucs 29 E3
Whitmore Staffs 49 G3
Whitnage Devon 16 B1
Whitnash Warwks 31 E6
Whitney-on-Wye Herefs 38 C1

Whitrigglees Cumb 71 E5
Whitsbury Hants 8 D5
Whitsome Border 81 E5
Whitson Newpt 28 B1
Whitstable Kent 23 F2
Whitstone Cnwll 14 C1
Whittingham Nthumb 81 F2
Whittingslow Shrops 38 D5
Whittington Derbys 51 E4
Whittington Gloucs 30 B2
Whittington Lancs 63 F3
Whittington Norfk 44 A2
Whittington Shrops 48 D3
Whittington Staffs 40 C4
Whittington Staffs 39 H4
Whittington Warwks 40 D3
Whittington Worcs 39 H2
Whittle-le-Woods Lancs 57 F4
Whittlebury Nhants 31 G4
Whittlesey Cambs 43 E2
Whittlesford Cambs 33 F3
Whitton Dur 65 G5
Whitton Lincs 60 C3
Whitton Nthumb 73 E6
Whitton Powys 38 C3
Whitton Shrops 39 F3
Whittonstall Nthumb 73 E2
Whitway Hants 19 F3
Whitwell Derbys 51 F4
Whitwell Herts 32 D1
Whitwell IOW 9 G2
Whitwell N York 65 F3
Whitwell Rutlnd 42 B3
Whitwell Street Norfk 44 D4
Whitwell-on-the-Hill N York 60 B6
Whitwick Leics 41 E5
Whitworth Lancs 58 A2
Whixall Shrops 49 E3
Whixley N York 59 E5
Whorlton Dur 65 E4
Whorlton N York 66 B3
Whyle Herefs 39 E2
Whyteleafe Surrey 21 F2
Wibsey W York 58 C3
Wibtoft Warwks 41 F2
Wichenford Worcs 39 G2
Wichling Kent 22 D1
Wick Dorset 8 D3
Wick Gloucs 17 H6
Wick Highld 110 D4
Wick V Glam 16 B6
Wick W Susx 10 D3
Wick Worcs 30 B4
Wick Airport Highld 110 D4
Wick St Lawrence Somset 17 E5
Wicken Cambs 33 G5
Wicken Nhants 31 H4
Wicken Bonhunt Essex 33 G2
Wickenby Lincs 52 C3
Wicker Street Green Suffk 34 C3
Wickersley S York 51 F5
Wickford Essex 22 C4
Wickham Berks 19 F4
Wickham Hants 9 G4
Wickham Bishops Essex 22 D6
Wickham Green Suffk 34 D5
Wickham Market Suffk 35 F4
Wickham Skeith Suffk 34 D5
Wickham St Paul Essex 34 B2
Wickhambreaux Kent 23 G2
Wickhambrook Suffk 34 B4
Wickhamford Worcs 30 C4
Wickhampton Norfk 45 G3
Wicklewood Norfk 44 D2
Wickmere Norfk 45 E5
Wickwar Gloucs 29 E2
Widdington Essex 33 G2
Widdrington Nthumb 73 F6
Widdrington Station T & W 73 F5
Wide Open T & W 73 F4
Widecombe in the Moor Devon 5 G4
Widegates Cnwll 4 D3
Widemouth Bay Cnwll 14 B2
Widford Essex 22 C5
Widford Herts 33 F1
Widmer End Bucks 20 C5
Widmerpool Notts 41 G6
Widmore Gt Lon 21 G2
Widnes Ches 57 E1
Widworthy Devon 6 D5
Wigan Gt Man 57 F3
Wigborough Somset 17 F1
Wiggaton Devon 6 C5
Wiggenhall St Germans Norfk 43 G3
Wiggenhall St Mary Magdalen
    Norfk 43 G3
Wiggenhall St Mary the Virgin
    Norfk 43 G3
Wiggens Green Essex 33 H3
Wigginton Herts 20 C6
Wigginton N York 59 G5
Wigginton Oxon 31 E3
Wigginton Staffs 40 D4
Wigglesworth N York 63 G2
Wiggonby Cumb 71 F4
Wighill N York 59 F4
Wighton Norfk 44 C5
Wigley Hants 9 E5
Wigmore Herefs 38 D3
Wigmore Kent 22 C2
Wigsley Notts 52 B2
Wigsthorpe Nhants 32 C6
Wigston Leics 41 G3
Wigston Parva Leics 41 F2
Wigthorpe Notts 51 G5
Wigtoft Lincs 43 E5
Wigton Cumb 71 F4
Wigtown D & G 69 F3
Wike W York 59 E4
Wilbarston Nhants 42 A1
Wilberfoss E R Yk 60 B5
Wilburton Cambs 33 F6
Wilby Nhants 32 B5
Wilby Norfk 44 D1
Wilby Suffk 35 F5
Wilcot Wilts 18 D3
Wilcott Shrops 48 D2
Wildboarclough Ches 50 B3
Wilden Beds 32 C4
Wilden Worcs 39 G3
Wildmanbridge S Lans 85 G1
Wildmoor Worcs 40 B1

Wildsworth Lincs 52 A5
Wilkesley Ches 49 F3
Wilkhaven Highld 107 H4
Wilkieston W Loth 86 B3
Willand Devon 6 B6
Willaston Ches 56 D1
Willaston Ches 49 F4
Willen Bucks 32 B3
Willenhall W Mids 40 B3
Willenhall W Mids 41 E1
Willerby E R Yk 60 D3
Willerby N York 67 F2
Willersey Gloucs 30 C4
Willersley Herefs 38 D1
Willesborough Kent 13 E6
Willesborough Lees Kent 13 E6
Willesden Gt Lon 21 E4
Willesley Wilts 18 B5
Willett Somset 16 C2
Willey Shrops 39 F5
Willey Warwks 41 F2
Willey Green Surrey 20 C1
Williamscot Oxon 31 F4
Willian Herts 32 D2
Willingale Essex 22 B6
Willingdon E Susx 12 B2
Willingham Cambs 33 F5
Willingham by Stow Lincs 52 B4
Willingham Green Cambs 33 H4
Willington Beds 32 D4
Willington Derbys 40 D6
Willington Dur 65 F6
Willington Kent 22 C1
Willington Warwks 30 D4
Willington Quay T & W 73 G3
Willitoft E R Yk 60 B3
Williton Somset 16 C3
Willoughby Lincs 53 F3
Willoughby Warwks 31 F6
Willoughby Waterleys Leics 41 F3
Willoughby-on-the-Wolds Notts 41 G5
Willoughton Lincs 52 B4
Willows Green Essex 34 B1
Willtown Somset 17 E2
Wilmcote Warwks 30 C5
Wilmington Devon 6 D5
Wilmington E Susx 12 A3
Wilmington Kent 21 H3
Wilmslow Ches 57 H1
Wilpshire Lancs 57 F5
Wilsden W York 58 C4
Wilsford Lincs 42 C6
Wilsford Wilts 18 D3
Wilsford Wilts 18 D1
Wilshaw W York 58 C1
Wilsill N York 58 C6
Wilson Leics 41 E5
Wilsontown S Lans 85 H1
Wilstead Beds 32 C3
Wilsthorpe Lincs 42 C3
Wilstone Herts 20 C6
Wilton Herefs 28 D5
Wilton N York 66 C5
Wilton N York 67 E2
Wilton Wilts 8 D6
Wilton Wilts 19 E3
Wilton Dean Border 80 B2
Wimbish Essex 33 G2
Wimbish Green Essex 33 G2
Wimbledon Gt Lon 21 E3
Wimblington Cambs 43 F2
Wimboldsley Ches 49 F5
Wimborne Minster Dorset 8 C3
Wimborne St Giles Dorset 8 C4
Wimbotsham Norfk 43 G3
Wimpole Cambs 33 E4
Wimpstone Warwks 30 D5
Wincanton Somset 17 H2
Winchburgh W Loth 86 B3
Winchcombe Gloucs 30 B3
Winchelsea E Susx 12 D4
Winchester Hants 9 G6
Winchet Hill Kent 12 C6
Winchfield Hants 20 B1
Winchmore Hill Bucks 20 C5
Winchmore Hill Gt Lon 21 F4
Wincle Ches 50 B3
Wincobank S York 51 E5
Windermere Cumb 62 D5
Winderton Warwks 31 E4
Windhill Highld 107 E1
Windlesham Surrey 20 C2
Windmill Cnwll 3 E6
Windmill Hill E Susx 12 B3
Windmill Hill Somset 17 E1
Windrush Gloucs 30 C2
Windsole Abers 102 B5
Windsor Berks 20 C3
Windsor Castle Berks 20 C3
Windsor Green Suffk 34 C4
Windsoredge Gloucs 29 F3
Windy Arbour Warwks 40 D1
Windygates Fife 86 D5
Wineham W Susx 11 E4
Winestead E R Yk 61 F3
Winfarthing Norfk 45 E1
Winford IOW 9 G2
Winford Somset 17 F5
Winforton Herefs 38 C1
Winfrith Newburgh Dorset 8 A2
Wing Bucks 32 B1
Wing Rutlnd 42 B2
Wingate Dur 73 G1
Wingates Nhants 31 F5
Wingerworth Derbys 51 E3
Wingfield Beds 32 C2
Wingfield Suffk 35 F6
Wingfield Wilts 18 A2
Wingham Kent 23 G1
Wingmore Kent 13 F6
Wingrave Bucks 32 B1
Winkburn Notts 51 G3
Winkfield Berks 20 C3
Winkfield Row Berks 20 C3
Winkhill Staffs 50 B2
Winkleigh Devon 15 F2
Winksley N York 65 F1
Winlaton T & W 73 F3
Winless Highld 110 D4
Winmarleigh Lancs 63 E1
Winnall Hants 9 G6
Winnersh Berks 20 B3
Winnington Ches 49 F6
Winscombe Somset 17 E4
Winsford Ches 49 F5

Winsford Somset 16 A3
Winsham Devon 15 E5
Winsham Somset 7 E6
Winshill Staffs 40 D5
Winshwen Swans 26 C2
Winskill Cumb 64 A6
Winslade Hants 19 H2
Winsley Wilts 18 A3
Winslow Bucks 31 H3
Winson Gloucs 30 C1
Winsor Hants 9 E4
Winster Cumb 62 D5
Winster Derbys 50 D3
Winston Dur 65 E5
Winston Suffk 35 E4
Winstone Gloucs 29 G4
Winswell Devon 15 E2
Winterborne Came Dorset 7 H4
Winterborne Clenston Dorset 8 B4
Winterborne Houghton Dorset 8 A4
Winterborne Kingston Dorset 8 B3
Winterborne Monkton Dorset 7 G4
Winterborne Stickland Dorset 8 B4
Winterborne Whitechurch Dorset 8 B3
Winterborne Zelston Dorset 8 B3
Winterbourne Berks 19 F4
Winterbourne Gloucs 28 D1
Winterbourne Abbas Dorset 7 G4
Winterbourne Bassett Wilts 18 D4
Winterbourne Dauntsey Wilts 8 D6
Winterbourne Earls Wilts 8 D6
Winterbourne Gunner Wilts 8 D6
Winterbourne Monkton Wilts 18 D4
Winterbourne Steepleton Dorset 7 G4
Winterbourne Stoke Wilts 18 C1
Winterburn N York 58 B5
Winteringham Lincs 60 C2
Winterley Ches 49 G5
Winterslow Wilts 9 E6
Winterton Lincs 60 C2
Winterton-on-Sea Norfk 45 G4
Winthorpe Notts 52 A1
Winton Cumb 64 C4
Winton Dorset 8 D3
Wintringham N York 67 E1
Winwick Cambs 32 C6
Winwick Ches 57 F2
Winwick Nhants 41 G1
Wirksworth Derbys 50 D2
Wirswall Ches 49 E4
Wisbech Cambs 43 F3
Wisbech St Mary Cambs 43 F3
Wisborough Green W Susx 10 D4
Wiseman's Bridge Pembks 25 E3
Wiseton Notts 51 H5
Wishaw N Lans 85 G1
Wishaw Warwks 40 C3
Wisley Gardens Surrey 20 D2
Wispington Lincs 52 D3
Wissett Suffk 35 F6
Wissington Suffk 34 C2
Wistanstow Shrops 38 D4
Wistanswick Shrops 49 F2
Wistaston Ches 49 F4
Wiston Pembks 24 D4
Wiston S Lans 78 C5
Wiston W Susx 11 E3
Wistow Cambs 33 E6
Wistow N York 59 G3
Wiswell Lancs 57 G6
Witcham Cambs 33 F6
Witchampton Dorset 8 C4
Witchford Cambs 33 G6
Witcombe Somset 17 F2
Witham Essex 22 D6
Witham Friary Somset 17 H3
Witham on the Hill Lincs 42 C4
Withcall Lincs 53 E4
Withdean E Susx 11 F3
Witherenden Hill E Susx 12 B4
Witheridge Devon 15 G3
Witherley Leics 41 E3
Withern Lincs 53 F3
Withernsea E R Yk 61 G3
Withernwick E R Yk 61 E4
Withersdale Street Suffk 35 F6
Withersfield Essex 33 H3
Witherslack Cumb 62 D4
Witherslack Hall Cumb 62 D4
Withiel Cnwll 3 F5
Withiel Florey Somset 16 B2
Withington Gloucs 30 B2
Withington Gt Man 57 H2
Withington Herefs 39 E1
Withington Shrops 49 F1
Withington Staffs 40 B6
Withleigh Devon 6 A6
Withybed Green Worcs 40 B1
Withybrook Warwks 41 E2
Withycombe Somset 16 B3
Witham E Susx 11 G5
Withypool Somset 15 G4
Withywood Bristl 17 G5
Witley Surrey 10 C5
Witnesham Suffk 35 E4
Witney Oxon 31 E1
Wittering Cambs 42 C2
Wittersham Kent 12 D4
Witton Norfk 45 F3
Witton Norfk 45 F5
Witton W Mids 40 C3
Witton Gilbert Dur 73 F2
Witton le Wear Dur 65 E6
Witton Park Dur 65 F6
Wiveliscombe Somset 16 C2
Wivelrod Hants 19 H1
Wivelsfield E Susx 11 F4
Wivelsfield Green E Susx 11 F4
Wivenhoe Essex 34 D1
Wiveton Norfk 44 D6
Wix Essex 35 E2
Wixford Warwks 30 C5
Wixoe Essex 34 B3
Woburn Beds 32 B2
Woburn Abbey Beds 32 B2
Woburn Sands Bucks 32 B2
Woking Surrey 20 D2
Wokingham Berks 20 B2
Wold Newton E R Yk 67 F1
Wold Newton Lincs 53 E5
Woldingham Surrey 21 F1
Wolf's Castle Pembks 24 D5
Wolfclyde S Lans 78 D6
Wolferton Norfk 43 H5
Wolfhill P & K 92 D3
Wolfsdale Pembks 24 D4
Wollaston Nhants 32 B5
Wollaston Shrops 48 D1
Wollaston W Mids 40 A2
Wollaton Notts 51 F1
Wollerton Shrops 49 F2
Wollescote W Mids 40 A2
Wolsingham Dur 73 E1
Wolstanton Staffs 49 H4
Wolston Warwks 41 E1
Wolvercote Oxon 31 F1
Wolverhampton W Mids 40 A3
Wolverley Worcs 39 G4
Wolverton Bucks 32 A3
Wolverton Hants 19 G3
Wolverton Warwks 30 D3
Wolverton Wilts 8 A6
Wolvesnewton Mons 28 C3
Wolvey Warwks 41 E2
Wolvey Heath Warwks 41 E2
Wolviston Dur 66 B5
Wombleton N York 66 C2
Wombourne Staffs 39 H5
Wombwell S York 51 E6
Womenswold Kent 23 G1
Womersley N York 59 F2
Wonford Devon 6 B5
Wonston Hants 19 F1
Wooburn Bucks 20 C4
Wooburn Green Bucks 20 C4
Wood Bevington Warwks 30 B5
Wood Dalling Norfk 44 D4
Wood End Gt Lon 20 D3
Wood End Herts 33 E2
Wood End Warwks 40 C1
Wood Enderby Lincs 53 E2
Wood Green Gt Lon 21 F4
Wood Hayes W Mids 40 B3
Wood Norton Norfk 44 D4
Wood Street Norfk 45 G4
Wood Street Surrey 20 C1
Wood Walton Cambs 32 D6
Wood's Corner E Susx 12 B4
Wood's Green E Susx 12 B5
Woodall S York 51 F4
Woodbastwick Norfk 45 F3
Woodborough Notts 51 G2
Woodborough Wilts 18 D3
Woodbridge Devon 6 D5
Woodbridge Suffk 35 F3
Woodbury Devon 6 B4
Woodbury Salterton Devon 6 B4
Woodchester Gloucs 29 F3
Woodchurch Kent 12 D5
Woodcombe Somset 16 B4
Woodcote Gt Lon 21 F2
Woodcote Oxon 19 H5
Woodcote Shrops 49 G1
Woodcroft Gloucs 28 D2
Woodditton Cambs 33 H4
Woodeaton Oxon 31 F2
Woodend Highld 89 H5
Woodend Nhants 31 G5
Woodend W Loth 85 H3
Woodend W Susx 10 B3
Woodend Green Essex 33 G2
Woodfalls Wilts 8 D5
Woodford Gloucs 29 E2
Woodford Gt Lon 21 G4
Woodford Gt Man 50 A5
Woodford Nhants 32 B6
Woodford Bridge Gt Lon 21 G4
Woodford Halse Nhants 31 F5
Woodford Wells Gt Lon 21 G4
Woodgate Devon 16 C1
Woodgate W Mids 40 B2
Woodgate W Susx 10 C3
Woodgate Worcs 30 B6
Woodgreen Hants 8 D5
Woodhall N York 64 D2
Woodhall Spa Lincs 52 D2
Woodham Bucks 31 G2
Woodham Surrey 20 D2
Woodham Ferrers Essex 22 C5
Woodham Mortimer Essex 22 C5
Woodham Walter Essex 22 C5
Woodhead Abers 102 D3
Woodhill Somset 17 E2
Woodhorn Nthumb 73 G5
Woodhouse Leics 41 F4
Woodhouse S York 51 E5
Woodhouse W York 58 D3
Woodhouse W York 59 E2
Woodhouse Eaves Leics 41 F4
Woodhouselee Mdloth 86 C3
Woodhouselees D & G 71 G6
Woodhouses Staffs 40 C5
Woodhurst Cambs 33 E6
Woodingdean E Susx 11 F3
Woodkirk W York 58 D3
Woodland Abers 103 E2
Woodland Devon 5 H4
Woodland Devon 5 F3
Woodland Dur 65 E6
Woodland Kent 13 F6
Woodland S Ayrs 76 B1
Woodlands Abers 95 G5
Woodlands Dorset 8 C4
Woodlands Hants 9 E4
Woodlands N York 59 E5
Woodlands S York 59 F1
Woodlands Somset 16 C3
Woodlands Park Berks 20 B3
Woodleigh Devon 5 G2
Woodley Berks 20 B3
Woodmancote Gloucs 29 G5
Woodmancote Gloucs 30 B1
Woodmancote Gloucs 29 E3
Woodmancote W Susx 10 B3
Woodmancote W Susx 11 E3
Woodmancott Hants 19 G1
Woodmansey E R Yk 60 D4
Woodmansgreen W Susx 10 B4
Woodmansterne Surrey 21 F2
Woodmanton Devon 6 B4
Woodnesborough Kent 23 G1
Woodnewton Nhants 42 C2
Woodplumpton Lancs 57 E6
Woodrising Norfk 44 D2
Woodseaves Staffs 49 G2
Woodsetts S York 51 F4
Woodsford Dorset 8 A3
Woodside Berks 20 C3
Woodside Fife 86 D6
Woodside Gt Lon 21 F2
Woodside P & K 93 E3
Woodstock Oxon 31 E2
Woodston Cambs 42 D2
Woodton Norfk 45 F2
Woodtown Devon 14 D3
Woofferton Shrops 39 E3
Wookey Somset 17 F3
Wookey Hole Somset 17 F4
Wool Dorset 8 B2
Woolacombe Devon 14 D5
Woolage Green Kent 23 G1
Woolaston Gloucs 28 D3
Woolaston Common Gloucs 28 D3
Woolavington Somset 17 E3
Woolbeding W Susx 10 C4
Woolbrook Devon 6 C4
Woolcotts Somset 16 B2
Wooler Nthumb 81 F3
Woolfardisworthy Devon 14 C3
Woolfardisworthy Devon 15 G2
Woolfords S Lans 86 A2
Woolhampton Berks 19 G3
Woolhope Herefs 28 D6
Woolland Dorset 8 A4
Woolley Cambs 32 D6
Woolley Somset 17 H5
Woolley W York 58 D2
Woolmer Green Herts 33 E1
Woolmere Green Worcs 30 B6
Woolminstone Somset 7 E6
Woolpit Suffk 34 C5
Woolstaston Shrops 39 E5
Woolsthorpe Lincs 42 A5
Woolsthorpe-by-Colsterworth Lincs 42 B4
Woolston Ches 57 F2
Woolston Hants 9 F4
Woolston Shrops 48 D2
Woolston Shrops 38 D6
Woolston Somset 16 C3
Woolston Somset 17 G2
Woolston Green Devon 5 H3
Woolstone Bucks 32 B3
Woolstone Gloucs 29 G5
Woolstone Oxon 19 E5
Woolton Mersyd 56 D2
Woolton Hill Hants 19 F3
Woolverstone Suffk 35 E3
Woolverton Somset 18 A2
Woolwich Gt Lon 21 G3
Woonton Herefs 38 D2
Woore Shrops 49 G3
Wootten Green Suffk 35 E5
Wootton Beds 32 C3
Wootton Kent 13 G6
Wootton Lincs 61 E2
Wootton Nhants 31 H5
Wootton Oxon 31 E2
Wootton Oxon 19 G6
Wootton Staffs 50 C2
Wootton Bassett Wilts 18 C5
Wootton Bridge IOW 9 G3
Wootton Courtenay Somset 16 B3
Wootton Fitzpaine Dorset 7 E5
Wootton Rivers Wilts 18 D3
Wootton St Lawrence Hants 19 G2
Wootton Wawen Warwks 30 C6
Worcester Worcs 39 H2
Worcester Park Gt Lon 21 E2
Wordsley W Mids 40 A2
Worfield Shrops 39 G5
Workington Cumb 70 D2
Worksop Notts 51 G4
Worlaby Lincs 60 D2
World's End Berks 19 G4
Worlds End Hants 9 H4
Worlds End W Susx 11 F4
Worle Somset 17 E5
Worleston Ches 49 F5
Worlingham Suffk 45 G1
Worlington Devon 15 G2
Worlington Suffk 34 A5
Worlingworth Suffk 35 E5
Wormald Green N York 58 D6
Wormbridge Herefs 28 C5
Wormegay Norfk 43 H3
Wormelow Tump Herefs 28 C5
Wormhill Derbys 50 C4
Wormingford Essex 34 C2
Worminghall Bucks 31 G1
Wormington Gloucs 30 B4
Wormit Fife 93 F2
Wormleighton Warwks 31 E5
Wormley Herts 21 F5
Wormley Surrey 10 C5
Wormshill Kent 22 D1
Wormsley Herefs 38 D1
Worplesdon Surrey 20 C1
Worrall S York 51 E6
Worsbrough S York 51 E6
Worsbrough Bridge S York 59 E1
Worsbrough Dale S York 59 E1
Worsley Gt Man 57 G3
Worstead Norfk 45 F4
Worsthorne Lancs 57 H5
Worston Devon 5 F2
Worston Lancs 57 G6
Worth Kent 23 G1
Worth Matravers Dorset 8 C1
Wortham Suffk 34 D6
Worthen Shrops 38 D6
Worthenbury Wrexhm 48 D4
Worthing Norfk 44 D4
Worthing W Susx 11 E2
Worthington Leics 41 E5
Wortley S York 50 D6
Wortley W York 58 D3
Worton N York 64 D2
Worton Wilts 18 C3
Wortwell Norfk 45 F1
Wotton Underwood Bucks 31 G2
Wotton-under-Edge Gloucs 29 E2
Woughton on the Green Bucks 32 B3
Wouldham Kent 22 C2
Woundale Shrops 39 G5
Wrabness Essex 35 E2
Wrafton Devon 15 E4
Wragby Lincs 52 D3
Wragby W York 59 E2
Wrangaton Devon 5 G3
Wrangle Lincs 53 F1
Wrangway Somset 16 C1
Wrantage Somset 17 E2
Wrawby Lincs 52 C6
Wraxall Somset 17 F6
Wraxall Somset 17 G3
Wray Lancs 63 F3
Wraysbury Berks 20 D3
Wrayton Lancs 63 F3
Wrea Green Lancs 56 D5
Wreay Cumb 71 G4
Wrecclesham Surrey 10 B6
Wrekenton T & W 73 F3
Wrelton N York 66 D2
Wrenbury Ches 49 E5
Wreningham Norfk 45 E2
Wrentham Suffk 35 H6
Wrentnall Shrops 38 D6
Wressle E R Yk 60 B3
Wressle Lincs 52 B6
Wrestlingworth Beds 33 E3
Wretton Norfk 44 A2
Wrexham Wrexhm 48 D4
Wribbenhall Worcs 39 G3
Wrinehill Staffs 49 G4
Wrington Somset 17 F5
Writhlington Somset 17 H4
Writtle Essex 22 B5
Wrockwardine Shrops 49 F1
Wroot Lincs 60 B1
Wrose W York 58 C4
Wrotham Kent 22 B2
Wroughton Wilts 18 D4
Wroxall IOW 9 G2
Wroxall Warwks 40 D1
Wroxeter Shrops 39 E6
Wroxham Norfk 45 F4
Wroxton Oxon 31 E4
Wyaston Derbys 50 C1
Wyberton East Lincs 43 E5
Wyboston Beds 32 D4
Wybunbury Ches 49 F4
Wychbold Worcs 30 A6
Wychnor Staffs 40 C5
Wyck Hants 10 B5
Wyck Rissington Gloucs 30 C2
Wycliffe Dur 65 E4
Wycoller Lancs 58 B4
Wycomb Leics 41 H5
Wycombe Marsh Bucks 20 C4
Wyddial Herts 33 F2
Wye Kent 13 E6
Wyke Dorset 8 A5
Wyke W York 58 C3
Wyke Champflower Somset 17 G3
Wyke Regis Dorset 7 G3
Wykeham N York 67 F2
Wyken Shrops 39 G5
Wyken W Mids 41 E2
Wykey Shrops 48 D2
Wylam Nthumb 73 E3
Wylde Green W Mids 40 C3
Wylye Wilts 18 C1
Wymeswold Leics 41 G5
Wymington Beds 32 B5
Wymondham Leics 42 B4
Wymondham Norfk 45 E2
Wynford Eagle Dorset 7 G5
Wyre Piddle Worcs 30 B4
Wysall Notts 41 G5
Wythall Worcs 40 C1
Wytham Oxon 31 F1
Wythenshawe Gt Man 57 G2
Wyton Cambs 33 E5
Wyton E R Yk 61 E3
Wyverstone Suffk 34 D5
Wyverstone Street Suffk 34 D5

Yeading Gt Lon 20 D3
Yeadon W York 58 D4
Yealand Conyers Lancs 63 E3
Yealand Redmayne Lancs 63 E3
Yealmpton Devon 5 F2
Yearsley N York 66 C1
Yeaton Shrops 48 D2
Yeaveley Derbys 50 C1
Yeavering Nthumb 81 E3
Yedingham N York 67 E2
Yelford Oxon 31 E1
Yelling Cambs 33 E5
Yelvertoft Nhants 41 G1
Yelverton Devon 5 F4
Yelverton Norfk 45 F2
Yenston Somset 17 H1
Yeoford Devon 15 G1
Yeolmbridge Cnwll 4 D5
Yeovil Somset 17 F1
Yeovil Marsh Somset 17 F1
Yeovilton Somset 17 F2
Yeovilton Fleet Air Arm Museum Somset 17 F2
Yesnaby Ork 111 g2
Yetminster Dorset 7 G6
Yettington Devon 6 C4
Yetts o' Muckhart Clacks 86 A6
Yielden Beds 32 C5
Yieldshields S Lans 77 G6
Yiewsley Gt Lon 20 D3
Ynysboeth Rhondd 27 F2
Ynysddu Caerph 27 G2
Ynyshir Rhondd 27 F2
Ynystawe Swans 26 C3
Ynysybwl Rhondd 27 F2
Yockleton Shrops 48 D1
Yokefleet E R Yk 60 C3
Yoker C Glas 84 D3
York N York 59 G5
York Minster N York 59 G5
York Town Surrey 20 B2
Yorkletts Kent 23 F2
Yorkley Gloucs 28 D3
Youlgreave Derbys 50 D3
Youlthorpe E R Yk 60 B5
Youlton N York 59 F6
Young's End Essex 34 B1
Yoxall Staffs 40 C5
Yoxford Suffk 35 G5
Ysbyty Ifan Conwy 55 F2
Ysbyty Ystwyth Cerdgn 37 F4
Ysceifiog Flints 48 B6
Ystalyfera Powys 26 D3
Ystrad Rhondd 27 F2
Ystrad Aeron Cerdgn 36 D2
Ystrad Meurig Cerdgn 37 F3
Ystrad Mynach Caerph 27 G2
Ystradfellte Powys 27 E4
Ystradgynlais Powys 26 D4
Ystradowen V Glam 27 F1
Ythanbank Abers 103 E3
Ythanwells Abers 102 C3
Ythsie Abers 103 E3

Zeal Monachorum Devon 15 F2
Zeals Wilts 8 A6
Zennor Cnwll 2 B3
Zouch Notts 41 F5

Z

Y

Y Felinheli Gwynd 54 D3
Y Ferwig Cerdgn 36 B2
Y Ffor Gwynd 46 D5
Y Gyffylliog Denbgs 48 B5
Y Maerdy Conwy 48 A4
Y Rhiw Gwynd 46 B4
Yaddlethorpe Lincs 52 B5
Yafforth N York 65 G3
Yalberton Devon 6 A2
Yalding Kent 22 C1
Yanwath Cumb 71 H2
Yanworth Gloucs 30 C2
Yapham E R Yk 60 B5
Yapton W Susx 10 C2
Yarborough Somset 17 E4
Yarburgh Lincs 53 E4
Yarcombe Devon 6 D6
Yard Devon 15 G3
Yardley W Mids 40 C2
Yardley Gobion Nhants 31 H4
Yardley Hastings Nhants 32 B4
Yardley Wood W Mids 40 C2
Yarkhill Herefs 28 D6
Yarley Somset 17 F3
Yarlington Somset 17 G2
Yarm N York 65 G4
Yarmouth IOW 9 F2
Yarnbrook Wilts 18 B2
Yarnfield Staffs 49 H3
Yarnscombe Devon 15 E3
Yarnton Oxon 31 F2
Yarpole Herefs 39 E3
Yarrow Border 79 F5
Yarrow Feus Border 79 F5
Yarrowford Border 79 G5
Yarwell Nhants 42 C2
Yate Gloucs 29 E1
Yateley Hants 20 B2
Yatesbury Wilts 18 C4
Yattendon Berks 19 G4
Yatton Herefs 38 D3
Yatton Herefs 28 D5
Yatton Somset 17 F5
Yatton Keynell Wilts 18 B4
Yaverland IOW 9 H2
Yaxham Norfk 44 D3
Yaxley Cambs 42 D2
Yaxley Suffk 35 E5
Yazor Herefs 38 D1